Frommer's®

Cuba

5th Edition

by Claire Boobbyer

WILEY

Wiley Publishing, Inc.

ABOUT THE AUTHOR

Claire Boobbyer is a travel writer, photographer, and editor who fell in love with Latin America more than 10 years ago after several backpacking trips around the region. She moved to Spain to learn Spanish and after a stint of working with wildlife in the Peruvian Amazon, she headed north to Central America. She first went to Cuba in 1998 to spend a newly reinstated Christmas Day holiday in Havana and has been returning ever since, improving her salsa dancing and Cuban accent each time she visits. Claire is the author of several other guidebooks on the region and has written articles about Cuba for newspapers and magazines; her photographic work has appeared in various guidebooks and alongside her travel articles. She is also the author of *Frommer's Cuba Day by Day*. For more information on Claire, visit www. claireboobbyer.com.

Published by:

WILEY PUBLISHING, INC.

111 River St.
Hoboken, NJ 07030-5774

ISBN 978-0-470-92173-9 (paper); ISBN 978-0-470-44894-6 (ebk); ISBN 978-1-118-01588-9 (ebk); ISBN 978-0-470-44914-1 (ebk)

Editor: Jennifer Polland
Production Editor: Lindsay Conner
Cartographer: Guy Ruggiero
Photo Editor: Richard Fox
Production by Wiley Indianapolis Composition Services

Front Cover Photo: Old cars passing the Gran Teatro Capitolio Habana Vieja Havana Cuba © David Noton Photography / Alamy Images
Back Cover Photo: View across the Viñales Valley from Hotel Los Jazmines © John Warburton-Lee Photography / Alamy Images

For information on our other products and services or to obtain technical support, please contact our Customer Care Department within the U.S. at 877/762-2974, outside the U.S. at 317/572-3993 or fax 317/572-4002.

Wiley also publishes its books in a variety of electronic formats. Some content that appears in print may not be available in electronic formats.

Manufactured in the United States of America

5   4   3   2   1

CONTENTS

10 EL ORIENTE 237

11 SANTIAGO DE CUBA 270

12 FAST FACTS 295

13 CUBAN SPANISH TERMS & PHRASES 301

Index 306

LIST OF MAPS

ACKNOWLEDGMENTS

Claire Boobbyer would like to thank the many Cubans across the country who gave her assistance on the ground, and always the warmest welcomes at their *casas particulares*. She would also like to thank Jen Polland, her editor at Frommer's.

HOW TO CONTACT US

In researching this book, we discovered many wonderful places—hotels, restaurants, shops, and more. We're sure you'll find others. Please tell us about them, so we can share the information with your fellow travelers in upcoming editions. If you were disappointed with a recommendation, we'd love to know that, too. Please write to:

Frommer's Cuba, 5th Edition
Wiley Publishing, Inc. • 111 River St. • Hoboken, NJ 07030-5774
frommersfeedback@wiley.com

AN ADDITIONAL NOTE

Please be advised that travel information is subject to change at any time—and this is especially true of prices. We therefore suggest that you write or call ahead for confirmation when making your travel plans. The authors, editors, and publisher cannot be held responsible for the experiences of readers while traveling. Your safety is important to us, however, so we encourage you to stay alert and be aware of your surroundings. Keep a close eye on cameras, purses, and wallets, all favorite targets of thieves and pickpockets.

FROMMER'S STAR RATINGS, ICONS & ABBREVIATIONS

Every hotel, restaurant, and attraction listing in this guide has been ranked for quality, value, service, amenities, and special features using a **star-rating system**. In country, state, and regional guides, we also rate towns and regions to help you narrow down your choices and budget your time accordingly. Hotels and restaurants are rated on a scale of zero (recommended) to three stars (exceptional). Attractions, shopping, nightlife, towns, and regions are rated according to the following scale: zero stars (recommended), one star (highly recommended), two stars (very highly recommended), and three stars (must-see).

In addition to the star-rating system, we also use **seven** feature icons that point you to the great deals, in-the-know advice, and unique experiences that separate travelers from tourists. Throughout the book, look for:

special finds—those places only insiders know about

fun facts—details that make travelers more informed and their trips more fun

kids—best bets for kids and advice for the whole family

special moments—those experiences that memories are made of

overrated—places or experiences not worth your time or money

insider tips—great ways to save time and money

great values—where to get the best deals

The following abbreviations are used for credit cards:

AE	American Express	DISC Discover	V Visa
DC	Diners Club	MC MasterCard	

TRAVEL RESOURCES AT FROMMERS.COM

Frommer's travel resources don't end with this guide. Frommer's website, **www.frommers. com**, has travel information on more than 4,000 destinations. We update features regularly, giving you access to the most current trip-planning information and the best airfare, lodging, and car-rental bargains. You can also listen to podcasts, connect with other Frommers. com members through our active-reader forums, share your travel photos, read blogs from guidebook editors and fellow travelers, and much more.

THE BEST OF CUBA

Cuba is unlike any other place on earth. What draws people to this fascinating Caribbean island is much more than beaches, sun, and cheap drinks, though there is plenty of all three for those who want them. One of the last Communist-bloc nations left, it doesn't suffer from the drab and desultory demeanor of its disappeared peers. Cuba's rich culture, unique political history, and continued survival through ongoing economic hardship make it one of the most eye-opening countries that experienced travelers can still discover. Seeing the best of Cuba means grooving to its intoxicating music, admiring at how Cubans improvise on a daily basis to make ends meet, and visiting a land in which the past 50 years seem to have passed by in some odd state of frozen animation.

THE best CUBAN EXPERIENCES

- **Patronizing Paladares and Casas Particulares:** The best way to appreciate Cubans, as well as, to have the opportunity to exchange ideas about Cuba and the outside world, is by stepping inside a *paladar* restaurant or a *casa particular*, the Cuban version of a simple bed-and-breakfast. These private initiatives, heavily taxed by the state, are one of the only ways Cubans can earn badly needed hard currency, and they allow travelers to interact with locals.

- **Exploring La Habana Vieja (Old Havana):** The streets and alleys of this colonial-era city center have been immaculately restored. You'll feel sucked back in time as you visit the plazas, churches, and forts here. See "What to See & Do," in chapter 5.

- **Spending an Afternoon at the Callejón de Hammel:** This short alley is lined with Salvador González's colorful murals and punctuated with scrap sculptures and shrines to Afro-Cuban deities. If you can make it on a Sunday afternoon in Havana, you'll be treated to a popular Afro-Cuban dance and music celebration. See "What to See & Do," in chapter 5.

- **Walking along Havana's Malecón:** Your best bet is to start in La Habana Vieja and work your way toward the Hotel Nacional in Vedado. Take time to stop and sit on the sea wall. If you time it right, you will reach the Hotel Nacional in the late afternoon—a good time to grab a cool drink and enjoy the setting sun from the outdoor terrace. See "What to See & Do," in chapter 5.

o **Celebrating Las Parrandas:** Near the end of the year, the little colonial town of Remedios gears up to host Las Parrandas, one of Cuba's grandest street parties and religious carnivals. Everything culminates on Christmas Eve in an orgy of drums, floats, and fireworks. See "Santa Clara," in chapter 8.

o **Hopping on a Steam Train to the Valley of the Sugar Mills:** The colonial mansions in Trinidad were built with the riches of a booming Cuban sugar trade of the 18th and 19th centuries. The best way to see the Valle de los Ingenios, an extraordinarily lush valley once home to 60 sugar mills, is aboard a vintage 1907 American steam train to one of the sugar estates, Manaca-Iznaga, where you can survey the valley's many shades of green. See "Trinidad," in chapter 8.

o **Following in Fidel's Footsteps:** Waging a guerrilla war against the Batista dictatorship, Fidel Castro and his young comrades hid out in the Sierra Maestra mountains in the late 1950s. Their small-scale rebel base camp was never discovered, but visitors today can hike a trail through remote cloud forest up to Comandancia de la Plata, the command post where Fidel turned a country on its head. See "Bayamo & the Sierra Maestra," in chapter 10.

o **Joining a Carnival Conga Line:** In the intense heat of summer, Santiago de Cuba explodes with the island's best carnival. Ripe with rumba music, conga processions, booming percussion, fanciful floats, and wild costumes, it's a participatory party. See "Carnival & Other Santiago Festivals," in chapter 11.

o **Beach time:** Lying on one of Cuba's white-sand beaches sipping a *mojito* (Cuban rum cocktail) before dipping into the sparkling waters of the warm Caribbean Sea is one of the most heavenly things you can do.

THE best HISTORICAL SIGHTS

o **Catedral de San Cristóbal and Plaza de la Catedral,** Havana (© 7/861-7771): Havana's cathedral and the plaza it sits on are perhaps Old Havana's most distinctive historical sites. The twin towers and worn baroque facade of this ancient church are beautiful both by day and night. See p. 114.

o **Museo de la Ciudad,** Havana (© 7/861-2876): Old Havana's preeminent museum displays colonial-era art and artifacts. Stroll the rooms, courtyards, and interior veranda of the former Palacio de los Capitanes Generales (Palace of the Captains General), which houses the museum. See p. 115.

o **Parque Histórico Morro y Cabaña,** Havana (© 7/863-7063 for El Morro, and © 7/862-0617 for La Cabaña): Across the harbor from Old Havana, the Morro & Cabaña Historic Park complex is comprised of two major forts charged with protecting Havana's narrow harbor entrance. There's a lighthouse, several museums, restored barracks, and batteries of cannons. See p. 121.

o **Cementerio de Colón,** Havana (© 7/832-1050): Columbus Cemetery is an impressive collection of mausoleums, crypts, family chapels and vaults, soaring sculptures, and ornate gravestones. All of the dead are laid to rest above ground, and you'll be awed by the surfeit of marble and alabaster. See p. 118.

o **Monumento Ernesto Che Guevara,** Santa Clara (© 42/20-5878): Featuring a huge sculpture of the revolutionary hero overlooking a vast plaza, this place is deeply revered by Cubans. Underneath the statue is a museum with exhibits detailing the life and exploits of "El Che," as well as a mausoleum holding his remains. See "Santa Clara," in chapter 8.

o **Trinidad:** The entire town of Trinidad qualifies as a historical site. The impeccably preserved relic—several blocks square of perfect pastel-colored mansions, churches, and cobblestone streets—is one of the greatest collections of colonial architecture in the Americas. See "Trinidad," in chapter 8.

o **Plaza San Juan de Dios,** Camagüey (© **32/29-1318**): This dignified square is the highlight of Camagüey's colonial quarter, one of the largest in Cuba with more than a dozen 16th-, 17th-, and 18th-century colonial churches. Marked by cobblestones and colonial houses with red-tile roofs and iron window grilles, the understated plaza is home to a 17th-century baroque church and hospital of the order of San Juan de Dios. See p. 232.

o **Museo El Chorro de Maíta,** Guardalavaca (© **24/43-0201**): This small museum site is a Taíno burial ground from the late–15th and early–16th centuries, the biggest and finest American Indian cemetery discovered in Cuba. The well-preserved remains of more than 100 members of the community reveal important clues about native groups after the arrival of the Spanish conquistadors. See "Guardalavaca," in chapter 10.

o **Casa Velázquez (Museo de Ambiente Historico Cubano),** Santiago de Cuba (© **22/65-2652**): Diego Velázquez founded the original seven *villas* (towns/settlements) in Cuba, and his 1515 mansion in Santiago de Cuba, the oldest house in the country and one of the oldest in the Americas, is still standing. Today it's a museum of colonial furnishings from the 16th to the 19th century. See p. 277.

o **Castillo El Morro,** Santiago de Cuba (© **22/69-1569**): Although nowhere near as expansive as its sister fort in Havana, this massive fortress is nonetheless quite impressive. You can almost feel like you're part of the history here while walking the mazelike alleyways. See p. 292.

THE best OF NATURAL CUBA

o **The Viñales Valley:** This broad, flat valley is punctuated by a series of limestone karst hill formations, or *mogotes*. The area provides great opportunities for hiking, mountain biking, bird-watching, and rock climbing, and there are plenty of caves to explore. See "Viñales," in chapter 6.

o **Las Terrazas:** This planned ecotourism project is set amid the Sierra del Rosario Biosphere Reserve. There are a host of trails and attractions here, including lakes, swimming holes, and a zip-line canopy tour. See "Sierra del Rosario Biosphere Reserve & San Diego de los Baños," in chapter 6.

o **Parque Nacional Ciénaga de Zapata:** The Zapata Swamp National Park is a massive expanse of mangroves, swamp, and wetlands housing an abundant variety of flora and fauna, including flamingos and Cuban crocodiles. The area is a mecca for bird-watchers, naturalists, and anglers. The diving is also superb. See "The Zapata Peninsula & Playa Girón," in chapter 7.

o **Parque Nacional Topes de Collantes:** The dense pine-covered mountains of the Sierra del Escambray lurk on the outskirts of Trinidad, and the Topes de Collantes National Park is a lovely, cool refuge from the town's stone streets. It's great for hiking, with several well-established trails, the best of which culminate in refreshing waterfalls. See "Trinidad," in chapter 8.

- **Baracoa:** Cuba's first settlement, overlooking a beautiful oyster-shaped bay, remains a natural paradise, with thick tropical vegetation, 10 rivers, and a distinctive flat-topped mountain called El Yunque, a UNESCO Biosphere Reserve. Travelers into rafting, beaches, and boating will also find ample opportunities to explore this isolated area. The Parque Nacional Alejandro de Humboldt around the Río Toa is rich in diversity. See "Baracoa," in chapter 10.

- **Sierra Maestra:** The highest and longest mountain range in Cuba, the Sierra Maestra is full of lore for Cubans—it's where Fidel Castro and his band of rebels hid out and waged guerilla warfare against the Batista government in the 1950s. Stretching across three provinces, its peaks are almost on top of the rocky southern coastline. The Gran Parque Nacional Sierra Maestra and Parque Nacional de Turquino are perfect for hikers and nature lovers. See "Bayamo & the Sierra Maestra," in chapter 10.

THE best OUTDOOR ADVENTURES

- **Landing a Marlin or Sailfish:** If you really want to emulate Ernest Hemingway, you'll head out to sea to fish. The waters off Cuba's coast are excellent for sportfishing year-round. Big game fish are best sought off the northern coast, while bonefish and tarpon are better stalked off the southern coast. Náutica Marlin (www.nauticamarlin.com) and Gaviota (www.gaviota-grupo.com) run a string of marinas with modern, well-equipped sport-fishing fleets all around Cuba's coastline.

- **Rock Climbing the Mogotes of the Viñales Valley:** Although in its infancy, rock climbing is a rapidly developing sport in Cuba, and Viñales Valley is the place to come and climb. More than 60 routes and 100 pitches have been marked and climbed, and more climbs are constantly being uncovered. See "Viñales," in chapter 6.

- **Scuba Diving at María la Gorda:** Cuba has many excellent dive destinations, but María la Gorda probably edges out the rest by having consistently excellent conditions, a variety of sites, an amazing setting, and an excellent dive operation. However, there's excellent diving off much of Cuba's coast, and if you want to combine diving with other attractions, you can do so from just about any destination on the island. See "María la Gorda," in chapter 6.

- **Bird-Watching in the Zapata Peninsula:** A dedicated (and lucky) bird-watcher might be able to spot 18 of Cuba's 24 endemic species in the swamps, mangroves, and wetlands of the Zapata Peninsula. In addition to the endemic species, ornithologists and lay bird-watchers can spot more than 100 other varieties of shore birds, transients, and waterfowl in this rich, wild region. See "The Zapata Peninsula & Playa Girón," in chapter 7. Other top bird-watching destinations include **La Güira National Park** (see chapter 6), as well as the areas around **Cayo Coco** and **Cayo Guillermo** (see chapter 9) and **Baracoa** (see chapter 10).

- **Hiking and Rafting in Baracoa:** Baracoa, long isolated by impenetrable tropical vegetation, steep mountains, and rushing rivers, is an adventurer's dream. El Yunque, a curiously flat-topped limestone mountain, is home to dozens of bird species, orchids, and unique tropical plants and forest; it's also great for climbing.

The Río Toa, the widest river in Cuba, is one of the few spots in Cuba for rafting, and Parque Humboldt offers new opportunities for walking and boating. See "Baracoa," in chapter 10.

o **Hiking Pico Turquino:** Pico Turquino, tucked within the celebrated Sierra Maestra National Park, is the highest peak in Cuba at just under 2,000m (6,562 ft.). The trail to the summit is swathed in cloud forest and tropical flora. Mountaineers in good physical condition can do the 15km (9-mile) round-trip journey in a day, but most camp overnight below the summit. The panoramic views of the coast and Caribbean Sea are breathtaking. See "Bayamo & the Sierra Maestra," in chapter 10.

THE best BEACHES

o **Playa Paraíso and Playa Sirena:** These two connected beaches are the most outstanding of the uniformly spectacular stretches of sand along the length of Cayo Largo del Sur. Located on the more protected western end of the island, these are broad expanses of glistening, fine white sand, bordering the clear Caribbean Sea. There's a simple beachside restaurant on Playa Paraíso, and not much else here—and that's a large part of their charm. See "Cayo Largo del Sur," in chapter 6.

o **Varadero:** This is Cuba's premier beach-resort destination, and it ranks right up there with the best in the Caribbean. We personally prefer some of the island's less-developed stretches of sand. But if you're looking for a well-run all-inclusive resort loaded with amenities and activities, Varadero is a good choice. The 21km (13 miles) of nearly uninterrupted beach here is fabulous. See "Varadero," in chapter 7.

o **Playa Ensenachos and Playa Mégano:** Located on the tiny islet of Cayo Ensenachos, which is part of la Cayería del Norte, these protected crescents of sand drop off very gently, allowing bathers to wade 90m (295 ft.) or more out into the calm, crystal-clear waters. You'll have to shell out big bucks to visit these beaches, either staying at the Occidental Royal Hideaway Ensenachos or paying its hefty day-use fee. Both of these beaches are astoundingly beautiful, but we slightly prefer Playa Mégano. See "Santa Clara," in chapter 8.

o **Playa Ancón:** A wonderful white-sand beach and close runner-up to the more spectacular beaches of Cuba, attractive Ancón has one huge advantage: It's just minutes from one of the country's true treasures, Trinidad, and perfectly positioned for those who'd like a bit of colonial culture with their sun and sand (or vice versa). With good diving and one very nice resort hotel, it's sure to be built up soon. See "Trinidad," in chapter 8.

o **Cayos Coco and Guillermo:** These tiny cays off the north coast, separated from the Cuban mainland by a long man-made causeway, are tucked into shallow waters that flow into the Atlantic. There's barely a sign of the "real Cuba," but what you do get is stunning, unspoiled beaches, excellent diving, and a full contingent of watersports. The most beautiful beach is Playa Pilar at the western tip of Guillermo. See "Cayo Coco & Cayo Guillermo," in chapter 9.

o **Cayo Jutías:** Beyond the tourist section, walk for miles along virginal sands backed by beautiful driftwood sculptures before reaching what's known as Playa de las Estrellas del Mar (Starfish Beach), where enormous burnt-orange starfish can be seen in the shallows. See "Another Nearby Island: Cayo Jutías," in chapter 6.

- **Guardalavaca:** Probably Cuba's prettiest resort area, Guardalavaca is a hot spot, but not overheated like Varadero. The area, a prime archaeological zone of pre-Columbian Cuba, is one of lush tropical vegetation, brilliant white sands, and clear turquoise waters. Long stretches of coastline are interrupted by charming little cove beaches, and some of Cuba's finest resort hotels are here. See "Guardalavaca," in chapter 10.

THE best RESORT HOTELS

- **Paradisus Varadero,** Varadero (℡ **45/66-8700**): This is the Sol Meliá's fanciest resort hotel in Varadero, with expansive grounds, a huge free-form pool, and all the activities and amenities you could hope for. There's a variety of dining options and they create the feel of an intimate, romantic getaway better than any of the other large resort hotels in Varadero. See p. 171.
- **Tryp Península Varadero,** Varadero (℡ **45/66-8800**): This is my top choice for a family resort in Varadero and an excellent all-around resort in its own right. The setting, facilities, and service are all tops, and the rooms are quite spacious and well equipped. The children's pools and play area are the best in Cuba. See p. 172.
- **Meliá Sol Cayo Santa María,** Cayo Santa María (℡ **42/35-0200**): This resort is yet another of the Sol Meliá's excellent all-inclusive properties. This one is located on a very beautiful and very isolated patch of beach in la Cayería del Norte. The facilities are certainly top-notch, and the setting is just spectacular. See p. 190.
- **Brisas Trinidad del Mar,** Península Ancón, Trinidad (℡ **41/99-6500**): This resort hotel on Playa Ancón has excellent sea and mountain views and is only minutes from the most beautiful colonial city in Cuba. The well-conceived design echoes the handsome architecture of Trinidad. See p. 206.
- **Meliá Cayo Coco,** Cayo Coco (℡ **33/30-1180**): Of the several fine hotels on Cayo Coco, Sol Meliá's top property on the cays is the most sophisticated and stylish, with cool bungalows overlooking a natural lagoon, elegant decor throughout, good restaurants, a beautiful pool area, and a great stretch of beach on a natural cove. See p. 222.
- **Sol Cayo Guillermo,** Cayo Guillermo (℡ **33/30-1760**): Relaxed and unpretentious, this lively resort hotel is less staid and prepackaged than many of the big hotels on the cays. The cheery bungalow-style rooms are perfect for a younger crowd. See p. 225.
- **Paradisus Río de Oro,** Playa Esmeralda (℡ **24/43-0090**): This sprawling Sol Meliá property hugs a rocky cliff has some of the most luxuriously designed grounds you'll find anywhere. Rooms are large, refined, and private. Sunbathers will have a hard time deciding between the terrific main beach, the nearly private small cove beaches, and the extraordinary pool area. See p. 245.
- **Hotel Cayo Levisa,** Cayo Levisa (℡ **48/75-6502**): Land one of the oceanfront bungalows here and you may never want to leave this idyllic little island resort. For those on a budget, these standard beachfront bungalows are a passport to paradise. See p. 149.
- **Villa Las Brujas,** Cayo Santa Maria (℡ **42/35-0199**): Perched on a rocky outcrop over the turquoise Caribbean, the reasonably priced, stylish, and comfortable villas here are connected by a raised, rugged wooden walkway through scrub and mangrove and face a long stretch of beautiful white-sand beach. Staff members are very friendly here, too. See p. 190.

- **Villa Maguana,** Playa Maguana (© 21/64-1204): This is not a resort, but an attractive rustic beach hotel fronting a private, pretty cove next to a 2km (1¼-mile) white-sand beach. This kind of rustic (but equipped) cabin accommodation is a rarity in Cuba. See p. 267.

THE best HOTELS

- **Hotel Florida,** Havana (© 7/862-4127): This is probably my favorite of the Habaguanex properties in Old Havana. The building features a wonderful open-air central courtyard, checkerboard marble floors, and oodles of colonial-era charm. The whole operation is elegant and refined, and located right on the pulse of things on busy Calle Obispo. See p. 93.
- **Hotel Saratoga,** Havana (© 7/868-1000): Set right on the Paseo del Prado, with stunning views of El Capitolio from many of its rooms, this hotel has the most comfortable and luxurious rooms of any hotel in or near La Habana Vieja. Add to that a wonderful rooftop pool and bar, and this hotel is clearly one of the top choices in the city. See p. 91.
- **NH Parque Central,** Havana (© 7/860-6627): This modern, upscale hotel dominates the northern end of Havana's small central park. It boasts luxurious spacious rooms with marble bathrooms and a lovely rooftop pool. Its ultramodern stylish annex, the NH Parque Central Torre hotel, is now open. See p. 91.
- **Hotel Los Jazmines,** Viñales (© 48/79-6205): With a spectacular setting on a hillside overlooking the Viñales Valley, this is the best option in town. If you land one of the third-floor rooms with a balcony, you'll forgive the somewhat smallish rooms and minimal amenities. Los Jazmines makes a great base for exploring this region. See p. 142.
- **Hotel La Unión,** Cienfuegos (© 43/55-1020): Housed in a marvelously restored colonial mansion right in the heart of downtown Cienfuegos, this is one of the nicest boutique hotels in the country. With a couple of interior courtyards, neoclassical furnishings, and architectural touches, La Unión captures the elegance and charm of Cuba's bygone era. It's worth the small splurge for one of the spacious junior suites. See p. 196.
- **Hostal Encanto del Rijo,** Sancti Spíritus (© 41/32-8588): The concept of small boutique hotels with historic character is catching on in Cuba, and this boutique hotel in Sancti Spíritus is among the best of its kind in the country. In a beautifully restored colonial mansion, it has massive rooms with restrained decor, and it just might rank as the best hotel bargain in Cuba. See p. 215.
- **Gran Hotel,** Camagüey (© 32/29-2093): In the heart of Camagüey's colonial quarter, this 1930s hotel has real old-world character, a selection of atmospheric bars, and a small terrace pool. The Gran Hotel offers tons of style at a bargain price—especially if you get one of the spacious corner rooms. See p. 233.
- **Hotel El Castillo,** Baracoa (© 21/64-5194): This hotel has history, charm, and a location to die for. Inside the walls of one of the town's oldest fortresses, up on a hill where the pool comes with splendid panoramic views of Baracoa and the bay, this is the kind of place you won't want to leave. Relaxed and unpretentious, it suits Baracoa perfectly. See p. 266.
- **Hotel Casa Granda,** Santiago de Cuba (© 22/65-3021): It's not Santiago's biggest or most expensive hotel, but the Casa Granda, in an elegant landmark building on Parque Céspedes in the heart of the city, is the place to stay if you want to be

in the heady mix that is the Oriente region's capital. Renovation has dramatically improved the rooms, and the terrace bars are among the best people-watching places in the city. See p. 281.

o **Hostal Basilio,** Santiago de Cuba (© 22/65-1702): This little hotel, operating under the boutique Hoteles E brand, is in a beautifully restored old home in the heart of downtown Santiago de Cuba. The good-size rooms have very high ceilings with ornate crown molding. Throughout the hotel, you'll find attractive tile work on the floors, wainscoting, and smart bathrooms. See p. 281.

THE best CASAS PARTICULARES

o **Casa de Evora Rodríguez,** Havana (© 7/861-7932): This top-floor "penthouse" belonging to the welcoming Evora has stunning panoramic views and the top-floor flat is full of potted plants. See p. 97.

o **Casa Lilly,** Havana (© 7/832-4021): On the 13th floor of a 1950s block of flats, this enormous flat has spectacular views of Vedado and the Malecón. The rooms are spacious and attractively decorated and guests share a nice living room. Run by Lilly and her family, this is a gorgeous place to stay. See p. 100.

o **Casa Luís and Marley,** Playa Girón (© 45/98-4258): This modern *casa,* with a front porch and back garden, offers two comfortable, well-equipped rooms and plenty of parking space. The family is friendly and serves great food. See p. 179.

o **Casa Amistad,** Cienfuegos (© 43/51-6143): Run by the super–friendly and knowledgeable Armando and Leonor, this colonial house with a wonderful front living room has two rooms and some hearty home-cooked food; the house is a stone's throw from Parque José Martí. See p. 197.

o **Hostal Casa Colonial Muñoz,** Trinidad (© 41/99-3673): Historic Trinidad is well stocked with beautiful colonial houses and rental rooms, but this one is distinguished by its impressive living room and ever-expanding facilities; its informative host is a photographer who knows Trinidad like the back of his hand. See p. 206.

o **Casa Font,** Trinidad (© 41/99-3683): A gorgeous late-18th-century colonial house in the heart of the old center, this warm and lovely family home has a great collection of antiques and a light, airy feel. For a *casa particular,* this is about as grand as it gets: chandeliers of Baccarat crystal, thick wood doors, colonial- and republican-era oil paintings, and *mampáras* (half doors in the Modernista design) enclosing bedrooms. See p. 206.

o **Hostal Florida Center,** Santa Clara (© 42/20-8161): This is a gorgeous 1876 colonial house filled with interesting historic furniture and blessed with a flourishing garden and welcoming host, Angel. The food served here is some of the best in Cuba. See p. 186.

o **Hostal Villa Colonial,** Remedios (© 42/39-6274): This lovely colonial house, with wonderful furniture and tiles, offers two rooms, one of which has an antique bronze bed decorated in mother of pearl panels. The friendly owners are very helpful. See p. 188.

o **Casa Xiomara,** Morón (© 33/50-4236): This modern, yet modest family home is one of the best *casas* in Cuba. There is one guest room in a small, independent *casita.* Indulge in Xiomara's wonderful food—especially the *flan de leche.* See p. 223.

- **Casa Daniel Salomón Paján,** Baracoa (℃ **21/64-1443**): This is one of the friendliest *casas* in Cuba. Daniel works at the museum and knows a lot about Baracoa's history. He has one comfortable room with a large bathroom and a central covered patio. See p. 267.

- **Casa Maruchi,** Santiago de Cuba (℃ **22/62-0767**): A lovely colonial house with a wonderful patio stuffed with orchids and other plants is run by the friendly Maruchi. Two chic, comfortable rooms with exposed brickwork, Spanish colonial furniture, lace bedspreads, and candlesticks are off the patio. See p. 282.

- **Casa Asensio,** Santiago de Cuba (℃ **22/62-4600**): Facility-wise, this house may be unrivaled in Cuba. It's a very large apartment with its own kitchen and a massive, private rooftop terrace. It's perfect for anyone planning to stay awhile to explore Santiago de Cuba in depth. See p. 284.

THE best RESTAURANTS & PALADARES

- **El Templete,** Havana (℃ **7/866-8807**): This is truly fine dining portside in Old Havana, with outside seating with roadside and harbor views and sophisticated interior dining. See p. 105.

- **Restaurante Castropol,** Havana (℃ **7/861-4864**): This is an architecturally bland yellow building on the Malecón, but it is nonetheless a surprising and welcome culinary find. See p. 108.

- **Gringo Viejo,** Havana (℃ **7/831-1946**): This homey *paladar,* decorated with knick-knacks, serves delicious food—including options for vegetarians. See p. 109.

- **Roof Garden Restaurant,** Havana (℃ **7/860-8560**): The creative French-inspired menu and stunning setting make this probably the best high-end dining option in Havana. Try for a window table on the elevated area ringing the restaurant. See p. 106.

- **La Cocina de Lilliam,** Havana (℃ **7/209-6514**): Lilliam Domínguez has raised the bar for *paladares* around Havana. Her delicious *criolla* cooking always makes the most of whatever ingredients are locally available, and her softly lit garden setting is stunning. See p. 110.

- **La Fontana,** Havana (℃ **7/202-8337**): This *paladar* serves up delicious international cuisine in an alfresco dining area with a waterfall and a fish pond. Service is classically old-fashioned and welcoming. See p. 110.

- **La Fonda de Mercedes,** Las Terrazas (℃ **48/57-8647**): Working out of her apartment's simple kitchen, Doña Mercedes Dache serves up wonderfully prepared *criolla* cuisine. Meals are served on large tables in an open-air terrace overlooking a mountain lake. If you come to Las Terrazas, don't leave without eating here. See p. 147.

- **Paladar Estela,** Trinidad (℃ **41/99-4329**): A colonial house with a pretty garden patio dining area, this private home restaurant in the heart of the historic quarter of Trinidad serves epic proportions of well-prepared Cuban specialties. See p. 208.

- **La Campana de Toledo,** Camagüey (℃ **32/28-6812**): Located on one of the most authentic and elegant colonial squares in Cuba, this handsome, rustic restaurant with a pretty patio is a great spot for a midday break from the heat or a relaxed dinner. Dishes are more imaginative than the basic Cuban fare at most state-run establishments. See p. 235.

- **Restaurant Isabella,** Camagüey (© **32/22-1540**): This is the first state-run restaurant in Cuba to show any modern artistic flair; it's decorated with director's chairs and old film posters. If this isn't enough to entice you inside, you'll be lured in by the pizzas, which are huge, thin, and packed with ingredients. See p. 235.
- **Hostal Florida Center,** Santa Clara (© **42/20-8161**): This is a popular *casa particular* serving dinners with enormous platters of delicious seafood and chicken, plus salads and fruit dishes. The garden is candlelit at night. See p. 187.
- **La Colonial,** Baracoa (© **21/64-5391**): The government seems to support the competition of private restaurants only nominally, and this is the last surviving *paladar* in Baracoa. The nicely decorated colonial house easily outclasses the state-run options in town, and it has good service and a changing menu with several fresh fish dishes. See p. 268.
- **Restaurant El Morro,** Santiago de Cuba (© **22/69-1576**): Perched along the cliff next to the El Morro fortress, with spectacular views of the Caribbean, this popular open-air restaurant is a good-value lunch spot. There are plenty of fish dishes and a fixed-price midday meal, all served under a canopy of hanging plants that help patrons beat the heat. See p. 287.
- **ZunZún,** Santiago de Cuba (© **22/64-1528**): One of the few upscale dining experiences in eastern Cuba, this elegant restaurant has several small, private dining rooms scattered throughout a large 1940s house in one of Santiago de Cuba's most pleasant suburbs. Attention to detail and presentation—dining elements seldom given much thought in Cuba—are a welcome surprise. It's best known for its top-quality seafood. See p. 286.
- **Paladar Salón Tropical,** Santiago de Cuba (© **22/64-1161**): One of the most elegant *paladares* in Cuba, this attractively decorated place offers a smorgasbord of tasty choices. It's just such a shame that the service is glacially slow. See p. 286.

THE best OF CUBAN MUSIC & NIGHTLIFE

- **Tropicana,** Havana (© **7/267-1010**): This is the original and still reigning cabaret show in Cuba. The Tropicana has been at it for over 60 years and it shows no signs of slowing down. The sea of lithe dancers, the exuberance of their costumes, and the sheer excess of it is worth the trip. It all occurs under the stars in the shadow of tall overhanging trees. See p. 130.
- **Casa de la Música Centro Habana,** Havana (© **7/860-8296**): With its massive dance floor and concert space in the heart of Centro Habana, this is currently considered the best salsa-dancing venue in town. The crowd is predominantly Cuban, and most of the folks can really dance. See p. 130.
- **Casa de la Música Miramar,** Havana (© **7/204-0447**): Housed in a beautiful, former Masonic Lodge Hall, this place is associated with the national recording label Egrem. It has nightly concerts that range from bolero to salsa to jazz in the in-house club, Diablo Tun Tun. Still, for me, the real treat here is the afternoon jam sessions, which take place daily from 4 to 7pm. See p. 130.
- **El Gato Tuerto,** Havana (© **7/838-2696**): The mood is dark and bohemian, although the decor mixes Art Deco and kitsch in equal measure. The nightly show usually features three or four distinct acts, which can range from sultry boleros to

up-tempo jazz. A storyteller, poet, or comedian might perform between sets. See p. 131.

o **La Zorra y El Cuervo,** Havana (© 7/833-2402): This is Havana's best jazz club, and that's saying a lot. The vibe is mellow and unpretentious in this compact basement club, but the music and acts are usually culled from the best Cuba has to offer. See p. 132.

o **Callejón de Hammel,** Havana. Between noon and 3pm each Sunday, this is the site of a weekly Afro-Cuban music and dance show and celebration headed up by the renowned folkloric group Clavé y Guaguanco. See p. 117.

o **Sábado de la Rumba at El Gran Palenque,** Havana (© 7/830-3060): Every Saturday, Conjunto Folklórico Nacional de Cuba hosts the weekly Sábado de la Rumba, a mesmerizing show of Afro-Cuban religious and secular dance and drumming; the show takes place at 3pm at El Gran Palenque. See p. 128.

o **Trinidad:** Trinidad's popularity has ensured a steady menu of live-music offerings. Cuban bands play under the stars on the steps of the **Casa de la Música** until more energetic dancing and music get underway inside. The **Palenque de los Congos Reales** regularly hosts an outstanding folkloric Afro-Cuban music and dance performance. Small, relaxed spots like the patio bars **La Canchánchara** and **Ruinas de Segarte** feature live *son.* If that's too traditional, then check out **La Cueva,** a funky dance club in a cave. See "Trinidad," in chapter 8.

o **Casas de la Trova,** Camagüey and Santiago de Cuba: Perhaps the country's two best *Casas de la Trova,* the traditional Cuban live-music spots, are in Camagüey and Santiago de Cuba. Camagüey's casa is agreeably low-key, while Santiago's is legendary, having given birth to dozens of Cuba's most respected musicians and bands. Both are great places to mix with locals, try out some dance moves, and sip a *mojito.* See "Camagüey" in chapter 9 and p. 289 in chapter 11.

o **Casa de las Tradiciones,** Santiago: This neighborhood music venue oozes charm and authenticity. It's not touristy and makes for a great night out regardless of the changing musical genre. See p. 289.

o **Ballet Folklorico Cutumba,** Santiago (© 22/65-5173): Try to see a performance by this extraordinary, exciting, and highly professional Afro-Cuban dance group; its base is in the old Cine Galaxia in Santiago. See p. 288.

o **Calle Antonio Maceo,** Baracoa: Tiny Baracoa rocks at night with its own little version of Bourbon Street. People spill out of a half-dozen cafes, bars, and live-music venues, shifting gears from traditional *trova* to *son* and dance music to full-throttle dance club. Amiable emcees entertain audiences with romantic poetry and humor. See "Baracoa After Dark," p. 269.

CUBA IN DEPTH

Cuba is an ongoing and enduring enigma. By any conventional measure, this Caribbean island should be a speck in the global geopolitical ocean. Yet for more than half a century, this nation of 11.4 million people has commanded the world stage in a manner wholly incommensurate with its small size and economic insignificance. A former colony of Spain and playground of American high rollers, Cuba struck out on its own in the late 1950s, and the nation remains a hot topic in the corridors of the world's power brokers. Fiercely independent but rarely free, and the unlikeliest of major players, Cuba arouses passions like perhaps no other nation.

For decades, those inflamed feelings have focused on the Communist regime that one man, Fidel Castro, brazenly engineered. Hated and worshiped in almost equal measure, Fidel Castro defied critics, confounded pundits, and frustrated his own followers. His brother, Raúl Castro, who became president in February 2008, walks the same walk with Cuba's unique brand of home-grown communism. However, Raúl has inherited a crumbling economy during a global recession that has forced him—and the government—to review some of Cuba's socialist policies.

Slowly, though, the world is learning that Cuba is more than a coveted property in a high-stakes game of Risk. Wider exposure to Cuban culture (especially its music and dance), the island's colonial treasures, and the Cuban people has given rise to a love affair that transcends international politics.

CUBA TODAY

Cuba was one of the major stories of the 20th century, from the stunning overthrow of the dictator Fulgencio Batista in 1959 by a ragtag revolutionary army to Fidel Castro's tenacious hold on power. And although virtually everything about Cuba is filtered through an ideological lens, Cuba is a fascinating living laboratory of social and political experimentation, and a test case for a people's perseverance. A defiant Fidel Castro weathered the fierce opposition of the U.S. government and the hostility of Cuban exiles in Miami, just 145km (90 miles) to the north. While some of his radical reform goals have been achieved, Cubans have also been greatly disheartened by the regime's abject failures. The Cuban people have been forced to make unfathomable sacrifices in the face of a poorly planned (and worse performing) economy and the ongoing American trade embargo.

Cuba was once the dazzling iconoclast, held in awe by much of Latin America for its willingness to stand up to the United States. In recent years, though, Fidel Castro found himself increasingly isolated, and few are those who don't believe that Cuba is a Communist dinosaur. Although Castro promoted foreign investment and joint ventures in oil, mining, and tourism, Cuba remains willfully individualistic.

The country's uniqueness is also the source of its phenomenal appeal. Cuba is a puzzling anachronism, a creaky and sputtering country caught in a tortuous time warp. Many of Havana's crumbling colonial buildings are little more than facades, propped up like a movie set. While most of the planet plunges ahead at a dizzying digital pace, Cuba crawls along in slow motion. Homes, which Cubans do not actually own but are instead given title to by the state, have only the most rudimentary appliances—if they have any at all. Vintage Chevy and Cadillac jalopies from the '40s and '50s, their chrome fenders pock-marked and their engines patched together with a hodgepodge of parts, lumber down the streets of dimly lit cities. In rural areas, even antique cars are a luxury; transportation is more commonly by oxen-led cart and rickety iron bicycle.

To many visitors, Cuba offers a mystifying, but welcome retreat from the whiz-bang of technology and convenience to which most of us have become accustomed. Groups of underemployed men while away the hours playing dominoes on card tables set up in the street. Septets of octogenarian musicians play traditional Cuban *son*, music with roots in the 1920s and whose rhythms are largely unaffected by outside influence and changing global tastes. Neighbors gather on doorsteps in the wilting heat of the late afternoon to chat and fan themselves, and they form friendly networks working together to solve problems of accommodations, transportation, plumbing, and electricity.

Many travelers, convinced that Cuba cannot forever remain a land of time travel, hasten to experience the country before it gets reeled in by a ravenous Western world. Cuba's tourist potential is almost unlimited, and the government has embraced tourism as its best and perhaps only hope to bring in hard currency and employ large numbers of people. The largest island in the Caribbean, Cuba is abundantly blessed with palm trees, sultry temperatures, hip-swiveling rhythms, stunning beaches, warm people, a surfeit of rum, and the world's finest hand-rolled cigars. In the mid-1980s, only about 250,000 visitors traveled to Cuba annually; in 2007, there were more than two million visitors. Tourism has now surpassed the source of Cuba's original wealth, the sugar industry, to become the country's top revenue earner. If all Americans were allowed to travel legally, politicians and hoteliers reason, Cuba might receive as many as 10 million visitors annually. Yet massive tourism is still a dream in Cuba. Most travelers still cling to package tours and tourist resorts clustered on beaches.

Modern Cuba is a tangled mass of contradictions. The centralized economy is dependent upon capitalistic joint ventures with foreign investors from Canada, Great Britain, Germany, Italy, and Spain. Plenty of Cubans survive only with the assistance of political and religious opponents of the regime who've fled the country and send hundreds of millions of dollars in hard currency each year to relatives. Until the change of head of state in February 2008, the socialist regime, ostensibly founded upon an egalitarian revolution, didn't allow its own citizens to step foot into certain tourist enclaves, including many resorts, hotels, and restaurants, and a long list of goods and services readily available to foreigners could not be enjoyed by nationals. Many of these goods still cannot be enjoyed by Cubans. Although now allowed to own mobile phones and computers, for example, these consumer goods are beyond the reach of the vast majority of Cubans. Start-up mobile-phone contracts cost CUC$40, but with average salaries of around CUC$10 to CUC$20 a month, owning a mobile phone is a pipe dream for most Cubans.

Cubans often fall back on an all-purpose national refrain to describe what their lives are like: *No es fácil.* It isn't easy. Cubans are specialists in what might be called the *arte de inventar,* the art of inventing solutions where there are none. That means fighting to make ends meet through odd jobs and hustling. Setting up neighborhood networks that distribute contraband goods, such as cigars nicked from the tobacco factory. Running illicit *paladares* in living rooms and backyards, serving black-market lobster or beef. Cuba is an entire nation jimmy-rigged and bandaged with duct tape.

Unless you're ensconced in a gleaming, all-inclusive beach resort, where the realities of Cuban life are whitewashed for the benefit of tourists, the grinding deficiencies of the Cuban economy and bottomless needs of the Cuban people are hard to ignore. Talk to almost any Cuban and he'll tell you about appallingly overcrowded housing and transport conditions, state rations that don't cover basic needs, the scarcity of basic commodities, and the CUC$10-to-CUC$20 monthly salaries paid in Cuban currency, the national peso, which then must be converted to the convertible peso (CUC) often at an unfavorable exchange rate. Workers trained by the state as engineers and doctors instead scramble for more lucrative positions as bellboys, while others cobble together a few dollars worth of hard currency from occasional, often extralegal, odd jobs. Ration booklets allow Cuban citizens to buy a certain amount of basic goods at highly subsidized prices in Cuban pesos. However, the rations allotted do not suffice: just 5 pounds of rice, 2 pounds of white sugar, 3 pounds of dark sugar, 1 packet of coffee, and half a pound of oil. Rations have been cut back since 2008, and supplies like cigarettes, beans, chicken, and some other products are difficult to get. A few other goods are available on an irregular basis, such as fish, ham, and toothpaste. Anything beyond those miserly provisions—the odd piece of beef, a pair of decent shoes—must be purchased on the black market or in hard currency–only stores.

Yet Cuba is remarkably free of the crushing poverty sadly common in Africa, India, and even other parts of Latin America. Housing is provided by the state—homeless people sleeping on the streets are nowhere to be seen in Cuba—and all citizens receive regular food rations. Many appear surprisingly well dressed, no doubt a privilege of possessing a job that earns a few dollars or having family members outside of Cuba who send money that helps ease the pain.

Fidel Castro took power in 1959 with a commitment to remake the nation by overhauling its economy, land ownership, education system, and healthcare. On a social agenda, Cuba has been remarkably successful. All Cubans receive free healthcare. However, most hospitals and pharmacies lack the most basic supplies, like aspirin and X-ray plates. The fabric and interior of some hospitals are appallingly outdated and back-up electricity generators for *apagónes* (power cuts) have been known to fail while operating theaters are in use. Compulsory state education through high school is free, and the national university system has produced some extremely accomplished professionals in medicine and the sciences. Average life expectancy rose from 57 years in 1958 to 77 in 2006—the highest in Latin America. Infant mortality, just 6.22 per 1,000 births, is the lowest in the region and equal to or better than many developed countries. Literacy rates are above 95% (the government claims to have erased illiteracy entirely), violent crime is almost nonexistent, and the pervasive sexism and racism of pre-revolutionary Cuba have given way to a more equitable landscape.

Those achievements receive less attention, though, than Cuba's strangled economy and continued political repression. Opponents of the socialist regime, both outside of Cuba and increasingly within the country, make the case that Cuba is a nation with no semblance of democracy. A single political party dominates all Cuban life. Cubans cannot speak freely, the media are state-owned and closely orchestrated by the Communist Party, and ordinary citizens have no rights to travel freely beyond Cuba.

Hundreds of thousands of Fidel Castro's early opponents fled Cuba in the early days of the Revolution, when the state was busy expropriating private property, land, and businesses. Since then, thousands more have tried, only a few successfully, to make it to U.S. shores, often in rickety *balseros* (rafts). The less daring, but equally hopeful form daily queues at the U.S. Interests Section in Havana and other foreign embassies, desperately hoping for exit visas. On three major occasions, including the Mariel Boatlift in 1980, Fidel Castro sought to relieve pressure by allowing large groups, many of them deemed "undesirables," to emigrate.

Although the U.S. trade embargo and travel restrictions are still firmly in place, there has been much focus on new U.S. President Barack Obama, and his policy towards Cuba. Obama's promise to close the U.S. prison at Guantánamo Bay in eastern Cuba (p. 260) has not been met, but he has relaxed rules on Cuban Americans visiting their families in Cuba (p. 34). In 2009 Obama also removed certain restrictions on food and medicines and offered to open a dialogue with Raúl Castro; Castro, in turn, said he was willing to talk to the president about "everything". However, since then, there has been little sign of the geopolitical thaw. The sanctions against Cuba have been renewed twice since spring 2009 and Cuba remains on the U.S.' state sponsors of terrorism list.

However, other promising strides have been made between the U.S. and Cuba. In 2010, a U.S. congressman from Minnesota, Collin Peterson, proposed the **Travel Restriction Reform and Export Enhancement Act,** which would lift restrictions on sales of agricultural goods and effectively end the travel ban for Americans wishing to go to Cuba. In June 2010, the House Agriculture Committee voted in favor of the bill, but this is the start of a long journey. The bill must go before the Foreign Affairs and Financial Services Committees before it goes to the full House. Only then can it go before the Senate. Track the bill's progress on www.govtrack.us/congress/bill.xpd?bill=h111-4645.

However, the Castros' regime still persists. Despite years of difficulty and isolation, *La Revolución,* now 52 years old, continues to be the nation's rallying cry and raison d'être. Schoolchildren don't become Boy or Girl Scouts, but Young Communist Pioneers. Secretive local chapters of the Committee for the Defense of the Revolution (CDR) keep tabs on dissenters and those not upholding the party line. Throughout the country, giant billboards function like government pep talks to convince a population more worried about shoes and food than ideology to stay on the path. Billboards proclaim quaint notions like VICTORIA DE IDEAS (A Victory of Ideas), VIVIMOS EN UN PAIS LIBRE (We Live in a Free Country), LA REVOLUCION SOMOS NOSOTROS (We Are the Revolution), and even the melancholy rationalization SOMOS

FELICES AQUI (We're Happy Here). Larger-than-life portraits of heroes and martyrs like Che Guevara (the roguish icon of revolution the world over), José Martí, Camilo Cienfuegos, and "Los Cinco" (five suspected spies convicted and imprisoned in the United States) guard the entrances to towns and are plastered on the walls of shops, offices, and homes. Perhaps fittingly, most of these billboards and portraits are now worn and faded.

Amid the extraordinary dilapidation of Havana and other decaying towns, it's near impossible for travelers not to wonder: What must this place once have looked like? Formerly grand, and now just badly faded and deteriorated buildings stand—if barely so—as harsh evidence of 5 decades of frustration, empty state coffers, and bankrupt promises of an idealistic, battle-hardened regime. Cubans are exhorted to fight on to bring the Revolution to fruition, but many Cubans, especially the young who've known nothing but Fidel, are weary of waiting. *Un año más*—one more year, they say.

When Raúl Castro replaced his ailing brother in early 2008, there was much talk of hope and great reforms. Many Cubans thought a corner had been turned. And although Raúl did implement some changes when he first took power, it seems that he has only recently started to rethink Cuba's socialist policies now that Cuba's economy is under serious duress. (For more information on the current state of Cuba's economy and politics, see "Cuba Under Raúl Castro," later in this chapter.)

Cuba, though, is as exhilarating as it is perplexing. One of the most exciting, mind-bending, and sensation-tingling countries you can visit, Cuba is a flood of indelible images. Many are inspiring, others heartbreaking. An open-air cafe with a smiling band of preternaturally cool musicians locked in a perfect groove. Huge crowds of hitchhiking Cubans gathered on the side of the road, desperate for a lift. Noisy Carnival rumbas and conga groups piercing the heat with Afro-Caribbean rhythms. Sexy couples with well-oiled hips gliding across dance floors. Those combative billboards forlornly pitched along the side of empty highways. Crowded *camellos,* crazy people-hauler flatbed trucks that look like urban transportation in a post-apocalyptic world. Mile-long lines for ice cream at Coppelia shops. Kids playing *pelota,* the national pastime of baseball, with a stick in the hollows of a ruined building.

But perhaps the truest picture of Cuba comes from the people themselves. Resilient and eternally patient Cubans somehow find the will to rise above devastating poverty, shortages, dense bureaucracy, and political authoritarianism. With wonderful senses of humor and hospitality like few others, they invite visitors into their cramped homes even if they've nothing to offer them. Schoolchildren, like an ad for the UN in identical maroon and mustard-colored uniforms, smile sweetly for photographs.

Cuba remains a quandary and a country full of potential. Hope can be seen in the painstaking restoration of landmark colonial buildings in La Habana Vieja, whose decrepitude only a few years ago was the perfect metaphor for Cuba. Now that the ailing Fidel Castro is mostly in the background, all eyes are firmly on Raúl Castro and the flurry of proposed reforms that he announced in summer 2010 to relieve the desperate economic situation in the country (see "Cuba Under Raúl Castro," later in this chapter).

LOOKING BACK AT CUBA

In the first half of the 20th century, the United States, the primary purchaser of Cuba's sugar, dominated the island's economy and to a considerable extent controlled its political processes. Until the 1950s, Cuba was besieged by political corruption and violence. Fulgencio Batista, though only a sergeant in the army, managed to dictate Cuba's internal affairs through a series of puppet presidents for nearly a decade before winning the presidency outright in 1940. Though Batista retired in 1944, he staged a military coup and returned to power in 1952. Batista's corrupt dictatorship, supported by the United States, overlooked growing poverty across the country while Batista fattened his overseas bank accounts.

Havana was effectively ruled by a group of millionaires more powerful than anywhere else in Latin America, a distortion that allowed Cuban officials to claim that Cuba had the second-highest per capita income in the region. The capital was overrun by brothels, casinos, and gangsters, with high rollers in zoot suits transforming the city into their personal playground. Meanwhile, most of the country was mired in poverty, and more than half of all Cubans were undernourished in 1950. The nascent republic's unequivocal dependence on the United States, corruption, and absence of social equality reinforced the seeds of discontent that had been planted as far back as the 1920s.

Guerrilla Warfare & Revolution

By the 1950s, the climate was ripe for revolution, though it would come in fits and starts. A band of young rebels attacked the Moncada Barracks, the country's second-most-important military base, in Santiago de Cuba on July 26, 1953 (the rebels would later take the date of the attack as the name for their movement, calling it the *Movimiento 26 de Julio*). The effort failed miserably, and many of the rebels were killed or later captured and tortured by the military. But the attack gave its young leader, a lawyer named Fidel Castro Ruz, the bully pulpit he needed. Jailed and tried for offenses against the nation, Castro's legendary 2-hour defense—presaging an uncanny ability to speak for hours at length about Cuba and the Revolution—included the now-famous words, "History will absolve me" (the title of Castro's revolutionary manifesto). Castro was imprisoned offshore on the Isla de la Juventud until May 1955, when Batista granted an amnesty to political prisoners.

Castro fled to Mexico, where he spent a year in exile planning his return to Cuba and the resumption of his plans to overthrow the government. The following year, Castro sneaked back to the southeastern coast of Cuba, along with a force of 81 guerrillas, including Ernesto "Che" Guevara and Castro's brother Raúl, aboard a small yacht, the *Granma*. The journey was beset by myriad problems and delays, including unfortunate weather, and Batista's forces were tipped off to the rebels' imminent arrival. Only 15 rebels reached their planned destination, the Sierra Maestra mountains. From such unlikely beginnings, the rebel forces evolved into a formidable guerrilla army, largely through the assistance of peasants who were promised land reforms in exchange for their support.

Following 2 years of dramatic fighting in the mountains and strategic points, Castro's insurrection gained strength and legitimacy among a broad swath of the Cuban population. Batista saw the end in sight and on January 1, 1959, he fled the country for the Dominican Republic. The combat-weary but triumphant rebels, known as the *barbudos* (the bearded ones), declared victory in Santiago de Cuba and then entered Havana a week later.

Cuba Under Fidel Castro

The new government immediately set about restructuring Cuban society: It reduced rents, instituted agrarian reform, and limited estates to 400 hectares (1,000 acres). As part of a comprehensive nationalization program, the government expropriated utilities, factories, and private lands. The fledgling government also embarked upon wide-ranging programs designed to eradicate illiteracy and provide universal healthcare and free schooling.

The Revolution's lofty aims were mitigated by cruder attempts to consolidate state power. The transition to a centralized, all-powerful state antagonized many Cubans, mostly elites. Castro placed the media under state control, as it remains today, and he promised elections that were never held. Local Committees for the Defense of the Revolution (CDRs) kept tabs on dissenters. In the early years of Castro's reign, many thousands of people suspected of opposing the Revolution were interrogated, imprisoned, or sent to labor camps, along with other social "undesirables," such as homosexuals and priests.

In just 3 years after the triumph of the Revolution, nearly a quarter of a million Cubans—mostly professionals and wealthy landowners—fled the country. They settled in nearby Florida and established a colony of conservative Cuban Americans, which, in the coming decades, achieved not only economic success, but also a level of political clout that was disproportionate to its size.

Washington, opposed to Cuba's political evolution and spurred on by politically active Cubans living in Miami, continued to try to isolate Castro in Latin America. Just 1 year after Castro took power, in 1960, the U.S. government launched a trade embargo against Cuba in retaliation for Cuba's state appropriations and seizures of the assets of U.S. businesses. The trade embargo, which Cuba terms a blockade, and travel restrictions later imposed on most U.S. citizens, continue to this day. In 1961, the United States broke diplomatic relations with Cuba, and CIA-trained Cuban exiles launched an attempt to overthrow the Castro government. The Bay of Pigs mission was an utter fiasco and a severe black mark against the Kennedy administration. Cuba's resistance strengthened Castro's resolve to stand up to the United States.

Castro had not revealed any Communist leanings in the decade since coming to power, but soon after the Bay of Pigs, Castro declared himself a Marxist-Leninist. Some historians have argued that the aggressive ploys of the U.S. government were fundamental in pushing the Cuban government into the arms of the American enemy in the Cold War, the Soviet Union and its Eastern bloc of potential trading partners. The USSR was only too eager to develop a strategic relationship with an ideological opponent of Washington in the backyard of the United States. By the end of the 1980s, the USSR dominated Cuban trade and provided Cuba with subsidies worth an estimated $5 billion annually.

In the fall of 1962, the Soviet Union under Nikita Khrushchev installed 42 medium-range nuclear missiles in Cuba. A tense standoff ensued when President Kennedy ordered a naval blockade on the island and demanded that the existing missiles be dismantled. The world waited anxiously for 6 days until Khrushchev finally caved to U.S. demands to turn back his ships. The possibility of a nuclear war was averted in return for a U.S. promise never to invade Cuba.

Another 200,000 people abandoned Cuba as part of the Freedom Flights Program between 1965 and 1971. In 1980, Castro lifted travel restrictions and opened the port of Mariel (west of Havana); during the Mariel Boatlift, at least 125,000 Cubans—many of whom Washington charged were criminals and drug addicts—made it to U.S. shores before President Carter forced Castro to close the floodgates.

The Special Period

Soviet trade and subsidies propped up Cuba's heavily centralized and poorly performing economy until the end of the 1980s. But the fall of the Berlin Wall and dismantling of the Soviet Union suddenly left Cuba in an untenable position, as supplies of food, oil, and hard currency were cut off while the U.S. trade embargo continued.

The Cuban government initiated a "Special Period" in 1990—a euphemism for harsh new austerity measures and hardship to be borne by the large majority of Cubans. Rationing of basic goods had existed for most of Castro's years in power, but limited government distribution now included many more necessities. During the Special Period and years since, most Cubans found it virtually impossible to subsist on rations alone.

Complicating the delicate situation was the 1992 Cuba Democracy Act, which broadened the U.S. embargo to cover a ban on trade with Cuba for foreign subsidiaries of U.S. companies. Though the U.S. government denies that its trade embargo can be blamed for the shortcomings in the Cuban economy and resulting shortages of food and medicine, many analysts believe that the embargo has greatly exacerbated the difficulties experienced by ordinary Cubans. Meanwhile, Castro held onto power and made few concessions, even using the U.S. trade restrictions to his advantage: They gave him something and someone to blame for Cuba's grinding poverty and lack of goods.

With the economy in shambles, the Cuban government has been forced to introduce a limited number of capitalist measures. Foreign investment, which has taken the form of joint ventures primarily in the fields of tourism and mineral and oil exploration, has been openly encouraged. Castro, with inescapable irony, legalized the U.S. dollar in 1993—even establishing state-owned, dollar-only stores, small-scale private enterprises like *casas particulares* and *paladares* (private homestays and restaurants), and the introduction of private farmers' markets. While these capitalist initiatives have benefited some Cubans, giving them access to hard currency (through jobs in tourism or relatives sending remittances from abroad), the dual economy has ultimately turned many other Cubans into have-nots, unequal in a socialist society.

In August 1994, in a frantic safety-valve measure designed to alleviate some of the economic pressure on the state, Castro lifted restrictions on those wishing to leave. More than 30,000 Cubans accepted the invitation and set out across dangerous waters to Florida on *balseros* (homemade rafts). Faced with the political embarrassment of an influx of poor Cubans, President Clinton abolished the standing U.S. policy granting automatic asylum to Cuban refugees. Instead, they were returned to the Guantánamo Bay Naval Base to await repatriation.

After Castro visited the Vatican in 1996, Pope John Paul II returned the favor. His visit to Cuba in 1998 prompted a relaxation of the government's harsh views of the

Catholic Church in Cuba. In late 1999, 6-year-old Elián González became the latest face of political animosity between the United States and Cuba. González survived for 2 days alone on a raft after his mother and other escapees had perished, only to become the object of an international tug-of-war. Castro and most Cubans, in huge demonstrations, demanded the boy's return to be with his father in northern Cuba. Castro's opponents in the United States sought to allow the boy to stay with distant relatives in Miami. After weeks of wrangling, the Immigration and Naturalization Service returned Elián to his father and Cuba, where he received a hero's welcome.

The normally quiet U.S. naval base at Guantánamo Bay has been in the news in recent years after Al Qaeda prisoners from the wars in Afghanistan and Iraq were taken to the base for interrogation and detention. Former President Jimmy Carter made a historic visit to Cuba in the spring of 2002, voicing support for Castro's call for an end to the trade embargo and travel restrictions while also criticizing the Cuban government's lack of democracy. Carter met with dissidents and gave an uncensored and at times harshly critical speech in front of Castro that was broadcast on Cuban television.

However, Carter's visit had little lasting effect. In 2003, Castro jailed some 75 prominent dissidents and government critics, imposing stiff sentences following abbreviated trials. In early 2004 and again in 2006, the Bush administration tightened the screws on U.S. citizens' right to travel to Cuba, virtually eliminating all educational and humanitarian licenses and severely reducing the amount of time and money that Cuban Americans can spend in Cuba.

In July 2006, Fidel Castro fell ill and withdrew from public life. His younger brother Raúl became acting president. Fidel Castro relinquished power in February 2008 and Raúl was unanimously elected as Cuba's new president by the country's National Assembly.

Cuba Under Raúl Castro

One of the first reforms that Raúl instituted following his election as Cuba's new president was the lifting of restrictions on Cubans owning TVs, DVD players, computers, and other electrical appliances. This was followed by a move to decentralize the state-run agricultural economy, including allowing farmers to till fallow land and to buy their own equipment. In June 2008, Raúl abolished the egalitarian wage system, allowing hard-working employees to earn a better salary, and raised the state pension. In July 2008, Raúl authorized land grants for private farming. This move was aimed at boosting agricultural production and reducing the amount of food that Cuba imports. Then Raúl lifted the restrictions on cellphone ownership and the prohibition preventing Cubans from staying in tourist hotels. However, freedom to travel abroad is still restricted and access to the Internet is also heavily restricted.

Like much of the world, Cuba suffered from the effects of the global recession: tourism was down and oil imports were limited because of a lack of cash. At the same time, Cuba was still reeling from spending millions of dollars that were needed to restore parts of the country battered by three hurricanes in autumn 2008. Cuba's economy has become so strained that in a rare nod to private property development, Cuba signaled that it would allow foreign companies to develop golf and leisure developments with 99-year leases. One of those companies celebrating this news is Britain's **Esencia** (www.esenciahotelsandresorts.com).

It seems that Cuba's crumbling economy has forced Raúl to review some of Cuba's socialist policies. Raúl has said that "We have to end forever the notion that Cuba is the only country in the world where you can live without working," and he has instituted some fairly radical reforms. On January 1, 2009, Cuba celebrated the 50th anniversary of the Revolution, and after this low-key celebration, government officials announced that Cubans with the financial means could build their own homes—a huge advance. Later that year, Castro leased millions of acres of uncultivated fertile state land to private farmers; this was followed, in April 2010, with news that barber shops and beauty salons could trade privately, joining private restaurants (*paladares*) and bed and breakfasts (*casas particulares*) as means of self-employment. Since fall 2010, Cubans have been permitted to sell home-grown products from their homes and kiosks; this signals the end of Cuba's roadside sellers, who would illicitly flag traffic down on the highway to sell items like cheese or fruit. Also in fall 2010, the Cuban government announced it would lay off more than a million state workers in the next few years. Some Cubans hoped that these unemployed state workers would be allowed to run small, private businesses—and indeed, the government soon after announced proposals to allow 178 forms of self-employment (*cuenta propia*), including *casa particulares*, *paladares*, some forms of transportation, and guiding services. As of November 2010, only the punitive tax codes had been issued; licenses to launch the new forms of self-employments were expected soon after. The Communist Party's media, *Granma* (www.granma.cubaweb.cu), is the best source of up-to-date information on this issue. Unfortunately, infrastructure issues, like electricity blackouts, transportation problems, food shortages, and rationing of air-conditioning and supplies still persist.

Cuba's economy is on its knees, pilfering from the state is widespread, and many Cubans are eagerly awaiting the prospect of self-employment licenses so that they can earn a decent living. However, it remains to be seen how these workers, who have only ever known state employment under the Castros, will manage and survive in private and self-employment.

CUBA'S ART & ARCHITECTURE
Architecture

Before the arrival of the Spaniards in 1492, Cuban Indians, such as the Siboney and Taíno, lived in *bohíos* (thatched huts). After Cuba was conquered by the Spaniards, the conquistadors imported Spanish and Moorish colonial styles. From 1511, conquistador Diego Velázquez de Cuéllar founded the seven *villas* (towns) of Cuba. Fortresses, homes, and buildings centered around courtyards in *Mudéjar* style, and, in later years, Baroque-influenced and neoclassical architecture bloomed. Havana's Old City is the Spanish colonial prize and a UNESCO World Heritage Site. For example, in La Havana Vieja, the Castillo de la Real Fuerza, built between 1558 and 1577, was the first fortress in the New World. The rest of La Habana Vieja (p. 114) is a treasure trove of Spanish colonial architectural excellence. Outside of La Habana Vieja, the historic core of Trinidad is an architectural gem and also a UNESCO World Heritage Site. Parts of Santiago de Cuba and Camagüey also preserve remarkable examples of Spanish architectural styles with the 16th-century Casa de Diego Velázquez in Santiago, named the oldest house in Cuba.

CUBA'S CONTEMPORARY ARTISTS

On a tumbledown street in Havana's Centro district is a wonder room of shoes. Artist **Liudmila López Domínguez** (1977–present) is fascinated by heels, and her studio is adorned with photos of shoes, bronze shoe sculptures, and an installation of shoes on white shelves that forms the colors and shape of the Cuban national flag. Femininity, sensuality, and female life inspire mixed-media artist Domínguez.

Artist **Enrique Baster** (1973–present) lives in a light and airy apartment in Vedado. Here, a large oil painting depicting the Hotel Nacional, towering above a forest of traffic lights, hangs on the living room wall. "The forest is difficult to get through," Baster explained, "and the traffic lights are saying you can go, you can't go, you can go . . . up to the Nacional." This powerful piece of art is a metaphor of the government rules that, prior to 2008, did not allow Cubans to enter their country's hotels. (This rule was later overturned by Raúl Castro.)

The work of **Rocío García** (1955–present) focuses around homoeroticism, a subject she has worked with for around 20 years. Some of her artworks are titled *Geishas* and *Hombres, Machos, Marineros.* Her living room is dominated by an enormous work which depicts broad-shouldered topless red men in black masks, black codpieces, and black boots. Rocío has enjoyed a long and prolific career and is considered one of the masters of contemporary Cuban painting. She also teaches at the Academy of Bellas Artes San Alejandro.

Raúl Castro Camacho, known as Memo, lives in Vedado. Paintings from a 2009 exhibition called *Entre Muros* line the walls of his bedroom. The instantly recognizable Havana Malecón appears as a circular labyrinth in one of these works, *Depresión Tropical.* Memo explained that "the Malecón is the border—a cultural, geographical and political border." Memo pushes boundaries by creating works that are strong political commentaries. His next exhibition, which will show in 2011 at Galería 23 y 12, is called *Penumbras,* a theme that reflects "la cosa está negra" (the thing is black), which refers to the subjects that Cubans cannot talk about publicly and do not know about—the country's political situation.

Artist **Eduardo Yanes Hidalgo** (1977–present), who lives in La Lisa, creates paintings that that depict chess pieces, which he uses to represent relationships of power, family, society, and the struggle between enemies.

It is clear that **Esterio Segura** (1970–present), who lives in the district of Playa, likes to play. His apartment is decorated with various installations from his *frustrada* (frustrated) series, depicting speakers and typewriters imprisoned in cages. Segura's pièce de résistance is a series of irreverent images that he is preparing for the 2012 Havana Art Bienal: *48 Entradas Victoriosas del Héroe a La Habana.* This audacious work consists of 48 framed drawings that portray Fidel Castro posing in various Kama Sutra-esque positions, having sex with the Virgin de la Caridad del Cobre. The 48 images represent the 48 years of power that Fidel was in power. Whether this art work will be approved for exhibition by the government remains to be seen.

See "Art-Havana," p. 124, for information on tours that takes visitors to the studios of Cuba's contemporary artists.

art IN CUBA

The history of *artes plásticas* (plastic arts) in Cuba dates back to 1818, with the foundation of the **San Alejandro Academy** (www.sanalejandro.cult.cu) in Havana. The Academy was created by French painter Juan Bautista Vermay (who painted the frescoes en el Templete in La Habana Vieja, see p. 105) to promote Fine Arts and work made by the black and mulata community. Thus begun a century of academic painting—mostly of landscapes and portraits—influenced by European models.

The 19th century brought new developments for Cuba: a national hymn, a national flag, and nationalistic sentiment; during this time, there was a backlash against academic national art, which gave way to modern art. In the 1930s, Cuban artists began to focus their attention on Cuban roots and the search for national values, resulting in a characteristically Cuban art. Some of these first-generation artists are Víctor Manuel (1897–1969), Carlos Enríquez (1900–1957), Eduardo Abela (1889–1965), Fidelio Ponce (1895–1949) and Wifredo Lam (1902–1982). Subsequently, the 1940s and 1950s brought abstract and expressionist art to Cuba.

Following the 1959 Revolution, art began to promote the ideals of the Revolution. For this reason, the 1960s witnessed an intense movement expressed through painting, poster art, and documentary photography that was attuned to the climate of enthusiasm that prevailed in Cuban society. During the 1970s, many artists born in the far-flung corners of the island began to graduate from new schools of art—like the National Art School founded in 1962 and the School for Art Instructors founded in 1961. Some of the artists that graduated during this era today are grand masters of Cuban art, such as Tomás Sánchez, Nelson Domínguez, Flora Fong, Flavio Garciandía, and Eduardo Roca (better known as CHOCO). They worked at a time when new artistic genres such as Pop Art, kinetic art, and photo realism began to enrich the island's art scene. The 1980s marked a period of thriving growth of the visual arts in Cuba. This was the first time that Cuban artists began to use diverse mediums such as art installations and performance and group art; it was also a time when artists portrayed subjects of political satire, which had previously been taboo.

Cuban modern art has continued to develop and has won both national and international acclaim. The variety of themes and styles of Cuban art today reveal a richness not reached in previous years. For more information on galleries, exhibitions, and artists, consult www.galeriascubanas.com, www.opushabana.cu, and www.cubarte.cult.cu.

—*Sussette Martínez Montero,* principal art curator and representative of Art-Havana (www.art-havana.com) in Cuba

Wonderful examples of art nouveau structures can be found in the Vista Alegre suburb of Santiago (p. 275), and the Havana suburb of Vedado (p. 84). An art deco highlight in Havana is the outstanding **Edificio Bacardí,** built by Esteban Rodríguez Castells and Rafael Fernández Ruenes in 1930 on the edge of La Habana Vieja, topped by the trademark bat symbol. Other highlights are the 1941 **Teatro América** building on Galiano in Centro and the ziggurat-topped **Edificio López Serrano,** designed by Ricardo Mira and Miguel Rosich in 1932 in Vedado. Other noteworthy

A Guide to Cuba's Architectural Details

While you're traveling through Cuba, keep an eye out for these architectural and decorative details that adorn the interiors and exteriors of Cuba's buildings:

o *Mediopunto* are stained-glass windows positioned above wooden doors, introduced in the mid-18th century. Some of the best examples are found on the facade of the Casa del Conde de Bayona and the Hotel Santa Isabel in La Habana Vieja (p. 114).

o *Mamparas* are half-door screens inlaid with plain or decorative glass that were installed in the houses of the rich.

o *Barrotes* are window grilles made of turned wood that date back to the 18th century.

o *Guardevecinos* are plain or decorative wrought-iron grilles that date back to the 19th century; these grilles served to divide neighbors' balconies.

o **Stone balustrades** (small posts that line the upper rail of a railing) line the roofs of many mansions; this became common in the 19th century.

o **Ornamental urns** line the roofs of many mansions; this became a popular feature in the 19th century. An example that has this feature is the Palacio Junco in Matanzas.

buildings in Havana are the 1952 **Tropicana cabaret,** by Max Borges Jr., and the 1957 **Hotel Habana Riviera,** by Igor Polevitzky and Philip Johnson, which was commissioned by Meyer Lansky.

The 1959 Revolution brought not only a change in the country's ideals and policies, but also a change in architectural styles. A crush of Brutalist Soviet blocks were erected, mainly in the form of residential buildings and hotels. Some of these structures evoke the style of famous Swiss architect Le Corbusier, with impersonal open-plan style buildings. Highlights of the post-Revolution period include Ricardo Porro's 1961 sensual and erotic **Instituto Superior de Atte** (continued until 1965 by Roberto Gottardi and Vittorio Garatti) and Mario Girona's 1966 **Coppelia** ice cream parlor.

THE LAY OF THE LAND

Cuba is the largest island in the Caribbean and is some 1,200km (745 miles) long; its greatest width is 210km (130 miles). There is about 6,073km (3,774 miles) of coastline and 345km (214 miles) of beach that shelters sea water that's an inviting 24°C (75°F) year-round.

Some 4,000 islands and islets offshore in both the north and south create an area of 110,992 sq. km (4,2854 sq. miles). There are two principal islands—both off the southern coast—the **Isla de la Juventud** and the tourist enclave of **Cayo Largo del Sur.** Most of the northern coast of the mainland is fringed by white sand beaches and palm trees with coral reefs just offshore; on the southern coast, black sand beaches can be found.

The interior of the island is dominated by three mountain ranges. In the west, stretching down the spine of Pinar del Río province is the **Cordillera de Guaniguanico;** in central Cuba is the **Sierra del Escambray** and in Oriente, the **Sierra**

Maestra, with Cuba's highest mountain, Pico Turquino at 1,974m (6,476 ft.). Waterfalls, such as **Salto del Caburní** in Oriente and **El Nicho** near Cienfuegos, abound. Limestone geology has meant that there are extensive cave networks in the country; those near Viñales, Santo Tomás, and the Cuevas del Bellamar near Matanzas are the most famous. In the World Heritage Site of the **Viñales Valley,** erosion left limestone stumps in its wake. These limestone round-topped mountains covered in clambering vegetation are scattered on the floor of the Valley, and are known as *mogotes.*

Cuba's landscapes are diverse and verdant (some 55 inches of rain fall a year) and include rolling sugar cane fields, tobacco plantations, coffee bushes, rivers, Royal Palms, river canyons, and forests bursting with bird life and orchids; across the country more than 300 protected areas have been established.

There are six UNESCO Biosphere reserves: Guanahacabibes Peninsula and Sierra del Rosario in the west, Parque Nacional Ciénaga de Zapata in the south at the Bay of Pigs; Parque Nacional El Caguanes in the north central area; Parque Nacional Baconao, east of Santiago, and Cuchillas del Toa near Baracoa.

Cuba is also rich in flora and fauna. Some 400 species of bird exist in Cuba (of which 21 are endemic). The most famous bird species is the **tocororo,** a trogon (*Priotelus temnurus*) and Cuba's national bird (it sports the colors of the national flag—red, white and blue). **Flamingos** (*phoenicopterus ruber*) stalk the marshlands of the Zapata peninsula and the saline flats along the north coast from Cayo Coco to Playa Santa Lucía. The smallest bird in the world, the **zunzuncito** (*Mellisuga helenae*), a hummingbird; the world's smallest frog (*Eleutherodactylus iberia*); and the world's smallest bat (*Natalidae lepidus*) all live in Cuba, along with the Cuban crocodile (*Crocodylus rhombifer*) and a rare creature called the Cuban Solenodon (*Solenodon cubanus*). Another unusual Cuban animal is the **jutía,** a tree-loving mammal that is like a cute rat when young. The most endearing of Cuba's fauna is the polymita picta snail, shaded in swirls of yellow, green, black, brown, and white; this rare snail is found near Baracoa.

Cuba is home to about 6,700 species of flora, including 74 endemic plants. A common sight is the **royal poinciana** (*flamboyán*), known for its starburst of red flowers; the mariposa, the white fragrant national flower; the ceiba tree; and enormous hibiscus flowers.

CUBA IN POPULAR CULTURE
Cuban Music

Perhaps no other nation—certainly no other nation of its size—is as spectacularly endowed musically as is Cuba. The seductive sounds of richly percussive Cuban music are, in many people's minds, Cuba's greatest export. In the late 1990s, a series of records and a documentary film brought a group of aging Cuban musicians to the world's attention. The unexpected popularity abroad of the Buena Vista Social Club and its individual artists—Ibrahim Ferrer, Compay Segundo, Rubén González, Eliades Ochoa, and Omara Portuondo—made traditional Cuban sounds very much in demand throughout Cuba and internationally. Buena Vista and company, though, is only the latest round of Cuban music to circle the globe, echoing the earlier mambo and cha-cha-chá crazes that took the United States and Europe by storm in the 1950s.

Within Cuba, music is a daily presence across the island, from rural areas and dusty provincial towns to the capital. It seeps out of cafes and *casas de la trova* (music clubs) in the midafternoon and thunders out of dance halls as the sun rises over the Malecón (promenade). The musical diet is a dizzying menu of styles with uncommon appeal, so emphatically tropical that you can almost hear the humidity in the vocals, chords, and percussion.

Cuba's musical heritage, an onomatopoeic stew of salsa, rumba, mambo, *son, danzón,* and cha-cha-chá, stems from the country's rich mix of African, Spanish, French, and Haitian cultures. The roots of contemporary Cuban popular music lie in the 19th century's combination of African drums and rhythms along with Spanish guitar and melody. Most forms of Cuban music feature Latin stringed instruments, African bongos, congas, and claves (wooden percussion sticks), and auxiliary instruments such as maracas and guiros.

The heartbeat of Cuban music is the clave, which refers to a distinctive rhythm and the instrument used to play it. While the actual instrument is not necessarily played in every song, all Cuban rhythms are built up from the simple concept of the clave. The perennial form of Cuban traditional music is *son* (literally, "sound"; pronounced *sohn*), a style of popular dance music that originated in the eastern, poorer half of the country known as El Oriente in the early 1900s.

You can and will hear live music anywhere you go in Cuba, but the best places for authentic traditional *son* and more modern styles are Havana, Trinidad, Camagüey, Santiago de Cuba, and Baracoa. The last three possess the best *casas de la trova* (music clubs) in the country, spots thick with sultry air, slowly rotating ceiling fans, and grinning octogenarians plunking away on weathered guitars and stand-up basses. Cubans seem only too happy to share the dance floor with tentative foreigners.

Books on Cuba

There's a wealth of books on Cuba's history and politics. For a good historical overview, try Jaime Suchlicki's ***Cuba: From Columbus to Castro and Beyond*** (Brasseys, 2002), or Richard Gott's ***Cuba: A New History*** (Yale University Press, 2005). More than 1,800 pages, Hugh Thomas's ***Cuba, or The Pursuit of Freedom*** (Da Capo Press, 1998) is far more comprehensive and fascinating, but it takes a while to read.

A unique account of post-revolutionary Cuba comes from a well-known Latin American journalist, Alma Guillermoprieto, who writes of the 6 months she spent in Cuba in the early '70s teaching dance. ***Dancing with Cuba: A Memoir of the Revolution*** (Vintage, 2005) is a portrait of the artistic world of Cuba in the '70s and a self-reflective memoir of the author's political awakening.

No reading list for Cuba would be complete without a biography or two of Fidel Castro and Che Guevara. The best are Leycester Coltman's ***The Real Fidel Castro*** (Yale University Press, 2005), Tad Szulc's ***Fidel: A Critical Portrait*** (Avon Books, 2000), and Jon Lee Anderson's ***Che Guevara: A Revolutionary Life*** (Grove, 1997). Another Fidel biography is ***Fidel Castro: My Life*** (Penguin, 2007) by journalist Ignacio Ramonet. Also worth a read are ***Guerilla Prince: The Untold Story of Fidel Castro*** (Little, Brown, 2002) by Georgie Anne Geyer, and ***The Life and Death of Che Guevara*** (Vintage, 1998) by Jorge Castañeda. There are also several volumes of writings worth looking into by both Fidel and Che. Che's own ***The Motorcycle Diaries: Notes on a Latin American Journey*** (Ocean Press, 2003) provides an interesting glimpse into the social and psychological genesis of this great revolutionary figure, although it deals with the period in Che's life prior to meeting Fidel and going to Cuba. The book was made into a very successful film (*The Motorcycle Diaries*) by director Walter Salles.

Another compelling perspective on the Revolution is offered by Enrique Oltuski, a former Shell Oil engineer and a leader in the 26th of July movement, in **Vida Clandestina: My Life in the Cuban Revolution** (Jossey-Bass, 2002).

Any exploration into Cuban literature should include the works of poets José Martí and Nicolás Guillén, as well as the novels and prose writings of Alejo Carpentier and José Lezama Lima. Prominent works that exist in English include Guillermo Cabrera Infante's **Three Trapped Tigers** (Marlow, 1997), and several of Reinaldo Arenas's novels and his best-selling autobiography **Before Night Falls** (Penguin, 1994), made into a stunning film by Julian Schnabel.

Also worth reading is Cristina García's novel, **Dreaming in Cuban** (Ballantine, 1993), which chronicles the lives of three Cuban women after the Revolution. If you like García's book, you might also enjoy Ana Menéndez's **Loving Che** (Atlantic Monthly Press, 2003), the story of one woman's quest to uncover the mysteries and romance of her mother's past.

New, interesting reads include the **Wildman of Rhythm: the Life and Music of Benny Moré** (University Press of Florida, 2009) by John Radanovich, and **The Sugar King of Havana: The Rise and Fall of Julio Lobo, Cuba's Last Tycoon** (Penguin Press, 2010) by John Paul Rathbone.

Of course, it goes without saying that you've already read Hemingway's **The Old Man and the Sea** (Scribner, 1952) and Graham Greene's **Our Man in Havana** (Heinemann, 1958).

Cuban Films

In addition to the poignant *Before Night Falls* and the excellent *The Motorcycle Diaries,* mentioned above, there are a host of wonderful films that can be rented prior to any trip to Cuba or bought while you are there from ARTex stores (www.cubacine. cu). One true classic film available on DVD is **Soy Cuba (I Am Cuba)** by the great Russian director Mikhail Kalatozov, who shot this Communist-era piece of social-realist propaganda in Cuba shortly after the Revolution. The film features a screenplay by Russian poet Yevgeny Yevtushenko and the Cuban writer and filmmaker Enrique Piñeda Barnet.

Cuba's own film industry has produced several fine films, including the celebrated *Fresa y Chocolate* (Strawberry and Chocolate), *Memorias del Subdesarrollo* (Memories of Underdevelopment), and *Muerte de un Burócrata* (Death of a Bureaucrat), all by Tomás Gutiérrez Alea. The animated comedy *Vampiros de la Habana* (Vampires of Havana) by Juan Padrón proved popular. Three of my favorite Cuban films are *Guantanamera* by Tomás Gutiérrez Alea and Juan Carlos Tabío, *Lista de Espera* by Juan Carlos Tabío, and *El Benny* by Jorge Luis Sánchez. Also look out for *Suite Habana* by Fernando Pérez.

For a good look into the conflict between Cubans in Cuba and their relatives and friends in the United States, check out *Azucar Amarga* (Bitter Sugar) by Leon Ichaso, or *Quién Diablos es Julieta* (Who the Hell Is Juliette?) by Carlos Marcovich. The movie *Buena Vista Social Club* documents the rediscovery and newfound fame of some of Cuba's great traditional musicians. The accompanying

Grammy Award–winning CD *Buena Vista Social Club* is as good a place as any to start listening to Cuban music.

Santería & Afro-Cuban Culture

Cuba's prominent African-influenced culture is one of the nation's defining characteristics. African culture brought by slaves and developed within the context of the Spanish colony has had a profound impact on religion, music, and indeed, virtually all of Cuban society.

One of the most salient aspects of Afro-Cuban culture is Santeria (also called *Regla de Ocha*). Frequently misunderstood and misinterpreted as a religious cult or form of voodoo, Santería is in fact a major syncretic and animistic religion that, by most estimates, has a greater following in Cuba than does Catholicism. Its practice is not restricted to Afro-Cubans or a certain socioeconomic class.

Havana's **Casa de Africa** museum, Obrapía 157, between San Ignacio and Mercaderes in La Habana Vieja (© 7/861-5798), has exhibits on Santería for those interested in learning more. The museum is open Tuesday through Saturday from 9am to 5pm and Sunday from 9am to 1pm. The **Museo de los Orishas**, Prado 615 between Monte and Dragones (© 7/863-5953), uses mannequins and performance to explain the Santería saints and practices. Through local contacts, Spanish-speaking visitors can sometimes arrange for a *santero* or *babalao* (high priest) to perform ritualistic divinations.

EATING & DRINKING IN CUBA

Do not come to Cuba for fine dining. While it's possible to minimize the pain, finding good food, service, and value is a challenge in Cuba. About 90% of restaurants that cater to tourists are run by large state-owned corporations, and as a whole, they are often overpriced and mediocre. Even the popular and highly touted restaurants here often suffer from inconsistency and indifferent service. *Note:* Be especially on the lookout for overcharging, either in the form of phantom charges or inflated prices.

In addition to hotel restaurants and official state-run tourist restaurants, the principal dining option in Cuba is the *paladar*. Like *casas particulares, paladares* are private homes that have been granted permission to serve foreign tourists. *Paladares* are small, with a seating limit of just 12, and subject to various limitations (although you will find in Havana that a few of the popular choices clearly do not adhere to the rules and are still operational). They cannot serve shrimp or lobster for instance, and cannot accept credit cards. They are also heavily taxed by the state. *Note:* In September 2010, the government announced plans that would permit *paladares* to accommodate up to 20 seats and to serve beef and shellfish; at press time, however, these proposals had yet to become a reality. However, Cubans are a creative lot and you will find *paladares* that have figured ways around many of these limitations. *Paladares* tend to open and close, move, or change their name or menu with great frequency. They also often run out of menu items, or simply can't find the raw materials to begin the day with. However, there are some dependable and long-standing *paladares*. In general, you should tip between 10% and 15%, keeping in mind that this represents a huge amount of hard currency for most Cubans. Some state restaurants add a 10% service charge to bills; this will not go to the waitstaff. Also, if you show up at a *paladar* on the recommendation of a taxi driver or *jinetero,* you can expect to pay a commission of between CUC$3 and CUC$5, which is often added to your bill after being paid to the driver or *jinetero* by the paladar.

Given the unique economic and social conditions of Cuba, there is little street food to speak of, aside from a few odd pizza and ice-cream vendors. Cuban street pizza has heavy dough, with a molten mess of sauce and gooey cheese topping, served as small individual discs on wax paper. Peanuts (*mani*) sold in newspaper cones and a peanut-and-toffee bar are also popular.

With a recent influx of foreign capital and a move toward modernization, fast-food chains have begun popping up around Cuba. The most prominent of these is **El Rápido,** which has numerous outlets serving fried chicken, burgers, hot dogs, microwave pizzas, and other fast-food staples. Another chain worth mentioning is **Pizza Nova,** which has several outlets in Havana and in various provincial cities. This chain specializes in thin-crust pizza and good pastas.

Local Cuisine

Cuban, or *criolla,* cuisine is a mix of European (predominantly Spanish) and Afro-Caribbean influences. The staples of the cuisine include roasted and fried pork, beef, and chicken, usually accompanied by rice, beans, plantains, and yucca. Oddly, Cubans do not eat large amounts of seafood, although fish and lobster dishes are on the menu at most tourist restaurants. In general, Cubans do not use aggressive amounts of spice or hot peppers, although onions, garlic, and, to a much lesser extent, cumin are used fairly liberally.

With the exception of breakfast, most meals are accompanied by some combination of white rice and beans. *Arroz moro,* or *moros y cristianos* (Moors and Christians), is the common name for black beans mixed with white rice. *Congrí* is a similar dish of red beans and white rice already mixed. Sometimes the rice and beans are served separately.

The national dish—which, unfortunately, you won't often find on restaurant menus, but it's worth sampling if you do—is *ajiaco,* a chunky meat and vegetable stew. *Ajiaco* comes from the Taíno word *aji* for chile pepper, although the dish is seldom prepared very spicy. You're much more likely to find *ropa vieja* (literally, "old clothes"), a sauté of shredded beef, onions, and peppers; or *picadillo,* a similar concoction made with ground beef and sometimes featuring olives and raisins in the mix.

La Bomba

If you want to order papaya, remember to call it *fruta bomba.* In Cuba, the word *papaya* is almost always used as pejorative slang referring to a woman's most private part.

If you're looking for a light snack, try a *bocadito,* literally a "little bite," which is what they call a simple sandwich, usually made of ham and/or cheese.

Aside from the excellent Coppelia ice creams, you'll generally find rather slim pickings for dessert. Flan is popular, but seldom outstanding. I feel similarly about *natilla,* a simple sweet pudding that usually comes in either chocolate or coconut flavors. Many dessert menus will feature some sort of sweet marmalade, usually *guayaba,* papaya, or coconut, accompanied by cheese. Unfortunately, the cheeses are generally bland and nondescript.

Wetting Your Whistle

Most Cubans simply drink water or any number of popular soft drinks, including Sprite and Coca-Cola, whose locally produced equivalents are called Cachito and Tu Cola, respectively. While many hotels and restaurants serve freshly squeezed orange juice for breakfast, you'll have a harder time finding other fresh fruit juices than you'd expect in the Caribbean tropics unless you are staying in a *casa particular*. One of the more interesting nonalcoholic drinks is *guarapo*, the sweet juice of freshly pressed sugar cane.

Cubans also drink plenty of coffee, and they like to brew it strong. Order *café espresso* for a straight shot, or *café con leche* if you'd like it mixed with warm milk. Ask for *café americano* if you want a milder brew.

Cuba produces a small handful of pretty good lager beers. Cristal, Bucanero, and Mayabe are the most popular. If you want something slightly darker and stronger, try a Bucanero dark. Cuba does produce excellent rums. Most visitors soon have their fill of *mojitos* (light rum with lime juice, fresh mint, sugar, and club soda) and daiquiris. Another popular cocktail is the *cuba libre* ("Free Cuba"), which is simply a rum and Coke with lime.

PLANNING YOUR TRIP TO CUBA

merican citizens are not allowed to travel directly to Cuba without a U.S. Treasury Department license. Travel is sometimes arranged through a third country instead (see "Entry Requirements," below). Once in Cuba, U.S. citizens will encounter no restrictions. All travelers must be aware that hurricanes may strike from June until November. Cuba has a very effective hurricane response operation. If planning to visit during an important carnival, make arrangements for your accommodations and rental car in advance; the supply of rental cars sometimes runs out. Be aware that if you have dietary restrictions, travel could be problematic as there is little variety in food in Cuba, and if you take regular medicines, bring them all with you. In fact, if you need anything in particular while you travel, bring it with you. There is very little to buy in Cuba.

For additional help in planning your trip and for more resources in Cuba, please turn to "Fast Facts," on p. 295.

WHEN TO GO

The tourist high season runs from December through March, coinciding with the winter months in most northern countries. It also coincides with Cuba's dry season. Throughout this season, and especially around the Christmas and Easter holidays, the beaches and resorts are relatively full, prices are somewhat higher, and it may be harder to find an available rental car or room. There is also a mini high season in July and August. Overbooking—a widespread problem in the Cuban tourism industry—is much more of a problem during the high season. During the low season, you can find discounts. Moreover, resorts and attractions are much less crowded. However, temperatures are somewhat higher throughout the low season, and periods of extended rainfall are not uncommon.

Climate

Cuba has two distinct seasons, rainy (May–Oct) and dry (Nov–Apr). The dry season is characterized by consistently sunny and temperate weather, with daytime temperatures averaging between 75° and 80°F (24°–27°C). However, temperature swings are greater during this period, and it can actually get somewhat chilly when cold fronts—or "northers"—creep down the eastern seaboard of the United States, particularly in the months of January and February. In contrast, the rainy season is overall a slightly warmer period in Cuba, with less dramatic same-day temperature swings. There's a small dry spell most years during August, which is also the hottest and most humid month to visit Cuba. The entire Caribbean basin is affected by an annual hurricane season (June–Nov), with September and October having the highest number of hurricanes.

Calendar of Events

Cuba has a packed schedule of festivals, congresses, and carnivals, and it seems like more are being held each year. If no specific contact information for a particular event is offered below, you can contact **Paradiso** (✆ **7/832-9538;** www.paradiso.cu), the tour agency arm of the national arts and cultural organization ARTex. Paradiso organizes theme tours and escorted trips based around most of the major festivals and cultural events occurring throughout the year. You can also find pretty good information at **www.cubatravel.cu** and **www.cubaabsolutely.com**.

For an exhaustive list of events beyond those listed here, check http://events.frommers. com, where you'll find a searchable, up-to-the-minute roster of what's happening in cities all over the world.

FEBRUARY

International Book Fair, Havana. This large gathering of authors, publishers, and distributors is really only of interest to those who can read in Spanish. But if you can, this is an excellent Latin American book fair. For more information, visit www.cubaliteraria. cu. Second week of February.

Habanos Festival, Havana. Cigar smokers won't want to miss this annual celebration of the Cuban stogie. Run by the official state cigar company, Habanos, S.A., events include lectures, factory visits, tastings, and a gala dinner with an auction of rare cigars. For more information, visit www.habanos. com. Late February.

MARCH

International Festival of "La Trova" Pepe Sánchez, Santiago de Cuba. If you like the sounds of traditional Cuban folk music, you'll want to hit this festival. Buena Vista Social Club member Eliades Ochoa organized a recent festival. Local Santiagueros are the heart of the festival, but singers and groups come from the entire island and throughout Latin America. Mid-March.

Celebration of Classic Cars, Havana. Recognizing the appeal of its huge fleet of classic American cars, Cuba has organized a weeklong celebration of these Detroit dinosaurs. Events include lectures, mechanical workshops, and parades. Owners from other countries are encouraged to bring their wheels to Cuba, and a caravan from Havana to another colonial city is usually orchestrated. Mid-March.

APRIL

Havana Bienal 2012, Havana. This is one of the premier Latin American art shows, bringing together and exhibiting a wide range of contemporary Latin American artists who work in a broad range of mediums and styles. Havana's celebrated arts' fair, forum, and festival takes place across a variety of venues in the capital. Each bienal has a different theme. Occurring every 3 years. www.bienalhabana.cult.cu. Throughout April.

MAY

May Day parades, nationwide. If you're in Cuba on May Day, the traditional socialist celebration of Labor Day, you'll want to join (or at least watch) one of the many parades and public gatherings. The big daddy of them all takes place at the Plaza de la Revolución in Havana, where more than 100,000 people usually gather to listen to the president's annual May Day speech. May 1.

International Blue Marlin Tournament, Havana. The Marina Hemingway is the fitting site for this annual big-game fishing tournament. Call ✆ **7/208-9920** ext. 223 or visit www.cubanacan.cu. Late May.

JUNE

International "Old Man and the Sea" Billfish Tournament, Playas del Este, Havana. Marina Tarará is the host to this annual big-game fishing tournament. Call ✆ **7/204-5088** or visit www.internationalhemingwaytournament.com for more information. Second week of June.

International Festival "Boleros de Oro," Havana. You'll be crying in your *mojito* (Cuban highball cocktail) . . . and loving it. Theaters, clubs, and concert halls across Havana will be filled with the sweet and melancholy sounds of bolero. Concerts are also staged in Santiago and other major cities. Late June.

JULY

Fiesta del Caribe/Fiesta del Fuego, Santiago de Cuba. This event features lectures, concerts, parades, and street fairs celebrating Afro-Caribbean culture. Speakers, guests, and musical groups from around the Caribbean are invited and each year the festival is dedicated to a Caribbean area or country. For more information, visit www.casadelcaribe.cult.cu; for reservations, contact **Paradiso** (✆ **22/62-0214;** paradisostgo@scsc.artex.cu). July 3–9.

Carnival, Santiago de Cuba. The most "African" city in Cuba throws an excellent annual carnival. Street parties and concerts are everywhere, and the colonial city is flooded with masked revelers and long conga lines. Second half of July.

AUGUST

Carnival, Havana. Although not nearly as colorful or charismatic as Santiago's Carnival, there's still a good dose of public merriment, street parties, open-air music concerts, and the occasional parade. For more information, visit www.sancristobal.cult.cu. August 3–15.

Carnival, Matanzas. Although not as massive or elaborate as Carnival celebrations in

Havana or Santiago, Matanzas still puts on a good party. The town has strong Afro-Cuban roots, and you'll experience this in body, flesh, food, and song throughout the week. Third week of August.

Symposia de Hip Hop Cubano, Havana. As Havana sizzles, hot Cuban hip hop music is performed and celebrated at various venues around Havana. The festival is based at the Casa de la Cultura de Plaza, Calzada and Calle 8, Vedado. For more information, contact the Cubana el Rap agency (✆ **7/832-3503**). Third week of August.

SEPTEMBER

Fiesta de la Virgen del Cobre, El Cobre, Santiago de Cuba. Cuba's national saint, the Virgin of Cobre, is revered by Roman Catholics and Santeros alike. There are pilgrimages to her altar in the small town of El Cobre, and celebrations in her honor nationwide. September 8.

OCTOBER/NOVEMBER

Days of Cuban Culture, nationwide. In yet another show of Cuba's omnipresent anticolonial spirit, the period traditionally marking Christopher Columbus's stumbling upon the New World is given over to celebrations of Cuban and Afro-Cuban culture. October 10–20.

International Festival "Matamoros Son," Santiago de Cuba. The silky sounds of Cuban *son* fill the streets and theaters of Santiago. This is a great chance to hear a solid week of some wonderful music. www.cultstgo.cult.cu Third week of October.

Havana International Ballet Festival, Havana. Alicia Alonso, amazingly, is still going strong as the director of the Cuban National Ballet, still one of the most highly regarded troupes on the planet. Alicia uses this cachet to stage a wonderful biennial international festival in the Gran Teatro de La Habana. For information, call ✆ **7/855-3084** or visit www.balletcuba.cult.cu. Occurring in even-numbered years. Late October–early November.

International Fishing Tournament, Jardines del Rey. This event was inaugurated in 2010 on Cayo Guillermo. Captured fish—Blue marlin, sailfish, dolphin fish, and wahoo—accrue points exchanged for silver prizes. For information, contact Jardines del Rey Marlin Branch at comercial@marlin.cco.tur.cu. Late October.

DECEMBER

International Festival of New Latin American Film, Havana. This is one of the premier film festivals in Latin America. A packed schedule of films is shown in theaters over a period of 10 days throughout Havana. For information, visit www.habanafilmfestival.com. Early December.

International Jazz Festival, Havana. This festival is organized by none other than Chucho Valdés. The event usually draws a handful of top international bands and soloists to share the stage and billing with a strong stable of Cuba's best jazz talents. Visit www.festivaljazzplaza.icm.cu. Third week of December.

Las Parrandas, Remedios. This extravagant public carnival features late-night parades with ornate floats, costumed revelers, and a serious amount of fireworks. The big event occurs on December 24, but between the preparations, practice runs, and smaller imitations in neighboring towns, you'll be able to catch some of the excitement throughout most of late December. Late December.

ENTRY REQUIREMENTS

Passports

All travelers to Cuba must possess a valid passport, a return ticket, travel insurance policy with medical coverage, and a visa or tourist visa. Unlicensed U.S. citizens may be allowed a stay of up to 90 days upon entry. British citizens are granted 30 days upon entry. This can be extended for another 30 days within Cuba. Canadian citizens are granted a visa for 90 days. This can be extended for 90 days only.

Visas

Tourist visas are generally issued by the ticketing airline or travel agent. (If you book a flight with Air Canada, the visa is included in the price.) In a worst-case scenario, the visa can usually be bought on the spot upon clearing Customs.

For U.S. and Canadian citizens, tourist visas cost around US$23/C$23, depending upon the issuing agent, and are good for up to 90 days although Customs agents will sometimes issue them for just 30 days, or until the date of your return flight, unless you request otherwise. They can be extended for another 30 days (90 days for Canadians) once you arrive in Cuba for an additional minimum CUC$25 fee. (The fee is related to your length of stay.) In order to extend your tourist visa, you must personally go to any immigration office in the country. An additional 90-day extension for Canadians can be granted once at any immigration office for a cost of approximately CUC$25. For further information in Canada, contact the Cuban Embassy at www.embacubacanada.net, the Cuban consulate in Toronto at cubacon1@on.aibn.com, or the Cuba tourist board in Canada at www.gocuba.ca.

In the U.K., if you buy a ticket for an independent flight, you will need to purchase a separate tourist visa. Some travel companies are charging exorbitant costs for this (up to £50). While the visa is also available from the **Cuban Embassy** in London for £15 plus postage (www.cubaldn.com), the cheapest, most efficient and reliable place to get a visa is directly from www.visacuba.co.uk. U.K. citizens are granted entry for 30 days. This can be extended once at any immigration office for an additional 30

WHAT TO pack

Pack everything you think you might need while traveling in Cuba. All consumer products in Cuba are either non-existent or scarce. Bring all medicines, special toiletries, contact lenses, special foods, reading materials, clothes, and sun protection. Opticians do exist, but pack a prescription just in case. Sun screen is available at resorts, but you'll pay exorbitant prices for it. Baseball caps can be found in some stores but proper sun hats can not. Bring sturdy luggage and locks; these cannot be replaced. Also, bring electricity adaptors and any unusual batteries.

days for CUC$25. It is then possible to request another 30 days but this must be referred to the provincial immigration office and there is no guarantee of success.

Note that when seeking a **tourist visa extension,** you need to purchase bank stamps (*sellos para la visa*) for the value of the extension you need before going to the immigration office. To avoid making unnecessary journeys, ask your hotel or *casa particular* to call the local immigration office and ask the price of the extension before heading to a branch of the Banco de Crédito y Comercio, the only bank authorized to sell the stamps.

In the event you need a specific work visa, or if your travel agent or airline will not provide you with the tourist visa, you should contact the Cuban consulate or embassy in your home country.

FOR RESIDENTS OF THE UNITED STATES

While it is not illegal for U.S. citizens to travel to Cuba, most are prohibited from spending any money in Cuba. This, in effect, is the "travel ban." The complicated prohibition, which allows for various exceptions, is governed by the U.S. Treasury Department and the Office of Foreign Assets Control (OFAC). For more information, visit www.treas.gov/offices/enforcement/ofac/programs/cuba/cuba.pdf.

The Treasury Department grants certain licenses. Some of these licenses are implicit, such as those for full-time journalists and government workers on official business. Other licenses must be applied for on a case-by-case basis with the U.S. Treasury Department. Since September 2009, **Cuban Americans** can now visit close relatives in Cuba for as long as they and want as often as they want, subject to per diem payment restrictions (http://aoprals.state.gov), currently US$179 per day for stays in Havana. See the U.S. Treasury Department rules for definition of close relative.

Travel arrangements for licensed travelers can be made by an authorized Travel Service Provider (TSP), and travel can be made directly from U.S. gateway cities on regular charter flights. There are hundreds of authorized TSPs. A couple of the most dependable are **ABC Charters** (© 305/263-6829; www.abc-charters.com) and the helpful **Tico Travel** (© 800/493-8426 in the U.S. or Canada, or 954/493-8426; www.destinationcuba.com). If you are unsure about the legality of any other service provider, visit www.treas.gov/offices/enforcement/ofac/programs/cuba/cuba_tsp.pdf.

Be careful about signing on for a "fully hosted" trip. According to the regulations, a U.S. citizen can travel to Cuba without violating the Treasury ban provided he or she does not pay for any goods or services, including food and lodging, or provide any services to Cuba or a Cuban national while in the country. This provision had been widely used by U.S. citizens to buy packages from Canadian, Mexican, or Bahamian tour agencies. However, the Treasury Department has caught on to this tactic and has declared any "fully hosted" trip that is clearly for pleasure or tourism is in violation of the regulations.

Failure to comply with Department of Treasury regulations may result in civil penalties and criminal prosecution upon return to the United States. For more information, contact the **Office of Foreign Assets Control,** U.S. Department of the Treasury, 1500 Pennsylvania Ave. NW, Treasury Annex, Washington, DC 20220 (© **202/622-2000;** www.treas.gov/ofac).

As far as Cuba is concerned, U.S. travelers are welcomed with open arms. In fact, as an aid to those seeking to circumvent the Treasury ban, Cuban immigration does not actually stamp U.S. passports, or any for that matter (but you should ask the officer to be sure)—instead, officers stamp the tourist visa. For current information on Cuban entry and Customs requirements, you can contact the **Cuban Interests Section** (© **202/797-8518**).

UNLICENSED TRAVEL   It is estimated that as many as 200,000 U.S. citizens travel to Cuba each year without a Treasury Department license. The vast majority of travelers use third-country gateway cities like Toronto, Montreal, Cancún, Mexico City, Nassau, George Town on Grand Cayman, or Kingston in Jamaica, and are never questioned or bothered by U.S. authorities upon return.

WHAT TO DO IF YOU GET BUSTED   Officially, U.S. citizens who violate the ban face up to 10 years in prison, $250,000 in criminal fines, and $65,000 in civil fines, but according to the Treasury, penalties range from $3,000 to $7,500. Just 21 people were penalized in 2006. If you are stopped upon returning from an unlicensed trip to Cuba and directly asked by the Customs and Immigration agents, you should give as little information as possible. United States citizens cannot be compelled to provide self-incriminating information. Furthermore, you cannot be denied reentry into the U.S. for traveling to Cuba. You will likely face a long and uncomfortable search and questioning session, and be sent on your way. This will probably be followed by the receipt of a pre-penalty notice from the OFAC. The letter will request specific information to prove or disprove your alleged travel to Cuba, and to threaten the various fines and penalties. At this point, you should contact the **Center for Constitutional Rights** (© **212/614-6470;** http://ccrjustice.org), which runs the Cuba Travel Project and works in conjunction with the **National Lawyers Guild** (www.nlg.org/cuba) to provide legal assistance to U.S. citizens facing prosecution for traveling to Cuba. Typically, after the initial pre-penalty letter, the OFAC offers to settle the case for a reduced fine in the neighborhood of $1,500 to $2,500. Many travelers have opted to go this route. A very, very small number of cases have ever fully gone to trial.

FOR CUBAN NATIONALS

The Cuban government doesn't recognize dual nationality of travelers from other countries who are Cuban-born or are the children of Cuban parents, particularly those who chose exile in the United States. The Cuban government requires some individuals whom it considers to be Cuban to enter and depart Cuba using a Cuban passport. Using a Cuban passport for this purpose does not jeopardize one's foreign

Some operators and guidebooks recommend lying if asked whether or not
you were in Cuba. If you lie, you then
place yourself at risk for perjury
charges, which in the end are easier for
the United States government to prosecute and are potentially more serious.
I recommend you say little or nothing
about your travel to Cuba, but I don't
recommend that you lie. Remember,
under U.S. law you have the right to
refuse to incriminate yourself.

citizenship; however, you will probably
have to use your home country's passport to exit and enter that country.
Other Cuban nationals and exiles just
need a visa, but acquiring this visa is
more complicated than acquiring the
simple tourist visa used by most other
travelers.

If you are Cuban-born or the child
of Cuban-born parents, you should
check with the Cuban embassy or
consulate in your country of residence, as well as your local immigration authorities. In Canada, contact
the **Cuban Embassy,** 388 Main St.,
Ottawa, Ontario, K1S 1E3 (✆ **613/
563-0141;** www.embacubacanada.net); there are also consulates in Montreal and
Toronto. In the U.K., contact the **Cuban Embassy,** 167 High Holborn, London,
WC1 6PA (✆ **0207/240-2488;** www.cubaldn.com). In the U.S., contact the
Cuban Interests Section, 2630 16th St. NW, Washington, DC 20009 (✆ **202/
797-8518**).

Customs

WHAT YOU CAN BRING INTO CUBA

You may bring in all manner of personal effects, including video and still cameras,
personal electronic devices, jewelry, and sports equipment. In addition, visitors
may bring in up to two bottles of liquor, a carton of cigarettes, and up to 10 kilo-
grams of medications, provided they are in the original packaging. You may now
import personal laptops, flash sticks, MP3 players, DVD players, film cameras,
and sports equipment, as well as walkie talkies, satellite equipment, and GPS
mechanisms. By law you may only import up to CUC$1,000 worth of any mer-
chandise, and there is a 100% duty on all but the first CUC$50 worth. In practice,
most visitors can freely bring in reasonable quantities of basic goods, like dried
foods, vitamins, pharmaceuticals, and household supplies, without them being
taxed or confiscated.

Note: You may bring unlimited amounts of cash, but you must declare quantities
in excess of US$5,000, as you may have trouble exporting large quantities of cash, if
discovered upon departure. For current and more detailed information, check out
www.aduana.co.cu.

WHAT YOU CAN TAKE HOME FROM CUBA

Travelers may export up to 50 cigars with no questions asked. Larger quantities can
be exported, provided you show proof that they were bought in official Habanos S.A.
outlets. There are restrictions on certain works of art, books, publications, and coins.
Consult www.aduana.co.cu for further information. Travelers are officially limited to
bringing home two bottles of rum or other spirits, although this limit is rarely
enforced. Still, if the Customs officials deem your purchases to be of a commercial
nature, you could face fines or confiscation.

To export works of art, you will need a permit from the **Registro Nacional de Bienes Culturales (National Register of Cultural Heritage),** Calle 17 no. 1009 between Calles 10 and 12, Vedado (© 7/831-3362). Theoretically, any reputable gallery or shop will provide you with this permit along with your purchase. Those buying artwork bought at the new artesanía market in Havana can purchase the permit for CUC$2 at a kiosk in the building.

Note: There's a CUC$25 departure tax. You must pay this in cash, so be sure to have it on hand.

For information on what you're allowed to bring home, contact one of the following agencies:

U.S. Citizens: U.S. Customs & Border Protection (CBP), 1300 Pennsylvania Ave., NW, Washington, DC 20229 (© 877/287-8667; www.cbp.gov). **Note:** U.S. travelers bringing back Cuban-made goods will be considered in violation of the Treasury embargo and their goods will be confiscated. It is also illegal for U.S. citizens to import Cuban products even if they never stepped foot on the island. It does no good to try to convince the Customs agent confiscating your stogies that you bought them in a cigar shop in Canada or Mexico or Costa Rica.

Canadian Citizens: Canada Border Services Agency, Ottawa, Ontario, K1A 0L8 (© **800/461-9999** in Canada, or 204/983-3500; www.cbsa-asfc.gc.ca).

U.K. Citizens: HM Customs & Excise, Crownhill Court, Tailyour Road, Plymouth, PL6 5BZ (© **0845/010-9000;** from outside the U.K., 020/8929-0152; www. hmce.gov.uk).

Australian Citizens: Australian Customs Service, Customs House, 5 Constitution Avenue, Canberra City, ACT 2601 (© **1300/363-263;** from outside Australia, 612/6275-6666; www.customs.gov.au).

New Zealand Citizens: New Zealand Customs, The Customhouse, 17–21 Whitmore St., Box 2218, Wellington, 6140 (© **04/473-6099** or 0800/428-786; www.customs.govt.nz).

Medical Requirements

Since May 2010, all visitors to Cuba must carry proof of medical insurance in order to enter the country. You must have all the vaccines recommended for international travel (tetanus, polio, diptheria, hepatitis A, and cholera). Vaccinations for yellow fever and cholera are not required unless you are arriving from a country where they are prevalent.

GETTING THERE & GETTING AROUND

Getting to Cuba

BY PLANE

Cuba has 10 international airports. Havana is by far the principal gateway, although there are numerous regularly scheduled and charter flights to Varadero (VRA) and Santiago de Cuba (SCU) as well. To a lesser extent, international charter flights from Canada and Europe service Cayo Largo del Sur (CYO), Cienfuegos (CFG), Santa Clara (SNU), Camagüey (CMW), Ciego de Avila (AVI), Holguín (HOG), and Cayo Coco (CCC).

It's roughly a 70-minute flight from Miami to Havana; 3 hours and 30 minutes from New York to Havana; 4 hours and 30 minutes from Toronto or Montreal to Havana; and 9–10 hours from London to Havana. Most of the principal Caribbean basin gateway cities—Cancún, George Town (Grand Cayman), Kingston, Nassau, and Santo Domingo—are between 30 and 90 minutes to Havana by air.

Airfares vary widely, depending on the season, demand, and certain ticketing restrictions. But, given the high number of charter flights and package tours to Cuba, combined with the stiff competition for vacation travel throughout the Caribbean, airfares are relatively cheap, and bargains abound. It really pays to shop around. If you wish to visit Cuba in July and August, a popular tourist season, book in advance because charter flights sell often out at this time.

Cubana (© 7/838-1039; www.cubana.cu) is Cuba's national airline and the principal carrier to the island, with regularly scheduled flights to a score of cities throughout the Americas, Europe, and Canada. (Cubana is code-shared with Aerocaribbean.) To find out which airlines travel to Cuba, please see "Airline Websites," p. 300.

There is no regularly scheduled service between the United States and Cuba, although there are numerous charter flights from Miami, and to a lesser extent from New York and Los Angeles. Licensed U.S. travelers are eligible to use these flights. For more information, see "Escorted General-Interest Tours" and "Special-Interest Trips," later in this chapter.

Getting into Town from the Airport

Cubataxis, the name for all official taxis in Cuba, line up outside the arrivals hall and you will be shepherded to the first in the queue. Despite it being illegal to carry passengers without using the meter, airport taxi drivers will refuse to use them and charge a flat fee of around CUC$20 to Vedado and CUC$25 to La Habana Vieja. The metered fee is around CUC$15. If you arrive at Varadero or Holguin airports, there will be taxis waiting as well as car rental options.

BY BOAT

When arriving by sea, contact the port authorities before entering Cuban waters 19km (12 miles) offshore on VHF channels 16 or 72, or HF channels 2790 or 2760. Skippers do not need to give advance notice or have a prior visa. A visa can be granted on arrival. All crew members must have current passports, and U.S. Treasury Department restrictions (see "Entry Requirements" and "Customs," earlier in this chapter) apply to all U.S. citizens. Skippers will also need to register their vessel upon arrival. A special permit, or *permiso especial de navegación,* is issued. This permit costs around CUC$50 depending on the length of the vessel.

Cuba has a network of state-run, full-service marinas, many run by Náutica Marlin (www.nauticamarlin.com) and Gaviota (www.gaviota-grupo.com). Marinas that function as official points of entry and exit include those in Jardines del Rey, María la Gorda, Cayo Largo del Sur, Cienfuegos, and Santiago de Cuba, as well as the Marina Hemingway in Havana and Marina Dársena in Varadero.

Good resources for any sailor planning to visit Cuba are Simon Charles's *The Cruising Guide to Cuba* (Cruising Guide Publications, 1997) and Nigel Calder's *Cuba: A Cruising Guide* (Imray, Laurie, Norie & Wilson, 1999). While a little dated, both books are full of invaluable information, tips, and firsthand experiences aimed at cruising sailors.

Getting Around

BY PLANE

Cubana (☏ 7/838-1039; www.cubana.cu) is the principal national and international carrier for Cuba. It is code-shared with **Aerocaribbean** (www.fly-aero caribbean.com). There's a full schedule of commuter flights connecting Havana and Varadero with the destination cities of Baracoa, Bayamo, Camagüey, Ciego de Avila, Manzanillo, Nueva Gerona (Isla de la Juventud), Guantánamo, Holguín, Santiago de Cuba, Las Tunas, Cayo Largo, and Cayo Coco. If you know you'll need an internal flight, try to have your travel agent or tour operator book it in advance. If not, you can easily book flights from almost any local tour operator.

BY CAR

Driving a rental car is an excellent way to travel around Cuba. (The legal age requirement is 21.) It gives you great flexibility and allows you to access beautiful off-the-beaten-track places. Many roads are in acceptable condition, while many are severely substandard. And, while there's very little traffic, you'll have to keep a sharp eye out for small and large chasms in the road, horse-drawn carriages, slow-moving tractors, scores of bicyclists, wandering dogs and fowl, and pedestrians taking over major roadways.

It is completely inadvisable to drive at night. It is very unsafe because there is no lighting on highways. Animal-drawn transport, some lorries, bicycles, and pedestrians are also not illuminated, giving rise to highly dangerous driving situations.

The speed limit for cars is 50kmph (31 mph) in the cities, 90kmph (56 mph) on the *carretera,* and 100kmph (62 mph) on the Autopista.

In all cities, there are *parqueos* where you can leave your vehicle attended for 24 hours. This costs from CUC$1 to CUC$2 a night. It may be unwise to leave the vehicle unattended in cities, as theft of wheels and wipers is not unknown.

There is a handful of state-run car-rental companies, with a large, modern fleet of rental cars to choose from. Prices and selection are rather standard, with an abundance of small, economy Japanese and Korean cars. A standard rental car should cost you between CUC$45 and CUC$85 per day, including insurance and unlimited mileage, depending on the model and the season. Low-season (*temporada baja*) prices are, obviously, cheaper. Some agencies start you off with a full tank of gas for which they charge you—in addition to the rental fee—then give no credit for any gas left in the tank upon the return of the car. Discounts are available for multiday rentals. It's always a good idea to have a reservation in advance, especially during peak periods, when cars can get a little scarce. However, there's a Catch-22 here, in that many of the state-run agencies don't have a trustworthy international reservations system. As is the case with rampant overbooking of hotel rooms, when demand outstrips supply, the car-rental agencies will often not honor your supposedly confirmed reservation.

Cubans may now drive rental cars and can be included on your insurance for an additional cost, as can a second foreign driver. Insurance is voided if an accident is shown to be caused by a driver under the influence of alcohol.

Some of the major car rental agencies in Cuba are **Cubacar** (☏ 7/273-2277), **Havanautos** (☏ 7/207-9898), **Micar** (☏ 7/204-7777), **Rex** (☏ 7/835-6830; www.rex.cu), **Transtur** (☏ 7/862-2686; www.transtur.cu), and **Vía Rent a Car** (☏ 7/861-4465; www.gaviota-grupo.com). All car rental agencies have desks at the Havana airport and at a host of major hotels around Havana and the rest of the country. If you book your car online, the best deals are usually found at the rental-car company websites, although all the major online travel agencies also offer rental-car reservation services. It may be cheaper to book your rental car before you arrive in Cuba.

All car-rental agencies in Cuba, except Transtur, offer insurance coverage for between CUC$10 and CUC$20 per day which must be paid in cash separately. Transtur, which runs Cubacar and Rex, charges a minimum CUC$15 for coverage for rentals that start in Havana. Most agencies carry a deductible of CUC$200 to CUC$1,000. Transtur's deductible is a minimum of CUC$350 on rentals that start in Havana. Some companies charge extra for picking a car up at an airport. Additional drivers will be charged between CUC$3 and CUC$10 per day. If you drop the car off in a different city than you picked it from, there will be a charge. Some companies do not cover theft, but this is a very minor problem in Cuba. If you hold a private auto insurance policy, you may be covered abroad for loss or damage to the car, and liability in case a passenger is injured. The credit card you use to rent the car also may provide some coverage. However, be sure to check whether or not your insurance company or credit card coverage excludes rental cars in Cuba. Moreover, this type of coverage probably does not cover liability if you caused the accident. Check your own auto insurance policy, the rental company policy, and your credit card coverage for the extent of coverage. Note that the daily insurance charge, if you pay it, is only payable in cash and never appears to be documented on official literature.

Be very thorough when checking out your car, and make sure that all accoutrements (like a spare tire, jack, and radio) are present and accounted for. Moreover, be sure to have the agent note every little nick and scratch, or you run a great risk of being charged for them upon your car's return. You will also be charged for small nicks caused by flying stones on some of Cuba's poorer roads. Gasoline costs about CUC$1.30 especial per liter (*por litro*), or CUC$1.15 regular per liter. Diesel is CUC$1.10 per liter. Gone are the gas shortages of several years ago. Service stations are plentiful and conveniently located on the major highways and on the outskirts of all major centers, as well as in major towns and cities. Tourist cars should use *gasolina especial*. Service stations are digitized.

Every car-rental agency will provide you with a basic road map. Alternately, you can try to get a copy of the **International Travel Map: Cuba** (ITMB Publishing; www.itmb.com) before arriving. The best road map is the Guia de Carreteras, but it is not widely available (p. 89).

While driving is generally easy and stress free, there are a couple of concerns for most foreign drivers here. First (and most annoying) is the fact that there are very, **very few road signs** and directional aids. This means that getting lost will happen. If you don't speak Spanish you will need a dictionary, phrases, paper and pen, and patience. Secondly, there's the issue of **hitchhikers.** Cuba's public transportation network is grossly overburdened and hitchhiking is a way of life. The highways sometimes seem like one long line, with periodic swellings, of people asking for a lift, or *botella*. While this is not dangerous, you should still be careful about whom you pick up as theft of belongings has been reported. It is not advisable to pick up hitchhikers after dark. However, the biggest hassle of offering rides is twofold: When you stop, you are likely to be swarmed by supplicants, who will want to stuff your car to the brink of its carrying capacity; and most hitchhikers are looking for relatively short hops, so once you pick up a load, you might find yourself suddenly making constant stops to let your passengers off—at which point there will almost certainly be a new rider immediately vying to snag the just-emptied seat. (You can, however, stop at an official *botella* point, identified by the mustard-yellow uniformed official with a clip-board.) However, that said, you will be providing the public-transport-starved Cubans with a much-needed ride.

Instead of driving your own rental car, an alternative option could be to hire a Cuban driver. In September 2010, the Cuban government announced plans that would allow Cubans to legally chauffeur tourists in their old American cars. At press time, the punitive tax codes for these new forms of self-employment had been announced, but no licenses had been issued

Note: Stop at all railroad crossings! It's the law, and it's also an important safety measure. Cuba's railroad network crisscrosses its highway system at numerous points. Trains rarely slow down and even rarer still are protective crossbars or warning lights. Police often hang out at railroad crossings, both to warn drivers when a train is coming and to dole out tickets to those who don't come to a stop.

One final note: If you have a minor accident you must go to a police station and get a signed report saying what happened and stating that you are not responsible for the damage (if that's the case). If the report does not state you are not responsible, you will be liable. If you are involved in a serious accident, whether or not you are to blame, you may be detained. If someone is killed, call your embassy for assistance and get a translator immediately.

BY TRAIN

The state-run train agency, **Ferrocuba** (℃ 7/861-4259), has offices in each train station. Havana is connected to Pinar del Río in the west, and Santiago de Cuba in the east by rail traffic. There are usually one or two trains a day heading west, and a half dozen or so heading east. Intermediate cities with regular service include Matanzas, Santa Clara, Ciego de Avila, Camagüey, Las Tunas, and Holguín. The principal train station, or **Estación Central,** is located in Havana at Calle Egido and Calle Arsenal, La Habana Vieja (℃ 7/861-4259).

Unlike the state-run bus service, there are usually seats available on most trains. However, most trains are in rather bad shape, with uncomfortable seats and limited amenities. Be sure to bring along some food and something to drink. Even if there's a cafeteria car onboard, which isn't always the case, you might not find any of the offerings particularly appealing, and they might just run out of food somewhere along the line. Moreover, train travel in Cuba is notoriously erratic, with frequent schedule changes and delays lasting up to 3 days. It is always best to check current schedules and conditions before buying a ticket and undertaking a train journey. If you are short on time and not looking for this kind of adventure, it would be wise to avoid all trains.

The most attractive rail option for travelers is the 12-hour express train to Santiago de Cuba, leaving Havana each evening at 6:05pm; the fare is CUC$50 to CUC$62. This train only makes stops in Santa Clara and Camagüey, and is the most modern and comfortable train in the whole national system.

BY BUS

For all intents and purposes, the only buses tourists will ride in Cuba are those run by **Víazul** (℃ 7/881-1413; www.viazul.com). (***Note:*** This website is not updated. Although the timetable and prices are incorrect, they are not hugely off the mark. If you plan a trip using the displayed timetable, your trip won't be completely thrown off kilter.) Víazul buses are modern and comfortable with lavatories on board. Now that many Cubans are using the service, it's more important to reserve at least several days in advance in high season. Víazul travels to most major tourist destinations in

Cuba. The main Víazul station is located in Nuevo Vedado, Havana, across from the metropolitan zoo. However, some of its routes, including the popular Viñales and Pinar del Río route, can be booked and boarded at the main bus terminal near the Plaza de la Revolución. For schedules and prices, see the regional chapters that follow. Children aged 5–12 pay half price; children 4 and under who do not occupy a seat travel for free.

You can also book Víazul tickets in the international airport in Havana and at Infotur offices around the country. Many tour agencies across the country are also now selling Víazul tickets at no extra cost to the purchaser. This is a great service, especially when many bus stations are a big sprint out of town. This also means travelers do not have to turn up early in order to purchase tickets before the bus departure. Note that in high season in some places, such as Baracoa, tickets are booked up well in advance and travelers are known to have been stuck for a few days; if you have a tight schedule, buy your return ticket for this route in Santiago de Cuba.

Note that it may not be possible to buy advanced tickets on some routes, for example Bayamo to Santiago. This is because the reservation system is not mechanized and the staff does not know if there is availability until the bus arrives. However, this likely will not be a problem.

MONEY & COSTS

THE VALUE OF THE CUBAN CONVERTIBLE PESO VS. OTHER POPULAR CURRENCIES

CUC$	US$	Can$	UK£	Euro (€)	Aus$	NZ$
1	$1.08	C$1.12	£0.70	€0.85	A$1.18	NZ$1.50

Frommer's lists exact prices in the local convertible peso currency. The currency conversions quoted above were correct at press time. However, rates fluctuate, so before departing consult a currency exchange website such as **www.oanda.com/convert/classic** to check up-to-the-minute rates.

Cuba is not a particularly cheap island to travel around for tourists and is not cheap at all compared to its neighboring Central American countries. You can reduce costs by traveling on the Víazul bus system and staying in *casas particulares* (private homes with rooms for rent), but note that single travelers rarely get a discount on a double room in a private house. You can easily pay out CUC$25 in a 2-week trip just on tipping the ubiquitous music bands that play in restaurants.

Although Castro has replaced the U.S. dollar with the **Cuban convertible peso, or CUC,** Cuba has always operated under a de facto dollarized economy. The CUC is an internationally unsupported currency, and it is, for all intents and purposes, pegged to the U.S. dollar. All of the CADECA branches and major banks will change U.S. dollars, euros, British pounds, and Canadian dollars.

There are, in fact, two distinct kinds of currency circulating in Cuba: the *moneda libremente convertible* ("convertible peso" or CUC), and the *moneda nacional* (Cuban peso or MN or CUP). Both are distinguished by the dollar $ symbol, leading to some confusion. Both the CUC and *moneda nacional* are divided up into units of 100 centavos. To complicate matters, the euro is also legal tender in many of the hotels, restaurants, and shops in several of the larger, isolated beach resort destinations.

Note: In this book, we list prices in the Cuban convertible peso (CUC$), but when an establishment only accepts the Cuban peso (MN) we also list prices in MN.

The convertible peso functions on a near one-to-one parity with the dollar—at press time, the official exchange rate was US$1=CUC$0.93 and £1=CUC1.43. However, U.S. dollars are penalized by a 10% surcharge on all money exchange operations into convertible pesos. For this reason, it is best to carry any hard currency you plan on spending in Cuba as euros, British pounds, or Canadian dollars. All of these are freely exchanged at all CADECA branches and most banks around Cuba. Be sure to bring relatively fresh and new bills. Cuban banks will sometimes refuse to accept bills with even slight tears or markings. Also, it is wise to bring a calculator with you and carefully monitor the exchange process, as tellers have been known to deliberately shortchange unsuspecting and overly trusting tourists.

Convertible pesos come in 1, 3, 5, 10, 20, 50, and 100 peso bills. Convertible peso coins come in denominations of 1, 5, 10, 25, and 50 centavos, and 1 peso. Although the government has long abandoned its official posture of a one-to-one parity between the Cuban peso (MN) and the U.S. dollar, the habit of converting *moneda nacional* prices directly into dollars is still common in many situations. Currently, Cuban pesos can be exchanged legally for CUC (and vice versa) at any CADECA money exchange office, some banks, and many hotels. The official exchange rate as of press time was around 24 Cuban pesos to the CUC. While opportunities for travelers to pay in Cuban pesos are few and far between, it is not a bad idea to exchange around CUC$1 to CUC$2 for pesos soon after arrival. It may be possible to pay for some meals, movie tickets, and other goods or services in Cuban pesos, and the savings are substantial. If "MN" is displayed on the prices, you should theoretically be paying Cuban pesos. However, in most cases, vendors will try to insist that any non-Cuban pay in convertible pesos, often at a one-to-one rate of exchange.

You can exchange any remaining convertible pesos for U.S. dollars, sterling, or euros at the airport before leaving. Do so, as the convertible pesos will be useless outside of Cuba.

Note: Cubans still often use the terms *peso* and *dollar* interchangeably. If you are quoted a price in pesos, it may not be the bargain you think it to be. To be clear, "*moneda nacional*" or "MN" always refers to Cuban pesos. Other terms for a CUC include *divisa*, *chavito*, *verde*, *guano*, and *fula*. Cash is known as *efectivo*.

Cuba's state banking system is trying to keep up with the rise in international tourism and joint business ventures. Both the **Banco de Crédito y Comercio** and **Banco Financiero Internacional** have opened up branches in most major business and tourist areas; most are open Monday through Friday from 8am to 4pm and a handful are open on Saturday mornings. These banks are the place to go for cash withdrawals off of your non-U.S.-issued credit cards. They'll also work for cashing traveler's checks or changing currency, but your best bet for money-exchange transactions is the national chain of *casas de cambio* (money-exchange houses), **CADECA, S.A.** You'll find CADECA branches in most major cities and tourist destinations, as well as at all the international airports. Don't be scared off by the long lines in front of most CADECA offices. These are invariably Cubans looking to buy Cuban Convertible Pesos, or CUC (*chavitos*). Foreigners wanting to sell dollars (*dólares*) and sterling (*Libra Esterlina*) for Cuban Convertible Pesos can almost always jump to the head of the line and walk right in, but ask beforehand. This is also the place to change your CUCs into national pesos (*moneda nacional*) for the odd purchase of *maní* (peanuts in a paper cone; $1MN), Granma newspaper, or a peso pizza and peso beer.

What Things Cost in Cuba	CUC$
Taxi from Havana airport to downtown	20.00–25.00
Bicitaxi ride from bus station to downtown	5.00
Double room in an all-inclusive beach resort, moderate	100.00–150.00
Double room in a provincial city, moderate	50.00–100.00
Room in a *casa particular*	20.00–35.00
Three-course dinner for one without wine, moderate	10.00–15.00
Bottle of beer	1.25
Mojito	2.50–5.00
Bottle of water (1.5 liters)	0.70–1.50
Cup of coffee	0.25–1.00
1 gallon/1 liter of premium gas	4.16 / 1.10
1-hour Internet card	6.00
Admission to most museums	1.00–5.00

Warning: Do not change money in the street. It is inevitable that you will be given a wad of useless national pesos instead of CUCs. Also, if you are offered the silver three-peso Che Guevara coin as a souvenir, note that it is worth three national pesos and not CUC$3; it can be obtained in a CADECA for $3MN.

MasterCard and **Visa** are widely accepted at hotels, car-rental agencies, and official restaurants and shops, with the caveat that they cannot be issued by a United States bank or financial institution. **Diners Club** is also accepted, although to a much lesser extent. **American Express** cards are not accepted anywhere on the island. It is always best to check with your home bank before traveling to see if your card will work in Cuba. If you have ignored all advice, contact **Asistur** (p. 48), which can advise you on a company in Santo Domingo that can arrange a transaction between your U.S. bank and Asistur.

You are fabulously ripped off when taking money out on your debit or credit card in Cuba. No matter what the country of origin of your card, your transaction will first be converted into dollars, thereby incurring a charge of up to a staggering 12.5%, before you are given the CUC. On a CUC$800 withdrawal, you'll pay a whopping CUC$100 fee. This also happens at ATMs where your request for CUC is converted to U.S. dollars at that day's exchange rate. You are then charged 3% of the transaction in dollars at the point of withdrawal.

Most *paladares* (private-home restaurants), *casas particulares* (private-home accommodations), and small businesses do not accept credit cards. In the more remote destinations, you should count on using cash for all transactions. Moreover, shaky phone connections and other logistical problems often get in the way of credit card usage. I actually saw some British travelers unable to use a card at a major hotel because the hotel was out of receipt tape, and the staff wasn't sure when the hotel would get more. Do not count on paying a hotel bill with a credit card unless it is a very expensive hotel and/or linked to an international chain such as Sol Melía.

If your credit card is lost or stolen while you're in Cuba, you can contact **Fincimex,** 3 Av 408 corner of Calle 6, Miramar, Havana (© **7/204-9252**). However, you're best off having written down in advance your issuing bank's telephone number and calling the bank directly. Banks will usually accept collect calls from anywhere in the world. You can also contact Asistur (p. 48).

Cuba has a modestly expanding network of ATMs (automated teller machines) associated with a string of banks, like the **Banco de Crédito y Comercio** and **Banco Financiero Internacional.** No credit or debit cards issued by U.S.-based companies will work at any of these machines. However, travelers from other countries can easily extract convertible pesos from ATMs at the international airport and most major tourist destinations. As with credit cards, it is always best to check with your home bank before traveling to see if your ATM card will work in Cuba.

Note: Remember that many banks impose a fee every time you use a card at another bank's ATM, and that fee can be higher for international transactions (up to $5 or more) than for domestic ones (where they're rarely more than $2 in the U.S.).

You can use your credit card to receive cash advances at ATMs. Keep in mind that credit card companies protect themselves from theft by limiting maximum withdrawals outside their home country, so call your credit card company before you leave home. And keep in mind that you'll pay interest from the moment of your withdrawal, even if you pay your monthly bills on time.

In Cuba, traveler's checks are accepted at most major hotels, government-run or chain restaurants, and major attractions, but far less readily than credit cards. The same prohibition against U.S. bank-issued tender applies to traveler's checks. If you are a die-hard fan of traveler's checks, **Thomas Cook** (visit www.thomascook.com to find your nearest branch) and **Visa** (℃ **0800/89-5078** in the U.K.) traveler's checks issued outside of the United States are still your best bet. Most banks, CADECA offices, hotels, and businesses charge commissions of around 3% and 4% on weekends for cashing traveler's checks.

STAYING HEALTHY
Staying Healthy

Despite ongoing economic troubles and shortages, Cuba's healthcare system remains one of the best in Latin America. The country takes extremely proactive steps toward preventive public health, and common tropical diseases like cholera and malaria are either uncommon or have been totally eradicated. You don't need any vaccinations to travel to Cuba, unless you are coming from a region with cholera or yellow fever, in which case the Cuban authorities will require proof of immunization.

Staying healthy on a trip to Cuba is predominantly a matter of common sense: **Know your physical limits** and don't overexert yourself in the ocean, on hikes, or in athletic activities. Cuba is a tropical country, so limit your **exposure to the sun,** especially during the first few days of your trip and, thereafter, from 11am to 3pm. (It is often much hotter in Cuba btw. 2–4pm than at midday.)

Contact the **International Association for Medical Assistance to Travelers (IAMAT)** (℃ **716/754-4883** or 416/652-0137 in Canada; www.iamat.org) for tips on travel and health concerns and for lists of local, English-speaking doctors. The website **www.tripprep.com**, sponsored by a consortium of travel medicine practitioners, also offers helpful advice on traveling abroad. You can find listings of reliable clinics overseas at the International Society of Travel Medicine website, www.istm.org.

Due to the U.S. embargo and other problems, common medicines are restricted or routinely unavailable in Cuba. It is wise to bring a full medical pack containing basic medicines. Travelers may also want to consider carrying ciprofloxacin if they are susceptible to stomach bugs that need treating with an antibiotic. Having said that, there is a well-established network of international health clinics in Cuba for emergencies, but it would still be better to bring what you can with you. All prescription medicines should be brought with you as well.

Regional Health Concerns

TROPICAL ILLNESSES   Cuba does experience dengue outbreaks from time to time and you would be wise to keep your ear to the ground about this.

DIETARY RED FLAGS   Overall, while **water** is potable throughout most of Cuba, I recommend you stick primarily to bottled water, just to err on the side of safety. Every hotel and restaurant catering to travelers will carry bottled water. Ask for agua mineral natural (still) or agua mineral con gas (sparkling water).

BUGS, BITES & OTHER WILDLIFE CONCERNS   There are no poisonous snakes in Cuba, which will put many minds at ease. In terms of **biting bugs,** your standard array of bees, wasps, mosquitoes, and sand fleas are present. Sand fleas are a slight nuisance at most beaches if there's no offshore breeze to clear them, particularly around sunrise and sunset. While there are also ticks and chiggers, so far Lyme disease is not considered a problem. Bring repellent and wear light, long-sleeved clothing.

SUN EXPOSURE   The tropical sun in Cuba is extremely fierce. The highest sun protection factor, hats, and protective clothing should be worn. Stay out of the sun between 11am and 3pm and drink plenty of water to avoid dehydration. Use a sunscreen with a high protection factor and apply it liberally. Remember that children need more protection than adults do.

EXTREME WEATHER   Hurricanes can occur between June and November in Cuba, but they do not arrive every year. The National Hurricane Center's website (www.nhc.noaa.gov) offers details on any storms in the Caribbean basin. It also has a hurricane preparedness section. In the event of a hurricane, Cuba has a very well-organized preparedness program. In the event of extreme danger, thousands can be evacuated, minimizing or avoiding deaths completely. Listen to all authorities in the event of an emergency.

During the rainy season, tropical storms with plenty of lightning are common. According to the Cuban Meteorological Institute, around 65 Cubans die each year from lightning strikes. During a storm, stay inside or in your vehicle. Move out of the sea and away from the beach and move away from high ground.

If You Get Sick

Cuba has a nationwide system of hospitals and clinics, as well as international clinics, and you should have no trouble finding prompt and competent medical care in the case of an emergency. (See the "Orientation" section of the individual destination chapters, or "Fast Facts" for specific recommendations. The system is entirely free for

Cubans, but foreigners are charged for services.) This is actually a significant means of income for the country; however, fees for private medical care are relatively inexpensive by most Western standards. If you are hospitalized, you may find that support staff, like nurses, are lacking. You may need to have someone bring your food, clothes, and other necessities, and if you are traveling alone, this could mean informally paying a Cuban—perhaps a *casa particular* owner you've met—to help.

The country has a network of pharmacies, though due to the U.S. embargo, certain medicines are restricted or often unavailable. That said, it is always a good idea to carry a sufficient supply of any necessary prescription medicines you may need (packed in their original containers in your carry-on luggage), and a small first-aid kit with basic analgesic, antihistamine, and anti-diarrhea medications. You might also bring a copy of your prescriptions, with the generic name of the medication in case the pharmacist doesn't recognize the brand name. Don't forget an extra pair of contact lenses or prescription glasses—although opticians are available if necessary.

If you suffer from a chronic illness, consult your doctor before your departure. For conditions like epilepsy, diabetes, or heart problems, wear a **MedicAlert identification tag** (© 888/633-4298; www.medicalert.org), which will immediately alert doctors to your condition and give them access to your records through MedicAlert's 24-hour hotline.

A full list of international clinics, international drugstores, and opticians is available on the **Servimed** website at www.servimedcuba.com. The **Clínica Central Cira Garcia,** Calle 20 no. 4101 on the corner of Avenida 41, Playa, Havana (© 7/204-2811; www.cirag.cu), is the largest center in the country catering to foreigners. It is also possible to have medical treatments, cosmetic surgery, and undergo drug-addiction programs in Cuba for a fraction of the cost elsewhere. All the details are listed under the Servimed website. Servimed is part of the agency Cubanacán.

Asistur, Prado 208 between Calles Trocadero and Colón (© **7/866-4499;** 7/866-8527 emergency number; www.asistur.cu) will help you with medical reports and the management of medical expenses if you end up in the hospital. Its addresses outside Havana are available on www.asistur.cu/mapa.html.

Called *farmacias* in Spanish, drugstores are relatively common throughout the country, although not necessarily well stocked. Those at hospitals and major clinics are often open 24 hours. Many hotels, particularly the larger ones, have either a small pharmacy or a basic medical clinic on-site. There's a 24-hour pharmacy at the international terminal of the José Martí International Airport (© 7/266-4105) in Havana.

We list **additional emergency numbers** in "Fast Facts", p. 295.

CRIME & SAFETY

Cuba is an extremely safe country. Street crime is relatively rare. With the recent upsurge in tourism, there have been some reports of pickpocketing and muggings in Old Havana and Centro Havana and around the gay hangouts in Vedado, but these are by far the exceptions to the rule. There's a strong security and police presence in most popular tourist destinations, and even outside the well-worn tourist routes, theft and assaults are quite uncommon. Having said that, news is heavily censored, so real crime statistics are unknown.

That said, you should still be careful and use common sense. Given the nature of Cuba's socialist system, a huge disparity in wealth exists between the average Cuban and any foreign visitor, even budget travelers. Don't flash ostentatious signs of wealth, and avoid getting too far off the beaten path, especially at night. Don't leave valuables unattended, and always use the safe in your hotel room or at the front desk.

Should you find yourself robbed, you will need a police report for insurance purposes. If you don't speak Spanish, go accompanied by a Spanish speaker; otherwise, you will make little headway.

The U.S. State Department (**http://travel.state.gov**) and the U.K. Foreign and Commonwealth Office (**www.fco.gov.uk**) issue updated advice for travelers.

Meddling in drugs and firearms brings stiff penalties. There are also prohibitions relating to blood products, obscene or pornographic literature, or any anti-state literature. Getting on the wrong side of the law is not advisable in any way.

Solo women travelers can go out at night with no fear for their safety, but it's always best to be careful. Walking home alone in small provincial towns is also quite safe. Also, see "Women Travelers," below.

SPECIALIZED TRAVEL RESOURCES

In addition to the destination-specific resources listed below, please visit Frommers. com for other specialized travel resources.

LGBT Travelers

Homosexuality is not illegal in Cuba, but in general, Cuba has a poor record on gay and lesbian rights, and while the situation has improved somewhat, there are still high levels of homophobia and broad societal rejection of gays and lesbians. For decades following the Revolution, gays and lesbians were closeted and persecuted. (Read Reinaldo Arenas' horrifying account in *Before Night Falls.*) The harsh measures they faced included forced labor and prison. The blockbuster movie *Fresa y Chocolate* (Strawberry and Chocolate) certainly brought the issue to the forefront, yet little has changed in the prevailing views of this macho society. However, Fidel Castro has now taken responsibility for the way homosexuals were treated in the 1960s and 1970s. There is only one openly accepted gay and lesbian establishment in Cuba (in Santa Clara, see p. 187), and few of the established gay and lesbian tour operators run trips to the island. However, **Out Adventures** (www.out-adventures.com), based in Canada and working with Intrepid travel, offers a "Comfort Cuba" tour.

Santa Clara is perhaps the most openly gay city in Cuba and there is an annual gay and transvestite carnival in the middle of May. In Havana, a transvestite entertains weekly at Cafe TV. Raúl Castro's daughter, Mariela Castro, heads the National Center for Sex Education and champions homosexual, bisexual, and transgender rights. In May 2008, the state-television network transmitted *Brokeback Mountain* on TV, the first time a gay film had been broadcast in Cuba. Cuba also held an anti-homophobia day for the fourth time in May 2010, promoted by Mariela Castro. The legalization of same-sex marriage has also been talked about, but so far no progress has been made. In addition, sex change operations were legalized in 2008, and in 2010, Cuba's first transsexual appeared in a documentary on the island publicly detailing her transition for the first time.

While travelers are generally not hassled in Cuba and given some leeway in terms of social mores, same-sex signs of physical affection are rare and frowned upon across the country. Gay and lesbian couples and singles should take the prevailing social climate into account when traveling in Cuba.

The documentary film, **Gay Cuba,** by Sonja de Vries (Frameline Films; www. frameline.org), is an honest look at the treatment of gays and lesbians in modern Cuba.

The International Gay and Lesbian Travel Association (IGLTA) (© 954/ 630-1637; www.iglta.org) is the trade association for the gay and lesbian travel industry, and offers an online directory of gay- and lesbian-friendly travel businesses.

Travelers with Disabilities

Most disabilities shouldn't stop anyone from traveling. There are more options and resources out there than ever before, and Cuba has been very forward-thinking in the recognition of the rights of people with disabilities. Still, overall, Cuba is not an easy country for them. While a few hotels are equipped for travelers with disabilities, these are far from the norm. Moreover, there's no private or public transportation service geared toward such travelers. The streets of Havana are rugged and crowded, and sidewalks, in particular, are often either totally absent or badly torn up. Provincial towns suffer from the same disrepairs. The Cuban people, however, are quite conscientious and embracing in their treatment of people with disabilities.

Asociación Cubana de Limitados Físicos-Motores (The Cuban Disabled Association), Calle 6 no. 106, between Avenidas 1 and 3, Miramar, Havana (© 7/ 209-3099; www.aclifim.sld.cu), is a Cuban organization charged with ensuring accessibility and lobbying for rights. The association is a member of the Disabled Peoples' International (DPI), and probably the best contact for travelers with disabilities in Cuba.

The Society for Accessible Travel & Hospitality (© 212/447-7284; www. sath.org) offers a wealth of travel resources for those with all types of disabilities and informed recommendations on destinations, access guides, travel agents, tour operators, vehicle rentals, and companion services.

Family Travel

Cuba is an excellent destination for families, particularly if you want an all-inclusive beach vacation with a broad range of tours, activities, and entertainment options. Toward this end, Varadero would probably be your top choice, with a wealth of watersports activities and land-based adventures, including nearby caves to explore. The beach destinations of Cayo Coco, Cayo Guillermo, and Guardalavaca are also worth considering. If you do go the all-inclusive route, be sure the resort you choose has a well-run children's program, with a full plate of activities.

If your children are old enough, they should enjoy the colonial wonders of La Habana Vieja (Old Havana), including its forts and castles. Hotels and attractions throughout Cuba often give discounts for children under 12 years old, as does the tourist bus service, Víazul.

However, hotels with regular, dependable babysitting service are few and far between. If you'll need babysitting service, make sure your hotel provides it before you leave home. To locate those accommodations, restaurants, and attractions that are particularly kid-friendly, refer to the "Kids" icon throughout this guide.

Women Travelers

Women should be careful when walking alone at night, both in Havana and in other more remote destinations. However, walking home alone at night in smaller provincial towns should be quite safe. Cuba is a somewhat typical "macho" Latin American nation, with an open and extroverted sense of sexuality. Single women can expect their fair share of catcalls, whistles, and propositions known as *piropo,* especially in Havana and Santiago. The best advice is to ignore the unwanted attention, rather than try to come up with a witty or antagonistic rejoinder. Cuban men are pretty persistent, but they should soon get the message if you ignore them. If they don't, say *"Déjeme en paz"* (Leave me in peace). If it gets out of control, a swear word will usually work.

Women travelers should check out the award-winning website **Journeywoman** (www.journeywoman.com), a "real life" women's travel-information network where you can sign up for a free e-mail newsletter and get advice on everything from etiquette and dress to safety; or the travel guide *Safety and Security for Women Who Travel* by Sheila Swan and Peter Laufer (Travelers' Tales, 2nd ed., 2004), which gives common-sense tips on safe travel.

Also, see the sections on "Safety," above, and "Single Travelers," below.

Multicultural Travelers

Africans and African-Americans used to be hassled quite regularly by the police as they were mistaken for Cuban citizens. Thankfully, with the change in apartheid rules in Cuba in February 2008, this is much less common. There is also the advantage of ethnically blending in and thus being less subject to hassle and scams. In Havana, multicultural attractions include Chinatown, Arabic societies, and synagogues. Mass is held in all churches across the country.

See also "Race Relations in Cuba," p. 53.

Senior Travelers

Cuba is a comfortable destination for senior travelers. Seniors are treated with deference and respect in Cuba. Moreover, it's a particularly safe country, with low levels of street crime, and the food and water are generally safe as well.

Mention the fact that you're a senior when you make your travel reservations—some of the hotel chains and package tour operators still offer discounts for seniors. However, don't expect to find specific senior discounts once you arrive in Cuba, where you will be lumped into the category of rich foreigner and gouged as much as possible, like all the rest.

ElderTreks (© **800/741-7956** in North America and 0808-234-1717 in the U.K.; www.eldertreks.com) is a Canadian-based company that arranges small-group (up to 16 people) adventure trips for those 50 and older to Cuba.

In the U.K., trips to Cuba are offered by **Saga,** The Saga Building, Enbrook Park, Folkestone, Kent, CT20 3SE (© **0800/096-0078;** www.saga.co.uk).

Single Travelers

Cuba is generally extremely safe for travelers. Single travelers face no real specific threats or dangers. That said, don't throw common sense out the window. Single travelers—and women in particular—should still be careful when walking alone at night, both in Havana and in other more remote destinations.

I have never felt unsafe traveling on my own and there are few other countries in the world, like Cuba, where I would consider taking an illegal taxi with a strange man for hundreds of kilometers down back roads. Remember also that there are severe repercussions for Cubans who commit crimes against tourists.

Perhaps the biggest issue facing single travelers is that of *jineterismo,* which is a way of life in Cuba. In its most disturbing form, it has become synonymous with prostitution. Sex tourism and prostitution flourish in Cuba, and single travelers of both genders and any sexual persuasion will encounter constant offers for companionship, and usually more. In some cases, the terms are quite clear and a cash value is set. In others, the *jinetera* or *jinetero* is just looking for some restaurant meals, drinks, store-bought clothing, food, daily necessities, and sometimes even a good time. Many are looking to cement relationships with foreign tourists that could lead to marriage and a means of improving their standard of living on a long-term basis, either on the island or abroad.

Single women of all ages, in particular, should not be naive about declarations of undying love. You could just be the desperately dreamed about ticket out of the country. Remember that most Cubans are not free to leave Cuba. If you do fall in love, the Cuban government cannot prevent the Cuban from leaving after marrying a foreigner but they make it difficult to grant the correct exit papers (waits of 3 years are not uncommon).

Vegetarian Travelers

Cuba is not a society geared up for vegetarianism. Vegetables are not plentiful, although fruits are widely available. Eggs are widely available and peanuts (*mani*) are sold on the street. Fish can be found in abundance. Travelers should locate the small vegetable markets (*agromercados*) where private trading of products is allowed. Rice and beans (*moros y cristianos*) are plentiful. Dairy products are not always available. Cartons of fruit juices and biscuits and tins of olives are always available in town supermarkets. In short, a vegetarian won't starve, but this is no place to come for any innovative cuisine.

RESPONSIBLE TOURISM

Although Cuba is home to beautiful beaches, forests, mountains, mangroves, and wetlands, the country is somewhat unsustainable. Cuba has suffered severe deforestation since the colonial era, and its increasing industrialization (using Soviet-era technology) polluted the environment. In the 1990s, however, the government established laws to protect the environment. Since then, organic farms have flourished, and the recent land reform that gives unused fertile land to private farmers is encouraging news. However, Cuba is still essentially a third world country and environmentally–friendly ventures, like recycling and researching alternative forms of energy, are not a visible priority in contemporary Cuba.

That said, Cuba has an excellent network of nationally protected natural areas, such as the Parque Nacional de Humboldt and the Viñales Valley. While traveling in these preserved areas, respect the environment by not dumping garbage, sticking to trails, and employing local guides; also, tip local guides (who are all employed by the state and earn no more than CUC$15–CUC$20 per month).

Cuba's only real ecotourism project is at Las Terrazas. It was a planned community project that has preserved local flora and fauna and forests and the population is all involved in exploiting its ecotourism potential.

Cuba is blessed with gorgeous beaches, and fortunately most beach areas are not overdeveloped—even though there are dozens of large all-inclusive resorts that line many of Cuba's beaches. The seas surrounding Cuba are pristine, and careful diving

race relations IN CUBA

The Cuban population is—very conservatively—estimated to be about one-third black or mixed-race (in reality, the percentage is probably closer to two-thirds or more). Cuba officially declares itself to be colorblind and, at least on the surface, the obvious mixed-race heritage and the strong presence of Afro-Cuban culture seem to support that notion. Though as a society, Cuba is much less racist and male dominated than it was before the Revolution, racism still exists, even if much of it is under the radar. Economic racism is widespread; relatively few black Cubans occupy positions of authority in the government, state enterprise, or tourism. Racist comments are as regrettably common as they are in other countries. Many Cubans assume blacks to be the majority of jineteros (male hustlers) and jineteras (female escorts), even though the reality is that hustling in Cuba is universal. Most Cubans also believe that the police harass blacks to a disproportionate degree, and travelers of African and Hispanic descent may experience the same. Spanish-speaking travelers accompanying Anglo-looking tourists are sometimes followed and questioned by police who ignorantly assume them to be Cuban hustlers working a beat. In fact, one other disturbing aspect of this situation is that black tourists are sometimes mistaken for Cuban jineteros and may be given a hard time by security personnel upon entering hotels, although now that it is legal for Cubans to enter and stay in hotels with foreigners, this should no longer happen.

—Neil E. Schlecht

and fishing operations are practiced, which helps preserve sealife. However, stone causeways run across miles of sea, connecting remote islands to the mainland, and thus bringing more visitors and in turn more pollution to the once isolated areas.

Although tourism is encouraged, the tourism industry props up a system of government that rules over a people who are not free. Visitors to Cuba can support the local economy by staying with local people through the system of *casas particulares* and eating at *paladares*. These bed and breakfasts and private restaurants support a large network of local people. Locals sell fruits and vegetables at *agromercados* throughout Cuba—and now from kiosks and their own homes.

Some state hotels—the Club Amigo chain in particular—now run partly on solar panels, and all houses, offices, and hotels in Cuba now use energy-saving light bulbs in a switch that was part of a nationally-enforced campaign a few years ago. However, most of the all-inclusive hotels serve imported food and pay their Cuban employees a mere CUC$10–CUC$15 a month. Do tip your maids, waiters, and tour guides (but not tour desk operatives who are taking their cut from the published prices of tours).

SPECIAL INTEREST & ESCORTED TRIPS
Special Interest Trips

There are plenty of options for a special-interest or theme vacation to Cuba. Popular themes include cigars, Ernest Hemingway, classic cars, bird-watching, diving, fishing, and Latin dance.

GENERAL RESOURCES FOR responsible travel

The following websites provide valuable wide-ranging information on sustainable travel.

- **Responsible Travel** (www. responsibletravel.com) is a great source of sustainable travel ideas; the site is run by a spokesperson for ethical tourism in the travel industry. **Sustainable Travel International** (www. sustainabletravelinternational.org) promotes ethical tourism practices, and manages an extensive directory of sustainable properties and tour operators around the world.

- **Carbonfund** (www.carbonfund. org), **TerraPass** (www.terrapass. org), and **Cool Climate** (http:// coolclimate.berkeley.edu) provide info on "carbon offsetting," or offsetting the greenhouse gas emitted during flights.

- **Greenhotels** (www.greenhotels. com) recommends green-rated member hotels around the world that fulfill the company's stringent environmental requirements. **Environmentally Friendly Hotels** (www.environmentallyfriendly hotels.com) offers more green accommodation ratings.

- **Volunteer International** (www. volunteerinternational.org) has a list of questions to help you determine the intentions and the nature of a volunteer program. For general info on volunteer travel, visit **www.volunteer abroad.org** and **www.idealist. org**.

- **GAP Adventures** ★ (℃ 800/708-7761 in the U.S. and Canada, or 0870/999-0144 in the U.K.; www.gapadventures.com) is a major international adventure and educational tour operator with a full plate of theme tours to Cuba.

- **Global Exchange** ★ (℃ 800/497-1994, ext 242; www.globalexchange.org) is a nonprofit organization working to increase international understanding by conducting small-scale tours that emphasize educational or social aid themes.

- **Paradiso** ★ (℃ 7/832-9538; www.paradiso.cu) is the tour agency arm of the Cuban arts and cultural organization ARTex. Paradiso organizes theme tours and escorted trips, including tours based around most of the major festivals and cultural events, as well as participatory learning trips with instruction in a variety of arts.

ADVENTURE TRIPS

Active tourism is still in its infancy in Cuba, but opportunities have opened up in the last few years. The island offers myriad opportunities to add a bit of adrenaline and adventure to your vacation. Watersports are the main draw here, and Cuba abounds with outstanding opportunities to fish, sail, snorkel, and scuba dive. For those looking for some dry-land adventure activities, there are great options for biking and rock climbing, and you might even be able to get on a diamond to play some baseball.

Most tour operators listed can arrange trekking tours. **Caledonia** (℃ 0131/621-7721; www.caledonialanguages.com) organizes trekking trips in the Sierra Maestra.

BASEBALL Baseball is the national sport and, after dancing and sex, Cuba's greatest national passion. Cuba's amateur players are considered some of the best in the world, and the premier players are aggressively scouted and courted by Major

League Baseball. The regular season runs November through March, and playoffs and the final championship usually carry the season on into May. Most major towns and cities have a local team. Some of the consistently better teams include Pinar del Río, Sancti Spíritus, Santiago de Cuba, Santa Clara, and of course Havana's Industriales. It's usually easy to buy tickets at the box office for less than 5 Cuban pesos, or ask at your hotel or casa particular and perhaps they can get you tickets in advance.

If you want to actually get out and play, you should be able to find a pickup game to join. Check out the website of **Baseball Adventures** (© 707/937-4478; www.baseballadventures.com), which offers fully hosted trips geared toward serious players looking to play and train with local Cuban pros.

Tip: If you're planning on playing, bring some extra equipment—balls, bats, and gloves—to leave behind. It'll be greatly appreciated and is a great means of getting into a game.

BIKING   With a local reliance on bicycles for everyday transportation and a relatively well-maintained road network serving a small motor vehicular fleet, Cuba is a great country to tour by bicycle. There are few local operations renting decent bikes in Cuba, so it's best to bring your own. I also recommend organized trips, as the logistics of traveling through Cuba still make it a bit difficult for independent bike touring. One dependable operation with regular bike tours and quality bike rentals in Cuba is **Wow Cuba** (© 800/969-2822 or 902/368-2453; www.wowcuba.com). Anyone thinking of bicycling in Cuba should pick up a copy of Wally and Barbara Smith's Bicycling Cuba: Fifty Days of Detailed Rides from Havana to Pinar Del Río and the Oriente (Backcountry Guides, 2002).

BIRD-WATCHING   Over 350 resident and migratory species of birds can be spotted in Cuba, including some 24 endemic species. Cuba is also home to the smallest hummingbird in the world, the endemic bee hummingbird. A couple of organized tour options are offered by the British company **Cuba Direct** (www.cubadirect.co.uk) and the Canadian operation **Quest Nature Tours** (© 416/633-5666; www.questnaturetours.com). Some of the best places to go bird-watching in Cuba include **La Güira National Park,** the **Zapata Peninsula, Cayo Coco** and **Cayo Guillermo, La Belen** reserve near Camagüey, the **Sierra Maestra** region, and **Baracoa.** Bird-watchers will want to bring a copy of Field Guide to the Birds of Cuba (Comstock, 2000), by Orlando Garrido et al.

FISHING   There's fabulous deep-sea sportfishing for marlin, sailfish, tuna, dorado, and more off most of Cuba's extensive coastline, while the Zapata Peninsula and Cayo Largo del Sur may just be some of the best and least exploited bonefishing spots left in the hemisphere. The mountain lake and resort of Hanabanilla is getting good grades as a freshwater ground for widemouth and black bass. There's a broad network of state-run marinas all around Cuba; the greatest number are run by **Grupo Empresarial de Náutica y Marinas Marlin** (www.nauticamarlin.com) and **Gaviota** (© 7/869-5774; www.gaviota-grupo.com). All offer sportfishing charters. For more information, see individual destination chapters. **Avalon** (http://cubanfishingcenters.com) runs a reputable operation; it operates out of **Jardines de la Reina, Isla de la Juventud,** and **Cayo Largo.**

GOLF   The country's only regulation 18-hole golf course is the **Varadero Golf Club** (© 45/66-8482; www.varaderogolfclub.com). The course is a relatively flat resort course, with lots of water, plenty of sand, great views, and almost no rough. Golfers will probably want to stay at the adjacent **Meliá Las Américas** (© 45/66-7600;

www.solmeliacuba.com), although you can make reservations and play here from any hotel in the area.

In Havana, there's the **Club de Golf Habana,** Carretera Vento Km 8, Capdevila, Rancho Boyeros (© 7/649-8918, ext. 111), which has a decent little 9-hole course.

HORSE-BACK RIDING Riding horses is possible in Viñales, around Trinidad and Guardalavaca, and on some beaches such as Cayo Guillermo. **Captivating Cuba** (www.captivatingcuba.com) can organize trips focused on horse-back riding.

KITE SURFING Great kite surfing can be found on Cayo Guillermo. You will need to bring all your own equipment though. Canadian hobbyists have been coming here for years.

MOUNTAIN & ROCK CLIMBING These sports are in their infancy in Cuba, but excellent opportunities abound, especially around the Viñales Valley. **Cuba Climbing** (www.cubaclimbing.com) can point you to the right rocks and answer any questions you might have.

SAILING Whether you take a day sail, or decide to go cruising the coastline for a week or so, opportunities to sail the clear waters off Cuba abound. The state-run marinas in Varadero, Jardines del Rey, Camagüey, Santiago, Cienfuegos, and Cayo Largo del Sur all offer charter sailboats, as well as a variety of day sailing options. See the individual destination chapters for more information.

SCUBA DIVING & SNORKELING There are fabulous scuba-diving and snorkeling opportunities on the coral reefs, ocean walls, and ancient wrecks that lie just off Cuba's coasts. **Isla de la Juventud, Los Jardines de la Reina, Santa Lucía, María la Gorda,** and **Playa Girón** are widely considered the absolute top scuba-diving destinations, but in each case, the majority of the accommodations options are either rustic or decidedly geared toward hard-core dive enthusiasts and almost no one else. You will also find perfectly acceptable dive opportunities and operations in **Varadero, Cayo Coco, Cayo Guillermo, Guardalavaca,** and **Cayo Largo del Sur,** as well as far more comfortable and varied accommodations. For more information, see specific destination chapters.

SURFING Cuba is not considered a world-class surfing destination, and there are very few Cuban surfers or surf tourists. Still, this is part of the charm of surfing in Cuba, and there are waves and breaks all along the island's long coastline, including right off the Malecón in Havana. For good information and a primer, check out **www.havanasurf-cuba.com**. You will definitely have to bring your own board, and I would recommend bringing a board (or two) that you wouldn't mind leaving behind for some very appreciative Cuban surfer.

TENNIS Many of the large-scale beach resorts have tennis courts. Almost all are outdoor courts, and very few are lit. If you're set on playing tennis on your trip, be sure to check in advance whether your hotel or resort has courts. Your options are much more limited in Havana, unless you're staying at one of the few city hotels with a court. Your best bet in Havana is to try to book a court at the **Occidental Miramar,** Avenida 5, between Calles 78 and 80, Miramar, Playa (© 7/204-8158), which has six courts; or head to the **Club Habana,** Avenida 5, between Calles 188 and 192, Reparto Flores, Playa (© 7/204-3300); or **Club de Golf Habana,** Carretera Vento Km 8, Capdevila, Rancho Boyeros (© 7/649-8820). Each have a few courts open to the general public. All charge around CUC$10 per hour.

LANGUAGE, MUSIC, AND PHOTOGRAPHY CLASSES

The **University of Havana** (www.uh.cu) offers language classes from CUC$100 a month starting on the first Monday of every month. A 60-hour Cuban culture class is offered every second month. The **University of the Oriente** in Santiago de Cuba (www.uo.edu.cu) also offers Spanish classes from CUC$231.

Caledonia (© **0131/621-7721;** www.caledonialanguages.com) offers Spanish courses in Havana and Santiago from £160 per week. **Caledonia** also offers fantastic music and dance trips to Cuba with prices starting at £1,995 for 2 weeks. (It is also possible to combine these activities with language classes.) Caledonia is tied to the Cuban Music School (www.jazzsummerschool.com/cuban_music_school). Caledonia is listed as a responsible travel operator by www.responsibletravel.com.

Cuba Direct also offers a variety of dance class options (www.cubadirect.co.uk/holidays/salsa-default.aspx).

If you're interested in photography, check **www.trinidadphoto.com** for workshop tours with British photographer Keith Cardwell. Tours are run in conjunction with Cuban photographer Julio Muñoz based in Trinidad. An 11-day tour costs £1,350 per person, excluding food and flights.

VOLUNTEER & WORKING TRIPS

The **Cuban Solidarity Campaign** (© **0208/800-0155;** www.cuba-solidarity.org/brigades.asp) runs international work brigades twice a year for up to 22 days from £945 per person, including all flights, accommodations, and food. See also **Global Exchange,** p. 54.

Escorted General Interest Tours

There are more than 100 licensed travel service providers in the United States; almost all offer charter flights and packages. Some of these operators arrange well-organized escorted general-interest tours. A couple of the best and most reputable are

- **ABC Charters** ★ (© **305/263-6829;** www.abc-charters.com) is an excellent travel service provider and charter company based in Miami.
- **Tico Travel** ★ (© **800/493-8426** in the U.S. or Canada, or 954/493-8426; www.destinationcuba.com) is a dependable company with operations throughout much of Latin America.

FROM CANADA

In addition to the agencies listed below, Canadian travelers and others using Canada as a gateway can check directly with **Transat Holidays** (© **866/322-6649** in the U.S. and Canada; www.transatholidays.com), the tour agency arm of one of the principal charter flight companies to Cuba.

- **Sol Meliá Cuba** (www.solmeliacuba.ca) is the Canadian-based tour agency arm of the Sol Meliá company.
- **Signature Travel** ★ (© **866/324-2883;** www.signaturevacations.com) is the largest tour and package operator in Canada, with offices in Burnaby, Mississauga, Montreal, and Winnipeg.

FROM THE U.K.

- **Captivating Cuba** (© **0844/412-9916;** www.captivatingcuba.com) offers package and tailor-made holidays from the UK.

- **Cuba Direct ★** (© 0844/415-5510; www.cubadirect.co.uk) is a good Cuban-owned operator running a variety of tours and selling flights.
- **Cubaism** (© 0800/298-9555; www.cubaism.com) offers a wide variety of flights, hotels, and other products.
- **W&O Travel ★** (© 0845/277-3355; www.wandotravel.com) took over Cuba specialists, Regent Travel, and offers great tours to Cuba.
- **Journey Latin America** (© 020/8747-8315; www.journeylatinamerica.co.uk) is a large U.K.-based operator for trips throughout the hemisphere, with often very good deals on airfare.
- **Thomas Cook ★** (© 0870/750-5711; www.thomascook.com) is a major U.K.-based operator for trips around the world, with excellent operations in Cuba.
- **Thomson** (www.thomson.co.uk) offers good-value packages and flights to Cuba.
- **The Holiday Place** (© 020/7644-1755; www.theholidayplace.co.uk) offers good package deals to Cuba.

FROM AUSTRALIA & NEW ZEALAND

- **Caribbean Bound** (© 02/9267-2555; www.caribbean.com.au) is a specialist in travel throughout the Caribbean.
- **Caribbean Destinations** (© 03/9571-3744; www.caribbeanislands.com.au) is another Australian-based specialist in travel throughout the Caribbean.

STAYING CONNECTED
Mobile Phones

In Cuba, cellular service is controlled by **Cubacel,** Avenida 5 and Calle 76, Edificio Barcelona, Centro de Negocios, Miramar (© 7/204-1640; www.cubacel.cu). Cubacel has offices at the José Martí International Airport and in Havana and most major cities and tourist destinations. Cubacel offers SIM cards for CUC$3 per day. You'll have to leave a deposit and purchase a prepaid calling card.

If you have a Cuban friend, you could organize a permanent contract through them: a CUC$50 charge activates an account that must be topped up every 2 months with a minimum of CUC$10. If there has been no activity in 3 months, the line dies. Cubacel works with both TDMA phones and GSM systems. Prepaid calling cards are sold in denominations of CUC$10, CUC$20, and CUC$40. Rates inside Cuba run between CUC10¢ and CUC60¢ per minute for outgoing calls, depending on the hour and the package. Rates to the rest of the world run between CUC$1.40 and CUC$1.83 per minute. Text (SMS) messages are free to receive, but cost CUC16¢ to send within Cuba and CUC$1to send abroad. (Remember to dial Cuba's country code of 53 before any area code and the number you wish to dial in the country before using your own phone.)

Note: Any phone with a SIM from a U.S. provider will not work in Cuba.

Internet & E-mail

In all cities outside of Havana, head to the main **Etecsa** telephone office where you will find a small bank of computers. A large number of hotels in the provinces and most beach resorts also offer Internet access. In Havana, outside of the Etecsa office in La Habana Vieja, all the top-end hotels offer internet access. The **José Martí**

International Airport in Havana also has Internet access. Internet access in most hotels and at Etecsa offices costs CUC$6 per hour for dial-up access. It is frequently frustratingly slow and is best avoided. You'll need to show your passport to register and get a card with a scratch-off log-in number and password, which will allow you to use any Etecsa computer around the country. It is valid for 30 days.

A handful of hotels have Wi-Fi (wireless fidelity) "hot spots." These include the Meliá Cohiba, the NH Parque Central, Hotel Saratoga, Hotel Chateau Miramar in Havana, and the Hotel Meliá Santiago in Santiago de Cuba. Charges are from US$8 an hour.

Wherever you go, bring a **connection kit** of the right power and phone adapters, a spare phone cord, and a spare Ethernet network cable—or find out whether your hotel supplies them to guests. Throughout Cuba, electricity is mostly 110-volt AC, and most outlets are U.S.-style two- or three-prong. However, many of the large hotels and resorts that cater primarily to Canadian and European clientele are wired for 220 volts.

Newspapers & Magazines

The nationwide Spanish-language daily, *Granma,* is a thin paper with sparse coverage of local and international news, and a strong party-line editorial bias. The paper is not nearly as widely available as daily papers in most other countries, but some street vendors and many hotels do have copies each morning. English-digest versions of *Granma* come out every few days and are available at many hotels. A handful of other daily and weekly newspapers are published, and are usually even harder to find than *Granma.* These include *Trabajadores, Juventud Rebelede,* and a host of regional rags.

Telephones

The phone numbering system inside Cuba is being modernized, but it remains confusing. Havana's city code is one digit. Other area codes are two digits; individual phone numbers can range from five to seven digits. You do not need to use the city or area code for local calls, but you must dial 01 followed by the city or area code for any long-distance call within Cuba or to a cellphone, except when calling to or from Havana. Calling from Havana to any other province or from a province to Havana, you would dial only a zero before the area code. Thus, a call from Trinidad to Pinar del Rio would start 01-48. A call from Havana to Pinar del Rio would begin 0-48. The same rules apply for a cellphone call. All Cuba cellphones begin with a 5. To dial a cellphone from a fixed line in Havana, dial 0-5, then the rest of the cellphone number. If you call a cellphone from any other province, dial 01-5, then the rest of the cellphone number. If you dial cellphone to cellphone, just dial 5, then the rest of the cellphone number.

To call Cuba: If you're calling Cuba from the United States:

- First dial 011, the international access code.
- Then dial 53, the country code.
- And last, dial the area code and then the number.

The whole number you'd dial for a number in Havana (area code 7) would be 011-53-7-XXX-XXXX.

To make international calls: To make international calls from Cuba, first dial 119 and then the country code (U.S. or Canada 1, U.K. 44, Ireland 353, Australia 61, New Zealand 64). Next dial the area code and number. For example, if you want to call the British Embassy in Washington, D.C., you would dial 119/1-202-588-7800. You can make collect calls to Canada, Spain, the U.S., France, Italy, and the U.K.

For directory and operator assistance: Dial Ⓒ 113 if you're looking for a number inside Cuba and for domestic help, and dial Ⓒ 180 for numbers to all other countries and for help with collect calls.

Nearly all hotels and some *casas particulares* have phones in their rooms. Dialing instructions should be available in rooms; if not, contact the reception desk. Cuba has a wide range of **public telephone booths** where Cuban pesos (*moneda nacional*) and a variety of cards can be used. Most older sky-blue phones have been phased out but where you see them—and the newer royal-blue phones with a coin slot—they will take *moneda nacional*. This is the cheapest option where you can talk for a very long time for 1 peso.

You can also buy pre-paid calling cards with set values; with these cards, you can make telephone calls by first dialing an access code (166), then dialing the number on your card, followed by the hash key, and then the phone number you want to dial. These cards are available in CUC and in *moneda nacional* and may be worth purchasing if you plan to make a lot of local calls on your trip. Note that international calls made from these calling cards run between CUC$1.50–CUC$1.80 a minute. To dial an international number from a CUC pre-paid calling card, you must dial 166 followed by the card code followed by the hash key, followed by 119 (international code) followed by the international area code, then the number you wish to call, followed by a hash key.

New royal-blue phones can be used for these calling cards expressed in CUC (from CUC$5) and *moneda nacional* (from $10MN). Only buy the CUC cards to make international calls, as making a local call with a CUC card means you are paying more than several times the peso amount.

Note that many public phone booths, especially in Havana, frequently break down. Those that are working suffer from long queues in Havana and, if you are in a rush, this may not be your best option.

Note that if you stay in a *casa particular* and wish to confirm your subsequent *casa* in another town, your *casa* owner will make this courtesy call for you. Pre-paid calling cards can be used from land lines in *casa* homes too.

TIPS ON ACCOMMODATIONS

Cuba's accommodations for tourists range from top-class historic **hotels** to budget, basic uniform blocks in the cities. These are complemented by ***casas particulares,*** a system of excellent value Cuban guesthouses where Cubans can rent out a few of their rooms to guests. At **beach resorts,** hotels range from top-class luxury to above-basic facilities at slightly inflated prices, with a few very good exceptions at the more reasonable/lower end of the market. In most areas, *casas particulares* are not permitted right on the beach, due to government restrictions. In rural areas, there is a mix of high-end to moderately priced attractive accommodations as well as some unattractive government hotels.

Hotels are either owned or run by the Cuban state or are run as joint ventures with foreign companies. There are no 100% foreign-owned hotels in Cuba.

Most hotel options in Cuba have been divvied up among a few large state-run chains: **Islazul** (www.islazul.cu), **Gaviota** (www.gaviota-grupo.com), **Cubanacán** (www.hotelescubanacan.com), **Gran Caribe** (www.gran-caribe.com), and **Haba-guanex** (www.habaguanexhotels.com). These chains generally stake out distinct territories. Habaguanex has near monopoly control over the hotel scene in La Habana Vieja in Havana. Their properties tend to be midrange to upper end, and most are in beautifully restored colonial buildings. Gaviota, Cubanacán, and Gran Caribe divvy up the remainder of the midrange to upper-end hotels around the country. Islazul runs the most economical hotels, although it has begun refurbishing some real gems in the colonial heart of some of Cuba's more interesting cities. Cubanacán is also upgrading properties with its Hoteles Encanto brand.

These large state-run companies have signed management contracts with international hotel chains, usually resulting in improved service and hospitality. While the international **Barceló** (www.barcelo.com), **NH Hoteles** (www.nh-hotels.com), **Iberostar** (www.iberostar.com), **Accor** (www.accor.com), and **Occidental** (www.occidental-hoteles.com) chains run a few hotels each, predominantly in Havana and Varadero, the major player is the Spanish **Sol Meliá** chain (www.solmeliacuba.com), which manages 24 midrange to high-end properties in Cuba.

Be prepared for some pitfalls when booking directly through hotel websites in Cuba. Many of the state-run chains—**Gaviota, Habaguanex,** and **Cubanacán**—have primitive or poorly maintained websites, and their online booking mechanisms can be cumbersome and inconsistent. You'll definitely do better with the larger international chains like **Sol Meliá** (www.solmeliacuba.com), **Occidental** (www.occidentalhotels.com), and **Barceló** (www.barcelo.com).

There are consistently competitive live availability deals offered on **www.cuba hotelreservation.com** ★★★, and hotels honor these reservations with good rooms.

Casas Particulares

Aside from official hotels and resorts, the other principal lodging option in Cuba is a *casa particular,* or private house. To meet demand and inject just a bit of economic relief (and nascent capitalism) into the system, the government has authorized certain households to rent out a maximum of two rooms. *Note:* In September 2010, the government announced plans that would allow *casa* owners to rent out their entire home as an independent rental property, and open a *paladar* in addition to running a *casa.* By November 2010, new punitive tax codes for these changes had been published but new licenses had not been issued. An official *casa particular* should display a small plaque or sticker declaring it to be a government sanctioned *casa.* The symbol is a blue capital "H" set on its side, with slightly bent horizontal lines, and the top horizontal line longer than the bottom one. (It also looks like an anchor.) It should also say *Arrendador Divisa.* This means the owner of the house is allowed to rent rooms for *divisa* (hard currency). Houses with red symbols can only rent to Cubans for *moneda nacional.*

Casas charge from CUC$15 to CUC$25 in the low season and CUC$20 to CUC$35 in the high season. The most expensive rooms are in houses in Vedado and Miramar in Havana. In addition to the season, price variations depend on the number of guests, the length of stay, your status (students often receive discounts), the location of the house in the country (for example, the more remote or less touristy the area, the cheaper it could be), and the amount of tax that owners pay on the room (this is dictated by the number of rooms they rent, the square meterage of their house that tourists use, and the location of their house). Those with impressive colonial homes often charge more.

During low season, do negotiate for a lower nightly rate and always try to negotiate a lower rate for a long stay. Note that it is very difficult to get a discount for single travelers. Pairs/couples and families with children under 18 who share the same room enjoy the most value.

On arrival, *casa* owners must ask for your passport and enter the information into a registration book that must be taken to the immigration office within 24 hours of your arrival. You will be asked to sign next to your information in this book. If you are not asked to sign or are not asked for your passport, your *casa* may not be legal. *Casas particulares* can have no more than two rooms for rent. Each room can only hold up to three adults and children under 18. The owners must pay a tax of between CUC$100 and CUC$250 per room per month, plus the now obligatory monthly gastronomic tax. At the end of the year, a further tax of between 10% and 30% is paid on the total annual earnings.

Most houses are quite modest—you are basically living with a Cuban family. Rooms for rent will either have their own private bathroom or a bathroom shared with other tourists, not with the family. Your room will most likely have air-conditioning. If there is no air-conditioning, you should pay less. The minimum facilities you will receive are clean sheets, towels, and toilet paper, probably a bedside lamp, a wardrobe closet, and a sideboard. Some *casas* now have security boxes, TVs, and stocked fridges. Most houses will provide locked rooms with a key. You may or may not be given the keys to the house depending on the rules of the owners. Some *casas* have independent entrances, which appeal to some travelers. Most colonial houses that often make the most attractive *casas* do not have en suite bathrooms due to the configuration of the houses.

Most *casas particulares* serve huge, varied, and tasty meals (breakfasts and dinners) at very reasonable prices, especially since the optional gastronomic tax of CUC$30 a month has become obligatory. The biggest advantage of staying in a *casa* is that it is a great way to meet and interact with Cubans, something you cannot really do at "official" hotels and resorts. Most owners will also bend over backwards to assist you with your plans—whether that means answering your questions, arranging transport, or making phone calls for you.

If you have a reservation for your *casa*, your hosts should honor it. Similarly, if you make a reservation, you must turn up; losing CUC$25 on a no-show is a small fortune to a Cuban. Please respect this system because those who don't are forcing some Cubans not to respect reservations. If you just turn up without a reservation and the house is full, the owner will farm you out to a friend or relative at a nearby house. You are not under any obligation to take these places, but they could save you a lot of hassle—just be prepared to pay a commission. Make sure they are legal houses, though. Even with a reservation, it is wise to make a follow-up confirmation by e-mail or by phone. *Casa* owners are happy to phone ahead to your next *casa* to tell the future host you are on your way.

Be aware that if you show up at a *casa particular* on the recommendation of a taxi driver or *jinetero*, either of them will expect a commission of between CUC$1 and CUC$5, which invariably is added onto the bill at your *casa particular*.

Warning: Be wary of *jineteros* (hustlers), who may try to dupe you into staying in a *casa* that they recommend so that they earn a commission. Sometimes *jineteros* will just tell you that the *casa* you have a reservation in is full; others will take you to the door, put the key in and pretend it's locked, saying that the owner is away; others will tell you the owner of the *casa* you have a reservation in has moved, died, or gone abroad and they can take you to a similar house nearby (from which they'll receive a commission). In this desperate economic climate, *jineteros* will stop at nothing until they collect a commission. Be on guard, and do not be deterred by these scams. If you have a reservation, be confident and insistent that you stay at the *casa particular* where you have a room reserved.

Frommer's has received reports of the occasional theft from *casas particulares*. This is an extremely rare occurrence, since renting rooms to tourists is the main source of hard currency for Cubans. Putting this at risk is, quite frankly, idiotic in Cuba's economic climate.

SUGGESTED CUBA ITINERARIES

Cuba is a big island—the largest in the Caribbean—and its attractions and charms run the gamut from the hustle and bustle of Havana, to the colonial grandeur of Trinidad and a host of other small and well-preserved old cities and towns, to the steamy, vibrant streets of Santiago, and the sparkling waters and white sands of a half-dozen or more top-notch beach destinations. So, you will need to plan well to make the most out of any trip here. The following itineraries should be used as rough outlines. Other options include specialized itineraries focused on a particular interest or activity. Bird-watchers could design an itinerary that visits a series of prime bird-watching sites. Latin dance or art enthusiasts could arrange a specialized trip to focus on these interests. And revolutionary history buffs could build a trip around visits to the Moncada barracks (Cuartel de Moncada) in Santiago, the Che Guevara Memorial (Monumento Ernesto Che Guevara) in Santa Clara, and the Bay of Pigs (Playa Girón). Feel free to pick and choose—you can combine a bit of one, with a smidgen of another, or come up with something entirely on your own.

THE REGIONS IN BRIEF

Cuba is probably the most intensely diverse island destination in the Caribbean, with everything from standard fun-in-the-sun beach resort getaways to colonial city circuits, myriad land and sea adventure opportunities, tobacco and classic-car theme tours, and a wide array of cultural and artistic offerings. There's a lot to see and do in Cuba, and most travelers will have to carefully pick and choose. This chapter will provide you with descriptions of the country's regions, along with itineraries that will help you get the most from your visit.

Cuba is the westernmost and largest of the entire chain of Caribbean islands, located at the convergence of the Caribbean Sea, the Gulf of Mexico, and the Atlantic Ocean just 145km (90 miles) south of Florida. They say that Cuba—if you use your imagination—looks something like a crocodile: The head is in the east, a line of small islands form the ridges along its back, the Sierra Maestra national park forms the front legs, the Zapata Peninsula forms the rear legs, and Pinar del Río province is the tail.

Cuba is in fact a closely linked string of archipelagos, made up of more than 4,000 separate little islands and cays.

Cuba's two major cities, Havana and Santiago de Cuba, are port cities with large protected harbors. Most of the island's other principal cities lie along its centerline, either right on or just off the Autopista Nacional (National Hwy.), the country's principal trade and transportation route.

HAVANA & PLAYAS DEL ESTE   **Havana** is Cuba's capital and the country's most important cultural, political, and economic hub. With a wealth of museums, antique buildings, old forts, the Malecón seaside promenade, and modern restaurants, clubs, and cabarets, Havana is one of the liveliest and most engaging cities in Latin America. Just east of the city center are some 15km (9 miles) of very respectable white-sand beach, the **Playas del Este.** While nowhere near as stunning as some of Cuba's more celebrated beach destinations, the Playas del Este are certainly a suitable alternative, either as a base for exploring Havana or as an easily accessible place for sun, sand, and sea.

VIÑALES & WESTERN CUBA   Comprising the new province of Artemisa and the most western province of Pinar del Río, western Cuba is a wonderfully rustic region of farms and forests, flanked by some beautiful and relatively underpopulated beaches. The only real city in the province, **Pinar del Río,** is of limited interest on its own, but it serves as a gateway to **Viñales** and the **Vuelta Abajo,** Cuba's premiere tobacco-growing and cigar-manufacturing region. Just north of Pinar del Río, Viñales is a pretty little hamlet in an even prettier valley, surrounded by stunning karst hill formations. Viñales is Cuba's prime ecotourist destination, with great opportunities for hiking, bird-watching, mountain biking, and cave exploration. On the far western tip of the island sits the tiny resort of **María la Gorda,** home to some of the best scuba diving in Cuba. Lying off the southern coast of this region in the Caribbean Sea are the island destinations of **Isla de la Juventud,** one of Cuba's top premiere scuba-diving destinations, and **Cayo Largo del Sur,** another long stretch of dazzling and isolated white sand.

VARADERO & MATANZAS PROVINCE   Matanzas is Cuba's second-largest province and home to its most important beach destination, **Varadero.** Boasting some 21km (13 miles) of nearly uninterrupted white-sand beach, Varadero is Cuba's quintessential sun-and-fun destination, with a host of luxurious all-inclusive resorts strung along the length of this narrow peninsula. In addition to Varadero, Matanzas province is home to the colonial-era cities of **Matanzas** and **Cárdenas.**

In the southern section of the province is the **Ciénaga de Zapata,** a vast wetlands area of mangrove and swamp, renowned for its wildlife-viewing, bird-watching, and fishing opportunities. This is also where you'll find the **Bahía de Cochinos (Bay of Pigs),** where the nascent Cuban revolutionary state defeated an invasion force trained, supplied, and abetted by the United States. The beaches of **Playa Girón** and **Playa Larga** serve as a base for access to some of Cuba's best scuba diving. Playa Girón also possesses, arguably, the most stunning colorful waters in Cuba.

TRINIDAD & CENTRAL CUBA   Beginning with the provinces of Villa Clara and Cienfuegos, and including the neighboring province of Sancti Spíritus, central Cuba is the start of the country's rural heartland. Vast regions of sugar cane, tobacco, and cattle ranges spread out on either side of the Autopista Nacional, which more or less bisects this region as it heads east.

SUGGESTED CUBA ITINERARIES

The Regions in Brief

The Regions in Brief

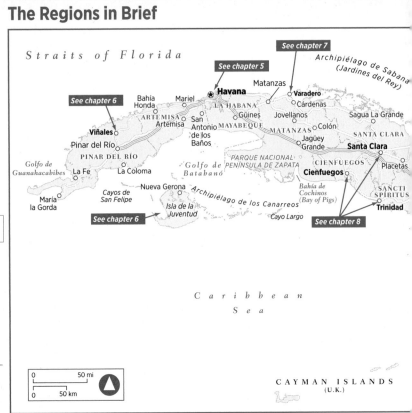

Trinidad is perhaps Cuba's quintessential colonial-era city, with beautifully maintained and restored buildings set on winding cobblestone streets. The cities of **Santa Clara, Cienfuegos,** and **Sancti Spíritus** are considered lesser lights on the tourism circuit, but all have ample charms of their own. Santa Clara is a lively university town, and is considered the "City of Che Guevara," with its massive memorial to the fallen revolutionary leader. To the north of Santa Clara lie the tiny and utterly charming colonial city of **Remedios** and the beautiful beach resorts of **la Cayería del Norte.** Cienfuegos is a charming port town with the country's second-longest seaside promenade. Sancti Spíritus is one of the original seven *villas* of Cuba, with some wonderful old historic churches and buildings, and a more natural feel than you'll find in other more touristy towns.

CAMAGÜEY & NORTHEASTERN CUBA This section of mainland Cuba is little more than a string of rural towns and small cities, anchored by two colonial-era cities. This is Cuba at its quietest, stuck in time and in no rush to break free. However, off the northern coast here lie a series of modern beach resorts built on long stretches of soft and silvery white sand, connected to the mainland by a long narrow causeway that seems to barely skirt the surface of the sea. The sister resort islands of

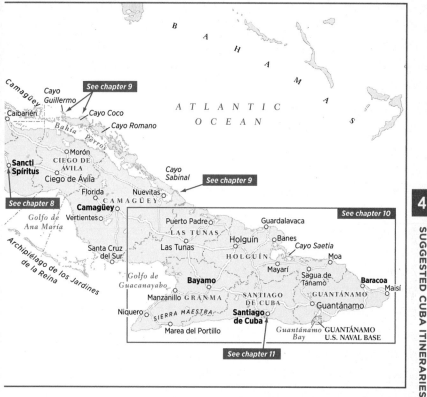

Cayo Coco and Cayo Guillermo are two of the finest and most popular resort destinations in Cuba. Several less-developed beach resorts stretch east along the coast on the string of islands making up the Archipiélago de Camagüey, better known as the Jardines del Rey (King's Gardens). The cities of **Ciego de Avila** and **Camagüey** are seldom explored colonial-era cities. The latter, in particular, has loads of charms and attractions, and is being restored to highlight much of its former glory. North of Camagüey is the tiny but growing beach resort of **Santa Lucía**. It's best known for its excellent scuba diving, offering a chance to dive with bull sharks.

EL ORIENTE   For most of the country's history, the whole eastern end of Cuba was known as El Oriente. Today, it is comprised of four separate provinces: Holguín, Granma, Santiago de Cuba, and Guantánamo. This is a large region with a host of gorgeous natural attractions, highlighted by the mountains of the **Sierra Maestra**— a mecca for naturalists and adventure travelers as well as those looking to follow in the revolutionary footsteps of Fidel and Che—and the very beautiful beaches of **Guardalavaca,** yet another of Cuba's premier beach resort destinations, with unimaginably fine white sand and calm turquoise waters. Of the cities here, only

Santiago de Cuba is a tourist draw in its own right, although visitors to **Holguín, Bayamo,** or **Baracoa** will experience Cuba at its most authentic.

SANTIAGO DE CUBA   This is Cuba's second largest city. Set between the Sierra Maestra mountains and the sea, Santiago is a vibrant city with a rich artistic and cultural heritage. Santiago is considered the heart of Cuba's Afro-Cuban and Afro-Caribbean heritage, which is expressed in the music, dance, and religion you'll find here. Santiago's Carnival celebrations are by far the best in Cuba, and some of the best in the entire Caribbean.

The city itself has a charming colonial-era center and a host of interesting museums and attractions, including José Martí's tomb and mausoleum, the original Bacardí rum factory, and the impressive Castillo del Morro protecting the city's harbor. Nearby sites worth visiting include the El Cobre shrine to the island's patron saint, La Virgin de Caridad, and the Gran Piedra, a massive rock outcropping allowing for great hiking and views.

4 CUBA IN 1 WEEK

This is a tough one. Many visitors are content to spend an entire week soaking up the rays and lying in the sand at an all-inclusive beach resort. I often devote an entire week to Havana. However, the following itinerary seeks to pack a handful of Cuba's top attractions into a concise, yet doable, week-long visit. You'll get a taste of the country's best big city and its top colonial-era town, as well as some time on the beach.

Day 1: Arrive & Settle into Havana

Arrive and check in to your hotel. Take an afternoon walk along the **Malecón** and have a sunset cocktail at the **Hotel Nacional de Cuba ★★** (p. 97). For dinner, head to either **La Fontana ★★** (p. 110) or **La Cocina de Lilliam ★★** (p. 110), two of the city's best *paladares*. Be sure to make a reservation as soon as you get to your hotel, because these places book up fast. After dinner, catch some jazz at **La Zorra y El Cuervo ★★** (p. 132) if you're not jet-lagged.

Day 2: Step Back in Time in Havana

Start the morning off in **La Habana Vieja** (p. 114). Visit the **Plaza de la Catedral, the Plaza de Armas, Plaza Vieja,** and **Plaza de San Francisco.** Be sure to tour the **Museo de la Ciudad ★★** (p. 115), the **Castillo de la Real Fuerza ★** (p. 114, and any other attractions that catch your attention. Have lunch at **La Bodeguita del Medio ★** (p. 105). After lunch, head toward **Parque Central** and visit **El Capitolio ★** (p. 117, and then later, either the Museo Nacional de las Bellas Artes ★★ (p. 115), or the **Museo de la Revolución ★** (p. 115). Finish up your afternoon strolling along the outdoor art exhibit that is **Callejón de Hammel ★★★** (p. 117), but if your second day is a Sunday, arrive here earlier for the Sunday rumba sessions. If you have a spare half-hour, drive by the **Plaza de la Revolución ★** to see the José Martí memorial and the iconic iron sculpture of the face of Che Guevara on the Ministry of the Interior building. In the evening, go to the **Tropicana ★★★** (p. 130) for dinner and a show.

Day 3: Trinidad

Head for Trinidad. Stay in one of the many glorious *casas particulares* right in the colonial center of this classic little city. Spend the afternoon touring Trinidad's colonial-era landmarks, including the **Plaza Mayor,** the **Plazuela El Jigüe,** the **Iglesia de la Santísima Trinidad,** and the **Museo Romántico ★★** (p. 203). For dinner, make a reservation at **Paladar Estela ★★** (p. 208) or **Sol y Son ★★**. After dinner, stroll around the Plaza Mayor and listen for where the action is. It might be a salsa or *son* band playing on the steps below the **Casa de la Música ★** (p. 207), or it might be in any one of several clubs nearby, including the excellent **Palenque de los Congos Reales ★★**.

Day 4: Checking in with Che

Spend the morning walking around Trinidad, and shopping at the various little street markets around town. From Trinidad, head north to **Santa Clara ★**, Che Guevara's city. Your first and most important stop here is the massive and impressive **Monumento Ernesto Che Guevara ★** (p. 184), set on the Plaza de la Revolución Che Guevara. In the early evening, head to **Parque Vidal,** the downtown heart and soul of Santa Clara. Stop in to tour the **Teatro La Caridad,** and then head to **Hostal Florida Center ★★** (p. 187) for dinner. After dinner, see if there's anything happening at **Club Mejunje ★★** (p. 187).

Days 5 & 6: Hit the Beach

From Santa Clara, head to **La Cayería del Norte ★★★** (p. 188), where you will find a handful of large, luxurious resorts on some of the finest beaches in Cuba. Be sure to stop for a bit in the tiny, colonial-era town of **Remedios ★★★** (p. 187) on your way. And then settle in for some serious relaxation. There's excellent snorkeling and scuba diving, as well as numerous opportunities to indulge in other watersports. Or you can just chill.

Day 7: Going Home

Return to **Havana** in time for your international connection. If you have extra time, head to the **Almacenes San José** market (p. 126) to do some last-minute shopping before you go.

CUBA IN 2 WEEKS

If you've got 2 weeks, you'll be able to hit all the highlights mentioned above, as well as some others, including Cuba's second city Santiago, a side trip to the gorgeous *mogotes* (limestone formations) and tobacco farms of the Viñales valley, and visits to Cienfuegos and Baracoa, two underappreciated Cuban cities. And, you get to do all this at a slightly more relaxed pace to boot. This itinerary starts off very similar to the 1-week version above, but soon diverges.

Day 1: Arrive & Settle into Havana

Arrive and settle in to your hotel. Spend the afternoon walking along the **Malecón ★★★** and have a sunset cocktail at the **Hotel Nacional ★★** (p. 97). After sunset, head over for dinner at **Los Doce Apóstoles ★** (p. 111)

Cuba in 1 Week & 2 Weeks

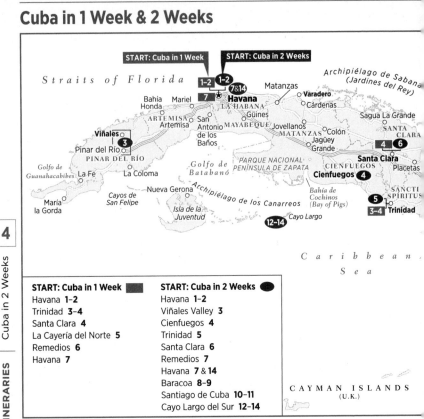

START: Cuba in 1 Week

START: Cuba in 2 Weeks

START: Cuba in 1 Week
Havana 1–2
Trinidad 3–4
Santa Clara 4
La Cayería del Norte 5
Remedios 6
Havana 7

START: Cuba in 2 Weeks
Havana 1–2
Viñales Valley 3
Cienfuegos 4
Trinidad 5
Santa Clara 6
Remedios 7
Havana 7 & 14
Baracoa 8–9
Santiago de Cuba 10–11
Cayo Largo del Sur 12–14

in the **Parque Histórico Morro y Cabaña** ★★ (p. 121). Stick around for the *cañonazo* (cannon-firing) ceremony.

Day 2: Step Back in Time

Start the morning off in **La Habana Vieja** ★★★. Visit the **Plaza de la Catedral,** the **Plaza de Armas, Plaza Vieja,** and **Plaza de San Francisco.** Be sure to tour the **Museo de la Ciudad** ★★ (p. 115), the **Castillo de la Real Fuerza** ★ (p. 114), and any other attractions that catch your attention. Have lunch at **La Bodeguita del Medio** ★ (p. 105). After lunch, head toward **Parque Central** and visit **El Capitolio** ★ (p. 117), then either the **Museo Nacional de las Bellas Artes** ★★ (p. 115), or the **Museo de la Revolución** ★ (p. 115). Finish up your afternoon strolling along the outdoor art exhibit that is **Callejón de Hammel** ★★★ (p. 117), but if your second day is a Sunday, arrive here earlier for the Sunday rumba sessions. If you have a spare half-hour, drive by the **Plaza de la Revolución** ★ to see the José Martí memorial and the iconic iron sculpture of the face of Che Guevara on the Ministry of the Interior building. In the evening, head to the **Tropicana** ★★★ (p. 130) for dinner and a show.

Day 3: The Viñales Valley by Day, Jazz at Night

Sign on for an organized day tour of the **Viñales valley ★★★**. You'll get to take in some of Cuba's best natural scenery, and also visit a tobacco farm and cigar-rolling facility. You'll probably also visit the Guayabitas liquor factory in **Pinar del Río** (p. 135), and take a quick tour through **La Cueva del Indio** (p. 140). This jam-packed day tour should still get you back to Havana in time for a dinner at one of the city's standout *paladares* (private home restaurants), followed by some hot jazz at **La Zorra y El Cuervo ★★** (p. 132) or the **Jazz Café ★** (p. 132).

Day 4: Cienfuegos, la Perla del Sur

Pick up a rental car and head for **Cienfuegos ★**, a bustling port city on the southern coast, with a compact, yet very attractive colonial-era core. Get to know the old center around **Parque José Martí,** visiting the **Catedral de la Purísima Concepción** and the **Teatro Tomás Terry ★** (p. 194). In the afternoon, head out to the Punta Gorda district and have a sunset drink on the roof of the **Palacio del Valle** (p. 198). For dinner, walk downstairs to the Moorish dining room or to the basement for the tapas bar (p. 198).

Day 5: Trinidad

From Cienfuegos, it's a short hop to **Trinidad** ★★★, with some beautiful scenery along the coast. Stay in one of the glorious *casas particulares* right in the colonial center of this classic little city. Spend the afternoon touring Trinidad's colonial-era landmarks, including the **Plaza Mayor,** the **Plazuela El Jigüe,** the **Iglesia de la Santísima Trinidad,** and the **Museo Romántico** ★★ (p. 203). For dinner, make a reservation at **Paladar Estela** ★★ (p. 208) or **Sol y Son** ★★. After dinner, stroll the area around the Plaza Mayor and listen for where the action is. It might be a salsa or *son* band playing on the steps below the **Casa de la Música** ★ (p. 209), or it might be in any one of several clubs nearby, including the excellent **Palenque de los Congos Reales** ★★.

Day 6: Checking in with Che

Spend the morning walking around Trinidad and shopping at the various little street markets around town. From Trinidad, head north to **Santa Clara** ★, Che Guevara's city. Your first and most important stop here is the massive and impressive **Monumento Ernesto Che Guevara** ★ (p. 184), set on the Plaza de la Revolución Che Guevara. In the early evening, head to **Parque Vidal,** the downtown heart and soul of Santa Clara. Stop in to tour the **Teatro La Caridad,** and then head to **Hostal Florida Center** ★★ (p. 187) for dinner. After dinner, see if there's anything happening at **Club Mejunje** ★★ (p. 187).

Day 7: Remedios and Back to Havana

In the morning, drive to the nearby charming town of **Remedios** ★★★ (p. 187). This is one of Cuba's smallest and best-preserved old colonial-era towns. Tour the **Iglesia de San Juan Bautista** ★★ (p. 188), with its intricately carved and ornate baroque altar, and stop for a cool drink or light lunch at the open-air **Café El Louvre** ★ (p. 188) right on the town's central plaza. Allow yourself a little over 4 hours to drive from Remedios back to Havana, where you'll turn in your rental car before taking a flight for the rest of your trip.

Days 8 & 9: Head East to Baracoa

From Havana, take a flight (booked well in advance) to **Baracoa** ★★★ (p. 261), the oldest, and arguably most beautiful city in Cuba. You'll definitely want to stay in the **Hotel El Castillo** ★★ (p. 266), with its commanding setting on a hillside over the city. Spend 1 day exploring the architecture and old-world charms of the city, and another hiking the lush forests around **El Yunque** ★★ or the **Parque Nacional Alejandro de Humboldt** ★★ (p. 265). Despite its diminutive size, Baracoa is a bustling little burg with excellent nightlife.

Days 10 & 11: Sweltering Santiago

In Baracoa, you can arrange for a transfer, Víazul bus, or private taxi to **Santiago de Cuba** ★★★, the island's second-largest city. If you want to be in the heart of downtown, choose the **Hotel Casa Granda** ★★ (p. 281), while if you're looking for more comfort, amenities, and facilities, you should book a room in the **Meliá Santiago de Cuba** ★★ (p. 283) or stay in some of the city's lovely *casas particulares*. You'll need 2 days to fully explore this colonial-era port city, with its host of historical and architectural attractions. Be sure to schedule at least 1 night at Santiago's fabulous **Casa de la Trova** ★★ (p. 289) or its even better **Casa de las Tradiciones** ★★★ (p. 289).

Days 12, 13 & 14: Hot Sun, Cool Sands, Clear Water

Finish your trip off with some downtime at an all-inclusive resort on **Cayo Largo del Sur** ★★★ (p. 156). You'll have to fly here from Havana, and you're best off just buying a 3-day/2-night package from any of the tour desks in Havana or Santiago. You should easily be able to arrange a flight from Santiago to Havana that connects with a flight to Cayo Largo; be sure that your flight back from Cayo Largo gets you into Havana in time for your international connection and flight home. If you have time pressures, opt for one of the top-end all-inclusives at Varadero ★★. Or, head north to the wonderful beaches of **Guardalavaca** ★★, a 4-hour drive from Santiago.

CUBA FOR FAMILIES

Most of Cuba's principal attractions—its art, architecture, history, music, cigars, and so on—are geared toward adults. There are, in fact, few attractions or activities geared for the very young. This is why I recommend families base themselves out of a town that has a large all-inclusive resort with a well-developed children's program. For my money, Varadero is the best bet, although a case can be made for Guardalavaca, as well. Both have a host of excellent all-inclusive resorts. If your children are worldly and inquisitive, feel free to swap out some resort days for the more cultural side trips to cities, destinations, and attractions described in some of the other itineraries in this chapter.

Day 1: Arrive in Varadero

Fly directly into **Varadero.** I recommend the **Tryp Península Varadero** ★★★ (p. 172), which has an excellent children's program and tons of activity and tour options. After settling into your room, check out the **children's program** and any **activities** or **tours** scheduled for the coming days. Feel free to adapt the following days' suggestions accordingly. Spend some time on the beach or at the pool.

Day 2: Take in an Attraction or Two

Varadero is chock-full of attractions geared toward the whole family. You can head to see the dolphin show at the local **Delfinario** (p. 195) or take a cruise up the main strip in a candy-pink gleaming classic American convertible (p. 167). If your family is adventurous, try the **Boat Adventure** ★, which is a fast and furious trip through the mangroves aboard sit-on-top motorized watercraft.

Day 3: A Trip to Trinidad

All of the hotel tour desks offer day trips to **Trinidad** ★★★. While some travel via bus, you should splurge and take a plane. Trinidad is an immaculately preserved colonial city, with a very compact central core that shouldn't tire or bore your children. In fact, they should get a kick out of the rough cobblestone streets, ancient architecture, vibrant street markets, and a real glimpse into everyday Cuban life.

Day 4: Parents' Day Off

Drop the kids off with the **children's program** for at least 1 full day and treat yourselves to some time alone. If you play golf, schedule a round at the **Varadero Golf Club** ★ (p. 166). Or, if you want to pamper yourself, take advantage of the excellent **spa services** right at the Tryp Peninsula Varadero. Pick up the kids and treat them to dinner off of the resort grounds. I recommend the **Mesón del Quijote** (p. 174), which is housed in a building with a medieval-style turret beside it.

Day 5: Head for the High Seas

Sign up for a day cruise on one of the many sailboats operating out of Varadero. These cruises head out to nearby cays, and include some snorkeling time, as well as lunch either on the boat or on some private little island beach.

Day 6: Parents' Night Off

This is your last day, so take advantage of the resort's in-house facilities and activities, but be sure to reserve a babysitter for the evening and make reservations for dinner and a show at the **Tropicana Matanzas** ★★ (p. 161).

Day 7: Heading Home

Use any spare time you have before your flight out of **Varadero** to buy last-minute souvenirs and gifts, or just laze on the beach or by the pool. The Centro Comercial de Hicacos has a children's toy shop.

COLONIAL TREASURES HIGHLIGHTS TOUR

Cuba's colonial cities are some of the best-preserved and architecturally intact examples to be found anywhere in the hemisphere. From the remarkable restored grandeur of Old Havana to the rugged realism of Trinidad to tiny Baracoa—one of the oldest colonial cities in the Americas—there's a wealth of history, culture, and overall beauty to be found in the country's colonial treasures.

Days 1 & 2: Havana

Follow the itinerary as described above in "Cuba in 2 Weeks."

Day 3: Cienfuegos

Pick up a rental car and head for **Cienfuegos** ★, a bustling port city on the southern coast, with a compact, yet very attractive, colonial-era core. Get to know the old center around **Parque José Martí,** visiting the **Catedral de la Purísima Concepción** and the **Teatro Tomás Terry** ★ (p. 194). In the afternoon, head out to the Punta Gorda district and have a sunset drink at the **Club Cienfuegos** (p. 195). For dinner, head to the historic old **Palacio del Valle** ★★ (p. 198).

Day 4: Trinidad

From Cienfuegos, it's a short hop to **Trinidad** ★★★, with some beautiful scenery along the coast. Stay in one of the many glorious *casas particulares* right in the colonial center of this classic little city. Spend the afternoon touring Trinidad's colonial-era landmarks, including the **Plaza Mayor,** the **Plazuela El Jigüe,** the **Iglesia de la Santísima Trinidad,** and the **Museo Romántico ★★** (p. 203). For dinner, make a reservation at **Paladar Estela ★★** (p. 208) or **Sol y Son ★★**. After dinner, stroll around the Plaza Mayor and listen for where the action is. It might be a salsa or *son* band playing on the steps below the **Casa de la Música ★** (p. 207), or it might be in any one of several clubs nearby including the excellent **Palenque de los Congos Reales ★★**.

Day 5: Sancti Spíritus

While its colonial center is modest in size and level of restoration, **Sancti Spíritus** nonetheless retains a wonderful sense of its former glory and receives far less tourist traffic than any other city on this tour. You'll definitely want to walk along **Calle Llano ★**, a narrow cobblestone alleyway of pastel-colored and tile-roof houses. You'll also want to have lunch or dinner at one of the outdoor patio tables overlooking the old stone **Puente Yayabo (Yayabo bridge),** which was built in 1825. Be sure to book a room at the **Hostal del Rijo ★★**, a comfortable hotel in a restored old mansion set on a quiet little plaza.

Days 6 & 7: Camagüey

Although far less celebrated—or visited—than Trinidad, **Camagüey ★★** just may be Cuba's richest colonial-era city, outside of Old Havana, in terms of art, architecture, and general ambience. The city's colonial core retains its highly irregular layout and an unequaled collection of impressive 16th-, 17th-, and 18th-century churches. The city's **Plaza del Carmen ★★** (p. 231) and **Plaza San Juan de Dios ★★★** (p. 232) are two impeccable and evocative city squares. Sitting right near the center of all the ancient action, the old **Gran Hotel ★** (p. 233) should be your first choice.

Day 8: Bayamo

Even though most of this city was deliberately torched in 1869 as an act of civil disobedience, it still makes a wonderful stop on a route taking in Cuba's principal colonial cities. Stay at the new refurbished boutique **Hotel Royalton ★★** (p. 255), which sits right on the central **Parque Céspedes ★★** or stay in one of the centre's friendly *casas particulares.* You'll also want to visit the **Casa Natal de Céspedes ★** (p. 254), the birthplace of the "father of the Cuban nation," and the only house on the square that escaped destruction from the fire.

Days 9 & 10: Santiago de Cuba

This is a colonial highlights tour, so you'll want to stay in the heart of downtown; choose either the **Hotel Casa Granda ★★** (p. 281), the **Hostal Basilio ★** (p. 281), or the private **Casa Maruchi ★**. You'll need 2 days to fully explore this beautiful colonial-era port city, with its host of historical and architectural attractions. Be sure to schedule at least 1 night at Santiago's fabulous **Casa de la Trova ★★★** (p. 289) or its even better **Casa de los Tradiciones ★★★** (p. 289). Turn in your rental car here in Santiago.

Day 11: Baracoa

From Santiago, take a Víazul bus or private taxi to **Baracoa ★★★** (p. 261), the oldest and arguably most beautiful city in Cuba. It's fitting to finish off this tour

Colonial Treasures

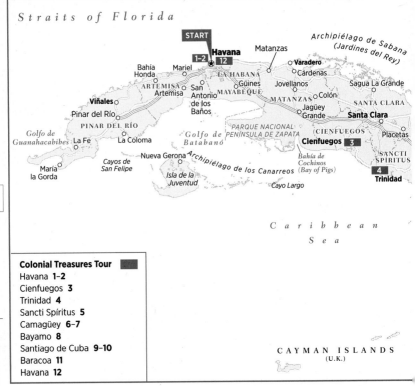

Colonial Treasures Tour
Havana **1–2**
Cienfuegos **3**
Trinidad **4**
Sancti Spíritus **5**
Camagüey **6–7**
Bayamo **8**
Santiago de Cuba **9–10**
Baracoa **11**
Havana **12**

in the oldest city on the island. You'll definitely want to stay in the **Hotel El Castillo** ★★ (p. 266), with its commanding setting on a hillside over the city. Spend your time here exploring the architecture and old-world charms of the city. Despite its diminutive size, Baracoa is also a bustling little city with excellent nightlife.

Day 12: Heading Home

From Baracoa, take a flight back to **Havana** in time for your international connection. If you have extra time, head to the **Almacenes San José** market (p. 126) to do some last-minute shopping before you go.

HAVANA IN 3 DAYS

Havana is an amazing—at times, overwhelming—city, overflowing with history, art, architecture, culture, nightlife, and more. Three days will allow you to visit its most important attractions, and maybe even discover some of its lesser-known charms.

Day 1: Start in the Old City

Start your day in La Habana Vieja. Visit the **Plaza de la Catedral,** the **Plaza de Armas, Plaza Vieja,** and **Plaza de San Francisco.** Be sure to tour the **Museo de la Ciudad ★★** (p. 115), the **Castillo de la Real Fuerza ★** (p. 114), and any other attractions that catch your attention. Have lunch at **La Bodeguita del Medio ★** (p. 105). Spend the afternoon exploring the area around Parque Central, which includes **El Capitolio ★** (p. 117), the **Museo Nacional de las Bellas Artes ★★** (p. 115), and the **Museo de la Revolución ★** (p. 115). Make a reservation in advance for the last tour of the Partagás cigar factory (p. 118). You will not have time to visit four attractions in one afternoon, so prioritize them beforehand.

As the day cools down, take a stroll on the **Malecón ★★★** (p. 86). If you've got the energy, you should be able to make the 20-minute walk to the **Hotel Nacional ★★** (p. 97) in time for a sunset *mojito* at their outdoor bar.

La Fontana 🍽 ★★

For dinner, visit the alfresco dining area of La Fontana (p. 110), a *paladar* known for its *parillada* and creative dishes.

Day 2: Vedado & Miramar

Start the morning strolling along the beautiful tombs and mausoleums of **Cementerio de Colón** ★★ (p. 118). From here, head over to the outdoor art exhibit that is the **Callejón de Hammel** ★★★ (p. 117). By now, you should have worked up enough of a sweat for a refreshing bowl of ice cream at **Coppelia** ★ (p. 119).

From Vedado, take a taxi to Miramar and the Playa district. Be sure to visit the **Maqueta de la Habana** ★ (p. 120), a rather impressive mock-up model of the entire city. Since you're out in this neck of the woods, have a late lunch at **La Cocina de Lilliam** ★★★ (p. 110), on the one hand because it's an excellent restaurant, and on the other, because your dinner tonight will be pedestrian at best (though the cabaret show will be unforgettable). After lunch, head to the **José Martí Memorial** (p. 119), and enjoy the panoramic view from the highest spot in Havana. Then, imagine the Plaza de la Revolución fit to bursting during a political rally and admire the iconic **image of Che Guevara cast in iron** ★ on the Ministry of the Interior building and the new image of Camilio Cienfugos on the Ministry of Communications building opposite the memorial.

Tropicana 🍵 ★★★

It's time to pull out all the stops and head to the Tropicana (p. 130) for dinner and a show. This place is the original and still the best cabaret show in Cuba. Stick around after the show for some serious salsa dancing in the adjacent Salón Arcos de Cristal club.

Day 3: More La Habana Vieja

Give yourself another day in La **Habana Vieja**—there's just no way you've seen it all in 1 day. Be sure to visit some of the art galleries and to spend some time shopping at the **Almacenes San José** indoor market (p. 126. Have lunch on one of the ancient plazas here. I recommend either the restaurant **Santo Angel** ★ (p. 106) or the **Cafetería El Portal** (p. 107). In the late afternoon, head over to the **Parque Histórico Morro y Cabaña** ★★ (p. 121) and explore the forts and museums at this complex.

Los Doce Apóstoles 🍵 ★

After touring the complex, grab an outdoor table near sunset at Los Doce Apóstoles (p. 111), and enjoy the view of Havana across the harbor from this restaurant. Be sure to finish your dinner in time for the *cañonazo* ceremony.

After dinner and the *cañonazo*, head to **Zorra y El Cuervo** ★★ (p. 132) for a late-night jazz concert.

HAVANA

t's hard to convey the wonder, sensuality, and alluring fallen beauty of Havana. It's hard to imagine a city with such rhythm and verve, a city at once so tremendously vibrant and at the same time laid-back—that is, until you've taken a lazy stroll along the Malecón, gotten lost in the time warp of La Habana Vieja's colonial cobblestone streets, taken a ride in a 1940 Dodge taxi through crumbling Centro Habana, danced salsa until dawn after catching the Tropicana floor show, or witnessed Afro-Cuban religious rituals on the street.

Originally established in 1514 on Cuba's southern coast, San Cristóbal de la Habana had been moved by 1519 to its present-day location on the island's north coast, at the mouth of a deep and spacious harbor with a narrow, protected harbor channel. Before long, Havana had become the most important port in the Spanish colonial empire, a natural final gathering place for the resupply and embarkation of the Spanish fleet before returning to the Old Country laden with bounty. By 1607, Havana had been declared the capital of colonial Cuba, and by the early 1700s, it was the third-largest city in the Spanish empire, behind Mexico City and Lima.

Subsequent centuries saw Havana grow steadily in wealth, size, and prominence. Havana was luckily spared the bulk of the violence and fighting that occurred in Cuba's Wars of Independence, and later revolutionary war. Following the sinking of the USS *Maine* in Havana harbor in 1898, a long period of direct U.S. control and indirect U.S. influence followed. This period saw the first indications of suburban sprawl and the growing importance of the western neighborhoods of Vedado and Miramar. This era was also marked by a strong presence of mob activity, with the likes of Al Capone, Meyer Lansky, and Lucky Luciano setting up shop in Havana.

Havana has been largely frozen in time in the wake of the 1959 Revolution. Decades of economic crisis and shortages have left much of Havana in severe decay and decomposition. The great exception to this rule is La Habana Vieja, where parts have been meticulously restored to much of its colonial glory, using a percentage of tourism receipts from the Old City hotels. Although the situation in Havana is beginning to change, with the recent boom in tourism and tourism-related growth, what new construction has occurred over the past 40 years has largely borne the drab architectural stamp of the former Soviet Union and its central state planning. Luckily, most of this has taken place outside the boundaries of the city center. Today, Havana, with some 2.5 million inhabitants, is the largest city in the Caribbean and Cuba's undisputed political, business, and cultural center.

ESSENTIALS

Getting There

BY PLANE

Arriving international passengers clear Customs on the ground level of Terminal 3 at the **José Martí International Airport** (✆ **7/266-4133;** airport code HAV). All of the major car-rental agencies have kiosks or booths just outside of Customs. There's also an **Infotur** kiosk (✆ **7/266-4094;** www.infotur.cu), where you can buy a map and pick up some brochures, and a **Víazul** kiosk (www.viazul.cu), where you can book advance bus tickets.

There's an ATM among all the booths and kiosks on the ground floor, and another on the second floor, where departing passengers check in. **Etecsa,** the national phone company, has booths with card-operated pay phones on this level, as well as on the second floor. You can either buy a card from them, or from one of the souvenir vendors on the second floor. Internet is also available.

Taxis wait in a long line just outside the ground-floor exit. In 2008, all taxis changed their name to Cubataxi and all are run by the Ministry of Transport. The rate to any hotel in downtown Havana is CUC$20 to CUC$25; airport taxis refuse to use their meters on this run.

Some charter flights and all national flights arrive at either Terminal 1 or 2. Both terminals also have Infotur offices or kiosks, an ATM, telephones, and taxis.

If you're driving from the airport, the main artery into Havana is Avenida de Rancho Boyeros. This will bring you to the Plaza de la Revolución and the towering José Martí Memorial. In general terms, if you continue straight, or roughly north toward the sea, you will hit the University of Havana and Vedado. Miramar and Playa will be to the left (west) and are best reached via the Malecón, while Centro Habana and La Habana Vieja will be to the right (east).

BY CAR

Entering Havana by car is a confusing mess. Almost none of the major arteries into downtown are marked. This is especially true of the Autopista Nacional coming in from the east, which dumps you unceremoniously into the midst of an urban mess of some of the city's outer neighborhoods. Similarly, while there is ostensibly a beltway, or *Circunvalación,* around the downtown area, it and its various exits are virtually entirely unmarked.

One good tactic for navigating Havana is to somehow find your way to the Malecón; from there, the entire city is relatively easily accessible. The main thoroughfare through Miramar and Playa is Avenida 5.

BY TRAIN

The principal train station, or **Estación Central,** is located in La Habana Vieja at Calle Egido and Calle Arsenal (✆ **7/861-4259**). There are always taxis waiting.

BY BUS

The main **Víazul** bus station (✆ **7/881-1413** or 7/881-5652; www.viazul.com) is located at Avenida 26 and Zoológico in Nuevo Vedado, on the outskirts of downtown.

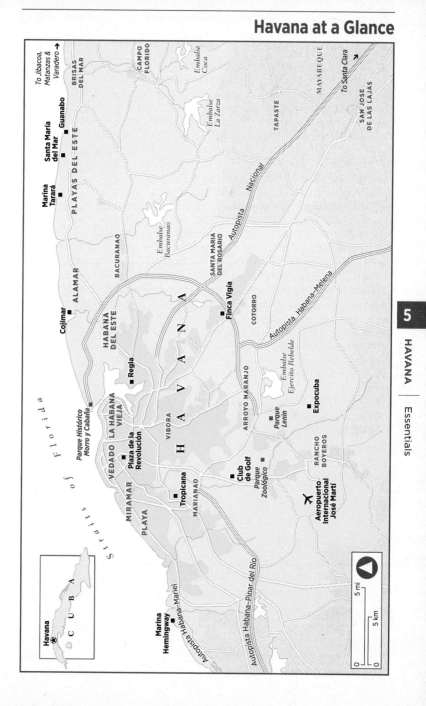

From here, it is a CUC$3 taxi ride to Vedado and CUC$4 to CUC$5 to La Habana Vieja. There are always taxis available at the station.

BY BOAT

Marlin's Marina Hemingway, Avenida 5 and Calle 248, Santa Fe, Playa (*ℂ* **7/204-1150** or 7/204-5088; www.nauticamarlin.com), is the principal port of call and official point of entry for clearing Customs and Immigration. When arriving by sea, contact the marina before entering Cuban waters (19km/12 miles offshore) on VHF channels 16 or 77. Commercial cruise ships dock at the Sierra Maestra Terminal in La Habana Vieja, just off the Plaza de San Francisco.

Visitor Information

Infotur (*ℂ* **7/866-3333;** www.infotur.cu), Calle Obispo, corner of Bernaza, is the official state-run tourist information agency. It has offices or kiosks in several strategic spots around Havana, and in each of the three terminals at the airport. It can provide you with some brochures and information, and can usually help you make reservations. Most of the kiosks also have a small selection of maps and various local tourist guides and books for sale.

There are a handful of large, state-run tour agencies that have desks at most hotels around town and these are actually more useful than Infotur in general; these include **Havanatur** (*ℂ* **7/204-8409;** www.havanatur.cu), **Cubanacán** (*ℂ* **7/208-6044;** www.cubanacan.cu), and **Cubatur** (*ℂ* **7/835-4155;** www.cubatur.cu). These are your best bets for information and tour bookings around the country. In Havana, the **San Cristóbal** agency, part of Habaguanex, Calle Oficios 110 bajos between Calles Lamparilla and Amarguar (*ℂ* **7/861-9171;** www.viajessancristobal.cu) also provides city tours that include some interesting sociocultural tours not offered by other agencies.

City Layout

Havana is a major city built around its ample and protected harbor. The oldest colonial-era buildings are closest to the harbor, and the bulk of the expansion heads out west from there. The city is bordered along its northern edge by the Caribbean Sea. The majority of Havana's denizens live in large, densely populated working-class neighborhoods to the south of the principal downtown business and tourist neighborhoods. While there are communities on the eastern side of the harbor, the most important neighborhoods and developments are all found on the western side. These communities are generally laid out in a series of abutting grids, although they often abut at odd angles.

While the streets in Vedado and Playa tend to be numbered or carry a letter designation, the neighborhoods of La Habana Vieja and Centro Habana have only named streets. To make matters more confusing, most of the streets in La Habana Vieja and Centro Habana have two or more names—those that appear on maps and street signs are often different from their common names. Wherever possible, I've tried to give the most common and popularly used name.

In La Habana Vieja and Centro Habana, street names are generally displayed on little plaques or signs attached to the sides of corner buildings at street intersections. The plaques tend to be hung relatively high, at about 3m (10 ft.) or so. In Vedado and

La Habana Vieja & Centro Habana

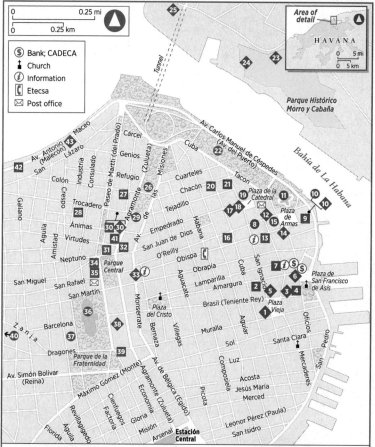

ACCOMMODATIONS ■
Hotel Ambos Mundos **13**
Hotel Conde de Villanueva **7**
Hotel Deauville **42**
Hotel del Tejadillo **21**
Hotel Florida **16**
Hotel Inglaterra **35**
Hotel Lido **28**
Hotel Los Frailes **4**
Hotel Plaza **32**
Hotel Raquel **2**
Hotel Santa Isabel **9**
Hotel Saratoga **39**
Hotel Sevilla **30**
Hotel Telégrafo **34**
NH Parque Central **31**
NH Parque Central La Torre **41**
Palacio O'Farrill **20**
Park View Hotel **27**

DINING ◆
Café del Oriente **6**
Café La Mina **14**
Café Taberna **3**
Cafetería El Portal **18**
El Bodegón Criollo **23**
El Floridita **33**
El Templete **10**
La Bodeguita del Medio **17**
La Divina Pastora **24**
La Dominica **12**
La Taberna de la Muralla **1**
Los Doce Apóstoles **25**
Los Nardos **38**
Restaurante Castropol **43**
Restaurant-Pizzeria El
  Asturianito **38**
Roof Garden Restaurant **30**
Santo Angel **5**

ATTRACTIONS ●
Castillo de la Real Fuerza **11**
Catedral de San Cristóbal **19**
Chinatown **40**
El Capitolio **36**
El Templete **10**
Fábrica de Tabaco Partagás **37**
Museo de la Ciudad **15**
Museo de la Revolución y
  Memorial *Granma* **26**
Museo de Arte Colonial **8**
Museo Nacional de Bellas
  Artes **29**
Parque la Maestranza **22**

Playa, you'll want to look lower, as most intersections feature a .5m-high (1½-ft.) concrete block in a sort of pyramid shape, with the street name engraved on it.

Street addresses are usually given as follows: Prado no. 22, e/Tejadillo y Empedrado; or 23 e/L y M. In the case of the first example, the address is for building 22 on Paseo del Prado, located between the cross streets Calle Tejadillo and Calle Empedrado. In the second case, the address is for an unnumbered building on Calle 23 between Calles L and M. Note that Cuban addresses frequently omit the word "Calle" or "Avenida." Also, Cubans usually refer to Avenida 5 as "Quinta Avenida," "5ta Avenida," or—most commonly—simply "5ta."

Neighborhoods in Brief

La Habana Vieja La Habana Vieja (Old Havana) is the historic colonial heart of Havana. Situated at the eastern edge of the city, in the area beginning around the Paseo del Prado, or Paseo de Martí, and the Parque Central, and extending to the Harbor Channel, it is a dense collection of colonial-era and neocolonial houses, mansions, churches, seminaries, and apartment buildings punctuated by a few picturesque plazas and parks. UNESCO declared La Habana Vieja a World Heritage Site in 1982, and today it is one of the most beautiful restored colonial cities in the world. You will find the city's greatest collection of museums and attractions here, as well as a broad selection of restaurants and beautifully restored boutique hotels. This is an area best explored on foot.

Centro Habana In many ways, Central Havana is little more than the necessary and neglected area connecting La Habana Vieja with Vedado. It is defined on its northern edge by the Malecón, the seaside pedestrian walkway that stretches from La Habana Vieja to the end of Vedado. The stretch of the Malecón (and everything inland from it) between the Hotel Nacional and La Habana Vieja is a study in decay and decomposition. Still, it is quite picturesque and charming in its own way. Centro Habana is primarily a residential area, although it does have a high concentration of *casas particulares* (private rooms for rent).

> **Beware:** I cannot stress enough the level of decay here. Balconies, crown molding, and other large chunks of brick, mortar,

and stone regularly drop off buildings here, sometimes injuring passersby below.

Vedado & the Plaza de la Revolución Beginning more or less at the Hotel Nacional and extending west to the Almendares River, and south to the Plaza de la Revolución, Vedado is a busy mix of middle- to upper-class houses and businesses. As the older sections of La Habana Vieja and Centro Habana began to overflow, residential and business growth centered on Vedado. Calle 23, or La Rampa, is the principal avenue defining Vedado, and it's where you'll find Coppelia, the Tryp Habana Libre (former Havana Hilton), and the Hotel Nacional. The broad Plaza de la Revolución sits on high ground on the southern edge of Vedado and houses several government agencies, in addition to the towering José Martí Memorial, the National Theater, and the National Library.

Playa This upscale residential district is located just west of Vedado, past the Almendares River. The most important neighborhood here is **Miramar,** home to many prominent businesses and most of the resident foreign community in Cuba. Almost all of the various embassies and diplomatic missions have set up shop in the various Batista-era mansions that make up this neighborhood. There are several large and luxurious, business-class hotels here, as well as many private rooms for rent in wonderfully maintained, neocolonial mansions.

Habana del Este & Playas del Este On the eastern banks of the harbor is Habana del Este, and about 11km (6¾ miles) farther east along the coast are the Playas del Este,

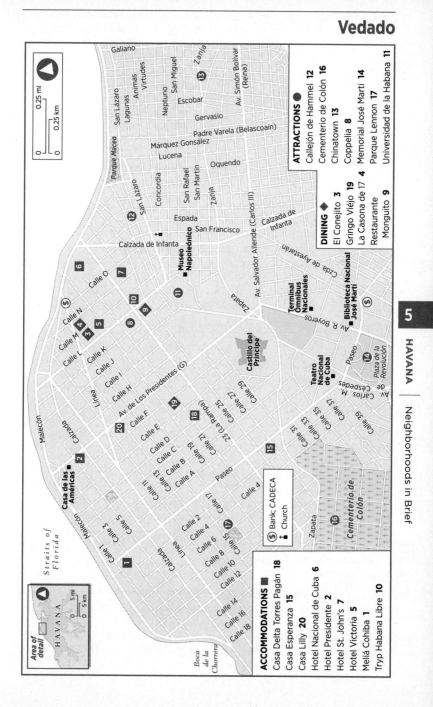

ATTRACTIONS ●
Callejón de Hammel **12**
Cementerio de Colón **16**
Chinatown **13**
Coppelia **8**
Memorial José Marti **14**
Parque Lennon **17**
Universidad de la Habana **11**

DINING ◆
El Conejito **3**
Gringo Viejo **19**
La Casona de 17 **4**
Restaurante
Monguito **9**

ACCOMMODATIONS ■
Casa Delta Torres Pagán **18**
Casa Esperanza **15**
Casa Lilly **20**
Hotel Nacional de Cuba **6**
Hotel Presidente **2**
Hotel St. John's **7**
Hotel Victoria **5**
Meliá Cohiba **1**
Tryp Habana Libre **10**

$ Bank, CADECA
✝ Church

5

HAVANA | Neighborhoods in Brief

or eastern beaches, which stretch on for about 15km (9 miles) of their own. Habana del Este and Playas del Este are connected to the rest of Havana by a tunnel running between La Habana Vieja and the area around the Morro Castle. There are also frequent little passenger ferries running between La Habana Vieja and the neighborhoods of Regla and Casablanca. The towns that comprise Habana del Este, Alamar, Cojímar, and Ciudad Panamericana are working class and industrial. The beaches of Playas del Este, on the other hand, are beautiful stretches of white sand fronting the sea. These beaches are popular with both Cubans and travelers alike.

Near the Airport The area near and around the airport is an industrial wasteland. There are no hotels or facilities for tourists here. Playa and Miramar, about a 15- to 20-minute drive away, are the closest neighborhoods for travelers looking for quick access to the airport; however, the extra time and distance to hotels in Vedado or La Habana Vieja are negligible.

Getting Around
BY TAXI

There is a host of different taxi cars with modern fleets geared toward the tourist trade. They have all been reunited under Ministry of Transport management and, although they continue to carry the names of the previous companies such as Panataxi, Taxi OK, and Transgaviota, they are now all called **Cubataxi** and can be called on a central number (© 7/855-5555-59). All tourist taxis have meters. (Taxi drivers claiming their meters are broken are gearing up to rip off tourists.) Rates vary somewhat, but most of the meters start at CUC$1 for the first kilometer and then charge between CUC$.50 and CUC$.85 for each additional kilometer. The most economical cabs are the yellow old-style Panataxis without air-conditioning, followed by the new yellow models with air-conditioning. Other options include horse-drawn carriages; the so-called **Coco Taxis** (© 7/873-1411), yellow, round, open-air two seaters powered by a motorcycle; and antique cars that range from a Ford Model T to a 1957 Chevy. Both the horse-drawn carriages and Coco Taxis cost from CUC$5 to CUC$10 per hour, with a minimum of around CUC$3. **Gran Car** (© 7/881-0992) is the only agent for antique-car rentals. Gran Car rates, with a driver, run CUC$25 per hour or CUC$125 per day, or CUC$30 per hour and CUC$150 per day for convertibles. A four-day trip (with 100km per day maximum) works out at between CUC$110 and CUC$135.

Peso taxis, *bicitaxis* (bicycle taxis), and freelance taxis are lesser options for most tourists. All are illegal for tourists, although it's the driver, not the rider, who is at risk. If you choose one of these options, be sure to fix your price beforehand, and don't be surprised if the driver is somewhat paranoid about the money transfer, and/or refuses to drop you off right at your hotel.

BY FOOT

Havana is a great town to walk around. It's almost entirely flat (although you need to keep an eye on the sometimes rough pavement) and safe (although there have been reports of muggings and pick-pocketing in Centro Havana). Early morning, late afternoon, and early evening are the prime times to walk. High heat and heavy humidity can make long walks, particularly around midday, a little uncomfortable. La Habana Vieja is best explored on foot, and a walk along the Malecón is obligatory. Attractions in Vedado and Miramar are a little spread out, making them less desirable to explore

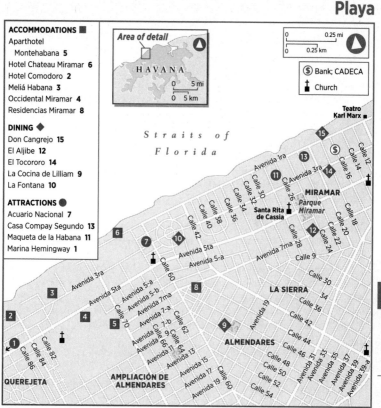

ACCOMMODATIONS ■
Aparthotel
  Montehabana **5**
Hotel Chateau Miramar **6**
Hotel Comodoro **2**
Meliá Habana **3**
Occidental Miramar **4**
Residencias Miramar **8**

DINING ◆
Don Cangrejo **15**
El Aljibe **12**
El Tocororo **14**
La Cocina de Lilliam **9**
La Fontana **10**

ATTRACTIONS ●
Acuario Nacional **7**
Casa Compay Segundo **13**
Maqueta de la Habana **11**
Marina Hemingway **1**

on foot, although a walk along La Rampa in Vedado, or Quinta Avenida (Av. 5) in Miramar, are both rewarding.

BY CAR

There's really no reason for tourists to rent a car to explore Havana. Taxis are plentiful and relatively inexpensive. Moreover, streets are poorly marked and it's a confusing city to navigate.

One exception would be to rent an antique car from **Gran Car** (© 7/881-0992). Gran Car's fleet runs from restored 1930s open-air Ford cruisers to classic 1950s Chevys, Buicks, De Sotos, and Studebakers.

If you do want to rent a modern car while in Havana, there is a host of options, including **Cubacar** (© 7/273-2277; cubacar@transtur.cu), **Havanautos** (© 7/207-9898; havanautos@transtur.cu), and **Rex** (© 7/835-6830 or 7/683-0303; www.rex.cu). All three are run by **Transtur** (© 7/862-2686 or 7/861-5885; www.transtur.cu). **Micar** (© 7/204-7777 or 7/204-8888) and **Vía Rent a Car** (© 7/861-4465; www.gaviota-grupo.com) are also options. All of the above companies have desks at the airport and at a host of major hotels around Havana. See "Getting Around" in chapter 3 for more information.

In general, traffic is much lighter than you'd find in most major urban areas. However, you do have to pay more attention to a wide range of obstacles, from pedestrians and bicyclists to horse-drawn carriages. While most roads in Havana are in pretty decent shape, it's not uncommon to come across huge potholes or torn-up sections of road with no markings or warnings. Moreover, street markings and signs are minimal, making navigation challenging.

BY BUS

For all intents and purposes, Havana's woefully overburdened urban bus system is not a viable option for tourists. Routes are overcrowded, and there are no readily available route maps and schedules.

Truly hearty travelers and independent souls can give the local buses a try. Your best bet is to query locals about routes and hours and where to find the appropriate stop. A large number of metro buses either originate or have a stop at the Parque de la Fraternidad, a block south of the Capitolio. A new bus service, known as *taxi rutero*, has begun, costing five Cuban pesos. Most buses are entered from the front, although some are still entered from the rear and use an honor system of passing your coins forward. Some have separate lines for those wanting a seat (*sentado*) and those willing to stand (*parado*). Fares run around 40 centavos to one peso in Cuban pesos (*moneda nacional*).

Transtur runs the red **HabanaBusTour** coaches (© 7/261-9015; www.transtur.cu) on two routes with a hop-on/hop-off service. Route T1 starts at Castillo de la Fuerza in La Habana Vieja and terminates at Restaurant La Cecilia (5th Avenida between Calles 110 and 112). T3 runs from Parque Central to Playas del Este. One ticket is valid for the whole day. Bus T1 costs CUC $5 and Bus T3 costs CUC$3. Children 5 and under travel free (one child per adult). Buses run daily from 9am to 7:30pm. All schedules are marked at the bright red bus stops.

BY MOTO

Visitors can rent mopeds (*motos*) to tour the city. This might be useful if you want to explore places that are off the beaten track or visit numerous places in one day. A one-day rental costs CUC$24, and a 5–12 day rental costs CUC$21 per day. *Moto* rental centers can be found at Galiano and San Rafael, Centro Habana (© 7/866-8634); Avenida Malecón and C, Vedado (© 7/834-6544); and Calle 3ra and 30, Miramar (© 7/204-0646).

[FastFACTS] HAVANA

Car Rentals See "Getting Around," above.

Currency Exchange Currency exchange offices are ubiquitous around Havana. There are branches of the state-run casa de cambio **CADECA** (© 7/855-5701) throughout Havana, as well as at the airport and in the lobbies of most major hotels.

Most banks will also exchange money.

Dentists Hospital Cira García, Calle 20 no. 4101, Playa (© 7/204-4300 or 204-2811; www.cirag.cu), and other major medical centers also provide dental care. If you want a specific recommendation, contact your embassy, or ask at

your hotel's front desk. Alternately, you can contact **Asistur** (© 7/866-4499; www.asistur.cu), which can help you with dental emergencies.

Doctors Cuba has a surfeit of doctors and many hotels catering to tourists have one or two on staff. If not, your hotel is still probably your best bet for a recommendation. You can also try contacting your embassy or **Asistur** (✆ **7/866-4499;** www.asistur.cu), which specializes in emergency medical care and insurance.

Drugstores Well-stocked drugstores are few and far between in Havana. There's a 24-hour pharmacy at the international terminal of the José Martí airport (✆ **7/266-4105**). The pharmacies at the **Hotel Sevilla** (✆ **7/861-5703**) in La Habana Vieja, and **Tryp Havana Libre** (✆ **7/838-4593**) in Vedado, are usually decently stocked. In Miramar, you can try the **Farmacia Internacional,** Avenida 41 and Calle 20 (✆ **7/204-2051**), also at Avenida 3 between Calle 78 and 80 (✆ **7/204-4515**) and Avenida 7 and Calle 26 (✆ **7/204-7980**).

Embassies & Consulates See "Fast Facts: Cuba," p. 295.

Emergencies Dial ✆ **106** for police; ✆ **104, 838-1185,** or 838-2185 for an **ambulance;** and ✆ **105** for the **fire department.** At none of these numbers can you assume you will find an English-speaking person on the other end. Also, you can try contacting **Asistur** (✆ **7/866-4499**), which specializes in emergency medical care for travelers.

Express Mail Services The main office of **DHL,** Calle 26 and Avenida 1, Miramar (✆ **7/204-1578;** www.dhl.com), will pick up and deliver anywhere in Havana. **EMS Cubapost,** Calle 21 no. 1009, between Calles 10 and 12, Vedado (✆ **7/831-3328**), is a Cuban-run express mail service with a desk at most post offices.

Eyeglasses Look for the word óptica. **Optica Miramar,** Avenida 7 and Calle 24, Miramar (✆ **7/204-2269**), is one of the better ópticas catering to foreign residents and visitors. It has a branch in downtown Havana at Calle Neptuno 411, between San Nicolás and Manrique (✆ **7/862-1292**), and another at Obispo 364 between Habana and Compostela. For contact lenses, try the **Centro de Contactología,** Obispo 359 between Habana and Compostela (✆ **7/860-8262**).

Hospitals Your best bet is **Hospital Cira García,** Calle 20 no. 4101, Playa (✆ **7/204-4300** or 7/204-2811; www.cirag.cu), which provides emergency services and long-term care. Another possibility is the **Hospital Hermanos Almeijeiras,** Calles San Lázaro and Belascoaín, Centro Habana (✆ **7/876-1000**).

Internet Access Internet access is becoming more common and available in Havana, but it can still be a frustrating experience to try to use the Internet. The most popular Internet cafe in town is located at **El Capitolio** (p. 117). The rate here is CUC$5 per hour, and the 14 machines here are often booked solid. Aside from this, your best options are the various hotels with business centers and/or Internet terminals in their lobbies; most of these charge CUC$6 an hour for use of the Internet terminals, and CUC$8 or more per hour Wi-Fi. Alternately, you can go to any **Etecsa** office. These offices sell disposable access cards at CUC$6 per hour, which are good at any Internet-equipped Etecsa office in the country for 30 days after first usage. There's one at Calles Obispo, corner of Calle Habana, in La Habana Vieja.

Maps The various Infotur booths and kiosks around town sell a pretty decent map of Havana for CUC$1; sometimes they'll even give you a copy for free. Most rental-car agencies and hotels can also give you a copy of the same, or a similar, map. The Cuban Geographic and Cartographic Institute publishes a couple of much more detailed maps of Havana, including the Ciudad de la Habana Mapa Turistica, which you can get at most tourist gift shops and Infotur kiosks. You'll also find good maps online at **www.cubaroutes.com** and **www.cubamapa.com.** The best road map to Cuba is the Guía de Carreteras published by Limusa; it can be bought at El Navegante, Calle Mercaderes 115 between

5

Obispo and Obrapía, La Habana Vieja.

Police Dial ☏ **106.** Although it's possible for someone who speaks English to be rounded up, do not expect to find an English-speaking person on the other end. In the event of serious danger, you are probably better off contacting your embassy (nonlicensed U.S. citizens should contact the U.S. Interests Section only as a last resort).

Post Office Most major hotels either have small post office branches, or will sell you stamps and post letters. This is generally your best bet, as the correos (public post office branches) are often crowded and inefficient. In La Habana Vieja, there's a correo on the west end of the Plaza de San Francisco. There's another on the side of the Gran Teatro toward the Capitolio. Both are open Monday through Saturday from 8am to 5pm.

Safety Havana is a very safe city. There's a strong police presence and street crime is uncommon, especially in tourist areas. But because streetlights are virtually nonexistent, it's wise to avoid the dark alleys and side streets of Havana after dark. Recently, there have been reports of muggings and pick-pocketing in Havana, so be aware of your surroundings. Solo female travelers should not walk alone through Centro Habana late at night, unless you're walking through Galiano or the pedestrian section of San Rafael. Popular tourist spots are relatively safe at night. Still, given the vast economic gap between Cubans and tourists, you should be careful about where you walk and whom you engage. It is best not to wear much jewelry or make other showy signs of wealth.

Taxis See "Getting Around," earlier in this chapter.

WHERE TO STAY

There's a wide range of hotel options and *casas particulares* (private rooms) for rent in Havana. Hotel options are divvied up among the large state-run chains. **Habaguanex** has monopoly control over the hotel scene in La Habana Vieja, and **Gaviota, Cubanacán,** and **Gran Caribe** own the remainder of the midrange to upper-end hotels around Havana. Of the international hotel chains, the major player in town is the Spanish-owned **Sol Meliá**, which manages three large, high-end properties in Havana. Given the fact that hotel chains control so much of the market, one major problem is a generalized lax attitude toward overbooking. Habaguanex and Gran Caribe are particularly notorious for this. Confirmed reservations at Gran Caribe's Hotel Nacional or Habaguanex's Santa Isabel have been shuttled off to one of their sister properties, usually with no compensation and little sympathy.

There are hundreds of *casas particulares* in Havana. The neighborhoods of Centro Habana, Vedado, and Playa have the greatest concentration of *casas particulares,* although La Habana Vieja is starting to catch up. In general, the rooms and homes are kept very clean, while the furnishings and amenities are quite simple. The rates average between CUC$20 and CUC$35 per room, and meals are often available at very reasonable prices. With the broad range of *casa particulares* and rapid turnover in the market, it's impossible to list a representative selection. I've tried to include the most dependable and long-standing options in each neighborhood below. In addition, you can check out www.cubacasas.net and www.casaparticular.info.

Given the compact nature of Havana, the proximity of its major attractions, and the wide availability of relatively inexpensive taxis, the neighborhood you choose is not a limiting factor. In general, most visitors will want to spend most of their time exploring La Habana Vieja, so the hotels there or nearby in Centro Habana are best for direct walking access. Large group and package tourists, as well as business travelers, are usually funneled toward hotels in Miramar and Playa, about a 10- to 15-minute ride away from most of the action, although the area is home to some of the better dining and nightlife spots. Vedado is a sort of middle ground, with plenty of accommodations and excellent dining choices, easy access to the rest of the city's attractions, and quite a few natural charms of its own.

La Habana Vieja

With few exceptions, all of the hotels in Old Havana are run by the Cuban chain **Habaguanex.** These are intimate boutique hotels in beautifully refurbished old buildings. I've listed my favorite Habaguanex hotels below, but there are others that are also nice; check www.habaguanexhotels.com for the complete listing.

VERY EXPENSIVE

Hotel Santa Isabel ★★ This is one of the most highly touted hotels of the Habaguanex chain, and it *is* a lovely little hotel, wonderfully located on the eastern end of the Plaza de Armas. Still, they're stretching things when they tout it as a top-tier luxury hotel. Sure, it's elegant and charming, and definitely a top choice in Old Havana, but the rooms and bathrooms are rather compact, and you won't find many of the amenities you'd expect at most luxury hotels. The rooms themselves are dark and understated, with high ceilings and iron bed frames. The junior suites have a small sitting room and extra television, as well as Jacuzzi jets in their standard-size tubs. However, the best rooms in the house, aside from the sumptuous Santovenia suite, are nos. 304 through 314, which come with large rooftop terraces overlooking the plaza.

Calle Baratillo 9 (btw. Calles Obispo and Narciso López), Plaza de Armas, La Habana Vieja. ℂ **7/860-8201.** Fax 7/860-8391. www.habaguanexhotels.com. 27 units. CUC$204–CUC$240 double; CUC$260–CUC$300 junior suite; CUC$320–CUC$360 Santovenia suite. Rates include breakfast. MC, V. Free valet parking. **Amenities:** Restaurant; 2 bars; babysitting; Internet; room service; smoke-free rooms. *In room:* A/C, TV, minibar.

Hotel Saratoga ★★★ This hotel has the most luxurious rooms and appointments of any La Habana Vieja property. Even the standard rooms are very spacious, with marble or tile floors, elegant furnishings, and all the modern amenities. Each comes with a tub and separate shower. Many have a private balcony and view over Havana's bustling streets. Several of the suites here are truly special. I like the Suite Capitolio, which is a corner unit with a fabulous view of the Capitol dome from the king-size bed. The Prado and Habana suites are also top-notch rooms. Despite having nearly 100 rooms, this place still feels like a boutique hotel. Two of the best features here are the delightful rooftop pool with stunning views and probably the best breakfast in Cuba.

Paseo del Prado 603, La Habana Vieja. ℂ **7/868-1000.** Fax 7/868-1001. www.hotel-saratoga.com. 96 units. CUC$300–CUC$362 double; CUC$424–$CUC466 Prado suite; CUC$516–CUC$570 Capitolio suite; CUC$714–CUC$786 Habana suite. Rates include breakfast. MC, V. Free parking. **Amenities:** Restaurant; 2 bars; small gym; rooftop pool; room service; smoke-free rooms; Wi-Fi. *In room:* A/C, TV, minibar.

NH Parque Central ★★ This modern, upscale hotel dominates the northern end of Havana's small Central Park. Behind a wall of glass doors fronting the park sits the large atrium lobby area. The rooms are spacious, with dark colors, thick fabrics, and fresh carpeting. The marble bathrooms even have a separate bathtub and shower. These are probably the most comfortable luxury rooms in La Habana Vieja, and the hotel has a broad array of amenities and services—although it lacks the old-world charm and sense of time travel provided by other hotels in this part of town. The suites are huge, and some have private balconies with nice views over the park and toward El Capitolio. Service is relatively efficient and attentive, something that cannot always be said about most other hotels in La Habana Vieja. The rooftop pool and surrounding views are priceless.

Calle Neptuno (btw. Calles Prado and Zulueta), La Habana Vieja. ℂ 7/860-6627. Fax 7/860-6630. www.nh-hotels.com. 227 units. CUC$270 standard double; CUC$325 superior double; CUC$330–CUC$550 suite. Rates include breakfast. MC, V. Free valet parking. **Amenities:** 2 restaurants; 2 bars; 2 lounges; babysitting; health club; Jacuzzi; small rooftop pool; room service; smoke-free rooms; Wi-Fi. *In room:* A/C, TV, hair dryer, minibar.

NH Parque Central La Torre ★★ This is the new cool kid on the block. It is connected by an underground tunnel to its sister hotel, the NH Parque Central (see above). It has an equally lovely—if not better—rooftop swimming pool than the Parque Central, and it boasts a guests-only sky-high bar with magnificent views. The roof is enclosed by a high glass wall, which offers fantastic views. The spacious standard rooms contain large double beds and rainbow-striped desk chairs. Watch out for interior rooms with no views. Habana Elegante, the Italian ground-floor dining room serves an expensive but tasty *funghi* risotto flavored with black truffles.

Calle Zulueta (btw. Calles Virtudes and Calles Animas), La Habana Vieja. ℂ 7/860-6627. Fax 7/860-6630. www.nh-hotels.com. CUC$280 double; CUC$340 junior suite; CUC$385 superior suite. Rates include breakfast. MC, V. **Amenities:** Restaurant; 2 bars; babysitting; rooftop pool; room service; Wi-Fi. *In room:* A/C, TV, minibar.

EXPENSIVE

Hotel Ambos Mundos ★ Hemingway claimed this was "a good place to write," and the room where he wrote parts of *For Whom the Bell Tolls* is a shrine to the late author, featuring his typewriter and photocopies of some drafts and notes; it's now a small museum (no. 511; daily 10am–5pm; CUC$2). The hotel is a good base for exploring La Habana Vieja. The rooms are simple and somewhat spartan, but they are clean and comfortable, and most have high French doors opening to some views of the bustling streets. A few even have small balconies. Most folks love the compact old, iron-grated elevator running up the inside of the central staircase; however, it's woefully inadequate to meet demand, so if you're staying on an upper floor, you might find waiting for it frustrating. Breakfast is served on the rooftop patio under shady arbors with a wonderful view of the harbor and La Habana Vieja; this is also a great spot for a refreshing drink any time of day or night. The lobby bar features live piano music.

Calle Obispo 153 (corner of Calle Mercaderes), La Habana Vieja. ℂ 7/860-9530. Fax 7/860-9532. www. habaguanexhotels.com. 52 units. CUC$130–CUC$160 double; CUC$160 minisuite. Rates include breakfast. MC, V. Street parking nearby. **Amenities:** Restaurant; 2 bars; babysitting. *In room:* A/C, TV, fridge.

Hotel Conde de Villanueva ★ This place is geared toward cigar freaks, and only true aficionados should stay here. The hotel features one of the better and most respected cigar shops in town, La Casa del Habano, which rents out private humidors so that regular clients can always have their own personal reserve. The rooms are large and soaked in old-world charm, not to mention the scent of tobacco—all are smoking rooms, of course. The better and more expensive rooms come with views over the street. The building dates back to the end of the 18th century, and features a large portrait of its namesake count in the entryway. A pet peacock roams the large central courtyard. The semiformal Vuelta Abajo restaurant serves good Cuban cuisine, and there's a wonderful, shady little park just across the street.

Calle Mercaderes 202 (btw. Calles Lamparilla and Amargura), La Habana Vieja. ✆ **7/862-9293.** Fax 7/862-9682. www.habaguanexhotels.com. 9 units. CUC$130–CUC$160 double; CUC$200–CUC$242 suite. Rates include breakfast. MC, V. Free parking. **Amenities:** Restaurant; bar; Internet; room service. *In room:* A/C, TV, minibar.

Hotel Florida ★★ 🛎 This is my favorite of the converted old colonial mansions in La Habana Vieja. Built in 1836 and turned into a hotel in 1885, the Florida is stately and elegant, but be aware that a couple of the rooms don't have any windows. However, if you do get one of the window rooms or one of the suites, you may find it hard to head out and explore the city. The rooms are decorated with a mix of imitation and real antique furnishings, wrought-iron beds, checkerboard marble floors, and tasteful framed prints. The entrance is right on the busy Calle Obispo, and it's possible to miss it amid all the hustle and bustle. The tranquil central courtyard provides immediate relief, surrounded by soaring stone columns connected by high arches.

If the Florida is full, the newly opened **Hotel Marqués de Prado Ameno** (253 O'Reilly btw. Cuba and Aguiar), with its cloistered courtyard, is accessed through the Florida and shares the same management. Its 16 spacious rooms with marble floors still retain parts of the original friezes.

Calle Obispo (corner of Calle Cuba), La Habana Vieja. ✆ **7/862-4127.** www.habaguanexhotels.com. 25 units. CUC$130–CUC$160 double; CUC$180–CUC$260 suite. Rates include breakfast. MC, V. Free valet parking. Amenities: 2 restaurants; 2 bars; Internet; room service. *In room:* A/C, TV, minibar.

Hotel Los Frailes ★ 🛎 While I find the staff dressed in mock monk garb a little bit cheesy (not to mention how hot and uncomfortable it must be for them), this is still a lovely little hotel located in the heart of La Habana Vieja. The rooms have high ceilings, smooth stucco walls, and heavy wooden beds. Unfortunately, most of the rooms here lack windows, and only two of the four minisuites come with queen-size beds (the rest come with two twins). The narrow central courtyard is engulfed in lush tropical foliage cascading down from the second-floor hallways, and features a murmuring fountain, traveling art expositions, and a Plexiglas viewing port into the building's 19th-century water-collection system.

Calle Teniente Rey 8 (btw. Calles Mercaderes and Oficios), La Habana Vieja. ✆ **7/862-9383.** Fax 7/862-9718. www.habaguanexhotels.com. 22 units. CUC$110–CUC$130 double; CUC$150–CUC$170 minisuite. Rates include breakfast. MC, V. Street parking nearby. **Amenities:** Bar; Internet; room service. *In room:* A/C, TV, minibar.

Hotel Plaza ★ Built in 1909, this is one of the more historic hotels in La Habana Vieja. Suite no. 216 is still rented out, replete with bat and ball and other memorabilia from one of its more famous guests, the Sultan of Swat, Babe Ruth. The building also served as the headquarters of *El Diario de la Marina* newspaper. However, historic charm is in greater supply than actual comfort or luxury; although rooms have attractive dark-wood furniture and quite a few have narrow, private balconies, they are a little spartan. You'll find just as many famous ghosts haunting the Hotel Sevilla (see below), while enjoying more comfortable accommodations in some, but not all rooms. The hotel underwent renovations throughout 2009, the year of its 100th anniversary. The lobby is worth checking out, for its intricate mosaic tile floor, bas-relief trim, and stained-glass atrium skylights. And, by all means, come by for an afternoon drink at the rooftop Solarium Bar ★★, with great views of Havana and the neighboring Bacardí building.

Calle Ignacio Agramonte 267, La Habana Vieja. © **7/860-8583** or 7/867-1075. Fax 7/860-8591. www. hotelplazacuba.com. 188 units. CUC$120 double; CUC$145 suite. Rates include breakfast. MC, V. Free valet parking. **Amenities:** 3 restaurants; 3 bars; Internet; room service. *In room:* A/C, TV, hair dryer, minibar.

Hotel Raquel ★ This is one of the newer additions to the Habaguanex chain, and yet another stunningly restored old building. The facade is a visual orgy of bas-relief work, while the centerpiece of the marble-tiled lobby here is a soaring stained-glass atrium ceiling. The third-floor rooms share a large rooftop terrace, with wonderful views over Old Havana. The rooms themselves are spacious and attractively decorated with lamp fixtures and headboards of artistically crafted iron. However, at these prices I'd expect more than a 13-inch television and two twin beds (only two of the standard rooms here have a queen-size bed, although the suites do come with a king-size bed). This is often called "the Jewish hotel" Because the restaurant features borscht and latkes, while various lobby displays pay homage to Cuba's small, but active Jewish tradition. In fact, many of the staff members are drawn from the local Jewish community.

Calle Amargura, at the corner of San Ignacio, La Habana Vieja. © **7/860-8280.** Fax 7/860-8275. www. habaguanexhotels.com. 25 units. CUC$85–CUC$100 double; CUC$230–CUC$250 suite. Rates include breakfast. MC, V. Free valet parking. **Amenities:** Restaurant; bar; gym; room service. *In room:* A/C, TV, minibar.

Hotel Sevilla ★★ This is the best of the three grand old hotels (Sevilla, Inglaterra, and Plaza) near the Parque Central. Plus, it's got a lovely street-level pool and well-equipped little health club, which the other old dames lack. Still, all three are easily eclipsed by the new Hotel Saratoga (see above). Some of the standard rooms are a bit small and lackluster, and it's definitely worth the splurge for a superior or junior suite—you'll get a lot more space. The hotel was actually built in two stages, and all of the current rooms are in the newer Biltmore addition, which dates from the 1920s. The original (ca. 1908) Grand Sevilla operates as a hotel training school, although the original ornate, Moorish-influenced lobby area is still working and quite impressive. The ninth-floor Roof Garden Restaurant (p. 106) is one of the top dining options in town.

Calle Trocadero 55 (corner of Calle Prado), La Habana Vieja. © **7/860-8560.** Fax 7/860-8875. www. gran-caribe.com. 178 units. CUC$99–CUC$149 double; CUC$149–CUC$201 junior suite. Rates include breakfast. MC, V. Free valet parking. **Amenities:** 2 restaurants; 2 bars; babysitting; health club; outdoor pool; room service. *In room:* A/C, TV, minibar.

Palacio O'Farrill This sumptuous restored property once belonged to 18th-century Irish slave trader and sugar baron Richard O'Farrill. The hotel features floors built from the 18th through the 20th centuries. The second floor rooms are the best in the hotel, with 3m- (10ft.-) high doors that open into huge rooms decorated with black-and-white pictures and simple furniture. The hotel is in an excellent location close to the cathedral.

Calle Cuba 102-108 (corner of Calle Chacón), La Habana Vieja. © **7/860-5080.** Fax 7/860-5083. www. habaguanexhotels.com. comercial@ofarrill.co.cu. 38 units. CUC$130–CUC$160 double; CUC$180–CUC$210. Rates include breakfast. MC, V. **Amenities:** Restaurant; bar; Internet. *In room:* A/C, TV.

MODERATE

Hotel del Tejadillo ★   It's hard to find a better located hotel in La Habana Vieja. Just a half-block from the Plaza de la Catedral and La Bodeguita del Medio, and about 2 blocks from the Malecón, this renovated old mansion provides decent value and ample colonial charm. The spacious rooms have high ceilings, comfortable new beds, and Oriental throw rugs. About half of them come with fully equipped kitchenettes. Most are set around a typical central courtyard, with a central fountain surrounded by lush tropical plants and large sculptures. The biggest drawback here is the fact that quite a few rooms have no windows. Breakfast is served in a little dining room, or in a separate open-air courtyard. There's a lively bar here and it's far enough removed from the rooms so as not to keep you up.

Calle Tejadillo 12 (corner of Calle San Ignacio), La Habana Vieja. ℭ7/863-7283. Fax 7/863-8830. www.habaguanexhotels.com. 32 units. CUC$85–CUC$95 double; CUC$110–CUC$130 junior suite. Rates include breakfast. MC, V. Street parking nearby. **Amenities:** Restaurant; bar. *In room:* A/C, TV, kitchenette (in some), fridge.

Park View Hotel 🌶   This is one of the newer additions to the Habaguanex stable and one of its better values. This old hotel, originally opened in 1928, has been entirely restored and remodeled. Rooms, while by no means large, are comfortable and inviting. Their biggest drawbacks are the tiny, 13-inch television sets and the smallish bathrooms, which have slightly cramped corner shower units. Three interior units on each floor have no window, while the end rooms are slightly larger and come with a small balcony overlooking the shady little park that gives this hotel its name. The seventh-floor restaurant serves up standard Cuban and international fare, but with a wonderful view over the Morro Castle.

Calle Colón (corner of Calle Morro), La Habana Vieja. ℭ7/861-3293. Fax 7/863-6036. www.habaguanexhotels.com. 55 units. CUC$80–CUC$90 double. Rates include breakfast. MC, V. Free valet parking. **Amenities:** Restaurant; 2 bars; Internet. *In room:* A/C, TV, minibar.

INEXPENSIVE

Due to Habaguanex's almost complete control of the area, there are no budget hotel options in La Habana Vieja. This is one of the best locations in Havana, and the following *casas particulares* are recommended. **Chez Nous** ★, Calle Teniente Rey 115, between Calles Cuba and San Ignacio (ℭ 7/862-6287; cheznous1@ceniai.inf.cu), is a friendly house and a stone's throw from Plaza Vieja. Its two rooms, furnished with colonial antiques, share a smart bathroom and there's a great terrace where you can take in the sun. **Casa Lisette y Orlando,** Calle Aguacate 509, Aptos 301 y 102 between Calles Sol and Muralla (ℭ 7/867-5768; lisettesobrino@yahoo.es), is a clean, modern, quiet apartment run by a lovely, friendly couple. **Casa Eduardo Canciano** ★, Calle Refugio 103 between Calles Prado and Morro (ℭ 7/863-0523; www.winpict.com/cuba/eduardo/eduardo_canciano.htm; eduardo.canciano@infomed.sld.cu), is a first-floor flat run by a friendly family. It has a wonderful Sevillana patio and Spanish wooden colonial windows. The large bedroom equipped with air-conditioning and a fan has an adjoining, original jet-black-and-yellow bathroom. The dining room is next to the sweet balcony overlooking the street. **Casa Mary,** Calle Cárcel-Capdevila No. 59, 2nd floor, between Calles Morro and Zulueta (ℭ 7/861-5911; http://xoomer.alice.it/gianni_franci; mariange2850@yahoo.com), is a flat with an enormous terrace overlooking El Morro. It is next to the Spanish Embassy in a quiet location. The two small rooms both have doors out onto the terrace, where you may lounge on painted iron chairs.

Centro Habana

With the exception of Hotel Deauville, all of the hotels listed here are either right on, or very close to, the dividing line between La Habana Vieja and Centro Habana, and so are convenient for exploring Old Havana.

EXPENSIVE

Hotel Inglaterra This is yet another of the more historic and better located hotels in Havana, although it's definitely showing its age—it's been in business since 1875. The ornate lobby, with its colorful Moorish mosaics, and the lively streetside cafe, are the best features here. Rooms are perennially desultory and dated. However, quite a few of the rooms do come with a small balcony overlooking the Parque Central, a nice perk. The rooftop bar is one of the few such perches to stay open relatively late (closed Sat), although the concrete balustrade obstructs the views when seated at your table.

Paseo del Prado 416 (in front of Parque Central), Centro Havana. ☏ **7/860-8595.** Fax 7/860-8254. www.gran-caribe.com. 83 units. CUC$120 double; CUC$175 suite. Rates include breakfast. MC, V. Free valet parking. **Amenities:** 3 restaurants; 2 bars; Internet; room service. *In room:* A/C, TV, minibar.

Hotel Telégrafo This restored hotel is actually over a century old, yet it has the boldest and most contemporary architecture and post-modern interior design in town. Instead of trying to recapture a sense of the past, this place offers a brash mix of Art Deco furnishings, playful light fixtures, and modern Cuban art and sculpture throughout the hotel. The rooms have soaring high ceilings, and proportionately high painted headboards. A majority have views over the Parque Central, although a few let out onto the interior courtyard. Unfortunately, the hyperhip interior design ends up leaving the rooms feeling a bit spartan and uninviting. The hotel's snack bar is located in a first-floor courtyard under ancient brick-and-stone arches in ruin, which set off a massive and intricate mosaic wall.

Calle Prado 408 (corner of Neptuno), Centro Havana. ☏ **7/861-1010.** Fax 7/861-4844. www.habaguanex hotels.com. 63 units. CUC$130–CUC$160 double; CUC$210–CUC$230 suite. Rates include breakfast. MC, V. Free valet parking. **Amenities:** Restaurant; bar; Internet; room service. *In room:* A/C, TV, minibar.

MODERATE

Hotel Deauville This place doesn't look like much from the outside and things don't get significantly better inside. The entire structure suffers from significant wear and tear, but all rooms recently had a makeover. It is located right on the Malecón and most rooms have a private balcony overlooking the sea. The views from the rooms on the higher floors are wonderful, and the corner rooms—with windows on two sides—are particularly nice. The Deauville does a brisk business in package tours, and is often full with French and German groups. The rooftop pool here is a popular spot. The hotel's advertised rates are a bit high for what you get, but if you're booked here as part of a package, or if you can get a lower rate, this is a pretty good option for a few days in Havana. The restaurants and inclusive buffet breakfast are embarrassments.

Calle Galiano 1 (btw. the Malecón and San Lázaro), Centro Habana. ☏ **7/866-8813.** Fax 7/866-8148. 144 units. CUC$68–CUC$82 double. Rates include breakfast buffet. MC, V. Street parking nearby. **Amenities:** 2 restaurants; 2 bars; dance club; Internet; outdoor pool. *In room:* A/C, TV.

INEXPENSIVE

There are literally hundreds of official and unofficial rooms for rent in private homes throughout Centro Habana. Many are quite dilapidated and run-down, but a few are well maintained and charming. Stunning views are enjoyed from the top-floor "penthouse" of **Casa de Evora Rodríguez,** ★ Paseo del Prado 20, 9th floor, between San Lázaro and Cárcel (✆ 7/861-7932; evorahabana@yahoo.com). Nearby is the super-friendly, modern apartment of a young couple, **Federico and Yamelis Llanes,** with a balcony overlooking Prado, Calle Cárcel 156 between Calles San Lázaro and Prado (✆ 7/861-7817; fllanes@gmail.com). Another great option with en suite rooms, incredible balcony views, and an independent kitchen and living room is the apartment of **Melba and Alberto,** ★ Calle Galiano 115, Apto 81, between Calles Animas and Trocadero (✆ 7/863-5178; barracuda1752@yahoo.es). **Casa 1932** ★, Calle Campanario 63 (bajos) between San Lázaro and Lagunas (✆ 7/863-6203; www.casahabana.net) is a beautifully furnished elegant colonial home run by the friendly Luís Miguel; Cuba's first jazz band, Orquesta Hermanos Castro, once lived here. Other options include the lovely **Casa Esther Cardosa,** Calle Aguila 367, between Calles San Miguel and Neptuno (✆ 7/862-0401; esthercv2551@cubarte.cult.cu), with a great terrace, and interesting furniture and prints on the walls. **Casa Viky,** Calle Barcelona 60, between Calles Aguila and Amistad (✆ 7/863-8923; mvictoriau@infomed.sld.cu), is a flat on the renovated Calle Barcelona, laid with gorgeous pink, blue, and cream Art Deco tiles. The elegant first room with two beds is equipped with handsome furniture and a chandelier and comes with an original 1950s bathroom that is shared with the other room. **Casa Isabel Gómez Durán,** Consulado 152 (altos) between Colón and Trocadero (✆ 7/860-1843; habana room@yahoo.com), is a newly renovated property with beautiful floor tiles, louvered shutters and modern bathrooms.

Hotel Lido 🛎 Although a block removed from the Prado, this is a much better bet than its nearby sister, the Hotel Caribbean. In general, the rooms are larger and more comfortable. Interior rooms lack windows and are a tad stuffy, but the end rooms have wonderful private balconies overlooking Calle Consulado. The fifth-floor rooftop restaurant serves uninspired budget fare, but has good views over Havana.

Calle Consulado 216 (btw. Calles Animas and Trocadero), Centro Habana. ✆/fax **7/866-8814.** www.islazul.cu. 64 units. CUC$36–CUC$43 double. Rates include breakfast. Street parking nearby. **Amenities:** Restaurant; bar. *In room:* A/C, TV.

Vedado & The Plaza de la Revolución Area
VERY EXPENSIVE

Hotel Nacional de Cuba ★★ Sitting on a high bluff overlooking the Malecón, this is Havana's signature hotel, and it's loaded with atmosphere. Two massive turrets loom overhead as you approach the entrance along its palm-lined driveway. The long, tiled lobby, with its high ceilings and heavy painted beams, is the heart and hub of this joint, and it's almost always bustling. The rooms themselves are large and well-appointed, although somewhat drab and showing their age. Over half the rooms have ocean views, although only a rare few have private balconies. The hotel has a vast lawn area on its high bluff that opens out toward the sea. My favorite spot here is the "Compass Card," an outdoor terrace made of marble inlaid in the pattern of a nautical compass. This is a great place to grab a table for a sunset drink overlooking the Malecón, with giant cannons protecting you on either side.

Calle O (corner of Calle 21), Vedado. ✆ **7/836-3564.** Fax 7/836-5171. www.gran-caribe.com. 457 units. CUC$170 double; CUC$215 suite; CUC$1,000 presidential suite. Rates include breakfast buffet. MC, V. Free valet parking. **Amenities:** 3 restaurants; 6 bars; babysitting; 2 lounges; cabaret; 2 outdoor pools; room service; lit outdoor tennis court; Wi-Fi. *In room:* A/C, TV, hair dryer, minibar.

Hotel Victoria ★★★   This little business-class hotel is one of the few boutique-style hotel options in Vedado. Overall, in this category the Hotel Presidente is a much nicer hotel, although the Victoria is closer to the action in Vedado. The cozy carpeted rooms are a bit on the small side, but they do have high ceilings. For a business-class hotel, the business center is a bit small, but Wi-Fi use is free for guests. Be careful here: The neighboring FOCSA building funnels the sea breezes right at the Victoria's entrance. When the winds are up, they can almost knock you off your feet.

Calles 19 and M, Vedado. ☎ **7/833-3510.** Fax 7/833-3109. www.gran-caribe.com. 31 units. CUC$80–CUC$100 double; CUC$130 suite. Rates include breakfast. MC, V. Free parking. **Amenities:** Restaurant; snack bar; bar; babysitting; lounge; small outdoor pool; room service. *In room:* A/C, TV, minibar, Wi-Fi.

Meliá Cohiba ★★   Sitting just off the Malecón, this hotel, with its sharp angles and alternating walls of stone and glass, is probably the most modernist building in Havana. Moreover, the Meliá Cohiba, along with its sister hotel, the Meliá Habana (p. 100), provide all the services and amenities luxury travelers are looking for in a top-rated hotel. Rooms are large and comfortable, and most have excellent views, particularly those on the higher floors. The executive floors and services here make this by far the best choice for business travelers, and it's got a wonderful outdoor pool and the best-equipped health club I've found at any hotel in Havana. The Cohiba has a wide range of restaurants and shops, and even its buffet restaurant is a treat, with live cook stations. The Habana Café ★ is one of the better club/restaurants in town, with a nightly floor show and live music. The executive floors and *Servicio Real* upgrade make this by far the best choice for business travelers.

Av. Paseo (btw. Avs. 1 and 3), Vedado. ☎ **7/833-3636.** Fax 7/834-4555. www.solmeliacuba.com. 462 units. CUC$180 double; CUC$200 junior suite; CUC$230 suite; CUC$100–CUC$185 supplement for *Servicio Real* upgrade. MC, V. Valet parking CUC$8 per day. **Amenities:** 4 restaurants; 4 bars; babysitting; well-equipped health club; Jacuzzi; 2 lounges; large outdoor pool; room service; sauna; smoke-free rooms; indoor squash court. *In room:* A/C, TV, hair dryer, minibar, Wi-Fi.

EXPENSIVE

Hotel Presidente ★★ ♙   This is an elegant Vedado hotel. The impeccable Victorian-style lobby features black-and-white marble floors, pink marble wainscoting, and real antiques. Some of the standard rooms are a bit compact, while others are quite spacious. About half (generally the even-numbered rooms) have good ocean views. On the 10th floor, you'll find two large suites with wonderfully inviting ocean-view terraces. There's a refreshing outdoor pool on the ground level, and a poolside bar and grill. While the hotel is just 2 blocks from the Malecón, it's not very close to much else.

Calle Calzada 110 (corner of Av. de los Presidentes), Vedado. ☎ **7/838-1801.** Fax 7/838-2956. www.hotelesc.com. 158 units. CUC$140 double; CUC$200 suite. Rates include buffet breakfast. MC, V. Free valet parking. **Amenities:** Restaurant; bar; Internet; outdoor pool, *In room:* A/C, TV, minibar.

Tryp Habana Libre ★★   Formerly the Havana Hilton, this historic landmark is the place Fidel Castro first called home following the fall of Batista. Rising high above Havana, this hotel provides some of my favorite views of the city and sea from most of its rooms. The two-story open lobby area, which underwent renovation in 2010, is striking, with its amoeba-shaped pool and massive modern sculpture surrounded by plants. The rooms themselves are large and comfortable, although they feel dated, despite the fact that most of the carpets and furniture are new. Of the dining and entertainment options, I find the famous Trader Vic's–style Polinesio an overpriced disappointment, although you might appreciate the 24-hour diner-style La Rampa Cafetería—I did. The 25th-floor Turquino Cabaret might not have the best floor show in town, but it does have the best view and regularly stages A-list concerts and performances.

Calles L and 23, Vedado. ℂ **7/838-4011.** Fax 7/834-6365. www.solmeliacuba.com. 572 units. CUC$122–CUC$170 double. Rates include buffet breakfast. Children 11 and under stay free in parent's room. MC, V. Valet parking CUC$6 per day. **Amenities:** 5 restaurants; 3 bars; babysitting; dance club; 2 lounges; Internet; outdoor pool; room service; smoke-free rooms. *In room:* A/C, TV, Internet, minibar.

MODERATE

Hotel St. John's 🍸 This is a perennially popular choice for budget and midrange travelers. Rooms are clean and simple. Most are pretty spacious and the furnishings are relatively modern. Rooms on the 9th floor and above have wonderful views. If you don't have a room on a higher floor, you can always spend time in the tiny rooftop pool or the new adjoining bar and events space. The hotel is right in the heart of Vedado, just a block off La Rampa.

Calle O No. 206 (btw. Calles 23 and 25), Vedado. ℂ **7/833-3740.** Fax 7/833-3561. www.gran-caribe. com. 87 units. CUC$54–CUC$80 double. Rates include breakfast buffet. MC, V. Street parking nearby. **Amenities:** 2 restaurants; 2 bars; dance club; outdoor pool. *In room:* A/C, TV.

INEXPENSIVE

Given that this is one of Havana's prime middle-class neighborhoods, there's a glut of *casas particulares,* many in wonderful old neoclassical and Art Deco homes and apartment buildings. The following are all recommended. **Casa Carlos Peña Avila,** Calle F 305, Apartment 3 between Calles 13 and 15 (ℂ **7/833-5992;** www.casavedado. bravepages.com; carlospecu@yahoo.com), owned by a very polite man, has two bedrooms furnished with antiques and modern bathrooms. **Casa María Elena Matos Fernández,** Calle 13 no. 106, between Calles L and M, Apartment 5 (ℂ **7/832-4346;** ernesto.mato@infomed.sld.cu) is a huge, smart flat with elegant proportions in an Art Deco building close to the Malecón. The one room has two beds and pretty floor tiles and an adjoining large 1950s bubble-gum pink bathroom. **Casa Luis Alberto Gómez Garcés,** Calle 15, no. 305 (bajos), between Calles H and I (ℂ **7/836-3954;** mroche@infomed.sld.cu), is a quirky house with its Spanish turret. It has one large room with a small kitchenette and an independent entrance. The room is next to a small patio. The main house interior decor is shabby chic with a chandelier, some choice pieces of furniture, and lovely hallway tiling. **Casa María D'García (Lola),** Calle I, no. 355, between Calles 17 and 19, Apartamento 1, 2nd floor (ℂ **7/832-1525;** lazaro.goenaga@infomed.sld.cu), has an attractive, nicely furnished room in a grand house on an atmospheric street. **Casa Jorge Coalla Potts,** Calle I between Calles 21 and 23, no. 456, Apto 11 (ℂ **7/832-9032;** www. havanaroomrental.com; jorgepotts@correodecuba.cu), is managed by Jorge and Marisel, helpful and very hospitable hosts. Their ground-floor apartment is in an excellent location in a handsome, modern white apartment building. **Casa Norma Alvarez Bustio,** Calle 25 359, Apartment D, between K and L (ℂ **7/832-2207;** hugovaldes@cubarte.cult.cu) is in an excellent location with one lovely room which shares a bathroom with the family. Norma is most welcoming.

Casa Delta Torres Pagán ★ This grand corner house is full of antiques. The front room is embellished with French chandeliers, a beautiful 18th-century grandfather clock, and 1930s huge glass lamps that were destined for the Hotel Nacional.

There are two rooms here (one with an independent entrance) but you'll want the larger interior room with an 18th-century bed. Delta is a great conversationalist and this is a fascinating place to stay.

Calle D No. 501 (btw. Calles 21 and 23), Vedado. ✆ 7/832-9078. 2 units. CUC$30 double. No credit cards. *In room:* A/C, no phone.

Casa Esperanza ★   This wondrous 1930s' house, fitted with fine furnishings, is owned by a delightful family. A large stained-glass peacock window towers over the elegant marble staircase that sits beneath a beautiful chandelier. There are two mini-apartments here, both with independent entrances. One is in the main house with a small outdoor balcony—this is the choice option. The other is off the back of the pretty patio, but it is darker and is equipped with modern furnishings.

Calle 27 No. 804 (btw. Paseo and Calle 2), Vedado. ✆ 7/831-1327. apiedra@infomed.sld.cu. 2 units. CUC$35 double. No credit cards. *In room:* A/C, TV, phone.

Casa Lilly ★★   On the 13th floor of this 1950s block, this enormous flat affords spectacular views of Vedado and the Malecón. The rooms are spacious and attractively decorated and guests share a spacious, minimally decorated living room enhanced by Asian influences. Breakfasts are served up on the elegant long dining table or on the wraparound terrace. Run by Lilly and her family, who work in film, this is a gorgeous place to stay.

Calle G, no. 301 (at the corner of Calle 13), 13th floor. ✆ 7/832-4021. www.casalilly.com. 2 units. CUC$35–CUC$40 double. No credit cards. Guarded parking available beneath the flats. *In room:* A/C, no phone.

Playa

VERY EXPENSIVE

Meliá Habana ★★   This modern luxury hotel is set on a coral ledge on the edge of the Caribbean. Its rows of balconies are draped with flowing ferns, and the building gets wider as it gets higher, giving it an inverted pyramid effect. Most of the rooms have excellent ocean views from their good-size private balconies. The rooms are large and comfortable. The most striking feature is the ground-level lagoon surrounded by lush tropical gardens and filled by man-made waterfalls set under soaring columns. The lagoon almost seems to blend into the free-form pool, which is billed as the largest in Cuba. As at the Meliá Cohiba, the executive floors and services are top-notch here, making it a good choice for business travelers. The hotel is the unofficial hub of the business scene in Miramar.

Av. 3 (btw. Calles 76 and 80), Miramar, Playa. ✆ 7/204-8500. Fax 7/204-8505. www.solmeliacuba. com. 397 units. CUC$172–CUC$194 double; CUC$260–CUC$280 junior suite; CUC$350–CUC$430 suite. MC, V. Valet parking CUC$4 per day. **Amenities:** 6 restaurants; babysitting; 3 bars; small exercise room; 2 lounges; large outdoor pool; room service; sauna; smoke-free rooms; 2 outdoor tennis courts. *In room:* A/C, TV, minibar, Wi-Fi.

EXPENSIVE

Hotel Chateau Miramar   This place is attempting to stake out the boutique business-class market. For lack of any competition, it is doing just that, although it doesn't have the warmth, charm, or personality I'd expect in a high-end boutique hotel; for anyone here on business, I'd recommend any of the large business-class hotels in town over this option. The standard rooms here are on the small side, while the junior suites and suites are more than ample. The decor is rather nondescript and impersonal. Most rooms come with a private balcony, and some of these are quite roomy. Suite no. 416 is the best room and view in the house, while any room with a number ending in 09 through 16 will have an ocean view. One of the more unique and appealing features here is the fact that each room comes with a 21-inch flatscreen television and Wi-Fi. The hotel is right on the waterfront, just behind the National Aquarium.

Av. 1 (btw. Calles 60 and 62), Miramar, Playa. © **7/204-1952.** Fax 7/204-0224. www.hotelescubanacan. com. 50 units. CUC$120 double; CUC$170 suite. Rates include breakfast. MC, V. Free valet parking. **Amenities:** Restaurant; snack bar; bar; lounge; outdoor pool; room service. *In room:* A/C, TV, minibar, Wi-Fi.

Hotel Comodoro   Located next to the Meliá Habana (see above), this complex has the feel of a South Florida condo community. The hotel rooms in the main building are acceptable, although I'd definitely opt for one of the one- or two-bedroom bungalows, which are housed in a series of two-story blocks spread around a maze of free-form pools. The bungalows all come with kitchenettes or full kitchens, making them a good option for longer stays. All of the rooms here have a balcony or patio. The Comodoro has a tiny patch of beach sand, which has been hauled in and set next to a natural pool created by a break wall just off the coast here. At press time parts of the hotel were undergoing renovation.

Av. 3 and Calle 84, Miramar, Playa. © **7/204-5551.** Fax 7/204-2089. www.hotelescubanacan.com. 300 units. CUC$118–CUC$137 bungalow; CUC$135–CUC$155 suite MC, V. Free parking. **Amenities:** 3 restaurants; snack bar; 3 bars; dance club; room service; natural saltwater pool; a series of free-form freshwater pools; watersports equipment/rentals. *In room:* A/C, TV.

Occidental Miramar ★★   This modern and massive luxury hotel is an impressive and imposing presence in the heart of Miramar's business district. It has nicer rooms than the Meliá Habana (see above), but it's 2 blocks from the sea and has fewer dining and entertainment options. The rooms are all at least junior suites, with one queen-size bed and a comfortable sitting area. The beds are some of the firmest I've found in Havana. Only the eight end-unit suites here have balconies, although these balconies are large. This place does a brisk business in group and conference travel.

Av. 5 (btw. Calles 72 and 76), Miramar, Playa. © **7/204-3584.** Fax 7/204-9227. www.occidental-hoteles. com/miramar. 427 units. CUC$110–CUC$130 double; CUC$160–CUC$300 suite. Rates include breakfast. MC, V. Free valet parking. **Amenities:** 3 restaurants; 2 bars; babysitting; children's center; well-equipped exercise room; lounge; large outdoor pool; room service; sauna; smoke-free rooms; indoor squash court; 6 outdoor tennis courts (2 lit). *In room:* A/C, TV, minibar, Wi-Fi.

MODERATE

Aparthotel Montehabana   While this place won't win any architectural or interior design awards, the spacious serviced apartments are convenient for long stays and are an extraordinarily good value for the location. The apartments have small, fully equipped kitchens, living rooms, and spacious bedrooms. Balconies, with not much of a view, come with sun loungers. The building also has large, standard hotel rooms. There's a bar, small supermarket, and Internet access on site. Guests can make use of the pool and tennis courts of the Occidental Miramar, a short walk away through the property.

Calle 70 (btw. Av. 5 and Av. 7), Miramar, Playa. © **7/206-9595.** www.gaviota-grupo.com. 177 units. CUC$75 double; CUC$85 studio apartment; CUC$95 double apartment; CUC$170 double apartment and double room. MC, V. Free valet parking. **Amenities:** Snack bar; bar; shuttle bus to city center; Wi-Fi. *In room:* A/C, TV; minibar.

INEXPENSIVE

As in Vedado and Centro Habana, there are scores of *casas particulares* and private rooms for rent in Playa. Given the fact that this was a popular upper-class residential neighborhood prior to the Revolution, most are housed in large, comfortable homes and apartments. In addition to the *casa* described below, you could try **Casa Gina,** Calle 86 no. 526, between Avenidas 5 and 7 ((*C* **7/203-4034**), or see if there's space at the Ministry of Education's **Hostal Icemar,** Calle 16 no. 104, between Avenidas 1 and 3 ((*C*/fax **7/203-7735**), a dependable budget option popular with students and backpackers, with additional three-bed apartments for rent. Doubles are CUC$44.

Residencias Miramar ★ This is an excellent *casa particular* with wonderful hosts. The rooms are clean and modern, and each comes with its own phone and a small fridge. Common areas include a comfortable living room, and a shady patio area amid well-tended gardens. Meals are served throughout the day for very reasonable prices, and host Eva can help arrange tours and activities, as well as arrange home-stays with friends in La Habana Vieja and Vedado.

Av. 7 no. 4403 (btw. Calles 44 and 46), Miramar, Playa. (*C* **7/202-1075.** evahabanasol@yahoo.com. 2 units. CUC$30 double. No credit cards. Free parking. **Amenities:** Restaurant. *In room:* A/C, TV, mini-fridge.

Near the Airport

There are no hotels at or truly near the airport. Luckily, the bulk of Havana hotels are just a 15- to 30-minute car ride away. The closest hotels to the airport are those in Playa.

Habana del Este & Playas del Este

The beaches of Playas del Este are quite beautiful. Moreover, the four long, consecutive beaches here are just a 15- to 25-minute taxi or car ride from La Habana Vieja, making it a good choice for combining your fun in the sun with some city pleasures. Of the most significant beaches, furthest east is **Guanabo,** which is where Habaneros decamp during weekends and the summer months. **Santa María del Mar** is closer to Havana, and is essentially a strip of hotels and villas. However, the hotel choices here are limited and rather desultory. While there are several all-inclusive resorts, offering a whole range of entertainment and activities options, they are far less polished and attractive than similar options in Varadero or other prime all-inclusive destinations. In fact, if you want a beautiful beach resort just a little bit farther east of Playas del Este, head to Breezes Jibacoa (see below). There are *casas particulares* in Santa María del Mar and Guanabo.

EXPENSIVE

Blau Club Arenal ★ Sandwiched between the Itabo lagoon and Playa Santa María, this is the best of the former Horizontes all-inclusives in this area, and it has become even better after being taken over by the Spanish Blau chain. The rooms are of good size and have plenty of windows or big, sliding glass doors opening onto private balconies or terraces. I think it's worth the slight splurge for one of the superior rooms or junior suites. The hotel does a brisk business in European group travel. The hotel was closed for renovation during summer 2010.

Laguna Itabo, btw. Santa María del Mar and Boca Ciega. (*C* **7/797-1272.** Fax 7/797-1280. www.blau hotels.com. 169 units. CUC$110–CUC$142 double. Rates are all-inclusive. MC, V. Free parking. **Amenities:** 2 restaurants; 3 bars; babysitting; dance club; small gym; large outdoor pool; 2 tennis courts; free watersports equipment. *In room:* A/C, TV, fridge.

Club Atlántico   Not to be confused with the Apartotel Atlántico, this is a comfortable and relatively modern, all-inclusive option that is the only hotel right on the beach in Santa María. The rooms are standard-issue affairs, mostly with two twin beds and a little balcony or terrace. The buffet meals here are nothing to write home about or look forward to, but on the upside, the all-inclusive rates include all your drinks and the use of nonmotorized watersports equipment. There's an inviting and refreshing, kidney-shaped pool that overlooks and lets out onto the beautiful beach here. Try for an oceanview third-floor room.

Av. Las Terrazas, Santa María del Mar, Playas del Este. ℰ 7/797-1085. www.gran-caribe.com. 92 units. CUC$100–CUC$150 double. Rates are all-inclusive. MC, V. Free parking. **Amenities:** Restaurant; snack bar; 2 bars; babysitting; Internet; outdoor pool; outdoor tennis court; free watersports equipment. *In room:* A/C, TV, minibar.

Villas Los Pinos ★   These independent villas are probably the plushest accommodations in Playas del Este and well suited to longer stays. The villas are a mix of two-, three-, and four-bedroom units in a series of two- and three-story buildings. Most villas come with their own swimming pool. The entire complex, moreover, borders a beautiful section of beach, but not all villas front the beach. The rooms vary considerably, but most are quite spacious, with rattan furnishings and well-equipped kitchenettes. Some have wonderful raised decks with ocean views. I like unit nos. 44 and 45 for their views, while no. 34 has its own squash court. For CUC$25 per day, you can hire your own cook and personal housekeeper.

Av. Las Terrazas 21 (btw. Calles 4 and 5), Santa María del Mar, Playas del Este. ℰ 7/797-1361. www.gran-caribe.com. reservas@complejo.gca.tur.cu. 70 units. CUC$125–CUC$167 2-bedroom villa; CUC$178–CUC$220 3-bedroom villa; CUC$230–CUC$248 4-bedroom villa. MC, V. Free parking. **Amenities:** 3 restaurants; 2 bars; babysitting; small exercise room; 20 outdoor pools; sauna; 2 outdoor tennis courts; watersports equipment rentals. *In room:* A/C, TV, kitchenette, fridge.

MODERATE

Hotel Tropicoco 🛈   This imposing, five-story hotel stretches on for a hundred yards or so in each direction from its blocky concrete lobby. This place hosts many group and package tours, and it's usually pretty lively. Still, it's hard not to find the Soviet-style architecture of this resort a little depressing, particularly the rectangular pool, wedged into an area in an alcove of the building. The whole complex has been remodeled and the rooms and facilities are in decent shape. Most of the rooms face the sea, although only a few have balconies, and overall they are unspectacular and on the small side. The best feature here is a beautiful and extremely popular section of beach just across the street.

Avs. Sur and Las Terrazas, Santa María del Mar. ℰ 7/797-1371. Fax 7/797-1389. www.hotelescubanacan.com. 188 units. CUC$58–CUC$87 double. Rates are all-inclusive. MC, V. Free parking. **Amenities:** 2 restaurants; 3 bars; large outdoor pool; small exercise room; sauna; watersports equipment rentals; in-room massage; babysitting; laundry service. Internet terminals. *In room:* A/C, TV, kitchenette, fridge.

INEXPENSIVE

Guanabo has a high concentration of *casas particulares.* Try the friendly home of **Felipa Ciruta,** Av. 9 48206 between Calles 482 and 484 (ℰ 7/796-4443; magciru@yahoo.es), or **La Gallega y Teresa,** Calle 472 7B07 A between 7B and 9 (ℰ 7/796-6860). At Santa María del Mar, set a kilometer back from the beach due to restrictions on beachfront *casas,* is the house of **Orlando Odio López,** Av. de las Banderas 909 between Calles 9na and 11na (ℰ 7/797-1219).

A Little Farther East

Breezes Jibacoa ★★   This plush, all-inclusive resort is set on a beautiful patch of beach, about halfway between Havana and Varadero. The hotel is less than an hour's drive from downtown Havana, making day trips, and even evening outings to the capital, convenient. The standard rooms are large, comfortable, and modern and many come with just one king-size bed. This resort is geared toward single adults and couples, and no children under 14 are allowed. The tropical oceanview rooms have a separate sitting area, fridge, and the best beach views in the house. All rooms come with a private balcony. A huge swimming pool is set in the center of the resort, and a wide range of activities is offered.

Playa Jibacoa. ☎ **47/29-5123.** Fax 47/29-5150. www.superclubscuba.com. 250 units. CUC$98 per person standard room; CUC$113 per person oceanview room. Rates are all-inclusive. MC, V. No children under 14 allowed. **Amenities:** 4 restaurants; 6 bars; free bicycles; cabaret; small, well-equipped gym; large outdoor pool; 2 tennis courts; free watersports equipment. *In room:* A/C, TV, fridge (in suite).

WHERE TO DINE

It has been said before, and it's worth repeating: Do not come to Cuba for fine dining. In addition to mediocre food and service in general, overcharging is attempted with disheartening frequency.

Paladares (private restaurants) are common in Havana. They are officially limited to no more than 12 seats, and cannot serve lobster or shrimp. Quite a few have established themselves as some of the better, long-standing restaurant options in Havana. In fact, the best of these outshine most of the official government-run options. La Guarida, once Havana's most famous *paladar,* closed. If you visit a *paladar* in a far-flung district on a weekend night, it may be wise to book your return taxi journey ahead of time, as taxis are scarce then.

Aside from the restaurants listed below, fast-food chains have started to pop up around Havana. The most prominent of these is **El Rápido,** which has numerous outlets serving fried chicken, burgers, hot dogs, microwave pizzas, and other fast-food staples. Another chain worth mentioning is **Pizza Nova,** Calle 248 and Avenida 5, Miramar (☎ **7/204-6969**), which also has outlets in Marina Hemingway and several provincial cities. This place has good thin-crust pizza and respectable pastas. Finally, for breakfast or a quick bite, look out for **Pain de Paris** storefronts, featuring a wide range of fresh-baked breads, croissants, and pastries, as well as simple sandwiches. For a coffee-and-cake pit stop, try the attractive **Café el Escorial** ★★, Mercaderes 317, corner of Muralla (☎ **7/868-3545**), where you can sit under the lemon-yellow arches, and sample the coffee, ice cream with amaretto, sandwiches, and cookies.

La Habana Vieja

In addition to the places mentioned below, budget travelers swear by the **Restaurante Hanoi** (La Casa de la Parra), Calles Teniente Rey and Oficios (☎ **7/867-1029**), although I was rather disappointed to find virtually no Vietnamese influence on the decidedly mediocre *criolla* and Chinese cuisine here. There's also the **Restaurante Europa,** Calle Obispo 112, corner of Aguiar (☎ **7/866-4484**), a former candy shop, serving up a host of adventurous sauces in well-presented food. The set menu for CUC$15 is a good value.

VERY EXPENSIVE

El Floridita ★ CRIOLLAN/INTERNATIONAL   This is by far the classiest of the many Hemingway hangouts in Havana. In fact, El Floridita is so upscale, I have a hard time imagining the rugged writer really enjoying this place. It'll cost you CUC$6 for a daiquiri in "The Cradle of the Daiquiri"—be sure to get it shaken, not blended. The bartenders' deep-red jackets blend perfectly with the plush decor. The long bar takes up a good portion of the front room. There's quieter and more formal seating in the back, although even if you land a table just off the bar, this place is never rowdy. The food here is acceptable, but can't justify the hefty price tags. If you do stick around for a meal, stick to the seafood. The sautéed shrimp, which is prepared table-side, is a good bet. This is a cool and refreshing place to stop for a drink on a hot afternoon.

Calle Obispo 557 (corner of Calle Monserrate). ⓒ **7/866-8856.** Reservations recommended. Main courses CUC$16–CUC$30. MC, V. Bar daily noon–11pm. Restaurant daily noon–11pm.

El Templete ★★ 🏮 INTERNATIONAL/SEAFOOD   This is truly fine dining portside with tables on the roadside overlooking the harbor and sophisticated interior dining inside. The eclectic menu notes dishes such as beef carpaccio with foie gras and red wine reduction, baby eels, and a delicious tuna crusted with sesame seeds and Marmitako sauce. This place has gained currency for those in the know and is a hot dining spot for government officials and other bigwigs; the service is excellent. The only drawback is that some of the outside tables are too close to the road.

Avenida del Puerto (corner of Narciso López). ⓒ **7/866-8807.** Main courses CUC$8–CUC$30. MC, V. Daily noon–midnight.

EXPENSIVE

Café del Oriente ★ INTERNATIONAL   This elegant little restaurant sits just off the Plaza San Francisco and, when the weather permits, has a few outdoor tables. Inside you'll find a cool, large room, with a beautiful patterned marble floor, high ceilings, and dark wainscoting on the walls. In the center of the restaurant is a large, U-shaped bar. The menu here is one of the more extravagant in Havana, but it isn't adventurous as it used to be. For the main course, I like the wild rabbit with oregano or the fish filet in lime coulis. Even if you don't take a full meal here, this is a great place to stop for a drink or cup of coffee while touring Old Havana.

Calle Oficios 112 (corner of Calle Armargura). ⓒ **7/860-6686.** Reservations recommended. Main courses CUC$9–CUC$22. MC, V. Daily noon–midnight.

La Bodeguita del Medio ★ CRIOLLAN   The "B del M," as it's also known, oozes history and suffers from overcrowding. Still, it's a must for any first-time trip to Havana. The collage of famous photos and signatures that crowd the walls here are legend. You'll definitely want a reservation (in high season), although even with a reservation, you'll probably end up waiting for a table—this place is just that popular. Tradition would have you start things off with a *mojito,* although the *mojitos* here are notoriously weak and unjustifiably expensive. Definitely order one with 3- or 5-year-old *añejo* rum if you plan on enjoying it. The food—simple and well-prepared Cuban dishes—is pretty good. The slow-roasted pork is my favorite, although the *ropa vieja* (shredded beef) gives it a run for its money. No matter what you order, make sure you have it served with plenty of yuca with *mojo* (gravy) and the *moros y cristianos,* black beans with rice. This place is crowded and rowdy, so don't come expecting anything less. There's live music in the squashed bar.

Calle Empedrado 207 (btw. Calles San Ignacio and Cuba). ✆ **7/867-1374.** Reservations recommended. Main courses CUC$12–CUC$16. MC, V. Daily noon–midnight.

La Domínica ★★ ITALIAN   This is the best Italian restaurant in town. Skip the formal and stuffy seating inside and grab one of the outdoor tables under a canvas umbrella on the old brick streets. If the band were playing "'O Sole Mio" instead of "Guantanamera," you might almost forget you're in Havana and think you were dining at a sidewalk trattoria in Rome. There's a wood-burning oven turning out excellent thin-crust pizzas. The pastas are cooked al dente and served in big portions. My favorite is the *penne alla putanesca,* which comes in a tomato cream sauce seasoned with anchovies and capers. For main dishes, I'd recommend the *saltimbocca alla Romana* (veal scallops wrapped in sage and prosciutto ham). Finish everything off with some *cassata sicilliana* (a cake dessert) and an espresso.

Calles O'Reilly and Mercaderes. ✆ **7/860-2918.** Reservations recommended. Main courses CUC$10–CUC$26); pizzas and pastas CUC$6–CUC$12. MC, V. Daily noon–11pm.

Roof Garden Restaurant ★★ 📖 FRENCH/INTERNATIONAL   Located on the top floor of the Hotel Sevilla, this is one of the finer restaurants in Havana, with arguably the finest setting. The large dining room has a massively high ceiling with intricate bas-relief work and moldings. The room is ringed by floor-to-almost-ceiling windows that are left open in all but the most inclement weather. Marble floors and huge chandeliers complete the ambience. The menu is one of the more adventurous in town, with main dishes such as king prawns in aged rum, squid ragout in its own ink, and a delicious lamb ragout *(cordero estofado)*. For starters, I recommend the salad of pickled duck with artichokes and poached egg in red wine. To finish off the night decadently, go for the profiteroles with ice cream and chocolate sauce. The set three-course meal at CUC$17 is a good value, as are the Cuban colonial cuisine dishes. This place is also known as the "Torre del Oro."

Calle Trocadero 55 (corner of Calle Prado). ✆ **7/860-8560.** Reservations recommended. Main courses CUC$9–CUC$32. MC, V. Daily 7–10:30pm.

Santo Angel ★ 📖 INTERNATIONAL   With a handful of outdoor tables right on the Plaza Vieja, as well as others on the broad covered veranda facing the plaza, this is arguably one of the most atmospheric restaurants in Old Havana. You'll definitely want to choose one of the aforementioned tables over those in the indoor dining rooms. The adventurous menu attempts to match the grandeur of the ambience, with mixed results. You can start things off with *malanga* (vegetable) soup and blue cheese or some seafood bisque. For a main dish, I like the lamb in red wine and honey. The chefs here are inconsistent, and at times I've left very pleased, while on other occasions I've been sorely disappointed.

Calle Teniente Rey 60, at the corner of Calle San Ignacio. ✆ **7/861-1626.** Reservations recommended. Main courses CUC$8–CUC$28. MC, V. Daily 11:30am–11pm.

MODERATE

Café La Mina CRIOLLAN   This popular place has a privileged location right on the Plaza de Armas. There's covered seating in three separate patios, with ferns and arbors and caged parakeets providing additional atmosphere, as well as several dining rooms spread through the interior of a couple of connected buildings. The food is standard and acceptable tourist fare. The combo *Caribeña La Mina* is a sauté of chunks of chicken, pork, and shrimp in a tasty sauce with a hint of rum. The

Traditional Cuban Combo comes with a *mojito,* black beans and rice, some grilled pork in *mojo* (gravy), and dessert. There's an attached ice-cream parlor and informal cafe. This is a good place to while away a few hours midday, or to take a break while walking around La Habana Vieja.

Calles Obispo and Oficios, Plaza de Armas. ✆ **7/862-0216.** Reservations not required. Main courses CUC$7–CUC$28. MC, V. Daily 24 hr.

Café Taberna 🦋 CRIOLLAN/INTERNATIONAL   This lively joint is housed in a beautifully restored, 18th-century building with high ceilings, just off the Plaza Vieja. Photos of Beny Moré and other popular mambo acts adorn the walls, and there's a long bar with an impressive wall of booze stacked behind it. The food is standard and uninspired fare, but this is one of the few places in La Habana Vieja that won't break your bank for a simple meal. The outdoor seating seems like an afterthought, and feels a little too far removed from the action.

Calles Mercaderes and Teniente Rey, Plaza Vieja. ✆ **7/861-1637.** Reservations not required. Main courses CUC$4–CUC$28. MC, V. Daily noon–midnight.

INEXPENSIVE

Cafetería El Portal CRIOLLAN   With seating on the large covered patio, and small tables set right on the Plaza de la Catedral, it's hard to find a spot with more character in La Habana Vieja. The menu is small, but this place is big on atmosphere. The only real splurge here is the lobster supreme in light vinaigrette, which, although small, is a decent deal at CUC$10. If you're hungrier, you can have a Cuban sandwich or a small steak, both of which will come with French fries. The *mojitos* here are acceptable and will run you CUC$3. The outdoor tables start getting some shade around 2pm, and all night long they provide wonderful views of the cathedral's lit bell towers. If you do opt for one of the pricier tables inside, be sure to snag one of the few tables on the second-floor balconies overlooking the plaza.

Calle San Ignacio 54 (corner of Calle Empedrado), Plaza de la Catedral. ✆ **7/867-1034.** Reservations not accepted. Main courses CUC$4–CUC$17. MC, V. Daily noon–midnight.

La Taberna de la Muralla ★ 🍴 GRILL   Havana's only brewpub is blessed with a beautiful setting on a corner overlooking Plaza Vieja. Grab a seat at one of the wrought-iron tables under a broad canvas umbrella on the edge of the plaza when the weather's right, or one of the heavy wooden tables on the covered patio or indoor dining room when it's not. The small and simple menu is made up almost entirely of grilled-to-order pork chops, chicken breasts, or fish filets, or kabobs of chicken, shrimp, lobster, or a mix of the three. Order a pint of the home-brewed amber or dark beer and admire the large copper brewing tanks just behind the bar. Large groups or heavy drinkers can order a *dispensa,* a tall, clear glass tube filled with beer, featuring a spout at the bottom and a thinner tube filled with ice running up its center. Service can be annoyingly slack when it's busy.

Calle San Ignacio (corner of Calle Muralla), Plaza Vieja. ✆ **7/866-4453.** Reservations not accepted. Main courses CUC$4–CUC$8. MC, V. Daily noon–midnight.

Los Nardos ★ 🦋 INTERNATIONAL/SPANISH   A small neon sign and a doorman mark the entrance to this hidden restaurant that serves up some of the largest and tastiest platters in Havana. Los Nardos, run by a cooperative, can be found on the top floor in the arches next to the Sala Kid Chocolate, conveniently located in the center of town opposite the Capitolio. Dine by candlelight—at lunch time and in the evening—on large wooden tables accompanied by a live band. The walls are impressively lined with wine vaults and trophies; colored-glass windows with candlelight cast an attractive light across the room. The servings of food are enormous: huge lobster platters or chicken with plenty of vegetables at very reasonable prices. It's extremely popular and you will almost always have to wait a short while to get served.

Paseo del Prado 565 (btw. Teniente Rey and Dragones, across from El Capitolio). © **7/863-2985.** Reservations not accepted. Main courses CUC$5–CUC$14. No credit cards. Daily 11:30am–11:30pm.

Restaurante-Pizzeria El Asturianito ★ 🍴 ITALIAN   Climb right to the very top of the Los Nardos building for this Italian-style eatery. It's run by the same crew as Los Nardos and it serves plenty of similar dishes, but without the waiting line, candlelight, ambience, and live music. However, the service and standards are the same and the seating is more spacious. Although there are Cuban platters served, you'll probably come for the Italian fare. There are 11 spaghetti dishes, plus lasagna. I recommend the great-value three-meals-in-one Juventud Asturiana pizza on a thin crust, which comes piled with ham, chorizo, salami, *camarones* (shrimp), tuna, and Bolognese sauce in separate quarters; the Bolognese sauce is a bit heavy for pizza, though.

Paseo del Prado 560 btw. Teniente Rey and Dragones © **7/863-2985.** Reservations not accepted. Main courses CUC$2.50–CUC$12. No credit cards. Daily noon–midnight.

Centro Habana

I am decidedly unimpressed with the Asian food available in Cuba. This goes for the handful of Chinese restaurants in Havana's little Chinatown, too. However, if you do venture to the block-long Cuchillo de Zanja, or just crave a change from *criolla* cooking, your best bets are **Los Tres Chinitos,** Dragones 355 (© **7/860-4318**) and **Viejo Amigo,** Dragones 356 between Manrique and San Nicolás (© **7/861-8095**).

EXPENSIVE

Restaurante Castropol ★ SEAFOOD/INTERNATIONAL   This restaurant is housed in an architecturally bland yellow building on the Malecón, but it's a surprising and welcome culinary find. The two floors offer different menus, but you'll want a balcony table on either floor at sunset. Start with an order of blue crab, pumpkin soup with serrano ham shavings, or fried malanga stuffed with pork crackling, and then continue with the delicious beer-scented ragout of shrimp, fish, octopus, and chicken or a roulade of fish fillet with salmon mousse. Service is impeccable. With the closure of Centro's famous La Guarida, Castropol is doing a good job of filling the culinary gap.

Malecón 107 (btw Genios and Crespo. © **7/861-4864.** Main courses CUC$8–CUC$35. No credit cards. Daily noon–midnight.

Vedado & the Plaza de la Revolución Area

In addition to the places listed below, you might try **Sierra Maestra** (© **7/838-4011**), which serves nouvelle Cuban cuisine in an elegant setting on the 25th floor of the Tryp Habana Libre hotel, or **Paladar Los Cactus de 33,** Av. 33 3405 between Calles 34 and 36 (© **7/203-5139**), which offers plain but filling dishes in elegant surroundings.

MODERATE

El Conejito INTERNATIONAL   The name means "little rabbit," but there's more than just a little bit of rabbit on the menu here: grilled, baked, *a la criolla*, or *ali oli* (in garlic *mojo*, or gravy) are just some of the treatments our furry friend gets—not to mention rabbit sausage, rabbit terrine, and rabbit ham for starters. Almost all the rabbit dishes are reasonably priced (CUC$4 to CUC$6.20). Avoid the house specialty, *conejo a la financiera*, which comes in a busy yet bland sauce, and stick to simpler preparations. There are also more traditional meat and seafood options. The place is modeled on an English Tudor pub, with brick walls and heavy, dark interior beams. There's a small attached bar that is usually quiet.

Calles M and 17. ☎ **7/832-4671.** Reservations not required. Main courses CUC$4–CUC$20. No credit cards. Daily noon–11pm.

Gringo Viejo ★★ CRIOLLAN/INTERNATIONAL   Despite the kitschy décor—it's decorated with knick-knacks and faux vines—and distracting music videos playing in the background, this homey *paladar* serves wonderful food and is professionally run. To start, work your way through octopus with garlic and pork tournedos in salsa cimmarona, and then try the succulent *cordero estofado* (stewed lamb), which is served with beans, red peppers, and olives. Vegetarians should try the corn stew.

Calle 21 No. 454 (btw. E and F). ☎ **7/831-1946.** Main courses CUC$8–CUC$12. No credit cards Daily noon–11pm.

La Casona de 17 CRIOLLAN/INTERNATIONAL   Housed in a yellow-and-pink Colonial-style mansion that was built in 1938, this restaurant exudes old-world charm, with its columns, white table cloths, and fine crockery. The specialty of the house is *arroz con pollo a la chorrera*, which is served in a ceramic dish accompanied by *petit pois* and peppers—just beware that you'll need to order this dish 50 minutes in advance. The 1938 fish fillet is a tasty and filling fillet of pargo, accompanied by prawns and topped with grated cheese. Service is exceptional considering it is a state-run restaurant.

Calle 17 No. 60 (btw. M and N). . ☎ **7/838-3136.** Main courses CUC$4.50–CUC$15. MC, V. Daily noon–midnight.

INEXPENSIVE

Restaurante Monguito 🍴 CRIOLLAN   This little joint has just five plastic tables with plastic lawn chairs in a narrow room. Plastic flowers in cheap vases, a couple of squawking parrots in the back, and kitschy, semiholographic nature scenes on the main wall complete the ambience. The *bistec uruguayo* (a kind of deep-fried pork *cordon bleu*) is huge, and the *pollo a la cacerola* (baked chicken in a tomato sauce) is excellent. Try to get a seat near one of the fans, because—despite the massive air-conditioning unit—this place can get a little stuffy, especially midday.

Calle L (btw. Calles 23 and 25, directly across from Tryp Habana Libre). ☎ **7/831-2615.** Reservations not accepted. Main courses CUC$4–CUC$7.50. No credit cards. Fri–Wed noon–11pm.

Playa

EXPENSIVE

Don Cangrejo ★ SEAFOOD   This oceanfront restaurant is one of the better and most dependable options for seafood in Havana. The menu is extensive, but your best bet is to stick to a piece of simply prepared fresh snapper or grouper. If you want something heavier, they prepare a lot of cheese and gratin sauces, often with shrimp, crab, or lobster thrown in. Weather permitting, the best seats are outdoors on the open-air patio right beside the water, and around the little courtyard swimming pool. The indoor seating is semiformal and heavily air-conditioned. If you're going to dine indoors, try to snag one of the second-floor window tables just off the little bar. The place has a decent and reasonably priced wine list and a knowledgeable sommelier. Nightly music shows are performed around the pool.

Av. 1 (btw. Calles 16 and 18). © **7/204-4169.** Reservations recommended. Main courses CUC$8–CUC$30. MC, V. Daily noon–midnight.

El Aljibe ★ CRIOLLAN   This popular tourist restaurant is a pleasant surprise. The fixed-price *pollo asado El Aljibe* is the way to go here; the slow-roasted chicken is served all-you-can-eat family style with white rice, black beans, fried plantain, French fries, and salad. This place serves busloads of people on a regular basis, and despite the assembly-line efficiency of the operation, you can still enjoy the pleasant open-air restaurant, with its thatched roof and rustic red-tile floors.

Av. 7 (btw. Calles 24 and 26). © **7/204-1583** or 7/204-4233. Reservations recommended. Main courses CUC$10–CUC$24. MC, V. Daily noon–midnight.

La Fontana ★ INTERNATIONAL/PARILLA   This *paladar* offers something different than the standard fare you often find in Havana. Its alfresco dining area has a waterfall and fish pond, and service is old-fashioned and welcoming. Try the barbequed octopus with pesto, shrimp ravioli in white sauce, chicken in beer, or Provencal lamb. There's live music at night and air-conditioned casita at the back of the property.

Calle 3 No. 305 (Corner of 46). © **7/202-8337.** www.lafontanahavana.info. Main courses CUC$9–CUC$23. No credit cards. Daily noon–midnight.

MODERATE

If you can't get a table at La Cocina de Lilliam (see below), **La Esperanza,** Calle 16 no. 105 between Avenidas 1 and 3 (© **7/202-4361**), is another excellent *paladar* set up in an old sprawling home in Miramar (Mon–Sat 7–11pm; CUC$13).

El Tocororo ★ CRIOLLAN/INTERNATIONAL   Like its progeny, La Finca, this is a place whose reputation precedes it, and whose actual performance can't quite justify the prices and renown. The food and service are fine, but they don't live up to the fanfare. There's no fixed menu, but if the waiter's suggestions don't hit the mark, ask and they may be able to accommodate your request. Almost anything can be prepared with whatever sauce or preparation you might desire. The restaurant is housed in an attractive old Miramar mansion; the decor is cluttered and eclectic, with Tiffany lamps, stained glass, assorted hanging plants, and carved parrots dominating the scene. There's also an attached little sushi bar and restaurant, **Sakura,** serving traditional and respectable Japanese cuisine, although sometimes certain ingredients are lacking.

Av. 3 and Calle 18. © **7/204-2209.** Reservations recommended. Main courses CUC$5–CUC$25; sushi CUC$6–CUC$12. MC, V. Mon–Sat noon–midnight.

La Cocina de Lilliam ★★ 🛈 CRIOLLAN   The elegant, softly lit outdoor garden seating here would be enough to recommend this family-run *paladar,* but the food is excellent as well. Lilliam Domínguez has a deft touch. Try the garbanzo, ham, and onion appetizer, and then opt for a piece of fresh fish, usually grouper or snapper, simply grilled. The menu varies, but order the *ropa vieja* if it's available, made with shredded lamb here instead of the traditional beef. This place is getting quite popular, so reservations are essential, especially if you want one of the outdoor tables.

Calle 48 no. 1311 (btw. Calles 13 and 15). ✆ **7/209-6514.** Reservations highly recommended. Main courses CUC$10-CUC$15. No credit cards. Sun-Fri noon-3pm and 7-10pm.

Habana del Este & Playas del Este

EXPENSIVE

La Divina Pastora SEAFOOD/CRIOLLAN   This place has a wonderful setting, just behind a battery of big cannons below the Fortaleza de la Cabaña, near the water and overlooking La Habana Vieja. However, you'll be paying extra for the setting, and most of the seating is indoors, with no views of the city. The food here, while acceptable, does nothing to justify the prices. You might as well order the lobster, as it's the only thing that costs more or less what you'd pay for it anywhere else—and you know they're fresh, since you get to pick your dinner from a large tank of live ones. If you're not especially hungry, check out the El Mirador bar next-door, which has better views from its outdoor tables, and a small, simple menu of sandwiches and light meals.

Parque Histórico Morro y Cabaña, Carretera de La Cabaña. ✆ **7/860-8341.** Reservations recommended. Main courses CUC$14-CUC$30. MC, V. Daily noon-midnight.

MODERATE

El Bodegón Criollo CRIOLLAN   A couple of huge wine casks hanging over the door mark the entrance to this, the principal restaurant at the Fortaleza de la Cabaña complex (see "Parque Histórico Morro y Cabaña," p. 121). The dining room occupies a long, wide, former storage room in the old fortress, with arched ceilings and brick floors. The food is simple and filling. I recommend the *grillada criolla*, which is a mixed plate of grilled beef, chicken, and pork served with *moros y cristianos* (black beans and rice). The grilled lobster is a good choice as well. Make a reservation for around 7pm if you want to eat and be out in time to snag a good spot for the nightly *cañonazo* (cannon-firing) ceremony. The Fortaleza de la Cabaña complex is popular with Cubans and actually has several restaurants—you might want to try the nearby La Fortaleza, a pesos-only *(moneda nacional)* restaurant that serves similar and slightly less-expensive food in a much less formal setting.

Fortaleza de la Cabaña. ✆ **7/861-9504.** Reservations recommended. Main courses CUC$5-CUC$20. MC, V. Daily noon-11pm.

La Terraza ★ SEAFOOD/CRIOLLAN   This place is de rigueur for any Hemingway tour of the island. The ghosts of Papa and his pal Gregorio Fuentes are omnipresent here—just saunter through the swinging saloon-style doors and look around. The small restaurant is actually somewhat unable to cope with its fame, but if you get here early or have a firm reservation, you won't have to wait to enjoy the well-prepared seafood, cool sea breezes, and a great view across the small plaza in Cojímar to the sea. The seafood paella is pretty good, and the lobster is usually fresh.

Calle 152 no. 161, Cojímar. ✆ **7/766-5151.** Reservations recommended. Main courses CUC$6-CUC$25. MC, V. Daily 11am-11pm.

Los Doce Apóstoles ★ CRIOLLAN   Set at the base of the Morro Castle, just behind a battery of 12 cannons—hence the name "The Twelve Apostles"—the setting is actually nicer than that at La Divina Pastora, with great views day or night at a collection of open-air patio tables. When it's raining or the sun's too strong, you can take a seat at one of the less picturesque, indoor tables. Stick to the reasonably priced *criolla* fare and, if you've come for dinner, hang around after you finish, as this joint often gets jumping after the *cañonazo* ceremony.

Parque Histórico Morro y Cabaña, Carretera de La Cabaña. © **7/863-8295.** Reservations recommended. Main courses CUC$8–CUC$28. MC, V. Daily noon–11pm.

INEXPENSIVE

In addition to the options listed below, try **Mi Cayito** at Laguna Itabo, Santa María del Mar (© **7/797-1339**) or **El Cubano** at Avenida 5ta and Calle 456, Boca Ciega (© **7/796-4061**), which serves lots of seafood.

Paladar Maeda ★ ☺ CRIOLLAN/ITALIAN   This attractive *paladar* has a quaint garden featuring a small fountain, and it's draped in ferns, palms, and tumbergia flowers. Dine alfresco or in the air-conditioned indoor dining room. The eclectic menu offers Italian dishes like pizza and spaghetti, as well as Cuban dishes such as chicken paella, chicken breast with creole sauce, and pork chops. Ask for the daily specials: we dined on delicious pargo in an orange and white wine sauce scattered with raisins and peanuts. There's a small children's menu.

Calle Quebec 115 (between 476 and 478), Guanabo. © **7/796-2615.** Main courses CUC$5–CUC$10. No credit cards. Mon–Sat 6p–11pm, Sun noon–11pm.

Paladar Piccolo ★ ITALIAN   Here, blue swinging doors lead to a leafy patio. Inside, paper money, pictures, and knick-knacks line the walls. This pizzeria, with a wood-fired pizza oven, is popular with Italians and locals and offers a variety of thin-crust pizza options. Ravioli and spaghetti also feature on the full menu. Die-hard Cuban comida fans can opt for roast pork or pork steaks. Foccaccia and red (Spanish) wine complete the ambience.

5th Avenue (btw. Calles 502 and 504), Guanabo. © **7/796-4300.** Main courses CUC$4.25–CUC$8.50. No credit cards. Daily noon–midnight.

WHAT TO SEE & DO

Havana is a city with a rich historical and architectural legacy. There are scores of sights and attractions, ranging from museums and churches to city squares and colonial forts—and more. There's easily a week's worth of worthy attractions. I've tried to select and describe the most important sights below.

At many attractions, a CUC$2 to CUC$5 fee is added on for the taking of photos, and as much as CUC$50 for shooting video. This policy seems to be applied somewhat erratically.

All of the major tour agencies offer **city tours.** These affairs generally take in as many attractions as can be fitted into the allotted time period. The most common tours include stops at the José Martí Memorial, a ride along the Malecón, and a walk around La Habana Vieja (including stops at a handful of churches and attractions, and, of course, La Bodeguita del Medio). Some include tours of any number of the attractions listed below, with perhaps a visit to El Morro or the Hemingway Museum thrown in, while others are theme based—castles and forts, churches, tobacco, art, or Hemingway, for example. Different tour agencies mix and match the various attractions at their discretion. If you want to see something specific, be sure it's on the tour you sign up for. The tours can range from 4 to 8 hours in length and cost between CUC$15 and CUC$50 per person.

A QUICK KEY TO HAVANA'S parks AND plazas

Any tour of La Habana Vieja will be oriented around the several colonial plazas or squares, and the Parque Central (Central Park). Although relatively close together, each is almost a world of its own. The principal attractions of each are described in greater detail below, but here's a general overview.

The smallest, **Plaza de la Catedral,** is probably the most visited. Named for the cathedral that defines its northern boundary, this compact cobblestone square is surrounded by a series of stunning, colonial-era buildings and former palaces. With the cathedral's bell towers lit up each night, this is a great plaza to visit after dark. Within a 1-block radius in any direction, you will find La Bodeguita del Medio, the Centro Wifredo Lam, and the Museo de Arte Colonial.

The **Plaza de Armas** probably has the densest concentration of historic buildings and attractions. Surrounding the shady urban park that now takes up the plaza, you'll find the Palacio de los Capitanes Generales and Museo de la Ciudad, the Castillo de la Real Fuerza, El Templete, and the Hotel Santa Isabel, housed in the former palace of the Count of Santovenia. Most days, the square is lined with stands set up by scores of used-book sellers.

The oldest plaza, **Plaza Vieja,** was first laid out in 1599 and was dubbed "Plaza Nueva" (New Square). It soon lost prominence to the better located Plaza de Armas and Plaza de la Catedral. In fact, for most of the last half of the 20th century, it served simply as a parking lot. However, it has recently been meticulously restored. At the center of the broad open square is a replica of an 18th-century fountain. Surrounding it are historic buildings representing 4 centuries of construction.

Near the waterfront, you'll find the **Plaza de San Francisco.** Asymmetrical in shape, this is the most open and uncluttered plaza in La Habana Vieja. Facing the Sierra Maestra ship terminal, it is anchored by the Fuente de los Leones (Lion's Fountain), which was carved in 1836 by Italian sculptor Giuseppe Gaggini, modeled after a sister fountain in the Alhambra in Granada, Spain. The area's former importance as a business center is quickly noted in the imposing facades of the Lonja de Comercio (Stock Exchange) and a couple of large banks and money exchange houses that dominate the northern side of the plaza. The southern edge is defined by the lovely, 16th-century Basílica Menor de San Francisco de Asís. Be sure to climb the bell tower here, the tallest church tower in Havana, for a wonderful view of La Habana Vieja and its harbor.

Parque Central marks the western boundary of La Habana Vieja. This is a popular local gathering spot, particularly known for its heated conversations about baseball. It is bordered on the west by the Paseo de Martí, or Prado, featuring El Capitolio and the Gran Teatro de la Habana. On the eastern edge, you'll find the Palacio del Centro Asturiano, which now holds the international collection of the Museo Nacional de Bellas Artes. Classic hotels that ring the park include the Hotel Inglaterra, Hotel Plaza, and the Hotel Telégrafo, as well as the modern Hotel Parque Central. A short stroll down the Prado will soon bring you to the Museo Nacional de Bellas Artes, Museo de la Revolución, and the Memorial Granma; while just 1 block in the other direction, heading toward La Habana Vieja on Calle Obispo, you'll hit El Floridita.

Calle Obispo is one of the most charming and distinctive streets in La Habana Vieja. This bustling pedestrian-only boulevard conveniently connects Parque Central and the nearby Capitolio with the Plaza de Armas and its many surrounding attractions, making it a classic route for any walking tour of La Habana Vieja.

The Top Attractions

LA HABANA VIEJA

In addition to the places mentioned below, there are scores of other interesting little museums and attractions. Moreover, many of the hotels and restaurants mentioned above (including El Floridita, Hotel Santa Isabel, and Hotel Ambos Mundos, to name just a few) are practically attractions in their own right, and worth a quick visit on any walking tour.

Castillo de la Real Fuerza ★ ☺ This well-preserved, 16th-century fort sits within a broad cloverleaf moat. This is the oldest fort in Havana, and the oldest surviving fort in the hemisphere. It was actually pretty much a failure, built too small and too far from the harbor entrance to be of much use. Still, crossing over the old drawbridge and walking around the ancient stone battlements gives you a great sense of history. The most distinctive feature of this compact fort is the weathervane, La Giraldilla, which has come to be the city's defining symbol. The original 1634 bronze sculpture is now on display in the entrance; a copy adorns the top of the fort's bell tower. Today, the fort also contains exhibits featuring items salvaged from shipwrecks, as well as replicas of Spanish colonial boats. Kids will love the chests that are stuffed with gold, necklaces, emeralds, and rings, but the standout exhibit is a huge four meter- (13 foot-) long model of the *Santísima Trinidad*, the largest naval ship of its time; it sank after the Battle of Trafalgar.

Calle O'Reilly 2 (at Av. del Puerto). ✆ **7/861-5010.** Admission CUC$1 adults, free for children under 12. Tues–Sun 9.30am–5pm.

Catedral de San Cristóbal ★★★ This is Old Havana's classic cathedral. The plaza fronting the cathedral and the church's baroque facade, with its asymmetrical towers, are the most visited attractions in La Habana Vieja. Inside, the cathedral is simple, almost to the point of austerity, thanks to a radical, 19th-century neoclassical makeover. Still, the vaulted ceilings, massive stone pillars, and modest collection of art and antiquities certainly make it worth a visit. Of these, the 17th-century wooden sculpture of Saint Christopher is interesting—note the shortened legs, which were cut in order to get the piece into place. Despite the official visiting hours listed below, the church is frequently closed tight. If you're lucky, you might be able to attend Mass here at 9am on Sunday.

Calle Empedrado 156, Plaza de la Catedral. ✆ **7/861-7771.** Free admission. Mon–Sat 9am–5pm; Sun (Mass) 9am–12:30pm.

El Templete A tall (and still growing) ceiba tree stands in front of this neoclassical Doric temple. The tree is the younger cousin of a fallen giant that stood here, on the site where local citizens celebrated the town's first Mass and town meetings in the early 1500s. Behind the tree stands the "little temple," which was built between 1754 and 1828. Inside, you'll find three large canvases by Jean-Baptiste Vermay depicting the inauguration of the temple, as well as depictions of those town meetings and masses. You'll also find a bust of the artist beside an urn containing his ashes.

Calles Baratillo and O'Reilly, Plaza de Armas. (☎ **7/861-2876.** Admission CUC$3 adults, free for children under 12. Daily 9am–6pm.

Museo de Arte Colonial ★★ Located in the cathedral square, this museum has a hidden collection of stunning artifacts. Of note is the collection of exquisite 19th century antique lace and linen gowns. Upstairs, under an attractive Moorish-style roof, is a veritable collection of riches: Baccarat and Opaline crystal, fans made from ostrich feathers and mother-of-pearl, Biscuit porcelain, carved bone- and ebony-topped walking sticks, leather chairs, and a charming 19th-century Italian porcelain ballerina sitting on a chair; her tutu is made from fabric.

Calle San Ignacio 61 (btw. O'Reilly and Callejón del Chorro). (☎ **7/862-6440.** Admission CUC$2; tour guide CUC$1; camera use CUC$1. Tues–Sat 8am–5pm, Sun 9am–1pm.

Museo de la Ciudad ★★ The Museum of the City is housed in the Palacio de los Capitanes Generales (Palace of the Captain Generals), a beautiful example of 18th-century Cuban baroque architecture, and one of the most important and well-preserved buildings in La Habana Vieja. The seat of Cuba's government for more than 100 years, the building now features a dozen or so rooms with polished marble floors and ornate architectural details, which have displays of colonial-era relics and arti-facts. It's worth the price of admission just to stroll along the broad second-floor interior veranda overlooking the lush central courtyard, with its white marble statue of Christopher Columbus. And don't miss the Throne Room, with its thick red-velvet draperies, an array of treasures, and plush throne built for use by Spain's visiting monarchs. Allow at least an hour to tour the museum.

Calle Tacón (btw. Calles O'Reilly and Obispo), Plaza de Armas. (☎ **7/861-2876.** Admission CUC$3 adults, free for children under 12. Tues–Sun 9:30am–5pm.

Museo de la Revolución y Memorial Granma ★ Housed in the former Presidential Palace, the Museum of the Revolution and *Granma* Memorial outline Cuba's history in copious detail, with an emphasis on its independence and revolu-tionary struggles. In addition to the history lessons, exhibits, and memorabilia, there are wonderful works of art and some stunning architectural details, including a rep-lica of Versaille's Hall of Mirrors, ornate bas-relief work, and interior decorations by Tiffany. Outside, you'll find several trucks, tanks, planes, and even a bit of a shot-down U2 spy plane, all surrounding the glass-enclosed *Granma*, the 18-meter (59-foot) motor launch that carried Fidel Castro, Che Guevara, and 80 other fighters to the island in 1956. Give yourself at least 1½ hours to see it all.

Calle Refugio 1 (btw. Calles Monserrate and Zulueta). (☎ **7/862-4091.** Admission CUC$5 adults, free for children under 12. Guided tours are given throughout the day and cost an additional CUC$2. Daily 10am–5pm.

Museo Nacional de Bellas Artes ★★ The National Fine Arts Museum fills three floors of this square-city-block building, and the design—with a central court-yard and zigzagging ramped stairwell—can make navigating the upper floors confus-ing, so allow yourself plenty of time. An extensive collection of Cuban art and sculpture is on display at the newly renovated main building here. Modern masters

LUIS POSADA CARRILES

On October 6, 1976, Cubana de Aviación flight 455 was blown up by plastic explosives, killing all 73 people aboard. The victims included Cuba's entire Olympic fencing team. The man implicated in the bombing, Luis Posada Carriles, is emblematic of the confusing and contradictory nature of U.S.-Cuba relations, and relevant in terms of the current War on Terror.

A former CIA operative and U.S. Army officer, the 82-year-old Posada Carriles took part in the failed Bay of Pigs invasion and later worked with the Nicaraguan contras to destabilize the Sandinista government. He has bragged, and later denied, being responsible for the Cubana airplane bombing, as well as a string of bombings at hotels and tourism facilities in Cuba in which several civilians and tourists were killed. Along with Orlando Bosch, he is implicated in the 1976 car bombing in Washington, D.C., that killed Chilean ambassador Orlando Letelier.

Posada Carriles has been jailed in both Venezuela and Panama. He broke out of jail in Venezuela in the mid-1980s, but was later arrested on charges of attempting to assassinate Fidel Castro at a 2000 regional summit in Panama. In July 2005, Posada Carriles was pardoned by outgoing President Mireya Moscoso. Between 2005 and May 2007, he was held in an immigration detention center as the result of his illegally entering the United States, after his requests for political asylum were denied. Charges were then dropped and he remains a free man. However, in June 2008, the Panamanian Supreme Court overturned the presidential pardon. This has opened up the possibility of extradition to Panama.

Posada Carilles represents an embarrassment to the United States. A self-proclaimed and proud "terrorist," he was seen as being coddled by the Bush administration, which refused to prosecute him under any terrorist statutes or grant extradition officially requested by both Cuba and Venezuela. However, during 2010, he was due to stand trial in Texas not for any alleged acts of terrorism but for lying to immigration authorities. In Havana, you can see him vilified along with George W. Bush and Adolf Hitler on propaganda billboards.

---

like Wifredo Lam, Raúl Martínez, Amelia Peláez, and René Portocarrero are well represented. The international collection is housed in a restored, early-20th-century gem of a building. This collection leans heavily on classical and neoclassical European works, with some fine portraits and still lifes from the Dutch Golden Age, although there are some American, Latin American, and Oriental works on display. Brits will be interested in Canaletto's 1751 painting of Chelsea College and the River Thames; the other half hangs in a National Trust property in Norfolk. Give yourself at least 2 hours to tour the collection in either building, or more if you want to get a good feel for the Cuban art collection.

Calle Trocadero (btw. Calles Zulueta and Monserrate) and Calle San Rafael (btw. Calles Zulueta and Monserrate). © **7/861-0241.** www.museonacional.cult.cu. Admission CUC$5 adults, free for children under 14. Combined museum entrance CUC$8. Tues–Sat 10am–6pm; Sun 10am–2pm.

Parque La Maestranza ☺ Located on the edge of La Habana Vieja, this 2-block stretch of city park is dedicated to the little ones. There are pony rides and a little train ride, as well as jungle gyms and inflatable rooms for romping around in. There are usually some clowns or mimes on hand, and balloons, popcorn, and soft drinks are for sale. This place is decidedly low-key and low-tech by Western standards, but the mix of mostly Cuban and some foreign kids don't seem to mind.

Calle Cuarteles (btw. Calle Tacón and Av. del Puerto). Admission CUC$2. Daily 9am–5pm.

CENTRO HABANA

Callejón de Hammel ★★★ 🎁 Nearly every inch of this narrow, 2-block-long alleyway is painted in bright colors, the work of painter Salvador González. Most are mural-size depictions of Afro-Cuban deities. There are also sculptures made from scrap and old bike parts, as well as a *Nganga,* a sacred place for the celebration of Palo Monte rituals centered on a giant cauldron. There are crafts and food for sale in this open-air bazaar, and González also has a small gallery here. Between noon and 3pm each Sunday, this is the site of a weekly Afro-Cuban music and dance show and celebration headed up by the renowned folkloric group Clavé y Guaguanco. (To locate this alleyway, see the "Vedado" map on p. 85.)

Callejón de Hammel, btw. Calles Espada and Aramburu. Free admission. Daily 24 hr.

Chinatown ✋ You'll see Havana's Chinatown touted in local literature, tour offerings, and other guidebooks. Overall, it's quite a disappointment. Occupying a small section of Centro Habana, it has few distinguishing features, a very small population of residents of Chinese descent, and none of the vibrancy of Chinatowns in cities like New York, San Francisco, or Toronto. A block-long pedestrian-only street, El Cuchillo de Zanja is packed with nondescript and unimpressive Chinese restaurants and shops. The biggest attraction here is the large, pagoda-style Dragon's Gate at the corner of Calle Dragones and Calle Amistad. Perhaps the most interesting attraction is the Iglesia de la Caridad, which features a statue of a Virgin that some say has Asian features. (To locate this area, see the "Vedado" map on p. 85.)

In the area bordered by Calles Dragones, Zanja, Rayo, and San Nicolás. Free admission. Daily 24 hr.

El Capitolio ★ Modeled after its U.S. cousin, the Cuban Capitol is a stunning architectural work of grand scale—it's actually a tiny bit taller and longer than the Washington, D.C. version. There's not a whole lot to see here, but it's worth climbing the steep steps and taking a quick tour. *Note:* El Capitolio was closed in late 2010 with no fixed reopening date. Its large scale and intricately inlaid marble floors are impressive. The entrance hall has a replica of a 25-carat diamond embedded in the floor from which all highway distances radiating out from Havana are measured. There's also the *Statue of the Republic,* a 17m-tall (56-ft.), 49-ton Roman goddess covered in gold leaf, which some claim is Jupiter. You can walk around the old parliamentary hall and, if you're lucky, visit the library. Regular guided tours are offered for CUC$1 per person. There are some arts-and-crafts galleries inside, as well as a simple restaurant and a popular Internet cafe.

Calle Prado (btw. Calles San José and Dragones). ✆ **7/861-5519.** Admission CUC$3 adults, free for children under 12. Daily 9am–5pm.

El Malecón ★★★ This oceanside pedestrian walkway stretches all the way from the Castillo de San Salvador de la Punta in La Habana Vieja to the Almendares River that separates Vedado from Miramar (about 7km/4¼ miles in total). No trip to Havana is complete without at least some time spent strolling and lingering along the Malecón, which is the social center for a wide range of Cubans. Throughout the day, you'll see children swimming and men fishing off the coral outcroppings that border

FROMMER'S FAVORITE HAVANA experiences

- Take a walk along the **Malecón,** and then, for a slight change of pace, grab a Coco Taxi or horse-drawn carriage for a different take on Havana's most popular promenade.

- Wander the streets of **La Habana Vieja.** Allow yourself to get lost in time and in the beautiful and dilapidated architecture of its colonial streets, buildings, and plazas.

- Visit the **Plaza de la Catedral** ★★★ at night, stopping to grab an outdoor table at **Cafetería El Portal** to sip a drink and soak in the sight of the **Catedral**

- **de San Cristóbal's** illuminated bell towers.

- Visit a **cigar factory** and enjoy the aromas of Cuba's top export being manufactured in timeless fashion before your very eyes.

- Head to the **Callejón de Hammel** to admire the street art and murals of this Centro Habana neighborhood. Try to come on a Sunday afternoon and you'll be able to enjoy the spectacle of an Afro-Cuban religious show and celebration.

- Pull out all the stops and treat yourself to dinner and a show at the **Tropicana.**

the walkway, and at night, you're sure to see lovers entwined on cozy perches and groups of revelers all along the seawall.

The section fronting Centro Habana is perhaps the most picturesque, with the crumbling facades and faded paint of neoclassical and neo-Moorish buildings and apartments lining the avenue that separates the Malecón from the city. If you've got the legs and time, a walk from the Hotel Nacional to La Habana Vieja (or vice versa) should only take you about 25 minutes. On rough days, you may have to time your steps—or cross the street—as waves break furiously over the seawall. Alternatively, you can hire a horse-drawn carriage or Coco Taxi for the trip.

Free admission. Daily 24 hr.

Fábrica de Tabaco Partagás ★ Founded in 1845, this is Cuba's largest and perhaps most renowned cigar factory, producing around 5 million cigars a year. The off-yellow-and-rust trimmed, neoclassical facade is resplendent in the Havana morning sunlight. (You can take your best photos of it from the west-side windows of El Capitolio.) Throughout the day, you can stop in and buy cigars from the well-stocked shop, La Casa del Habano.

Calle Industria 524 (behind the Capitolio). ✆ **7/862-4604.** 45-min. guided tour CUC$10; reservations recommended. Tickets must be bought at the hotel desks of nearby hotels. Mon–Fri 9–11am and noon–1:30pm. No photography allowed.

VEDADO

Cementerio de Colón ★★ A miniature city of mausoleums, crypts, family chapels and vaults, soaring sculptures, and ornate gravestones, Columbus Cemetery covers 55 hectares (136 acres). Designed by Spanish architect Calixto de Loira in the mid-1800s, it is laid out in grids around a central chapel. The main entrance features a large sculpture of Faith, Hope, and Charity in Carrara marble. There's also a large monument to fallen soldiers of the Revolutionary Armed Forces, and an impressive stainless steel sculpture capping a memorial to the martyrs of the 1957 attack on

⊗ Imagine

Beatles fans will want to stop by the little **Parque Lennon (Lennon Park)** at Calles 17 and 6 in Vedado, where you'll find a life-size statue of John Lennon seated on a park bench. The "smart Beatle" is quite revered here, and there is an annual open-air concert in this park every December 8, featuring a wide range of prominent Cuban musicians, singing his songs and commemorating his assassination on that day.

Batista's Presidential Palace. One of the most popular graves is that of La Milagrosa (The Miraculous One). The story goes that when Amelia Goyri de la Hoz died in childbirth in 1901, she was buried with her stillborn daughter placed at her feet. When the tomb was opened a few years later, the baby was found in her arms. Amelia is now considered the protector of pregnant women and newborn children. Pilgrims paying homage must not turn their backs to the tomb upon leaving. Brief guided tours are available (for free, but a tip is generally expected), or you can buy a little guidebook with a detailed map (CUC$5) at the entrance.

Calles Zapata and 12. ✆ **7/832-1050.** Admission CUC$1 adults, free for children under 12. Daily 8am–5pm.

Coppelia ★ ◩   Made famous in Tomás Gutiérez Alea's hit film *Fresa y Chocolate* (Strawberry and Chocolate), this is the main branch of the Cuban national ice-cream company. At the center of the block-long complex is a postmodern building of curving concrete and glass, surrounded by a series of open courtyards with wrought-iron tables, where customers are served bowls of the frozen nectar. There are actually a dozen or so small booths selling cones and bowls spread around the park. Still, Coppelia is yet another glaring case of tourist apartheid: Cubans form long lines to wait their turn at a table or stand while tourists, who are paying in hard currency and not Cuban pesos, are always taken to the head of the line, or shown to a separate convertible peso stand. There are usually only two or three flavors available on any given day; if you're there on a rum raisin day, you're in for a treat. Ice cream in wrappers for tourists starts at about CUC$1.30; it costs a couple of pesos in *moneda nacional*.

Calles 23 and L. ✆ **7/832-3450.** Tues–Sun 10am–10pm.

Memorial José Martí   The 109m (358-ft.) marble tower here is the highest point in Havana. At the base of the tower is a massive statue of the poet and national independence hero José Martí. Inside the base is a small museum dedicated to Martí featuring manuscripts, memorabilia, portraits, and other informative displays. An elevator takes visitors up to a series of lookout rooms atop the tower, providing far-reaching panoramic views of Havana. The lookout is by far the most interesting and popular attraction here, although there's also a little theater where concerts and poetry readings are sometimes held. The memorial sits in the Plaza de la Revolución, host to all political rallies, and faces the Ministry of Interior building with the iconic image of Che Guevara's face cast in iron ★ as well as the Ministry of Communications, which depicts the face of Camilo Cienfuegos, also cast in iron.

Plaza de la Revolución, Nuevo Vedado. ✆ **7/859-2347** or 7/859-2347. Admission museum CUC$3 adults, CUC$1.50 children under 12; mirador CUC$2 adults, CUC$1.50 children under 12. Mon–Sat 9am–5pm.

Universidad de la Habana   The compact campus of Havana's main university sits on some high ground in Vedado close to the former Havana Hilton. The broad staircase leading up to the school, with its signature *Alma Mater* statue of a seated woman with outstretched arms, is a popular gathering spot for students, and you can sometimes catch impromptu concerts here. There are a couple of unimpressive museums on campus—those of Natural Sciences and Montane Anthropology—as well as the nearby and slightly more interesting **Museo Napoleónico,** Calle San Miguel 1159, at the corner of La Ronda (© 7/873-6564), with its large collection of Napoleonic-era memorabilia. (**Note:** This museum was closed in late 2010 and may reopen mid-2011).

Calles L and 27, La Ronda. © **7/879-3488.** Free admission to the university; CUC$3 for museums. Mon–Fri 9am–noon, 1–4pm.

PLAYA

Acuario Nacional ☺   A few years ago, the National Aquarium got a major face-lift and improvements are ongoing. It's not Sea World or the Baltimore Aquarium, but this is a pretty spiffy attempt for Cuba. A variety of tanks and pools re-create all the major water habitats of Cuba, and sea lion and dolphin shows are presented throughout the day. There are a couple of simple cafeteria-style restaurants, and one pseudo-fancy option, the Gran Azul Restaurant, with a huge Plexiglas wall opening onto a large tank where two sad and claustrophobic dolphins swim. This place is very popular with Cuban families and school groups, so it's a great place to mingle.

Av. 3 and Calle 62, Miramar. © **7/202-5872** or 7/203-6401. www.acuarionacional.cu. Admission CUC$7 adults, CUC$3 students and children under 12. Winter Tues–Sun 10am–6pm. Summer Tues–Sun 10am–10pm. Dolphin shows are 11am, 3pm and 5pm. Sea lion shows are noon, 2pm, and 4pm.

Casa Compay Segundo   The megafamous Buena Vista Social Club star who died in 2003 lived in this house for the last six years of his life. It is filled with memorabilia, his awards, newspaper articles, and dozens of photographs that his fans will love. His preserved bedroom provides a rare glimpse of photos taken in his youth.

Calle 22 no. 103 (btw. Avs. 1 and 3), Miramar, © **7/202-5922.** www.compaysegundo.es. Mon–Fri 9am–4pm.

Maqueta de la Habana ★   I was prepared to dislike this miniature display of Havana, but left oddly impressed. The realistic scale model of the city takes up almost 144sq. m (1,550 sq. ft.). You can walk around it on the ground level, or climb a narrow interior balcony that rings three walls here. There's usually some traveling art exhibition on the walls surrounding the model. A guide can be hired for CUC$5 to CUC$10. This is not to be confused with a similar (and much smaller) scale model of Old Havana, found in Old Havana, of course.

Calle 28 113 (btw. Avs. 1 and 3), Miramar. © **7/202-7303.** Admission CUC$3; CUC$2 to take photos; CUC$5 to take video. Mon–Sat 9:30am–5pm.

OUTSIDE DOWNTOWN

Museo Ernest Hemingway   I have mixed feelings about the experience of visiting this place, since visitors are not allowed into the former home of the famous writer. Sure, you get a bit of the feel for Hemingway, but you also end up feeling like a Peeping Tom. Nevertheless, it is an interesting visit. Circling the ground floor, you can see the house more or less as it was when Hemingway was living and writing

The *Cañonazo*

The cañonazo (cannon blast) ★ is a picturesque ritual that takes place at La Fortaleza de San Carlos de la Cabaña every night. An honor guard in 18th-century military garb emerges from the barracks at about 8:40pm and conducts a small parade to a bank of cannons overlooking Havana's harbor channel. With pomp and circumstance, the cannon is loaded and fired precisely at 9pm. About 1,000 people show up each night, the vast majority of them Cubans. Arrive early if you want a good vantage point. The blast itself is quite loud—you can hear it in most parts of Havana—so protect your ears. You can combine the ceremony with a meal at one of the nearby restaurants.

here. There's a copious collection of books, paintings, and stuffed animal heads. In addition to an old typewriter, the works of art by Picasso, Miró, and Klee are some of the more prized possessions. There's a small tower separate from the main house with some rooms with rudimentary exhibits, and you can even climb it for a better view all around. In the surrounding gardens, you can see Papa's pet cemetery and the author's dry-docked fishing boat, *Pilar.*

Finca la Vigía, San Francisco de Paula, Carretera Central Km 12.5. ℗ **7/891-0809.** Admission CUC$3 adults, free for children under 12; CUC$1 for a guide; CUC$5 to take photos; CUC$50 to take video. Mon–Sat 10am–5pm; Sun 10am–1pm.

Parque Histórico Morro y Cabaña ★★ Located across the harbor channel from La Habana Vieja, this historic park of forts, battlements, and barracks was responsible for the protection of Havana for centuries. The complex is actually made up of two separate forts, or attractions: the Castillo del Morro and La Fortaleza de San Carlos de la Cabaña.

The Morro Castle, or "El Morro" as it is most commonly known, is the first fort you'll come to after crossing under the harbor channel tunnel. Sitting on the point overlooking Havana's narrow harbor channel, it was built between 1589 and 1630 and served as an important line of defense against pirate attacks and naval invasions. In addition to its ramparts, barracks, and banks of cannons, El Morro has a series of exhibition rooms and minimuseums. You can walk the fort's ancient streets and even climb the still-functioning, 19th-century lighthouse here. El Morro affords excellent views of Havana and the curve of the Malecón, and there are several restaurants and bars here.

About a kilometer (½-mile) away, and separated by a deep ravine, is the larger La Fortaleza de San Carlos de la Cabaña, more popularly referred to as simply "la Cabaña." Built between 1764 and 1774, in response to the British invasion, the long fort is a miniature city, with a high perch overlooking the harbor channel and La Habana Vieja. As at El Morro, there are several exhibition halls and a handful of restaurants, bars, and gift shops here. One of the more popular exhibition halls is the **Comandancia de Che Guevara,** a room where the revolutionary leader briefly set up a command post after storming the fort in January 1959. Be sure to stop in at the cigar shop, which features the longest cigar in the world, an 11m (36-ft.) stogie that hangs above your head and is duly registered in the Guinness Book of World Records.

There are separate entrance fees for each attraction. A taxi to the complex from Havana costs between CUC$5 and CUC$7. You can walk between the two forts— it's about a 15-minute walk that's only moderately strenuous if you stick to the high ground—or you can take a taxi between the two for under CUC$2.

Carretera de La Cabaña, Habana del Este. ℰ **7/863-7063** for El Morro; ℰ **7/862-0617** for La Cabaña. Admission El Morro CUC$5 adults, free for children under 12; La Cabaña CUC$6 adults before 6pm, CUC$8 adults after 6pm, free for children under 12. El Morro daily 8am–8pm; La Cabaña daily 10am–10pm.

OUTDOOR PURSUITS

BASEBALL   Baseball is the national sport and the greatest national passion. Cuba's amateur players are considered some of the best in the world, and the premier players are aggressively scouted and courted by the Major Leagues. The regular season runs November through March, and playoffs and the final championship usually carry the season on into May. **Industriales,** the main Havana team, plays at the **Estadio Latinoamericano,** Calle Zequeira 312, Cerro (ℰ **7/870-6526**). It's usually easy to buy tickets at the box office for less than 5 Cuban pesos, or ask at your hotel and perhaps they can get tickets for you in advance—although for these, you'll probably end up paying CUC$1 to CUC$2.

BIKING   Despite the fact that so much of Havana's transportation is conducted on bicycles, there are no rental agencies or outlets for tourists wishing to get around town by bike. Your best bet for bicycling in Cuba is to bring your own set of wheels and head outside Havana.

GOLF   While the only regulation 18-hole course in the country is located in Varadero (see chapter 7), the Club de Golf Habana, Carretera Vento Km 8, Capdevila, Rancho Boyeros (ℰ **7/649-8918**, ext. 111), has a decent little 9-hole course for true golf junkies. A round of 9 holes will run you CUC$20. Each hole actually has two sets of tees, so you can really play 18 holes, and fake the impression that it's a regulation course. A round of 18 holes costs CUC$30. Club rental is an extra CUC$10 and a caddy will cost you CUC$5. Open daily 9:30am–6:30pm.

GYMS   There are no chains of modern gyms in Havana. Visitors looking for a regular workout on modern gym equipment or an aerobics class should stick to the larger hotels with well-equipped facilities (see "Where to Stay," earlier in this chapter). If you're not staying at one of these hotels, you can use the facilities at the Meliá Habana or Meliá Cohiba for CUC$10.

  Club Habana, Avenida 5, between Calles 188 and 192, Reparto Flores, Playa (ℰ **7/204-5700** or 7/204-3300; www.cpalco.com), has a decent gym and will let guests use the facilities for CUC$20 to CUC$30 per day.

JOGGING   The Malecón is a fabulous place to jog. Early mornings and early evenings, when the heat has somewhat abated, are best. You'll have to watch your step in certain sections where the sidewalk is torn up or deteriorated, but overall this is the choice route for jogging. Farther afield, joggers could try **Parque Lenin,** Calle 100 and Carretera de la Presa (ℰ **7/644-3026**), which is open Tuesday through Sunday from 9am to 5:30pm. This massive park is a major recreational area for locals and has several trails and internal roadways good for jogging.

SCUBA DIVING   While the diving is nowhere near as good as you'll find in more dedicated dive destinations in Cuba, it's certainly possible to do some underwater exploring out of Havana. Your best bet is to head over to **Club Acuario,** Avenida 5 and Calle 248, Santa Fe, Playa (ℰ **7/204-1150**), La Aguja; **Marlin Diving Centre,** Marina Hemingway, corner Avenida 5 and 248, Playa (ℰ **7/204-6848;** www.nautica marlin.com); **Centro Internacional de Buceo,** Club Habana, Avenida 5 between Calles 188 and 192, Playa (ℰ **7/204-5700** ext. 406; www.cpalco.com); or **Marina Tarará,** Vía Blanca Km 18, Playa Tarará, Habana del Este (ℰ **7/797-1500**), located

18km (11 miles) east of the city. It costs between CUC$50 and CUC$85 for two tank dives, including equipment and lunch. You might also consider a day trip to Varadero or Playa Girón for generally better conditions, and not much more cost.

SPORTFISHING   It's easy to follow in Hemingway's wake and try your luck at landing a big one. As with diving, your best bet is to head over to **Club Acuario,** Avenida 5 and Calle 248, Santa Fe, Playa (☎ **7/204-1150**), or **Marina Tarará,** Vía Blanca Km 18, Playa Tarará, Habana del Este (☎ **7/797-1500**). Depending on the size of the boat and number of fishermen, a half-day of sportfishing costs between CUC$150 and CUC$500, while a full day will run you between CUC$400 and CUC$1,400, including gear and lunch.

SWIMMING   If your hotel does not have a swimming pool, most of the larger hotels allow nonguests use of their pool facilities for a price. Rates generally range between CUC$5 and CUC$18 per person. The nicer options include the Meliá Habana and Club Habana in Playa; the Hotel Nacional and Meliá Cohiba in Vedado; and the NH Parque Central, Hotel Saratoga, and Hotel Sevilla in La Habana Vieja.

Although it's possible to use the small beach at the Club Habana, the nearby Playas del Este is your best bet for some beach time. Most tour agencies and hotel tour desks offer a day trip to Playa Santa María del Mar for CUC$25 to CUC$40, including round-trip transportation, lunch, and often free run of the facilities at one of the all-inclusive hotels out there. However, you can also get there on your own steam using the HabanaBusTour (see p. 88).

Note: Do not be tempted to join the locals you see swimming off the coral outcroppings just below the Malecón. The coral is jagged and sharp, and the seas can get suddenly rough. Moreover, in recent years there have been complaints that the water is very polluted.

TENNIS   Unless you're staying at one of the few Havana hotels with a court, your options are limited. Your best bet is to try to book a court at the Occidental Miramar, Avenida 5, between Calles 78 and 80, Miramar, Playa (☎ 7/204-8158), which has six courts; or head to the Club Habana, Avenida 5, between Calles 188 and 192, Reparto Flores, Playa (☎ 7/204-3300); or Club de Golf Habana, Carretera Vento Km 8, Capdevila, Rancho Boyeros (☎ 7/649-8820), each of which has a few courts open to the general public. All charge around CUC$10 per hour.

SHOPPING

The Shopping Scene

Havana is by no means a great shopping city (although it is the best in Cuba). Given the reality of the Cuban economy, all shops selling any goods above and beyond the basic necessities are by default geared entirely toward tourists, a small community of foreign diplomats and workers, and an even smaller community of Cubans earning enough hard currency to afford such luxuries. Hence, it's a challenge to find interesting shops with unique local items at good prices. In general, stores throughout Havana are open from 9am to 5pm, 7 days a week. Some may open earlier and close later, particularly in heavily trafficked tourist areas. Virtually none close for lunch.

All shops selling to tourists operate exclusively with Cuban convertible pesos. Most are run by big, state-owned enterprises. The most common stores belong to the **Caracol** chain, which is geared primarily to tourists, while the **Tiendas Panamericanas** chain specializes in household and domestic items aimed at foreign residents.

In recent years, modern malls have begun popping up. Everything stated above holds true for the merchandise you'll find here.

ARTex ★ (📞 7/204-0813; www.soycubano.com) is the state-run company in charge of managing Cuba's artistic export products (hence the name "ARTex"). Its job runs the gamut from promoting Cuban musicians and artists abroad to marketing their goods and negotiating contracts. ARTex operates a series of storefronts around the country, either stand-alone affairs or shops placed in prominent hotels or tourist attractions. Depending on the size and location, these usually carry a good selection of Cuban music, Cuban films, tourist T-shirts, and kitschy arts and crafts. The better ones have decent quality drums and percussion instruments, as well as art prints and posters. In Miramar, head to ARTex's **Bazar Volveré,** Calle 3, between Calles 78 and 80 (📞 7/204-5370); in Vedado, check out **Habana Sí,** Calle 23 no. 301, at the corner of Calle L (📞 7/838-3162), across from the Tryp Habana Libre.

Shopping A to Z
ART GALLERIES

Art-Havana ★★★　A half-day or one-day tour with curator Sussette Martínez is a fascinating and compelling experience that takes in visits to the studios of contemporary artists in Cuba. The tour is geared to people who are interested in collecting Latin American art and for those wanting to learn more about contemporary art in a wider sociocultural context. 📞 7/267-7989. www.art-havana.com. Tour costs CUC$35–CUC$50.

Galería Acacia　This gallery is the place to go for high-end contemporary Cuban art, and a good place to see who the up-and-coming hot artists are. Calle San José 114 (btw. Calles Industria and Consulado), Centro Habana. 📞 **7/863-9364.** www.galerias cubanas.com.

Galería Víctor Manuel　This place has a pretty good selection of modern decorative paintings, crafts, and a few pieces that could qualify as real artwork. Given its prime location and popularity, don't expect anything to come cheap. Calles San Ignacio and Callejón del Chorro, Plaza de la Catedral, La Habana Vieja. 📞 **7/861-2955.**

La Casona　Located in a series of rooms over two floors of the Casa de los Condes de Jaruco on Plaza Vieja, this wonderful gallery has similar works to those found at Víctor Manuel, but the selection is better, and there's less of a cattle-car mass-market feel to the place. Calle Muralla 107 (corner of Calle San Ignacio), Plaza Vieja, La Habana Vieja. 📞 **7/863-4703.** www.galeriascubanas.com.

Centro Wifredo Lam ★　This little museum and gallery is dedicated to the memory of Cuba's most treasured modern artist, Wilfredo Lam. The center features traveling exhibits. Open Monday through Friday from 10am–5pm. Calle San Ignacio 22 (corner of Calle Empedrado). 📞 **7/861-3419.** Admission free.

BOOKS

On Plaza de Armas, you'll find multiple stalls selling second-hand and antiquarian books, including many with revolutionary and political themes. (You can also find coins, stamps, and other Revolution memorabilia.) Bargain very hard. **Anticuaria El Navío,** Calle Obispo 119, between Oficios and Mercaderes (📞 7/861-3187), is a dusty old store selling expensive, rare and unusual books.

CERAMICS

Terracota 4   This working studio-cum-gallery in La Habana Vieja features the works of Amelia Carballo, Angel Norniella, and José Ramón. The pieces show a wide range of influences and utilize wide-ranging techniques. One or more of the artists is usually on hand, and sometimes you'll get a chance to see them working. Calle Mercaderes (btw. Calles Obrapía and Lamparilla), La Habana Vieja. ✆ **7/866-9417.**

CIGARS

Cigars are Cuba's most-prized product. The word *Cubans* is synonymous with the highest quality cigars on the planet. Locally, they are called *puros* or *habanos*; the latter is the name of the country's official cigar company. All of the various brands—Partagás, Cohiba, Romeo y Julieta, Punch, and so on—are marketed by Habanos S.A. Cigars not officially sold by Habanos fall into the various categories of black- and gray-market stogies. Habanos markets its product through a series of storefronts, usually called something like La Casa del Tabaco or La Casa del Habano. Official sales are also held at shops at most cigar factories, as well as at many higher-end hotels, restaurants, and attractions around town. ***Beware:*** Black- and gray-market cigars sold on the street or by *jineteros* (hustlers) are falsely marked, lower-quality cigars.

Cuban cigars range widely in size and shape. Prices range from around CUC$30 to CUC$50 per box for the smallest, lowest-quality *puros*, to over CUC$400 per box for the more coveted cigars. Most shops sell only complete boxes, although certain cigars are often available individually, or in boxes of five.

The best **La Casa del Habano** shops are those in the Hostal Conde de Villanueva at Calle Mercaderes 222, La Habana Vieja (✆ 7/862-9293); the Partagás cigar factory at Calle Industria 524, behind El Capitolio (✆ 7/862-4604); and in the Quinta y 16 shopping minicomplex at Avenida 5 and the corner of Calle 16, Miramar (✆ 7/204-7973). Another nice one in La Habana Vieja is the **Casa del Ron y Tabaco Cubana,** Calle Obispo and Calle Bernaza (✆ 7/867-0817), where you can combine two of Cuba's greater pleasures—smoking cigars and drinking rum.

FASHIONS

Perhaps the most distinctive clothing items a traveler can buy include T-shirts with the image of Che Guevara on the front, and the revolutionary's signature green *boina* (beret) with a little red star in front.

Men might want to pick up a *guayabera* or two. This cool, pleated, and embroidered tropical shirt comes in a variety of (mostly) solid colors, and in both long- and short-sleeve versions. As a rational alternative to heavy suits and ties in a tropical clime, *guayaberas* are appropriate for everything from informal occasions to high-level government and business meetings (in Cuba, at least). You'll find *guayaberas* for sale all over; some of the typically touristy gift shops even carry them. One good place to shop for a guayabera is **El Quitirín,** Calle Obispo and San Ignacio (✆ 7/862-0810). For a more upscale selection, head over to Miramar and shop at **Le Select,** Avenida 5 and Calle 28 (✆ 7/207-9681); or **Joyería Quinta y 16** (see "Jewelry," below).

For clothes try, **Galería Comercial Comodoro,** Avenida 3 between Calles 80 and 84, Playa (✆ 7/204-6177), which houses Mango, Adidas, Converse, Benetton, and Clarks stores, or **Paul and Shark,** Muralla between Mercaderes and San Ignacio, Plaza Vieja, La Habana Vieja.

HANDICRAFTS

Cuba doesn't have a particularly strong tradition in producing handicrafts, but the rise in tourism has seen local artisans quickly making up for lost time. Tourist gift shops as well as the street markets discussed below are well stocked with locally produced handicrafts. The best buys are woodcarvings and statues, papier-mâché masks and religious figures, and simple jewelry made from shells and seeds. You'll also find a host of Afro-Cuban percussion instruments for sale. Drums you'll find include the two-headed, hourglass-shaped *bata* drums; paired bongos, carved African-style religious drums; and congas, the modern salsa backbone. *Shékeres* (gourd shakers) and *claves* (two wooden sticks used to play the fundamental rhythm in various Cuban genres) are also available.

The Calle Tacón market, which was a large crafts market, has closed, and all vendors have moved to the **Almacenes San José,** which is now Havana´s largest craft market, offering clothing, paintings, tourist souvenirs, ceramics, baseball bats, jewelry, and a multitude of other products. It is open daily 9am–5pm.

JEWELRY

There are few good jewelry shops in Cuba, which has no real history of producing fine jewelry. You'll find a plethora of simple, artisan-produced necklaces, bracelets, rings, and earrings at most tourist shops and street markets. If you look hard enough, you'll actually find some well-made and attractive pieces. Unfortunately, the nicest jewelry being produced in Cuba is usually made with tortoiseshell or black coral, both natural resources slow to replenish and easily endangered by overharvesting.

Joyería Quinta y 16   This is the trendiest jewelry shop in the trendiest little mini-mall in Havana's trendiest neighborhood. Come here if you want to drop a wad of cash for some strands of gold, silver, and diamonds, although the selection is far from inspiring. Av. 5 and Calle 16, Miramar. ⊙ **7/204-7963.**

MUSIC

Music is one of Cuba's greatest exports. Many CDs available in Cuba are also widely available abroad or via the Internet. Most CDs in Cuba sell for between CUC$8 and CUC$15. However, be careful: Unless you are shopping at one of the official state-run stores, the CDs you buy may be low-quality bootlegs.

If you're looking for salsa, pick up a disc or two by Los Van Van or NG La Banda. Fans of Cuban folk music should definitely stock up on recordings by Silvio Rodriguez and Pablo Milanes. Jazz fans will want some Chucho Valdés with Irakere, and Gonzalo Rubalcaba, while those looking to groove to some Afro-Cuban sounds should check out Síntesis, Los Muñequitos de Matanzas, Yoruba Andabo, and Clavé y Guaguanco. For *son* and mambo, pick up discs by Adalberto Alvarez y su Son, or the classic rereleases of Beny Moré and Peréz Prado. Finally, since you've probably already got a copy of *Buena Vista Social Club,* you might stock up on solo albums by its various members: Compay Segundo, Rubén Gonzales, Eliades Ochoa, and Omara Portuona. If you enjoy Reggaeton, Eddy-K or Gente de Zona is your group.

Egrem (www.egrem.com.cu) is the national recording industry's signature label, the home of many prominent Cuban musicians. Egrem has a series of storefronts around the country called **Casa de la Música Egrem.** You can also buy discs at one of the many **ARTex** shops around Havana, or you can shop the ARTex catalog online at www.mallcubano.com.

Casa de la Música Habana   Housed in a classic old apartment building in Centro Habana, this is the nicest and best stocked of the Egrem storefronts. It also features daily concerts at 5 and 10pm. Calle Galiano (btw. Calles Concordia and Neptuno), Centro Habana. © **7/860-8296.**

Longina Música   This ARTex shop has an excellent selection of CDs and cassettes, as well as sheet music, magazines, and one of the better stocks of Afro-Cuban drums, shakers, and claves you'll find. Calle Obispo 360, La Habana Vieja. © **7/862-8371.**

La Habana Si   This modern store, opposite the Hotel Habana Libre, sells musical instruments, CDs, DVDs, and souvenirs. The staff is quite helpful. Calle 23 (corner of L), Vedado. © **7/838-3162.**

PERFUME

Habana 1791   This attractive shop in Old Havana sells traditional perfumes and aromatherapy distillations in faux-vintage glass jars and vials. The place is sometimes marketed as a "perfume museum." Calle Mercaderes 156 (corner of Calle Obrapía), La Habana Vieja. © **7/861-3525.**

RUM

After cigars, rum is one of Cuba's signature products. Cuba produces several fine rums. The most commonly sold brand, Havana Club, comes in white and dark varieties of various vintages and ages. The premier rum in Cuba is Havana Club's 15-year-old Gran Reserva. This sells for anywhere from CUC$75 to CUC$100 per bottle. It's good, but I don't think it's worth the price tag. However, their 7-year-old Añejo Reserva is a fine rum at around CUC$12 per bottle. Other good rums include Ron Varadero, Matusalém, Ron Caney, Ron Santiago, and Ron Mulata.

STREET MARKETS

A small street market occurs daily in Vedado in a small open area on the south side of La Rampa, at Calle 23 between Calles M and N. The market, which is open daily from 9am to 5pm, has less artwork than the market at Almacenes San José (see "Handicrafts," above), but it has plenty of woodcarvings and simple jewelry for sale.

   Note: Cubans don't really have a firm grasp on this capitalism thing. Moreover, given the huge gap between the peso and hard currency economies, Cubans often have a hard time understanding the true value of the convertible peso. Prices are often grossly inflated for tourists, on the principle that they "must all be rich." Bargaining is possible at street markets, but it's not necessarily a fluid and enjoyable process. Still, if you think something is overpriced, definitely feel free to offer whatever you believe to be fair, or whatever you are prepared to pay.

5

HAVANA | Shopping

HAVANA AFTER DARK

Some would say Havana only really gets going after dark, when the slow pace and heat-induced stupor of the day finally wears off. This is a vibrant and truly cosmopolitan city with scores of bars, dance clubs, and theaters to choose from. If your footwork is not so fancy, show up at the **Museo del Ron** (www.havanaclubfoundation. com; CUC$10 for 2-hour classes) for dance classes between Monday and Friday from 10am to 4pm.

The Performing Arts

Cuba has a strong tradition in the performing arts. Cuban musicians, playing in a range of styles, are world renowned. The **Cuban National Ballet ★** (✆ 7/866-0142; www.balletcuba.cult.cu) has been garnering international accolades for decades, under the direction of Alicia Alonso. There's an active theater scene (and plenty of movie theaters), both of which are popular with locals, given the scant offerings of Cuban television. The major venues for the classical performing arts are the **Teatro Nacional de Cuba,** Paseo and Calle 39, Vedado (✆ 7/879-3558), which specializes in theater performances by local and visiting companies; the **Gran Teatro de La Habana,** Paseo de Martí and Calle San Rafael, Centro Habana (✆ 7/861-3077, ext. 115), which is home to the Cuban National Ballet, as well as a prime venue for concerts and dance performances; and the **Teatro Amadeo Roldán,** Calle Calzada, between Calles D and E, Vedado (✆ 7/832-1168), which is home to the National Symphony Orchestra. Other important and working theaters include the **Teatro Mella** (✆ 7/833-5651), **Teatro Karl Marx** (✆ 7/203-0801), and the **Café Teatro Brecht** (✆ 7/832-9359).

Visit **www.cubaescena.cult.cu** and **www.paradiso.cu** for a rundown of annual festivals and events. **Paradiso** (✆ 7/832-9538), the tourism arm of the Ministry of Culture, publishes the highly elusive *Cartelera* magazine (✆ 7/836-4931), a free periodic bilingual magazine with listings for movies, theaters, bars, and live music, which is sometimes available at the front desk of hotels in Havana. For good up to date information in English, consult *Cuba Absolutely* (www.cubaabsolutely.com).

Your best bet for any advance planning is to go online or call the venue when you are in Havana. You can call any of the theaters listed above directly for performance schedules and ticket information.

◉ Feel the Beat

The **Conjunto Folklórico Nacional de Cuba (Cuban National Folklore Group)** hosts the weekly **Sábado de la Rumba,** a mesmerizing show of Afro-Cuban religious and secular dance and drumming. The 2-hour shows (CUC$5) are presented every Saturday at 3pm, at **El Gran Palenque,** Calle 4, between Calzada and Avenida 5 in Vedado. Call ✆ 7/830-3060 or 7/830-3939 for more information.

Similar shows are offered Thursday through Sunday at 10pm by the group **Obbara** at the Palacio de la Artesanía, Calle Cuba 64, between Calles Peña Pobre and Cuarteles, La Habana Vieja.

The Cabaret, Club & Dance Scene

I'll bet Havana has more floor shows per capita than Las Vegas. In addition to the clubs and cabarets listed below, there are nightly and entirely respectable cabaret shows at the Habana Riviera's **Copa Room,** Paseo and Malecón, Vedado (📞 **7/836-4051**); ARTex's **Patio de la Casa 18,** Calle 18, between Avenidas 5 and 7, Miramar (📞 **7/204-1212**); and the **Cabaret Nacional,** Calle San Rafael and Paseo de Martí, La Habana Vieja (📞 **7/863-2361**).

There's also a vibrant flamenco show at **Hotel Mesón de la Flota,** Mercaderes 257 between Amargura and Teniente Rey, La Habana Vieja (📞 **7/863-3838;** shows at 12:30pm and 8:30pm).

Habaneros love to dance and party, and you'll find a wild dance and club scene here. In fact, dance aficionados come to Havana from all over to learn the basic steps, fine-tune their moves, and watch the locals strut their stuff. Most clubs don't get going until after 10pm, and most stay pretty vibrant until the wee hours of the morning. While salsa is king in Cuba, most of the popular dance clubs catering to travelers have been putting some house, techno, Reggaeton, and other modern dance tunes into the mix. Dress codes are somewhat casual, but locals still like to put on the ritz as much as possible before a night of dancing, so bring some finery if you plan to hit any of the more popular clubs.

For a schedule of events at Havana's Casas de la Música, visit **http://promociones. egrem.co.cu** or **www.pmmfiesta.com**.

Cabaret Parisien   Located at the Hotel Nacional, this venerable cabaret show is a vibrant and extravagant spectacle. Still, it will always play second fiddle to the Tropicana, which trumps it in terms of size and setting. Nevertheless, the show here is less expensive, and certainly more convenient, if you're staying at the hotel or in Vedado. Calle O (corner of Calle 21). 📞 **7/836-3663.** Show CUC$35; dinner packages from CUC$55.

Café Cantante Mi Habana   Top acts often perform at this popular club. They also have a much more informal dance scene happening every afternoon between 4 and 7pm. This is a place where locals come to mix it up with foreigners who are in town specifically to learn how to salsa. Teatro Nacional, Paseo and Calle 39, Plaza de la Revolución. 📞 **7/878-4275.** Cover CUC$5–CUC$10.

Café Fresa y Chocolate   Located in the Cuban Institute of Cinematographic Arts and Industry (ICAIC), this terrace bar is the place to spot Cuban actors, filmmakers, and other art folks. There are live music performances—including a popular trova night—over weekends. Calle 23 btw. 10 and 12, Vedado. 📞 **7/836-2096.** Cover CUC$1.

Café TV   With its monochromatic décor, this place pays tribute to Cuban TV. There are nightly cabaret, comedy, and live music shows. On Tuesdays, Maricohnci, a transexual, entertains. Shows from 10pm. Edificio Focsa, Calle 17 corner of N, Vedado. © 7/834-54499. Cover CUC$10.

Casa de la Música Centro Habana ★★   This place, with its massive dance floor and concert space in the heart of Centro Habana, is currently considered the best salsa-dancing venue in town. The crowd is predominantly Cuban, and most of the folks can really dance. About half of the cover is usually applied to your food and drink tab. Calle Galianao 225, btw. Neptuno and Concordia. © 7/860-8296. Cover CUC$5–CUC$20.

Casa de la Música Miramar ★★   Housed in a beautiful, former Masonic Lodge Hall, this place is associated with the national recording label Egrem. It has nightly concerts that range from bolero to salsa to jazz in the in-house club, Diablo Tun Tun. Still, for me, the real treat here is the afternoon jam sessions, which take place daily from 4 to 7pm. Calle 20 (corner of Calle 35), Miramar. © 7/204-0447.

El Rincón del Bolero ★   If you're looking for a slightly mellower scene, this is your spot. One of several bars and restaurants at the Dos Gardenias complex, this place specializes in the sad and sultry songs of bolero, and usually features some fine performers. Dos Gardenias, Av. 7 and Calle 26, Miramar, Playa. © 7/204-2353.

El Sauce   This hugely popular local venue showcases a variety of musical talent. Hip-hop and salsa are current favorites. Avenida 9 btw. Calles 120 and 130, Playa. © 7/204-7061.

Habana Café   This place is loosely modeled after the Hard Rock Cafe chain. There's an old propeller fighter dangling overhead and a vintage 1957 Chevy in the middle of the joint. There's a good-size dance floor, and the evening's entertainment is part cabaret, part revue show, and part dance party. The atmosphere is far less formal and far livelier than you'll find at most other cabarets. In the Meliá Cohiba, Paseo, btw. Avs. 1 and 3, Vedado. © 7/833-3636, ext. 2630. www.cohiba-habanacafe.com. Cover CUC$20 (includes CUC$10 worth of food and drink).

Salón Rojo   This is the entertainment emporium of the Hotel Capri, a famous hotel from the pre-Castro era built with mafia money by Meyer Lanksy (which was undergoing renovation at press time), and it is often used by PMM (www.pmmfiesta.com) to stage the latest en vogue acts. Calle 21 between N and O, Vedado. © 7/833-3747. Cover CUC$10.

Salón Turquino   Located on the top floor of the Tryp Habana Libre, this dance club is one of the hotter and more popular dance spots in Havana. The views are great, there's a nightly cabaret show at 10:30pm, and the club periodically features top-billed live bands. Tryp Habana Libre, 25th floor, Calles L and 23, Vedado. © 7/834-6100. Cover CUC$10–CUC$20.

Tropicana ★★★   Accept no substitutes. This is the real deal. It's expensive—in fact, overpriced—but if you're going to see a cabaret show in Havana, it should be at the Tropicana. First opened in 1939, this open-air dinner theater is still the defining cabaret show in Cuba, if not the world. You enter the lush garden theater after passing the club's signature sculpted *Fountain of the Muses*. Dinner service starts around 8pm and is an uninspired, but acceptable affair. The show itself begins around 10:30pm. Once the show begins, the stage and verdant surroundings become an orgy of light, color, spectacular costumes, and pulsating movement. Scores of scantily clad showgirls and dancers seamlessly weave together a series of different numbers. The

2-hour-long spectacle covers most of the bases of popular Cuban show and dance music, from *son* to bolero to *danzón* to salsa, with a bit of Afro-Cuban religious music thrown into the mix. After the show, you can continue the celebration by dancing the night away at the adjoining Salón Arcos de Cristal.

Virtually every hotel and tour agency in Havana can book you a night at the Tropicana; some include dinner and a bottle of rum at the nightclub, others are just for the show (including a complimentary *cuba libre,* a rum-and-Coke drink), or include dinner first at El Ajibe or another Miramar restaurant. Packages with transportation and dinner are only slightly more than for the show alone, and are therefore a decent deal. Since it's open air, rain cancels the function. You'll get your money back on a rainout, but they offer no guaranteed reservations for a makeup show. Calle 72 (btw. Calles 41 and 45), Marianao. ✆ **7/267-1010.** reserves@tropicana.gca.tur.cu. Show CUC$50–CUC$60; packages with transportation and dinner from CUC$70.

The Bar Scene

In addition to the bars listed below, **La Bodeguita del Medio** (p. 105) **and El Floridita** (p. 105) are two famous watering holes. I also enjoy the rooftop bar at the **Hotel Ambos Mundos** (p. 92).

The **gay scene** is concentrated around Calle 22 at the corner of Infanta in Vedado, and at Casa Balear on Sunday nights (after 11pm) at Calle 23 at the corner of G in Vedado.

Bar Dos Hermanos   This is a slightly seedy port bar, but well within the safety net of restored La Habana Vieja. A few *jineteras* and a *conjunto* (small musical band) are usually in attendance. There are tables scattered across two rooms, and a long, wooden bar with a good selection of call liquors. This place is open 24 hours. Av. del Puerto 304 (corner of Calle Santa Clara), La Habana Vieja. ✆ **7/861-3514.**

Café Monserrate   I like the relaxed vibe at this popular bar, which attracts a mix of travelers and Cubans. The club's signature drink, the *coctel Monserrate,* is a tasty blend of rum, grapefruit juice, mint, sugar, and grenadine that gives the *mojito* a run for its money. There's usually live music here, as well as *jineteros* and *jineteras.* Calles Monserrate and Obrapía, La Habana Vieja. ✆ **7/860-9751.**

Café O'Reilly   While this bar and restaurant combo occupies two floors of this decaying building in Old Havana, all the action happens on the second floor. French doors open onto a small veranda, giving a good view of the folks strutting by on the street below. The food is mediocre, but the ambience is energetic, without feeling forced. Calle O'Reilly 203 (corner of Calle San Ignacio), La Habana Vieja. No phone.

Café París   This place is almost always crowded and rowdy. The *conjunto* plays loud, and the patrons try to top them. Known as a *jinetera* hangout, this is still a good place to go for a good time. Open noon to midnight. At the corner of Calle San Ignacio and Calle Obispo, La Habana Vieja. No phone.

Club Imágenes   This place is done up like an upscale piano bar. The lighting is dark and the mood more subdued than you'll find at other joints. Still, they put on a nightly show, and even get things pumped up with karaoke now and again. The small menu here includes a selection of tapas. Calzada 602 (corner of Calle C), Vedado. ✆ **7/833-3606.** CUC$5 minimum.

El Gato Tuerto ★   This hyperhip little club attracts a good mix of travelers and Cuban intelligentsia. The mood is dark, with walls of mirrors behind the tiny stage, and a long bar running the length of the longest wall. The club is small, so either reserve a table in advance or get here early. The entertainment runs the gamut from old-style bolero to *nueva trova* and modern jazz. Performers range from mediocre to top-notch. On most evenings, Alden Night, a melodramatic storyteller and poet, serves as master of ceremonies. The admission is applied to your first drink, so ask for the call liquor first. Calle O (btw. Calles 17 and 19), Vedado. ℃ **7/838-2696.** Cover CUC$5.

Jazz Café ★   This place feels a little too slick and modern to be a jazz club, with chrome-trimmed tables and chairs, a curving wall of windows, and fairly bright lighting. But a jazz club it is, and next to La Zorra y El Cuervo (see below), this is the top spot to search out Cuba's best and brightest jazz talents. Third level of the Galerías Paseo mall, Avs. Paseo and 3, Vedado. ℃ **7/838-3556.** CUC$10 minimum.

La Zorra y El Cuervo ★★   This is the premier jazz club in Havana and the first place to check if you want to catch any of the A-list jazz performers while you're in town. Modeled after an English pub, the basement-level bar space is small and cozy and relatively plain. The standard cover might double if someone like Chucho Valdés is playing. La Rampa, Calle 23 no. 155 (btw. Calles N and O), Vedado. ℃ **7/833-2402.** Cover CUC$10.

Lluvia de Oro ★   Open noon to midnight, this is a raucous and rowdy bar in the heart of Old Havana. There's often live music and a lively mix of tourists, locals, *jineteros,* and *jineteras.* Calle Obispo no. 316 (corner of Habana), La Habana Vieja. ℃ **7/862-9870.**

Piano Bar Delirio Habanero   This subdued and low-lighted club is a good place for a quiet and romantic evening. It's on the fourth floor of the Teatro Nacional, and the walls of glass windows offer great nighttime views of Havana. The *criolla* cuisine is decent here. Teatro Nacional, Paseo and Calle 39, Plaza de la Revolución. ℃ **7/878-4275.**

VIÑALES & WESTERN CUBA

W estern Cuba is a pastoral and underdeveloped region, with some stunning scenery. When folks talk about western Cuba, they mean Pinar del Río and the new province of Artemisa.

The area has been the inhabited continuously for over 4,000 years, beginning with Guanahatabey, Ciboney, and Taíno indigenous tribes that settled this section of the island prior to the Spanish arrival. In addition to the province of Pinar del Río, the general geographic area of western Cuba also includes the Archipiélago de los Canarreos (the Canary Archipelago), considered a "special municipality." The two largest islands of the chain, Isla de la Juventud and Cayo Largo, are developed for tourism.

Pinar del Río province is Cuba's prime ecotourism destination. Rock climbing, spelunking, mountain biking, hiking, and bird-watching are all excellent in this area. **La Güira National Park,** the **Guanacahabibes Peninsula,** and the **Sierra del Rosario Biosphere Reserve** make this one of Cuba's richest and wildest areas. The small hamlet of **Viñales** is widely considered one of the most beautiful places in the country, and it is rapidly becoming the region's center for nature and adventure tourism. At the far western tip of the island, **María la Gorda** is one of Cuba's signature scuba-diving destinations. And the diving at **Cayo Levisa, Isla de la Juventud,** and **Cayo Largo** isn't too shabby either. To top it all off, Cayo Largo has some of the nicest and least-crowded beaches in Cuba.

Pinar del Río province is also Cuba's most heralded tobacco-growing region. Cigars made from tobacco grown in the **Vuelta Abajo** area, just west of the city of Pinar del Río, are coveted the world over.

Note: Pinar del Río sustained direct hits from Hurricanes Gustav and Ike in September 2008, resulting in considerable damage to much of the province, especially Viñales and Isla de la Juventud. Housing took a serious hit in Isla de la Juventud, with many homes completely destroyed. Many of the *secadores* (traditional thatched-roof tobacco leaf drying huts) in the Valley were flattened, and many homes are still being rebuilt. The fishing industry there was severely damaged and some roads that were destroyed have still not been repaired, but tourist operations have rebounded.

6 PINAR DEL RÍO

174km (108 miles) SW of Havana

Pinar del Río, the provincial capital, is named for the pine trees that grow along the banks of the Río Guamá, where the city is set. Originally founded as Nueva Filipina (New Philippine), it was re-christened Pinar del Río in 1774 and is one of the last major cities founded by the Spanish in Cuba. Pinar del Río is an animated little city of around 150,000, with a university, several hospitals, and some industries. The city's architecture is a mix of colonial and neoclassical in varying states from finely restored to post revolutionary decay. The city's major attractions can easily be visited in a day, and you'd be better off giving more time and attention to the province's less urban destinations, although the city provides a glimpse of a town unfettered by major tourism.

Essentials

GETTING THERE

BY BUS   The **bus station** (© 48/75-5255) is located at Calle Adela Azcuy, between Avenidas Colón and Comandante Pinares. **Víazul** (© 7/881-1413 in Havana, or **48/75-2572** in Pinar del Río; www.viazul.com) has buses at 9am, 12:40pm, and 2pm from Havana to Pinar del Río. The trip takes 2 hours and 40 minutes and costs CUC$11 each way. This bus continues on to Viñales. If you pick the bus up here, it costs CUC$6 to Viñales. From Havana to Viñales, buses cost CUC$12 one-way. Víazul buses to Havana leave Pinar del Río at 8:50am, 2:50pm, and 6:50pm daily.

BY CAR   Take the Autopista Nacional (A4) west to Pinar del Río. It's a straight shot, and the Autopista actually ends as it enters Pinar del Río. To get on the Autopista Nactional from Havana, drive south out of Havana on Av. Independencia. At the spaghetti junction at Alturas de la Habana, turn right on Av. San Francisco (Calle 100). At a second spaghetti junction, turn left (west) onto the unsigned Autopista (A4) for Viñales. (Just before Pinar del Río, there's a sign marked Las Ovas to the east/right: this is the western route, a winding cross-country shortcut to Viñales.) Two alternative routes are the old Carretera Central, which runs roughly parallel to the newer Autopista, and connects Havana with Pinar del Río, and the Circuito Norte or "northern circuit," a road that runs from Havana to Mariel to Bahía Honda. At La Palma, you'll want to head south on the Viñales highway and then on to Pinar del Río. Both of these routes are two-lane affairs that are slower and more picturesque than the Autopista. On either of these, slow-moving ox carts and trucks combine with bicycle traffic, pedestrians, and potholes to slow you down—not a bad thing if you want to take in some of the scenery. I recommend integrating the Circuito Norte route into an itinerary that encompasses Pinar del Río, Viñales, and either Cayo Levisa or Cayo Jutías.

GETTING AROUND

You can easily walk to most places in Pinar del Río. Taxis are also readily available all around town, and are either at hand, or can be called, at most hotels and *casas particulares*. Call **Cubataxi** (© 48/75-8080) for a cab ride. If you want to rent a car, contact **Havanautos** (© 48/77-8015), who has an office at the Islazul Hotel Pinar del Río, or **Cubacar** (© 48/77-8278).

<table>
<tr><td>

Watch Out

</td></tr>
<tr><td>

If you're driving a rental car, you will be swarmed by bicycle-riding *jineteros* (hustlers) offering you *casas particulares* and *paladares* (private-home rooms and restaurants) as soon as you enter town. They will latch on to your car at any traffic light, stop sign, or slow

section and follow alongside if their pedaling can keep pace as you drive through town. For some reason, they are particularly aggressive in Pinar del Río. If you want to lessen the attention, you might have to roll up your windows and shake your head a lot.

</td></tr>
</table>

ORIENTATION

The Autopista Nacional ends and turns into Calle Martí as it enters Pinar del Río from the east. As you enter town, you'll see the Hotel Pinar del Río on your right. The heart of downtown is straight ahead. At the western end of downtown, you'll find the small, triangular-shaped Plaza de la Independencia. The main north-south byway, Calle Isabel Rubio, is also the old Carretera Central, and bisects Calle Martí by the post office.

Havanatur, on Calle Osmani Arenado at Martí, is an excellent resource for tourist information. For currency exchange, there's a **CADECA** on Calle Gerardo Medina, next to the local Coppelia ice-cream outlet and at Martí 46, virtually opposite the post office. On the same street, 2 blocks east of Coppelia, there's an **Etecsa** phone office where you can make local, national, and international calls and connect to the Internet. The main **post office** is located at the corner of Calle Martí and Calle Isabel Rubio (© 48/75-5916); it's open Monday through Sunday from 8am to 8pm. The **León Cuervo Rubio hospital** (© 48/75-4443) is at the junction of the Carretera Central and the Viñales highway.

What to See & Do

The principal attraction in town is **Fábrica de Tabacos Francisco Donatién** (© 48/77-3069), Calle Antonio Maceo, just off the Plaza de la Independencia. Several fine brands are rolled at this renowned cigar factory. You can walk through the timeless rolling station, where a caller reads news and short stories to keep the rollers interested. You'll also visit rooms where the final selection and grading, labeling, and boxing take place. You can buy some of the wares here, or at the well-stocked **Casa del Habano** across the street. The factory is open Monday through Friday from 9am to noon and 1 to 4pm and Saturday from 9am to noon. Admission is CUC$5, and includes a guided tour that lasts about 15 to 20 minutes.

The other main attraction in Pinar del Río is the **Casa Garay Fábrica de Guayabitas del Pinar** (© 48/75-2966), Calle Isabel Rubio, 3½ blocks south of Calle Martí. This little factory produces the town's signature Guayabita del Pinar liquor. They produce two types, *dulce* (sweet) and *seco* (dry). Both are cane liquors distilled with the fruit berries of a local bush. I like the *seco* quite a bit. It's a good-quality sipping liquor that, if you stretch your imagination, is almost brandylike. The factory is open during the same hours as Fábrica de Tabacos Francisco Donatién. Admission is free and usually includes a quick guided tour and a stop at the tasting room. Bottles of Guayabita are on sale for around CUC$4.

smoke 'EM IF YOU GOT 'EM

When Christopher Columbus first visited Cuba, he found the local population smoking a local herb, *cohiba,* through a pipe, or *tobago.* They called the act of smoking *sikar.* He brought back some samples, and it wasn't long before millions of Europeans were smoking tobacco rolled into cigars and cigarettes. Tobacco was grown commercially in Cuba as early as the 16th century, and by the late–17th century, it was the country's most important export crop. By all accounts, the finest cigars in the world come from Cuba. And of the Cuban cigars available, the crème de la crème are made with tobacco grown in the **Vuelta Abajo,** the low plains spreading west from the city of Pinar del Río.

Most of the tobacco grown in Cuba is grown on small farms. Seeds are planted each year beginning in late October and throughout November to stagger the harvest. In a little over a month, seedlings are transplanted to the fields or *vegas.* Plants are carefully tended and regularly topped to stimulate leaf growth lower down. The highest-quality wrapper leaves, *capa,* are grown in semi-ishade under protective mesh. Harvesting takes place from January through April. Leaves are classified by plant type, growing region, growing condition (sun or shade), and where they grow on an individual plant. All go through an intensive and carefully monitored process of drying, sorting, preparing, fermenting, aging, and finally, rolling. Real care is taken in handling the prized *capas.* Lesser-quality leaves end up as *capote* (binders) and *tripa* (filler).

Throughout Vuelta Abajo, you'll pass field after field planted with tobacco and see the traditional high-peaked, thatched-roof drying sheds. Tobacco from the Vuelta Abajo region is shipped to various factories in the region and around Cuba. The finest brands—Cohibas, Partagas, Romeo y Julieta, Montecristo, Robaina, H. Upmann, Corona, and Hoyo de Monterey—are all made with tobacco from Vuelta Abajo.

Aside from the city's two main draws, you can easily spend a few hours walking around town, and perhaps stopping in at either the **Museo Provincial de Historia (Museum of Province History)** at Calle Martí 58 (© 48/75-4300), or the **Museo de Ciencias Naturales (Museum of Natural Sciences)** at Calle Martí and Avenida Pinares (© 48/75-3087). Neither contains exhibits or collections of great interest, although the latter is housed in a wonderful old building with ornate Moorish architecture. You could also check out the **Teatro Milanés** (© 48/75-3871), Calles Martí and Colón, a striking 19th-century theater that is open for visits during the day, and sometimes hosts evening concerts and performances. Admission to each of the above attractions is $5MN.

Where to Stay

I personally recommend staying in Viñales (see below) and visiting the attractions in Pinar del Río on a day trip.

There is a host of *casas particulares* in Pinar del Río. Most charge between CUC$15 and CUC$25 per person and usually offer reasonably priced meal options. The **Casa de Tebelio and Mayra,** Calle Colón between Mariana Grajales and Juan Gualberto Gómez, 50m (164 ft.) from the bus station (© 48/77-8050), is a nice *casa* that offers one room for rent, an attractive garden, and two terraces.

MODERATE

Hotel Vueltabajo ★ This is by far the best option in downtown Pinar del Río. The hotel occupies a large and meticulously restored old mansion in the heart of the city. The rooms are simply furnished and there is little in the way of decor. Still, the rooms are very spacious and all have immensely high ceilings. It's worth the very slight splurge for the rooms with views and small balconies. Only four rooms here have king-size beds; the rest have two twin beds. The suite is not worth the extra cost, as the seating area is uncomfortable.

Calle Martí 103, Pinar del Río. ✆ 48/75-9381. www.islazul.cu. 39 units. CUC$55 double. Rates include breakfast buffet. MC, V. **Amenities:** Restaurant; bar. *In room:* A/C, TV, fridge.

INEXPENSIVE

Hotel Pinar del Río Serving both Cuban and international guests in equal measure, this is by far the largest hotel in town. It's uninspired and largely unappealing. It is perennially run-down, and I'm not sure it's ever seen better days. Still, the rooms are adequate. The hotel has a broad range of facilities and services, and it's an acceptable option if you're staying in Pinar del Río for a night or two. The several bars and in-house dance club make it a lively joint. In fact, be sure you get a room as far from the club as possible, or you might not sleep much; the fifth-floor rooms are quieter. The pool is open to visitors for CUC$10 per person, CUC$8 of which can be spent on food and drink.

Calle Martí, Pinar del Río. ✆ 48/75-5070. www.islazul.cu. 149 units. CUC$24–CUC$30 double. Rates include breakfast buffet. MC, V. **Amenities:** 2 restaurants; 3 bars; dance club; outdoor pool. *In room:* A/C, TV.

Hotel Aguas Claras This countryside hotel with the rooms in casitas spread about the grounds is much more idyllic than anything in town. The focus is around the pool and pool bar, popular with locals on weekends (visitors can pay CUC$2 to use the pool), so you may want to opt for more tranquil casitas up the hill. The casitas are a mix of one-level with two rooms or two-levels with four rooms. The rooms are small with two single beds. A river runs through the property and there's a field you can frolic in; at the center of the field is a picturesque green-and-white *casa del campo* (country house) with two rooms for rent.

Km 7.5 Carretera a Viñales. ✆ 48/77-8427. www.cubamarviajes.cu. 50 units. CUC$36–CUC$40 double. Rates include breakfast buffet. No credit cards. Free parking. **Amenities:** Restaurant; bar; outdoor pool; horseback riding. *In room:* A/C, TV, minibar.

Where to Dine
MODERATE

Rumayor ★ CRIOLLAN This is probably the best dining option in Pinar del Río. Run by the Islazul chain, it's both a restaurant and nightly cabaret. The specialty here is slow-smoked chicken, and it's excellent. There are also several fish and meat dishes. Of these, the *cherna frita,* a fried fish in a garlic sauce, is good. The main dining room is indoors in a dark room decorated with Afro-Cuban motifs. Service is quick and attentive, a relative rarity in Cuba.

On the Viñales hwy., 1km (½ mile) north of town. ✆ 48/76-3007. Reservations not required. Main courses CUC$6–CUC$26. MC, V. Daily noon–9:40pm.

INEXPENSIVE

La Casona 🍴 CRIOLLAN This is certainly the most atmospheric place to eat in Pinar del Río proper. About 13 heavy wooden tables with bench seating fill up the main dining room in this old colonial building. High ceilings, modern sculpted wall hangings, and long French doors that open onto the street give this place its character. The food is mediocre and simple. Avoid the pastas and stick to the roasted chicken or sandwiches. In the evenings, they open up a little patio beer garden with live music and an informal atmosphere.

Calles Martí and Colón. ✆ **48/77-8263.** Main courses CUC$1–CUC$5. MC, V. Daily 11:30am–11:30pm.

Pinar del Rio After Dark

Rumayor ★ (see review above) offers up a nightly cabaret-style show in its large outdoor amphitheater space. The show here leans more on Afro-Cuban dances and traditions than the shows in Havana, and is less ornate, but it's still a pretty good spectacle. The show starts at around 11pm and finishes at 1am on Saturdays only. Admission is CUC$5, which includes one drink per person.

Alternately, you could see what's happening at **La Casona** (see review above), the dance club at Hotel Pinar del Río, or **Café Pinar,** Calle Vélez Caviedes 34 (✆ **48/77-8199**). You can also see what's playing at the old **Cine Praga,** Calle Gerardo Medina, next to the Coppelia ice-cream parlor. Admission is just a couple of pesos, and you should be able to pay with Cuban pesos.

VIÑALES ★★★

200km (124 miles) SW of Havana; 26km (16 miles) N of Pinar del Río

Viñales is an extremely picturesque town in the heart of Cuba's prime tobacco-growing region. The town itself sits in the center of a flat valley surrounded by stunning karst hill formations known locally as *mogotes.* The *mogotes* are irregularly shaped, steep-sided geological formations that rise as high as 300m (984 ft.) and have bases ranging from just a few hundred yards in diameter to as much as a couple of kilometers in length. The *mogotes* are part of the Sierra de los Organos mountain chain, and were formed by eons of erosion. Many consider this to be the most naturally beautiful spot in Cuba and the view of the Viñales Valley from any of the surrounding hillsides is stunning, particularly at sunrise or sunset. The Viñales Valley is a great spot to bicycle around, and there are good options for bird-watching, hiking, and in particular, rock climbing and spelunking.

Essentials

GETTING THERE Víazul (✆ **7/881-1413** in Havana; www.viazul.com) has daily buses at 9am, 12:40pm, and 2pm from Havana to Viñales, via Pinar del Río. The trip takes 3 hours and 15 minutes and costs CUC$12 each way. Víazul buses depart Viñales for Havana daily at 8am, 2pm, and 6pm, and pass through Pinar del Río about 40 minutes later, before continuing on to the capital. You can hire a taxi to Havana for between CUC$80 and CUC$90 for up to four people, and you can also hire a taxi to Cienfuegos and Trinidad. The **bus station** (✆ **48/79-3195**) is located at Salvador Cisnero 63, just across the street from the town's main plaza.

To get here **by car,** take the Autopista Nacional (A4) west to Pinar del Río (see above for how to find it). From Pinar del Río, it's another 26km (16 miles) north on the well-marked Carretera Viñales. Entering Pinar del Río from the Autopista, you'll want to turn right at the post office, on Calle Isabel Rubio, and follow the signs for

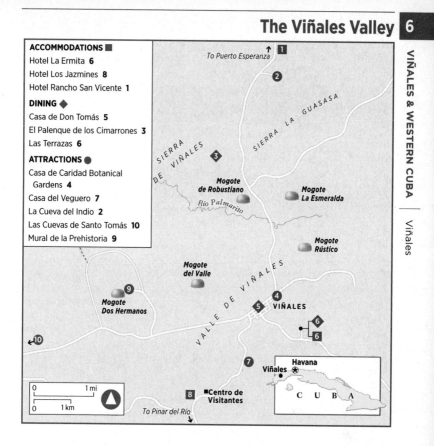

ACCOMMODATIONS ■
Hotel La Ermita 6
Hotel Los Jazmines 8
Hotel Rancho San Vicente 1

DINING ◆
Casa de Don Tomás 5
El Palenque de los Cimarrones 3
Las Terrazas 6

ATTRACTIONS ●
Casa de Caridad Botanical
 Gardens 4
Casa del Veguero 7
La Cueva del Indio 2
Las Cuevas de Santo Tomás 10
Mural de la Prehistoria 9

To Puerto Esperanza

SIERRA LA GUASASA

SIERRA DE VIÑALES

Mogote
de Robustiano

Mogote
La Esmeralda

Río Palmarito

Mogote
Rústico

Mogote
del Valle

VALLE DE VIÑALES

Mogote
Dos Hermanos

VIÑALES

Havana
Viñales ✪

C   U   B   A

0   1 mi
0   1 km

■Centro de
 Visitantes

To Pinar del Río

Viñales. Or, alternatively, just before Pinar del Río, there's a sign marked Las Ovas to the right (west). Take the western route, a winding cross-country shortcut to Viñales.

GETTING AROUND   Taxis can be hired in Viñales, or called from your hotel. They tend to congregate around the central plaza. A cab to any of the local attractions costs between CUC$2 and CUC$6. You can hire a cab for a full-day trip to anywhere around the region for around CUC$30. If you'd rather rent a car, **Transtur** (© **48/79-6060**) has an office downtown just off the central park, and **Havanautos** (© **48/79-6330**) has an office diagonally opposite the Viñales Cupet gas station. Mopeds (*motos*) can now be rented from a place next to the Casa Don Tomás (© **48/79-6300**) for CUC$23 a day. The Viñales Bus Tour has 18 stops and is a hop-on/hop-off service for CUC$5 a day.

This is a good region to bicycle around. The valley itself is almost perfectly flat and most of the major attractions can be reached along well-paved roads. You can rent bikes in pretty good shape for CUC$5 to CUC$10 per day from your *casa particular* or Cubanacán offers a 1-day guided biking tour in the valley for CUC$20 with lunch included. Horse riding can also be arranged through agencies for CUC$5 per person per hour.

What to See & Do
OUTDOOR ADVENTURES

Caves abound in this area and are one of the major attractions in and around Viñales. **La Cueva del Indio (the Indian's Cave; ✆ 48/79-6280)** is the most popular cave and it's become a real tourist trap. Located about 5km (3 miles) north of Viñales at Km 33 on the Carretera de Puerto Esperanza, this cave gets its name from the fact that indigenous remains were found here. Only 1km (½ mile) or so of the extensive cave system here is open to travelers. A well-lit path leads from the entrance through a few small and narrow galleries to a tiny dock on an underground river. Here, you board a small rowboat powered by an outboard engine for a quick trip of about 180m (591 ft.) up and down this river, before exiting the cave at a dock area crowded with souvenir stands and a little snack bar. The entrance fee is CUC$5, and I don't think it's justified. Moreover, when the buses arrive, the line to get in is long and slow. It is open daily from 8am to 5pm.

Those with an interest in more serious spelunking should head to **Las Cuevas de Santo Tomás ★**. With over 45km (28 miles) of connected tunnels, chambers, and galleries, it's the largest explored cave system in Cuba. Some of these chambers and galleries are quite massive, with impressive stalagmite and stalactite formations. Unlike La Cueva del Indio, this cave system has been left in its natural state and you must visit it with headlamps and flashlights. So far, a relatively simple 1km (½-mile) section has been opened for guided tours, although more adventurous spelunking tours are in the works. Visits here, including a guide and equipment, cost about CUC$10, and are best booked in advance with the new **Centro de Visitantes,** located on the highway into Viñales, just beyond the Hotel Los Jazmines (open 8am–5:30pm daily; ✆ 48/79-3157). Those with their own transport can pitch up; last departure into the cave is 3pm.

In addition to caving, the limestone mountains and karst formations of Viñales make for excellent **rock climbing.** Although climbing is still in its infancy as a sport in Cuba, the Viñales Valley is rapidly becoming a mecca for local and visiting climbers. So far, over 300 routes have been identified and climbed in the area. Some carry colorful names, such as "Razor's Edge" and "Friday 13th." A few attest to some of the hazards of the area, such as "Feeding Mosquitoes" and "Poison Oak, Guano, and Spines." For more information, check out **www.cubaclimbing.com**.

Unless you plan on scaling several *mogotes* (steep geological formations), most of the **hiking** here is on gentle, well-groomed trails. There are several popular trails and routes, although you must hire an official guide to hike most of these. One of the most popular hikes is a simple walk through the *fincas* (farms) of the valley just outside of town. This provides wonderful views of the surrounding *mogotes*, and allows for encounters with the local farmers and a firsthand view of the tobacco-growing process. More athletic forays into the nearby forests and hills include hikes to and around the valley, hikes up **Coco Solo Mogote** and **el Palmarito,** as well as climbs to the summits of several other *mogotes*. Guided hikes should run you between CUC$6 and CUC$10 per person, depending on the route and length of the hike. Do-it-yourself hikers can wander the dirt roads and byways of the Viñales Valley, but must stay off the marked trails of **Viñales National Park.** For more information on guides and organized hikes, ask at your hotel, or check with **Centro de Visitantes (✆ 48/79-3157;** open 8am–5:30pm daily), on the highway into Viñales, just beyond the Hotel Los Jazmines. It offers three options: a sociocultural trail through the valley, a flora-and-fauna trail, and a trip to the Cueva de Santo Tomás with departures at 9:30am and

2:30pm daily, for CUC$6 to CUC$10 per person. The caves were closed in late 2010 due to lighting problems but should have reopened by the time you read this.

There are few well-defined trails for serious **mountain biking,** although there are plenty of dirt roads you can explore all around. Horseback riding can be arranged through the Hotel La Ermita or in the town's agencies.

ATTRACTIONS & ORGANIZED TOURS

The Viñales Valley is part of the heart of Cuba's tobacco-growing region and a great place to take a tobacco tour. Typical tours start at the **Casa del Veguero,** a small farm that grows and dries the primary material, followed by a visit to the nearby de-veining station, or *despalilladora.* Here, you'll see workers handle and sort the prized leaves for *capas,* or outer layers. You might also be given a quick tour of a final curing station, where the leaves emit an ammonia gas that will make your eyes tear. Finally, you'll visit a local cigar shop, **El Estanco.** However, you'll have to go into Pinar del Río if you want to visit an actual cigar factory.

Feel free to pass up the ✋ **Mural de la Prehistoria (Prehistoric Mural;** ✆ **48/79-6260).** Sure it's big, but this over-hyped attraction can't quite cut it as kitsch, is decidedly uninteresting as art, is woefully inadequate as narrative, and is just not impressive enough in execution to merit all the attention. Despite some fresh paint, which restored—and even improved on—the vibrant colors of artist Leovigildo González Morillo's original work, this massive mural lacks the style and weight of the works of his mentor, Diego Rivera. The mural is located 4km (2½ miles) west of Viñales and is open daily from 8am to 7pm. The CUC$1 admission is waived if you eat at the on-site restaurant.

One of the nicer attractions in Viñales is the little **Casa de Caridad Botanical Gardens ★** at the northeastern end of town. The lush gardens feature a mix of ornamental and medicinal plants and flowers, as well as orchids, bromeliads, palms, and fruit trees. If you're really lucky, you'll be able to munch on some freshly har-vested fruit. No admission is charged, but donations are accepted.

📎 **Avoid the Crowds**

Viñales is an extremely popular desti-nation for day trips out of Havana. If you're staying here, try to visit the vari-ous attractions early, before the buses arrive, and then spend the afternoon walking around town, hiking a more remote trail, or lazing around your hotel.

Cubanacán and **Havanatur** have offices right off the town's main square and offer a variety of tour options (the latter is not recommended due to poor customer service), from where you can book organized tours of the Viñales Valley. These jam-packed full-day tours cost CUC$28 per person and usually include a visit to the Casa del Veguero, El Estanco, the Mural de la Prehistoria, the Cueva del Indio, and El Palenque de los Cimarrones, with lunch at one of the last three places, as well as a sunset cocktail at Hotel Los Jazmines. Other tour options include day trips to Pinar del Río (CUC$36), Cayo Levisa (CUC$29), Cayo Jutías (CUC$22), and María la Gorda (CUC$35).

Where to Stay
MODERATE

The hotels below do a brisk business with tour groups. It is essential that you have a reservation in advance.

Hotel La Ermita   Similar in style and setting to Hotel Los Jazmines (see review below), this is a lovely and modest hotel set on the hillside just above the town of Viñales. There are excellent views from the grounds and restaurant here, although only 12 rooms have the area's signature view. Those that do, such as second-floor corner room no. 64, are real steals. The rooms themselves are a little more spacious than those at Hotel Los Jazmines. Those in the newer buildings have a private porch or balcony, with a couple of heavy Adirondack chairs. There's a popular kidney-shaped pool in the center of the grounds and a poolside barbecue restaurant that I prefer to the hotel's principal buffet option. Even if you don't stay here, I recommend coming for sunset and perhaps staying for dinner at their Las Terrazas restaurant (see "Where to Dine," below).

Carretera de La Ermita Km 1.5, Viñales, Pinar del Río. ℭ **48/79-6071.** Fax 48/79-6069. www.hoteles cubanacan.com. 62 units. CUC$67–CUC$74 double. Rates include breakfast buffet. MC, V. **Amenities:** 2 restaurants; 2 bars; Internet; outdoor pool; tennis court. *In room:* A/C, TV.

Hotel Los Jazmines ★   I give this hotel the nod over its nearby sister Hotel La Ermita, if only because you have much better odds of landing a room with a view. Most of the rooms are housed in two, three-story buildings set on a hillside overlooking the Viñales Valley. All are clean and comfortable, if a tad on the small side, and feature French doors opening onto a little balcony from which you can soak in the sights. Touches of gingerbread wrought-iron work and stained glass give the place a sense of elegance. If possible, request one of the third-floor rooms in the newer block, nos. 301 to 316. Sixteen duplex *cabañitas* (cabins) are located in a row heading downhill from the pool. These are a little bit smaller than the standard rooms, but are charming nonetheless and were recently renovated, following the 2008 hurricanes.

Carretera de Viñales Km 25, Viñales, Pinar del Río. ℭ **48/79-6205.** Fax 48/79-6215. www.hoteles cubanacan.com. 78 units. CUC$60–CUC$74 double. Rates include breakfast buffet. Rates lower in off season. MC, V. **Amenities:** 2 restaurants; 2 bars; Internet; outdoor pool. *In room:* A/C, TV.

Hotel Rancho San Vicente ★ 🌡   Located about 270m (886 ft.) north of the Cueva del Indio, this quiet nature hotel can almost be considered a spa. A half dozen or so semi-private soaking pools (CUC$5 for 30 minutes) are fed by tepid mineral springs, and massages are available at very reasonable prices. Most of the clean and comfortable rooms are actually individual little bungalows, with two twin beds and a tiny front porch. By far, the best rooms are the 20 new units housed in a series of two-story wooden buildings spread around the grounds. The whole complex is set amid a lovely, shady grove of pine, palm, and fruit trees. There's good bird-watching here, although the hotel doesn't afford any of the classic views for which Viñales is so famous. However, the bucolic charm offered by this hotel surpasses the grounds that other nearby hotels offer.

Carretera de Puerto Esperanza Km 33, Viñales, Pinar del Río. ℭ **48/79-6111.** Fax 48/79-6265. www. hotelescubanacan.com. 53 units. CUC$55–CUC$58 double. Rates include breakfast. MC, V. **Amenities:** Restaurant; bar; Internet; outdoor pool. *In room:* A/C, TV.

INEXPENSIVE

There is a host of *casas particulares* in Viñales, which for some reason are called *villas* here. Most are on either the main street through town or on the street 1 block southeast and parallel to it. All charge between CUC$20 and CUC$25 per room and usually offer reasonably priced meal options. I recommend **Casa Oscar Jaime Rodríguez,** Adela Azcuy 43 (ℭ **48/79-3381;** oscarjaime59@gmail.com), with its friendly family and communal areas; **Garden House,** Salvador Cisneros 44

(© 48/79-3297), for its lovely garden and big porch; **El Relojero,** off Adela Azcuy on Orlando Nodarse 7 (© 48/69-5429), with its welcoming family; **Casa Lumino and Heriberto,** Calle Orlando Nodarse 3 (© 48/69-6952) for Lumino's great cooking; **Villa El Cafetal**, Adela Azcuy Norte Final s/n (© 52/23-9175), a lovely house run by Martha Martínez that sits at the trail head to the *mogotes* and is surrounded by a garden of coffee and fruit trees; and **Villa Sol,** behind the Banco Nacional (© 48/69-5591 or 52/83-2018; deborahsusana7@yahoo.es), with one independent room.

Where to Dine

In addition to the places listed below, there are official—and uninspired—restaurants at most of the major tourist attractions, including the Mural de la Prehistoria and the Cueva del Indio. If you're staying at either Hotel Los Jazmines or Hotel La Ermita, you'd probably do well to venture away from their buffets and try one of the a la carte options. All *paladares* in Viñales have been closed by the government, although *casas particulares* are permitted to serve meals to their guests, and most will accept other diners with a certain amount of discretion.

Casa de Don Tomás CRIOLLAN/SPANISH   This is probably the most popular restaurant in Viñales. Although the restaurant—which is located in a restored 1889 colonial mansion—was destroyed by the 2008 hurricanes, it has been restored and is now in a finer state than before. The restaurant's signature dish, *Las Delicias de Don Tomás,* is a paella-like dish of Spanish rice cooked featuring bits of chicken, pork, fish, ham, and even lobster. It's usually slightly overcooked and underseasoned. Instead, opt for a simpler pork steak in *criolla* sauce, or the hefty portion of fried chicken. The house drink is called a *Trapiche,* and it's made of rum, pineapple juice, and honey, and served with a sliver of sugar cane. Traditional Cuban music is played by the Guacachason quintet.

Calle Salvador Cisnero 140 (the main street in Viñales). © 48/79-6300. Reservations not accepted. Main courses CUC$5-CUC$14. No credit cards. Daily 10am-10pm.

El Palenque de los Cimarrones ★ CRIOLLAN   This is definitely a tourist trap catering to tour groups. However, the food is surprisingly good, and the show and setting are interesting and informative, without being too kitschy. You reach the restaurant after paying a CUC$1 entrance fee and walking about 270m (886 ft.) through a narrow cave that bisects one of the area's signature *mogotes*. At the end of the path, you come to a re-creation of one of the nomadic homes set up by runaway slaves who lived and hid in these caves. The restaurant is a series of interconnected *ranchos* (thatched huts), each decorated and representing a different orishá, or Afro-Cuban deity. The main dish here is a slow-roasted chicken seasoned with oregano, cumin, garlic, and lime juice—it's excellent. And, the yellow rice with bits of ham, bacon, sausage, and peas puts Casa de Don Tomás's version to shame. The restaurant is only open for lunch, but the bar located in the cave at the entrance is open 24 hours. This spot also serves as a popular dance club on Saturday (see "Viñales After Dark," below).

Km 36 on the highway to Puerto Esperanza, north of Viñales. © 48/79-6290. Reservations not required. Main courses CUC$5-CUC$5.80 No credit cards. Daily 11am-4pm.

Las Terrazas CRIOLLAN   This hotel restaurant has a wonderful perch above and view over the Viñales Valley. The view itself is worth the price of admission, and the food is pretty good as well, but the price of a bottle of Cuban wine is a shock—a staggering CUC$13. Standard Cuban cuisine is featured here, but there are a few twists. You can get turkey fricassee, which is turkey meat stewed in a tomato and white-wine sauce. I like the chicken Viñales, which is a boneless breast served au gratin. Arrive in time for the sunset over the valley.

At the Hotel La Ermita, Carretera de La Ermita Km 1.5. ☏ **48/79-6071.** Reservations recommended. Main courses CUC$4.85–CUC$9.85. MC, V. Daily 7am–10pm.

Viñales After Dark

Viñales has a couple of low-key little bars on the main road through town and, if you're lucky, there might be a concert taking place at the local **Casa de la Cultura,** or the hugely popular **Patio de Polo Montañez ★**, both of which are right on the central plaza, just off the church, or at the nearby smaller ARTex venue, **Patio del Decimista.** Sol del Valle and its leader, who plays the recorder through his nose, is worth seeking out. The scene at either Hotel Los Jazmines or Hotel La Ermita is dependent upon the type of groups and guests in residence. The **Discoteca Las Cuevas** is located at the entrance to El Palenque de los Cimarrones (see review above). Flashing lights and loud music get an atmospheric boost from the hanging stalactites. There's a cabaret-style show here on Saturday beginning around 9pm; admission is CUC$3.

SIERRA DEL ROSARIO BIOSPHERE RESERVE & SAN DIEGO DE LOS BAÑOS ★

Soroa: 87km (54 miles) W of Havana; San Diego de los Baños: 120km (75 miles) W of Havana

The mountainous region between Havana and Pinar del Río is another prime destination in the country's budding ecotourism industry. With both the **Sierra del Rosario Biosphere Reserve** and **La Güira National Park,** as well as ecotourism projects in **Soroa** and at **Las Terrazas,** the area offers a wealth of opportunities to explore the flora and fauna of Cuba's inland mountain forests.

Sierra del Rosario Biosphere Reserve

Declared a UNESCO biosphere reserve in 1985, the 25,000-hectare (61,776-acre) **Sierra del Rosario** encompasses a mountainous area of rapidly recovering, secondary tropical deciduous forests, cut with numerous rivers and waterfalls. Nearly 100 species of birds can be spotted here, including over half of Cuba's 22 endemic species. Currently, there are few trails and facilities in the reserve, which is not open to individual exploration and trekking. Most activity is confined to two tourism developments, **Las Terrazas** and **Soroa,** which are connected by a loop of paved roads, which begins and ends on the Autopista Nacional.

ESSENTIALS
GETTING THERE & GETTING AROUND The only public transportation to Las Terrazas is the once-a-day Víazul drop-off leaving Havana at 9am and arriving at Las Terrazas at 10:35am, returning at 4:30pm. If you want to spend more time, you will either have to rent a car, hire a taxi, or come with an organized tour (which can be booked at any major tour operator or hotel tour desk). Las Terrazas is about 75km

(47 miles) west of Havana. Take the Autopista Nacional (A4) west to Km 51. Here you'll see the sign and turnoff for Las Terrazas on your right. The heart of the complex is about 8km (5 miles) from the turnoff. About halfway there, you'll hit the entrance, where you have to sign in and pay an entrance fee of CUC$4 per person, although this is waived for guests at the hotel here.

To get to Soroa, continue through Las Terrazas or on the Autopista until the town of Candelaria at Km 62. The turnoff here is marked and it's another 8km (5 miles) to Soroa.

ORIENTATION The main offices at Las Terrazas are at Rancho Curujey (see below); the community and Hotel Moka are a couple of kilometers away. Everything is well marked and connected by paved roads. If you don't have a reservation at Hotel Moka or its affiliated accommodations, you'll have to check in at Rancho Curujey before undertaking any tours or explorations of the reserve. The reserve gets busy in the high season and on weekends; reservations are recommended, even for day visits.

WHAT TO SEE & DO

Las Terrazas ★ (© **7/204-3739** in Havana, or 48/57-8555 on-site; www.lasterrazas.cu; open 9am–6pm) is a neat and organized project designed around a working community. The community and Hotel Moka are set just above the shores of the diminutive **Lago San Juan.** There are a half dozen or so trails and swimming holes, along with a smattering of other attractions, including the **Cafetal Buenavista,** an abandoned coffee plantation, and a few artists' and artisans' studios. If you're lucky, you might spot one of the area's endemic lizards or amphibians, including the world's second-smallest frog.

Officially you must have a guide to hike any of the trails here. Guides can be provided either by Hotel Moka or by the offices at Rancho Curujey (© **48/57-8555,** ext 221 or 7/204-3739 in Havana; reserva@terraz.co.cu or reservas@commoka.get. tur.cu). The trails around the **Cafetal Buenavista** make for a good couple of hours of gentle hiking, and the restaurant here makes the whole thing rather convenient. Another popular hike is the slightly more rugged **La Cañada del Infierno (the Gorge of Hell),** which follows a mountain river down beyond the ruins of yet another coffee plantation, ending at the Santa Catalina sulfur springs. A guide costs between CUC$12 and CUC$39 per person, depending on the group size and length of your hike.

The newest attraction and adventure here is a zip-line and harness-style **Canopy Tour.** The tour features five platforms connected by long steel cables, which you traverse with a climbing-style harness and pulley setup. The cables crisscross the little lake here two times. The tour takes about 50 minutes and costs CUC$25 per person, or CUC$15 if you are staying at the hotel.

Fans of the brilliant Polo Montañez can stop off at the **Peña Polo Montañez** (closed Mon) where the singer used to live. The small house overlooking the lake contains dozens of newspaper cuttings, his guitar, and his hat. His brother, Luis Borrego, is usually hanging around talking to visitors.

Soroa is a small community with one basic mini-resort (see "Where to Stay," below). The area's claims to fame are a lovely 22m (72-ft.) waterfall and a wonderful botanical garden. You reach the base of **Salto de Soroa** after a gentle hike of around 250m (820 ft.). There's a small pool here fit for wading. If you're more adventurous, you can hike or hire a horse for CUC$5 to ride the steep 1.8km (1-mile) trail to the natural lookout, El Mirador. The rainbow that sometimes forms in the mist of this waterfall has earned the whole town the moniker *El Arcoiris de Cuba* (the Rainbow of Cuba). The entrance to the trails is just a few hundred yards from the hotel, on the road to Havana; admission costs CUC$3 per person for those not staying at the hotel. Another nearby road leads up to a hilltop lookout called **El Castillo de las Nubes,** where you'll find a derelict building built to resemble a small fortress.

With more than 6,000 species of tropical plants and flowers from around the world, including 700 species of orchids, the **Jardín Botánico Orquideario Soroa ★** (ⓒ **48/52-3871**) is a must-see for anyone passing through Soroa. The compact grounds are well tended and pleasant and there are usually at least 20 or so species of orchids in bloom (most flowering blooms are btw. Dec and Apr). There's also a good chance of hearing and spotting the national bird, the tocororo. Admission is CUC$3 and includes a 15- to 20-minute guided tour. Open 8:30am to 4:30pm daily.

A 1-day taxi trip to this area from Havana costs around CUC$80.

WHERE TO STAY
Expensive

Hotel Moka ★   This is the principal hotel in Las Terrazas and the nicest ecolodge in Cuba. The first-floor rooms have vaulted redbrick ceilings, while those on the second floor have high-pitched ceilings. Each of the well-lit and spacious rooms has colorfully tiled floors and a small balcony; however, there are no queen- or king-size beds. The marble bathrooms come with a bathtub-to-ceiling window overlooking the forest. The restaurant serves food that is neither spectacular nor imaginative, and I recommend that you take some meals at the nearby La Fonda de Mercedes and Buena Vista restaurants. You can also rent small villas, attached to the homes of local residents, on the little lake below the hotel. These are charming; there are also rustic one-roomed cabins (reached by a ladder) next to the Río San Juan.

Autopista Nacional Km 51, Las Terrazas. ⓒ **48/57-8600** at the hotel, or 7/204-3739 in Havana. Fax 7/204-5305. 26 units, 5 villas. CUC$64–CUC$110 double; CUC$50–CUC$85 villa; CUC$25 cabin. Rates include breakfast. MC, V. **Amenities:** Restaurant; bar; horse rental; Internet; small outdoor pool; tennis court. *In room:* A/C, TV, minibar.

Moderate

Hotel & Villas Soroa   The clean and compact rooms at this mini-resort are not nearly as nice as those at Hotel Moka; however, the best rooms are those set up the stairs around the pool (nos. 16–24). Most have either two or three full-size beds, although a few have queen-size beds. The furnishings are simple and spartan. This place has a fair amount of group traffic and is also popular with Cubans, especially on weekends, when they gather around the large pool and the sound system is at full throttle. This is a good base for exploring Soroa, but I wouldn't recommend more than a night or two here. One advantage is that the pool can be used by day-trippers for CUC$10, and CUC$7 of that can be spent on food and drink; there's also a very well-stocked (food) shop on the premises.

Carretera de Soroa Km 8, Pinar del Río. ⓒ **48/52-3534.** www.hotelescubanacan.com. 49 units. CUC$53–CUC$65 double. Rates include breakfast buffet. **Amenities:** 2 restaurants; 3 bars; outdoor pool. *In room:* A/C, TV.

Inexpensive

Casa Estudio de Arte, Carretera Soroa Km 8½, next to the primary school (ⓒ **48/59-8116;** infosoroa@hvs.co.cu) is run by Aliuska, and the spacious bedroom available for rent was once the art studio of her husband, painter Jesús.

WHERE TO DINE

La Fonda de Mercedes 🏠 CRIOLLAN   This is clearly the top dining option in Las Terrazas, even though there are only six items on the menu. The best dish is the Camagüey-style lamb, which is served shredded and cooked in wine, although the grilled chicken a la Pinareña, which is seasoned with orange juice, garlic, and cumin, is also good. There are only five large wooden tables on the open-air patio of Doña Mercedes Dache's apartment in this residential block of housing just below Hotel Moka, so reservations are a good idea.

Edificio 9, Apto. 2, Las Terrazas. ✆ **48/57-8647.** Reservations recommended. Main courses CUC$6.45–CUC$8. No credit cards. Daily 9am–9pm.

San Diego de los Baños & La Güira National Park

Just west of the Sierra de los Rosario, in the foothills of the Sierra de los Organos, you'll find La Güira National Park and San Diego de los Baños. **La Güira** is a small park that is nonetheless a favorite stop for bird-watching tours and general sightseers. **San Diego de los Baños** is a tiny back-of-beyond town built on the edge of a lovely river and some natural mineral springs. The springs, which have been closed for some time, had been famed for their medicinal properties for centuries. Today only basic spa treatments and physical therapy are available.

GETTING THERE & GETTING AROUND

There is no regular or reliable public transportation to San Diego de los Baños. You will either have to rent a car, hire a taxi, or come with an organized tour. San Diego de los Baños is located about 133km (83 miles) southwest of Havana. Take the Auto-pista Nacional (A4) west to Km 102. You should see the sign and turnoff to your right. From here, it's another 21km (13 miles) to town. A taxi from Havana to San Diego de los Baños costs CUC$70 one-way. A few taxis are available in town. They charge from CUC$3 to CUC$5 one-way to La Güira.

WHAT TO SEE & DO

San Diego de los Baños is a tiny town built on the edge of a lovely river and some natural mineral springs. The **San Diego de los Baños Spa** (✆ **48/54-8812**) is a relatively desultory facility that shows the wear and tear it has borne over the years. This place does a heavy business in therapeutic and vacation care for Cubans. A host of physical and occupational therapists, and doctors, are on staff here. If you're staying at El Mirador next-door (see "Where to Stay & Dine," below), you'd do well to stop in for a massage (CUC$10–CUC$25). *Note:* At press time, the springs were closed.

La Güira National Park is 5km (3 miles) west of San Diego de los Baños. You enter the park through the grand gates of the former Hacienda Cortina. There are some ruins and tended gardens near the entrance, as well as a restaurant. There are no marked trails and no signs, but a heavily potholed road leads through the park (keep going straight) and up to the **Cueva de Los Portales** (marked by a Campismo sign; ✆ **63-6749**), a small cave complex from which Che Guevara coordinated the Cuban defense forces during the Cuban missile crisis. The latter is probably the most interesting site in the area, and a must-see for anyone on the Che trail. Inside, you can tour the compound and see where Che hung his hammock for afternoon siestas, where he and the men took target practice, where they cooked and ate, and where they played chess. You can even peek into the tiny room where the revolutionary icon slept during those troubled times. Admission is CUC$1; it's the same price for a guide and to take pictures. Note that the nearby campsite is not open to international visitors.

WHERE TO STAY & DINE

Hotel El Mirador   This little hotel is a surprisingly neat and well-run option in this neck of the woods. The rooms are all set in a two-story building above and behind the pool and reception. All of the rooms are clean and comfortable, with good light (but more so on the first floor) and well-kept rattan furnishings, though the bathrooms are a tad small and the beds a bit soft. There are well-tended gardens and grounds and a midsize pool. The main restaurant is actually pretty good for a Cuban chain hotel in the middle of nowhere; it serves unimpressive, but acceptable, international fare. Hotel El Mirador does a mixed business of tourists and Cubans, and the pool and poolside bar are both usually lively.

San Diego de los Baños, Los Palacios, Pinar del Río. ⓒ **48/54-8866.** www.islazul.cu. 30 units. CUC$37–CUC$41 double; CUC$55 suite. MC, V. **Amenities:** Restaurant; poolside grill; 2 bars; outdoor pool. *In room:* A/C, TV.

CAYO LEVISA ★

113km (70 miles) W of Havana; 53km (33 miles) N of Viñales

Cayo Levisa is an isolated little island accessible only by boat. The island is around 3km (1¾ miles) long and just several hundred yards wide at most points. The entire northern shore of Cayo Levisa is one long stretch of white sand fronting a calm and startlingly turquoise blue sea. The beach is backed alternately by small stands of pine trees and stretches of thick mangrove. There's excellent bird-watching and scuba diving here. Cayo Levisa is part of the Archipiélago de los Colorados, which includes Cayo Paraíso, an even smaller little island reputed to have been a favorite fishing haunt of Ernest Hemingway.

Several Havana, Pinar del Río, and Viñales tour agencies run day tours to Cayo Levisa, so the island's resort and beaches can fill up with 50 to 100 extra visitors between 10:30am and 5pm in high season. But if you spend the night, you'll feel like you've got the island to yourself.

Getting There

Hotel Cayo Levisa (see "Where to Stay & Dine," below) runs two **boats** daily to Cayo Levisa leaving from Palma Rubia at 10am and 6pm. The trip takes 30 minutes. It may be possible to hire a boat to take you out if you miss the morning trip, but don't count on it. Return boats from Cayo Levisa leave for Palma Rubia at 9am and 5pm. If you don't have a prearranged tour to the island, the boat ride will run you CUC$10 per person round-trip.

To get to Palma Rubia from Havana by **car,** drive the northern highway from Mariel to Bahía Honda and continue on for another 40km (25 miles) west to Palma Rubia. If you're coming from Viñales, drive north to La Palma and then another 21km (13 miles) northeast to the embarkation point.

There is no regular or reliable **bus service** to Palma Rubia or Cayo Levisa. You could hire a **taxi** from Havana (CUC$75 each way) or take a tour from Viñales or Pinar del Río (CUC$25), but make sure you prearrange a pickup for your return trip if you come by taxi, or you could have trouble getting out of Palma Rubia.

Fun On & Off the Beach

The beach encompasses 450m (1,476 ft.) on either side of the main lodge and is excellent for **sunbathing** and **swimming,** with broad stretches of soft sand and a gentle entry into the sea that allows you to walk out literally hundreds of yards before it gets too deep. The water can get a little rough and the weather cool when cold fronts blow through in the winter months, but this is the exception rather than the rule.

Cayo Levisa is an excellent destination for **diving** and **snorkeling.** There's a good dive operation on-site (cayolevisa@cubanacan.co.cu) and some 23 identified dive sites within a 45-minute boat ride of the island. Most of the sites are less than 15 minutes away, and some are excellent for snorkeling. Rest stops often include a packed lunch at some deserted little island. Two tank dives per day will run you CUC$72, including equipment, and multiday packages are available. Rental of snorkeling equipment costs CUC$5 per day.

If you're looking to follow in Papa Hemingway's footsteps, take a day trip to **Cayo Paraíso.** This small island is about 10km (6 miles) east of Cayo Levisa. There's a small bust of Papa and a little shack that functions as a bar and grill, where you can buy lunch and drinks. The trip costs CUC$20, including transportation, snorkeling, and refreshments. Snorkeling gear will run you an extra CUC$5. There have been reports of the dive/excursion boat being broken on several occasions. Check with Cubanacán before setting off.

Where to Stay & Dine

Hotel Cayo Levisa ★ 🎁 If you land one of the oceanfront bungalows here, you may never want to leave this idyllic little resort. I prefer the older rooms, which are individual bungalows, built in two rows parallel to the shore and staggered so they all get an ocean view. The rooms themselves are rather spartan, although they are relatively spacious with two twin beds. The newer rooms are slightly more plush, but you sacrifice a bit of privacy. Scuba diving and snorkeling are the prime activities here, although you can organize a game of beach volleyball, or get an open-air massage from the resident massage therapist under the shade of palm trees at the water's edge. The little restaurant serves good fresh seafood and *criolla* (Cuban creole) cuisine at reasonable prices.

Cayo Levisa, Pinar del Río. ② **48/75-6502.** Fax 48/75-6506. www.hotelescubanacan.com. 33 units. CUC$126–CUC$150 double. Rates include all food but not drinks. Round-trip transportation from Palma Rubia $15. No credit cards. **Amenities:** Restaurant; bar. *In room:* A/C, TV, minibar (in some).

Another Nearby Island: Cayo Jutías

A little bit west of Cayo Levisa, you can find similar attractions and isolated wonder at **Cayo Jutías ★**. Unlike its nearby sister, Cayo Jutías is connected to the mainland by a 8km (5-mile) *pedraplén,* or low-lying causeway. The island is a popular destination for day trips out of Pinar del Río and Viñales. Aside from the 8km (5 miles) of deserted white-sand beach, there's an open-air beachside restaurant serving standard *criolla* fare at reasonable prices. There's a *náutico* (nautical) center from which excursions are arranged to Starfish Beach—a real highlight with dozens of enormous starfish—and to Isla Mégano, among others, for CUC$5 to CUC$17 per person. You can also walk to Playa de los Estrellas del Mar, an isolated stretch of beach that will take you past sculpted driftwood; it takes about 2 hours each way to walk along the coastline, but beware that there is no shade and no water. Fishing trips can also be arranged for CUC$40 to CUC$45 an hour. You can also rent pedal boats, kayaks, and snorkel gear.

To get to Cayo Jutías from Havana, drive the northern highway from Mariel to Bahía Honda and continue west to Santa Lucía. If you're coming from Viñales, drive north to San Vincente, then continue to San Caetano and Santa Lucía. The *pedraplén* to Cayo Jutías begins about 5km (3 miles) northwest of Santa Lucía. The toll for the *pedraplén* is CUC$5 per person (open 10am–6pm daily). All of the major tour agencies offer day trips to Cayo Jutías from Viñales and Pinar del Río for CUC$22 per person, including lunch.

MARÍA LA GORDA & GUANACAHABIBES NATIONAL PARK ★

306km (190 miles) SW of Havana

María la Gorda is a tiny beach and dive resort on the eastern end of the Bahía de Corrientes (Current Bay), which is formed by the long, curving Peninsula de Guanacahabibes. If you want to get away from it all, this is a good choice. The one hotel here caters almost exclusively to divers and dive groups, although it's also a good base for naturalists looking to explore the flora and fauna of the Guanacahabibes Peninsula, which UNESCO has declared an International Biosphere Reserve. The beach and hotel are named for a legendary Venezuelan beauty who was marooned here by pirates. María allegedly gained quite a reputation for her fleshy charms. She's long gone, but if you're looking to admire raw physical beauty, the sunsets here are some of the best in Cuba.

Essentials

GETTING THERE   There is no regular **bus service** to María la Gorda. If you are coming, check with the Gaviota hotel chain, which runs the only hotel here (see "Where to Stay & Dine," below)—they can arrange transportation to and from Havana, leaving daily at 8am and returning at 2pm, for CUC$60 per person one way, or CUC$100 round-trip. (It becomes cheaper the larger the group.)

To get here by **car,** take the Autopista Nacional (A4) west to Pinar del Río. From Pinar del Río, it's another 94km (58 miles) to María la Gorda on the old Carretera Central passing through the prime tobacco-growing towns of San Juan y Martinez and Isabel Rubio, and then continuing on to Sandino and La Fe. There are two left turns on the route without signs, so you will need to seek directions. You'll hit the water at Bahía de Corrientes at La Bajada. The road to the left leads 14km (8¾ miles) to María la Gorda. The road to the right heads out the peninsula another 59km (37 miles) to Cabo de San Antonio.

The **Marina María la Gorda** (✆ **48/75-0123**) is an official entry and exit port for yachts. When arriving by sea, contact the marina before entering Cuban waters (19km/12 miles offshore) on VHF channels 16 or 19, or HF channel 2760. Theoretically, there's a Customs and Immigration officer on 24-hour duty, and water, electricity, and fuel can be had while tying up to the small pier here.

GETTING AROUND   Vía Rentacar (✆/fax **48/77-8131**) has a car- and scooter-rental desk here. A four-door compact car with air-conditioning will run you between CUC$55 and CUC$80 daily, including insurance and unlimited mileage, while scooters go for CUC$24 per day; hourly rates are available.

Fun On & Off the Beach

The beach right in front of the hotel quickly hits coral and rock outcroppings as soon as it meets the water. In fact, sand is at a premium here. You'd definitely be wise to bring along a pair of waterproof aquatic shoes or sandals. The best beach for sunbathing and swimming is about 1km (½ mile) southwest of the hotel near an abandoned marina. There are also some excellent beaches out toward Cabo San Antonio on the Guanacahabibes Peninsula.

Scuba diving ★★★ is the principal activity here, and this is one of the top dive destinations in Cuba. More than 50 dive sites are within a 1-hour boat ride of the resort, and many are much, much closer. Visibility is excellent and the waters of the bay here stay calm year-round. The place has a bit of a reputation for whale sharks that apparently congregate near here in October and November. However, my dive master had been working here for almost 2 years and had yet to see a whale shark. What you will see are fabulous coral and sponge formations, colorful tropical fish, turtles, eels, barracuda, and rays. It costs CUC$42 per dive, including a complete equipment package. The boat goes out at 10:30am, noon, and 3pm. There are also nightly scuba dives for CUC$40. Multiday dive packages are available for CUC$135. Snorkelers can reach some decent coral outcroppings in 3 to 7.5m (10–25 ft.) of water within 90 to 180m (295–591 ft.) of the coast. Mask, fins, and snorkeling will cost you CUC$12 per day.

Depending on boat availability, half-day **fishing** trips can also be arranged for between CUC$150 and CUC$250 for up to four persons, with your own equipment only. Possible catches range from tarpon to bonefish to a variety of deepwater fish.

Aside from the watersports mentioned above, the other main attraction here is exploring the nearby **Guanacahabibes National Park ★**. There are three trails in the park, and you must have a guide to hike any of them. The land here is flat and you'll find a mix of lowland scrub, pine forests, and mangrove, dotted with numerous little lakes and lagoons. There are quite a few endemic bird, lizard, and mammal species. This was also the last refuge of Cuba's indigenous tribes as the Spaniards completed their conquest, and several small archaeological sites have been uncovered. There's a little lighthouse, Faro Roncali, at the point at Cabo San Antonio, wild sandy beaches, and a park ranger station (Estación Ecológica; © **48/75-0366**; open 9am–5pm daily) at La Bajada. It costs CUC$6 to CUC$10 per person to hike the trails (starting at 9am; insect repellent required), including a multilingual guide, depending upon which trail you hike. Specialist trips for the same price can be organized for snorkelers, bird-watchers, spelunkers, and photographers. If you just plan on driving your car out the road to Cabo San Antonio and visiting some of the beaches here, you may be able to get away without a guide; however, as a rule, they are averse to foreigners roaming around the park unaccompanied. The road to Cabo San Antonio is bordered by huge stretches of jagged rock called *dientes del perro* (dog's teeth). The beaches and vegetation are wild and this is only really a trip to be made if you want to stay at the truly remote **Villa Cabo San Antonio** (©/fax **48/75-7655**; www.gaviota-grupo.com; CUC$51–CUC$76 double). You can book the excursions from Villa María La Gorda (see below), too. Tours from Pinar del Río and Viñales include a bag lunch and cost CUC$40 and CUC$45 respectively.

Where to Stay & Dine

Villa María La Gorda   Also known as the International Diving Center, this place is run by the Cuban Gaviota chain, and exists somewhere in that gray area between a no-frills dive camp and a modern resort. The rooms are adequate and fairly spacious, if nothing fancy. You'll want to land one of the older oceanfront units, if possible, but the newer rustic wooden bungalows, set back from the beach, are also pleasant, quiet, and spacious. The wooden walkways attract monstrous iguanas that will keep children fascinated. The resort's restaurants are uninspired, although there are really no other options around. (I actually spied quite a few guests buying cookies and crackers at the little gift shop here and calling it a meal.) Still, the main buffet restaurant does have a great setting, just steps from the water; the a la carte restaurant does not operate in low season.

Península de Guanacahabibes, Pinar del Río. ⓒ/fax **48/77-8131** or 48/77-8077. www.gaviota-grupo. com. 55 units. CUC$84 double. Rates include breakfast buffet and dinner. CUC$5 extra for oceanview room. MC, V. **Amenities:** 2 restaurants; bar; full-service dive shop. *In room:* A/C, TV, fridge.

ISLA DE LA JUVENTUD

162km (101 miles) S of Havana

Isla de la Juventud hangs like an apostrophe off the southern coast of Cuba and is the largest and westernmost island in the Archipiélago de los Canarreos. Sometimes referred to as the Island of a Thousand Names, it was called variously Siguanea, Guanaja, and Camarco by the early indigenous populations. The island was later christened El Evangelista by Columbus, Parrot Island by pirates, and Isla de Pinos (Isle of Pines) throughout most of the 19th and 20th centuries. Some even call it Treasure Island, claiming Robert Louis Stevenson used it as a model for his book of the same name. Following the Cuban Revolution, it was renamed Isla de la Juventud, or Isle of Youth, after a slew of secondary schools and colleges were built here to educate both Cuban and foreign students.

For travelers, Isla de la Juventud's primary attraction is its stellar scuba diving. The one working hotel serving foreigners caters almost entirely to divers. Other attractions include some of the most elaborate and best-preserved indigenous cave paintings in the entire Caribbean basin and the eerie prison buildings where Fidel Castro was incarcerated.

Essentials
GETTING THERE
BY PLANE **Cubana** has three daily flights to **Rafael Cabrera Mustelier Airport** (ⓒ **46/32-2300;** airport code GER) on Isla de la Juventud from José Martí International Airport in Havana. Fares cost CUC$43 each way. Demand is often very high, as the flights are quicker and cheaper than the ferry, so be sure to make your return reservation as far in advance as possible.

Regular public buses connect the airport and Nueva Gerona, 6.5km (4 miles) away. These are marked SERVICIO AEREO. The official fare is 1 peso, but foreigners are usually charged CUC$1. A taxi between the airport and downtown costs around CUC$5 to CUC$7.

BY BUS & FERRY Isla de la Juventud is connected to the mainland by regular ferry service between Nueva Gerona, on the island, and the town of Batabanó, on the coast 71km (44 miles) south of Havana. Several types of ferries make the trip. You'll definitely want to book one of the two high-speed modern catamaran ferries. Either of these will make the trip in between 2 and 3 hours, and costs CUC$50 each way. These ferries depart Batabanó daily at 8am, with return trips leaving Nueva Gerona at 11am. The ferries often have varying schedules, according to demand. The company, **Empresa Viamar,** which books all of the vessels, has a desk in the main Astro bus terminal in Havana (© **7/870-1841** or 47/588-240 in Batabanó, or 46/32-4415 in Nueva Gerona). Here, you can buy a bus-ferry combination ticket, which I highly recommend. Buses leave the terminal for Batabanó four times a day and cost $5MN (CUC$0.17). Sometimes the connections at the Batabanó end do not work like a fine Swiss watch. In Nueva Gerona, the ferry terminal and dock are approximately 4 blocks east of Calle José Martí (© **46/32-4415**). It is highly recommended that you buy a return ticket at the time of purchase and that you buy tickets at least a day or two in advance, because schedules are subject to change.

GETTING AROUND

Taxis are plentiful on Isla de la Juventud and around Nueva Gerona (**Cubataxi;** © **47/32-3121**). Rides around town, out to the airport, or to one of the nearby beaches costs between CUC$2 and CUC$7. A trip down to the Hotel El Colony costs CUC$18 to CUC$22. There are three or four daily buses between Nueva Gerona and the Hotel El Colony. A full day with a driver cost from CUC$60 to CUC$80. If you want to rent a car, **Cubacar,** Calle 32 corner of 39 (© **46/32-6666**); **Havanautos,** Calle 32 and 39 (© **46/32-4432**); and **Transtur,** at the ferry terminal and Hotel El Colony (©/fax **46/32-6666**), have offices on the island. Havanautos also rents mopeds.

There are also numerous horse-drawn taxis, which generally charge from CUC$1 to CUC$2 for short rides, or between CUC$4 and CUC$6 per hour.

ORIENTATION

The main city, **Nueva Gerona,** sits near the northern tip of the island on the banks of the Río Las Casas, while the better beaches and scuba-diving locations are on the southwest and southeastern shores. The **Hotel El Colony** (see "Where to Stay & Dine," below) is located on the shores of Siguanea Bay, on the central western coast of the island. The southern third of the island is an almost entirely uninhabited area of swamp and mangrove.

There are several banks and a **CADECA** office (Calle José Martí corner of Calle 20) in Nueva Gerona. There's a **post office** at Calle José Martí corner of Calle 18, a 24-hour **Farmacia José Martí** on Calle José Martí and Calle 24, and an **Etecsa** Telepunto phone and center at Calles 41 and 28. All of the above are located either on or within a 1- or 2-block radius of the Calle José Martí pedestrian mall.

The downtown offices of **Cubanacán** (© **46/32-6369**) and **Ecotur** (© **46/32-7101**) are your best sources of local information, and where you should head to book a tour to the attractions listed below.

What to See & Do

The island's most publicized attraction is the **Presidio Modelo (Model Prison;** © **46/32-5112),** located about 5km (3 miles) east of Nueva Gerona. The massive, five-story, circular prison blocks are dire and imposing, the remaining metal brackets whining in the silence, and even brief visits give you an idea of how uncomfortable they must have been. This is the prison where Fidel Castro and other surviving conspirators were sent following the failed Moncada raid. There's a small museum in the block where Fidel and his compadres did time, and you can even visit the Comandante's former cell, no. 3859. The museum is open Monday through Saturday from

8am to 4pm, and Sunday from 8am to noon; admission is CUC$2. There's an extra CUC$3 charge for taking photos, and a CUC$15 fee for taking video.

If you're spending much time in downtown Nueva Gerona, you might want to stop in at the **Museo Provincial** (✆ **46/32-3791**) on the park. Housed in an old building dating from the 1830s, this museum features a wide range of exhibits illustrating the island's history from pre-Columbian times to the modern era. Admission is CUC$1.

Nueva Gerona's **downtown park,** the Parque Julio Antonio Mella, is a great place to hang out, with some strategically placed benches for sitting and watching the townsfolk stroll on by. There's a pretty little colonial, mission-style church, **Nuestra Señora de los Dolores,** on the northern edge of the park, and the snazzy-looking Art Deco **Cine Caribe** on the eastern edge. Beginning at the park's western edge and running north for 5 blocks, Calle 39, also known as **Calle José Martí,** is a pedestrian-only street. This is where most of the town's shops, restaurants, and bars are located, and it's the site of the town's nightlife.

About 27km (17 miles) south of Nueva Gerona is an interesting botanical garden dubbed **La Jungla de Jones,** or the Jungle of Jones (✆ **46/39-6246**). A rather unkempt attraction, the gardens nonetheless have a broad and varied collection of tropical flora. Admission is CUC$3. Farther south, beyond the town of La Fe, you'll find the **Criadero de Cocodrilos,** a crocodile-breeding project. The facilities are basic, but there are hundreds of these impressive reptiles here, ranging in size from little tots to monstrous adults. The facility is open daily from 8am to 5pm, and the CUC$3 entrance fee will get you a brief guided tour.

On the southeastern coast of Isla de la Juventud, 59km (37 miles) from Nueva Gerona is the **Cueva de Punta del Este ★**, a small complex of caves with more than 200 ancient pictographs well preserved on its walls. This cave system has been called the Sistine Chapel of Caribbean indigenous art. The paintings are of abstract and geometric patterns and are thought to have both religious and celestial significance. There's a pretty white-sand beach here as well, so you can combine a visit to the caves with some beach time. There's no entrance fee to the caves, but you'll need a special permit and guide to enter this area; your best bet is to visit as part of an organized tour, which can be arranged at your hotel or with **Cubanacán** (✆ **46/32-6369**) or **Ecotur** (✆ **46/32-7101**) in town.

On the Beach & Under the Sea

Isla de la Juventud is one of Cuba's premier **dive destinations ★★★**, and the diving here is wonderful. The waters are crystal clear, and there are walls, corals, caves, and even a few wrecks. The **Centro Internacional de Buceo Colony** (✆ **46/39-8181**) is the main dive operator on the island, with its dive center at the small marina a few kilometers beyond the Hotel El Colony (see "Where to Stay & Dine," below). Most trips head to **Punta Francés ★★**, a national maritime park, with a beautiful stretch of white-sand beach fronting a calm and protected sea on the southwestern tip of the island. From here, many of the island's best dive sites are easily accessible. There are a couple of long piers out into the calm waters here. One has a buffet restaurant and bar at the end of it. On shore, there's a small park station, with bathroom facilities and some picnic tables. The park station also has several hundred chaise lounges, which are taken out and spread along the beach whenever a cruise ship pulls in for a day tour. When this happens—once or twice a week—this quiet, isolated beach becomes a swarming mass of up to 1,500 sun worshipers. When the cruise ships aren't around, you'll have the joint almost to yourself. Dive trips cost CUC$60 for a two-tank dive, including a full-equipment package. However, if you stay here for any length of time, you are best off buying a multiday, multidive package. Day-trippers can take the boat ride out for between CUC$8 and CUC$30; the higher fees include lunch.

Fishing can also be arranged through **Avalon** (© **72/04-7422** in Havana; www. avalonfishingcenter.com), which runs packages based out of the Hotel Rancho El Tesoro or on the live-aboard boat, the *Perola*. Abundant bonefish, tarpon, and permit are among the dozens of fish species encountered here.

The most popular beaches close to Nueva Gerona are the white-sand **Playa Paraíso** and the dark-sand **Playa Bibijagua.** These beaches are 5km (3 miles) and 8km (5 miles) east of town, respectively, and both are served by regular bus service from town. Oddly, the dark-sand Playa Bibijagua is the more popular spot, although neither is a prime beach destination by any standard.

Where to Stay & Dine

In addition to the hotel listed below, there are many *casas particulares* in Nueva Gerona. You'll definitely be offered a few as soon as you set foot on the island, whether you arrive by sea or by air. Check out the offerings of whomever gives you the best vibe, or head to either **Villa Peña,** Calle 10 no. 3710, between Calles 37 and 39, Nueva Gerona (© **46/32-2345**), which offers clean, air-conditioned rooms with meals for between CUC$20 and CUC$25 per person, as well as reasonably priced rides around the island, or **Elda House,** Calle 43 2004 between 20 and 22, Nueva Gerona (© **46/32-2774**).

Hotel El Colony   This is primarily a dive resort, and I only recommend it for hard-core divers. The hotel itself was built in two stages. The original horseshoe-shaped, two-story main building feels perpetually run-down. The newer "bungalows" are in better shape. These rooms are in one- and two-story blocks, and are spacious and modern, with two firm double beds, wicker furniture, and a small private balcony. The buffet restaurant is mediocre and overpriced. The nicest feature is the long pier and the Mojito Bar & Grill that sits at the end of it.

Carretera Siguanea Km 42 (49km/30 miles southwest of Nueva Gerona), Isla de la Juventud. © **46/39-8181.** reservas@colony.turisla.co.cu. 77 units. CUC$88–CUC$108 double. Rates include breakfast buffet. MC, V. Taxis to or from Nueva Gerona or the airport CUC$18–CUC$22; public buses make the run 3 times daily for 2 Cuban pesos. **Amenities:** 2 restaurants; 2 bars; outdoor pool; watersports equipment. *In room:* A/C, TV.

Isla de la Juventud After Dark

Start your evening with a stroll and mingle on Calle José Martí. If you get tired of that, you can check out what's playing at the **Cine Caribe,** Calle 37 and Calle 28, or stop in at the **Caberet El Patio,** Calle 24 between Calles Martí and 37, which offers up this island's somewhat anemic version of a traditional cabaret show (admission CUC$3), and then becomes a dance club. Other spots right on Calle Martí include the neighboring **Casa de las Mieles** and **Nuevo Café Virginia,** which are good options for a few drinks. The latter sometimes has live music and dancing. Or you can see if there's any live music or performance at the **Casa de la Cultura,** on Calle 24 at the corner of 37.

CAYO LARGO DEL SUR ★★★

177km (110 miles) S of Havana; 120km (75 miles) E of Isla de la Juventud

Cayo Largo del Sur—or more simply, Cayo Largo—is the second-largest island in the Archipiélago de los Canarreos, and the only other island in the chain to support any population or tourism activity. The island's primary attraction is its uninterrupted kilometers of pristine white-sand beach, perhaps the best in Cuba. The island also provides fabulous scuba-diving and snorkeling opportunities, excellent wildlife viewing, and great bonefish, tarpon, and deep-sea fishing.

Cayo Largo has a long and rich history as a stomping and fishing ground for nomadic Caribe and Siboney indigenous populations. It was also visited by Christopher Columbus on his second voyage in 1494, and used as a base and stopover point by pirates and corsairs, including Sir Francis Drake, Henry Morgan, and Jean Lafitte.

Over three-quarters of all visitors to Cayo Largo come direct on charter packages to the island, never even setting foot on mainland Cuba.

Essentials

GETTING THERE The modern **Juan Vitalio Acuña Airport** (© 45/24-8141; airport code CYO) accepts international traffic. Charter flights arrive here from Canada and Europe regularly throughout the year, with greater frequency during the high season. There are also daily flights here from Havana by **AeroCaribbean** (© 45/24-8364 or © 7/879-7524 in Havana). These are best booked in Havana with any of the many tour agencies (for contact information, see "Getting Around," in chapter 3). Fares are CUC$108 and run around CUC$137 for the day tour. A taxi from the airport to any hotel on the island costs around CUC$6.

The **Marina Internacional Cayo Largo del Sur** (© 45/24-8212; www.nautica marlin.com) is an official port of entry to Cuba. If you're arriving by sea, contact the marina before entering Cuban waters (19km/12 miles offshore) on VHF channel 16 or 19.

GETTING AROUND There's a shuttle that periodically runs a route connecting the marina and all the major resort hotels here; fare is CUC$1. Taxis are also readily available on Cayo Largo. A ride anywhere on the island costs between CUC$2 and CUC$10. You can also rent a car or scooter from **Transtur** (© 45/24-8245), which has desks at most of the hotels on the island, as well as at the airport. Rates run about CUC$8 per hour for the first hour on a scooter, and about CUC$3 per hour for each additional hour; it's CUC$60 per day for a small jeep, including your first tank of gas and insurance.

Fun On & Off the Beach

Most visitors to Cayo Largo spend most of their time sprawled out on the 25km (16 miles) of uninterrupted white-sand beach. While the beaches fronting most of the hotels here are some of the finest to be found in the Caribbean, both **Playa Paraíso ★★★** and **Playa Sirena ★★★** on the western end of the island deserve special mention. Protected from the prevailing southeasterly trade winds, these beaches are broad expanses of some of the finest white sand to be found, and they are fronted by calm, clear Caribbean waters of postcard-perfect blue hues. Most of the beaches here are clothing optional, and the large number of European and Canadian visitors to Cayo Largo make topless and nude sunbathing quite common. Shade can be at a premium here, so you'll want to park your towel or beach mat close to a coconut palm, or under a beach umbrella or one of the thatched-roof *palapas* that are spread around. Be fore-warned, demand usually far exceeds supply. If you have a portable beach umbrella or shade device, I highly recommend you bring it to Cayo Largo. The marina runs a basic restaurant and grill on Playa Sirena, and you can also rent Hobie Cats and windsurfers there. Playa Paraíso is almost entirely undeveloped, with a few thatched-roof A-frame structures on the sand for shade.

Full- and half-day **boat trips,** either on large sailing catamarans or converted fishing boats, are a popular activity here. The trips usually include a stop at Cayo Iguana, a small island with a large population of endemic iguanas, as well as some snorkeling on the barrier reef. These trips often stop at a spot called the *piscina natural* (natural pool). This slightly submerged sandbar is a beautiful and protected spot for a refreshing swim. These trips cost from CUC$69 to CUC$73 per person, including lunch. Most of the all-inclusive resorts on the island allow guests unlimited use of small sailboats, catamarans, and windsurfers. You can rent a larger cruising sailboat for the day, or even overnight, from the marina. Boats go for between CUC$250 and CUC$600 per day, with a skipper and crew.

Right beside the marina is a small turtle breeding and protection project, **La Granja de las Tortugas.** You can visit the facility and usually see various young turtles in holding tanks or protected nests. The farm is open daily from 9am to 6pm; admission is CUC$1. Between April and September, the folks here occasionally offer nighttime trips to see the nesting turtles lay eggs. Inquire at your hotel or at the farm for details.

There's great **bonefishing** on the shallow flats and mangroves all around Cayo Largo. Tarpon, permit, Jack Crevalle, snook, and barracuda are also plentiful. Serious fishermen should contact **Avalon** (www.cubanfishingcenters.com), which offers 7-day packages, or contact the **marina** (© **45/24-8212**; nautica.marina@repgc.cls.tur.cu). With rich coral reefs, steep walls, and numerous wrecks, Cayo Largo has excellent **scuba diving** and **snorkeling,** and unlike two of the island's nearby celebrated dive spots, María la Gorda and Isla de la Juventud, you can actually stay in a very comfortable hotel here. Scuba-diving and snorkeling trips are run by the **International Dive Center** at the marina here (© **45/24-8214;** buceo.marina@repgc.cls.tur.cu), but can be booked by any hotel on the island. A two-tank dive trip costs CUC$60, with a full equipment package costing an additional CUC$15. Avalon has opened **Villa Marinera** (www.cubandivingcenters.com), a new dive center with accommodations. Whale sharks can be seen around October and November and at a new dive site, Cayo Blanco, it's possible to dive with dolphins.

Nightlife on Cayo Largo is pretty much limited to the bars, dance clubs, and revue shows at its all-inclusive hotels.

Where to Stay & Dine

I find the hotel listed below to be the best choice by far on Cayo Largo, but the Sol Meliá company has another property just next door, the **Sol Pelícano** (© **45/24-8333;** www.sol-pelicano.com), which is another good option geared more toward families. The **Hotel Playa Blanca** (© **45/24-8080** on Cayo Largo; www.gran caribe.com) is a nice resort that is now run by **Gran Caribe,** which has incorporated the more rustic options here, including the **Villa Lindamar, Villa Coral,** and **Villa Soledad** into the Playa Blanca complex. Of these, Villa Coral, with a lively small-village feel, and Villa Lindamar, with its spacious A-frame bungalows, are the best.

Sol Cayo Largo ★★ 🎁 This is an animated and, at the same time, romantic all-inclusive resort set amid rolling dunes and limestone outcroppings bordering a stretch of Cayo Largo's fabulous Lindamar beach. The two-story blocks of rooms are done in a Cape Cod style, with faux stressed paint that gives the place a worn and lived-in feel. The rooms are quite spacious and comfortable, with either one king- or two queen-size beds and a private balcony or terrace. I think it's worth the CUC$20 supplement for one of the 60 oceanview standard rooms. All of these are located on the second floor and come with some added amenities, including a little nightstand CD player, stocked minibar, and—my favorite feature—an inviting, siesta-inducing, Yucatán hammock strung on the balcony. The junior suites come with a connecting sitting room and an extra TV.

Cayo Largo del Sur, Archipiélago de los Canarreos (6km/3¾ miles from the airport). ℂ **45/24-8260.** Fax 45/24-8265. www.sol-cayolargo.com. 296 units. CUC$190–CUC$270 double. Rates are all-inclusive. Children 2 and under stay free in parent's room; children 3–12 stay for half-price in parents' room. MC, V. **Amenities:** 5 restaurants; 4 bars; babysitting; children's programs; dance club; health club; Internet; large free-form outdoor pool; 2 lit outdoor tennis courts; nonmotorized watersports equipment. *In room:* A/C, TV, fridge.

VARADERO & MATANZAS PROVINCE

An easy ride from Havana, Matanzas is Cuba's second-largest province, and the site of its principal beach destination: Varadero. In addition to Varadero, the province is home to the colonial-era cities of Matanzas and Cárdenas, as well as the Ciénaga de Zapata, a vast wetlands area of mangrove and swamp taking up most of the southern half of the province. The southern section of Matanzas province also holds great historical and sentimental value to modern Cubans, as it was here, in the Bahía de Cochinos (Bay of Pigs), that the nascent Cuban revolutionary state defeated an invasion force trained, supplied, and abetted by the United States. Today the area draws divers for the stunning clear waters and colorful coral. Matanzas remains an important agricultural region with huge sugar plantations, as well as citrus groves and cattle ranches.

MATANZAS

98km (61 miles) E of Havana; 40km (25 miles) SW of Varadero

Matanzas is a city of many names: City of Bridges, City of Rivers, and the Venice of Cuba. They all refer to the fact that the city is divided by two major rivers, and connected back by a series of pedestrian, auto, and rail bridges. Due to its slow pace and laid-back nature, Matanzas is also sometimes called Cuba's Sleeping Beauty. However, the city is probably most proud of its moniker as the Athens of Cuba, a name reflecting Matanzas's important cultural tradition and history. The first *danzón*, a languid and lyrical original dance and musical form, was originally composed and played in Matanzas in 1879 by native son Miguel Faílde, and Matanzas has a rich legacy of prominent poets, writers, painters, and musicians. Still, today's reality is that aside from its beautiful old city center, Matanzas is a relatively unappealing industrial port city of only passing interest to travelers. While it is a popular destination for day trips out of Havana and Varadero, there are no hotels or notable restaurants in Mantanzas.

Essentials

GETTING THERE

BY PLANE   The nearest airport is Varadero's **Juan Gualberto Gómez International Airport** (© **45/24-7015;** airport code VRA), located more or less midway between Varadero and Matanzas. See "Varadero," below, for more information.

BY BUS   The **bus station** is located at the corner of Calzada de Esteban and Calle Terry. **Víazul** (☏ **7/881-1413** in Havana, or 45/29-1473 in Matanzas; www.viazul. com) has three buses daily for Varadero, stopping in Matanzas to drop off and pick up passengers. The buses depart Havana daily at 8am, 10am, noon, and 6pm. The trip takes about 2 hours to Matanzas, and the one-way fare is CUC$7. The return bus for Havana leaves Matanzas at 8:55am, 12:15pm, 4:25pm, and 6:50pm.

BY TRAIN   One interesting alternative means of reaching Matanzas is the **Hershey Train ★**, a legacy of the famous chocolate company's formerly vast network of sugar plantations in Cuba. This slow-moving electric train leaves from Havana's **Casablanca Station** (☏ **7/862-4805**). The Hershey Train station in Matanzas is located at Calle 67, in Reparto Versalles, just north of the Río Yumurí (☏ **45/24-7254**). This scenic trip takes between 3 and 4 hours, making numerous stops, and costs CUC$3. There are three departures daily in each direction, leaving more or less simultaneously from each terminal station at roughly 5am, 11:30am, and 5pm. However, the train rairly departs regularly each day because of deteriorated service; call ahead to find out the schedule.

BY CAR   Matanzas is connected to Havana by a modern coastal highway, the Vía Blanca, which begins as you exit the tunnel connecting La Habana Vieja with Habana del Este. It's a straight shot and scenic drive that generally takes around 90 minutes.

GETTING AROUND

You can easily visit all the principal sites in downtown Matanzas on foot. **Taxis** are readily available in Matanzas, and tend to gather around the Plaza de la Vigía and Plaza de la Libertad. A taxi out to the Castillo de San Severino from downtown should cost around CUC$2–CUC$3 each way.

ORIENTATION

Matanzas is divided into three distinct sections by the Yumurí and San Juan rivers. All let out onto the broad bay, Bahía de Matanzas. The northern section and the first you'll reach coming in on the Vía Blanca from Havana is **Reparto Versalles.** The central section, **Reparto Matanzas,** is where you'll find the city center and most of the local attractions. Heading south and out of town toward Varadero is **Pueblo Nuevo.**

The main **post office** is located at the corner on Calle 85 between Calles 288 and 290. There's an **Etecsa** center at Calles 28 and 83 (☏ **45/24-3123**). There's a **CADECA** branch on Jovellanes and Milanés (☏ **45/25-3558**).

What to See & Do

Matanzas has a very compact city center, and a few hours of walking around are generally enough to get a good feel for the place. There are two small plazas that anchor the social and cultural life of Matanzas, the **Plaza de la Vigía** and the **Plaza de la Libertad.** Both are within 5 blocks of each other in Reparto Matanzas, the central section of the city.

Probably the most visited site in Matanzas is the stunning neoclassical **Teatro Sauto ★★**, on the Plaza de la Vigía (☏ **45/24-2721**). The theater, which was finished in 1863, is the design of Italian architect and artist Daniel Dal'Aglio, who also painted the beautiful frescoes that adorn the ceiling. Dance, theater, and classical music performances are still regularly held here, and it's worth checking to see if there's anything playing while you're in town. Otherwise, you may be able to take a guided tour of the theater; CUC$2 between 9am and 5pm daily.

The other main attraction in town is the **Museo Farmacéutico** ★, Calle 83 no. 4951, Plaza de la Libertad (☎ **45/24-3179**). Seemingly little has changed here since its founding in 1882 by the French pharmacist Ernesto Troilet. Porcelain jars of potions and elixirs are stacked high in beautiful floor-to-ceiling wood cabinets. The museum is open daily from Monday to Saturday 10am to 5pm and on Sunday from 10am to 2pm; admission is CUC$3.

At the head of the harbor, close to the downtown center, you'll find a couple of small stretches of beach, where there will almost always be a few locals swimming, fishing, and sunbathing. However, the harbor is quite industrial and I'd highly recommend you head over to Varadero for some more inviting beaches.

Out on the northern edge of the bay is the **Castillo de San Severino,** Avenida del Muelle. Built in 1734, this small fort served as a line of defense, slave-trading post, and long-standing prison. It's been restored and is definitely worth a visit, if for nothing other than the great view of Matanzas Bay. The Castillo is open Mon–Sat 9am–5pm and Sun 9am–1pm; admission is CUC$2.

On the outskirts of the city, you'll find the **Cuevas de Bellamar** ★, Finca La Alcancia (☎ **45/26-1683**), a cave complex of nearly 3km (1¾ miles) of galleries and passageways, with intricate stalactite and stalagmite formations, indigenous pictographs, and several underground streams and rivers. You can tour the first kilometer or so of caves for CUC$5 per person, including a guide. This section is lit, so no equipment or flashlights are needed. The caves are located 5km (3 miles) southeast of Matanzas, off a well-marked access road. They are open daily from 9:30am to 4:15pm.

Where to Stay & Dine

There are currently no hotels catering to travelers in Matanzas, and no restaurants worthy of a hearty recommendation. Most folks—and I recommend this—come here on day trips from either Havana or Varadero. There is a handful of *casas particulares* congregated around the downtown center. **Casa Alma,** Calle Milanés (C/83) 29008 between 290 and 292 (☎ **45/24-2449;** hostalalma@gmail.com), is a lovely colonial home with well-preserved *mediopuntos* (semi-circular stained glass windows positioned above wooden doors). The most happening spot in town is the **Café Atenas,** Calle Magdalena and Calle Milanés, Plaza de la Vigía (☎ **45/25-3493**), a simple 24-hour cafe and snack bar, with an easygoing ambience and comfortable seating both indoors and outdoors on a cool patio.

Matanzas After Dark

Matanzas is a quiet city without much nightlife, with one notable exception. The younger sister to the venerable Tropicana in Havana, **Tropicana Matanzas** ★★, Autopista del Sur Km 4.5 (☎ **45/26-5380**), seeks to provide the classic Tropicana cabaret experience to the thousands of tourists who come to Cuba and never venture far from Varadero. I don't know why they didn't just build it in Varadero, but whatever the reason, it is located on the outskirts of Matanzas, about a 20-minute drive from Varadero. Like its famous sibling, this is a large open-air theater with extravagant nightly performances. The artistic direction is shared between the two venues, and the show here is quite up to snuff. Scores of scantily clad showgirls and dancers seamlessly weave together a series of different numbers. Costumes are tight-fitting, garish, and often feature gravity-defying headgear. The spectacle covers most of the bases of popular Cuban show and dance music, from *son* to bolero to *danzón* to salsa, with a bit of Afro-Cuban religious music thrown into the mix. The 90-minute show starts around 10:30pm each night. After the show, you can continue the celebration by dancing the night away at the adjoining dance club.

Virtually every tour agency in Varadero can book you a night at the Tropicana Matanzas; packages include a complimentary *cuba libre* (cocktail with rum and Coke). All include round-trip transportation. Tickets for the show are CUC$49. Since it's open-air, rain cancels the function. You'll get your money back on a rainout, but there are no guaranteed reservations for a makeup show.

VARADERO ★★

140km (87 miles) E of Havana; 40km (25 miles) NE of Matanzas

Varadero is Cuba's most renowned and popular beach destination (with prices to match). Varadero is the common name for the entire length of the Hicacos Peninsula. The peninsula, which takes its name from a local spiny cactus, is 21km (13 miles) long, with a nearly continuous broad band of fine white sand fronting a clear blue sea. Backed by mangroves and the calm waters of Cárdenas Bay, it is less than a mile at its widest point. Large resort hotels take up a large percentage of the entire length of this peninsula. There are three distinct parts of the peninsula: the far eastern end is home to the most expensive, remote upscale resorts where the beaches are quieter. Downtown, from Calles 10 to 64, is part of Varadero town; this is dominated by a cluster of mostly cheaper hotels that are on and off the beach. (This is also the most popular with Cuban visitors.) During the summer months, this beach is extremely busy. At the far western end are a handful of medium-sized and moderately priced hotels. The beach here is lovely and remarkably empty even in the height of summer.

Home to indigenous populations and a base camp for itinerant Taíno and Carib fishermen, Varadero was largely ignored throughout the Spanish colonial period. While it was first developed as a summer retreat by some 10 families from Cárdenas in 1887, its real potential as a tourist destination was realized relatively late. The first hotel was built here in 1910, and U.S. industrial magnate Irénée Dupont built his Xanadú Mansion here in 1928. A small cadre of celebrities and gangsters followed, including Al Capone. Still, at the time of the Revolution, there were only three hotels in Varadero. Today, there are more than 55, with more than 15,000 rooms . . . and construction continues. ***Note:*** Examine your bills carefully to make sure that you are not overcharged in all shops, bars, and taxis.

Essentials

GETTING THERE

BY PLANE　The **Juan Gualberto Gómez International Airport** (✆ **45/24-7015;** airport code VRA) is located 18km (11 miles) west of Varadero, roughly midway between Matanzas and Varadero. Direct charter and scheduled commercial flights arrive in Varadero from Montreal, Toronto, Vancouver, Cancún, Nassau, Montego Bay, and most major European hubs. The major international carriers servicing Varadero include **Air Canada, Air Europe, Condor, Martinair, Monarch, Edelweiss, Sobelair, Lauda Italia, Air Lib, Eurofly, Corsair, Star Airlines, Sky Service,** and **LTU.** A taxi between the airport and Varadero costs CUC$25. If you coincide with a Víazul departure, it will cost you CUC$6 to the bus station and an additional CUC$2 on another Víazul bus to your hotel. **Cubana** (✆ **45/61-1823**) has an office at Av. 1 at Calle 55. **Aerocaribbean** (✆ **45/61-1470**) is based at Av. 1 at Calle 23.

BY BUS Víazul (✆ 7/881-1413 in Havana, or 45/61-4886 in Varadero; www.
viazul.com) has four buses daily for Varadero, leaving Havana at 8am, 10am, noon,
and 6pm. The trip takes 3 hours to Varadero. The return buses for Havana leave
Varadero at 8am, 11:25am, 3:30pm, and 6pm. The fare is CUC$10 each way. Víazul
also has a daily bus from Varadero to Trinidad via Santa Clara leaving at 8:15am (6
hr.; CUC$20 each way). The bus to Trinidad via Cienfuegos leaves at 2:55pm (4 hrs;
CUC$20). The return buses leaves at 9am and 2:50pm. The bus to Santiago leaves
at 9:25pm (15 hr.; CUC$49 each way). The return bus leaves Santiago at 8pm. The
bus station is located at Calle 36 and the Autopista del Sur.

In addition, most of the hotels and tour agencies in Havana can arrange transportation on periodic transfer buses to Varadero, including a pickup at your hotel. In a
similar vein, all of the hotels and tour agencies in Varadero can book you on similar
buses heading back to the hotels and airport in Havana. The fare is CUC$25 to
CUC$35 each way.

BY CAR Varadero is connected to Havana by a modern, four-lane, coastal highway,
the Vía Blanca, that begins as you exit the tunnel connecting Habana Vieja with
Habana del Este. It's a straightforward, scenic drive to Matanzas. The highway then
threads its way through Matanzas, generally hugging close to the coast, and continues
on the final 40km (25 miles) to Varadero. About 13km (8 miles) outside of Varadero
there's a tollbooth (CUC$2 per vehicle each way). The trip generally takes around 2
hours. A taxi from Havana to Varadero costs around CUC$80–CUC$100; a taxi from
Matanzas/Cárdenas costs around CUC$20.

GETTING AROUND

Taxis are plentiful in Varadero. A trip from one end of the peninsula to the other costs
from CUC$15–CUC$17, and most trips to other places in the area cost CUC$2 to
CUC$10. If by some chance you can't flag one down, or there's none hanging around
your hotel, you can call **Cubataxi** (✆ 45/61-4444 or 45/61-1616). Watch for
rogue *taxistas* who refuse to use the *taximetro*. Víazul now offers a transfer from the
station to any hotel in Varadero for CUC$2 after the long-distance buses pull in. As
in Havana, open-air **Coco Taxis** are also available for CUC$25 per hour. In theory,
they should charge CUC$.50 a kilometer, but they often cost more than a metered
taxi. A **horse-and-carriage ride** costs CUC$10 for a city tour.

Sol Melía operates a free **open-air tourist train** between various points of the
peninsula. The **VaraderoBeachTour buses** (✆ 45/66-8992) that ply a loop from
one end of Varadero to the other operate a day pass, with unlimited use of the route;
it costs CUC$5 per day.

One of the best ways to get around Varadero is on a **scooter.** Rental agencies
abound. Most rent modern, easy-to-use Vespa-style scooters for CUC$12 for two
hours, and CUC$24 per day.

There are a host of **car-rental agencies** at the airport and around town. Virtually
every hotel either has a car-rental desk, or can easily facilitate renting a car. Contact
Cubacar (✆ 45/61-1875 or 45/66-7359; www.transturvaradero.com) or **Transtur** (✆ 45/61-1435) for more information.

ORIENTATION

Infotur, a network of information offices, has offices at Calle 13 and Av. 1 (✆ 45/66-
2961; vardirec@enet.cu), and in the Cento Comercial Hicacos at Av. 1 between
Calles 46 and 48 (✆ 45/66-7049). **Cubatur, Cubanacán,** and **Havanatur** have
offices all over Varadero and in the hotels. **CADECA** (✆ 45/66-7870) is at the

Varadero

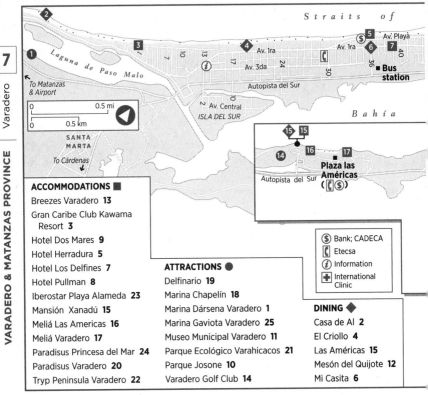

ACCOMMODATIONS ■

Breezes Varadero **13**

Gran Caribe Club Kawama
  Resort **3**

Hotel Dos Mares **9**

Hotel Herradura **5**

Hotel Los Delfines **7**

Hotel Pullman **8**

Iberostar Playa Alameda **23**

Mansión Xanadú **15**

Meliá Las Americas **16**

Meliá Varadero **17**

Paradisus Princesa del Mar **24**

Paradisus Varadero **20**

Tryp Peninsula Varadero **22**

ATTRACTIONS ●

Delfinario **19**

Marina Chapelín **18**

Marina Dársena Varadero **1**

Marina Gaviota Varadero **25**

Museo Municipal Varadero **11**

Parque Ecológico Varahicacos **21**

Parque Josone **10**

Varadero Golf Club **14**

ⓢ Bank; CADECA

Ⓒ Etecsa

ⓘ Information

✚ International
  Clinic

DINING ◆

Casa de Al **2**

El Criollo **4**

Las Américas **15**

Mesón del Quijote **12**

Mi Casita **6**

airport and Avenida Playa between Calles 41 and 42, and at Avenida 1 corner of Calle 59. **Banco Financiero Internacional** (𝄐 **45/66-7002**) is at Avenida 1 and Calle 32. The **Banco de Crédito and Comercio** (𝄐 **45/61-2616**), Avenida 1 (btw. Calles 35 and 36) has a Visa ATM. The **Clínica Internacional Varadero,** Avenida 1 and Calle 61 (𝄐 **45/66-7711**), is open 24 hours for emergency and routine medical care. It also has a 24-hour pharmacy. **Etecsa** has an office with Internet access (open daily) at the corner of Avenida 1 and Calle 30.

WHAT TO SEE & DO

This is a beach destination and, aside from lying on the beach and swimming in the clear waters of the Straits of Florida, most of the attractions and activities here are either found or conducted on or under the water. The nicest spot to visit in "downtown" Varadero is the **Parque Josone,** Avenida 1 between Calles 55 and 58 (𝄐 **45/66-7228**), a beautifully maintained little city park with cool, shady grounds and gardens. There are paths winding around and over little lakes with fountains, several restaurants, and food stands, and the park is dotted with gazebos and park benches. The park is open daily from 9am to 11pm.

If it's raining, or you just can't take any more sunbathing, active adventures, or shopping, you could make a quick visit to the **Museo Municipal Varadero,** Calle

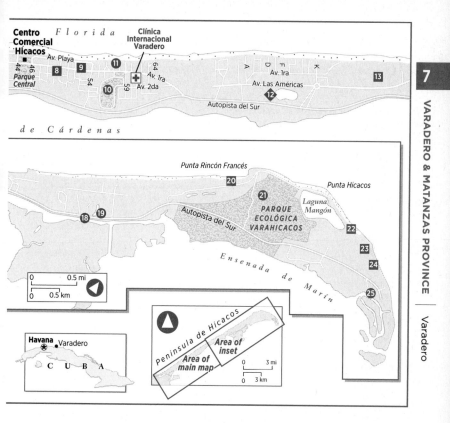

57 and Avenida de la Playa (℃ **45/61-3189**). Open daily from 10am to 7pm (CUC$1), the exhibits inside are of less interest and appeal than the beautiful old building that houses the collection. The perfectly maintained blue-and-white, two-story wooden building, built by architect Leopoldo Abreus from Cienfuegos, has a gingerbread trim and red-tile roof; it is a tribute to colonial Caribbean architecture.

Near the Marina Chapelín, on the ocean side of the road, you'll find the **Delfinario,** Autopista Sur Km 12 (℃ **45/66-8031**). Open daily from 9:30am to 5pm, this attraction offers a 40-minute show with trained dolphins at 11am and 3:30pm. Admission is CUC$15; it's CUC$5 extra to take photos and CUC$89 for a 15-minute swimming session with the dolphins if booked through a hotel. While this place is highly touted by tour agencies, I personally find this type of attraction—and this one in particular—to be depressing and on the cruel side.

If you want a bird's-eye view of things, the **Centro Internacional de Deportes Aéreos,** Vía Blanca Km 1.5, off a little side road across from the Marina Dársena (℃ **45/66-7256**), offers parachute jumps and ultralight flights. Tandem parachuting costs CUC$160 per person. Ultralight flights start at CUC$45 for 10 minutes. You can also usually find ultralight flights leaving from different spots up and down the beach.

Take a Detour

At 110m (361 ft.), the **Bacuanayagua Bridge** ★ is the highest in Cuba. It spans the beautiful Yumurí Valley. Most tourist buses will stop here for a quick break and photo opportunity, and if you are driving, you'll probably want to do so as well. A rugged side road leads off the highway if you want to explore this largely undeveloped valley. The bridge is located 7km (4¼ miles) west of Matanzas, right on the Vía Blanca en route from Havana to Matanzas and Varadero.

The **Varadero Golf Club** ★ (© 45/66-8482; www.varaderogolfclub.com) features a lovely little resort course, with plenty of water, few trees, and almost no rough. There are beautiful views of Cárdenas Bay from most holes. Greens fees run CUC$70 for a round, plus an extra CUC$50 for a cart. Club rental will cost you CUC$50. You can play a twilight round of 9 holes for CUC$48 after 4pm.

A large swath of the eastern end of the peninsula is protected as the **Parque Ecológico Varahicacos (Varadero Ecological Park).** There are some gentle paths through the scrub forests here, and you can visit a series of small caves, some of which contain ancient indigenous pictographs. The park is broken up into two sections, with a small area close to the major hotel district, and the larger section farther east. It's open daily from 9am to 4:30pm; admission is CUC$3.

FUN ON & UNDER THE WATER

If you want to take out a Hobie Cat, windsurfer, paddle boat, or sea kayak, chances are your hotel will have them, either as part of your all-inclusive package or for hire. If not, simply hit the beach and walk a bit until you find some for rent.

There are three main marinas on Varadero: **Marina Gaviota Varadero,** at the far eastern end of the Autopista del Sur (© 45/66-7755); **Marina Dársena Varadero,** at the western end of the Autopista del Sur (© 45/61-4448); and **Marina Chapelín,** Autopista del Sur Km 12.5 (© 45/66-7550). The latter two also operate under the umbrella name of **Marlin** (© 45/66-8000; www.nauticamarlin.com). At any of these, you can charter a sailboat, organize a fishing excursion, or arrange to go scuba diving. Moreover, the tour agencies and hotel activities desks can book any of these activities.

FISHING   The waters off Varadero provide the opportunity to go deep-sea fishing (© 45/66-7565) for marlin, sailfish, tuna, snapper, dolphin, and more. Rates are CUC$340 for a boat for up to four fisherman. Non-fisherman pay CUC$30.

Fishing trips can also be arranged to the **Ciénaga de Zapata** area in southern Matanzas province. See "The Zapata Peninsula & Playa Girón," later in this chapter, for more details.

SAILING   There are many charter sailboat options available at each of the marinas mentioned above. The most popular outfit, **Seafari** ★, Marina Chapelín (© 45/66-8338), has a fleet of broad and comfortable catamarans. A range of cruise options is available, from half-day and full-day cruises to simple sunset sails. Many of the sailing adventures make stops at the small, uninhabited cays off the eastern coast of the peninsula, including Cayo Blanco; these trips can include lunch on one of the cays, as well as snorkeling adventures on close-in coral reefs. Rates are CUC$63–CUC$75 for a full day. Many of these boats are outfitted with a bar or two and carry either a live band or loud, recorded dance music. Some boats head out for a floating sunset party or a raging dance party under the moonlight.

The popular **Boat Adventure ★**, Marina Chapelín (✆ **45/66-8440**), is a 2-hour tour on small, sit-on-top motorized watercraft, or Aqua-Rays, through the canals and mangroves backing the peninsula. A guide leads a caravan of the small craft, which can hold up to two adults. This tour leaves roughly every hour, with a total of eight departures daily; it's CUC$41 per person.

The **Discover Tour (Jeep & Boat Safari;** ✆ **45/66-8000)** involves speedboating up the Rio Canimar, swimming in the Saturno Cave, visiting Matanzas, and off-roading in jeeps for CUC$73.

SCUBA DIVING & SNORKELING Most of the large hotels on Varadero either have their own dive operations or can arrange scuba-diving and snorkeling trips around the area. Scuba diving and snorkeling off Varadero is generally pretty good, although rarely spectacular. There's an assortment of sites, including a black coral bed, various coral reefs, and wrecks. True aficionados prefer the diving found in southern Matanzas province off the coasts of Playa Larga and Playa Girón. It's about a 90-minute drive from Varadero, and all of the dive operations here offer trips to these dive spots, an especially good choice if a northern wind is blowing and the waters are rough off of Varadero. If your hotel can't arrange this for you, contact **Centro Internacional de Buceo Barracuda,** Calle 59 and Avenida 1 (✆ **45/61-3481;** www.nauticamarlin.com). Dives are CUC$50 and Open Water courses CUC$365. Two new dive centers have opened: **Acua** (✆ **45/66-8063**), located at the western end of the peninsula, and **Marina Chapelín** (✆ **45/66-8871**), located at the eastern end of the peninsula. There is a recompression chamber at Varadero.

One popular scuba-diving and snorkeling site worth mentioning is the **Cueva de Saturno,** located outside of Matanzas, on the road to the airport. This large cave houses a large deep *cenote* (pool) that can be explored with a mask and snorkel. The cave is open daily from 9am to 6pm; admission is CUC$5, or CUC$10 with lunch and an alcoholic drink. Most agencies and hotels can arrange a half-day trip for CUC$30 per person including snorkeling at **Playa Coral** where squid can be seen.

ORGANIZED TOURS

All of the tour agencies in town offer a host of guided excursions to the principal cities and attractions within striking distance of Varadero. Options include half-day tours to Matanzas or Cárdenas, day tours to Havana or Trinidad, and overnight excursions to Cayo Largo, Cayo Coco, or Santiago de Cuba. Rates run around CUC$15 for half-day tours and from CUC$49 to CUC$99 for full-day excursions. Overnight trips vary widely depending on the means of travel (air or bus) and the type of accommodations. Your best bet for booking any of these is to check at your hotel, or contact helpful **Cubatur,** Av. 1 at Calle 33 (✆ **45/61 4405**); **Cubanacán,** Calle 24 between Av. 1 and Avenida de la Playa (✆ **45/66-7061;** www.cubanacan.cu); **Gaviota Tours,** Calle 56 and Avenida de la Playa (✆ **45/61-1844**); or **Havanatur,** Avenida de la Playa, between Calles 33 and 34 (✆ **45/66-7589**).

Gran Car (✆ **45/61-0555**),offers various trips for CUC$166 to CUC$187, including a day trip spent tooling around Havana in a classic car. The trip includes a tour of La Habana Vieja, with stops at the four major plazas, as well as a visit to a cigar factory, the Plaza de la Revolución, and a stop at the Hotel Nacional. Classic car trips start at CUC$30 for 1 hour; CUC$35 for a convertible classic. Classic cars, with drivers, are available for longer hire, but visitors are not allowed to self-drive an American classic car.

Shopping

There's no lack of souvenir stands, T-shirt outlets, and overpriced hotel gift shops here, but good shopping options are limited. For clothes, shoes, beach accessories and toiletries head to the **Centro Comercial Hicacos** (Parque del 8000 Taquillas) at Av. 1 between Calles 44 and 46. There are several outdoor arts and crafts markets around Varadero; the best, **Artesanía,** is at Avenida 1 and Calle 12. The **Plaza de los Artesanos** at Avenida 1 between Calles 46 and 47 is also good. **ARTex** has stores at each of these sites, as well as at Avenida 1 and Calle 35. At each, you will find a broad (and standard) collection of trinkets, T-shirts, musical instruments, posters, and CDs.

Taller de Cerámica Artística, Avenida 1 between Calles 59 and 60 (✆ 45/66-7829), is a working pottery studio and factory with a broad selection of finished goods for sale. Some are quite good and quite expensive. The work ranges from abstract and artistic to purely functional. You can usually watch a potter at work while shopping.

For a dense collection and variety of shops, **Plaza las Américas,** Autopista Sur Km 11 (✆ 45/66-8181) has a modern mini-mall and convention center with clothing boutiques and T-shirt shops, along with an art gallery and a music shop thrown in. There's even a small supermarket here, and several restaurants.

If you want cigars, the best-stocked shop in Varadero is **Casa de los Tabacos,** Avenida 1 and Calle 38 (✆ 45/61-4719). They usually have one or two rollers making fresh stogies here, and there's a comfortable bar for enjoying their wares, while sipping a glass of rum or a strong espresso.

Where to Stay
HOTELS

Most of the hotels on Varadero operate as all-inclusive resorts. Still, there are a few options for those who just want a room and breakfast, and the ability to pick and choose where they eat the rest of their meals. You can also purchase a day pass at many of the local all-inclusive resorts for between CUC$30 and CUC$80, which will allow you access to their facilities, including meals and endless drinks.

Expensive

Mansión Xanadú The former mansion of Irénée Dupont de Nemours is now a medium-end boutique hotel but its 1930s grandeur feels a little dated, and almost dingy in some instances. Moreover, the fact that it is such a tourist attraction takes away any real sense of intimacy. Still, you will be staying at what was once, and in some respects still is, the most luxurious address in town. The rooms are spacious and meticulously maintained, with marble floors, Persian rugs, and antique furnishings. Most have narrow, intricately carved wooden balconies overlooking the ocean. All of the rooms are on the second floor, and on the third floor, there's a lively bar with good views. The hotel is right on the Varadero golf course and guests enjoy unlimited privileges at the course. The hotel sits on a rocky outcropping a hundred or so yards from the beach, and while

Stake Your Claim

At some resorts, finding a chaise longue under a shady *palapa* is a cut-throat endeavor. You will either have to stake out your turf early, or find a local worker who, for a small gratuity, will save you a prime spot.

there's no pool or beach right here, guests can use both at the nearby Meliá Las Américas.

Carretera Las Américas Km 8.5, Varadero. ℰ **45/66-8482.** Fax 45/66-8481. www.varaderogolfclub. com. 6 units. CUC$150 double. Rates include full breakfast and unlimited greens fees. MC, V. **Amenities:** Restaurant; bar; room service. *In room:* A/C, TV, minibar.

Inexpensive

In 1998, the Cuban government outlawed *casas particulares* in Varadero, wanting to steer all business to the official state-owned hotels and resorts. The ban is still in effect, although there are folks who will rent out rooms in private houses. Still, since it's not legal, they don't like to advertise or call attention to themselves. If you really want to find a *casa particular,* ask a taxi driver or tour guide, or walk around the area between Calle 13 and Calle 64 in the heart of Varadero's downtown, and you should be able to find something.

Hotel Dos Mares   This little hotel is housed in an old, three-story Spanish-style stucco building. The rooms here are a tad dark, but they are clean and comfortable. However, they come with big, wall-mounted air-conditioning units that can be a bit loud. The good news is that you're centrally located and the beach is less than 90m (300 ft.) away.

Calle 53, btw. Avs. 1 and Playa, Varadero. ℰ **45/61-2702.** Fax 45/66-7499. www.islazul.cu. 34 units. CUC$34–CUC$40 double. Rates include breakfast. No credit cards. **Amenities:** Restaurant; bar. *In room:* A/C, TV.

Hotel Herradura ♠   This bare-bones budget hotel has an unbeatable location, right on the beach, with rooms overlooking the sea. Only in Cuba could you have a beach-view room on prime seafront land for such a bargain. The hotel staff is really friendly and the breakfast served is acceptable. Rooms are spartan and outdated, but are air-conditioned and have cable TV. They share a huge living room, with fridge and balcony, with one other mini-apartment. At these prices, you can't complain about sharing the balcony or the view.

Av. Playa between Calle 35 and 36, Varadero. ℰ **45/61-3703.** www.islazul.cu. 75 units. CUC$36–CUC$44 double. Rates included breakfast. MC, V. **Amenities:** Restaurant; bar. *In room:* A/C, TV.

Hotel Pullman ♠   This old hotel probably has the most personality of any budget hotel in Varadero. It's across the street from the beach, in a three-story stone building, with some pretty decorative masonry work crowning it. The compact rooms are all clean and well maintained, and the hotel is well located in the heart of Varadero's little town. There's a charming patio restaurant here, and a couple of the rooms even share a nice veranda.

Av. 1, btw. Calles 49 and 50, Varadero. ℰ **45/61-2702.** Fax 45/66-7499. www.islazul.cu. 16 units. CUC$34–CUC$40 double. Rates include breakfast. No credit cards. **Amenities:** Bar. *In room:* A/C, TV.

ALL-INCLUSIVE RESORTS

There are literally scores of large, all-inclusive resorts in Varadero. I've listed my top choices. In addition to the places listed below, good options include the **Barceló Marina Palace** (ℰ **45/66-9966;** www.barcelomarinapalace.com), **Brisas del Caribe** (ℰ **45/66-8030;** www.belivehotels.com/hotel/ES/home.jsp), **Coralia Club Playa de Oro** (ℰ **45/66-8566;** www.accorhotels.com), **Iberostar Varadero** (ℰ **45/66-9999;** www.iberostar.com), **Sandals Royal Hicacos Resort & Spa** (ℰ **800/545-8283** in the U.S. or Canada, or 45/66-8844; www.sandalshicacos. com), and **Sol Palmeras** (ℰ **45/66-7009;** www.solmeliacuba.com).

The rack rates listed below are actually the high end of what you might pay. In fact, you should expect to pay much less. Most of these hotels sell the bulk of their rooms to wholesalers and package tour operators, who in turn sell quite attractive all-inclusive packages. Competition is fierce, and it pays to shop around. However, as this is a segment of the industry that depends on volume, some resorts try to make up for the low prices by skimping on food and drink quality, and upkeep. So be careful: If you come across a resort not listed here at a deal that seems too good to be true . . . it just might be.

Note: Since so much of the market here is European, many of the large resort hotels operate either exclusively on 220-volt electricity or a combination of 110-volt and 220-volt electricity. Regardless, bring the proper adapters with you.

Very Expensive

Meliá Las Américas ★★ Located just off the clubhouse of Cuba's only 18-hole golf course, this upscale hotel should be a golfer's top choice. The Meliá Las Américas is a large resort hotel, with the bulk of its rooms in the five-story main building, as well as one- and two-bedroom bungalows in a series of smaller buildings spread around some lush gardens amid a maze of swimming pools and ponds. Still, the rooms in the main building are all large, spacious, and well maintained, and I'd choose them over the bungalows, if only for their comfortable balconies with views over either the Straits of Florida or the golf course and bay. The hotel sits right on a small section of beautiful beach and next to the Plaza las Américas mall, making it one of the more strategically located hotels in Varadero. It boasts a sushi restaurant, a rarity in Cuba.

Autopista del Sur, Carretera Las Morlas, Varadero. (✆ **45/66-7600.** Fax 45/66-7625. www.solmelia cuba.com. 340 units. CUC$327–CUC$442 double; CUC$208–CUC$458 suite; CUC$400–CUC$651 Grand or Presidential suite. Rates are all-inclusive. MC, V. Children under 18 not allowed. **Amenities:** 5 restaurants; snack bar; 5 bars; 18-hole golf course; small, well-equipped health club; Internet; 4 outdoor pools; room service; smoke-free rooms; nonmotorized watersports equipment. *In room:* A/C, TV, hair dryer, minibar.

Meliá Varadero ★★ This large hotel sits on a rocky outcrop with small sections of fine beach on either side. Seven pyramid-like spokes extend off a massive and lush central atrium lobby. Rooms are large, contemporary, and comfortable. All come with either a king-size bed or two twin beds and a private balcony with a couple of sitting chairs. While the bathrooms aren't exactly small, some are a bit narrow, with the toilet and bidet a bit close to the tub and shower. Almost all of the rooms have some view of the water; the farther out on each spoke you go, the better the view. The hotel is just off the Plaza las Américas complex, so between the in-house arcade and the neighboring mall, you'll have a few more shopping and dining options.

Autopista del Sur Km 7, Carretera Las Morlas, Varadero. (✆ **45/66-7013.** Fax 45/66-7012. www.melia-varadero.com. 490 units. CUC$220–CUC$310 double; CUC$350–CUC$450 suite. Rates are all-inclusive. Children under 2 stay free in parent's room; children 3–12 stay for half-price in parent's room. MC, V. **Amenities:** 4 restaurants; snack bar; 6 bars; babysitting; bikes; children's center and programs; small gym; Internet; Jacuzzi; outdoor nightly show; large outdoor pool; room service; 2 lit outdoor tennis courts; nonmotorized watersports equipment. *In room:* A/C, TV, hair dryer, minibar.

Paradisus Princesa del Mar ★★ The rooms, facilities, and grounds here are all quite grand. There's a sort of modern plantation styling throughout and lovely white parasols and gazebos with wafting curtains surrounding the pool. The best rooms here are the Royal Service suites, which almost qualify as a hotel within the hotel, and are collected together in the Hilltop Hideaway. All of these come with ocean or lagoon views, private Jacuzzis—some on the balcony—and a host of other perks. The rest of the rooms are extremely attractive with handsome linens, and can all be considered junior suites, at the very least. The decor is subdued and elegant. The resort has a wide range of dining options, activities, facilities, and entertainment programs.

Autopista del Sur, Carretera Las Morlas, Varadero. © **45/66-7200.** Fax 45/66-7201. www.solmeliacuba. com. 434 units. CUC$330–CUC$450 double; CUC$472–CUC$530 Royal Service suite. Rates are all-inclusive. MC, V. Children under 18 not allowed. **Amenities:** 7 restaurants; snack bar; 6 bars; dance club; well-equipped health club; Internet; Jacuzzi; 2 large outdoor pools; room service; smoke-free rooms; sauna; spa; 4 lit outdoor tennis courts; watersports equipment. *In room:* A/C, TV, hair dryer, minibar.

Paradisus Varadero ★★★   Set at the eastern end of the peninsula on a gorgeous and remote section of beach, this is the Sol Meliá chain's fanciest hotel in Varadero and part of its high-end brand Paradisus. Most rooms here are large junior suites with sunken sitting rooms that exit onto either a private terrace or balcony. Only a small percentage of the rooms here have an ocean view. A few suites have separate sitting areas and extra half-bathrooms. About half the units come with king-size beds, and the rest come with two twins. The two Garden Villas, set on a point of land just above the ocean, feature separate dining and sitting rooms, a full kitchen, a private lap pool and Jacuzzi, and a private three-story tower with a fabulous lookout. Service is attentive and friendly. Sol Meliá now offers extra services at this hotel through its Royal Service program.

Autopista del Sur Km 15, Rincón Francés, Varadero. © **45/66-8700.** Fax 45/66-8705. www.solmelia cuba.com. 344 units. Royal Service 81 units. CUC$330–CUC$450 double; CUC$583–CUC$646 Royal Service suite; CUC$1,500 Garden Villa. Rates are all-inclusive. Children under 2 stay free in parent's room; children 3–12 stay for 75% of adult rate in parent's room. MC, V. **Amenities:** 7 restaurants; 6 bars; babysitting; snack bar; bikes; cabaret; children's center and programs; health club; Internet; Jacuzzi; 7 outdoor pools; room service; smoke-free rooms; spa; 3 lit outdoor tennis courts; extensive watersports equipment. *In room:* A/C, TV, hair dryer, minibar.

Expensive

Breezes Varadero ★   This adults-only resort is part of the SuperClubs chain, and sits on a beautiful section of beach near the western edge of the Varadero Golf Club. All rooms are either junior suites or suites; my favorites are the juniors housed in a separate three-story building on the eastern edge of the property. Some of the third-floor units here have excellent ocean views, but others are a bit too close to the popular dance club. I'd avoid the Tropical Suites, which have relatively uninviting separate sitting rooms. Overall, there's an exuberant party vibe here. The expansive grounds are filled with tropical trees and flowers, most of which are marked; there's also an orchid garden. All watersports are included.

Carretera Las Américas Km 3, Varadero. © **45/66-7030.** www.superclubscuba.com/brand_breezes/ resort_var. 265 units. CUC$78–CUC$184 double; CUC$83–CUC$189 suite. Rates are all-inclusive. MC, V. Children 13 and under not allowed. **Amenities:** 4 restaurants; snack bar; 8 bars; bikes; dance club; small gym; Internet; outdoor nightly show; large outdoor pool; 2 lit outdoor tennis courts; watersports equipment. *In room:* A/C, TV, hair dryer, minibar.

Iberostar Playa Alameda ★★★   Located on the eastern edge of the peninsula, this is one of the more upscale resorts in Varadero. The rooms here are housed in a series of three-story units spread around the resort's expansive grounds. The rooms are all junior suites, with two twin beds or one king-size bed, separate sitting areas, separate tub and shower units, walk-in closets, and either a balcony or terrace. Thick iron headboards, marble-topped tables, and large Italian tiles lend the rooms a fair amount of class. A broad pedestrian-only avenue leads from the reception and restaurant area to the large complex of pools, which includes a well-designed children's pool and play area. The resort's dance club and nightly cabaret theater are well removed from the rooms, so noise isn't a problem at night. There's an inviting bar with a lookout tower down by the beach. The restaurants, health center, and pool underwent renovations in 2010.

Las Morlas Km 15, Punta Hicacos, Varadero. ✆ **45/66-8822.** Fax 45/66-8833. www.iberostar.com. 391 units. Rates are all-inclusive. MC, V. **Amenities:** 7 restaurants; 2 snack bars; 4 bars; babysitting; bikes; children's programs; concierge; dance club; health club; Jacuzzi; 2 pools; sauna; smoke-free rooms; 2 lit outdoor tennis courts; nonmotorized watersports equipment. *In room:* A/C, TV, hair dryer, minibar.

Tryp Península Varadero ★★★ ☺

This is my first choice for a family resort in Varadero. The facilities are top-notch, and the children's area is a standout, with a large children's pool area that's a virtual amusement park, with several fountains, an island castle, a crocodile slide, and a spouting whale. There's a separate area for toddlers, a large game room, and a beached galleon that serves as the jungle gym playground area. The rooms, housed in a series of attractive three-story Key West–style buildings, are all junior suites, with rattan furniture and a host of amenities. Most have two twin beds, although a small percentage have king-size beds, and there are five suites. The whole complex is tied together by a series of wooden decks and bridges and concrete walkways passing over ponds and skirting a large lagoon. Located toward the far eastern end of the peninsula, the hotel is on a beautiful stretch of beach.

Autopista del Sur Km 17.5, Punta Hicacos, Varadero. ✆ **45/66-8800.** Fax 45/66-8805. www.solmelia cuba.com. 591 units. CUC$230–CUC$300 double; CUC$355-425 suite. Rates are all-inclusive. Children 2 and under stay free in parent's room; children 3–12 stay for half price in parent's room. MC, V. **Amenities:** 4 restaurants; snack bar; 2 bars; babysitting; bikes; children's center and programs; disco; health club; Jacuzzi; 3 outdoor pools; room service; spa; 2 lit outdoor tennis courts; extensive watersports equipment. *In room:* A/C, TV, hair dryer, Internet, minibar.

Moderate

Gran Caribe Club Kawama Resort 🏊

One of the oldest resort hotels in Varadero, the Gran Caribe has, over time, become one of the best midrange all-inclusive options in the area. Built between 1930 and 1947, the original resort still stands as a series of two-story stone buildings built around a central courtyard. Inside, the rooms are modern, with attractive furnishings and good-size balconies, but no ocean views. The massive limestone blocks used to construct the buildings are polished and buffed on the inside, giving the interiors a cool and comforting feel. A host of newer units have less character, but are equally comfortable, and most are either right on or just off the beach; some of these do have ocean views. Part of the price savings here is reflected in the tiny 13-inch television sets and the rather insipid buffet meals. The resort is set on a nice stretch of beach toward the western end of the peninsula.

Av. 1 and Calle 1, Reparto Kawama, Varadero. ✆ **45/61-4416.** Fax 45/66-7334. www.gran-caribe.com. 336 units. CUC$94–CUC$132 double. Rates are all-inclusive. MC, V. **Amenities:** 4 restaurants; 2 snack bars; 4 bars; lounge; dance club; exercise room; Internet (in lobby); sauna; nightly show; 5 pools; nonmotorized watersports equipment. *In room:* A/C, TV, minibar.

Hotel Los Delfines 🏊

This is a pretty little hotel complex and a pretty decent value. The beachfront resort was built in several stages, with a midsize swimming pool at its center. Rooms are standard issue, but they're clean, spacious, and comfortable, and everything is well maintained. For some reason, this 100-plus-room resort almost feels intimate, especially when compared to all the monster all-inclusives that are the rule of the roost here. The buffet restaurant is situated in an attractive stone house that was once a guesthouse belonging to the Bacardí family. The meals are unspectacular, but the hotel is in the heart of Varadero's downtown, close to plenty of dining and entertainment options. Since the rates are so low, you might not mind splurging on a meal out.

Av. 1 btw. Calle 38 and Calle 39, Varadero. © **45/66-7720.** Fax 45/66-7729. www.islazul.cu. 103 units. CUC$100–CUC$120 double, all-inclusive. MC, V. **Amenities:** 2 restaurants; 2 bars; outdoor pool; children's pool. *In room:* A/C, TV, minibar.

Where to Dine

Since most hotels in Varadero are all-inclusive, most folks take the majority of their meals at their hotels. However, it's natural to want some variety when faced with a week or more at one resort, even if it has several dining options.

The restaurants inside **Parque Josone** are dependable, if unspectacular options; of these, the little lakeside Italian restaurant **Dante** (© **45/66-7228**) is my top choice. **Esquina Cuba** (© **45/61-4019**) is an attractive choice in an open-sided *ranchón* with a classic American car inside the restaurant. The generous portion of garlic chicken breast is a good option. **La Mallorca,** Avenida 1 at Calle 62 (© **45/66-77746**), offers a good-value platter of battered shrimp. **La Vicaria,** Avenida 1 at Calle 37 (© **45/61-4721**), is a very popular spot for light, inexpensive bites, in a pleasant open-air setting. **Coppelia** is a good option located in the Centro Comercial Hicacos (Parque del 8000 Taquillas). The cute blue-and-yellow **Ranchón Cielo-Mar,** next to the municipal museum, is a good spot for a drink with a view. If you'd like to mingle with the locals, try **Cafeteria El Caribeño,** Avenida 1 between Calle 30 and 31.

EXPENSIVE

Las Américas ★ INTERNATIONAL   Arguably the most elegant restaurant in town is found at the most exclusive address in town, occupying a couple of ground-floor rooms and the oceanfront veranda of the Mansión Xanadú. The best seats are those on this veranda, at heavy wooden tables set with heavy china. The food is old-school French and Continental fare, adequately done, but no more. Service is semi-formal and inattentive at times. There's a good, fairly priced wine list. Several hotels offer discount coupons here, so be sure to ask your concierge.

At the Mansión Xanadú, Carretera Las Américas Km 8.5. © **45/66-7388.** Reservations required. Main courses CUC$12–CUC$45. MC, V. Daily noon–4pm and 7–10:30pm.

MODERATE

Casa de Al ★ 🏠 CRIOLLAN/SEAFOOD   Located on a pristine stretch of beach, this stone and wood house is the most atmospheric place to dine in Varadero. Al Capone lived here from 1928–29 and used it as a base to run black market rum from Cárdenas to the U.S. A secret tunnel lies behind a locked door. The management's sense of humor is evident: "mafiosa soup," "Godfather salad," and "lucky Luciano" filet mignon are featured on the menu. There's also "high explosive pudding" (a bread-and-butter concoction) and "cold-blood ice cream." The "Don shrimp," in garlic and butter, is delicious. With white tablecloths and good service, this is a wonderful option for a leisurely and or romantic lunch with vistas of the sapphire sea through the arches.

Av Kawama near Club Kawama. © **45/66-8018.** No credit cards. Main courses CUC$7–CUC$19. Daily 10am–10pm.

Mesón del Quijote ♦ SPANISH/SEAFOOD Located on a small hillside between the Autopista and the beach resorts, the dining room of this popular restaurant is in a small building set beside the turret of a three-story imitation medieval castle. There are plenty of windows to enjoy the limited views afforded from its modest perch. I found the paella to be disappointing, but the seafood and lobster are fresh and well prepared. If you don't order one of the many lobster entrees, try the fresh fish filet with olive oil. There's pork in brandy sauce and chicken breast in pepper sauce for those not inclined toward fish dishes.

Carretera Las Américas, Reparto La Torre. ✆ **45/66-7796.** Reservations recommended. Main courses CUC$6.75–CUC$25. MC, V. Daily noon–11pm.

Mi Casita ★ CRIOLLAN/SEAFOOD Antique clocks, religious statues, enormous vases, and glass chandeliers are artfully arranged in this new restaurant. Sit on French chairs at tables laid with Italian cutlery and lace tablecloths and dine on grilled lobster or *criolla* cuisine. A consommé is served to all guests. If you don't opt for the seafood, I recommend the *ropa vieja y cerdo* (a mix of pork and sautéed, shredded beef, onions, and peppers), accompanied by salted potatoes in wine and salad. This is still an atmospheric place to eat (although the white plastic window frames seriously detract) and the wait staff is very friendly.

Av. 1 and Calle 36. ✆ **45/61-2545.** Main courses CUC$2–CUC$25. MC, V. Daily noon–10:45pm.

INEXPENSIVE

El Criollo ★ CRIOLLAN This popular place is probably your best bet for straight-ahead Cuban cuisine in Varadero. The restaurant is housed in an old building that re-creates the vibe of a typical Cuban country home. You'll definitely want a table on the large, open-air veranda under a gently sloping red-tile roof. Simple roast chicken and pork dishes are reasonably priced and well prepared. Even the lobster dishes are a good value here. This restaurant is not to be confused with El Bodegon Criolla, a weak imitation of Havana's signature La Bodeguita del Medio.

Av. 1 and Calle 18. ✆ **45/61-4794.** Reservations recommended. Main courses CUC$4–CUC$18. No credit cards. Daily noon–10:45pm.

Varadero After Dark

Almost every hotel here has some form of nightly entertainment, usually a Broadway theater review or local cabaret-style show. These can vary from sadly comic to totally professional. Most give way to a dance party. By far, the biggest and best cabaret show, the **Tropicana Matanzas** ★★, is located about 20 minutes away on the outskirts of Matanzas; see "Matanzas After Dark," earlier in this chapter for details. Other cabaret options include the **Cabaret Continental** at Varadero Internacional (✆ **45/66-7038;** cover CUC$25); the **Mambo Club** at Gran Hotel, Carretera Las Morlas Km 14 (✆ **45/66-8565;** cover CUC$10); and the **Palacio de La Rumba** at the Hotel Bella Costa, Avenida Las Américas (✆ **45/66-8210;** cover CUC$10).

The new Egrem-run **Casa de la Música,** Avenida Playa between Calle 42 and 43 (✆ **45/66-7568**), kicks off at 10:30pm with different shows and turns into a disco afterward. Admission is CUC$10. It's open Tuesday to Sunday.

Perhaps my favorite place for a show is the new **La Comparsita** ★★, Calle 60 and Avenida 3 (✆ **45/66-7415**), which is a lovely open-air space that evokes the feel of a colonial-era courtyard. There are good sightlines from all the tables here and an excellent nightly show from 10:30pm with wide-ranging Cuban music and dance styles. Admission is CUC$3. The place also has a happening bar upstairs.

Cueva del Pirata, Autopista Sur Km 11 (☎ **45/66-7751**), is a midsize cave that has been converted into a popular cabaret and dance club. Lights create eerie shadows among the stalactites. The cabaret show begins around 10:30pm from Monday to Saturday and has a pronounced Afro-Cuban emphasis. It's followed by dancing to either a live band or a DJ. Admission is CUC$10.

The **Mirador,** atop the Mansión Xanadú (☎ **45/66-8482**), is a good spot for a quiet drink with a nice view.

A Side Trip to Cardenas

Located 18km (11 miles) southeast of Varadero, Cárdenas is a small, quiet city with beautiful colonial-era architecture and a timeless quality. Horse-drawn carriages and bicycles far outnumber cars on the streets here. Cárdenas is known as Cuba's "Ciudad Bandera" (Flag City), as it was here, in 1850, that the national flag was first flown. Because it's so close to Varadero, Cárdenas is popular—we'd say almost overrun—with day tours.

The city center is quite compact, and you can easily see most of the sights in a couple of hours while strolling around. There are several small squares and parks in Cárdenas. The diminutive **Parque Colón,** Avenida Céspedes, between Calles 8 and 9, has an important statue of Christopher Columbus dating from 1862. Fronting it is the beautiful **Catedral de la Concepción Inmaculada ★**, which is famous for its stained glass. In another main park, **Parque Echeverría,** sits the **Museo Casa Natal José Antonio Echeverría,** Calle Jenes 560, between Calzada and Coronel Verdugo (☎ **45/52-4145;** Tues–Sat 9am–6pm, Sun 9am–1pm; admission CUC$1. This beautiful old home features tributes to various independence fighters and revolutionary heroes, including the museum's namesake, a murdered revolutionary student hero who was born here in 1932. The town's main market, **Plaza Molokoff,** Calle 12 and Avenida 3, is housed in an interesting two-story, L-shaped iron building, topped with a large dome. Out by the water's edge is the **Arrechabala Rum Factory,** where the brand Havana Club was born and where present-day Varadero and Buccanero rums are made. Tours of the factory are given daily between 9am and 4pm; admission is CUC$2.

Cárdenas is the birthplace and home of Elián Gonzalez, the little boy who became the center of an international custody dispute in late 1999 when he washed up on the shores of Miami after his mother died at sea. While you're unlikely to see Elián, almost anyone in town will point out his humble home. There's always at least one guard out front. The **Museo Batalla de Ideas (Museum of the Ideological Battle)**, Calle Vives 523 at the corner of Coronel Verdugo (☎ **45/52-3990**), is housed in a beautifully restored old building, and features exhibits honoring the child celebrity, alongside numerous other displays documenting Cuba's revolutionary battles. The centerpiece here is a statue of a young Cuban boy, dressed in the uniform of the Young Pioneers, tossing away a Superman doll. The museum is housed in a beautifully restored old firehouse. Admission is CUC$1, and a guided tour is CUC$2. It will cost you an additional CUC$5 to take photos and CUC$15 to take videos. Open Monday to Saturday, from 9am to 6pm and Sunday 9am to 1pm.

Very few travelers stay in Cárdenas, and there are currently no hotels or official *casas particulares* accepting foreign tourists in the city, although that may change. There's regular public bus service between Varadero and Cárdenas, but it's geared primarily to commuting Cuban workers. A taxi from Varadero to Cárdenas costs around CUC$15–CUC$20.

THE ZAPATA PENINSULA & PLAYA GIRÓN ★

202km (126 miles) SE of Havana; 194km (121 miles) S of Varadero

The Zapata Peninsula juts off the southern coast of Matanzas province, and is surrounded by stunning colorful waters. The peninsula itself is almost entirely uninhabited; most of it is protected as part of the **Parque Nacional Ciénaga de Zapata (Zapata Swamp National Park)** ★, a haven for bird-watchers and naturalists. The eastern edge of the peninsula is defined by the Bahía de Cochinos (Bay of Pigs), the site of the failed 1961 U.S.-backed invasion of Cuba. The Bay of Pigs, and Playa Girón in particular, is a sort of national shrine to this stunning David-over-Goliath victory. Just off the shore, all along the Bay of Pigs and toward the east, the coast drops off steeply for 305km (1,000 ft.) or more, making this a true haven for scuba divers and snorkelers. The waters near Playa Girón—shades of sapphire, aquamarine and lapis lazuli—evoke a picture-perfect postcard of paradise.

Note: Bring plenty of mosquito repellent. Since this is an area of vast swampland, mosquitoes can be fierce, particularly if there's no wind. I also pack lightweight, long-sleeved shirts and pants.

Essentials

GETTING THERE   The nearest **airport** is in Varadero; see "Varadero," earlier in this chapter, for complete details. There is no dependable **public transportation** to this area, although most tour agencies in Havana and Varadero offer trips here.

The Zapata Peninsula and the beaches of Playa Larga and Playa Girón are connected to the Autopista Nacional—and each other—by a well-maintained two-lane highway. If you're coming **by car,** get off the highway at the exit for Australia and Jagüey Grande, and head south for 17km (11 miles) to Boca de Guamá. From there, it's another 13km (8 miles) to Playa Larga, and 34km (21 miles) to Playa Girón. If you arrive at Jagüey Grande on the Víazul bus, drop in at the **Cubanacán** office (© **45/91-3224**) at the junction inside the restaurant (open from 8am to 8pm) to arrange a local taxi or, if you are staying in a *casa particular*, arrange a pick-up with them beforehand. A taxi to Playa Larga is CUC$20 and to Playa Girón, CUC$30.

GETTING AROUND   Public transportation is very sporadic and unreliable in this area. Most visitors either have their own rental car or come on a guided tour. **Cubacar** is based at both Playa Larga and Playa Girón (© **45/98-4126**), so if you end up here without wheels, you can easily rent some to get around. (There's a gas station at Boca de Guamá and close to Jagüey Grande.) Local taxis also can be hired at either of the hotels listed below. **Cubataxi** (© **45/98-4199**) is based at Playa Girón. The new **Guamá Bus Tour** costs CUC$3 and runs between Playa Girón and Boca de Guamá, departing twice a day in each direction (departs Playa Girón at 9am and 2pm; departs Boca de Guamá at 10:30am and 3:30pm).

ORIENTATION   Heading south from the highway, you come first to Boca de Guamá. Continuing on, the road hits the head of the bay at Playa Larga and then follows the coast, in a southeasterly direction to Playa Girón. There are small communities in both Playa Larga and Playa Girón, but aside from the resorts, restaurants, and few attractions, there's little of interest to travelers along the road. Look out for the tiny palm-studded island of Cayo Piedra that can be seen offshore near Playa Girón—it's Fidel's favorite (and private) holiday home.

Battle Marks

As you walk along the beaches of Playa Girón and Playa Larga, and drive the coastal road connecting them, you will notice tall concrete monuments marking the spots where a Cuban soldier died in the fighting. You may also notice many low-lying concrete machine gun nests, with their open rears for easy entry and thin front slits for wide-angle aiming. Many of these machine gun nests have been destroyed by recent hurricanes, but if you spot one, feel free to try it on for size—it makes a unique photo opportunity.

What to See & Do

Most organized tours and independent travelers make a stop at **Boca de Guamá** (© 45/91-5551), a contrived tourist attraction, built as a re-creation of a Native American village on a series of small islands at the center of the large **Laguna del Tesoro (Treasure Lake)**. Boat tours of the lake and canals (CUC$12 for 1 hr between 9am and 4pm) are available. On one small island in the middle of the lake, you'll be able to walk among 32 life-size figures of Taíno Indians sculpted by the late Cuban artist Rita Longa. You can also dine on crocodile meat (CUC$15) at **El Colibrí,** a decent little tourist restaurant here. You can stay at the **Guamá Hotel** (© 45/95-9100; www.hotelescubanacan.com; CUC$42–CUC$58 double) here (hotel guests need to pay CUC$12 for the round-trip boat ride). The hotel features a series of individual circular bungalows built on stilts over the lagoons. The rooms are spartan, but the setting is pleasant and there's a pool.

At the entrance to Boca de Guamá, you'll find a roadside mini-mall of shops and a small zoo with crocodiles, *jutías* (an endemic ratlike creatures), and other animals (open 9:30am–5pm daily; CUC$5). Just down the road from there, you'll find a much more authentic and formidable breeding and conservation crocodile farm: the **Criadero de Cocodrilos** (© 45/91-5562). If you've never seen a crocodile up close, you will be awed by the size, power, and prehistoric aspect of these impressive reptiles. Admission is CUC$5 (open from 8am–6pm daily) and includes a brief guided tour. A series of walkways will carry you past numerous pens of around 4,000 crocs of all ages and sizes. You can't exactly pick out your dinner, but it doesn't take much imagination to figure out where all the crocodile meat is coming from—at least you know it's fresh.

If you go to Playa Girón, it's worth taking a quick tour of the little **Museo Playa Girón** (© 45/98-4122). Two rooms inside this simple building contain a series of photos, relics, and a written history detailing the Bay of Pigs invasion and battles, as well as some local history. A 15-minute documentary video (in Spanish) is shown throughout the day, and outside you can see tanks, heavy artillery, and a U.S. plane. The museum is open daily from 8am to 5pm; admission is CUC$2 for adults. It is an additional CUC$3 for a guide, CUC$1to see the documentary, CUC$1 to take photos and CUC$5 to film. Unfortunately, the written explanations are in Spanish only.

Just south of Jagüey Grande is the community of Central Australia where you'll find a decommissioned sugar factory and the **Museo Memorial Comandancia de la FAR** (© 45/91-2504). It was Fidel Castro's command post during the 1961 Bay of Pigs invasion. It's open Tuesday to Sunday 9am–5pm, and costs CUC$1.

the BAY OF PIGS

On April 16, 1961, an invasion force of 1,400 Cuban exiles, trained and backed by the United States, landed at several beach points along the Bay of Pigs in an ill-fated attempt to overthrow the Castro regime. They were quickly met by Cuban forces, led by Fidel Castro himself, and soon defeated. Fighting lasted less than 72 hours. Though they were entirely trained and supported—and even escorted—by the U.S. military and CIA, the invaders were left to fight on their own. President Kennedy was reluctant to commit any direct U.S. forces to the fight. The lack of air support and several serious tactical blunders contributed to the rout. The battle took the lives of some 160 Cubans and around 120 mercenary fighters. Some 1,195 of the invading troops were captured, and most of them were released 20 months later in a bartered exchange with the U.S. government for food, medical supplies, and hospital equipment. Today, the Bay of Pigs continues to be a source of great pride to Cuba's communist government and supporters, and an equally bitter pill for anti-Castro exiles and opponents.

OUTDOOR ACTIVITIES

You'll need a permit to enter **Zapata Swamp National Park**. The park station and entrance (© 45/98-7249; pnacionalcz@enet.cu) is located just north of Hotel Playa Larga. It is open daily from 8am–4pm. The permit costs CUC$10 per person, a guide costs extra, depending on the length and type of excursion. Trips include **Refugio de Fauna Bermejas, Las Salinas, Río Hatiguanico, La Turba** and **Sendero espeleolacustre.** The state-run tour center has naturalist, birding, and fishing guides familiar with this area; English, French, German and Russian is spoken. In addition, all of the hotels and tour agencies in the area can arrange bird-watching excursions and fishing trips with local guides. You can also take a 7-hour kayaking trip through the swamplands of the Quinto Canal with Cubanacán (© 45/91-3224; comercial@peninsula.cyt.cu).

BIRD-WATCHING ★★★   The Zapata Peninsula is probably Cuba's richest bird-watching destination. Some 18 of Cuba's 21 endemic bird species can be spotted here, as well as large flocks of resident waterfowl and seasonal migrants. The Zapata wren, Zapata sparrow, and Zapata rail are just some of the endemic species. Hurricane Michelle flattened much of the forest here, and it's currently much harder to spot some species, including the bee hummingbird, (the world's smallest bird) which in the past were quite common. Several trails through and around the national park are available to birders. A local guide we recommend is **Orestes Martínez Garcías** (El Chino; © 45/98-7373 or 52/53-9004; chino.zapata@gmail.com), who has more than 30 years experience as an ornithological guide; he charges a minimum of CUC$12 for two hours.

FISHING ★★★   Fishing for bass, trout, tilapia, tarpon, permit, bonefish, and the bizarre looking *manjaurí* (alligator gar, a type of fish) is excellent in this area. Prime fishing sites include the saltwater flats and mangroves of **Las Salinas de Brito** on the eastern edge of the peninsula, the **Hatiguanico River** deep within the national park, and the lagoons of **Boca de Guamá.** Rates range from CUC$25 to CUC$50 per person for a simple outing, and from CUC$200 to CUC$500 per day for a boat, guide, tackle, and lunch for up to three people. Ask at your hotel or any tour agency for details.

SCUBA DIVING & SNORKELING ★★   The waters off the coast between Playa Larga and Playa Girón offer some of Cuba's best scuba diving; there are 20 immersion points in the area, six cenotes, and four sunken fishing boats to explore. A steep wall, rich in coral and sponges, plunges to depths of over 300m (984 ft.). There are numerous caves to explore and visibility is typically excellent. In many cases, the drop-off is within 90 to 180m (295–591 ft.) off shore. The dive shops at both of the hotels here typically load people and gear into small buses or trucks and drive to one of numerous put-in points all along the shoreline. The dive shops will also collect guests from the *casas particulares*. Both **Hotel Playa Girón** and **Hotel Playa Larga** have full-service dive facilities on-site and offer a full menu of multiday dive packages. The **Octopus Diving Center** also operates at Playa Larga. Contact Francisco Veulens at **Naútica** (✆ **45/98-7284**) or Pepe at **Hotel Playa Girón** (buzo@hpgiron.co.cu) for more diving information. A one-tank dive costs CUC$25, a cenote dive costs CUC$40, and an open water course costs CUC$365, including equipment and transport. Snorkeling, with transport and equipment (available from the dive centers), costs CUC$5 per day or CUC$3 for 1 hour. There is talk of expanding the maritime national park to include a section of the sea beyond—watch this space.

Along the coastal road between Playa Larga and Playa Girón is the **Cueva de los Peces**, a lovely cenote where visitors can dive and snorkel (entrance is CUC$1). Near Playa Girón is the **Punta Perdiz,** a small beach area with some good snorkeling and a restaurant. At **Caleta Buena** ★, part of the Hotel Playa Girón, there is good snorkeling, a dive center, and a beach with chaise lounges; wear sandals because you'll have to cross the *dientes del perro* (dog's teeth rocks) to access the water. Entrance costs CUC$12, which includes lunch and drinks (open from 9:30am–5pm). See also Caleta Buena, p. 180.

Where to Stay & Dine

Most visitors to this area take all their meals at their hotels. The few available alternatives include the restaurant at Boca de Guamá, and a couple of simple state-run roadside restaurants geared to tourists between Playa Larga and Playa Girón. The best of these is the **Cueva de los Peces,** Carretera Playa Larga a Girón Km 18 (✆ **45/98-4183**), with good seafood and *criolla* cuisine. There is a handful of *casas particulares* in both Playa Larga and Playa Girón. One of the best *casas particulares* in the country, with incredible food, is **Casa Luís and Marley** ★★, Carretera a Cienfuegos at Carretera a Playa Larga, Playa Girón (✆ **45/98-4258;** casa@hpgiron. co.cu). Marked by cream-and-blue columns topped with lions, this is a modern *casa* with a front porch, back garden, two comfortable and well-equipped rooms, and ample parking space. The family is very friendly and offers some of the best food and service the country. **Casa Enrique Rivas Fente,** Caletón, Playa Larga (✆ **45/98-7425**), is a very professionally run *casa* with excellent home-cooked food, two rooms that share a bathroom, and a large living room. **Casa Ernesto Delgado Chirino,** Caletón, Playa Larga (✆ **45/98-7278;** ernestodccz@yahoo.es), has a small apartment with a separate entrance at the back of the house with a double and single bed and a kitchenette with fridge. There's no beach in front of this house but the little fishing boats bob outside.

Hotel Playa Girón   Originally designed and built as a residential community, this place is now a midsize all-inclusive resort. The rooms are housed in a series of one-, two-, and three-bedroom ranch bungalows and duplexes. Recent remodeling has greatly improved the furnishings and decor here, but rooms still feel a bit lackluster. Still, this place is really only for hard-core divers or bird-watchers, because if you're looking for a week of sun and fun at an all-inclusive, Cuba has many more appealing options. The beach is acceptable here and the water is lovely but the view is obscured by a very ugly large breakwater. The best feature is the resort's **Caleta Buena ★**, a recreation area based around a series of natural pools in the coral and rock, located about 8km (5 miles) from the hotel. There's a grill restaurant, some sailboats, paddleboats, and windsurfers.

Playa Girón, Montemar Natural Park, Matanzas province. ✆ **45/98-4110.** www.hotelescubanacan.com. 282 units. CUC$52–CUC$65 double. Rates are all-inclusive. MC, V. **Amenities:** 2 restaurants; snack bar; 2 bars; bikes; dance club; outdoor pool. *In room:* A/C, TV.

Hotel Playa Larga   The entire complex here feels rather depressing, despite ongoing efforts to spruce things up. The problem, as far as I'm concerned, is the inherently desultory Soviet-era architecture, but the paint job—peach melba and duck-egg blue—has greatly improved the aesthetics of this very large complex. Some rooms are compact with modern furnishings; others are casitas that feature two bedrooms adjoined by a small sitting area. There is a mix of bed sizes across all the accommodations. The small patch of beach here is acceptable with a lively atmosphere, but it doesn't compare to other premier beaches. This place is best for serious divers and bird-watchers, and even they would probably do better at the Hotel Playa Girón (see above). Non-guests can use the pool for CUC$6.

Playa Larga, Montemar Natural Park, Matanzas province. ✆/fax **45/98-7294.** www.hotelescubanacan. com. 68 units. CUC$48–CUC$64 double. Rates include breakfast. MC, V. **Amenities:** Restaurant; snack bar; 2 bars; dive center; Internet (CUC$10 per hour); outdoor pool; 1 outdoor tennis courts; watersports equipment rental. *In room:* A/C, TV.

TRINIDAD & CENTRAL CUBA

C entral Cuba is an area rich in both historical and natural attractions. It is home to several wonderful colonial-era cities, as well as isolated and pristine beaches. Heading east from Matanzas into Cuba's central heartland, you first hit Villa Clara province, which is devoted largely to sugar cane, citrus, tobacco farming, and cattle ranching. The provincial capital, Santa Clara, a lively university town, is often called Che Guevara's City and features an impressive monument and plaza dedicated to the fallen revolutionary. To the north of Santa Clara lie the tiny and well-preserved colonial-era city of Remedios and the stunningly beautiful beach resort destination of la Cayería del Norte.

Abutting Villa Clara to the south is Cienfuegos province. The city of Cienfuegos is affectionately known as *La Perla del Sur* (The Southern Pearl). Cienfuegos is a busy port city with a pretty, colonial-era center and the country's second-longest seaside promenade, or Malecón. Cienfuegos is connected to Trinidad by a pretty coastal highway, and is definitely worth a visit on a loop trip around the region.

The province of Sancti Spíritus is the only one in Cuba to count two of the original seven *villas* (towns) in Cuba among its offerings. The preserved colonial city **Trinidad,** tucked in the southwest corner of the province, is the highlight of a visit to the central section of the country, or all of Cuba for that matter. The provincial capital, **Sancti Spíritus,** isn't a great deal larger than Trinidad, and though it is more ramshackle and rough around the edges, lacking Trinidad's remarkable collection of perfectly preserved architecture, it is still worth a visit to see a couple of its colonial highlights.

SANTA CLARA ★

270km (168 miles) E of Havana

Santa Clara was founded in 1689 by settlers from Remedios looking for a site inland that would be less vulnerable to pirate attack. Heading east from Havana, Santa Clara marks the start of Cuba's central region. The city is strategically located on the island's spine, right on the main highway and train lines, and is the capital of Villa Clara province. Santa Clara is home to one of Cuba's principal colleges, la Universidad Central de las Villas (Las Villas Central University), and it played an important role in both the independence and revolutionary wars. Thanks to the latter, Santa Clara is known as Che Guevara's City. Today, it is also home to several industrial factories, the legacy of Guevara's tenure as Minister of Industry and his special relationship with this city. In addition to being an interesting destination in its own right, Santa Clara serves as the gateway to the colonial treasure of **Remedios ★★★** and the up-and-coming beaches of **la Cayería del Norte (the Northern Cays) ★★★**.

Essentials

GETTING THERE

BY PLANE Santa Clara's **Abel Santamaría Airport** (✆ **42/21-4402;** airport code SNU) accepts both national and international flights. The latter are predominantly international charter flights bringing tourists on package tours to la Cayería del Norte.

BY BUS Víazul (✆ **7/881-1413** in Havana, or **42/22-2523** in Santa Clara; www.viazul.com) travels daily to Santa Clara on the Havana–Santiago de Cuba, Varadero-Trinidad, and Havana-Holguín lines. From Havana, the bus departs at 9:30am, 3pm, and 10pm arriving at 2:10pm, 7:10pm, and 2:05am respectively; the fare is CUC$18. From Santiago, departure times are 3:15pm and 10pm, arriving at 3:20am and 8:30am respectively; the fare is CUC$33. From Varadero to Trinidad, the bus leaves at 8:15am and arrives at 11:30am; the fare is CUC$11. From Trinidad to Varadero, the bus departs at 2:50pm and arrives at 5:45pm, costing CUC$8. From Holguín to Havana, the bus departs at 9:20am and arrives at Santa Clara at 5:50pm, costing CUC$27. From Havana to Holguin, the bus departs at 9:20am and arrives at 12:40am, costing CUC$18. From Santiago to Varadero the bus departs at 10:35pm and arrives in Santa Clara at 7:40am, costing CUC$38. The main **bus station** is on the western edge of town, on the Carretera Central, between Independencia and Oquiendo.

BY CAR Santa Clara sits right on the Carretera Central, and just off the Autopista Nacional, 270km (168 miles) east of Havana. It's a straight shot on the highway and generally takes about 3½ hours.

⚠ AUTOPISTA scam

Many visitors to Cuba rent a car in Havana and set off looking for the Autopista A1. However, the Autopista isn't marked or easily identifiable, so some visitors spend hours negotiating their way out of the city, leaving themselves as easy targets for scam artists. Some wily Cubans flag tourist cars down (identifiable by the T-branded red license plate) and offer to escort them to the correct turn off. One report Frommer's received suggested that the Cubans did escort the tourists to the right exit, but then demanded CUC$40 for their troubles. Another report suggested that Cubans returned the travelers to the same (wrong) spot but still demanded CUC$20. We have also heard reports that some Cubans are stealing signposts to divert and charge tourists. To avoid the scam, drive down the road you believe is the Autopista and then ask somebody if you're on the right road. If you are on the wrong road, it is easy to make a safe U-turn.

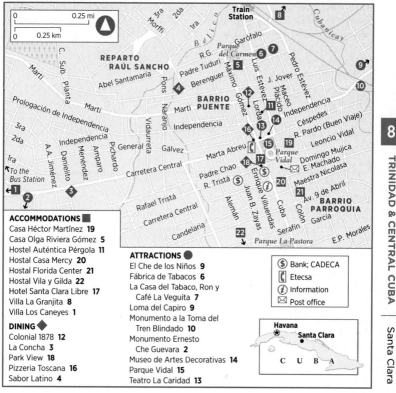

Santa Clara

ACCOMMODATIONS ■
Casa Héctor Martínez **19**
Casa Olga Riviera Gómez **5**
Hostel Auténtica Pérgola **11**
Hostal Casa Mercy **20**
Hostal Florida Center **21**
Hostal Vila y Gilda **22**
Hotel Santa Clara Libre **17**
Villa La Granjita **8**
Villa Los Caneyes **1**

DINING ◆
Colonial 1878 **12**
La Concha **3**
Park View **18**
Pizzeria Toscana **16**
Sabor Latino **4**

ATTRACTIONS ●
El Che de los Niños **9**
Fábrica de Tabacos **6**
La Casa del Tabaco, Ron y
   Café La Veguita **7**
Loma del Capiro **9**
Monumento a la Toma del
   Tren Blindado **10**
Monumento Ernesto
   Che Guevara **2**
Museo de Artes Decorativas **14**
Parque Vidal **15**
Teatro La Caridad **13**

$ Bank; CADECA
C Etecsa
ⓘ Information
✉ Post office

Havana
★
Santa Clara
C U B A

GETTING AROUND

Taxis are plentiful and inexpensive in Santa Clara. If you can't find one on the street or if your hotel can't hook you up, call **Cubataxi** (✆ **42/22-2555**) or hop on a horse and carriage or *tuk-tuk* (bicycle or motorbike with a carriage).

Car-rental agencies in Santa Clara include **Havanautos** (✆ **42/21-8177**), **Cubacar** (✆ **42/20-2040**), **Micar** (✆ **42/20-4570**), and **Rex** (✆ **42/22-2244**). Mopeds are available from Havanautos.

ORIENTATION

Parque Vidal, also called Plaza Mayor, is Santa Clara's center. In addition to having the greatest concentration of colonial-era buildings, most of the city's banks, businesses, and tourism operators are based within a 2-block radius of the park. The city is ringed by a beltway, or *Circunvalación.*

Infotur can be found at Calle Cuba 68 between Candelaria and E. Machado (✆ **42/22-7557**). **Cubanacán,** Colón 101 corner of Maestra Nicolasa (✆ **42/20-5189**), **Cubatur,** Marta Abreu 10, between Máximo Gómez y Villuendas (✆ **42/20-8980**), **Havantur,** Máximo Gómez between Independencia and Alfredo Barreras (✆ **42/20-4001**), and **Paradiso,** Independencia and L. Estevez (✆ **42/20-1354**), can supply you with information and arrange a wide range of tour and onward-travel options. There are a couple of banks and a **CADECA** branch near the Parque Vidal.

For medical emergencies, head to the **Hospital Arnaldo Milian (Hospital Nuevo,** ✆ **42/27-0069)** on Circunvalación and Av 26 de Julio. **Farmacia Internacional** (✆ **42/20-8069)**, Colón 106 between 9 de Abril and M. Nicolasa. Ring 104 for emergency.

Internet is at the ETECSA building, Martha Abreu and Villuendas and is open daily from 8:30am to 7pm.

What to See & Do

Santa Clara is a great town to walk around. Thanks to the university here, the city has a bit of a typical college-town vibe. The heart of the city is the central **Parque Vidal.** The double-wide streets ringing the park are pedestrian-only and often crowded with locals and lovers strolling in leisurely circles. There's a separate 5-block-long pedestrian-only mall (the Boulevard), a block behind the **Teatro La Caridad** (✆ **42/20-5548),** where you'll find a series of shops and restaurants aimed at travelers and dollar-spending Cubans. The active and ornate 19th-century theater, modeled after the Paris Opera, often features concerts and shows, and is worth a quick tour (CUC$1) during the day. It was restored recently; check out the *cartelera* or visit the box office for a schedule.

The biggest attraction in town is the **Monumento Ernesto Che Guevara ★**, Plaza de la Revolución Che Guevara (✆ **42/20-5878),** which features a huge sculpture of the revolutionary hero, overlooking a vast plaza where massive demonstrations and music concerts are often held. Underneath the statue is a museum with exhibits detailing the life and exploits of "El Che" and a separate mausoleum holding Guevara's remains, as well as tombstones (and some of the remains) of 37 other revolutionary fighters killed alongside Guevara in Bolivia. This place is deeply revered by most Cubans, so don't joke or take it lightly. The monument is located on the western outskirts of the city and is open Tuesday through Sunday from 9am to 5:30pm; no cameras or video cameras are allowed.

Behind the mausoleum is a new cemetery where the remains of those who fought with Che in the 8th column from the Sierra Maestra up to Santa Clara are interred. Interestingly, the graves of those comrades who have yet to die have already been erected.

Another popular revolutionary landmark is the **Monumento a la Toma del Tren Blindado (Armored Train Monument)** at Carretera Camajuani and the train line. It's a small park built around the spot where Che Guevara and his soldiers derailed an armored train during the critical battles for control of Santa Clara in 1958. In addition to the five cars and some sculptures, there's a tiny museum in this pleasant open-air park. The museum is open Monday to Saturday from 9am to 5:30pm; admission is CUC$1. About 450 meters (1,476 feet) northeast past the monument, on Ave. de la Liberación or Carretera de Camajuani, is **El Che de los Niños,** a bronze statue by Casto Solano that's located in front of the building that was once Che's barracks during the capture of Santa Clara; today this building is the seat of the Provincial Committee of the Cuban Communist Party. If you continue another 500 meters (1,640 feet) northeast and make a right turn at a gas station, you'll see signs to the **Loma del Capiro,** a group of three small peaks, where the first skirmish between Che's troops and Batista's troops took place on the December 29, 1958; there is a monument on the summit.

CHE GUEVARA

Perhaps no one person, not even Fidel Castro, is so clearly representative of the Latin American revolutionary movement in both image and deed as Ernesto "Che" Guevara. In broad terms, Cubans respect and fear Castro, but they love Che Guevara. Fidel gave the Revolution its brains and brawn, but Che gave it sex appeal.

Born June 14, 1928, in Rosario, Argentina, to a middle-class family, he set off on a motorcycle trip through the Americas in 1953, having just graduated with a medical degree. (For a good glimpse into this period of his life, see the 2004 film *The Motorcycle Diaries*.) In 1954, he got caught in the crossfire of the CIA-supported overthrow of Guatemala's democratically elected leftist president Jacobo Arbénz. Exiled to Mexico in the aftermath of the coup, he met fellow exile Fidel Alejandro Castro Ruz. The two hit it off immediately, and soon, Guevara was a principal figure in the Cuban revolutionary struggle.

Despite chronic asthma and an overall weak constitution, Guevara was famous for his gritty work ethic and dogged determination. Guevara led the decisive December 1958 battles to seize Santa Clara, and was later rewarded with several high posts in the new revolutionary government, including Minister of Industry and president of the National Bank. As the story goes, Fidel Castro, in need of someone to head up the National Bank said, "We need a good economist." Hearing him incorrectly, Guevara said, "I'm a good communist." Despite the misunderstanding, he was given the post. However, Guevara soon tired of the bureaucratic life of politics and government, and embarked on a crusade to spread the Revolution and liberate the rest of the world. A falling-out with Castro, never fully clarified, may have also been behind his renewed revolutionary wanderings.

In 1966, after a brief foray in the Congo, Guevara went to Bolivia—namesake of Simón Bolívar, an early Latin American freedom fighter and Pan-American nationalist—and began organizing a guerilla army. However, the United States military and CIA were already on his trail, and on October 8, 1967, Guevara was caught by a unit of the Bolivian army, aided by U.S. "advisors." After consultations with Washington, the injured Guevara was summarily executed in the remote highlands of Bolivia.

Santa Clara has an excellent **Fábrica de Tabacos** ★ at Calle Maceo 181 (© **42/20-2211**). The factory occupies a full city block and produces high-quality Montecristo, Partagas, Romeo y Julieta, Punch, and Robaina cigars. It's open Monday through Friday from 9 to 11am and 1 to 3pm. A 20-minute guided tour costs CUC$4 per person, but the ticket can only be bought at one of the three principal tour agencies in town (see "Orientation," above). Across the street, there's a well-stocked shop, **La Casa del Tabaco, Ron y Café La Veguita** ★, Maceo 176-A (© **42/20-8952**). The cigar sommelier here, Marilín Morales Bauta, is quite charming and one of the premier experts in the field. It is open Monday to Saturday from 9am to 5pm.

The **Museo de Artes Decorativas,** Parque Vidal (© **42/20-5368**), is in an 18th-century house whose last owner was named Clara Cartas. The house is stuffed full of Baccarat crystal and chandeliers, including a "spaghetti" chandelier. Its other unusual items include a rocking chair with a carved protruding face at its tip to stop the nanny from falling asleep and a wall plate imprinted with the image of the

Crystal Palace in London. It is open Monday to Thursday 9am to 6pm, Friday 1 to 10pm, and Sunday 6 to 10pm. Admission is CUC$2.

Where to Stay

There are scores of *casas particulares* (private rooms for rent) in Santa Clara. Most are within a block or two of either the Parque Vidal or the Plaza del Carmen. Recommended *casas particulares* in Santa Clara include: **Hostal Florida Center** ★★ Calle Maestra Nicolasa (Candelaria) 56, between Colón and Maceo (☎ **42/20-8161;** ar3840@enet.cu), a gorgeous 1876 colonial house full of interesting historic furniture and blessed with a flourishing garden and a welcoming host, Angel—as well as some of the best food served in Cuba; **Hostal Casa Mercy,** Calle E Machado 4 (San Cristóbal) between Cuba and Colón (☎ **42/21-6941;** iselmm@gmail.com), run by the friendly Mercedes and Omelio with two bright rooms, a terrace, a cocktail menu, good food, and a book exchange; **Casa Olga Rivera Gómez,** Calle Evangelista Yanes 20 between Máximo Gómez and Carolina Rodríguez (☎ **42/21-1711;** www.betterhostal.4t.com; zaidabarreto2006@yahoo.es), a lovely house with a roof terrace and beautiful floor tiles, fronting Plaza del Carmen and its church; **Casa Héctor Martínez,** Calle Rolando Pardo (Buen Viaje) 8 between Maceo and Parque (☎ **42/21-7463**), a smart house close to all the action, with a small patio garden, hammock, and interesting objects and books; **Hostal Vilo y Gilda,** Ave. 9 de Abril 106 between JB Zayas and Alemán (☎ **42/20-7215;** www.viloygilda.com), owned by a friendly retired couple, offers one air-conditioned room facing a patio full of ancient areca palm trees; and **Hostal Auténtica Pérgola,** Luis Estévez 61 between Independencia and Martí (☎ **42/20-8686;** carmenrt64@yahoo.es), a restored colonial house with beautiful mosaic floors, large ensuite rooms, and a pergola and fountain in the plant-filled interior patio.

MODERATE

Villa La Granjita   Octagonal one- and two-story thatched-roof buildings scattered around rural grounds make up this quiet hotel that is around 4km (2½ miles) from the city center. Rooms are on the small side, but are comfortable and most have balconies; some have views toward the inviting pool. The hotel also has green credentials (solar power heats the water). A clutch of royal palms tower over the entrance and the hotel keeps a mini-farmyard, which children will love.

Carretera de Maleza Km 2.5 ☎ **42/21-8190.** Fax 42/21-8149. www.hotelescubanacan.com. 65 units. CUC$56–CUC$62 double; CUC$66–CUC$88 suite. Rates include buffet breakfast. MC, V. **Amenities:** Restaurant; snack bar; bar; outdoor pool; dance club; gift shop. Internet terminals. *In room:* A/C, TV, fridge.

Villa Los Caneyes ★   Built to resemble a Taíno Indian village, this mini-resort is the most comfortable option in Santa Clara. Most of the rooms are housed either in large, round, six-unit structures or in individual bungalows. All are clean and roomy enough, although some have pretty low ceilings. The nicest rooms by far are in the two-story "H" block; two of these are actually two-room suites. The grounds are planted with tall trees and flowering plants, and there's good bird-watching all around. The buffet meals are unspectacular, to say the least. This place does a brisk business in tours, so don't be surprised if you're sharing it with a large group or two. Like the Villa La Granjita (see above), it's located about 5km (3 miles) from downtown, so if you're staying here, you can't just wander around Santa Clara at will—you'll either be taking taxis or you'll need your own wheels.

Av. de los Eucaliptos and Circunvalación, Santa Clara. ℰ/fax **42/21-8140.** www.hotelescubanacan. com. 96 units. CUC$60–CUC$62 double; CUC$74–CUC$80 suite. Rates include buffet breakfast. MC, V. **Amenities:** Restaurant; snack bar; bar; outdoor pool; game room; gift shop. *In room:* A/C, TV, fridge.

INEXPENSIVE

Hotel Santa Clara Libre This ugly 10-story hotel fronting Parque Vidal is currently the only true hotel option right in Santa Clara. It definitely has seen better days. The rooms are dingy and only just acceptable; anything above the fourth floor should give you a good view, but the place does suffer from regular water supply problems. If you really want to stay here, it would be worth forking out the extra CUC$10 for the suite (no. 414) where Fidel once stayed and whose walls are lined with photographs. There's a rooftop bar here and a disco.

Parque Vidal 6, Santa Clara. ℰ **42/20-7548.** www.islazul.cu. 145 units. CUC$24 double; CUC$36 suite. Rates include buffet breakfast. MC, V. **Amenities:** 2 restaurants; bar. *In room:* A/C, TV.

Where to Dine

Dining options are rather scant and uninteresting in Santa Clara apart from the dinner at Hostal Florida Center. Most folks end up eating at their hotel, particularly those staying at either Villa Los Caneyes or Villa La Granjita or in their *casa particular.* There's little to recommend right around Parque Vidal, although for a quick and inexpensive bite, the **Pizzería Toscana, Colonial 1878,** and the air-conditioned bliss of **Park View,** all on or just off the park, would do in a pinch. The Palmares-run **La Concha,** on Carretera Central at the corner of Calle Danielito (ℰ **42/21-8124**), is a dependable though unexciting option near the Che Guevara Monument. By far the best place to eat is the **Hostal Florida Center ★★** (ℰ **42/20-8161**), a popular *casa particular* with enormous platters of delicious seafood and chicken, plus salads and fruit dishes. The garden is candlelit at night. Stop by to reserve in advance. **Sabor Latino,** Esquerra 157 between Julio Jover and Berenguer (ℰ **42/20-6539**), is a friendly *paladar* serving up large portions of all the favorite meat and fish staples.

Santa Clara After Dark

The **Bar La Marquesina,** just off the Teatro La Caridad, is a good bar, and it's open 24 hours daily. It usually draws a mix of college students, locals, and tourists; there's a small group that plays nightly. The open-air bar **Europa,** Boulevard and L. Estévez, offers great people-watching opportunities and a shady corner spot. With an artsy bohemian vibe, **Club Mejunje ★★**, Calle Marta Abreu 12 (ℰ **42/28-2572**), is probably my favorite spot, featuring regular concerts, poetry readings, gay night on Saturday, and theater pieces put on in their brick-walled, open-air courtyard. Cover CUC$2.

   Bar Club Boulevard, Independencia 225 between Maceo and Unión (ℰ **42/21-6236**), is the most upscale joint in Santa Clara (closed Mon). This Cubanacán property features live music, the occasional cabaret show, and a popular dance club.

   Casa Mercy, E. Machado (S. Cristóbal) 4 between Cuba and Colón, offers cocktail hour on its terrace between 7 and 10:30pm, where you can choose from some 20 cocktails.

A Side Trip to Remedios

The tiny old city of **Remedios ★★★** is considered one of Cuba's colonial highlights. It's 45km (28 miles) northeast of Santa Clara on a direct two-lane highway. There's not a whole lot to see in Remedios, but that's part of its charm. The small Plaza Martí sits at the colonial center of Remedios, watched over by the beautiful **Iglesia de San Juan Bautista** ★★, with its stunning baroque-style altar covered in 22-karat gold and celebrated pregnant Madonna statue (open Mon–Fri 9am–noon and 2–5pm and Sat 2–5pm).

For several weeks at the end of each year, the quiet town of Remedios becomes the site of one of Cuba's great street parties and religious carnivals, **Las Parrandas.** The infectious revelry keeps things lively throughout the holiday season. Everything culminates on Christmas Eve in an orgy of drums, floats, and fireworks. The whole thing allegedly began in 1820, when the local priest sent some altar boys out to bang on pots and pans and scare some parishioners into the midnight Advent Masses. It later evolved into a sort of battle of the bands and fireworks between two sections of the small town. Today, the festivities drag out over the weeks leading up to Christmas Eve, and have even spread into neighboring hamlets. Still, Plaza Martí in Remedios is the place to be, and the night to be there is December 24. Be prepared to stay up late, and bring some ear protection. If you're not here near year's end, pop in at the **Museo de las Parrandas,** Calle Máximo Gómez 71, where you can get an idea of the pageantry by examining the small display of photos, costumes, and floats. It's open Tuesday through Saturday from 9am to noon and 1 to 6pm and Sunday from 9am to 1pm; admission is CUC$1. No visit to Remedios would be complete without at stop at the atmospheric **Café El Louvre** ★ (✆ 42/39-5639), which is set on a corner facing the town's central plaza and church.

For trips to the cay, contact **Cubacar,** Carretera Caibarien (✆ 42/39-5555).

Currently, the only hotel option in Remedios is the quaint and modest 10-room **Hotel Mascotte,** now rebranded as a Hoteles E hotel, Máximo Gómez 114, between Calle Margal and Avenida del Río (✆ 42/39-5144; www.hotelescubanacan.com; CUC$60 double), which faces the small central park here. The same Hoteles E chain will eventually open the Hotel Barcelona just two blocks away. However, there are also various *casas particulares* within a few blocks of the central park. Of these, head first to ★ **Hostal Villa Colonial,** Calle Antonio Maceo 43 between Avenida General Carrillo and Fe de Valle (✆ 42/39-6274; www.cubavillacolonial.com), which has a gorgeous front room, two guest rooms, and friendly owners; or to the delightful **Hostal el Patio** ★, Calle José Antonio Peña 72, between Antonio Romero and Hermanos García (✆ 42/39-5220); or to **La Paloma,** Balmaseda 4 between Máximo Gómez and Ramiro Capablanca (✆ 42/39-5490), which faces the main square and boasts huge bathrooms, but has no real outdoor space; or to **Casa Rivero Méndez (Hostal El Chalet),** Calle Brigadier González 29, between Independencia and José Antonio Peña (✆ 42/39-6310), a 1950s house with Art Deco ironwork, two rooms, parking and a terrace.

La Cayeria del Norte

About 8km (5 miles) east of Remedios, you'll hit the small coastal town of Caibarién where Virginia from **Villa Virginia,** Ciudad Pesquera 73 (✆ 42/36-3303) will give you a grand welcome and help you with transport if necessary. Just outside of Caibarién, you'll come to the toll (CUC$2 each way) for the 50km (31-mile) *pedraplén,* or causeway, that leads out to **la Cayería del Norte** ★★★, a small string of tiny islands, mangrove swamps, and coral reefs with some of the nicest beaches in Cuba. There's the small Aeropuerto Las Brujas (✆ 42/35-0009) close to the toll; **AeroCaribbean** operates charter flights to here.

While the beaches on both Cayo Las Brujas and Cayo Santa María are spectacular, perhaps the premier beaches in this area are **Playa Ensenachos** ★★★ and **Playa**

Mégano ★★★, both on Cayo Ensenachos. The protected waters here are as crystal clear as you can imagine, and you can usually wade out a couple hundred yards without the water getting much above your waist. However, these once public beaches are now the exclusive domain of guests at the new **Royal Hideaway Ensenachos** (see "Where to Stay & Dine," below). The hotel charges half the price of their rack rate for a day pass that includes access to its beach and facilities, and can be bought at their reception desk. Villa Las Brujas charges a bargain CUC$15. From Santa Clara taxis charge CUC$65 for a day trip, including Remedios. Public beaches include La Salina, Punta Madrugilla, which is good for snorkeling, and Perlas Blancas.

Aside from premier beaches, the hotels listed below offer a wide range of watersports activities, nature tours and bird-watching outings into the mangroves here, and organized tours to Remedios, Santa Clara, and beyond.

The **Marina Cayo Las Brujas** (© 42/35-0013/0213; www.gaviota-grupo.com; gaviotatourscsm@enet.cu) is next to Villa Las Brujas and offers catamaran cruises, diving, and aquabike tours.

In addition to the resorts listed below, the **Barceló Cayo Santa Maria Beach Resort,** the newest and largest property on these cays, has partly opened with 624 rooms. This massive megaresort (with more sections under construction) will eventually offer 2,780 rooms across four hotels. All three of the Sol Meliá properties (Meliá Cayo Santa María, Meliá Las Dunas, and Sol Cayo Santa María) share the delightful **Aguas Claras Spa.**

WHERE TO STAY & DINE
Expensive

Meliá Cayo Santa María ★★   This resort is a slight step up from its sister Sol property next-door—the whole operation is slightly larger, slightly more luxurious, and slightly more elegant. The rooms, facilities, and setting are wonderful, although only 28 rooms have sea views. The rooms themselves are quite spacious, with large wrought-iron furnishings, large checkerboard-tile floors, and private balconies. There is a variety of dining options, of which we recommend the Mediterranean restaurant, and a stream of activities and entertainment options throughout the day and night. The beach in front of the hotel is a long, beautiful stretch of soft white sand fronting a turquoise sea. The guests at this hotel can use the facilities at the Sol Cayo Santa María resort, but not vice versa. This is now an adults-only hotel.

Cayo Santa María, Villa Clara province. © **42/35-0500.** Fax 42/35-0505. www.melia-cayosantamaria. com. 358 units. CUC$280–CUC$350 double; CUC$360–CUC$430 suite. Rates are all-inclusive. No children allowed. MC, V. **Amenities:** 6 restaurants; 3 bars; bikes; cabaret; health club; Internet; 2 outdoor pools; room service; smoke-free rooms; spa; 2 outdoor tennis courts; extensive free watersports equipment. *In room:* A/C, TV, minibar.

Meliá Las Dunas   This vast complex of more than 900 rooms is like a minicity that requires golf buggies to move around; the farthest room is some 200m (656 ft.) from the lobby. If you like the impersonal and don't want to see the same face twice, then this is the place for you. Those who have difficulty with a lot of walking and want something more intimate should consider the other two Meliás (Meliá Cayo Santa María or Sol Cayo Santa María). All the main services are close to the lobby, while the rooms are either ringed around the kids' pool for families or the adults' pool in two residential zones. The gardens are as lush as you would expect. Only a disappointing 53 rooms have sea views, but rooms are in the same style and layout as the Meliá Cayo Santa María, only they feature more attractive, light-wood furniture. Superior rooms are closer to the lobby; the standard rooms are only a little smaller.

Cayo Santa María, Villa Clara province. ✆ **42/35-0100.** Fax 42/35-0105. www.melia-lasdunas.com. 925 units. CUC$240–CUC$300 double; CUC$280–CUC$340 suite. Rates are all-inclusive. MC, V. **Amenities:** 7 restaurants; 3 snack bars; 5 bars; bikes; childrens' and teenage programs; cabaret; gym; Internet; 3 outdoor pools; room service; spa; 2 outdoor tennis courts; extensive free watersports equipment. *In room:* A/C, TV, minibar.

Meliá Sol Cayo Santa María ★★   Although neighboring resorts have upped the ante some, this is still one of my favorite all-inclusive options in Cuba. The facilities and service are excellent, the location is spectacular, and the place manages to provide a sense of isolation and escape, despite the fact that there are some 300 rooms here. The rooms themselves are quite comfortable, with plenty of space, large windows, modern furnishings, and private balconies. Only 82 rooms have ocean views, and these are the choice rooms here, obviously. The entire complex is relatively compact and easy to navigate. The beach in front of the hotel is long and almost immediately deserted, just 91m (299 ft.) or so away from the hotel, and of the three Meliá hotels here, it has the loveliest stretch of sand. The large percentage of European and Canadian tourists here has made it a comfortable place for topless and nude bathing. Close by is the private and beautiful house of Villa Zaida del Río bounded by verandas with two rooms, a private pool, Jacuzzi and solarium, dining, and butler service.

Cayo Santa María, Villa Clara province. ✆ **42/35-0200.** Fax 42/35-0505. www.solmeliacuba.com. 301 units. CUC$158–CUC$230 double; CUC$500 villa. Rates are all-inclusive. Children 2 and under stay free in parent's room; children 3–12 stay for half price in parent's room. Rates lower in off season; higher during peak weeks. MC, V. **Amenities:** 4 restaurants; 3 bars; babysitting; bikes; cabaret; children's program; dance club; gym; Internet; children's pool; large free-form outdoor pool; smoke-free rooms; spa; extensive free watersports equipment. *In room:* A/C, TV, fridge.

Occidental Royal Hideaway Ensenachos ★   This massive resort has top-notch facilities and virtually total dominion over two of the best beaches on the entire island, the namesake Playa Ensenachos and neighboring Playa Mégano. The resort is divided into three sections: the Royal Hideaway, Royal Spa, and Royal Suites; however at press time the Royal Suites were closed. All the rooms are large, modern, and luxurious, with marble floors and a private balcony or porch. Every block of rooms at the resort has its own private concierge. The resort's spa facilities are lovely (a 7-day minimum stay is required for the Royal Spa). The elegance and luxury here are over the top and the staff can be very snooty. Some guests have complained that the food is sub-par for a five-star hotel billing.

Cayo Ensenachos, Villa Clara province. ✆ **42/35-0300.** Fax 42/35-0301. www.occidental-hoteles.com. 506 units. Royal Hideaway: CUC$320 double. Royal Spa: CUC$360 double. Rates are all-inclusive. Children 12 and under not allowed. MC, V. **Amenities:** 6 restaurants; 2 snack bars; 4 bars; bikes; cabaret; health club; Internet; 4 Jacuzzis; 4 outdoor pools; room service; smoke-free rooms; spa; 2 outdoor tennis courts; extensive free nonmotorized watersports equipment. *In room:* A/C, TV, hair dryer, minibar.

Moderate

Villa Las Brujas ★ 🏨   Perched on a rocky outcrop over the turquoise Caribbean, the individual and duplex villas here are connected by a raised, rugged wooden walkway through scrub and mangrove. At the end of the row of buildings, there's a long stretch of beautiful white-sand beach, which is seldom crowded, as there are so few rooms here. The rooms themselves are spacious and well-appointed, with marble bathrooms, and separate sitting areas—making them all like minisuites. All but five have ocean views. Of these, the second-floor units have the best views. The restaurant, El Farallón, serves respectable *criolla* fare and fresh seafood; a fire destroyed the restaurant in 2010, but it was slated to reopen by the end of that year. This is one of the few beach resorts in Cuba that has the feel of a boutique hotel. Watersports equipment can be rented from the nearby marina. Staff members are very friendly.

Cayo Las Brujas, Villa Clara province. (© **42/35-0199.** Fax 42/35-0599. www.gaviota-grupo.com. 24 units. CUC$81–CUC$91 double. MC, V. **Amenities:** Restaurant; bar; 2 outdoor Jacuzzis. *In room:* A/C, TV, minibar.

CIENFUEGOS ★

256km (159 miles) SE of Havana; 67km (42 miles) S of Santa Clara

Known as *La Perla del Sur* (the Southern Pearl), Cienfuegos is an uncharacteristically calm and inviting port city. Although Columbus visited the deep and protected harbor here on his second voyage, and the Spanish built the Castillo de Jagua in 1745, it wasn't until 1819, when a group of French colonists settled here, that Cienfuegos began to grow and develop. The French influence continued through most of the city's history, particularly throughout the 19th century, when Cienfuegos became a major shipping point for sugar, tobacco, and coffee. As trade with the United States increased, Cienfuegos lost some of its strategic importance to the northern ports of Havana and Matanzas.

Nevertheless, today Cienfuegos is still a busy port, with an assortment of heavy industry and important sugar-producing plantations surrounding it. In fact, the industrial smokestacks, high-tension electrical towers, and an abandoned nuclear plant significantly mar the landscape. However, the historic center, a UNESCO World Heritage Site since 2005, the beautiful bay and harborfront buildings, the charming wooden homes of Punta Gorda, and the Malecón make it a wonderful city to explore and enjoy.

Essentials
GETTING THERE
BY PLANE   Only international flights from Miami and Canada now use the small **Jaime González International Airport** (© **43/55-2047;** airport code CFG) located 5km (3 miles) northeast of downtown. A taxi from the airport to downtown costs CUC$6.

BY BUS   **Víazul** (© **7/881-1413** in Havana or **43/51-8114** in Cienfuegos at the bus station; Calle 49 between Av 56 and 58; www.viazul.com) has three daily buses to Cienfuegos (actually an intermediate stop on the Trinidad route) leaving Havana at 8:15am, 1pm, and 2:30pm, and arriving at 12:30pm, 5:10pm, and 6:50pm respectively. Buses return to Havana at 9:10am, 4:50pm, and 8:10pm. The fare is CUC$20. From Cienfuegos to Trinidad, the fare is just CUC$6, and the ride takes around 1½ hours. A bus also leaves Viñales at 8am daily and arrives in Cienfuegos at 3:20pm before heading to Trinidad; on the return route from Trinidad, the bus stops at Cienfuegos at 9:40am before heading to Viñales (CUC$32). Cienfuegos is also on two other routes linking Trinidad with Varadero. The direct bus from Varadero leaves at 2:50pm and arrives in Cienfuegos at 6:10pm; the return bus departs at 10:30am, and the fare is CUC$16. The second Varadero route stops at Santa Clara. It leaves Varadero at 8:15pm and arrives in Cienfuegos at 12:50pm; the return departure is at 4:30pm. The Santa Clara–Cienfuegos leg costs CUC$6.

BY CAR   From Havana, take the Autopista Nacional east. (See "Autopista Scam," earlier in this chapter.) There are several possible turnoffs for Cienfuegos. The first and most popular is at Aguada de Pasajeros. This route is marked (at km 170, there is a gas station and cafe) and will bring you through the towns of Rodas and Abreus, before leading you into Cienfuegos. If you continue farther on the Autopista Nacional, your next turnoff will be at Cartagena (km 230). If you are coming from Santa Clara, you can take the turnoff at Ranchuelo (km 255), which is a straight shot into Cienfuegos, passing through the attractive center of Palmira). The trip should take 3½ to 4 hours from Havana.

GETTING AROUND

Taxis are readily available around Cienfuegos. Most rides will cost between CUC$1 and CUC$3. If you can't find one, call **Cubataxi** (© **43/51-8454**). Tourists are technically not supposed to use the common horse-drawn taxis, as they are not licensed to carry foreigners, though some drivers will let you ride but will only accept CUC$1 or CUC$2. There are also plenty of bicycle-powered cabs around town; the same prohibitions will apply but they will risk taking you for a few CUC$s.

Car-rental agencies in Cienfuegos include **Havanautos,** Calle 37 at the corner of Avenida 18, Punta Gorda (© **43/55-1211**), and **Cubacar** at the Hotel Jagua (© **43/55-2014**) and at the Trade Center, Av 50 between Calles 35 and 37 (© **43/55-2166**).

ORIENTATION

There are two main areas you should be concerned with in Cienfuegos: the **historic center** of town that contains the city's central park, Parque José Martí, and other historic buildings; and **Reparto Punta Gorda,** a slightly newer section that heads out on a narrow strip to the southern point of the city, where you'll find the Hotel Jagua and the Palacio del Valle. Calle 37, or Prado, is the main north-south street and runs all the way to the tip of Punta Gorda. For a long stretch, it runs along the seafront, earning it the moniker the "Malecón" (boardwalk). It is bisected by Avenida 54, an east-west street, also called the "Bulevar," which is pedestrian-only for several blocks between the Parque José Martí and Prado.

The principal tour agencies in town are **Cubanacán,** with two locations on Calle 39 between Av. 54 and 56 (© **43/55-1242**) and on Av. 54 no. 2903 between Calles 29 and 31 (© **43/55-1680**); and **Havanatur,** Avenida 54 between Calles 29 and 31 (© **43/55-1639**).

There's a **Banco Financiero Internacional** at the corner of the Bulevar and Calle 29 (© **43/55-1625**), and the Banco Popular de Ahorro, Avenidas 54 and 33, which has two ATMs; there's a **CADECA** branch on Avenida 56 between Calles 33 and 35 (© **43/55-2164**). The **Clínica Internacional,** Calle 37 no. 202, between Avenidas 2 and 0, Punta Gorda (© **43/55-1622**), is a small, modern facility that can handle most emergencies and medical needs, and has a 24-hour pharmacy. The **post office** is located at Avenida 56 between Calles 37 and 35 (© **43/51-5622**). There's an **Etecsa** office at Calle 31 between the Bulevar and Avenida 56 (© **43/51-3046**), which has Internet access.

What to See & Do

IN TOWN

The **Parque José Martí,** formerly the Plaza de Armas, is the historic center's hub. It's a broad city park with a gazebo/bandstand at its center and a little Arco de Triunfo (Arc of Triumph) dating from 1902 at its western end. Surrounding the park, you'll find Cienfuegos' most interesting historical buildings. The stylish 1918 **Palacio Ferrer** (© **43/51-6584**), on one corner here, is the city's Casa de la Cultura. This is a good

Cienfuegos

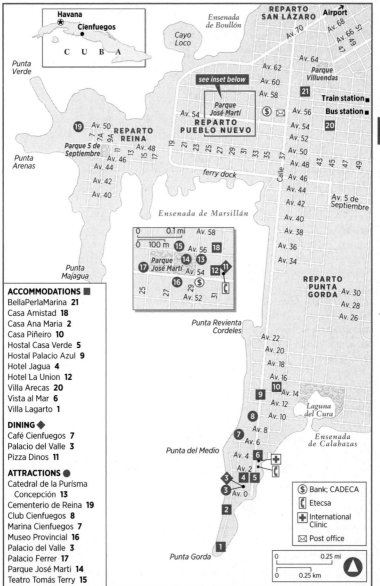

ACCOMMODATIONS ■
BellaPerlaMarina **21**
Casa Amistad **18**
Casa Ana Maria **2**
Casa Piñeiro **10**
Hostal Casa Verde **5**
Hostal Palacio Azul **9**
Hotel Jagua **4**
Hotel La Union **12**
Villa Arecas **20**
Vista al Mar **6**
Villa Lagarto **1**

DINING ◆
Café Cienfuegos **7**
Palacio del Valle **3**
Pizza Dinos **11**

ATTRACTIONS ●
Catedral de la Purísima
  Concepción **13**
Cementerio de Reina **19**
Club Cienfuegos **8**
Marina Cienfuegos **7**
Museo Provincial **16**
Palacio del Valle **3**
Palacio Ferrer **17**
Parque José Marti **14**
Teatro Tomás Terry **15**

place to find out if there are any interesting art exhibits or concerts going on while you're in town. You should also check out the view of the city from the rooftop cupola here; admission is CUC$0.50. The building is undergoing renovation but it's possible to climb the cupola. On the eastern end of the park, you'll find the **Catedral de la Purísima Concepción,** a beautiful neoclassical church finished in 1870. The church features wonderful stained-glass work imported from France. On the north side of the park is the **Teatro Tomás Terry ★** (✆ **43/51-3361;** www.azurina.cult. cu). Inaugurated in 1890, the theater has been wonderfully maintained. It has been declared a national monument, and stars such as Enrico Caruso, Sarah Bernhardt, and Anna Pavlova performed here. Check to see if there will be any performances while you're in town; if not, you can tour the facility during the day. Admission is CUC$1 and includes a quick, guided tour. Across the park, on its south side, is the small **Museo Provincial,** which is only of interest to die-hard museum and local-history buffs.

Out on the end of Punta Gorda, past the Malecón, is the historic old **Palacio del Valle ★★** (✆ **43/55-1003 ext. 830**), an eclectic architectural masterpiece, which covers vast stylistic ground in its compact floor plan. The centerpiece here is the Salón Comedor (dining room), which dates to 1917 and tries to imitate the intricate Moorish stucco and tile work of Spain's Alhambra. Other rooms are done variously in baroque, neoclassical, and Gothic styling. The whole thing operates as a restaurant (see "Where to Dine," below), and there's also a wonderful third-floor rooftop balcony bar and lookout, as well as a tapas bar and wine cellar with live music in the basement.

At the very tip of Punta Gorda, there's now **La Punta,** a small garden, snack bar, and bar open late.

Cienfuegos has two picturesque cemeteries, featuring elaborate marble head-stones, mausoleums, and aboveground burial crypts. The **Cementerio de Reina ★** is the older of the two and located on the western extreme edge of the city beyond the downtown center. The **Cementerio Tomás Acea** is in an eastern suburb of the city and features an elaborate entrance modeled after the Parthenon in Greece.

ON THE OUTSKIRTS OF TOWN

Popular tours from Cienfuegos include visits to the **Castillo de Jagua** (✆ **43/59-6402;** open Mon–Sat 9:30am–5pm, Sun 9:30am–1pm; admission CUC$1), which is located on the western flank of the narrow entrance to the harbor. Built between 1738 and 1745, the little fort sits on a hill above the quaint fishing village of Perché. Although the moat is dry, you still enter the castle by crossing the wooden drawbridge. Inside, there are some basic museum-like exhibits. You reach the castle by driving to the Hotel Pasacaballos, then parking and taking the constant little ferry across; the cost one-way is CUC$1. More convenient is the thrice daily ferry from the dock at Avenida 46 between Calles 23 and 25. It departs at 8am, 1pm, and 5:30pm, and returns at 6:30am, 10am, and 3pm; cost is CUC$0.50.

The **Jardín Botánico Soledad ★**, Calle Central 136, Pepito Tey, Cienfuegos (✆ **43/54-5334**), was begun by U.S. sugar magnate Edwin Atkins in 1904, and taken over by Harvard University in 1919. With more than 2,000 species of plants covering some 90 hectares (222 acres), it is the largest and most extensive botanical garden in Cuba. The grounds are beautiful to walk around, and there's usually good bird-watching here, although everything tends to be overgrown and unkempt, and markings are sorely lacking. The gardens are 17km (11 miles) east of downtown, via the road to Trinidad. The garden is open daily from 8am to 4:30pm; admission costs CUC$3.

BENNY MORÉ

Maximiliano Bartolomé Moré, better known as Benny Moré and perhaps most descriptively dubbed "El Bárbaro del Ritmo" (The Rhythm Barbarian), is Cienfuegos' pride and joy. Born in the nearby hamlet of Santa Isabel de las Lajas on August 24, 1919, Moré was probably the greatest Cuban singer and bandleader of his time. He sang and composed in a variety of genres, from mambo to *son* to cha-cha-chá.

Tall and thin, with a velvet-smooth voice, Moré was the epitome of the debonair Cuban bandleader of the '40s and '50s. Although he never enjoyed the overseas success of Xavier Cugat or Pérez Prado, in Cuba, Benny Moré is considered the king. His life and voice were immortalized in the 2006 movie, *El Benny*. His bronze statue stands on Cienfuegos' main thoroughfare, Prado.

Near Playa Rancho Luna is the **Delfinario** 🖐 (**Dolphin Show;** ✆ **43/54-8120**). Captive trained dolphins perform several times daily here. Although the amphitheater around a penned-in saltwater lagoon is spiffy, we find these types of shows and facilities depressing. The main pool and side pens here are particularly small and shallow. This place is open Thursday through Tuesday from 8:30am to 4:30pm, and has a reasonably priced little restaurant. Shows are at 10am and 2pm. Admission is CUC$10 for adults and CUC$6 for children. It will cost you an extra CUC$1 to take photos, CUC$2 to shoot video, and CUC$3 to get a kiss from a dolphin. A 15- to 20-minute swimming session with a dolphin costs CUC$50; a show is included in this price. Cubanacán offers a package for CUC$45.

Farther away is **El Nicho ★**, in the Escambray mountains, a series of waterfalls (some up to 15 meters high) from which you can plunge into a natural pool; the scenery is lovely; there's a restaurant on-site. Agencies organize trips for CUC$30 although you can arrange private transport through local casas that works out cheaper.

ON & BELOW THE WATER

While Cienfuegos sits on a large and beautiful protected bay, the best (and really the only) beach is 17km (11 miles) away at **Playa Rancho Luna.** The beach here is a long expanse of white sand, although the sand isn't quite as fine and silky as that found at some of Cuba's more famous beaches. You can book scuba-diving trips out of the **Faro Luna Diving Center** (✆ 43/54-8040; buceocom@nautica.cfg.cyt.cu) or with the **Whale Shark Diving Center** at Hotel Rancho Luna (✆ **43/54-8020**) or book through Cubanacán in town. Dives are CUC$30.

Marina Cienfuegos, Calle 35 between Avenidas 6 and 8, Punta Gorda (✆ **43/55-1699** or 43/55-1241; www.nauticamarlin.com), is your one-stop shop for all nautical needs. Here you can charter a sailboat or sportfishing excursion, book a cruise around the harbor, rent a Hobie Cat or windsurfer, and go fishing and diving. The elegant 1920s-built **Club Cienfuegos** entertainment complex, Calle 35 between Avenidas 8 and 12 (✆ **43/55-1275**), has a small patch of sand with a little swimming area in front of it; some locals and tourists use it as a place to sunbathe and cool off. Several international regattas, fishing tournaments, and speedboat races are held in Cienfuegos each year. Check with the marinas or your hotel for details.

Shopping

The best shop in town is the **Galería Maroya,** which has two locations, on Av. 54 no. 2506 between Calles 25 and 27, located on the southern flank of the Parque José Martí, and on Av. 54 between Calles 35 and 37 in the Bulevar. Both branches of this shop feature a broad selection of Cuban arts and crafts, with a decent representation of local works. There's an excellent cigar shop, **Casa del Habano El Embajador,** at Avenida 54 between Calles 33 and 35. There's an **ARTex** shop on the Bulevar (Av. 54 btw. Calles 35 and 37) stocking a selection of typical souvenirs, and it usually has a good selection of CDs, including some by Benny Moré. Much more interesting is the **Galería Tizón,** Av. 62 no. 4523 between Calles 45 and 47 (℃ **43/51-5173;** santimar@cfg.rimed.cu), a private house that features works by painter and engraver Santiago Hermes, sculptor Alaín Moreira who works with bronze, and Adriel Hernández, a photographer and designer who offers a fascinating metal interpretation of the Cuban coat of arms.

Where to Stay

IN CIENFUEGOS
Expensive

Hotel La Unión ★ 🎒   This hotel, housed in a marvelously restored mint-green 1869 colonial mansion right on the Bulevar a block off of the Parque José Martí, is one of the nicest boutique hotels in the country. The standard rooms are small, so you might consider an upgrade to one of the 10 junior suites, which are quite spacious. The neoclassical furnishings are elegant, and the service is attentive, but some repair work is needed in the rooms. The inviting pool here is located in an interior courtyard, with a fragment of an old arched brick wall and a couple of sculpted lions standing guard over it. The open-air central courtyard bar is another great space to hang out and relax, as is the rooftop bar. The main restaurant (ca. 1869) is merely acceptable, with uninspired buffets and a limited a la carte menu. The pool bar/cafe service is unacceptably slow.

Calle 31 (corner of Av. 54), Cienfuegos. ℃ **43/55-1020.** Fax 43/55-1685. www.hotellaunion-cuba.com. 49 units. CUC$100 double; CUC$110 junior suite; CUC$130 suite. No seasonal variations in rates. MC, V. **Amenities:** Restaurant; snack bar; 2 bars; small exercise room; Jacuzzi; outdoor pool; room service; sauna. *In room:* A/C, TV, hair dryer, minibar.

Moderate

Hostal Casa Verde   This little hotel recently opened on the bay. Despite opening under the Hoteles Encanto brand, it lacks charm and has poor service. That said the rooms feature stylish dark wood furnishings, handsome stand alone mirrors, and smart pine green bedspreads. Two upstairs rooms have bay views but much of the glass is frosted; only two rooms come with king-size beds. While the suite also has bay views, it is large and impersonal. A small bar fronts the bay.

Calle 37 4 between Ave 0 and 2. ℃ **43/55 1003** ext 840. www.gran-caribe.com. 8 units. CUC$98–CUC$120 double; CUC$120–CUC$140 suite. No seasonal variations in rate. MC, V. **Amenities:** Bar/snack bar; smoke-free rooms. *In room:* A/C, TV, hair dryer, minibar.

Hotel Jagua   This seven-story hotel is situated out on the end of Punta Gorda, just across from the Palacio del Valle. The modern rooms are spacious, comfortable, cool, and bright, with a large sliding-glass door to let in light, white tile floors, and plenty of amenities. However, we have received reports of air-conditioning and hot water being rationed between 8am and 4pm. Those on the higher floors of the main building have wonderful views over the city and harbor from private balconies. Only 20 of the rooms come with king-size beds; the rest have two twin beds. There's a large rectangular pool at the center of this complex.

Calle 37 no. 1, Punta Gorda. ℂ **43/55-1003.** Fax 43/55-1245. www.gran-caribe.com. 149 units. CUC$85–CUC$105 double. CUC$125–CUC$150 suite. MC, V. **Amenities:** 2 restaurants; bar; snack bar; cabaret; Internet; children's pool; outdoor pool; watersports equipment rental. *In room:* A/C, TV, hair dryer, minibar.

Inexpensive

Cienfuegos has scores of good *casa particular* options. You'll find no shortage of *jineteros* (hustlers) offering to show you a room. You'll find the greatest concentration of *casas particulares* all along and near the Prado (Av. 37), as well as surrounding the Parque José Martí and on Punta Gorda. In addition to the Hostal Palacio Azul listed below, dependable and clean choices include:

○ **Casa Amistad,** Av. 56 no. 2927, between Calles 29 and 31 (ℂ **43/51-6143;** armando@apc.cf.rimed.cu), a colonial house with a wonderful front living room, two rooms, and some hearty home-cooked food (it's a stone's throw from Parque José Martí).

○ **Villa Arecas,** Av. 54 no. 4317 between Calles 43 and 45 (ℂ **43/51-6606** or **524-52415;** arteaga@jagua.cfg.sld.cu), run by the very welcoming Dr. José Arteaga Herrera and his wife María Elena, who will offer you a piña colada on arrival.

○ **BellaPerlaMarina,** Calle 39 no. 5818 at Av. 60 (ℂ **43/51-8991,** bellaperlamarina@yahoo.es) which offers two rooms—one of which has an extraordinary bronze bed carved with mounted horses in flight—and helpful advice from owner Waldo, who will help organize excursions.

○ **Casa Piñeiro,** Calle 41 no. 1402 between Avenidas 14 and 16, Punta Gorda (ℂ **43/51-3808;** www.casapineiro.com), an enormous house with friendly owners and a great outdoor oven.

○ **Vista al Mar,** Calle 37 no. 210 between Avenidas 2 and 4, Punta Gorda (ℂ **43/51-8378;** www.vistaalmarcuba.com; gertrudis_fernandez@yahoo.es), in the southern part of the city offers a small, sea-front patio.

○ **Villa Lagarto,** Calle 35 no. 4B (ℂ **43/51-9966;** villalagarto_16@yahoo.com), run by the very friendly Tony and Maylin, with two breezy, comfortable top-floor rooms, a seawater pool, and a garden overlooking the sea right at the tip of Punta Gorda.

○ **Casa Ana María,** Calle 35 no. 20 (ℂ **43/51-3269**), an old colonial home, also out on Punta Gorda, with dark rooms. Hostess Ana María Font D'Escoubet prepares filling meals and can help arrange tours and activities around Cienfuegos.

Hostal Palacio Azul ★ ✈ This restored waterfront building is good value, offering clean and comfortable rooms just off the Malecón, out near the tip of Punta Gorda. Rooms in the 1920s building have high, decorated ceilings and beautiful tiled floors (ca. 1921). A grand marble staircase leads up to the second floor, where you'll find my favorite room, Dalia, a corner unit with a view of the Club Cienfuegos, the harbor, and the nightly sunset. All but two rooms come with a private little balcony. There's a solarium on the roof.

Calle 37 no. 1201, btw. Avs. 12 and 14, Punta Gorda. ℂ **43/55-5828.** Fax 43/55-1020. www.hotelescubanacan.com. 7 units. CUC$60 double. No seasonal variations in rate. Rate includes breakfast. MC, V. **Amenities:** Restaurant; bar; room service. *In room:* A/C, TV, minibar.

NEAR CIENFUEGOS

The only true beach hotel close to Cienfuegos is **Club Amigo Rancho Luna** (✆ **43/54-8012;** www.hotelescubanacan.com); however, this is a rather mediocre place catering to package-tour groups of folks who must be unaware that they have scores of better options all over Cuba. Still, if you want to go swimming for a few hours or the day, the beach here will certainly do. **Finca Los Colorados,** Carretera Rancho de Luna, Pasacaballos Km 18 (✆ **43/54-8044**), a *casa particular,* is on the road close to the lighthouse.

Where to Dine

In addition to the places listed below, you can get acceptable pizza and pastas at **Pizza Dinos,** Calle 31 between Avenidas 54 and 56 (✆ **43/55-2020**).

Café Cienfuegos CONTINENTAL/SEAFOOD   This is the most refined dining option in Cienfuegos—but that isn't saying too much. The elegant, second-floor dining room is part of the Club Cienfuegos complex. While not as ornate or elaborate as the Palacio del Valle (see below), the ambience here is still very pleasant, and the food is a bit better. While there is an assortment of steak, pork, and poultry dishes, we recommend you stick to the fresh fish and seafood. If you have an aversion to meat, you should note that the Paella Cienfueguera will come with more chicken than seafood. The large, first-floor open-air bar area is set underneath a modern tent structure, with soaring spires. This is a great place to catch the sunset before heading in for dinner.

Calle 37 (Prado) btw. Aves. 8 and 10, Punta Gorda. ✆ **43/51-2891.** Reservations recommended in high season. Main courses CUC$6.25–CUC$38. No credit cards. Daily noon–10pm.

Palacio del Valle CONTINENTAL/SEAFOOD   The food is not nearly as spectacular as the setting, but the luxurious and ornate surroundings just about make up for it. Music and entertainment in the main dining room are provided by the charismatic María del Carmen Iznaga Guillén, the niece of the great Cuban poet Nicolás Guillén. She is a genuine character, and worth a visit just to see and hear her play. The cuisine here is uninspired, but acceptable. This place, now belonging to the Hotel Jagua, is the de rigueur stop in town and there's a cattle-car feel to the operation at times. My favorite draw here is the rooftop bar, with its fabulous views over the harbor. There is also a tapas bar and wine cellar with live music in the basement.

Calle 37 (Prado) and Av. 0, Punta Gorda. ✆ **43/55-1003.** Reservations recommended in high season. Main courses CUC$9–CUC$25. No credit cards. Daily noon–10pm.

Cienfuegos After Dark

The biggest draw in town is the **Club El Benny,** Av. 54 no. 2907 (the Bulevar) between Calles 29 and 31 (✆ **43/55-1674**). There's a nightly cabaret show here (admission CUC$3 Fri–Sun and CUC$2 Mon–Thurs) that features the classic sounds and songs of the club's namesake. The place also serves as one of the city's most lively dance clubs. The other popular spot to dance the night away is the **Guanaroca Disco** at the Hotel Jagua, Calle 37 no. 1, Punta Gorda (✆ **43/55-1003**). There's also music nightly at the large, open-air bar at the **Club Cienfuegos** (✆ **43/51-2891**). A local **Casa de la Trova** (Patio del ARTex, also known locally as El Cubanísimo), at Avenida 16 and Calle 35 (✆ **43/55-1255**), has nightly concerts (admission CUC$2). Next to the city's historic theatre is the **Patio Terry,** Av. 56 between Calles 27 and 29 (✆ **43/51-0770**), where traditional music can be heard Tuesday to Sunday (admission is CUC$2).

For a quieter time, pick out a sidewalk table at the **Palatino Bar,** overlooking the Parque José Martí at Av. 54, corner of Calle 27; or saddle up to a seat at the little hole-in-the-wall local hangout **Don Luis** on Calle 31, across from the Hotel La Union. At night, locals hang out on the Malecón near Punta Gorda.

TRINIDAD ★★★

334km (208 miles) SE of Havana; 261km (162 miles) S of Varadero; 649km (403 miles) W of Santiago de Cuba

Tiny Trinidad is, quite simply, one of the finest colonial towns in all the Americas. Wholly disproportionate to its diminutive size, Trinidad ranks as one of Cuba's greatest attractions. A few square blocks of cobblestone streets, pretty pastel-colored 18th- and 19th-century houses, palaces, and plazas, Trinidad's colonial-era core can be toured in just a few hours. However, its serenity is so soothing that many visitors are easily coaxed into much longer stays. Magically frozen in time and tastefully scruffy where it needs to be, the city has streets that are more populated by horse-drawn carts than automobile traffic, and old folks still crouch by windows, behind fancy wrought-iron grilles, to peer out at passersby.

Founded in 1514 on the site of a native Taíno settlement, Villa de la Santísima Trinidad was the fourth of Diego Velázquez's original seven **villas** (towns). Trinidad quickly grew and later prospered in princely fashion from the sugar-cane industry concentrated in the outlying Valle de los Ingenios. The sugar boom that took root by the mid-1700s created a coterie of wealthy local sugar barons, who built magnificent estates in the valley and manor houses in town and imported thousands of African slaves to work the fields. Trinidad's golden age, though, proved to be short-lived. Slave uprisings on plantations, intense European competition, and, finally, independence struggles throughout the Caribbean all took their toll on the Cuban sugar industry.

When the bottom dropped out of sugar by the 1860s, Trinidad's economy collapsed and the town drifted into obscurity. Its economic failure in the late-19th century is a true blessing in the 21st: Trinidad escaped further economic development and modernization that surely would have obscured the colonial nucleus that UNESCO honored as a World Heritage Site in 1988. Even in the 1950s, in prerevolutionary, capitalist Cuba, the beauty and historical value of Trinidad prompted the government to declare it off-limits to further development.

Essentials
GETTING THERE
BY PLANE   Chartered **AeroCaribbean** light-aircraft flights from Havana, Cienfuegos, and Varadero arrive in Trinidad at the little **Aeropuerto Alberto Delgado,** Carretera Casilda Km 1.5 (✆ **41/99-6393;** airport code TND), a couple of kilometers beyond the historic center of Trinidad. A taxi from the airport to Trinidad costs around CUC$5.

BY BUS   The bus terminal, or **Terminal de Omnibuses** (✆ **41/99-4448**), in Trinidad is on Gustavo Izquierdo between Piro Guinart and Simón Bolívar, close to the Plaza Mayor.

The quickest and best bus service to Trinidad is **Víazul** (✆ **41/99-4448** in Trinidad; www.viazul.com). From Havana, buses depart daily at 8:15am, 1pm, and 2:30pm, arriving at 2:10pm, 6:45pm, and 8:25pm respectively; the fare is CUC$25 one-way. From Varadero, buses leave at 8:15am and 2:50pm and arrive in Trinidad at

2:25pm and 7:45pm respectively; the fare is CUC$20 one-way. From Santiago de Cuba, buses leave at 7:30pm and arrive at 7am the following day; the fare is CUC$33 one-way. Return buses leave Trinidad for Havana at 7:30am, 3:20pm, and 6:30pm; for Varadero at 9am and 2:50pm; and for Santiago at 7:40pm. A new bus from Viñales leaves at 8am and arrives in Trinidad at 4:55pm; the return bus departs at 8am and the one-way fare is CUC$32.

BY CAR   From Havana, the fastest route is to drive along the Autopista Nacional to Santa Clara (about 4 hr.), and then drop down through Jibacoa to Trinidad along the local road south. (See "Autopista Scam," earlier in this chapter.) Another option is to continue on the Autopista Nacional to Sancti Spíritus (perhaps stopping for a look, if you're not planning an overnight visit there), and circle back southwest to Trinidad for a scenic drive through the Valley of the Sugar Mills (see "Side Trips from Trinidad," later in this chapter). If you're driving in from Cienfuegos, there are actually two routes. We prefer the coastal road, which gives you some good sea views as you get close to Trinidad. From Santiago de Cuba, start out northwest on the unfinished Autopista Nacional and then take the Carretera Central through Bayamo, Camagüey, Ciego de Ávila, and Sancti Spíritus. The journey from Santiago to Trinidad takes about 8 hours.

GETTING AROUND

Getting around Trinidad is a simple affair. Almost everything of interest in town is clustered around the Plaza Mayor in the historic center. The streets of old Trinidad were made for exploring on foot, and you can easily get around the whole of the old city, and most of the newer parts just beyond the colonial core, very easily on foot.

BY TAXI   State-owned, registered taxis are available for travel back and forth between Playa Ancón and Trinidad, up the hill to Hotel Las Cuevas, or private hire for excursions. Call **Cubataxi** (© **41/99-2214**). Taxis charge CUC$8 to Playa Ancón. Little yellow **Coco Taxis,** slightly slower, non-air-conditioned three-wheel vehicles, charge CUC$4.

BY CAR   Though it is far easier to sign on for an organized tour to visit the surrounding area, including Topes de Collantes in the Sierra del Escambray, you might choose to rent a car to explore central Cuba or travel to more distant destinations. The drive northeast to Sancti Spíritus through the Valle de los Ingenios is particularly alluring. The major car-rental companies are **Cubacar** (© **41/99-6110**) and **Vía Rent a Car** (© **41/99-6388**). Rates range from CUC$45 to CUC$80 per day for a standard four-door to CUC$80 and up per day for a 4WD vehicle.

BY BICYCLE   Locals sometimes rent out bikes (usually functional cruisers for CUC$2–CUC$4 per day) that you can use to get back and forth to the beach. However, be forewarned: It's downhill, then flat on your way to the beach, but the final few kilometers coming home will be uphill. The best place to ask is at your *casa particular*. **Ruinas del Teatro Brunet** (© **41/99-5547**) rents out bikes for CUC$3 a day.

BY BUS   The **Trinidad Bus Tour** starts at the Transtur office on Lino Pérez between Maceo and Francisco Cadahía. It departs at 9am, 11am, 2pm, 4pm, and 7pm and picks up at a few stops in town, including the Cubatur office, before heading to Playa La Boca and the hotels on Playa Ancón. It returns from the beach at 10:15am, 12:15pm, 3:15pm, 5:15pm, and 8:15pm. The fare is CUC$2 per person.

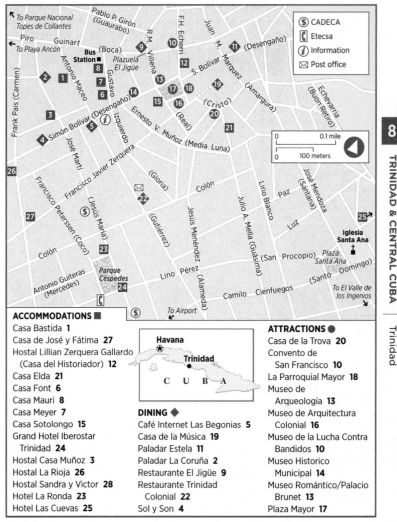

ACCOMMODATIONS ■
Casa Bastida **1**
Casa de José y Fátima **27**
Hostal Lillian Zerquera Gallardo
(Casa del Historiador) **12**
Casa Elda **21**
Casa Font **6**
Casa Mauri **8**
Casa Meyer **7**
Casa Sotolongo **15**
Grand Hotel Iberostar
Trinidad **24**
Hostal Casa Muñoz **3**
Hostal La Rioja **26**
Hostal Sandra y Victor **28**
Hotel La Ronda **23**
Hotel Las Cuevas **25**

DINING ◆
Café Internet Las Begonias **5**
Casa de la Música **19**
Paladar Estela **11**
Paladar La Coruña **2**
Restaurante El Jigüe **9**
Restaurante Trinidad
Colonial **22**
Sol y Son **4**

ATTRACTIONS ●
Casa de la Trova **20**
Convento de
San Francisco **10**
La Parroquial Mayor **18**
Museo de
Arqueología **13**
Museo de Arquitectura
Colonial **16**
Museo de la Lucha Contra
Bandidos **10**
Museo Historico
Municipal **14**
Museo Romántico/Palacio
Brunet **13**
Plaza Mayor **17**

ORIENTATION

The streets of Trinidad go by both original colonial and newer, post-Revolution names. Locals usually don't know both; what one person may call Boca another calls Piro Guinart. Streets are haphazardly labeled. Many longtime residents use the old names, but most businesses and institutions adopt the newer names, which are used in this section. Be prepared to encounter some confusion if asking for an address, though Trinidad is so small that it's nearly impossible to be lost for long.

Your best bets for information about Trinidad and nearby excursions are any of the major state-run travel agencies. **Cubatur** (© 41/99-6314; www.cubatur.cu), is at Antonio Maceo at the corner of Francisco Javier Zerquera, as well as at Maceo at the corner of Bolívar and in the Hotel Ancón (p. 207). More helpful is **Cubanacán,** located on José Martí between Francisco Javier Zerquera and Colón (© 41/99-6142), and at Cafe Las Begonias where the employees are extremely helpful. **Infotur** is inside the Restaurante Santa Ana, but keeps irregular hours and is too far out of the center to be of any use.

Banco de Crédito y Comercio is located at José Martí 264 between Colón and Francisco Javier Zerquera (© 41/99-2405). It's open Monday through Friday from 8am to 3pm and Saturday from 8am to 11am. A **CADECA** is at José Martí 166 (© 41/99-6263); its hours are Monday through Saturday from 8am to 6pm and Sunday from 8am to 1pm.

For medical attention, go to the 24-hour **Clínica Internacional** located at Lino Pérez 103, at the corner of Reforma (© 41/99-6492). There's a pharmacy in-house too. **Etecsa Internet terminals** are at the Etecsa office on Lino Pérez (on the east side of Parque Céspedes, between José Martí and Miguel Calzada). There are also Internet terminals inside the Cafetería Las Begonias.

The main **post office** is situated at Antonio Maceo 418, between Colón and Francisco Javier Zerquera. It is open Monday through Saturday from 8am to 7pm.

What to See & Do

Unquestionably, the greatest attraction in Trinidad is the town itself, which constitutes one of the finest colonial centers in the Americas and, justifiably, has been designated a UNESCO World Heritage Site in its entirety. The town's cobblestone streets contain a treasure-trove of small and grand colonial homes, churches, and quiet squares. Walking aimlessly about the curving streets of the old town is unmatched in Cuba for tranquillity and charm. About the only feature not authentically colonial is the neon cross that crowns the church on Plaza Mayor. Remarkably, as quaint as it is, Trinidad feels like a real town where Cubans live and work, rather than the film set it first appears to be.

A good way to get your bearings in Trinidad is to trace a path from the **Plaza Mayor,** the heart of the old town, heading west on Echerri and then down Piro Guinart to **Plazuela El Jigüe,** a quiet and pretty little square. Then head down Peña to Simón Bolívar and east on Antonio Maceo, the closest thing there is to a main drag in Trinidad.

A couple blocks south of here, along Lino Pérez, is **Parque Céspedes,** the focal point of the "new" town (though newer than the colonial core of Trinidad, it remains anything but shiny and modern).

Northeast of the old town, following Fernando H. Echerri to José Mendoza for several blocks, you'll reach **Plaza Santa Ana** and the ruins of **Iglesia Santa Ana,** which looks ancient, but dates only to 1812. On the square is a former 19th-century prison, **Real Cárcel,** which today houses a touristy restaurant and souvenir shop.

AROUND THE PLAZA MAYOR ★★

The neo-baroque, 19th-century Plaza Mayor, elaborately adorned with serene sitting areas, statuary, towering palm trees, and gardens enclosed by white wrought-iron fences, is one of Cuba's most beautiful plazas. It's ringed by magnificent palaces and pastel-colored houses with red-tile roofs and wood shutters. On the northwest corner is the cathedral, Iglesia de la Santísima Trinidad, which most locals refer to as **La Parroquial Mayor.** The cathedral, completed in 1892, replaced the original 17th-century church that was destroyed in 1812 by a hurricane. The new construction, completed at the end of the 19th century, is rather simple on the outside, but the restored interior reveals a Gothic vaulted ceiling and nearly a dozen attractive carved altars. The cathedral can be visited Monday through Saturday from 10:30am to 1pm. Mass is at 9am on Sunday.

The highlight of the Plaza Mayor, and the most evocative reminder of Trinidad's glory days, is the lovingly restored **Palacio Brunet,** Fernando H. Echerri 52 at the corner of Simón Bolívar. The colonial mansion dates to 1704 (the second floor was built in 1808) and houses the **Museo Romántico ★★** (© 41/99-4363). Its splendid collection of period antiques culled from a number of old Trinitario families convincingly evokes the life of a local sugar baron in the 1800s. Don't miss the enormous kitchen, covered in *azulejo* (glazed ceramic tiles), with a wood-burning stove. The views from upstairs are marvelous. The museum is open Tuesday through Sunday from 9am to 5pm. Admission is CUC$2; allow about 45 minutes for your visit.

In a pale yellow colonial building on the west side of the main square, **Museo de Arqueología** (© 41/99-3420) features a collection that encompasses natural sciences and pre-Columbian Cuba. It's mostly an uninspired hodgepodge of exhibits, though; you'll find bones of Indian natives and slaves, glass-enclosed stuffed animals, and a 19th-century kitchen, which, though interesting, is hard to classify as either archaeology or natural science. It is currently closed and has no scheduled reopening date.

On the east side of the Plaza Mayor, in a squat, sky-blue mansion once belonging to the Sánchez Iznaga family, the **Museo de Arquitectura Colonial** (© 41/99-3208) features moderately interesting exhibits that trace the development of Trinidad, including examples of woodwork and ironwork, maps, models, and photographs. What is on display, though, can hardly compare to the real-life exhibits beyond the museum's doors. It's open Monday, Thursday, Saturday, and Sunday from 9am to 5pm. Admission is CUC$1.

The former Palacio Cantero, an 1830 palatial residence built by a noted sugar baron, houses the **Museo Histórico Municipal ★,** Simón Bolívar 423 between Peña and Gustavo Izquierdo (© 41/99-4460). In addition to antiques and 19th-century furnishings, there are bits and pieces of slave history, old bank notes, and exhibits of revolutionary Cuba. For many visitors, though, the highlight is the climb up the narrow and rickety wooden stairs to the tower, which has terrific bird's-eye views of Trinidad and the surrounding area. The museum is open Saturday through Thursday from 9am to 5pm; admission is CUC$2. Allow about an hour for your visit, a bit longer if you want to linger over the views.

The second of Trinidad's two major towers is the picturesque, yellow-and-white domed bell tower belonging to the former 18th-century **Convento de San Francisco (Convent of Saint Francis of Assisi),** Fernando H. Echerri at Piro Guinart. Today the building hosts the dogmatic, but rather fascinating **Museo de la Lucha Contra Bandidos** (© 41/99-4121), which focuses on revolutionary Cuba and the continuing "struggle against bandits." Exhibits document Fidel's battles against counterrevolutionaries—the *bandidos* in question—who sought to overturn the regime's ideals by winning support among *guajiros* (poor rural farmers) and fighting in the Sierra del Escambray in the 1960s. In addition to newspaper reports, you'll find machine guns, military maps, a CIA radio, and photos of the ragtag principals who

Be careful. I've received reports of *jineteros* (husslers) meeting incoming buses and taxis with the names of tourists they've gleaned from friends inside the bus or taxi company. They then proceed to tell the tourists either that their reservation at a specific *casa particular* has been canceled, or that they are taking them to that *casa,* when in fact they are bringing them to a different *casa* altogether. Some locals have also resorted to putting up copied house signs and numbers to deceive people. *Jineteros* have also been known to enter a false key into the door of the house that tourists have booked at only to be told that the door is locked and so the casa owner is not there and they should therefore come to the *jinetero's* casa or *jinetero's* friend's casa. If you have and trust your confirmed reservation at a *casa particular,* make sure you know the exact address and location of the house, and distrust touts who take you elsewhere. Beware of people who wish to escort you—especially *jineteros* on bicycles. However, not all folks are distrustful; many are *arrendadores* (owners of legal *casas particulares*) who have not had the good fortune to be listed in a guidebook. Don't dismiss them all; just check that they have a genuine license.

finally, and quite extraordinarily, overthrew the Batista government in 1959. As is the case with the Museo Histórico, though, the biggest draw may be the panoramic views from atop the bell tower. The museum is open Tuesday through Sunday from 9am to 5pm; admission is CUC$1. Allow 45 minutes or so, including the visit to the tower.

Where to Stay

Trinidad has an abundance of *casas particulares*—around 380 at last count, including several in fine colonial homes that rank as excellent bargains and are particularly appropriate accommodations in this beautifully preserved old town. Visitors who arrive on the Víazul bus are confronted by a rabble of dozens of card- and placard-waving folks hoping to get you to follow them to their homestays. They are perfectly innocuous and, for the most part, honest folks just trying to make a buck. Not all the *casas* are officially registered, however, and many are not as close to the colonial center as you might wish to be. Have a map ready so they can show you clearly where their houses are located. If you already have the name of a *casa,* don't mention that you are looking for "José" or "María" (for example); the homeowner you're talking to will morph into that person in no time. Houses in the old center of town generally charge CUC$25 to CUC$35 per double; those a bit farther out (usually no more than a 15-min. walk from the Plaza Mayor) charge CUC$20 to CUC$25 per double. Alternatively, you could stay at one of the large resorts on Playa Ancón, 12km (7½ miles) away.

IN TRINIDAD

The venerable old **Hotel La Ronda,** José Martí no. 239 (© **41/99-2248;** www. hotelescubanacan.com), has been closed for some time for extensive remodeling. It is expected to open as an elegant little downtown boutique hotel run by Cubanacán, but an opening date is not known. A new hotel is under construction on a hill outside of town.

Very Expensive

Grand Hotel Iberostar Trinidad ★★ Facing the quiet Parque Céspedes, this restored and remodeled old building is now a beautiful and luxurious hotel in the heart of colonial Trinidad. A stately air pervades this place, from the large lobby area, with its soaring atrium ceiling and central fountain and broad marble staircase, to the rooms, restaurant, and all the rest. The rooms are spacious and tastefully done, with a broad range of amenities. The junior suites are somewhat bigger, with a separate tub and shower, and walk-in closet. My favorite rooms are the second-floor standard units, nos. 106 through 111, with balconies facing the park. No children under 15 are allowed.

Calle José Martí 262 (at Calle Lino Perez), Trinidad. ✆ **41/99-6073.** Fax 41/99-6077. www.iberostar. com. 40 units. CUC$172–CUC$290 double; CUC$220–CUC$250 suite. Rates include breakfast. MC, V. Children under 15 not allowed. **Amenities:** Restaurant; bar; room service; Wi-Fi (free). *In room:* A/C, TV, minibar.

Moderate

Hotel Las Cuevas ★ Perched on a hill 1.6km (1 mile) north of (and up above) the old colonial core of Trinidad, this hotel is named for the caves that dot the hillside. Built in the 1950s, the hotel is surprisingly large, featuring rows of concrete bungalow-style rooms, a round pool, and a fantastic underground cave dance club (a short distance from the property). The remodeled rooms are very comfortable, with exposed stone walls and good bathrooms. While it's a little inconveniently located up a steep hill (a quiet setting many will appreciate), you can easily walk (downhill) to the restaurants and nightlife of Trinidad, and then take a taxi home. The hotel is popular with tour groups.

Finca Santa Ana, Trinidad. ✆ **41/99-6133.** Fax 41/99-6161. www.hotelescubanacan.com. 109 units. CUC$84–CUC$91 double; CUC$99 suite. Rates include breakfast. MC, V. **Amenities:** 2 restaurants; 2 bars; dance club; nightly show; outdoor pool; outdoor tennis court. *In room:* A/C, TV, minibar.

Inexpensive

In addition to the *casas* reviewed below, following are some other recommended options. **Hostal La Rioja** ★ Frank País 389 between Simón Bolívar and Francisco Javier Zerquera (✆ **41/99-4589** or 527-11776; tereleria@yahoo.com.mx), is run by the superfriendly and welcoming Teresa; it has a rooftop bar with city views. **Casa Mauri,** Gustavo Izquierdo 119 between Simón Bolívar and Piro Guinart (✆ **524-74272;** www.hostalcasamauri.com) is an enormous house run by Miguel A Suárez del Villar Mauri that dates back to the 1920s. The colorful house offers two rooms—one of which boasts an ancient bathtub. The welcoming **Casa Bastida** ★ Maceo 537, between Simón Bolívar and Piro Guinart (✆ **41/99-6686;** www.hostalbastida. com), boasts wonderful rooftop views. One room has a cute balcony overlooking the street and there's an attractive communal dining area under a bamboo roof. **Casa Elda,** Jesús Menéndez 166, between Fernando Hernández Echerri and Ernesto Valdés Muñoz (✆ **41/99-3283;** mdleon@pol1tdad.ssp.sld.cu), is run by a friendly couple; the two rooms can be connected and both rooms now have ensuite bathrooms. **Hostal**

Check in Before You Check In

In Trinidad, if you make a reservation with one of the more popular *casas particulares,* it's a very good idea—if not essential—to reconfirm your reservation a couple of days in advance. *Casas* often let out rooms that haven't been reconfirmed.

Liliana Zerquera Gallardo (**Casa del Historiador**), Fernando Hernández Echerri 54 (☏ **41/99-3634**), a lovely colonial home, has two rooms, one quite small with a tiny bathroom. There is also **Casa Sotolongo,** Real 33 between Francisco Javier Zerquera and Simón Bolívar (☏ **41/99-4169**), which is located right on the main plaza, and **Casa de José y Fátima,** Francisco Javier Zerquera 159 between Frank País and Fco Peterson (☏ **41/99-6682**), which has comfortable rooms with a balcony, in a colonial house with a gorgeous blue porch. **Hostal Sandra y Victor,** Maceo 613, between Piro Guinart and Pablo Pichs Girón (☏ **41/99-6444;** www. hostalsandra.com), has two modern rooms and a great terrace with a rustic bar.

Casa Font ★★   A gorgeous, late-18th-century colonial house with a green facade, just a few steps from the bus station and in the heart of the old center, this family home has a great collection of antiques and a light, airy feel. For a *casa particular,* this is about as grand as it gets: chandeliers of Baccarat crystal, thick wood doors, colonial- and republican-era oil paintings, and fan-shaped slat windows above doors. Out back is a pretty courtyard with a well. One room has a bed dating from 1800, richly decorated with mother-of-pearl, and a lovely tiled bathroom; the other room has two beds and feels more contemporary. There are also stunning *modernista mampáras* doors (half doors in the Modernista design) in the house.

Gustavo Izquierdo 105 (btw. Piro Guinart and Simón Bolívar), Trinidad. ☏ **41/99-3683.** viatri@slg. mymdw.net. 2 units. CUC$25 double. No credit cards. *In room:* A/C, no phone.

Casa Meyer ★   A few paces from Casa Font, this is another spectacular, 200-year-old colonial home, with a garden courtyard. The house has very high, wood-beamed ceilings and very nice antiques, though it is a bit darker than Casa Font. One bedroom is huge, with antique beds, one decorated with mother-of-pearl, while the new room set back in the garden is just as nice and perhaps even more tranquil, with a huge, bronze four-poster bed. An original pram and 1903 gramaphone grace the main front room.

Gustavo Izquierdo 111 (btw. Piro Guinart and Simón Bolívar), Trinidad. ☏ **41/99-3444.** www.hostalcasa meyer.com. 2 units. CUC$20–CUC$25 double. No credit cards. *In room:* A/C, no phone.

Hostal Casa Colonial Muñoz ★   This charming place is run by English-speaking Julio and his wife Rosa. A breezy and centrally located colonial house built in 1800, it has two bedrooms with en-suite bathrooms and a shady patio, plus a rooftop terrace with fantastic views. Julio is a photographer and has considerable advice on Trinidad's cultural scene; check out his collection of slides and pictures adorning the house. Julio also offers photographic workshops. This place is popular and advance reservations are a must.

José Martí 401 (corner of Santiago Escobar), Trinidad. ☏/fax **41/99-3673.** www.casa.trinidadphoto. com. 2 units. CUC$30–CUC$35 double. No credit cards. *In room:* A/C, minibar, no phone.

IN PLAYA ANCÓN

Brisas Trinidad del Mar ★   The fanciest beach hotel in the general area of Trinidad, this place is semi-luxurious and easygoing. For those looking to combine beach time, great sea and mountain views, and easy access to Cuba's finest colonial city, this is without doubt the best option. The all-inclusive hotel imitates the famed colonial architecture of nearby Trinidad, with pastel colors and pastel-colored imitations of the town's more famous landmarks, including the San Francisco tower and the Plaza Mayor. The hotel is on one of the best sections of Playa Ancón, and it has a great pool and all the services one could want, including language and dance classes and diving.

Rooms are handsomely outfitted, nicely decorated with pale yellow walls and blue accents. If there's a drawback, it's that the food can be pretty average and bland.

Península Ancón, Trinidad. ☎ **41/99-6500.** Fax 41/99-6565. www.hotelescubanacan.com. 241 units. CUC$110–CUC$165 double. Rates are all-inclusive. MC, V. **Amenities:** 3 restaurants; 2 bars; snack bar; children's center and programs; gym; Internet; Jacuzzi; outdoor pool; room service; sauna; scooter and bike rental; 2 outdoor tennis courts. *In room:* A/C, TV, hair dryer, minibar.

Hotel Ancón   While this place definitely plays second fiddle to the neighboring Brisas Trinidad del Mar, the Hotel Ancón is nonetheless a good option for travelers looking for plenty of services and amenities on the beach at a reasonable price. The older-style hotel—a large Soviet block plunked down on the sand—is pretty uninspiring, and rooms are moderate in size and simply decorated (bare bones, even). About half of the rooms have oceanview balconies, and these are a definite plus. Still, we recommend you ask for a room in the newer wing, although these are in no way new, having been built in 1995. Rooms here have either mountain or sea views, balconies, and slightly more space. Activities include salsa and language classes, volleyball, aerobics, and more.

Carretera María Aguilar, Playa Ancón, Trinidad. ☎ **41/99-6120.** www.hotelescubanacan.com. 279 units. CUC$110–CUC$140 double. Rates are all-inclusive. MC, V. **Amenities:** 4 restaurants; 5 bars; Internet; nightly show; outdoor pool; sauna; 2 outdoor tennis courts. *In room:* A/C, TV, minibar.

Where to Dine

The dining scene in Trinidad is one of the more enjoyable ones in the country—which, admittedly, is not saying much—not so much for the excellence of its restaurants, but for the low-key atmosphere and a mix of both pretty good state-run establishments and *paladares* (private restaurants). Plenty of self-appointed guides will make their presence known, trying to lead you to an unofficial *paladar;* these are safe and often quite good, even if illegal (though that status has no consequence for you—feel free to dine wherever you like).

In addition to the restaurants listed below, the state-run **Plaza Mayor** (☎ 41/99-6470) is an acceptable option serving a decent buffet, in a beautifully restored old home and an even more beautiful courtyard.

EXPENSIVE

Grand Hotel Iberostar Trinidad INTERNATIONAL   The Grand Hotel's restaurant is the only place with fine dining in Trinidad. The main course is a la carte, but the starters and dessert are a little odd for such an expensive menu; however, you get the variety and no doubt avoid the wastage that is the curse of many Cuban resort hotels. Try the beef carpaccio with spicy tomato and the rarely-to-be-found Danish blue and manchego cheeses. For main courses, the grilled filet of *pargo* (snapper) with Parmesan vegetables or the candied tenderloin steak tournedos in red wine with fresh marrow and creamy potatoes are recommended.

Calle José Martí and Calle Lino Perez. ☎ **41/99-6073.** www.iberostar.com. Prix-fixe menu CUC$28 for hotel guests, CUC$35 for non-guests. MC, V. Daily 12:30–3pm and 7–10pm.

MODERATE

Casa de la Música CRIOLLAN   It's not an obvious place to eat, perhaps, but one of Trinidad's best spots for live music also has a restaurant attached, and if you're lucky enough to score one of the tables on the terrace, you'll be within earshot of the band playing on the platform on the steps below. The restaurant is, on the whole, no better or worse than other state-run places in town. It serves the standard main courses—grilled chicken, pork, and fish, as well as lobster and a couple of inexpensive sandwiches. We also like this spot for lunch.

Fernando H. Echerri 3. (℃) **41/99-6622.** Reservations not accepted. Main courses CUC$3.50–CUC$26; sandwiches CUC$1.50–CUC$3. Daily 10am–10pm.

Paladar Estela ★★ 🎒 CRIOLLAN Enter through an elaborately decorated colonial house, 2 blocks north of the cathedral, into this private restaurant. It has a handful of tables set in an exuberant backyard garden setting, with tons of flowering plants, including red *estrella de navidad,* and a wall festooned with vines. Portions are nearly as voluminous as the flora, and light eaters can share one dish between two people. Dishes include roast pork *a la cubana,* fried chicken, grilled fish, and ham omelet. However, my favorite is the perfectly spiced *ropa vieja* made with shredded lamb. All are served with *moros y cristianos* (black beans and rice), salad, fried banana, crackers, and fruit.

Simón Bolívar 557. (℃) **41/99-4329.** Reservations not accepted. Main courses CUC$8–CUC$10. No credit cards. Mon–Fri 7–10pm.

Paladar La Coruña ★ CRIOLLAN A pleasant private home restaurant with just two tables on the patio just beyond the living room, under a welcome ceiling fan, this is another of Trinidad's excellent *paladares.* It has an oral menu only, but you can already guess what's served: chicken, pork, grilled fish, and paella. Meals begin with a salad and veggie plate, and the main course is served with a heaping mound of rice and beans, followed by a small plate of bananas and mango. Tables are very informal, with plasticized tablecloths and wood chairs upfront. One wall of the *paladar* is decorated with souvenir money from customers around the world.

José Martí 430. No phone. Reservations not accepted. Main courses CUC$8–CUC$10. No credit cards. Daily 11am–11pm.

Restaurant El Jigüe CRIOLLAN El Jigüe (*Hee*-gweh) is a brightly lit, nearly formal dining room in a handsome, airy colonial house. It sits on one of the old town's prettiest and tiniest squares, next to a massive shade tree. Just a block from the Plaza Mayor, the restaurant has high-backed chairs, white and plum tablecloths, and prominent chandeliers, which lend it an elegance not often seen in official restaurants in Cuba. Its specialty is *pollo El Jigüe,* which comes in a clay pot with pasta and cheese and is served with salad and coffee. Other dishes worth checking out are grilled fish, standard chicken, and lobster.

Rubén Martínez Villena 69 (corner of Piro Guinart), Plazuela El Jigüe. (℃) **41/99-6476.** Reservations not required. Main courses CUC$7.50–CUC$24. Daily 11am–10:30pm.

Restaurante Trinidad Colonial CRIOLLAN This state-owned restaurant is more notable for its setting than its menu. It's in a pretty, mauve-colored house set back from the street, with a couple of tables in a sunny courtyard and more inside surrounded by chandeliers, fading oil paintings, and enormous dressers. The standard dishes of grilled fish, pork filet, grilled shrimp, and lobster are decent-size portions, but are a bit unexciting. The *filete de pescado Trinidad Colonial,* grilled fish topped with grated carrot, potato, and melted cheese, is small in size, but surprisingly good.

Antonio Maceo 55. (℃) **41/99-6473.** Reservations not required. Main courses CUC$6–CUC$15. Daily 9:30am–10:45pm.

Sol y Son ★★ CRIOLLAN One of Trinidad's long-standing *paladares,* this place is housed in an art- and furniture-bedecked, 19th-century house that could double as an antiques store. Out back, on the porch of a very attractive, verdant courtyard, the restaurant offers one of the more extensive menus among private restaurants. Choose from soups, spaghetti, a long list of fish (including a breaded filet stuffed with cheese), and grilled and roasted chicken and pork dishes. Check out the *cerdo borracho* (drunk pork), which is grilled and doused with rum and the house cocktail made from seven-year-old rum and honey. The patio has mounted ceiling fans and, during the day, you should do your level best to sit beneath one, as it can get very hot.

Simón Bolívar 283 (btw. José Martí and Frank País). (✆ **41/99-2926**. Reservations not accepted. Main courses CUC$6–CUC$10 No credit cards. Daily 12:30pm–3pm; dinner from 7pm.

INEXPENSIVE

Café Internet Las Begonias LIGHT FARE   Once one of Trinidad's better restaurants, Las Begonias is now not much more than a snackateria, with 10 glass-topped tables on a red-tile floor, open to the street. Still, it's good enough for breakfast or a cheap light lunch. It serves mostly *emparedados* (sandwiches), pizzas, and hamburgers, as well as the ubiquitous fried chicken. This place has an Internet café attached.

Corner of Simón Bolívar and Maceo. No phone. Reservations not accepted. Main courses CUC$1.50–CUC$3.50. No credit cards. Daily 8am–10pm. Internet service 9am–8:30pm.

Shopping

Trinidad, given its starring role on the tourist circuit, is one of the better shopping towns in central and eastern Cuba (though far from a shopper's paradise). In addition to the requisite cigar and music shops, several of Trinidad's atmospheric, cobblestone streets are converted daily into **street markets** featuring handicrafts, lace, and clothing items. While lace and clothing are the main attractions, you can also find interesting woodcarvings, musical instruments, masks, and a host of ceramic works. The street with the most variety tends to be Peña, near the Museo Municipal de Historia tower, while most of the lace and textile merchants, who occasionally have good *guayabera* shirts (simple, short-sleeved cotton shirt, with pockets and pleats, worn by men), tend to cluster on the small streets just east of the Plaza Mayor.

The art gallery on the south side of the Plaza Mayor, **Galería de Arte ARTex,** has two floors of contemporary art, much of it very accessible, and the traditional souvenir renderings of Trinidad.

The place for cigars and tobacco paraphernalia in town, **La Casa del Tabaco,** has two branches and carries all the finest Cuban cigars, carefully stored. The shop at Lino Pérez 296 (at the corner of José Martí) is open daily from 10am to 6pm; the branch on Francisco Javier Zerquera (at the corner of Maceo), is open daily from 10am to 6pm.

Many of the ceramic wares you'll see for sale around Trinidad are produced by the Santander family, whose history in this art form goes back generations. You can visit their small factory, **El Alfarero Casa Chichi,** Andrés Berro 51, between Abel Santamaría and Pepito Tey (✆ **41/99-3146**), although it's best to call in advance and tell them you're coming.

The most complete Cuban CD store in town, **ARTex,** is annexed to the Casa de Música on Fernando H. Echerri, where you'll find nightly performances of live music. The clerks will usually play just about anything you want to hear.

Trinidad After Dark

While most of Trinidad's old-town streets are coffin-quiet after dark, several joints bop with live Cuban music nightly. One of the best spots to sit outside, have a *mojito* or beer, and hear good traditional bands is the small plaza midway up the steps leading to the **Casa de la Música ★**. The dance floor is usually a good mix of polished, semiprofessional locals and foreigners whose hips are somewhat less smoothly oiled. The steps are often overflowing with people checking out some free music under the stars from 8:30pm until midnight. Inside the Casa de la Música, a more raucous environment prevails until the wee hours for a cover charge of CUC$1. Just around the corner on Fernando H. Echerri, **Palenque de los Congos Reales ★★** has an open-air stage where you can sometimes catch Grupo Folclórico performing Afro-Cuban music and dance (performances aren't regularly scheduled). At other times, there may be a standard *trova* or *son* group playing. It's open daily from 10am to 1am, and until 10pm on Saturday. The **Casa de la Trova,** Fernando H. Echerri 29, a block east of the Plaza Mayor, is the traditional spot to listen to Cuban bands and try out a few dance steps; it's open daily from 10am to 1am, and there's a cover charge of CUC$1. A similar spot is **Casa Fisher** (ARTex), on Lino Pérez 306 between José Martí and Francisco Cadahía, but the scene here can be hit-or-miss.

The **Ruinas del Teatro Brunet ★**, Maceo between Zerquera and Simón Bolívar, puts on a nightly Afro-Cuban cabaret-style show in the spacious courtyard of the ruins of the city's first theater. Another bar set in a delightful open-air courtyard in the ostensible ruins of a colonial home, the **Ruinas de Segarte ★**, Jesús Menéndez s/n between Callejón Gado and Juan Manuel Marquéz, is an intimate affair and open from 10:30am to 1:30am daily, and also has live music most nights.

La Canchánchara, Rubén Martínez Villena at Pablo P. Girón, sometimes has a few musicians assembled, but it's mostly just a little open-air courtyard bar in an atmospheric colonial house, a good place to kick back in old wooden chairs and have a *mojito* or the eponymous house drink, made with *aguardiente* (firewater), lime, and honey. It's open daily from 8:30am to 2am (but no food is served).

Club Amigos de la Parranda, Rubén Martínez Villena 59 (Patio del Templo de Santeria Yemaya) is home to a group of older guys who play traditional music and accept suggestions from the public. Donations are, obviously, gratefully received. It's open daily 10am–midnight.

One of the most unusual nightspots in Cuba has to be the dance club carved out of a deep two-level cave, **Discoteca Ayala,** also called La Cueva (© **41/99-6133**). Though it can be deadly hot, and the kitsch factor is undeniable, it's still pretty cool to dance to blasting disco-salsa tunes as colored lights bounce off stalactites. The crowd on weekends is largely Cuban. Now if they could only install air-conditioning to go with the lights and sound system, nocturnal spelunking would be even more appetizing. To get there, you can either walk up a path leading directly behind the cathedral, off Juan Manuel Márquez, or take the longer route from Hotel Las Cuevas (it's not actually on the premises of the hotel, though it's under the same management). It's open Tuesday to Sunday 10pm to 2am (later Fri–Sat); admission is CUC$3.

Side Trips from Trinidad

Though the colonial streets of Trinidad are the main draw, the town is perfectly situated for quick trips to the beach (one of the best on the southern coast) and gorgeous surrounding countryside, which includes the Sierra del Escambray mountains and a picturesque valley that was once home to the sugar plantations that made Trinidad wealthy in the 18th and 19th centuries.

PLAYA ANCÓN ★

Though it can't quite compare with Cayo Largo, Varadero, Cayos Coco and Guillermo, Cayo Santa Maria, or Guardalavaca—Cuba's prettiest and most prestigious beaches—Playa Ancón is still a very beautiful beach with one distinct advantage over those other, isolated stretches of sand: the proximity to Trinidad. At just 13km (8 miles) from town, Ancón, a 3km (2-mile) strip at the end of a peninsula, is a quick and easy ride to and from Trinidad, so beach lovers can stay here and visit the colonial wonder of Trinidad at their will. The beach is made up of wonderful white sand, and there's good snorkeling and diving at some 30 offshore dive sites. Both the Brisas del Mar Trinidad and Playa Ancón hotels (p. 210), as well as the major travel agencies in town, offer diving and snorkeling excursions beginning at CUC$45 per person in addition to watersports. **Cayo Blanco** is a tiny offshore island reputed to be one of the best dive spots, with a huge variety of coral. Local operators also offer "seafari" expeditions to Cayo Blanco, with boat trips to the island, lunch, and snorkeling. Trips depart from the Marina Nautica Marlin (© **41/99-6205**).

Northwest of Playa Ancón, about 8km (5 miles) from Trinidad, is **La Boca,** a small fishing village that's the popular beach spot among locals. Few tourists make it to La Boca, though there are a couple of *casas particulares* that rent rooms, including the **Hostal Vista al Mar,** Calle Real 47 (© **41/99-3716**), a cute royal-blue bungalow overlooking the beach. The best room is at the front of the house.

To get to Playa Ancón, take a taxi or Coco Taxi. Alternatively, energetic folks can rent a bike; see "Getting Around," earlier in this section.

VALLE DE LOS INGENIOS ★★

Trinidad got rich off the sugar trade back in the 18th and 19th centuries, and the Valle de los Ingenios (Valley of the Sugar Mills) was one of the most productive sugarcane growing areas in all of Cuba. The gorgeous, verdant valley is no longer king of the sugar trade, which once supported 60 mills, but for visitors, it makes a wonderful day trip. The zone has been declared a UNESCO Cultural Heritage Site. A 1907 American steam train, especially for tourists, departs daily for the valley, making the journey out to one of the old sugar estates, **Manaca-Iznaga,** in just over 30 minutes from Trinidad. However, the train has broken down several times in the last year; a replacement bus costs CUC$19, but it's not nearly as atmospheric. The old manor house (Casa Hacienda) remains and is now a pretty good tourist restaurant; however, the main attraction is the fantastic, 45m-high (148-ft.) pointed tower, built in 1845, which visitors can ascend (for a fee of CUC$1) for spectacular views of the surrounding area. A huge bell once hung here and tolled for the toiling slaves in the fields, signaling the beginning and end of their working days. There's a surprisingly good little restaurant in a hacienda-style home here, that serves up a filling lunch for between CUC$4 and CUC$8.

If it's working, the steam train departs Trinidad daily at 9:30am, leaves Manaca-Iznaga at 1:30pm, and returns back in Trinidad around 2pm. Tickets (CUC$10 round-trip) can be purchased from any tour operator around town, or directly at the **train station** 1km (½ mile) from the center of Trinidad on Calle Antonio Guiteras Final (© **41/99-3348**).

PARQUE NACIONAL TOPES DE COLLANTES (SIERRA DEL ESCAMBRAY) ★★

Northwest of Trinidad, along dangerously curving roads, are the thickly pine-covered mountains of the Sierra del Escambray, a beautiful range that cuts across central Cuba. From Trinidad, the Topes de Collantes National Park, which covers 175sq. km (68 sq. miles), is the main draw, a cool refuge from the heat that usually bakes the stone streets of Trinidad. It's a splendid area for hiking, though a sad and lifeless resort village of Soviet-style hotels also provides therapeutic spa treatments.

Of the several well-established trails, the most popular route is **Salto del Caburní,** a hike that begins near a graffiti-covered house, the Casa de la Gallega (where simple lunches are served), and terminates in a great 75m (246-ft.) waterfall and swimming hole. The clearly marked trail, through dense forests of palm, pine, and eucalyptus trees, is fairly challenging, with several steep descents, often along a muddy, narrow path. The water in the deep green pool makes for a brisk swim. Another popular hike, which also has a waterfall as its reward at the end, is **Salto Vega Grande.** Each of these trails is a 4km (2.5-mile) hike each way.

The Topes de Collantes resort, about 20km (12 miles) from Trinidad, welcomes mostly Cubans; but several of its hotels accept foreign guests. Of these, the top choice is **Villa Caburní** (✆ 42/54-0189; www.gaviota-grupo.com). The massive and rather unattractive **Kurhotel Escambray** (✆ 42/54-0180; www.gaviota-grupo.com) is most notable as a sort of lakeside spa offering a variety of therapies, including hydrotherapy. Still, it's hard to recommend this place, when most visitors have access to such vastly better services at home. Reservations for these hotels must be made at an office at the resort complex or by phone (✆ 42/54-0117) or at a tourism desk in town.

Though it's possible to rent a car and explore the region on your own, paying a CUC$6.50 entrance fee at the Topes de Collantes resort (**Complejo Turístico Topes de Collantes;** ✆ 42/54-0193/0219; reserva@topes.com.co.cu; run by Gaviota), hikers are advised to sign on for organized bookings, since many trails are not well marked. The Trinidad travel agencies, such as Havanatur and Cubatur, offer Sierra del Escambray jeep excursions for CUC$29 to CUC$37 per person.

SANCTI SPÍRITUS

70km (43 miles) NE of Trinidad; 386km (240 miles) E of Havana

Sancti Spíritus lies smack-dab in the middle of the island and is the capital of the province of the same name. Perched on the banks of the Río Yayabo, the old town is a warren of corkscrew streets, many lined with fine, if weathered, colonial homes. Like Trinidad, the town was one of the original seven *villas* founded by Velázquez in the early 16th century. Today, Sancti Spíritus is a small and not greatly significant, mostly modern provincial capital with an unassuming, lived-in feel. Though much of the city is run-down, it is beginning to renovate some of its more important colonial buildings, including one of the finest house-museums and one of the best-preserved colonial churches in the country, with the hopes of attracting a greater percentage of the travelers that stop off in nearby Trinidad.

Essentials
GETTING THERE
BY BUS **Víazul** (✆ 7/881-1143 in Havana; www.viazul.com) has daily buses to Sancti Spíritus on the Havana–Santiago de Cuba line leaving at 9:30am, 3pm, 6:15pm, and 10pm. From Havana, the trip takes just over 5 hours. The fare is CUC$23. Víazul also makes the 1-hour trip to Sancti Spíritus directly from Trinidad (✆ 41/99-4448; CUC$6) daily at 8am on the Trinidad–Santiago de Cuba route. From Santiago, buses leave at 9am, 3:15pm, 7:30pm, and 10pm, and the trip takes around 10 hours. The fare is CUC$28.

The bus terminal in Sancti Spíritus (✆ 41/32-4142) is located at Carretera Central Km 388, between Circunvalación and the Carretera de Jíbaro. Taxis charge CUC$2 or CUC$3 for a ride to the center of town.

Sancti Spíritus

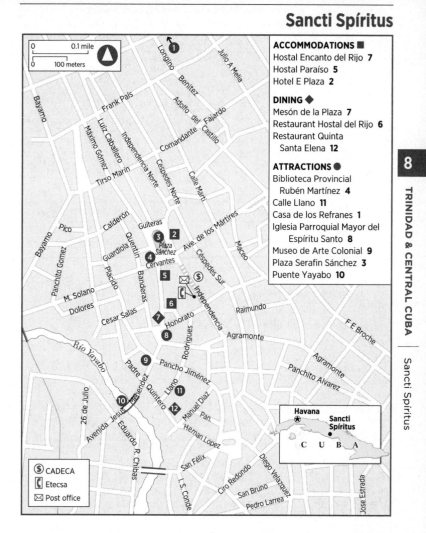

ACCOMMODATIONS ■
Hostal Encanto del Rijo **7**
Hostal Paraíso **5**
Hotel E Plaza **2**

DINING ◆
Mesón de la Plaza **7**
Restaurant Hostal del Rijo **6**
Restaurant Quinta
 Santa Elena **12**

ATTRACTIONS ●
Biblioteca Provincial
 Rubén Martínez **4**
Calle Llano **11**
Casa de los Refranes **1**
Iglesia Parroquial Mayor del
 Espíritu Santo **8**
Museo de Arte Colonial **9**
Plaza Serafín Sánchez **3**
Puente Yayabo **10**

BY CAR   Driving from Havana, the fastest route is along the Autopista Nacional (A1) to Santa Clara, and then continuing along the Carretera Central to Sancti Spíritus (about 5 hr.). (See "Autopista Scam," earlier in this chapter.) The short drive from Trinidad, along the Circuito Sur, is one of the prettiest in Cuba, as the road rolls through fields of sugar cane with the Sierra del Escambray looming in the background. From Santiago de Cuba, start out northwest on the unfinished A1 and then take the Carretera Central through Bayamo, Camagüey, and Ciego de Avila (about 6 hr.).

GETTING AROUND
Call **Cubataxi** (© **41/32-2133**) for a taxi, or hop aboard one of the horse-drawn *coches* (carriages), which officially only accept pesos, but most will accept an offer for the fare of CUC$1 to CUC$2. Unlicensed taxis also circulate on the streets of Sancti

Spíritus. To rent a car, call **Cubacar** (📞 **41/32-8533**). Rates are about CUC$55 to CUC$85 per day for a standard four-door car.

ORIENTATION

For a relatively small town, Sancti Spíritus is rather spread out. However, you're unlikely to spend much time beyond the old town, where you can easily walk everywhere. You'll only need a taxi (or horse-drawn *coche*) for getting to the bus terminal, train station, or your hotel, if you choose to stay at one of the inconveniently located, large hotels on the outskirts of town.

The closest Sancti Spíritus comes to having a tourist information office is the travel agency **Cubatur** (📞 **41/32-8518**), Máximo Gómez 7 on the west side of Plaza Sánchez. Cubatur also offers hotel discounts and discounted set meals at various restaurants in the city, including Quinta Santa Elena and Restaurant Mesón de la Plaza; ask for details.

The **Banco Financiero Internacional,** Independencia 2 between Plaza Sánchez and Honorato (📞 **41/32-8479**), is open Monday through Friday from 8:30am to 3:30pm. The **CADECA** branch at Independencia 31 (📞 **41/32-8535**) is open Monday through Saturday from 8am to 4:30pm and Sunday from 8am to 11:30am.

If you need medical attention, **Hospital Provincial Camilo Cienfuegos** is located on Carretera Central at Bartolomé Masó (📞 **41/32-4017**).

You can make long-distance or international phone calls or log on for CUC$6 per hour with the Etecsa card at the **Etecsa** office on Independencia 10 Sur between Plaza Sánchez and Honorato opposite the CADECA; it's open daily from 8:30am to 7:30pm. The main **post office** is now in the same building.

What to See & Do

It won't take much more than a morning or afternoon to check out Sancti Spíritus's principal attractions. The old town is very untouristy and unassuming, and perfect for an easygoing stroll.

Calle Llano ★ is the most atmospheric street in Sancti Spíritus, a bent-elbow cobblestone alleyway (one of the only remaining stone streets in town) of pastel-colored and tiled-roof houses. It's often very still, except for a few kids playing stickball. **Puente Yayabo,** the bridge over the river at the southern edge of the old town, is a 19th-century take on a European Romanesque stone bridge. Locals don't pause long enough to wonder whether a medieval-style bridge built in 1825, in a town not founded until well into the 16th century, looks odd or not; they bound over it at great speed, on bicycles, in horse-drawn wagons, and in 1950s Chevys on their way to and from the Colón residential district.

The main hub of life in Sancti Spíritus is **Plaza Serafín Sánchez,** a large public square with a handful of fine colonial buildings in various states of disrepair mixed in with bland modern constructions. It certainly doesn't qualify as one of Cuba's most attractive plazas, but it is perennially busy with cars buzzing around and people meeting up. One of the most notable edifices on the square, on the corner of Solano and Máximo Gómez, is the **Biblioteca Provincial Rubén Martínez,** an early-20th-century library that looks more like the local opera house. The main sights in town are a short walk south of here.

Perhaps Sancti Spíritus's most splendid colonial home, **Museo de Arte Colonial** ★★, Plácido 74 at Jesús Menéndez (📞 **41/32-5455**), is the city's standout attraction. The opulent former palatial mansion of one of Cuba's most elite families, the Valle-Iznaga clan, who fled Cuba after the Revolution, it became the property of the state in 1961. Ninety percent of what you see inside, from furniture to paintings, is original. Though the family obviously kept an impressive collection of Limoges porcelain, French gilded mirrors, Italian marble tables, and Baccarat crystal chandeliers here, this wasn't their primary residence; the house was used mostly to host family members in transit, so the furnishings were rather eclectic. The three bedrooms are decorated in grand style, though, with handmade lace, embroidered sheets, and hand-painted glass. Note the gorgeous and very Cuban leather *sillón fumador* (smoking chair) and, in the music room, the mid-18th-century American piano, one of only two of its type in Cuba. In the tearoom is the family seal, which says a lot about the arrogance of the rich and powerful: *"El que más vale no vale tanto como Valle vale"* ("He who has the greatest worth isn't worth as much as a Valle is worth"—playing off the Spanish word for "worth" with the family surname). The museum is open Tuesday through Saturday from 9am to 5pm and Sunday from 8am to noon. Admission is CUC$2 with a guided tour in English, Spanish, or French; there is a fee of CUC$1 to take photos and taking video costs CUC$1.

Iglesia Parroquial Mayor del Espíritu Santo ★, Jesús Menéndez between Honorato and Agramonte, is one of the best-preserved colonial churches in Cuba and the oldest building in Sancti Spíritus. A small, faded blue church with a tall bell tower, the austere construction dates to 1680. The church's massive ceiling beams are impressive, as is the blue-and-yellow painted nave. Though the church is unlikely to wow most visitors, it is a quietly evocative, authentic colonial sight that recalls a day when Sancti Spíritus may have looked more like Trinidad. It's open Tuesday through Saturday from 9 to 11am and from 2 to 5pm; admission is free.

If you have occasion to be north of downtown, take a peek at the curiosity that is the so-called **Casa de los Refranes (House of Aphorisms).** The bricks that make up the exterior of the modest roadside house are covered with hundreds of sayings and slogans, some banal and others philosophical (they look like graffiti, but they're actually baked in a ceramic-like process). The house belonged to Tomás Alvarez but since his death his niece opens the house, on Carretera Central just past the bus stop and up the road from Villa Los Laureles hotel, on Saturdays and Sundays.

Where to Stay

Sancti Spíritus has one of the best new boutique hotels in Cuba, as well as a good collection of *casas particulares* clustered within easy walking distance of the old town's main attractions. **Hostal Paraíso,** Máximo Gómez 11 Sur between Honorato (Parque Honorato) and Cervantes (℃ **41/33-4658** or **52/71-1257;** hectorluis paraiso64@gmail.com), has two comfortable rooms—one in an old doctor's consulting room where an original glass cabinet is embedded in the wall. **Hostal Las Américas,** Carretera Central No. 157 Sur, between Cuba and Cuartel (℃ **41/322-984;** hostallasamericas@yahoo.es), run by Pedro Hernández Castro, has two air-conditioned guest rooms with TVs and an attractive garden full of fruit trees.

Hostal Encanto del Rijo ★★ ✦ This handsomely restored, light-blue colonial mansion on Plaza Honorato del Castillo is part of a growing trend in elegant boutique hotels, and best of all, it's a steal. The house was in complete ruins just several years ago, but it has been completely redone and now exudes colonial character and charm. The rooms are huge, especially nos. 5, 6, 7, and 8, which look out onto the plaza and have balconies with views of the tower of La Parroquial church. The accommodations have restrained decor, with sedate colors and old photos of Sancti Spíritus. Ceilings are so high that chirping birds often flutter in and fly around in the public rooms in the morning. The two-story structure is built around a lovely patio with a fountain, where you'll find the hotel's excellent little restaurant. There's also a nice cafe and bar that opens onto the plaza.

Honorato del Castillo 12, Sancti Spíritus. © **41/32-8588.** Fax 41/32-8577. www.hotelescubanacan.com. 16 units. CUC$64 double; CUC$80 suite. **Amenities:** Restaurant; bar; room service. *In room:* A/C, TV, minibar.

Hotel E Plaza   This small hotel right off Plaza Sánchez has been remodeled into a Hoteles E boutique hotel by Cubanacán. It has a rooftop terrace and *mirador* with long views of Sancti Spíritus and an interior courtyard which provides a cool retreat away from the heat of the sun. Local artists' exhibits decorate the public areas. Rooms have high ceilings and the largest rooms face the plaza and the street.

Independencia 1 (Plaza Sánchez), Sancti Spíritus. © **41/32-7102.** Fax 41/32-8577. www.hoteles cubanacan.com. 25 units. CUC$54 double. Rates include breakfast. MC, V. **Amenities:** Restaurant, bar; room service. *In room:* A/C, TV.

Where to Dine

Mesón de la Plaza ★ CRIOLLAN   Set on one of Sancti Spíritus's most attractive plazas, this handsome 1850s house is open to the street and has two rooms with high ceilings and picnic-style tables with benches. The restaurant is very clean, well man-aged, and popular, especially with a lunchtime tourist crowd. It breaks out of the Cuban restaurant doldrums with a couple of house specialties: garbanzo soup with bacon, pork, and sausage; and *ropa vieja* (shredded beef), served in an earthenware pot. Those two dishes, plus a glass of excellent and refreshing sangria, make for a very good meal, but you might also opt for grilled shrimp or fish filet. **Note:** The restaurant is apt to close early at night, around 9pm, if there are no customers.

Máximo Gómez 34, Plaza Honorato. © **41/32-8546.** Reservations recommended for lunch. Main courses CUC$4.80–CUC$9. Daily 9am–10:45pm.

Restaurant Hostal del Rijo ★★ CRIOLLAN   Set in an airy central courtyard beside a stone fountain and surrounded by an abundance of potted plants, this res-taurant features wrought-iron furniture and an overall elegant ambience. Aside from the wonderful environs, this place also has a creative and deft young chef, who takes chances with local ingredients and dishes—an uncommon occurrence at most state-run restaurants. We recommend the roast pork in a fruit glaze, or the *camarones casilda* (shrimp cooked in white wine). You'll even find a fairly decent and reasonably priced wine list here. The *serrano helado,* an espresso coffee with vanilla ice cream, grenadine and syrup, is a delicious way to end your meal. Breakfast can also be served to non-guests for CUC$5.

Honorato del Castillo 12, Sancti Spíritus. © **41/32-8588.** Main courses CUC$3.50–CUC$18. Daily 7am–10:30pm.

Restaurant Quinta Santa Elena ★ CRIOLLAN   This restaurant near the river and Puente Yayabo occupies a lovely colonial home with handsome rooms and a relax-ing grand terrace that opens onto the garden backyard, with river views. Popular with groups, especially at lunch, it features traditional Cuban music and good meals and service. Standard dishes like fried fish filet and pork and beef steaks are enlivened by a twist, of *vaca frita,* a traditional dish of roast beef, accompanied by white rice and vegetables.

Padre Quintero (btw. Llano and Manolico Díaz). © **41/32-8167.** Reservations recommended for lunch. Main courses CUC$5.50–CUC$9. Daily 10am–10pm.

CAMAGÜEY & THE NORTH-EASTERN COAST

T he extraordinary, powdery, dazzling white beaches of Cayo Coco and Cayo Guillermo, the cays that lie off the mainland and jut into the deep aquamarine blue of the Atlantic Ocean, are the primary attractions of Ciego de Avila province. It is a remote area, but one with the infrastructure and natural gifts that make it perfect for idyllic sun, sand, and sea holidays. The namesake provincial capital Ciego de Avila and other towns and cities in this province hold few attractions for visitors.

A little farther east, the predominantly flat, low-lying Camagüey province, southeast of Ciego de Avila, is the largest in the country, though it is also the least densely populated. It occupies the widest swath on the island, 120km (75 miles) from the Atlantic coast to the Caribbean coast. Camagüey, the provincial capital, is Cuba's third-largest city, after Havana and Santiago de Cuba, and is a fine colonial city marked by dozens of churches that is worth exploring. Its architectural wealth was recognized by UNESCO in 2008.

CAYO COCO & CAYO GUILLERMO ★★

98km (61 miles) N of Ciego de Avila; 550km (342 miles) E of Havana; 270km (168 miles) NE of Trinidad; 202km (126 miles) NW of Camagüey

One of Cuba's premier beach destinations, distinguished by some of the most pristine sand and water on the island, Cayo Coco and Cayo Guillermo are cousin cays (*cayos*) reached by crossing a 27km (17-mile) *pedra-plén,* or man-made causeway, that extends from the mainland over the shimmering, shallow waters of the Atlantic. The cays share some of the same attributes as Varadero, but with a more isolated and natural feel, and without the interminable string of hotels.

Though these cays were explored way back in 1514, when Diego Velázquez named the stretch of islands and cays along the north coast **Jardines del Rey (the King's Gardens),** Cayo Coco was only developed for tourism in the early 1990s. The development on its neighboring cay, Guillermo, is newer still. Until construction of the causeway in 1988, the Cayos remained completely isolated, exclusively known to local fishermen, adventurous sailors like Ernest Hemingway, and pirates who would stow their treasures.

The cays are part of the Archipélago de Sabana-Camagüey, which extends 300km (186 miles) along the north coast and consists of some 400 large islands and small cays. Cayos Coco and Guillermo, the most developed of the entire stretch, are populated by just a handful of resort hotels—although more are planned. The unspoiled beaches have spectacular white and powdery sand and the waters are a classic Caribbean-style crystal-line turquoise. The area's natural gifts are some of the best in Cuba: nearly 400km (250 miles) of coral reefs, plus an ecotourist's bundle of lagoons, marshes, and one of Cuba's most abundant populations of birds, with more than 200 species. The latter includes one of the Americas' largest native colony of pink flamingos, estimated at upwards of 10,000 birds, which often appear as a gauzy pink haze shimmering on the horizon (except in May, when they venture close to the causeway), as well as herons, pelicans, black and white egrets, white ibis, and other tropical species. The white ibis, known as "coco" in Cuba, gave the cay its name. The waters off the cays are flush with grouper, snapper, and mackerel, while deeper off the coast, fishermen find marlin and swordfish.

A third cay—east of Cayo Coco, Cayo Romano, and the beaches out on Cayo Paredón Grande (tiny despite its name)—is the next bull's-eye targeted for Cuban hotel development in the archipelago, although no construction has yet begun. For now, the main resorts are Cayo Coco and Cayo Guillermo, and they're quite popular with Canadian, British, and Argentine travelers, as well as a good number of other nationalities. The focus for most guests is trained squarely on the beaches, swimming pools, watersports, dining and drinking, in-house activities, and nightly entertain-ment; rare is the traveler who comes seeking something else. If you have other activities in mind, your sense of isolation could be significant, although for those who get antsy, all the hotels offer local excursions as well as day trips and overnights to Trinidad, Santa Clara, Cienfuegos, Camagüey, and Havana.

Essentials

GETTING THERE

BY PLANE   The **Aeropuerto Internacional Jardines del Rey,** Carretera a Cayo Coco (✆ **33/30-9165**; airport code CCC), accepts international flights from Canada, Argentina, and the U.K. There are twice-daily domestic flights on **AeroCaribbean** (✆ **33/30-9106**) from Havana for CUC$108.

The hotels offer airport pickup services for clients. If you have not prearranged transportation to your hotel, there are usually a couple of state-owned taxis hanging about. The fare from Aeropuerto Internacional Jardines del Rey is about CUC$10–CUC$15 to Cayo Coco and CUC$15–CUC$25 to Cayo Guillermo.

BY BUS   If you're traveling independently to the cays from within Cuba, getting there on your own without a rental car or legal taxi is complicated. The only bus services that travel across the checkpoint are those belonging to official tour operators, such as **Cubanacán, Cubatur,** and **Havanatur.** All of these operators offer package deals and transportation options to the cays from all of their major operational points, including Havana, Santiago, Varadero, Trinidad, Santa Clara, Cienfuegos, and Camagüey.

A more complicated way to the cays is to take a **Víazul** bus (✆ **33/22-5109**; www. viazul.com) to Ciego de Avila, and then hire a taxi all the way to the cays for CUC$60 to CUC$75. All Víazul buses on the Havana-Santiago route stop in Ciego de Avila. The fare is CUC$27 from Havana, and CUC$24 from Santiago. Make sure you hire a state

Cayo Coco & Cayo Guillermo

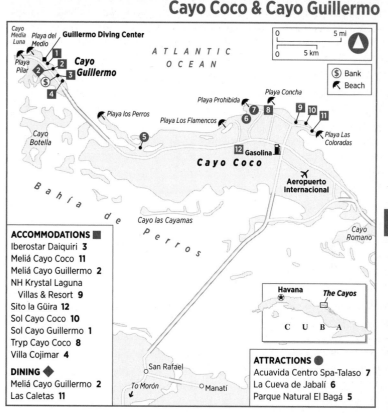

ACCOMMODATIONS ■
Iberostar Daiquiri **3**
Meliá Cayo Coco **11**
Meliá Cayo Guillermo **2**
NH Krystal Laguna
  Villas & Resort **9**
Sito la Güira **12**
Sol Cayo Coco **10**
Sol Cayo Guillermo **1**
Tryp Cayo Coco **8**
Villa Cojimar **4**

DINING ◆
Meliá Cayo Guillermo **2**
Las Caletas **11**

ATTRACTIONS ●
Acuavida Centro Spa-Talaso **7**
La Cueva de Jabalí **6**
Parque Natural El Bagá **5**

cab, as a driver with his own car is still not allowed to transport foreigners to the cays. The nearest town to the cays with legal *casas particulares* is Morón (p. 223).

BY CAR/TAXI   To drive to the cays, head north out of Ciego de Avila toward the city of Morón, and follow the signs out to the cays. You can pick up a taxi in either Ciego de Avila or Morón, the two nearest cities of note. Call **Cubataxi** (✆ **33/26-6666** in Ciego de Avila and **33/50-3290** in Morón). A taxi from Trinidad costs CUC$100. A taxi from Morón to Cayo Coco is CUC$45 and to Cayo Guillermo CUC$55–CUC$65. From Ciego to Avila to Morón is CUC$15. One has to pass a guarded checkpoint with a toll each way of CUC$2 to access the *pedraplén* that bridges the distance between the mainland and the cays. Remember that if you travel from Morón to the cays for the day you will need to show your passport at the check point. There are rental offices in Morón and Ciego de Avila.

GETTING AROUND

You won't get very far on foot. The cays are deceptively large, and there's no place to go on foot anyway, unless you want to visit an adjacent hotel. The best way to get around the cays is by **moped.** Most of the hotels have mountain bikes (free for guests) and mopeds that rent for CUC$25 a day.

There is a tourist bus, Jardines del Rey Bus Tour, which makes the entire circuit from one end of Playa Coco to Playa Pilar at the far end of Playa Guillermo. The bus runs six times a day in each direction, and costs CUC$5.

All of the hotels can call you a cab, or you can try **Cubataxi** (© 33/30-1414) on Cayo Coco. If you prefer to drive yourself, there are car-rental companies located on both Cayo Coco and Cayo Guillermo, and most hotels have agencies on the premises. **Havanautos** has an office at Calle Libertad between Honrato del Castillo and Maceo, Ciego de Avila (© 33/21-2570) and at Av.Tarafa, Morón (© 33/50-2115); **Cubacar** has an office at the bus terminal in Ciego de Avila (© 33/22-5105) and in the Hotel Morón in Morón (© 33/50-2028). All have operational centers on Jardines del Rey. Due to high demand and isolation, rates are relatively expensive on the cays, about CUC$80 to CUC$100 per day for a standard four-door vehicle. You're sometimes better off renting a car in Ciego de Avila or Morón before traveling to the cays.

All the hotels offer a variety of **organized excursions,** either directly or through tour representatives, which transport guests by bus or minibus from one cay to the other, or to other destinations, such as Playa Pilar on Cayo Guillermo. You're probably just as well off using whatever operator is working out of your hotel, or you can call **Cubanacán** (© 33/30-1225), **Cubatur** (© 33/30-1029), **Ecotur** (© 33/30-8163), Gaviota Tours (© 33/30-2260), or **Havanatur** (© 33/30-1371) to set something up.

ORIENTATION

Banco Financiero Internacional is in the Servicupet at the Rotonda at the entrance to Cayo Coco (© 33/30-1252) and at the **Iberostar** in Cayo Guillermo (© 33/30-1607). For medical attention, go to **Clínica Internacional Cayo Coco** (© 33/30-2158), next to the Villa Gaviota on Cayo Coco. The Hospital General Docente de Morón has a designated foreigners' ward.

Several of the hotels have Internet access for their guests. International and domestic mail can be handled at any of the hotels.

What to See & Do

Cayo Coco is the better known of the two cays, probably due to its earlier development. The best-known **Cayo Coco beaches** ★★ are **Playa Larga** and **Playa Las Coloradas. Playa Los Flamencos,** a few kilometers west, is a slightly more isolated and quieter beach, and beyond this is **Playa Prohibida.** They're among the most stellar beaches to be found in all of Cuba. In the interior of the cay are lagoons and marshlands, havens for the local bird and animal populations.

Cayo Guillermo is connected to Cayo Coco by a 15km (9-mile) *pedraplén*. **Cayo Guillermo beaches** ★★ (**Playa El Paso, Playa del Medio,** and **Playa Larga**) are every bit as spectacular as those on Cayo Coco; in fact, at low tide, the crystal-clear waters are so shallow that you can comfortably wade out several hundred meters. The landscape is very similar to Cayo Coco, but Guillermo boasts the most spectacular beach of either cay, and perhaps the entire northern coastline, if not the country: **Playa Pilar** ★★★, long ago explored by Ernest Hemingway and today a popular day trip for hotel guests on both cays. Playa Pilar features high sand dunes, a new attractive blue and white walkway and a restaurant on the beach serving up seafood (from CUC$6.50–CUC$15) and other dishes from CUC$3. Sun loungers are charged at CUC$2 a day. Just one kilometer away is **Cayo Media Luna,** a popular spot for snorkelers.

papa & THE CAYOS

Ernest Hemingway's love of sailing and deep-sea fishing is well documented, a great source of his love affair with Cuba. The novelist was one of the first to explore Cayo Guillermo; in the '30s and '40s, Hemingway used to set sail off the coasts of the northern cays in dogged pursuit of marlin and swordfish in the Atlantic. The celebrated beach on Cayo Guillermo, Playa Pilar, is even named for the author's beloved fishing boat, *Pilar.* In an episode befitting his he-man, roguish character, Hemingway enlisted his crew and boat to hunt for Nazi submarines off Cuba's northern cays at the height of World War II (according to some, the island was awash with Nazi sympathizers and agents). Papa's companion was, as ever, Gregorio Fuentes, the model for the aged fisherman in *The Old Man and the Sea.*

In Hemingway's novel *Islands in the Stream,* the main character looks longingly across the bay at Cayo Guillermo, asking rhetorically, "See how green she is and full of promise?" Evidently the Cuban authorities, intent on developing the cays a half century after Hemingway first explored them, feel the same way.

DIVING & OTHER WATERSPORTS

With long, pristine stretches of coral reef, and warm, crystal-clear waters, the cays are one of the best diving spots on the planet. There are 28 dive sites, including five superior sites easily accessible from the cays, which range in depth from 4 to 30m (13–98 ft.). All the hotels on Cayo Coco and Cayo Guillermo can organize diving excursions, but you may wish to directly consult one of the main outfits, like **Blue Diving** (© 33/30-8180 or 33/30-8179; bluediving@marlin.cco.tur.cu), which has a dive center at the Meliá Cayo Coco, right on the beach; **Coco Diving** (© 33/30-1020; cocodiving@marlin.cco.tur.cu), which has a dive center at Tryp Cayo Coco, and **Green Moray** at Meliá Cayo Guillermo (© 33/30-1627; greenmoray@marlin.cco.tur.cu), which offers certified programs, several dive packages, and diving excursions to Playa Santa Lucía and Trinidad. A two-tank dive is CUC$74, including equipment.

Most of the hotels have their own catamarans, sailboards, and other vehicles and facilities for watersports; kite surfing and paragliding are also possible. **Marlin Jardines del Rey** on Cayo Coco (© 33/30-1221 or 33/30-1411) has a wide range of watersports programs, including "seafari" catamaran trips to Paredón Grande, east of Cayo Coco and a complement of kayaks and windsurfing boards. The **International Marina** on Cayo Guillermo (© 33/30-1737/1323) has a six-vessel pier and similar capabilities and facilities, including diving and sportfishing trips. Full-day catamaran trips run about CUC$75 per person; half-day trips are CUC$43. **Boat Adventure** ★ (© 33/30-1516) offers small speedboat 2-hour trips (self-driven, with a guide) through a maze of mangrove canals, marshes, and wetlands of Cayo Guillermo, a scenic trip with stops for snorkeling. There are four departures daily; the cost is CUC$41 per person. Private boat charters are also possible but expensive, costing about CUC$300–CUC$500. Fishing is available from CUC$90 for a half-day; fly fishing is CUC$129 for a half-day excursion east of Cayo Paredón Grande. Call © 33/30-2139 for information or contact **Ecotur** at © 33/30-8163.

ORGANIZED TOURS

All the hotels offer day trips to remote beaches, including the finest in the cays, **Playa Pilar,** as well as **flamingo tours, jeep tours,** and **city tours** by minibus to

Morón, Ciego de Avila, Santa Clara, Trinidad, and Camagüey, or to Havana (CUC$189–CUC$289) and Cienfuegos by plane. Other options include **sugar cane tours** that take visitors to a decommissioned sugar factory that now produces sweets, tours of the **Criadero de Crocodrilos** (crocodile breeding center), a boat trip on Redonda lagoon (see below; CUC$65), and visits to **Sitio La Güira** (a purpose-built dude ranch). Horseback treks and jeep safaris (CUC$69) through the interior of the cays and to Morón are also available. A popular trip is to **Laguna de la Leche ★**, a massive lake on the outskirts of Morón with plenty of pelicans and other native birds. The lake's name comes from the water's murky, milky appearance (caused by limestone deposits). Another, much smaller lake that's worth a visit is **Laguna La Redonda,** where you'll find thick mangroves, swamps, and funky woodlands growing out of the still waters. It's best seen by *lancha* (motorboat) tour leaving from the entrance of the little restaurant (CUC$4 for a 45-minute trip). On a cruise, you'll see huge spider webs, massive mounds of termites in trees, and thick Spanish moss. Both lakes are most often visited in combination with a city tour of Morón.

One of the only true attractions here, aside from the beaches and nature, is the **Parque Natural El Bagá** (© **33/30-1062,** ext. 103), an interesting little complex that features a series of nature trails and lookouts through mangroves and litoral forest, and on raised platforms over lagoons. There is also a small reconstruction of an ancient indigenous village, with periodic live shows of local actors engaged in re-creations of Taíno dances. (**Parents, be forewarned:** The women in the shows are topless.) A wonderful stretch of beach is also right here. Admission to the whole complex is CUC$25.

To explore the region on your own, you can take a **tourist train** from Tryp Cayo Coco to Sitio La Güira, Flamingo Beach, and Jabalí Cave (CUC$12). **Palmares Aeroclub** (© **33/30-1054**) offers paragliding and ultralight flights (small, single-seater airplanes) from the hotels, CUC$30.

TIME FOR SOME PAMPERING

Although nowhere near as opulent as many modern spas, the **Acuavida Centro Spa-Talaso** (© **33/30-2158;** www.servimedcuba.com) offers a wide range of massage and spa treatments. Options range from mud baths and seaweed scrubs to full-body massages and a host of water-based treatments. The large facility has five pools in a range of sizes and temperatures. Some are freshwater pools, while others take advantage of the neighboring seawater. There's a salon on the premises. It's open Monday to Saturday from 9:30am to 7pm.

Where to Stay & Dine on Cayo Coco

Almost all visitors to Jardines del Rey come as part of an all-inclusive package and take all their meals at their hotels. If you want to take a break from your hotel fare, check out the simple shack, **Ranchón Playa Prohibida,** located out on Playa Prohibida, where a full lobster meal, with rice and beans and two good-size tails, will run you around CUC$15. If you're out at Playa Pilar, try **Ranchón Playa Pilar,** which serves similar fare at similar prices. **Ranchón Cuba Libre,** right on the beach between Iberostar Daiquirí and Meliá Cayo Guillermo, and **Ranchón Media Luna,** in Cayo Guillermo, offer seafood and creole food; dishes run about CUC$6 to CUC$15.

VERY EXPENSIVE

Meliá Cayo Coco ★★★　This elegant flagship of the Meliá chain is the top hotel on Cayo Coco and one of the finest hotels in Cuba. This adults-only hotel is popular with honeymooners. The property is hip and stylish throughout, chic for an

A STOPOVER IN morón

Located 37km (23 miles) north of Ciego de Avila, Morón (Moh-*rohn*) is the small gateway city to the cays, and home to most of the 3,500 Cubans who work at the resort hotels. With just a few dusty streets traveled by bicycles, horse-drawn carriages, and antique American autos, charmingly low-key Morón is most notable for its splendid, but dilapidated collection of colonial buildings that line the main street, **Calle Martí.** Most visitors arrive by bus or taxi from Ciego de Avila or Camagüey or on an organized tour from one of the hotels on the Cayos. Though Morón possesses a **Municipal Museum,** Calle Martí 374 (℘ **33/50-4501;** admission CUC$1) with pre-Columbian artifacts and idols, and an evocative **1920s railway station,** most travelers are content to stroll up and down Martí, absorbing the relaxed local flavor. The town mascot is the cock of Morón, a bronze statue placed at the foot of a clock tower near the Hotel Morón (the cock crows twice daily).

Some visitors decamp to Morón as a less-expensive alternative to the all-inclusive luxury hotels on the cays. The large, unattractive, and uninviting **Hotel Islazul Morón,** Avenida de Tarafa (℘ **33/50-2230;** www.islazul.cu) has a pool; double rooms cost CUC$36 to CUC$42. The best lodging options are the *casa particulares.* **Casa Xiomara,** Calle 8 no. 2-C, between Calle Sordo y Calle C (℘ **33/50-4236;** marlene@ moron.cav.sld.cu), is a modern, modest family home that offers one excellent air-conditioned guest room in an independent *casita.* Dine on Xiomara's wonderful food—try the *flan de leche*—while relaxing under hibiscus flowers and mango trees.

Easily the best dining spot in Morón is **Restaurante Paraíso Palmeras,** Calle Martí 382 (℘ **33/50-2030** ext.117), whose house speciality is paella Valenciana. **Restaurante-Bar La Fuente,** Calle Martí 189 between Libertad and Ignacio Agramonte (℘ **33/50-5758**), is a charming, upscale restaurant with original art on the walls and an open central patio and fountain that serves salads, omelets, and main courses like grilled fish and lobster for CUC$13 to CUC$20. At night, visit **Patio el Gallo,** Calle Libertad between Narciso López and Martí, for traditional Cuban music, comedians, and artistic shows.

all-inclusive beach hotel. The resort has 76 fantastic bungalow rooms built out over a natural lagoon, separate from the other facilities and very private. Superior standard doubles on the lagoon have refined decor and unscreened balconies. In this case, we actually prefer the first-floor units, as they have fabulous private balconies close to the lapping water. The hotel's excellent stretch of beach, Playa Las Coloradas, fronts a pretty, protected bay. The hotel's Las Caletas restaurant is a beautiful open-air affair built on a dock over the lagoon.

Cayo Coco, Jardines del Rey. ℘ **33/30-1180.** Fax 33/30-1195. www.solmeliacuba.com/cuba-hotels/ hotel-melia-cayococo. 250 units. CUC$190–CUC$240 double. Rates are all-inclusive. MC, V. Children under 18 not allowed. **Amenities:** 5 restaurants; snack bar; 4 bars; bikes; dive shop; fitness center; Internet; Jacuzzi; outdoor pool; room service; sauna; scooter rental; smoke-free rooms; 2 lit outdoor tennis courts; watersports equipment. *In room:* A/C, TV, hair dryer, minibar.

EXPENSIVE

NH Krystal Laguna Villas & Resort ★★   One of the newer hotels on the cays and one of the largest in Cuba, this resort is made up of two conjoined complexes, connected by a system of asphalt walkways. The grounds are extensive and chock-full of facilities, including three amphitheaters and a host of restaurants and bars. Half of the rooms are corporate-style blocks, while the others are very attractive, wooden cabin casitas built over a natural lagoon. The latter, considered the "villas" here, are the best feature of the hotel, and have living rooms with a sofa bed, two-room bathrooms, high ceilings, and open balconies overlooking the lagoon. The standard rooms are housed in large blocks with an apartment-complex feel, and all are junior suites with a connected sitting room. The beach, hidden behind the lagoon, isn't visible from the property; to get to the sands on Playa Larga, you've got to walk about 5 minutes.

Cayo Coco, Jardines del Rey. ✆ **33/30-1470.** Fax 33/30-1498. www.nh-hotels.com. 690 units. CUC$150–CUC$190 double; CUC$210–CUC$270 villa. Rates are all-inclusive. Children 2 and under stay for free in parent's room; children 3–12 stay for CUC$35 per day in parent's room. MC, V. **Amenities:** 2 restaurants; 2 bars; babysitting; free bikes; children's center and programs; concierge; dance club; gym; Jacuzzi; 4 outdoor pools; sauna; scooter rental; 3 lit outdoor tennis courts. *In room:* A/C, TV, fridge.

Sol Cayo Coco ★ ☺   Yet another of Sol Meliá's hotels on Cayo Coco, this is probably the best-suited hotel on the cay for families. Constructed in 1997, the large hotel has a very relaxed feel. Families make up a great percentage of clients, and the kids' club, minigolf, soccer field, and kid's corner restaurant are tailored to youngsters. It's the only hotel on the cays with two beaches—it sits on a nice expanse of Playa Las Coloradas and also offers guests access to a sensational, secluded section of Playa Larga reached by crossing a bridge over a river to spectacularly limpid, shallow waters. Rooms are a good size, with an airy, beachy feel, and almost all of them have sea views. Much of the hotel, including 100 guest rooms, underwent renovations in 2009. The hotel's Nautical Club is one of the largest in Cuba, with more than 10 catamarans and other watersports facilities.

Cayo Coco, Jardines del Rey. ✆ **33/30-1280.** Fax 33/30-1285. www.solmeliacuba.com/cuba-hotels/hotel-sol-cayococo. 270 units. CUC$152–CUC$215 double. Rates are all-inclusive. Children under 2 stay free in parent's room; children 3–12 stay for half price in parent's room. MC, V. **Amenities:** 4 restaurants; 6 bars; 1 snack bar; babysitting; free bikes; children's center and programs; dance club; gym; Internet; Jacuzzi; 2 outdoor pools with 1 section devoted to children; sauna; scooter rental; 2 lit outdoor tennis courts; watersports equipment. *In room:* A/C, TV, hair dryer, minibar.

Tryp Cayo Coco ★★   The granddaddy of all the Cayo hotels is the Tryp Cayo Coco, built in 1996 and restructured and remodeled in recent years. The resort has smart, cheery double rooms, with red-tile floors, headboards, and mirrors. The rooms are adorned with big, colorful pillows and vibrant tropical paintings above the beds, and all have open-air balconies. Many of the rooms have sea views. The buildings and restaurants are spread out across the extensive property whose public spaces are the least intimate of those on the two cays. The pool areas are ample, with lots of greenery. There is even a small pond area with some resident flamingos.

Cayo Coco, Jardines del Rey. ✆ **33/30-1300.** Fax 33/30-1386. www.solmeliacuba.com/cuba-hotels/hotel-tryp-cayococo. 508 units. CUC$120–CUC$238 double. Rates are all-inclusive. Children under 2 stay free in parent's room; children 3–12 stay for half price in parent's room. MC, V. **Amenities:** 7 restaurants; babysitting; 7 bars; 1 snack bar; bikes; children's center and programs; dance club; dive center; gym; Internet; Jacuzzi; 2 outdoor pools; sauna; scooter rental; 3 lit outdoor tennis courts; watersports equipment. *In room:* A/C, TV, hair dryer, minibar.

INXPENSIVE

Sitio La Güira   This rustic, ranchlike property is unique for Cuba. This rural compound, which stages a mini-circus with animal shows, offers four guest rooms: Two of the rooms are in newly refurbished cabañas and come with a private bathroom.

The other two cheaper rooms share a bathroom and are located in rustic *bohíos* (thatched huts) with fans. There's a restaurant on site too. The whole complex is set back from the beach so you'll need your own transport to get there.

Carretera a Cayo Guillermo Km 7, Cayo Coco. ✆ **33/30-1208.** www.palmarescuba.com. 4 units. CUC$25–CUC$30 double. Rates include breakfast. **Amenities:** Restaurant. *In room:* A/C (in 2 rooms), fan (in 2 rooms).

Where to Stay & Dine on Cayo Guillermo
VERY EXPENSIVE

Meliá Cayo Guillermo ★★   This imposing luxury hotel wraps around the extensive pool area, with several restaurants and bars scattered about the property, including an open-air grill restaurant down by the beach. The section of beach the hotel fronts is one of the finest on the cays, with thick palm trees sprouting out of pristine white sand. The hotel has a beautiful, long wooden pier that extends out into the surf, where you can venture for total privacy, as well as a couple of shaded *palapas* set out in the sea, grazing the shallow waters. Rooms are second only in elegance to the Meliá Cayo Coco, and a recent remodeling has really spruced them up substantially. Suites are very large bungalows with a sitting area, backyard, and Jacuzzi, while junior suites have two rooms and two bathrooms. Recently renovated rooms are decorated in yellow, beige, and cream décor. The grounds are lush and luxurious, and feature several lotus gardens.

Cayo Guillermo, Jardines del Rey. ✆ **33/30-1680.** Fax 33/30-1685. www.solmeliacuba.com/cuba-hotels/hotel-melia-cayoguillermo. 291 units. CUC$190–CUC$364 double; suite CUC$226–CUC$386. Rates are all-inclusive. Children under 2 stay free in parent's room; children 3–12 stay for half-price in parent's room. MC, V. **Amenities:** 3 restaurants; 4 bars; babysitting; free bikes; dance club; children's center and programs; dive center; fitness center; Jacuzzi; outdoor pool; sauna; scooter rentals; smoke-free rooms; 2 lit outdoor tennis courts; watersports equipment. *In room:* A/C, TV, hair dryer, minibar.

EXPENSIVE

Iberostar Daiquirí ★★   This large resort hotel sits on a beautiful section of beach. Run by a Spanish chain, the hotel has several long, three-story blocks constructed around a large pool surrounded by gardens, as well as a host of smaller three-story buildings spread around their ample grounds. The rooms are a good size with modern and tasteful terracotta-toned decor, tile floors, and multicolored bedspreads. Every room has two full beds, a sofa bed, and either a balcony or terrace. The better rooms have views of the ocean. The pool bar is behind a curtain of water. The Iberostar has an excellent children's program and a host of available activity and tour options; staff are among the friendliest on the cays. The free minibar is replenished every two days.

Cayo Guillermo, Jardines del Rey. ✆ **33/30-1650.** Fax 33/30-1641. www.iberostar.com. 312 units. CUC$150–CUC$170 double. Rates are all-inclusive. MC, V. **Amenities:** 3 restaurants; 4 bars; babysitting; bike rental; children's center and programs; dance club; gym; outdoor pool; 2 outdoor tennis courts; sauna; scooter rental; watersports equipment. *In room:* A/C, TV, minibar (free).

Sol Cayo Guillermo ★★   Although its nearby sister, the Meliá Cayo Guillermo, may be a bit swankier, this is still my favorite place to stay on Cayo Guillermo. This well-designed hotel, with a new pool, has plenty of personality and a relaxed and intimate vibe. All the accommodations are loosely described as bungalows, although there are a few two-story blocks and duplex units here. The rooms are bright, decorated in cheery blue beach tones. They have beamed, peaked wooden ceilings, and nice tile-and-marble bathrooms. The best rooms are the individual bungalows set close to the beach, although the second-floor superior rooms are also a good bet, with large private balconies, some equipped with hammocks. The grounds are very nicely designed and maintained, and the beach is a wonderful long stretch of white sand. The hotel is popular with a broad range of travelers, from honeymooners and families to singles and retirees.

Cayo Guillermo, Jardines del Rey. ✆ **33/30-1760.** Fax 33/30-1748. www.solmeliacuba.com/cuba-hotels/hotel-sol-cayoguillermo. 267 units. CUC$152–CUC$310 double. Rates are all-inclusive. Children under 2 stay free in parent's room; children 3–12 stay for half price in parent's room. MC, V. **Amenities:** 4 restaurants; 4 bars; babysitting; bikes; children's center and programs; dance club; fitness center; Jacuzzi; 2 outdoor pools (one for children); scooter rental; smoke-free rooms; steam room; 2 lit outdoor tennis courts; watersports equipment. *In room:* A/C, TV, hair dryer, minibar.

MODERATE

Villa Cojímar The oldest of the four Cayo Guillermo hotels (built in 1992), this Gran Caribe hotel is in the process of upgrading its rooms and facilities. Renovations, which are slated to finish in 2011, will include 48 new Brazilian-style wooden cabañas with two rooms each, a new beach restaurant, and repairs to the grounds. Some rooms have already been renovated and are now quite modern and attractive, although overall this hotel still lags far behind the competition in terms of style, facilities, and amenities. That said, it's one of the cheapest options on the cays, it's right on the beach, and the rooms are certainly acceptable. The beach is small but beautiful, with a wooden pier stretching out into the sea.

Cayo Guillermo, Jardines del Rey. ✆ **33/30-1712.** www.gran-caribe.com. 212 units. CUC$82–CUC$115 double. Rates are all-inclusive. MC, V. **Amenities:** 3 restaurants; snack bar; 3 bars; babysitting; bikes; children's club; dance club; fitness center; 2 outdoor pools (one for children); scooter rental; nightly show; 2 outdoor tennis courts; watersports equipment. *In room:* A/C, TV, hair dryer, minibar.

Jardines del Rey After Dark

Most folks simply take advantage of the bars and nightly shows at their all-inclusive resorts. The Sol Cayo Coco has one of the largest, most atmospheric, and liveliest dance clubs of the large resorts, **Salsatheque** (open Tues and Thurs, CUC$7). The disco at **La Cueva de Jabalí ★** (✆ 33/30-1206; open Tues and Thurs; CUC$20, including drinks), 5 kilometers (3 miles) from the Cayo Coco hotel strip, is set in the belly of a small underground cave. Bring insect repellant to fight off the mosquitos inside the cave. Another alternative is **La Bolera** (✆ 33/30-1697), a four-lane bowling alley that also serves as a bar and cabaret, located near the Meliá Playa Guillermo.

Farther South: Jardines de la Reina

South of Ciego de Avila is the protected pristine chain of islands known as the **Archipiélago de los Jardines de la Reina ★★**. Here, there are hundreds of uninhabited virgin cays, but the real attraction lies under the water with some of the best diving and fishing in the Caribbean. There are some 80 dive sites that offer the possibility of seeing whale sharks, hammerhead sharks, bull sharks, and hawksbill turtles, among others. (Whale shark high season runs Aug–Jan, with the peak months being Oct–Dec.) Anglers can hope to catch an abundance of bonefish, tarpon, permit fish, horse eye jacks, mutton snapper, and silky sharks. There is only one authorized diving and fishing operation based out of Júcaro, south of Ciego de Avila: **Avalon** (www.cubandivingcenters.com or www.cubanfishingcenters.com), which runs 6-day diving and fishing packages on four live-aboard boats or the floating hotel, La Tortuga. Prices start at CUC$1,478 in low season (including accommodations, meals, transfers, dives, and park fee).

CAMAGÜEY ★★

553km (344 miles) E of Havana; 110km (68 miles) E of Ciego de Avila; 328km (204 miles) W of Santiago de Cuba

One of Cuba's most historic and important cities, Camagüey is an excellent place to visit to get a feel for Cuba's colonial-era grandeur. Founded as the sixth of Cuba's original seven *villas* in 1514—as a port town originally named Santa María del Puerto del Príncipe—the city was later moved to a different spot by Diego Velázquez himself in 1516 and transplanted again to its present, inland location in 1528. The town didn't receive its final name, which means "Son of the Tree" in the Taíno language, until after the conclusion of the Spanish-American War in 1898.

Camagüey retains a strong colonial imprint, with a highly irregular layout and warren of narrow, bending streets and alleyways, handsome colonial houses, two of the most dignified colonial plazas in Cuba, and an unequaled collection of impressive, if evocatively dilapidated 16th-, 17th-, and 18th-century churches. In fact, Camagüey is often called *la ciudad del Barroco* (city of baroque) or *la ciudad de las iglesias* (city of churches). Another symbol of the city is the *tinajón*, a massive terra-cotta water jug used in the 18th and 19th centuries to collect rainwater. These now largely decorative items can still be seen in the serene gardens and courtyards of the city's colonial houses. Its historical and architectural wealth was recognized by UNESCO in 2008 and the historic core is now a World Heritage Site.

Travelers intent on experiencing the cultural offerings of urban, interior Cuba should not skip Camagüey. The birthplace of Cuba's national poet, Nicolás Guillén, Camagüey claims some of the strongest artistic and literary traditions in Cuba and one of the country's most vital cultural scenes, with an active community of plastics artists and the internationally renowned Camagüey Ballet. Camagüey is also recuperating its distinguished historical character, plowing ahead with invaluable restoration work of the city's classic colonial structures. The 1998 visit of Pope John Paul II gave the city added impetus to refurbish its crumbling set of colonial churches. Yet, it is not just a museum set piece—it's a lively city that explodes with a vibrant cultural life and fiestas. Travelers could conceivably blow through and see the principal attractions in a day, but Camagüey requires at least 2 or 3 days or more to unfurl its significant charms and visit the nearby beaches and ecological attractions.

Essentials

GETTING THERE

BY PLANE You can fly from Havana to Camagüey on **Aerocaribbean** (© **32/29-1338**) four times a week for CUC$89; there are also international charter flights from Canada. Flights arrive at **Aeropuerto Internacional Ignacio Agramonte,** Carretera Central Nuevitas Km 8 (© **32/26-1010;** airport code CMW), 9km (6 miles) west of the city. A local bus runs from the airport to Parque Casino and back, but a taxi is probably your best bet. A taxi from the airport to the city is CUC$6.50.

BY BUS Víazul (© **7/881-1413** in Havana, or **32/27-0396** in Camagüey; www.viazul.com) travels daily to Camagüey on the Trinidad–Santiago de Cuba and Havana–Santiago de Cuba lines. From Havana, the bus departs at 9:30am, 3:15pm, 6:15pm and 10pm, and the ride takes about 9 hours; the fare is CUC$33. From Santiago, departures are at 9am, 3:15pm, 6:15pm, 7:30pm and 10pm, and the ride to Camagüey takes about 7½ hours; the fare is CUC$18. From Trinidad, the bus leaves at 7:40pm and arrives at 12:15am; the fare is CUC$15. From Varadero, the bus leaves at 9:25pm, arriving at 5am (CUC$25).

The main bus terminal for long-distance buses, the **Terminal de Omnibuses** (✆ **32/27-1668**) is located 2km (1¼ miles) southeast of the city, at Carretera Central 180 at the corner of Calle Perú. Taxis/bicitaxis charge CUC$4 from the terminal to the city center. For buses to locations within Camagüey province, there is a separate **Terminal Municipal** (✆ **32/28-1525**), several blocks north of the old center, near the intersection of Padre Olalla and Avenida Carlos J. Finlay (just north of the railway station).

GETTING AROUND

The labyrinthine layout of Camagüey's old town is extremely complicated, though it is pretty compact. The best way to get to know the historic center is on foot. In fact, in and around Camagüey, you will mostly depend on leg power, though bicitaxis may be necessary to get back and forth between a couple of the hotels.

BY TAXI　There are a few taxis around town. Call **Cubataxi** (✆ **32/28-1247**) for local and long-distance hire. Bicycle-powered rickshaws also function as taxis around the historic center. A taxi to Playa Santa Lucía is CUC$60.

BY CAR　A car isn't necessary if you are planning to stay put in Camagüey, but if you're looking to go beyond the city, the major car-rental companies are **Havanautos** (✆ **32/27-2239**) and **Cubacar** (✆ **32/28-7067**); the latter is in the Hotel Plaza and in Parque Casino. There are also company offices in the airport. Rates are about CUC$45 to CUC$85 per day for a standard four-door car.

ORIENTATION

There's a new **Infotur** office on Plaza de los Trabajadores at Ignacio Agramonte 448 (✆ **32-25/6794**); there's also an Infotur office at the airport.

You'll find a **Banco Financiero Internacional** (✆ **32/29-4846**) at Independencia 221, at Plaza de Maceo. It's open Monday through Friday from 8:30am to 3pm. There is a **CADECA** (✆ **32/29-5220**) at República 353, open Monday to Saturday from 8am to 6pm and Sunday from 8am to 1pm. The above branches are two of the most centrally located ones, but you'll find several other banks and money exchange houses around the city.

If you need medical attention, **Servicios Médicos Internacionales** is located at Ignacio Agramonte 449, opposite the church of La Merced (✆ **32/33-6370**).

An **Etecsa** Telepunto telephone and Internet center is on Calle República 453; it's open daily from 8:30am to 6:30pm. The main branch of **Correos** is at Ignacio Agramonte 461; it's open Monday through Saturday from 7:30am to 8pm.

Most of the major Cuban tour agencies operate several tour desks around Camagüey, and at all the major hotels. **Cubatur** operates at Ignacio Agramonte 421 (✆ **32/25-4785**). **Havanatur** (✆ **32/28-8604**) and **Islazul** (✆ **32/29-2550**) were both moving their offices to unspecified locations at press time, but are currently located next to the church on Plaza de los Trabajadores. Cultural promoter **Paradiso** at Ignacio Agramonte 413 (✆ **32/28-6059;** esme@sccm.artex.cu) can arrange trips to see ballet rehearsals and a ballet shoe factory for CUC$5; you can also tour local artists' studios (CUC$5). It also offers city tours, and courses in dance, singing, and ceramics.

What to See & Do

Camagüey's *casco histórico* (old quarter) is the primary draw, and most sights of interest are within easy walking distance of its epicenter, just north and west of the

Camagüey

ACCOMMODATIONS ■
Casa Los Vitrales **22**
Casa Manolo **5**
Casa Xiomara & Rodolfo **6**
Gran Hotel **12**
Hotel Islazul Colón **4**
Hotel Islazul Plaza **3**
La Casa de Caridad **11**
Reyes y Carolina **17**

DINING ◆
Café de la Ciudad **21**
Don Ronquillo Restaurant **10**
La Campana de Toledo **23**
Restaurante Isabella **14**
Salón Caribe **12**

ATTRACTIONS ●
Casa de la Trova **19**
Casa Natal del Mayor
  (Ignacio Agramonte) **8**
Casa Natal Nicolás Guillén **13**
Casino Campestre **25**
Hospital de San Juan de Díos **24**
Iglesia de Nuestra Señora de la Merced **9**
Iglesia de Nuestra Señora del Carmen **16**
Iglesia San Juan de Díos **24**
La Catedral **20**
Museo Provincial General Ignacio Agramonte **2**
Parque Agramonte **18**
Plaza del Carmen **15**
Plaza San Juan de Díos **24**
Teatro Principal **7**
Tifereht Israel Synagogue **1**

Hatibonico River. The historic zone represents one of the largest colonial sectors in Cuba, spread over 300 hectares (741 acres), and Camagüey boasts more than a dozen colonial churches. As in Havana, the office of the city historian is actively engaged in restoring as many of the city's historic buildings as it can manage, and by law, all businesses in the district contribute 2% of their revenues toward the restoration cause. During 2010, Calle Maceo was being converted into a pedestrian boulevard and the Plaza Maceo was being repaired.

Parque Agramonte, which occupies the spot where the old Plaza de Armas existed in 1528, shortly after the transfer of the city to its present location, is the best place to get your bearings. In its center is a bronze and pink granite equestrian statue of the most famous citizen of Camagüey, Ignacio Agramonte. Each corner of the park is marked by a tall royal palm, planted to pay tribute to four local martyrs of the struggle for independence, who were executed in the square by Spanish forces for treason. The park is an agreeable spot, with elegant street lamps and marble benches popular with locals. It is flanked by attractive colonial houses, including the **Casa de la Trova** (where live traditional Cuban music can be heard daily), and the early-18th-century **Catedral** on the south side. The church is a good example of the city's ongoing efforts to resurrect neglected historic buildings. Dedicated to Nuestra Señora de la Candelaria, patron saint of Camagüey, the cathedral has been transformed, in the span of less than 3 years, from a dull and uninspiring church to an attractively austere house of worship, showing off beautiful *vigas* (wood ceiling beams). It is open Monday to Friday from 8–11:45am and 2–5pm, Saturday 3–4pm and Sunday 8–11:30am. Climb the tower (CUC$5) for wonderful photo opportunities.

Calle Maceo, just north of Parque Agramonte, is the city's principal shopping avenue, a busy pedestrian artery stuffed with shops and bars. The other principal reference point of downtown Camagüey is the much-trafficked, but disappointingly pedestrian **Plaza de los Trabajadores (Workers' Square).** On it are two of the city's more important sights: the birth house of Ignacio Agramonte, and the church of La Merced.

Southeast of the historic core, across the unspectacular Hatibonico River, lies **Casino Campestre,** the largest natural city park in Cuba. Inaugurated in 1860, it was transformed into a public park at the beginning of the 20th century. Its tall, shady royal palms, public monuments, and children's attractions make it a favorite with Camagüeyanos. Nearby, on the other side of the Cándido González baseball stadium, is the **Plaza de la Revolución,** a massive but cold square honoring Cuba's revolutionary legends past and present: Agramonte, Che, and Fidel. Pope John Paul II said Mass at this spot in 1998.

THE TOP ATTRACTIONS

Casa Natal del Mayor (Ignacio Agramonte)   Ignacio Agramonte y Loynaz, Camagüey's favorite son and the national hero of the independence struggle—known to all as "El Mayor"—was born December 23, 1841, in this pale yellow 18th-century house. Agramonte's birthplace displays classical colonial elements, both baroque and Hispanic-*mudéjar* (Hispanic-Moorish). The house, now a national monument, may interest those with a thirst for Cuban history; others may simply be interested in viewing the lovely carved wooden ceilings upstairs and smattering of period furnishings (only some are original to the house) of an authentic colonial house. A number of artifacts aim to reveal Agramonte's boyhood life here and his later achievements, with documents including love letters to Amalia Simoni (who would later become his bride), photographs, newspaper accounts of battles, and Agramonte's pistol.

Ignacio Agramonte 459, Plaza de los Trabajadores. ☎ **32/29-7116.** Admission CUC$2. Tues–Sat 9am–4:30pm; Sun 8:30–11am.

Casa Natal Nicolás Guillén   Camagüey's most important literary figure, considered Cuba's national poet, was born in this house, which stands as a simple tribute to his life and enduring work. Guillén, born here in 1902, only lived in the house for 2 years, though he returned to Camagüey after studying law in Havana and worked as a journalist for a local paper. The house now functions primarily as a research and cultural center, with occasional poetry readings and concerts. A smattering of photographs, personal memorabilia, and copies of a handful of poems connect the house to the life and work of Guillén.

Calle Hermanos Agüero 58 (btw. Cisneros and Príncipe). ✆ **32/29-3706.** Free admission. Mon–Fri 8am–5pm.

Iglesia de Nuestra Señora de La Merced ★   The most significant structure on the rather plain Plaza de los Trabajadores is this massive, 18th-century brick church, Camagüey's most distinguished and, in its day, the largest in Cuba. A chapel existed on this spot in 1601; the present structure dates to 1748 (it was reconstructed in 1848 and again in 1909 after a fire). The old convent still houses a rapidly decreasing number of nuns. The church is an eclectic architectural mix. Adorning the ceiling are surprising Art Nouveau murals, added in the 20th century. Also of note are the painted wood, neo-Gothic altar and the **Santo Sepulcro,** a 1762 casket elaborately fashioned from 25,000 silver coins and carried high by eight men during Easter processionals. Down narrow stairs behind the principal altar is a mysterious crypt, the remains of an extensive underground cemetery. Most of it was closed off after fire damage, but six macabre tombs with skeletons remain and are on creepy view alongside a small museum of 18th- and 19th-century objects uncovered at the church.

Av. Agramonte 4 (Plaza de los Trabajadores). ✆ **32/29-2783.** You'll have to tip to see the catacombs, as they're padlocked. Free admission to the church. Mon–Sat 8am–1:30am and 3m–5pm; Sun 8am–1am and 4:30–6pm. Access to the catacombs Mon–Sat 9am–1pm.

Museo Provincial General Ignacio Agramonte   Several blocks north of the historic center of the city, Camagüey's largest and most important museum houses the second-largest collection of paintings in Cuba, bettered only by the Museo de Bellas Artes in Havana. The museum concentrates on Cuban fine arts (from the early 19th c. to contemporary works), but also packs in moderately interesting collections of natural history and archaeology. There is also a selection of decorative arts, including furnishings and porcelain from the colonial and Republican periods. The natural history rooms display native Cuban species, such as sharks, fish, and exotic fauna. These exhibits may be interesting for kids bored with Cuban history and fine art, but you've surely seen better. The building itself is worth a look around, as it features a handsome patio with a wealth of indigenous trees and *tinajones* (large ceramic pots).

Av. de los Mártires 2 (btw. Ignacio Sánchez and Rotario). ✆ **32/28-2425.** Admission CUC$2 adults, free for children under 12. Tues–Sat 10am–1pm and 2–5pm; Sun 10am–1pm.

Plaza del Carmen ★★ 📷   A narrow, pedestrian-only street of pastel-colored colonial row houses opens onto an irregularly shaped square. Renovations have revamped the 18th-century square with street lamps, huge *tinajones* (clay pots used for storing water), and slightly larger-than-life sculptures of locals in various poses of daily work and pleasure by ceramicist Martha Jiménez. The restored spot has done much to uncover a classic Camagüey colonial plaza.

Not long ago, the church and convent at the end of the open square stood roofless, in utter ruins. The baroque-style **Iglesia de Nuestra Señora del Carmen,** which dates to 1825, is now immaculately restored. It is the only church in Camagüey, and

Camagüey has one of the more active, if still tiny, Jewish communities in Cuba, and many Jewish visitors from overseas visit the city's small synagogue, **Tifereht Israel**, Calle Andrés Sánchez 365, between Capdevila and J. de Agüero, La Vigía (✆ **32/28-4639**). Inaugurated in 1998, the synagogue serves just a handful of families, and the community is in the process of restoring the small Jewish cemetery in the city, which had suffered from neglect. It's best to call beforehand as visits are preferred after 5pm, although the synagogue is open all day.

indeed in the whole eastern half of Cuba, topped by two towers. The church is open Tuesday to Saturday 8am–noon and 3–5pm. The early-19th-century **Monasterio de las Ursalinas (Ursuline Convent)** next-door is now an architectural showpiece distinguished by handsome arches framing the expansive patio. Built in 1829, the convent later became a refuge for hurricane victims and a school for the poor. In the years following the Revolution, it served several purposes; most recently, it was a nondescript warehouse. The building was taken over in 1999 by the city historian's office, and today the convent is a beauty, with thick mustard-yellow columns, *tinajones* (large round clay pots), and *mediopunto* (semi-circular stained glass windows above wooden doors). You may visit the courtyard if the door is open.

Plaza del Carmen. Daily 24 hr.

Plaza San Juan de Dios ★★★ A national monument and one of the most remarkable colonial relics in Cuba, this elegant and serene square looks like a meticulously designed movie set. Its charms are subtle, but undeniable. The colonial arches, cobblestones, and houses with red-tile roofs and window grilles speak volumes about Camagüey's colonial past. The square, whose present design dates to 1732, holds great significance for Cubans: The body of the national independence war hero Ignacio Agramonte was brought here, after being burned by the Spaniards, for identification in 1873.

On one side of the square are the 17th-century church and hospital of the order of San Juan de Dios. **La Iglesia San Juan de Dios** features a baroque colonial interior with dark-toned woods and the original brick floor. The church adjoins the handsome **Hospital de San Juan de Dios**, established to serve the poor. Padre José Olallo Valdés (1815–89), who furthered that mission, has been beatified by the Catholic Church and is on his way to being made a saint. Off one side of the cloisters are the remains of Agramonte, making the buildings even more of a sacred place for Camagüeyanos. The city now puts on art exhibits, concerts, and historical displays, such as old pharmaceutical objects, in one corner of the hospital. The understated, but noble colonial structure contains a notable courtyard, thick doors, and an elegant wood staircase. Climb the stairs to the tower from which there is a splendid view of all the church belfries spread across the skyline of the *centro histórico*.

Plaza San Juan de Dios. ✆ **32/29-1318**. Admission CUC$1. Mon–Sat 9am–4pm.

Shopping

You'll find *artesanía* (handicrafts) stands set up on **Plaza San Juan de Dios** Friday through Sunday. Another spot for handicrafts is **Centro/Galería ACAA**

(**Asociación Cubana de Artesanos Artistas**), just off the Plaza de los Trabajadores at Calle Padre Valencia 2 (ℂ **32/28-6834**), which features exhibits and sales, including clay and ceramics, with artisans working out back.

If you want to visit an **artist's studio,** we highly recommend the work of the amiable husband-wife team Joel Jover and Ileana Sánchez. Their home studio is Calle Martí 154, on the north side of Parque Agramonte (ℂ **32/29-2305;** jover@pprincipe. cult.cu). They also have a **gallery** on Plaza San Juan de Dios. Another well-known and very welcoming artist is Oscar Rodríguez Lasseria, a talented **ceramicist** whose studio is on Calle Luis A Varona (Vista) 420, between Alfredo Adán and 25 de Julio (ℂ **32/28-1400** or 32/28-6909; lasseri@pprincipe.cult.cu), a bit removed from the *centro* in La Vigía district. Oscar conducts invitational seminars with ceramics artists from around the world. *Note:* If you purchase any artworks in Camagüey, you'll need to take them to the **Registro de Bienes Culturales,** Avenida de la Libertad 112 (ℂ **32/29-2877 or 32/28-5382**) to get official permission and documentation to export them from Cuba; fees vary.

Check out the **Casa del Tabaco** in the Galería Colonial, Ignacio Agramonte 406 (ℂ **32/28-3944**), for a fine selection of Cuban cigars. The gentleman in the shop is very willing to educate customers about the fine art of Cuban tobacco. He'll tell you that Fidel used to smoke a Cohiba Lancero (which goes for about CUC$350 a box).

Pick up CDs and tapes of Cuban music at any **ARTex** shop. Perhaps the best one is within the Casa de la Trova, on Calle Cisneros (ℂ **32/29-1357**). Other branches are on República 38 and Ignacio Agramonte 109. Those interested in Cuban memorabilia, stamps, and coins should drop in at Ignacio Agramonte 433 between Lopez Recio and Independencia.

Mercado Agropecuario Hatibonico is the largest *agromercado* (agricultural market) in the province, with mangos, bananas, garlic, *chiles,* and a plant nursery.

Where to Stay

Camagüey has an appealing supply of attractive and affordable hotels—most owned and operated by the Cuban Islazul chain—and several have undergone extensive restorations that have brought back their old-world charm. For visitors interested in homestays, there is a host of excellent private accommodations.

MODERATE

Gran Hotel ★ Camagüey's most classic hotel dates from 1939. Its clubby, old-world feel is accentuated by an abundance of watering holes—this midsize hotel has four bars, including the Piano Bar, a great dark place that's one of the best cocktail lounges in Cuba. Another good bar is the spot on the rooftop. There's more to the Gran Hotel than places to wet your whistle, though. It has a medium-size terrace pool that features a nightly show that's part water ballet; a top-floor restaurant with panoramic views; and a handsome, breezy lobby with an old elevator of beautiful wood. The rooms are nicely appointed and have high ceilings. A handful of corner rooms (nos. 1 and 7 on each floor) are the prize, though; they are larger, with separate, but small, sitting rooms and handsome dressers.

Maceo 64 (btw. General Gómez and Ignacio Agramonte), Camagüey. ℂ **32/29-2093.** Fax 32/29-3933. www.islazul.cu. 72 units. CUC$52–CUC$58 double. Rates include buffet breakfast. MC, V. **Amenities:** Restaurant; cafeteria; 2 bars; Internet; nightly show; small outdoor pool. *In room:* A/C, TV, minibar.

INEXPENSIVE

There are many excellent *casas particulares* in Camagüey. **Casa Los Vitrales,** Calle Avellaneda 3, between General Gómez and Martí (ℂ **32/29-5866;**

requejobarreto@gmail.com), is a centrally-located colonial casa in a former seminary run by a very helpful family. The rooms are spacious and quiet, the breakfasts are filling, and there is a lovely courtyard. **La Casa de Caridad** 🎁 ☺, Calle Primelles 310A between Bartolomé Masó and Padre Olallo (℗ **32/29-1554;** carmita1@enet.cu) has two ensuite rooms with fridges. The real draw of this house is the huge courtyard-garden with attractive white wrought-iron furniture and beautiful hanging white flowers. **Reyes y Carolina,** Calle Damas 221 between Horca and Medio (℗ **32/29-8907**), is filled with kitschy toys. There are two rooms—the one upstairs has more light—and there's a huge roof terrace. **Casa Manolo,** Santa Rita 18, between República and Santa Rosa (℗ **32/29-4403;** yohsbany@hotmail.com), has two bedrooms with ensuite bathrooms; one is larger with a bathtub, the other with shower. **Casa Xiomara & Rodolfo,** Oscar Primelles 615, between Lugareño and San Ramón (℗ **32/28-1948;** cubarentur@gmail.com), has an amazingly large and well-equipped apartment that's a very nice option for two couples or a family traveling together.

Hotel Islazul Colón ★ 🗡 Opened in 1927 by Catalan owners, the lobby—decorated with colorful glazed tiles, columns, and a marble staircase—features a handsomely restored, antique dark-wood bar. Though some of the rooms are smaller than those at the Hotel Plaza (see below), they have high ceilings, colorful tile floors, and fairly elegant appointments. The five "matrimonial" rooms at the back off the patio are the largest and have queen-size beds. Other rooms off the long, airy hallway that leads to the street are less appealing and only have either two or three twin beds. The rooms at the end of the hallway—nos. 201 and 235—do have small balconies overlooking the street, though, and they're larger than others along the hall. The open-air grill restaurant in the patio is a good place for a bite to eat. The lobby bar should be your last stop of the evening; it's a splendid spot for a *mojito.*

Calle República 472, between San José and San Martín, Camagüey. ℗ **32/25-4878.** Fax 32/28-3346. www.islazul.cu. 48 units. CUC$38–CUC$44 double. Rates include continental breakfast. MC, V. **Amenities:** Restaurant; bar. *In room:* A/C, TV.

Hotel Islazul Plaza 🗡 Built in 1907, this place is a little funky, but cool for the right kind of traveler—one who values uniqueness over strict adherence to hotel standards. Each of the 67 large rooms is different, with sizes and shapes determined by the structure of the building. Most are newly refurbished, with new furniture, tile floors, and new, but tiny TVs. Try to get a room with a private balcony on the north- or west-facing side of the building; although rooms on the interior, with views of the patio, are quieter than those facing the street, but they do suffer from bar noise. The most unusual option is no. 221, from which the first radio transmission in Cuba was broadcast in 1924; the original microphone is in the room along with photographs on the walls. The main restaurant, El Dorado, is, surprisingly enough, almost elegant.

Van Horne 1 (btw. República and Avellaneda), Camagüey. ℗ **32/28-2457.** www.islazul.cu. 67 units. CUC$32–CUC$38 double. Rates include continental breakfast. MC, V. **Amenities:** Restaurant; cafeteria; bar. *In room:* A/C, TV.

Where to Dine

In addition to the places listed below, **Café Callejón de la Soledad** (℗ **32/29-1961**) is an atmospheric outdoor cafe on a cobblestone alley, just beside the 18th-century Iglesia de Nuestra Señora de la Soledad.

Café de la Ciudad ★ 🍴 CAFÉ/COFFEEHOUSE   This café is located in a gloriously restored Spanish colonial building, and it features huge, old black-and-white photos of the city. Try a cup of café Mambí (CUC$0.35); you can watch staff prepare this drink by grinding coffee beans, then mixing them with boiling water, criollo cheese, and honey. Grab a window seat and a cup of coffee, and watch children playing in the park. There are dozens of coffee concoctions, chocolate bar options, and a great toasted ham and cheese sandwich.

Parque Agramonte, Calle Martí at Cisneros. ✆ **32/28-8412.** Sandwiches CUC$2. No credit cards. Daily 10am–10pm.

Don Ronquillo Restaurant ★ CRIOLLAN Tucked back in the Galería Colonial, this upscale colonial-style restaurant is one of the best in town. The restaurant has a breezy feel, lemon-yellow walls, and mural paintings at either end. The menu offers a nice assortment of well-prepared dishes, including breaded shrimp, chicken *cordon bleu,* and a juicy steak "Mayoral" in a red-wine sauce. Unusual for a Cuban restaurant outside of Havana or the beach resorts, it has a pretty decent wine selection.

In Galería Colonial, Calle Ignacio Agramonte 406 (btw. República and Lopez Recio). ✆ **32/28-5239.** Main courses CUC$6–CUC$12. No credit cards. Daily noon–9:30pm.

La Campana de Toledo ★ CRIOLLAN Although it's a tad touristy, this elegantly rustic restaurant still ranks as the city's most enjoyable dining experience. The gorgeously restored, 18th-century house has a lovely patio with great shade trees and several tables out by the aged bell (which gives the restaurant its name). The well-prepared dishes go beyond the standard offerings: Try *picadillo a la Habanera* (beef hash), the house specialty; *boliche mechado,* beef stuffed with fatty bacon and served with French fries; or choose from among a number of salads and grilled fish. Service is excellent. The restaurant is most popular for lunch, but at night, the patio is illuminated and the square is wonderfully quiet.

San Juan de Dios 18 (btw. Ramón Pinto and Padre Olallo), Plaza San Juan de Dios. ✆ **32/28-6812.** Reservations recommended. Main courses CUC$4.20–CUC$18. MC, V. Daily 10am–10pm.

Restaurant Isabella ★ 🍴 ITALIAN/PIZZA This is the first state–run restaurant in Cuba to show any modern artistic flair. Named in honor of local actress Isabel Santos, the restaurant is decorated with royal blue director's chairs imprinted with famous names on the backs and glass-topped tables. Film posters line the wall at one end, while old film reels hang on the other. The low metallic lighting and set lights create a cinematic ambience. If this isn't enough to entice you inside, you'll be lured in by the pizzas, which are huge, thin, and packed with ingredients—plus, they're a good value. If pizza isn't your thing, choose from the director's clapboard menu, which lists spaghettis, pastas, and lasagna.

Calle Ignacio Agramonte btw. Independencia and Lopez Recio. ✆ **32/22-1540.** Main courses CUC$3–CUC$10. Daily 11am–10pm.

Salón Caribe ★ 🍴 INTERNATIONAL/CRIOLLAN This sophisticated, top-floor restaurant of Camagüey's coolest hotel has panoramic views of the city. Surprisingly elegant, it has faux-crystal chandeliers, large mirrors, cool breezes, and black-and-white tile floors. During the day, there's lunch a la carte with a variety of soups, fish, and Creole fried chicken; there's also a good-value buffet dinner for CUC$12.

In the Gran Hotel, Maceo 67 (btw. General Gómez and Ignacio Agramonte). ✆ **32/29-2314.** Main courses CUC$3.50–CUC$7.50. MC, V. Daily noon–3pm and 7–10pm.

Camagüey After Dark

There's a **Cartelera Cultural board** (www.pprincipe.cult.cu) with weekly events listings posted in a building at 432 Ignacio Agramonte.

Built in 1850, the neoclassical **Teatro Principal,** Padre Valencia 64, between Tatán Mendéz and Lugareño (☎ **32/29-3048**), is an elegant showpiece with a grand marble staircase and chandeliers. The theater often showcases the distinguished **Ballet de Camagüey ★★**, which celebrates the Festival de Ballet in February. Camagüey's **Casa de la Trova ★★**, Salvador Cisneros 171 (☎ **32/29-1357**), is one of the liveliest in Cuba, with good bands and great local crowds. It's open Tuesday through Thursday from noon to 6pm and 9pm to midnight; Friday and Saturday from noon to 6pm and 9pm to 1am; and Sunday from 11am to 4pm and 9pm to 1am. Admission is CUC$3 and includes CUC$2 worth of drinks. **El Cambio,** Calle Martí and Independencia, is an atmospheric small bar on the main park, whose walls are plastered with graffiti.

Excursions From Camagüey

Some 110 kms (68 miles) north of Camagüey are the white sands and aquamarine seas of **Santa Lucía.** There are a handful of hotels and a dive school along the 21-km (13-mile) stretch of fine white sand. At the western end is **Playa Los Cocos,** which is known for its **bull sharks** that feed in the area from July to September and February to March. Along this north coast are **Cayo Sabinal, Cayo Cruz,** and **Cayo Romano.**

For tours to Bonita Beach (CUC$55) or snorkeling tours (CUC$25), contact **Cubanacán** (☎ **32/33-6449**) or **Ecotur** (☎ **32/33-6109**) at Playa Santa Lucía. The bull sharks tend to appear around the turning of the tide, so dives are timed to coincide with the turning of the tides to give visitors the best chance to see the sharks; many dives include a visit to the Mortera wreck, a Spanish galleon that sunk in 1905. Contact **Shark's Friends Diving Center** (☎ **32/36-5182**) between Hotel Be Live Brisas Santa Lucía and Gran Club Santa Lucía for information. There are some 34 dive sites with dives from CUC$30.

At Playa Los Cocos, **Restaurante Bar Bucanero** (☎ **32/36-5226**) serves seafood and slices of smoked beef under a thatched roof. Los Cocos is very popular with locals and has a more authentic feel than the hotel strip.

There's a gas station, bank, shops, an Etecsa office, car rental office, and international clinic at Santa Lucía. There is no public transport to and from Santa Lucía but a workers' bus leaves for the city bus station at 3:20pm and 5:20pm ($10MN/CUC$0.35) from a spot just beyond El Rápido on the hotel strip.

WHERE TO STAY

Day passes are available for many Santa Lucía hotels, but considering its distance from Camagüey, most visitors opt to spend the night in the area.

Hotel Be Live Brisas Santa Lucía ☺ This is the most comfortable of the large hotels on the stretch, evoking the feel of a Spanish courtyard. The hotel has a spacious pool and an alluring thatched-roofed pool bar; plus, it lies next to the beach, which is a draw because several other hotels in the area are located further from the beach. Rooms are filled with distressed pine-green furniture; note that only 14 of the rooms have sea views. A kids' club and children's pool will keep the tots entertained, as will the nice new alfresco cafe near the pool. Local artisans set up market stalls in the atmospheric lobby daily.

Playa Santa Lucía, Nuevitas. ☎ **32/33 6317.** Fax 32/36-5142. www.belivehotels.com. 408 units. CUC$80–CUC$120 double. Rates are all-inclusive. MC, V. **Amenities:** 4 restaurants; cafeteria; 2 bars; children's programs; gym; Internet; 2 pools; sauna; tennis court; watersports equipment. *In room:* A/C, TV, minibar.

EL ORIENTE

Prior to the 1959 Revolution, the eastern half of Cuba was a single province, straightforwardly called El Oriente, or the East. Most Cubans still refer to everything east of Camagüey—a region much more scenically and historically interesting than most of central Cuba—as El Oriente, even though it is now composed of the distinct provinces of Holguín, Granma, Santiago de Cuba, and Guantánamo. The region is less known and visited than the western half of Cuba, but every bit as rewarding for travelers (and perhaps more so). The farther east you go, the more emphatically Caribbean it feels. The region's remarkable landscapes include the north coast's exuberant banana and coconut groves, stunning aquamarine seas off Guardalavaca, densely wooded peaks of the Sierra Maestra, and tropical rainforest on the east coast.

The wars of independence began in El Oriente in the 1860s, and nearly a century later, Castro concentrated his power base in the inaccessible **Sierra Maestra.** Quiet but dignified **Bayamo,** which played a pivotal role in Cuba's revolutionary struggles, is the capital of Granma province. The gorgeous beaches and warm seas of **Guardalavaca,** part of Holguín province, make it the fastest-growing resort area in Cuba, while tiny, remote **Baracoa,** where Columbus first dropped anchor at the extreme northeastern edge of Guantánamo, is one of the most beautiful, rugged spots on the island. The former capital city of the Spanish colony, **Santiago de Cuba,** is not only known as a vibrant musical center, but also as the cradle of the Revolution; see chapter 11 for full coverage of Cuba's "Second City."

The eastern end of Cuba was especially hard hit from Hurricanes Gustav and Ike in September 2008. More than 100,000 people were evacuated from Guantánamo province, including the popular tourist spot of Baracoa. In Holguín, the main areas affected were Banes and Gibara, and repairs to those damaged towns are still ongoing.

GUARDALAVACA ★★

56km (35 miles) N of Holguín; 190km (118 miles) NW of Santiago de Cuba; 258km (160 miles) NE of Camagüey

Guardalavaca's white sands, hidden coves, stunning aquamarine seas, and underwater life make it a top beach destination. And though the beaches are lined with all-inclusive resort hotels that gaze out over some of the finest beaches in Cuba, Guardalavaca remains charmingly low-key. Its location, close to historic towns and cities, also makes it a good base for inland exploration. As a result, Guardalavaca is one of the hottest destinations on the island.

Guardalavaca is both a bucket-term for a series of neighboring beaches north of Holguín and the namesake for one small town and specific beach. Guardalavaca is the finest, and really the only resort cluster in the eastern half of the island. Guardalavaca's appeal is its stunning, three-stripe canvas of intensely green tropical vegetation, stone-white sand, and pristine turquoise seas well protected by coral reefs.

When Not to Come to Guardalavaca

The month of May in Guardalavaca is heavy with tropical rains, as is the early part of June. August is sweltering and too humid for all but the most committed sun worshipers.

Christopher Columbus first sailed around the coast at Guardalavaca, landing just to the west at the Bay of Bariay in late 1492. He declared it "the most beautiful land that human eyes have ever seen." Columbus may have been given to hyperbole, repeatedly touting the unrivaled virtues of the places where he dropped anchor, but his assessment of Guardalavaca remains pretty accurate. The area was originally home to several indigenous groups, and today it is recognized as Cuba's archaeological capital, primarily for the discovery of the 15th-century Arawakan Indian village and burial site near Guardalavaca, one of the most important pre-Columbian sites in the Caribbean. The *bohíos* (thatched-roof huts) that dot the thickly wooded hills still evoke a sense of Caribbean discovery more than 500 years later.

The town of Guardalavaca remains a dusty country backdrop to the resort hotels that now dwarf it. The foundations of Guardalavaca's resort development were laid in the late 1970s: Fidel Castro himself inaugurated the first hotel here, swimming laps in its large square pool. "Guardalavaca" now denotes not only the eponymous town and beach, but is also used to refer to the entire resort, strung along several nearby beaches and continuing to expand. Playa Esmeralda and Playa Pesquero (also known as Costa Verde) are the two newest and most exclusive beaches to be developed.

The backdrop to the beaches is a bucolic region thick with sugar-cane fields, grazing cattle, and luxuriant, rolling hills sprinkled with royal palms. The zone is being touted as an ecotourist paradise; in addition to scuba diving at a dozen dive sites, hiking, biking, and horseback-riding trips are primed to take off in the near future. A dozen nature preserves, including one declared a UNESCO World Biosphere Reserve, dot the region. Side trips from Guardalavaca are easy to arrange.

Essentials

GETTING THERE

BY PLANE The gleaming **Aeropuerto Internacional Frank País,** Carretera Central Vía Bayamo Km 11.5 (*©* **24/47-4774;** airport code HOG), is about 70km (43 miles) south of Guardalavaca, and 14km (8¾ miles) south of Holguín, the provincial capital. The airport is about an hour from hotels in and around Guardalavaca. Both national and direct international flights from Canada, the U.K., Switzerland, the Netherlands, Italy, Finland, and Germany (via **Air Canada** and 5 other Canadian airlines, **Condor, Thomas Cook, First Choice, Blue Panorama,** and various package charters) arrive at the airport here. The main domestic carrier is **AeroCaribbean** (*©* **24/46-8556** in Holguín, or 7/879-7524 in Havana; www.aero-caribbean. com), which offers daily flights from Havana for CUC$105 each way.

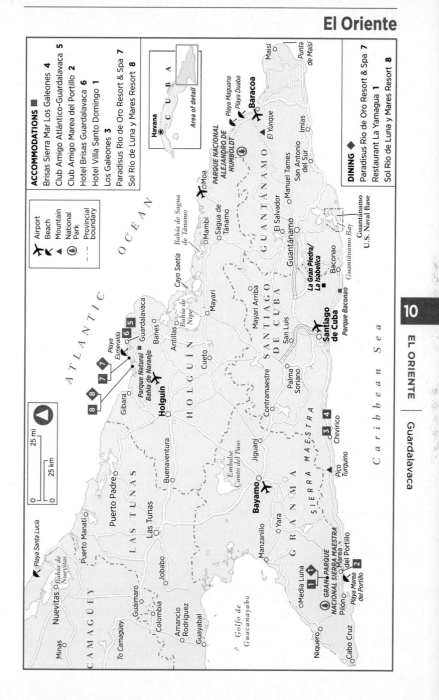

ACCOMMODATIONS ■
Brisas Sierra Mar Los Galeones **4**
Club Amigo Atlántico-Guardalavaca **5**
Club Amigo Marea del Portillo **2**
Hotel Brisas Guardalavaca **6**
Hotel Villa Santo Domingo **1**
Los Galeones **3**
Paradisus Rio de Oro Resort & Spa **7**
Sol Rio de Luna y Mares Resort **8**

✈ Airport
⚲ Beach
▲ Mountain
Ⓝ National Park
--- Provincial boundary

DINING ◆
Paradisus Rio de Oro Resort & Spa **7**
Restaurant La Yamagua **1**
Sol Rio de Luna y Mares Resort **8**

Area of detail

10

EL ORIENTE | Guardalavaca

The relatively expensive all-inclusive hotels pretty much have a lock on the splendid beaches around Guardalavaca. If you would like to visit the beaches and spend the day there without paying for the privilege of sleeping at one of the hotels, you can design a day trip from Holguín if you have a rental car. (*Note:* If you don't have your own wheels and have to take a taxi, the cost could equal the cost of staying in one of the less-expensive all-inclusive hotels, and you'd have to travel 1½ hr. back to your hotel in Holguín, making it hardly worth the effort.) The major hotels sell day passes, generally from CUC$15 to CUC$25, that allow you to use the facilities, including pool and beaches, and eat and drink all you wish.

The hotels all have airport pickup services (buses and minibuses) for clients. If you have not prearranged transportation to your hotel, there are usually a couple of state-owned taxis hanging about. Rates run between CUC$35 to CUC$45 to Guardalavaca, CUC$15 to Holguin, CUC$22 to Gibara, and CUC$60 to Bayamo.

BY BUS Víazul (✆ 24/42-2111 in Holguín, or 7/881-1413 in Havana; www.viazul.com) travels to Holguín on its Havana-Santiago and Trinidad-Santiago lines. From Havana, the buses depart at 8:40am, 3:15pm, 6:15pm, 8:30pm, and 10pm, and the ride takes between 9 and 12 hours; the fare is CUC$44. From Varadero, the bus departs at 9:25pm and arrives at 8.35am, costing CUC$40. From Trinidad (✆ 41/99-4448), the bus leaves at 7:40pm and arrives in Holguín at 3:30am; the fare is CUC$26. From Santiago, departures are at 9am, 3:15pm, 7:30pm, 8pm, and 12:50pm, arriving at 1:10pm, 7:25pm, 11pm, 11:30pm, and 6:40pm, respectively; the fare is CUC$11.

The main bus station in Holguín is located on Carretera Central between 20 de Mayo and Independencia (✆ 24/42-2111), just west of downtown. No state taxis wait at the bus station.

During summer months, **Transtur** (✆ 24/43-0273) may run Saturday and Sunday return buses from La Begonia restaurant on Parque Calixto García between 8:30am and 5pm for CUC$5.

BY CAR/TAXI The easiest way to get to Guardalavaca, if you don't have a prearranged bus service to take you from the airport, is by rental car or state-owned **Cubataxi** (✆ 24/47-3155). Getting from the airport, through the city of Holguín, out onto the highway to Guardalavaca is quite confusing. One of the best ways to navigate it is to hire a local tout for a few CUCs to ride with you until you're on your way.

Note that if you arrive by Víazul and have not pre-booked a Cubataxi car you will be reliant on the green Lada that eagerly awaits visitors. This is not a legal way to travel but clearly the two guys that take people up to Guardalavaca—and have been doing so for years—are paying off the right people. They will quote a fare higher than the state cab fare of CUC$35—bargain them down.

Guardalavaca's beauty and proximity to areas of interest, including Baracoa, make it one of the better areas in Cuba to rent a car for some regional sightseeing. Car-rental agencies in Holguín include **Cubacar** (✆ 24/46-8559; www.transtur.cu), **Transgaviota** (✆ 24/42-1602), and **Rex** (✆ 24/46-4644). Almost all of these have desks at the airport, as well as at one or more beach resorts. Car rentals average from CUC$45 to CUC$60 per day for a standard economy car.

10

Guardalavaca

EL ORIENTE

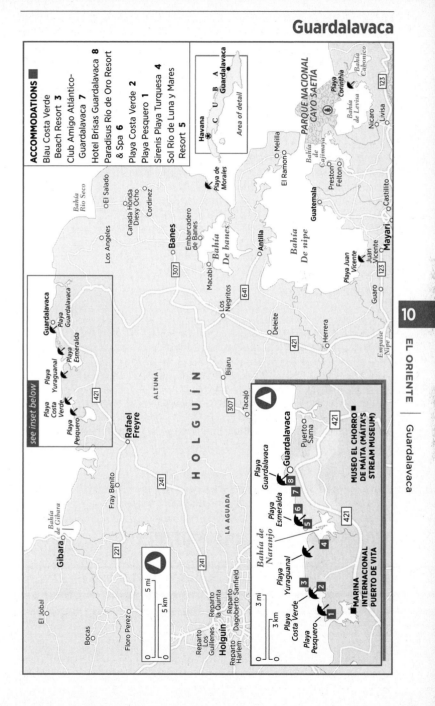

GETTING AROUND

Playa Guardalavaca is small enough that you can easily walk from any of the hotels here to the La Roca dance club and the restaurants in town. Playa Esmeralda is about 3km (1¾ miles) from Guardalavaca, a manageable walk. The rest of the beaches and attractions are quite far.

The best way to get around the beaches of Guardalavaca is by **bicycle** (if you're feeling fit) or **moped** (*moto*). Most of the hotels have mountain bikes (free for guests) and mopeds that rent for CUC$18 a day. There are also *coches* (carriages) but this isn't a cheap way to travel.

Any of the hotels can arrange a taxi for side trips in the area. You can also call directly **Cubataxi** (© **24/43-0139**) on Playa Guardalavaca; taxis to Esmeralda cost CUC$5, Pesquero CUC$12, Gibara CUC$35, and Banes CUC$25. All the hotels also offer excursions either directly or through tour operator representatives.

Each of the major hotels has representatives of one or more car-rental agencies on the premises. You could also contact **Cubacar** (© **24/46-8559** in Holguín, © **24/43-0389** on Playa Guardalavaca, or © **24/46-8414** at the airport; www.transtur.cu).

One interesting alternative for touring the area is the **Guardalavaca Bus Tour** that runs a hop-on/hop-off service in the area that now includes Chorro de Maita. The fare is CUC$5 for the day.

ORIENTATION

The best sources of **visitor information** are the Guardalavaca hotels themselves and the representatives of the major tour operators (Havanatur, Cubatur, and Cubanacán) that operate out of the hotels. In Holguín, **Infotur,** Edificio Pico Cristal, C/Libertad esq Martí (© **24/42-5013**), can sell Guardalavaca hotel packages and Víazul bus tickets.

Currency exchange and **postal services** are available at any of Guardalavaca's hotels. There are a couple of grocery stores, a photo processing store, and a branch of the cigar store La Casa del Habano.

For medical assistance, contact **Clínica Internacional,** Calle 2 no. 15, Playa Guardalavaca (© **24/43-0312**). It has a pharmacy on the premises; pharmacies are also located in the **Paradisus Río de Oro** hotel (p. 245), Hotel Costa Verde, Hotel Sirenis Playa Turquesa, and Hotel Playa Pesquero.

What to See & Do

Most folks come here on all-inclusive packages, and many are content to spend their entire time in a chaise longue on the beach or beside the pool. However, a wide range of tours and activities are available for the more active.

BEACHES, DIVING & OTHER WATERSPORTS

The spectacular beaches around Guardalavaca are this resort area's main attraction. Tracing the coast are more than 1,200km (746 miles) of pure white beaches lined by royal palm trees, framed by exuberant vegetation, and fronting some of the clearest, most inviting waters of Cuba. The best beaches are **Esmeralda, Pesquero, Yuraguanal,** and **Guardalavaca**—all of which have major hotels lining them—and small **Don Lino.** Many of the beaches are long and wide expanses of sand, but the jagged coastline is also peppered with tiny coves that are nearly private. Near the gentle arc of Esmeralda is a series of tiny cove beaches that in practice are almost exclusively for the guests of the Paradisus Río de Oro hotel (p. 245).

Guardalavaca has a dozen excellent dive sites, including Canto Azul, Laberinto, Cuevas 1–3, Sierena, and Pesquero Sponges, and is well-known for its abundant and vibrant sponges. **Eagle Ray** (© **24/43-0316;** marlin.hlg@tur.cu) is on Playa Guardalavaca, and **Sea Lovers Scuba Diving Center** (© **24/43-0132**) is on Playa Esmeralda. They offer dive packages and diving gear rental. Certification programs are also provided with several dive packages; a single dive costs CUC$45 and an open water course costs CUC$365. It is recommended to go direct to the dive centers to book as hotel reps take a large commission cut. Transfers from the hotels are included in the price.

The most popular watersports are sailing, kayaking, wind surfing, canoeing, and pedal boating. Most of the hotels have their own catamarans and other vehicles and facilities for watersports. **Marina Internacional Puerto de Vita** (© **24/43-0445**) operates catamaran cruises around the coral reef beyond the cays for either a half- or full day. **Marlin,** behind La Roca (© **24/43-0491**), has a wide range of watersports programs, including seafaris with snorkeling to Playa Pesquero, and yacht rentals for sportfishing. Other excursions that can be booked from tour desks include a seafari to Cayo Saetía (CUC$69), a snorkeling trip on a catamaran (CUC$59), a speedboat adventure (CUC$29), a trip to Fidel Castro's birthplace at Birán (CUC$89), and ultralight flights (CUC$150).

Note: While masks are new and tend to fit well, the snorkels these companies use tend to be cheap and do not fit well; bring your own if you plan to do a lot of snorkeling.

PARQUE NATURAL BAHIA DE NARANJO

The **Bahía de Naranjo,** about 5km (3 miles) west of Guardalavaca, is a 1,000-hectare (2,471-acre) nature park of mangrove swamps and thickly wooded wilderness. Within the park, visitors can take boat rides. There are plenty of man-made attractions to round out the more ecologically oriented offerings. The **aquarium** at Cayo Naranjo, a sliver of an island reached by boat, isn't really a large-scale aquarium in the traditional sense; it's part of a *parque recreativo* (tourist complex), but it does feature tropical fish as well as a daily marine show at noon and, best of all, an opportunity to swim with dolphins for CUC$79, which includes transport and guide from the hotels. While we are normally fairly appalled by the conditions of most dolphin attractions, including others around Cuba, this place has some of the largest natural ocean pens you'll find anywhere. You'll also find watersports and a seafood restaurant with an Afro-Cuban show. The park is open daily from 9am to 3pm.

ON DRY LAND

One of the most popular activities on dry land here is **horseback riding.** There's plenty of wide-open terrain and wonderful sea views to be enjoyed. However, be sure to bring plenty of sunscreen as protection from the often-brutal sun here. Most hotels can arrange a riding excursion for you. There are stables in front of Hotel Club Amigo Guardalavaca (© **24/43-0780**).

BANES

A slow-moving, dusty little town about 30km (19 miles) southeast of Guardalavaca, Banes is best known for its unlikely association with the towering figures of 20th-century Cuba. Fulgencio Batista, whose government the rebels deposed in 1959, was born here in 1901. Fidel Castro and his brother, Raúl, were born nearby in Birán. The hotels and tour operators in Guardalavaca arrange guided excursions to Banes, though if you wish to go independently, you could easily do so by rented moped or taxi.

Fidel married the daughter of the conservative mayor of Banes in 1948 at the small **Iglesia de Nuestra Señora de la Caridad,** on a plaza at the edge of the park. (They divorced 6 years later.) Of perhaps greater significance in town is the **Museo**

Indocubano ★, Av. General Marreo 305 (ⓒ **24/80-2487**), specializing exclusively in Cuba's pre-Columbian history. Its collection is among the best in Cuba; among the 20,000 or so items, exhibits include fragments of ceramics, jewelry, tools, and a valuable 13th-century gold "idol of Banesa," just 4cm (1½ in.) high. The museum is open Tuesday through Saturday from 9am to 5pm, and Sunday from 8am to noon; admission is CUC$2.

Tucked into the hills of the Banes zone are 96 archaeological sites from the Native American groups that once populated the area. **Museo El Chorro de Maíta (Maíta's Stream Museum)** ★, Cerro de Yaguajay (ⓒ **24/43-0201**), represents the largest and most important discovery of a Native American cemetery in Cuba. The community dates from 1490 to 1540. The burial ground contains the remarkably well-preserved remains of 108 Taíno men, women, and children (62 are on display), including a single Spaniard, most likely a friar, whose body is marked by a cross. A *cacique* (tribal chief), lying in a fetal position, is distinguished by a copper medal placed on his shin. Several skulls are deformed, the result of a beautification practice that involved applying two pieces of wood to the head with ropes. Found among the remains were Spanish ceramics and jewelry and objects crafted from gold, copper, coral, and quartz; many are displayed in cases. The museum is open daily from 9am to 5pm. Admission is CUC$2.

Where to Stay

The entire area is developed around the all-inclusive resort concept, and visitors have no other options. Playa Guardalavaca was the original beach resort developed in the late 1970s, but today, resort hotels are distributed on several beaches along the coast. Principal among them are Playa Esmeralda, Playa Turquesa, and Playa Pesquero, where the hotels are more upscale than Guardalavaca, and the beaches even finer. Guardalavaca is dominated by Cubanacán properties, for the most part older and more affordable than newer hotels in other parts. The non-resort area of Guardalavaca, where there are a few restaurants, shops, a taxi stand, market, and a large park, are due to be bulldozed at the end of 2010 to make way for a new five-star hotel complex: the Albatross. La Roca, La Rueda, and the market will be preserved and El Ancla will be incorporated into the hotel complex. The Spanish chain Sol Meliá has concentrated its hotels in a row along Playa Esmeralda. Playa Pesquero is gaining another hotel near Blau Costa Verde.

PLAYA GUARDALAVACA

Club Amigo Atlántico-Guardalavaca Over the years, several neighboring projects here have been fused into one massive all-inclusive resort. The oldest hotel at this resort, the Atlántico, was built in 1976 and its age shows in its basic structure. Three large, '70s Soviet-style blocks are situated around a square old-style pool. However, the newer section of villas is considerably nicer and closer to the beach, and really should be your first and only choice here. These large, tastefully decorated villas are much more modern, with marble bathrooms and small terraces; some have good sea views. The pool is much better as well. But the rooms and the grounds still can't compare with nicer properties in the area. The hotel has only a tiny cove beach with a statue of Christopher Columbus; you have to walk along a boardwalk to get to the real public beach. On the whole, it's a decent if unexciting hotel that clings to its glory days as the first property on the beach, when Fidel himself swam in the pool.

Playa Guardalavaca, Banes, Holguín. ⓒ **24/43-0180.** Fax 24/43-0200. www.hoteles cubanacan.com. 747 units. CUC$62–CUC$91 double; CUC$86–CUC$CUC115 villa. Children 12 and under stay free in their parents' room; children 3–12 pay 70% of full price to stay in a separate room. Rates are all-inclusive. MC, V. **Amenities:** 4 restaurants; 2 snack bars; 4 bars; babysitting; bike rental; children's programs; concierge; dance club; gym; Internet; nightly show; 4 outdoor pools for adults; 4 outdoor pools for children; sauna; outdoor tennis court; watersports equipment. *In room:* A/C, TV.

Hotel Brisas Guardalavaca ★   Like a couple of other all-inclusive beach hotels in the area that have upgraded their facilities, this hotel is a hybrid: part standard resort hotel with a big and rather uninteresting block structure, and part more intimate villa-style accommodations. The two sections are connected and considered one property, but guests would be wise to draw a firm distinction; the one-star rating we have given applies only to the villas, which are much more striking. Mediterranean in style and set amid pleasant gardens, the 98 pastel-colored, red-tile-roof villas are large and luxurious, with balconies. The atmosphere is one of tranquillity, with easy access to an attractive stretch of beach. The standard hotel next-door, built in 1994, doesn't fare well in comparison. Rooms aren't very inspiring for the price, but many of them have good sea views.

Playa Guardalavaca, Banes, Holguín. ✆ **24/43-0218.** Fax 24/43-0418. www.hotelescubanacan.com. 231 units. CUC$100–CUC$116 double. Rates are all-inclusive. MC, V. **Amenities:** 4 restaurants; snack bar; 5 bars; babysitting; bikes; children's programs; concierge; dance club; Internet; Jacuzzi; nightly show; 2 outdoor pools for adults; 2 outdoor pools for children; 2 lit outdoor tennis courts; watersports equipment. *In room:* A/C, TV, hair dryer, minibar.

PLAYA ESMERALDA

Paradisus Río de Oro Resort & Spa ★★★   One of the finest and most luxurious all-inclusive resort hotels in Cuba, this Sol Meliá flagship hotel is perched above a low, rocky cliff overlooking Playa Esmeralda. Set amid lush, meticulously landscaped gardens are handsome two-story blocks of rooms and slightly more exclusive casitas, consisting of two apartments with separate terraces and outdoor showers. The rooms are very large and well-appointed, with separate sitting areas, balconies, and large bathrooms with heated floors. Of these, those on the second floor have higher ceilings than those below, and those on the corners have larger balconies. There are also two massive, private oceanview villas, with private swimming pools, that are easily the top accommodations in Guardalavaca. Walkways wend through lush vegetation and around ponds; scattered about the grounds are private sitting areas and hammocks strewn lazily between trees. All the specialized restaurants are in high demand, so it's a good idea to make reservations for the duration of your stay upon arrival.

The superb main beach is a short walk down some stairs built into the cliff, but the hotel also features three nearly private, tiny cove beaches accessed through the gardens (few guests seem to know about them). A serene, blue wood bridge over a large pond leads to the other two Meliá hotels on Esmeralda. This hotel accommodates adults only and it offers spa facilities that include some open-air massage gazebos built out over the ocean.

Carretera a Guardalavaca, Playa Esmeralda, Holguín. ✆ **24/43-0090.** Fax 24/43-0095. www.solmelia cuba.com. 354 units. CUC$258-480 double; CUC$490 superior suite; CUC$800 villa. Rates are all-inclusive. MC, V. Children are not allowed. **Amenities:** 8 restaurants; 5 bars; bikes; disco; gym; Internet; Jacuzzi; nightly show; outdoor pool; room service; sauna; smoke-free rooms; spa; 3 lit outdoor tennis courts; watersports equipment. *In room:* A/C, TV, hair dryer, minibar.

Sol Río de Luna y Mares Resort ★★ ☺   This complex consists of two formerly separate Sol Meliá properties on Playa Esmeralda joined at the hip. Formerly the Río de Luna and Río de Mares, they've merged—and guests at either one are free to use the facilities at both—but the two hotels deserve to be thought of separately, since they're slightly different in character and design. We prefer the Río de Luna, which was built in 1992. It has a sedate, open-air lobby and medium-size pool, and the overall design of the hotel is more intimate. Suites have two rooms, with two bathrooms and a large balcony or small terrace. The Río de Mares, while somewhat newer, has a slightly more impersonal feel, with rooms built in large wings in a U-shape around the pools. However, the rooms on the third and fourth floors here have excellent views, and the junior suites are immense, with massive terraces. The rooms are all very cute and playfully rustic. The long stretch of beach fronting the two hotels is superb. The accommodating staff, wide range of activities, facilities, and a well-run children's program make this an excellent choice for families.

Carretera a Guardalavaca, Playa Esmeralda, Holguín. ☎ **24/43-0060.** Fax 24/43-0065. www.solmelia cuba.com. 464 units. CUC$230 double; CUC$267 suites. Rates are all-inclusive. Children under 2 stay free in parent's room; children 3–12 stay for half-price in parent's room. MC, V. **Amenities:** 6 restaurants; 10 bars; babysitting; bikes; children's center and programs; dance club; gym; Internet; Jacuzzi; nightly show; 2 outdoor pools; sauna; spa; 2 lit outdoor tennis courts; watersports equipment. *In room:* A/C, TV, hair dryer, minibar.

PLAYA PESQUERO & PLAYA YURAGUANAL

Blau Costa Verde Beach Resort ★★ ☺   This resort has a decidedly tropical feel, with blinding bright orange and blue colors. The huge concrete structure you drive up to, though, is not the most attractive. It consists of six big building blocks, with three open-air restaurants built around a large figure-eight pool. Rooms are cheery with an ocean theme, but not overly large, and TVs are rather small. Some rooms have distant beach views. The sands are a 50m (164-ft.) walk away, but the beach is lovely, and the water has amazing crystal-clear turquoise tones. A kids' club, kiddie pool, playground, shallow "children's beach," and child care will appeal to families. The food here is actually pretty good for a large-scale all-inclusive.

Playa Pesquero, Rafael Freyre, Holguín. ☎ **24/43-3510.** Fax 24/43-0515. www.blau-hotels.com. 309 units. CUC$122 double. Rates are all-inclusive. Children under 3 stay free in parent's room; children 4–14 stay for half price in a separate room. MC, V. **Amenities:** 4 restaurants; snack bar; 3 bars; babysitting; bikes; children's center and programs; concierge; dance club; gym; Internet; Jacuzzi; nightly show; outdoor pool for adults; outdoor pool for children; sauna; smoke-free rooms; 2 lit outdoor tennis courts; watersports equipment. *In room:* A/C, TV, hair dryer, minibar.

Sirenis Playa Turquesa ★★ ☺   This large resort is set above a beautiful broad beach and next to some lovely natural forests. Perhaps the most distinctive features here are the seven swimming pools, several connected in cascading fashion by waterfalls. Rooms are large, modern, and well kept. They have large, cool, ceramic tile floors in a checkerboard pattern, and stylish wrought-iron headboards over the beds. All have private balconies, although many of these are quite compact. The grounds here are lush and shady. There are several good a la carte dining options, as well as the ubiquitous large buffets. The pizza and ice-cream stand on the beach is a big hit here. This hotel has an extensive array of watersports and activities, and an excellent children's program.

Playa Yuraguanal, Rafael Freyre, Holguín. ☎ **800/858-2258** in the U.S. and Canada, or 24/43-3540. Fax 24/43-0545. www.sirenishotels.com. 531 units. CUC$125 double; CUC$200 suite. Rates are all-inclusive. Children under 2 stay free in parent's room; children 2–12 stay for CUC$51 in parent's room. MC, V. **Amenities:** 5 restaurants; 2 snack bars; 6 bars; babysitting; children's center and programs; concierge; dance club; gym; Internet; Jacuzzi; nightly show; 7 outdoor pools; sauna; smoke-free rooms; 8 lit outdoor tennis courts; watersports equipment. *In room:* A/C, TV, minibar.

Playa Costa Verde ★★ ☺ 🗝   Originally built for and run by the Jamaican SuperClubs chain, this attractively designed property is now managed by the Cuban

Gaviota company. The resort is an excellent value for families, with whom it is extremely popular. Although rooms do not have sea or beach views, they are quite large, with very nice decor in bright greens and deep blues, tile floors, and balconies or terraces. They represent some of the best-equipped and best-designed rooms I've seen among high-end beach hotels in Cuba. In addition to the beautiful rooms, this hotel has a wide range of activities and an excellent children's program. A spectacular section of Playa Pesquero is a 5-minute walk from the pool over a bridge and through wetlands. The Japanese restaurant here is especially worthy of mention.

Playa Pesquero, Rafael Freyre, Holguín. **24/43-3520.** Fax 24/43-3525. www.gaviota-grupo.com. 480 units. CUC$230 double; CUC$290 suite. Rates are all-inclusive. 1 child under 12 stays free in parent's room; 2nd child stays for 50% MC, V. **Amenities:** 4 restaurants; snack bar; 9 bars; babysitting; bikes; children's center and programs; concierge; dance club; fitness center; Internet; Jacuzzi; nightly show; 2 outdoor pools; 4 lit outdoor tennis courts; watersports equipment. *In room:* A/C, TV, hair dryer, minibar.

Playa Pesquero ★★ ☺ This massive hotel is one of the largest in Cuba. Your experience here begins with a fabulous open-air lobby with lily pools, large sculptures, and several romantic sitting areas. The rooms are all in two-story blocks spread around the massive grounds ringing the large free-form pool, gym, and entertainment area. Rooms are all spacious and cheery, and all have a private balcony or porch. The superior rooms are really junior suites, and the extra space and sitting area is quite nice. This resort has a whole host of organized activities and entertainment options, as well as a broad selection of restaurants and bars. Of the a la carte restaurants here, La Gondola is particularly appealing, with a series of private dining gazebos spread around a small re-creation of Venice's canal system, replete with a real gondola. Be sure to reserve one of these in advance if you're looking for a romantic dinner.

Playa Pesquero, Rafael Freyre, Holguín. **24/43-3530.** Fax 24/43-0535. www.gaviota-grupo.com. 912 units. CUC$280 double; CUC$360 suite. Rates are all-inclusive. Children under 2 stay free in parent's room; children 3–12 stay for half price in same room. MC, V. **Amenities:** 7 restaurants; 2 snack bars; 6 bars; babysitting; children's center and programs; dance club; fitness center; Internet; 4 Jacuzzis; sauna; nightly show; massive outdoor pool; 3 lit outdoor tennis courts; watersports equipment. *In room:* A/C, TV Internet (in some), minibar.

Where to Dine

Few visitors eat anywhere besides their all-inclusive hotels, of course. However, if you're just day-tripping to Guardalavaca, or you can't take another hotel buffet, check out **El Cayuelo,** near the Las Brisas hotel on Playa de Guardalavaca (**24/43-0736**), which serves decent *comida criolla* (Cuban creole food), or **El Ancla,** Playa de Guardalavaca (**24/43-0381**), for seafood. Other tourist restaurants in the zone include **Mongo Viña,** on the road to Playa Pesquero with a pastoral view (**24/43-0915**), as well as **Restaurante Cayo Naranjo** (**24/43-0132**) and **Yaguajay Restaurant** (**24/43-0422**), both within the tourist complex of Parque Natural Bahía de Naranjo.

Guardalavaca After Dark

All of the all-inclusive hotels provide free nightly entertainment of varying quality; as a general rule, the stages, dancers, and musicians increase in quality along with the price, so expect the nightly cabaret at the Río de Oro to far outclass what Club Amigo puts on. Some are well-produced, professional, lively affairs and give you a pretty good time. Others are, well, cheesy and embarrassing. Most hotels change the program every night over a 1- or 2-week schedule, so if you want to drop in every night, you'll at least see a new presentation (the musicians and dancers, though, may very well be the same).

When the tourist-targeted entertainment gets to be too much, head for the one place where you can be assured of spotting (and maybe even interacting with!) locals. For those who need a break from packaged entertainment, the **Disco La Roca** (© **24/43-0167;** CUC$3 cover) in Guardalavaca is the place to be outside of the hotels. It is partly open air and has good beach views.

Side Trips from Guardalavaca

The following are the most common and easily accessible side trips from Guardalavaca. Though it may seem unfair to characterize the largest city and provincial capital, Holguín, as a day trip from the beach, the fact of the matter is that the overwhelming majority of visitors to this section of northeastern Cuba have sun and surf on their minds.

HOLGUÍN

56km (35 miles) SW of Guardalavaca; 734km (456 miles) E of Havana; 134km (83 miles) NW of Santiago de Cuba

The provincial capital, officially called San Isidoro de Holguín, may be known across Cuba as the "city of parks," but it doesn't get a whole lot of tourist traffic, which also makes it appealing. Holguín is a pleasant but unremarkable city with only a modicum of attractions. Still, it makes a good day trip for resort visitors who would otherwise see nothing of Cuba save Guardalavaca's all-inclusive hotels and brilliant beaches.

Holguín, the fourth-largest city in Cuba, has a compact center that's easy enough to get around; visitors can manage the highlights in an unhurried day. The city's few elegant plazas, colonial buildings, and small dose of museums do not rival the highlights of Trinidad or Camagüey, and much of the city's historical character has been subsumed by industrial expansion. The great majority of the city's buildings date from the 19th and 20th centuries.

Pleasant **Parque Calixto García** (also called Parque Central), named for a 19th-century patriot, represents the heart of the city. The hero of the wars of independence is paid tribute with a large marble statue in the park's center. Benches are usually occupied by locals watching the town and time pass by. Two nearby churches of note are the domed **Iglesia de San José** (on Plaza Carlos Manuel de Céspedes), which has an unusual baroque interior to go with its remade neoclassical facade, and the imposing 18th-century **La Catedral de San Isidro de Holguín** (Calle Manduley, on Parque de las Flores), which features *mudéjar* (Moorish-style) carved wooden ceilings.

Of special note in Holguín is the unusual **Familia Cuayo Fábrica de Organos,** Carretera a Gibara 301 (© **24/42-4162**), a studio that still produces handmade *órganos pneumáticos* (air-compression organs) with hand-cut music sheets, and restores musical instruments—perhaps the very last of a breed. Eighteen workers make only four organs per year. A large organ, for which there is today a very limited market, costs about CUC$23,148. It would be wise to call before visiting because in summer 2010, work on the organs had ceased. Another interesting stop is the **Fábrica de Muñecas,** Carretera a Gibara 562 e/Narcisco López y Cervantes, Cuba's only doll factory; here, clay dolls—dressed in 46 different costumes—are made for the tourist trade. It's open Monday to Friday 7am–5:30pm; tips are appreciated.

La Loma de Cruz (Hill of the Cross), 3km (1¾ miles) north of the city, can be climbed by ascending the nearly 500 steps to the top, where there's a wooden cross that was placed there in 1790. Though the often-windy hill has excellent views of Holguín in the flat valley and the surrounding countryside, the hilltop is a little forlorn. The **Mirador de Mayabe** is the other acclaimed viewpoint, about

10km (6 miles) from the city center. On the hill, **Cerro de Mayabe,** is a hotel and restaurant.

Holguín's **Cabaret Nuevo Nocturno** ★, Carretera Central Vía Las Tunas, km 2.5 (✆ **24/42-9345**), is an open-air cabaret show. Its Corazón Caribeño show (Wed–Mon, 9pm–2am) is very professional and entertaining, considerably better than the ones put on nightly by the all-inclusive hotels in Guardalavaca. Afterward, the stage becomes a hopping dance club. Admission is CUC$10, or you can buy a package at any of the hotel tour desks for around CUC$30, which includes transportation from your hotel and a cocktail.

The **Villa Liba,** C/ Maceo 46 esquina 18 (✆ **24/42-3823;** marielaygoa@cristal. hlg.sld.cu), is a 1950s mansion, decorated with original furniture, that has been converted into a wonderful *casa particular.* Relax on the interior patio fragranced by mariposa flowers. The owner, Jorge Mezerene, who is of Lebanese descent, cooks with organic ingredients and is known for his vegetarian food. His wife Mariela is a yoga and reiki practitioner who can offer massages to guests.

For details on getting to Holguín, see "Getting There," earlier in this section.

GIBARA
35km (22 miles) N of Holguín

A sleepy, charming, early-19th-century provincial port, **Gibara** ★—sometimes referred to as *La Villa Blanca,* or the White Village, due to its one-time whitewashed appearance—is home to a number of fine colonial buildings. Unfortunately, Hurricane Ike pummeled Gibara in 2008, and many historic attractions are still waiting to be restored. Today, Gibara, a modest fishing town, has great scenery and overlooks a wide natural bay, with a very tranquil atmosphere. Two pretty little beaches and a *malecón* (promenade) line the picturesque bay, and inland is the **Silla de Gibara,** a flat-topped mountain that locals claim is the hill described by Columbus when he first happened upon Cuba (it is much more probable that he landed in Baracoa, much farther east of here, and that the mountain described in his journal is El Yunque).

On the top of Los Caneyes hill are the ruins of an old fortress, which protected merchants involved in trade with Europe and the U.S. (a 30-min. walk up the hill rewards hikers with excellent views of the town and bay). Trade soon diminished with the introduction of the railroad, and the fortunes of Gibara suffered, leading to an exodus of a significant portion of its population. Gibara's moment in the sun is still reflected in the handful of grand mansions and public buildings.

The main plaza, Calixto García, is marked by an attractive yellow church, **San Fulgencio,** which dates back to 1850 and has red-tiled cupolas and African oak trees. Of greatest interest is the **Museo de Artes Decorativas,** Independencia 19 (✆ **24/43-4687**), housed in an impressive neoclassical house constructed in 1872. The sumptuous mansion, which once belonged to an elite merchant, was severely damaged by the hurricane and has yet to reopen. Its saved features include huge mediopunto stained-glass windows, yellow and blue tiles, and quality period furnishings. Museum staff may be happy to show you the unique-in-Cuba 1910 *alfiletero,* an egg-shaped needle store with a tiny panorama of a Jordanian scene viewed through a tiny pin-sized viewer in its "shell." Also of note is the well-known mixed media picture, *La Copa del Amor* (1872), which features human hair. Lovers Adolfo Ferrin and Ygnacia Nates were separated as he traveled for work. On his return he found his betrothed gravely ill. After 17-year-old Ignacia died (of typhus), local businessman Adolfo asked her father if he could cut some of her hair to incorporate into a picture.

La Copa del Amor depicts the tomb of Ygnacia in the Gibara cemetery, shaded by the branches of the sauce llorón tree. The tree, with its branches—made of hair and tree—is seen as a tree of tears. After a visit to the cemetery, climb the steps to the *mirador* for an attractive view of the town's rooftops.

Gibara holds the annual **Festival Internacional del Cine Pobre** (www.cubacine.cu/cinepobre) in April, and there's the **Cine Jibe** on the main plaza, the star screen in town.

The **Hostal La Muralla** near Parque Colón, Calle Joaquin Aguero 77 (© 24/84-4848; rfalegret@gmail.com), is a comfortable place to stay with a great back patio, plentiful food, and a relaxing bedroom.

For all intents and purposes, there's no public transportation available to tourists connecting either Holguín or Guardalavaca to Gibara. This is just as well, since it is quick and convenient to take a taxi there and back for around CUC$22 to CUC$24. Gibara is also featured as a day trip by most of the tour operators in Guardalavaca and can be visited with **Cubatur** from Holguín (© 24/42-1679) for CUC$10 per person (minimum four people)

CAYO SAETÍA

130km (81 miles) SE of Guardalavaca

This pristine cay, on the eastern side of the Bahía de Nipe, isn't terribly easy to get to, but if isolated and totally unpopulated, sugar-white cove beaches and wild game are of interest to you, it might be worth the effort. This erstwhile exclusive game resort was once the private stomping and hunting grounds of Cuba's military and political brass. The cay has an exceptional roster of flora and fauna, which includes not only deer and wild boar, but also a wild collection of exotics such as antelopes, ostrich, water buffalo, and zebras. Most excursions include snorkeling, boat rides, jeep safaris, horseback riding, and lunch on the beach. While this place is billed as an ecotourist getaway, this seems to include stalking semicaptive and imported game under the rubric of "ecotourism." There's only one hotel on the cay, **Villa Cayo Saetía ★** (© 24/51-6900; www.gaviota-grupo.com), with just a dozen simple, yet tasteful rooms and cabanas. Cayo Saetía is about 90 minutes from Guardalavaca by jeep and just 20 minutes by helicopter (the preferred method of transport). Contact **Gaviota Tours** (© 24/43-0434), which runs the place, or any of the hotels or travel agencies in Guardalavaca. A great option is to take the catamaran cruise around the coast to the cayo, and enjoy lunch and a jeep safari among the wild animals, CUC$69.

BAYAMO & THE SIERRA MAESTRA ★

757km (470 miles) E of Havana; 201km (125 miles) E of Camagüey; 127km (79 miles) W of Santiago de Cuba; 73km (45 miles) S of Holguín

Granma province is unusually easygoing and lethargic, even by the standards of stifling hot and dry eastern Cuba, but its retiring pace and unassuming nature belie a turbulent, indelible role in modern Cuban history. Bayamo, the capital of the province, and the densely forested, impenetrable mountains of the Sierra Maestra at the extreme southwest corner of the Oriente region have long been at the forefront of political turmoil and rebellion. The otherwise unassuming region may just be the place where Cuba's independent streak runs deepest.

Bayamo, one of Cuba's original seven *villas* and today a midsize city and the capital of Granma province, is considered the birthplace of Cuban independence. The *himno nacional,* or national anthem, was first sung here after the city was seized by the Liberating Army and became the capital of the Republic at Arms in 1869. South of Bayamo, the Sierra Maestra, a national park comprising a spectacularly verdant and rugged range that reaches right down to the Caribbean coast, is where Fidel Castro and his band of rebels sneaked back into Cuba in 1956 after a period of exile in Mexico. The rebels hid in the mountains, depending upon the assistance of sympathetic *guajiros* (peasants), and based their long-shot revolution there, covertly raising the antenna of Radio Rebelde and scoring decisive victories on the road to eventual triumph. How influential was the province as a turning point in 20th-century Cuban politics and society? Important enough that, after the Revolution, it received the name of the yacht in which Fidel and his brothers in arms sailed from Mexico, and the government-owned and operated national daily newspaper is also named after the boat: Read all about it in *Granma.*

Today, Bayamo and the Sierra Maestra are considerably better known for their historical associations than they are as travel destinations. Bayamo is pleasant and peaceful, but its citizens and well-maintained colonial structures don't really try too hard to impress visitors, making it a tranquil stopover. Meanwhile, much of the Sierra Maestra remains difficult to penetrate due to controlled access. However, it is relatively simple and rewarding to trace the revolutionary steps of Fidel and Che Guevara, visiting the fascinating installations of the rebel group—preserved as they were in the tense days of the late 1950s—tucked high in the mountains. The dramatic coastline that bends around the southeastern base of the Oriente, where the mountains scrape the edge of the sparkling Caribbean, makes an excellent, if time-consuming, ground approach to Santiago de Cuba, and is worth the trip for the scenic value alone. Hurricane damage has blasted the roads in part but it is passable if a little hair-raising at times. A handful of package tourism hotels are perched on the rocky coast, where the sands aren't much to speak of, but the incomparable sea and mountain views, and diving and hiking opportunities—not to mention very favorable package prices—more than compensate for that.

Essentials

GETTING THERE

BY PLANE   You can fly from Havana to Bayamo on **Aerocaribbean** (© **23/42-3916** in Bayamo, or 7/879-7524 in Havana; www.cubajet.com) on Tuesday and Friday; the fare is CUC$104 one-way. Flights arrive at **Aeropuerto Carlos Manuel de Céspedes,** Carretera a Holguín (© **23/42-7514;** airport code BYM), 10km (6 miles) north of the city. By registered taxi, the trip to town is about CUC$5–CUC$8.

BY BUS   Víazul (© **23/42-4036** in Bayamo, or 7/881-1413 in Havana; www.viazul.com) is the most convenient mode of transportation for traveling to Bayamo from Havana and Santiago, and major cities in between. On the Trinidad–Santiago de Cuba line, the bus departs Trinidad at 7:40pm and arrives in Bayamo at 4:50am; the fare is CUC$26. Buses from Santiago bound for points west leave at 9am, 3:15pm 7.30pm, 8pm. and 10pm, and stop in Bayamo 2 hours and 10 minutes later; the fare is CUC$7. On the Havana-Santiago line, there are daily departures at 9:30am, 3:15pm, and 10pm; the trip from Havana is roughly 14 hours and costs CUC$44. On the Varadero-Santiago line the bus leaves Varadero at 9:25pm, and arrives at 9:55am, costing CUC$44.

Sometimes you're told there are no spaces on the bus by the ticket office in Bayamo; wait to speak to the bus driver, who may tell you that there are seats left.

The main bus terminal for long-distance buses, the **Terminal de Omnibuses,** is located on the outskirts of downtown, on Carretera Central near Avenida Jesús Rabi, on the road to Holguín. Horse-drawn carriages and unregistered taxis await passengers to ferry them downtown for CUC$3 (far is higher at night).

GETTING AROUND

The compact old town of Bayamo is very simple to get around on foot. You're only likely to need a taxi to get back and forth to your hotel, if you stay out at the large Hotel Sierra Maestra, or to get to the airport or bus station to move on. Contact **Cubataxi** (© 23/42-4313) for local and long-distance taxis. Alternatively, you can take a horse-drawn or bicycle taxi anywhere in town for CUC$1 to CUC$2. It's sometimes difficult to locate a Cubataxi at night, so a bicitaxi might be the only option.

Getting to the Sierra Maestra mountains is rather more complicated, necessitating a rental car, hired *carro particular,* or organized excursion. If you wish to explore the Sierra with any degree of independence, or make the coastal drive to Santiago de Cuba, your own wheels are virtually indispensable. There are **Transtur** offices within the Servi-Cupet gas station on Carretera Central (© **23/42-7375**) and in the Sierra Maestra Hotel (© **23/48-2990**). Transgaviota are based in the Hotel Royalton (© **23/42-7372**). Rates are about CUC$45 to CUC$85 per day for a standard four-door compact car.

To get to the Sierra Maestra for a day's hike it's often cheaper to organize the excursion with a *casa particular* than it is to go with a state travel agency.

ORIENTATION

Bayamo's historic center sits on a high bluff overlooking the Bayamo River. For information about excursions in the province, visit one of the major tour operators. **Cubanacán** has an office inside the Hotel Royalton, and **Havanatur** (© **23/42-7672**) has an office on the western side of Parque Céspedes. The tour desk at the Hotel Sierra Maestra is also a good place to get information and arrange tours and car hire.

A **Banco de Crédito y Comercio** branch is on General García between Saco and Perucho Figueredo. It's open Monday through Friday from 8am to 3pm and on Saturday from 8 to 11am. There is a **CADECA** on Saco No. 5 between Donato Mármol and General García; it's open Monday through Saturday from 8am to 6pm and Sunday from 8am to 1pm.

For medical attention, go to **Hospital General Carlos Manuel de Céspedes,** Carretera Central on the way to Santiago de Cuba (© **23/42-2144**). There's also a Servimed **Farmacia Internacional** inside the Hotel Sierra Maestra.

The main **post office** is on the west side of Parque Céspedes. It's open Monday through Saturday from 8am to 8pm. An **Etecsa** telepunto center with Internet access is at General García 109; it's open daily from 8:30am to 7:30pm and until 9pm on Saturdays.

Bayamo

The second Spanish city founded in Cuba in 1513, as Villa de San Salvador de Bayamo, is small and quiet for a provincial capital. The laid-back town welcomes relatively few visitors, except for day-trippers, and locals refrain from hassling foreign visitors—unless it involves singing the Cuban national anthem for you, the city's pride and joy.

Bayamo

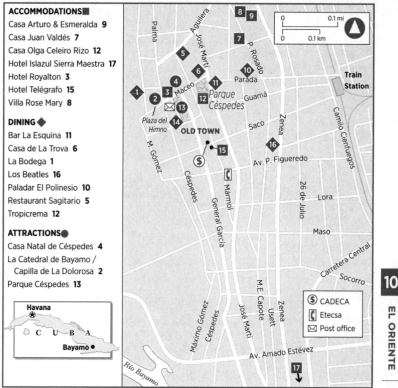

ACCOMMODATIONS■
Casa Arturo & Esmeralda **9**
Casa Juan Valdés **7**
Casa Olga Celeiro Rizo **12**
Hotel Islazul Sierra Maestra **17**
Hotel Royalton **3**
Hotel Telégrafo **15**
Villa Rose Mary **8**

DINING◆
Bar La Esquina **11**
Casa de La Trova **6**
La Bodega **1**
Los Beatles **16**
Paladar El Polinesio **10**
Restaurant Sagitario **5**
Tropicrema **12**

ATTRACTIONS●
Casa Natal de Céspedes **4**
La Catedral de Bayamo /
   Capilla de La Dolorosa **2**
Parque Céspedes **13**

Bayamo grew wealthy in the 17th and 18th centuries from contraband and later sugar and cattle. Many of the local elite were privileged enough to send young men off to Spain and France to study, and a number of them returned with enlightened ideals about colonialism and a strong desire for Cuban independence. Carlos Manuel de Céspedes (1819–74) was a wealthy businessman who, in 1868, freed his slaves and formed a small army that set about achieving that goal. The movement was known as the *Grito de Yara,* a call for independence or death. His forces succeeded in capturing Bayamo and giving life to the War of Independence against Spain. The rebels held Bayamo for 3 months until it was evident that the superior numbers of Spanish troops would soon defeat them. Rather than surrender, the rebel army audaciously chose to burn the city, in the ultimate act of sedition. Most of the city was wiped out by this act of self-immolation in 1869.

WHAT TO SEE & DO

Parque Céspedes ★★ is the focal point of downtown Bayamo. It's an exquisite, peaceful square flanked by tall royal palm trees. The light-blue and pink building at one end of the square, which housed a pharmacy, is where the great blaze began. At one end of the plaza is a marble bust of the independence fighter Perucho Figueredo, which carries the words and music to "La Bayamesa" (later the national anthem), imploring followers not to fear "a glorious death" and encourages Cubans that to "die for the homeland is to live." At the other end of the plaza is a stately granite and bronze statue of Carlos Manuel de Céspedes. Ringing the square are handsome, pastel-colored, arcaded colonial-style (post-1869) buildings. Had the city not been consumed by fire, in all likelihood it would resemble the remarkable colonial core of Trinidad.

Next to the Hotel Royalton on the north side of the square, the **Casa Natal de Céspedes ★**, Calle Francisco Maceo Osorio 57 (© **23/42-3864**), the birthplace of the "father of the Cuban nation," is the only house on the square that escaped destruction from the fire. The significance of it alone being saved is not lost on Cubans. Today it is a museum, open Tuesday through Friday from 10am to 6pm, Saturday from 10am to 3pm and 8 to 10pm, and Sunday from 10am to 3pm and 8 to 10pm; admission is CUC$1. The house has been lovingly restored; the two-story building holds a chronological exhibit about the Céspedes family, elegant 19th-century colonial furnishings, objects belonging to Céspedes (such as his ceremonial saber), and a few odds and ends that help piece together the story of Bayamo's independent streak (including the original printing press that produced the first newspaper of free Cuba, *El Cubano Libre,* in 1868). The standout item, however, is the extraordinary, huge four-poster bronze bed complete with two oval shields depicting towns in mother-of-pearl decoration; the imagery changes as you glance at the depictions from left to right. Céspedes is remembered for refusing to trade his surrender for the life of his son, who was captured by the Spanish army; the Cuban patriot replied in writing that all Cubans were his sons and he could not be expected to trade their independence for the life of one man. The Spaniards promptly shot his son Oscar.

Just west of the museum and Parque Céspedes, dominating a small open square called **Plaza del Himno,** is **La Catedral de Bayamo** (or La Catedral del Santísimo Salvador), an immense, ocher-colored, 16th-century church that succumbed to the 1869 fire. Rebuilt several times over the course of its life, the church was recently magnificently restored. It features a high-peaked wood-beam ceiling and, above the altar, an attention-getting battle mural commemorating a pivotal local episode when the parish priest blessed the rebel army flag. This blurring of the lines between church and state was not the only overtly political statement to take place in the cathedral; the first singing of the revolutionary anthem was staged here in 1869. The cathedral is open to visitors daily from 9am to 1pm and from 3 to 5pm. To one side of the cathedral, the small chapel **Capilla de La Dolorosa (Chapel of the Lady of Sorrows),** which dates to 174, is distinguished by a lovely Moorish-style, carved wooden ceiling and fine baroque altarpiece; it was only one of three important buildings to survive the 1869 blaze (the others were the Casa de la Trova and Céspedes' home).

Heading south from Parque Céspedes, Calle General García has been turned into a pleasant pedestrian mall, with several shops, simple restaurants, and tour agency offices.

WHERE TO STAY

Quite a few *casas particulares* can be found in the old center of Bayamo. **Casa Arturo & Esmeralda,** Calle Zenea 56A between William Soler and Capote (© **23/42-4051;** www.casa-bayamo.com) offers two air-conditioned rooms with TVs and minibars, located in a modern, welcoming house. **Casa Olga Celeiro Rizo,** Calle Parada 16 (Altos) between Martí and Mármol (© **23/42-3859;** yaimara.grm@infomed.sld.cu), is a friendly house with two comfortable, air-conditioned rooms and a great terrace overlooking the pleasant Francisco Maceo Osorio plaza; Olga can help with

dear GRANMA

In early December 1956, Fidel Castro, his brother Raúl, Ernesto (Che) Guevara, and a group of idealist revolutionaries, including some who had previously stormed the barracks in Santiago de Cuba and Bayamo, sailed back to Cuba from exile in Mexico with weapons and an audacious plan: to overthrow, once and for all, the Batista government. They set sail aboard a yacht christened the *Granma*, purchased from a couple of Americans in Veracruz. The stealth journey was beset by all manner of hitches, including bad weather and scarce provisions. Just 82 men disembarked at Las Coloradas beach 2 days later than planned, with few weapons and virtually no supplies.

Batista forces had been tipped off to the operation, and prompt aerial bombing killed about half the rebels; the others fled for the mountains in small groups. After suffering an ambush, only 16 men remained, and when the survivors eventually met up at Cinco Palmas in the Sierra Maestra, only a dozen men remained. They had but eight rifles to their names. Against

monumental odds, they nonetheless began to plan their offensive. Batista, no doubt convinced that the attempted sedition had been effectively quashed, announced to the world that Castro and the other leaders had been killed and withdrew government forces from the area—a fatal mistake.

Crafty Castro slowly but surely began to gain adherents and advance the rebel cause of the 26th of July movement. Astonishingly, a band of just over a dozen fighters at the campaign's inception—propped up by a growing network of *guajiros* (poor rural farmers) and vast, inaccessible terrain—somehow ended up toppling the Batista regime just 2 years later.

Today, the spot where the rebels landed ashore, at the southwestern tip of Cuba near Cabo Cruz, is a national park, Parque Nacional del Desembarco del Granma (admission CUC$5; open daily 7am–6pm). A monument features a replica of the Granma; the real vessel is in the Museo de la Revolución in Havana.

excursions. **Villa Rose Mary,** Pío Rosado 22 between Ramírez and Avenida F.V. Aguilera (© **23/42-3984;** www.cubahostal.com; varezsanchez@yahoo.es), is an attractive house with two comfortable, clean, air-conditioned rooms. **Casa Juan Valdés,** Pío Rosado 64 between Ramírez and N López (© **23/42-3324**), has an upstairs floor with a bedroom, bathroom, kitchenette, and sitting room. It's inexpensive, and would be great for a family.

In addition to the hotels listed below, another good option and excellent value is the former training school **Hotel Telégrafo,** Calle José Antonio Saco 108 (© **23/42-5510;** www.ehtgr.co.cu), which is in the heart of downtown. It has 12 double rooms, each with air-conditioning, a TV, and a small refrigerator. The hotel is now part of the newly branded Royalton; at press time, it was closed for renovations, but it is slated to reopen in December 2010.

Hotel Royalton ★ Set facing Parque Céspedes, this small hotel has been refurbished under Cuba's boutique Hoteles Encanto brand. Dating to the 1940s, four of the rooms have small balconies with great plaza views; and despite the small bathrooms, these rooms are the top choice. Off to one side of the lobby is the dependable **Restaurant Plaza,** which has a nice sidewalk terrace and serves a generous plate of fried chicken with excellent French fries, as well as beef steak. Prepare to wait for a table and a menu—there are just two menus for 72 seats!

Calle Maceo 53, Bayamo. © **23/42-2246**. 33 units. CUC$50–CUC$60 double. Rates include breakfast. MC, V. **Amenities:** Restaurant; bar. *In room:* A/C, TV, minibar.

Hotel Islazul Sierra Maestra   Located 2km (1¼ miles) from Parque Céspedes, this large and friendly hotel has an excellent outdoor swimming pool and a quiet, relaxed feel. Rooms are smallish, but well-appointed, with air-conditioning and TV, and most have a balcony of some sort. Most rooms are in a large, nondescript three-story block of a building backing the pool. My favorite rooms are in the separate cabaña section of two-story units. At night, this place has a decent bar scene and probably the liveliest dance club in town (open Wed–Sun 8pm–2am).

Carretera Central Km 1.5 on the way to Santiago de Cuba. © **23/42-7970.** www.islazul.cu. 132 units. CUC$30 double. MC, V. **Amenities:** Restaurant; bar; large outdoor pool. *In room:* A/C, TV.

WHERE TO DINE & DRINK

Only a few *paladares* remain in Bayamo. Aside from the place listed below, **Paladar El Polinesio,** Parada 125 between Pío Rosado and Capotico (© 23/42-3860) is the second-best restaurant in town. There's also a **Dino's Pizza** at General García 111, and a host of restaurants along pedestrian Calle General García that are open noon to 10pm. For dessert, stand in line with locals at the ice-cream parlor **Tropi-crema,** located just off the southwest corner of Parque Céspedes.

The loveliest place to kick back with a cerveza is **La Bodega** at 34 Plaza del Himno (© 23/42-1011). This sweet bar and café has a lovely view of the river, and is the perfect spot for a drink at sunset. There is usually live music until 1am.

The small, air-conditioned **Bar La Esquina,** on the corner of the small, shaded Francisco Maceo Osorio plaza, is a cool spot for a drink. At the other end of the plaza on Calle Maceo is the **Casa de La Trova,** which has regular live performances. **Los Beatles,** Calle Zenea between Saco and Figueredo (closed Mondays), is a new outdoor venue that hosts cover bands; sip a *mojito* for CUC$5 per glass.

Restaurant Sagitario ★ CRIOLLAN   This place serves large and well-prepared meals in a pleasant backyard patio. The house specialty is pork steak cooked with cheese; the *pargo* (red snapper) is also good. Service here is friendly and downright efficient.

Calle Mármol 107 btw. Maceo and Francisco Vicente Aguilera. © **23/42-2449**. Main courses CUC$6–CUC$7. No credit cards. Daily noon–11pm.

Sierra Maestra ★★

Cuba's highest and longest mountain range stretches about 140km (87 miles) west to east, across three provinces: Granma, Santiago de Cuba, and Guantánamo. Its highest peaks are only several kilometers from the coastline, making for some exciting views, whether you're perched up in the mountains or cruising along the coast. The entire range forms part of the **Gran Parque Nacional Sierra Maestra,** and its thickly forested, rugged terrain, with steep, deep green mountains swathed in wispy clouds, is impenetrable for most traffic, though the area is splendid for hikers. While there are many trails just begging to be explored, until recently most remained closed to the public; hard-core hikers should perhaps anticipate encountering some closed trail heads. The heart of the Gran Parque is a park-within-a-park, the **Parque Nacional de Turquino ★**, which includes Turquino, the nation's highest summit at just under 2,000m (6,562 ft.).

Deep folds and craggy ravines make these mountains very inaccessible, and they are, not surprisingly, very sparsely populated, with only small numbers of *guajiros* (poor rural farmers)—many of whose families once gave shelter and support to the rebels in their midst—living very simply in *bohíos* (thatched-roof huts) with no electricity or running water. Also tucked away in the mountain range are dozens of endemic species of birds and plants.

Unless you're a physically prepared hiker with all your own equipment and several days or more for hikes, your best bet is to head to Turquino Park, where there is, at least, minimal infrastructure; there's also the lasting legacy of Fidel Castro and his committed band of rebels, which formed the **Comandancia de La Plata,** a base command for their guerrilla war in 1956 after returning from exile in Mexico (see "Dear *Granma*," above). The two main trails into the mountains are the **Pico Turquino Trail** and the **La Plata Trail;** the latter visits the rebels' base camp.

The road south from Bayamo is a long, lush, tropical adventure; it cuts through beautiful sugar-cane fields where pigs, peacocks, and machete-wielding farmers roam, with the rounded, green peaks of the Sierra Maestra looming in the background. **Villa Santo Domingo,** 65km (40 miles) south of Bayamo by a good road, is where you'll find the entrance to the national park, as well as a rustic hotel and restaurant that serve as a perfect base camp for those who want to trace the trail of Fidel and Che, ascend Pico Turquino, or just explore the rugged beauty of the national park. The **Hotel Villa Santo Domingo** (© 23/56-5568; www.islazul.cu), where Fidel and his brother Raúl have been frequent guests in the past (Fidel favored cabin no. 6), sits down a bit on the left side of the road, on the banks of the Yara River. The 20 attractive little cabins have twin beds, private bathrooms, air-conditioning, TVs, solar-powered hot water, and fridges. They cost CUC$34 to CUC$37 double, including breakfast. Also on the grounds are a good restaurant and outdoor grill, as well as a bar, and video/game room. Even for those not staying at the hotel, the rustic, open-air **Restaurant La Yamagua** is the best place to eat in the area if you didn't bring your own provisions. For groups, the restaurant does a good *parrillada* (barbecue) of *cerdo asado* (roast pork), salad, rice, dessert, and coffee for CUC$14 per person. The menu includes standards of *comida criolla* (Cuban creole food), several different preparations of chicken, and pork steak.

HIKING IN THE SIERRA

Hiking deep into the Sierra Maestra is a superbly rewarding experience for any hiker, but—given the mountains' historic role in the success of the Revolution and the fact that much of the Sierra remains a military zone—the Cuban government zealously protects access to it. By law, you need permission and a guide to explore the national park. Remember, Fidel's cronies hid from Batista's forces and the CIA for more than 2 years in the dense forest of the Sierra, so finding your way around is a complicated task. Park authorities don't look kindly upon foreigners seeking to explore the park on their own.

Guides can be contracted at the official entrance to the national park, the **Centro de Visitantes,** about 200m (656 ft.) along the road beyond the Hotel Villa Santo Domingo. It is open daily from 7:30 to 10am. Visitors now pay a minimum CUC$20 fee to enter the park, which includes a guide for hikes into the Sierra. An additional CUC$5 is payable to take pictures of La Comandancia. This also is the spot to arrange for treks and bird-watching. You will need to arrive with all necessary gear, as no one in the area rents equipment. The center offers a number of different hikes and prices. All prices are per person and include a guide:

- Comandancia La Plata del Ejército Rebelde (see below): CUC$20
- Palma Mocha, a 1-day trek toward Pico Turquino: CUC$20
- Aguada de Santo Domingo to Pico Turquino, includes 1 night in the Aguada refuge, which has beds and mattresses, but you'll need a sleeping bag: CUC$33
- Santo Domingo–Aguada–Pico Turquino–La Majagua–Las Cuevas, includes 2 nights of camping: CUC$40

To gain access to the Pico Turquino or La Plata trail, hikers must either climb or take a 4WD (CUC$5 return) that takes 15 minutes one-way, or a tough-as-nails flatbed truck (CUC$5 return) that takes 45 minutes one-way; the trip is up a treacherously steep paved road, with thrilling hairpin turns, to **Alto de Naranjo,** 5km (3 miles) from the visitor center. A minimum number of 10 to 12 hikers is usually required for the truck service.

Places to get more information about trekking in the Sierra Maestra are **Agencia de Reservaciones del Campismo (Cubamar),** General García 211, Bayamo (✆ **23/42-4200**), and **Islazul,** General García 207, Bayamo (✆/fax **23/42-3273**), which runs the Villa Santo Domingo hotel at the entrance to the park. However, it is much cheaper to arrive independently at the national park or with a hired *carro particular* (private Cuban's car) to arrange a hike than it is to book through Cubamar whose prices are exorbitant.

Pico Turquino ★★

The hike to Pico Turquino, the highest summit in Cuba, requires a minimum of 2 nights in the area (1 night camping). The trek from Alto de Naranjo is about 15km (9 miles). Experienced, fast hikers can do the ascent and descent in a day, but most people choose to camp overnight at the *refugio* (refuge), several kilometers below the summit. The trek through an amazing array of tropical ferns, vines, and dense cloud forest, punctuated by the sharp calls of unseen birds, is terrific, with stunning panoramic views all around, and is only really difficult at the steep end. It gets quite cold at night, so make sure you're prepared with proper clothing and equipment.

Comandancia de la Plata ★★

Though not nearly as challenging a hike—you can do the 6km (4 miles) up and back in about 3 hours—the trail to La Plata perched on a mountain ridge reverberates with thrilling history, no matter on which side of the political fence you fall. Visiting the rudimentary installations of Fidel Castro's rebel base camp is a remarkable experience. When you learn the story of the rebellion and visit the crude installations from which Fidel directed his offensive, it's hard not to have at least some appreciation for why this man clung so tenaciously to power and the ideals of the Revolution: Look what he did to get there.

After about 20 minutes on the trail, about 800m (2,625 ft.) above sea level, hikers come to the **Alto de Medina,** a small wooden house. At the entrance to the base camp, it was the checkpoint building. Farther up along the trail, you come to a **small museum** about the revolutionary guerrilla warfare waged in these mountains. You'll see what, at one time, was a small hospital, and eventually, you'll arrive at the huts where Fidel lived with his *compañera* (partner) Celia Sánchez. Fidel never allowed anyone but Celia inside the shack; the bench outside the door where he conducted interviews is still there. Ingeniously constructed under the cover of thick forest, the installations make it quite apparent how the rebels eluded capture and assassination.

The hilltop rising above the camp is where the guerrillas covertly erected the antenna to broadcast their rebel message on the nascent Radio Rebelde.

The Coastal Road to Santiago de Cuba

The Sierra Maestra stretching down to the rocky beaches and black sands of the south coast, against the sparkling blue waters of the Caribbean, is one of the most dramatic sights in Cuba. To trace the coastline to Santiago de Cuba is to take the scenic route; it's a roundabout way to get to your destination, for sure, but well worth it if you're a fan of rugged, bravura landscapes. The road and bridges suffered damage from the 2008 hurricanes, but are still passable—ask about the status of the road in Niquero, Pilón, or Santiago before setting out on your trip, and take it slow. It takes around 8 to 9 hours from Pilón to Santiago and is the most scenic drive in the country. If you're pressed for time and headed to Santiago, the inland route from Bayamo is much more direct.

The coastline is remarkably absent of any sort of villages or installations for long stretches at a time: It's just you, the open road (watch for rockslides), and the sea to your right and Sierra Maestra to your left. While you can usually make the trip in any normal sedan, a four-wheel-drive vehicle is recommended for the added clearance, if nothing else. The beaches, such as they are, range from passable soft gray stone to forbidding big black rock.

A smattering of large resort hotels are located at certain points along the coast, and while it's a stretch to describe them as beach resorts, they do offer splendid sea views, a host of watersports, and plenty of trekking opportunities. Most are package tourism confines, aimed largely at seniors. Canadian charter planes fly direct to Manzanillo, then the hotels bus in groups of 100 vacationers or more for an inexpensive, week-long, coastal Cuban vacation. Whether those guests arrive expecting fine, white, powdery Caribbean sand we don't know (we certainly hope not). Although we were initially turned off by the notion of an all-inclusive hotel hovering illogically on "beaches" that suffer so in comparison with those along the north coast, we do admit that there are a couple of hotels that wouldn't be awful places to vacation, as long as your expectations are simple, such as the **Club Amigo Marea del Portillo,** Carretera Granma Km 12.5, Pilón (© **23/59-7081;** www.hotelescubanacan.com).

From Marea del Portillo, the road continues another 40km (25 miles) or so to Santiago de Cuba province. The views take in desertlike landscapes, the massive dry mountains of the Sierra Maestra, black rocky beaches, and large waves crashing ashore; it's a highly scenic drive. The only village of any real size is **Chivirico,** a small fishing settlement about 75km (47 miles) outside of Santiago de Cuba. The best hotel en route to Santiago de Cuba is the all-inclusive **Brisas Sierra Mar Los Galeones ★** (© **22/32-9110;** www.hotelescubanacan.com), a massive, multitiered hotel overlooking a sandy brown beach. Though the overall facilities are fairly impressive—there are four restaurants, five bars, two tennis courts, a fitness room, and a large swimming pool—the rooms are standard and uninspiring, with ugly flowered curtains and tiny TVs. There are plenty of better all-inclusive hotels in other parts of Cuba, but this place does combine well with a visit to Santiago. Rates are CUC$118 to CUC$148 double, all-inclusive. **Los Galeones ★** (© **22/32-6160**) is a small, pretty hotel that has been recently refurbished; the hotel is located atop a peak, and offers outstanding views. From here, it's another hour or so to Santiago; see chapter 11 for full coverage.

GOIN' (OR NOT) TO gitmo

On the radio in Guantánamo city and along the road to Baracoa, the unmistakable sounds of English-speaking DJs and American pop music can be heard, seemingly out of nowhere. The programming is courtesy of the U.S. government, emerging from behind barbed-wire fences at the base at Guantánamo Bay, known to American military personnel as "Gitmo." The base is an eyebrow-raising anomaly in revolutionary Cuba, as it's probably the least likely spot in the world for the U.S. to have a naval base. Washington continues to hold an indefinite lease on the base, which was established in 1903 as a reward for the U.S. role in the Spanish-American War—making it the oldest overseas American naval base.

Pursuant to the original agreement, signed by President Theodore Roosevelt, which called for an annual payment of 2,000 gold coins (worth US$4,085 in 1903), the U.S. government continues to send rent checks for that original amount, even though Fidel Castro has never cashed a single one since 1959. Castro understandably would rather forgo the paltry sum than lend legitimacy to the American presence in Cuba. A 1934 treaty that reaffirmed the lease of the base stipulated that both the U.S. and Cuba must mutually agree to terminate the lease—and when was the last time Washington, D.C., and Havana agreed on anything?

Though it has official missions (refueling and reconnaissance), in peace times the Guantánamo base has existed primarily to continue to poke thorns in Castro's side. That was, until 2001, when the U.S. military decided to send Al Qaeda prisoners captured in the conflicts in Afghanistan and Iraq to Guantánamo. Since then, the base has been a source of international news and controversy. Most of the detainees continue to be held and interrogated without access to lawyers or the filing of any formal charges.

Cubans have grudgingly learned to live with the base. They no longer expect a U.S. invasion at any moment, and the U.S. now returns those Cubans who, rather than attempting to cross the Atlantic, try to escape Cuba by crossing over to the American base. Only a small handful of Cuban workers still cross military checkpoints every day to get to their jobs on the base.

Gitmo has about 3,000 full-time residents who, though surrounded on three sides by Cuba, live as if they were in American "suburbotopia," with typical suburban homes, U.S. products, American cars, cable TV, a golf course, and, of course, a McDonald's. However, this gated community has a sign (on the Cuban side) that reads REPUBLICA DE CUBA, TERRITORIO LIBRE DE AMERICA (Republic of Cuba, Free Territory of America).

The Road to Baracoa

Guantánamo province, by virtue of a Cuban song seemingly known the world over ("Guantanamera") and an attention-getting, anachronistic U.S. military base, gets more ink and initial interest than it probably deserves. The easternmost province on the island only has one true draw, but it's one of the highlights of Cuba: the tiny tropical town of Baracoa. The only real reason to stop over in the sweltering and unappealing city of Guantánamo is to visit the distant lookout trained at the contentious **American naval base** isolated on Cuban soil. That's as close as you'll get—and honestly, outside of the novelty factor, there's nothing much to see.

The parched landscape of the southern coast begins to change gradually in color along the spectacular 40km (25-mile) road **La Farola ★★★**, which courses southeast of Santiago and wends its way through the mountains along the route to Baracoa. Things get more and more lush, with thick tropical vegetation and beautiful views at every turn. *Be forewarned:* In addition to its beauty, this is a tight and winding road with a seemingly endless series of white-knuckle hairpin turns. Baracoa, isolated from the rest of Cuba before the building of the road, is a beguiling little town, known for its chocolate and coconut and connections to Columbus. It's been known to bewitch more than a few travelers into staying much longer than they'd planned.

BARACOA ★★★

236km (147 miles) NE of Santiago de Cuba; 150km (93 miles) NE of Guantánamo; 332km (206 miles) E of Holguín

Swathed in generous tropical vegetation—royal palms, coconut palms, coffee bushes, and cacao plants—and refreshed by 10 rivers, Baracoa is perhaps the most picturesque spot in all of Cuba. The historic town sits on a lovely oyster-shaped bay, **Bahía de Miel (Honey Bay) ★★★**, and the landmark flat-topped mountain known as **El Yunque (the Anvil)** looms in the background.

Not only is Baracoa, for my pesos, the most beautiful place on the island, it's also the oldest. That Baracoa was the first settlement established by Diego Velázquez in 1511—making it the second oldest colonial city in the Americas—is not in doubt. Christopher Columbus is thought to have first landed at this spot in late November 1492, and locals claim that he planted a wooden cross here to mark his arrival. (The cross, carbon-tested for age, is temporarily on display in the priest's house next to the Asunción church in town while the church undergoes renovation.)

After its founding, Nuestra Señora de la Asunción de Baracoa remained the capital of the new Spanish colony for just 4 years; when Velázquez moved the capital west to Santiago, on a bigger and deeper bay, Baracoa's isolation had already begun. The small fishing and farming village remained virtually cut off from the rest of Cuba, with no true road in until the 1960s, when a scenic roller coaster of a highway was cut through the mountains.

For such a small, isolated settlement, Baracoa is loaded with things to do and see. It swims with possibilities for hiking, rafting, swimming, and boating. Baracoa really shines the first week of April, when heady street parties (part of a *semana de cultura,* or cultural week) commemorate the date General Antonio Maceo disembarked at nearby Playa Duaba in 1895, marking the beginning of Cuba's War of Independence. The greatest pleasure Baracoa offers, though, is just being here. Most people make the trek just to take in its extraordinary beauty, tranquillity, and abundant charms. A UNESCO Biosphere Reserve, the tropical seaside town is tucked into green hillsides covered with cocoa and coconut groves, and surrounded by beaches lined by royal palms. As the abundant greenery attests, Baracoa is huddled in the midst of the wettest region in Cuba. In 2011, Baracoa will celebrate the 500th anniversary of its founding.

Essentials
GETTING THERE
BY PLANE There are flights on Thursday and Sunday on **Cubana/Aerocaribbean** and flights on Fridays with **Aerogaviota** from Havana to Baracoa; however,

flights are often booked weeks ahead. Fares are CUC$135 one-way. The Cubana/
Aerocaribbean office is at Calle José Martí 185 (📞 **21/64-5107**). Flights arrive at
the small **Aeropuerto Gustavo Rizo** (📞 **21/64-5376;** airport code BCA), west of
the bay near the Hotel Porto Santo and about 4km (2½ miles) west of downtown. By
taxi, the trip to town costs CUC$5.

Should the Baracoa flights be full, Moa, 38km (24 miles) down the road, has
flights on Monday from Havana, for CUC$117; flights operate Tues–Wed and Fri–
Sun from Havana to Guantánamo, for CUC$117.

BY BUS   Most visitors arrive overland; the ride from Santiago de Cuba is especially
spectacular, if lengthy. A **Víazul** bus (📞 **22/62-8484** in Santiago, or 21/64-3880 in
Baracoa; www.viazul.com) departs Santiago daily at 7:45am and arrives in Baracoa at
12:35pm; the fare is CUC$15. The bus stops in Guantánamo. The same bus departs
Baracoa at 2:15pm and arrives in Santiago at 7:05pm. The route is very popular,
especially in high season; make reservations for the trip at least several days in
advance, as these buses sell out frequently and fast.

The Baracoa **Terminal de Omnibuses** (📞 **21/64-3880**) is located at the end of
José Martí near Avenida de los Mártires, diagonally opposite the La Punta restaurant.

BY CAR   You can drive to Baracoa from either Santiago de Cuba, along the scenic
La Farola highway (see "The Road to Baracoa," above), or from Guardalavaca/Holguín
along the northern coastal road through Moa (although this latter road is hideously
bad in places, but passable). Allow 3½ to 4 hours for either route.

GETTING AROUND

You can easily get around most of Baracoa on foot or *bicitaxi* (bicycle carriage). To
reach the beaches, rivers, and mountains around Baracoa, you'll either need to contract a taxi, rent a car, or sign on for an organized excursion. **Cubataxi** (📞 **21/64-
3737**) makes local and long-distance runs.

A car is a good idea if you really want to do some independent exploration of the
surrounding area, or travel to, say, Santiago de Cuba or Guardalavaca. There's a
Cubacar desk in the Havanatur office (📞 **21/64-5358;** www.transtur.cu), and **Vía
Rent a Car** (📞 **21/64-5137**) has offices in Cafe El Piropo/El Parque (📞 **21/64-
1671**) and at the airport (📞 **21/64-1665**). *Motos* can be rented from this company
too. Rates are CUC$45 to CUC$60 per day for a standard four-door compact car.

ORIENTATION

There is a new **Infotur** office at Maceo 129A (📞 **21/64-1781**); you can book excursions and hotels here, and use the Internet. The **Havanatur** office at Martí 202
(📞 **21/64-5358;** www.havanatur.cu) can also provide travel information. Other tour
agencies include **Cubatur,** Maceo, corner of Pelayo Cuervo (📞 **21/64-5306**) next
to the church; **Gaviota Tour** in Café El Piropo/El Parque (📞 **21/64-5164**), and
EcoTur, Coronel Cardoso 24 (📞 **21/64-3665;** ecoturbc@enet.cu), which specializes in outdoor trips in the area.

A **Banco de Crédito y Comercio** branch is on Calle Antonio Maceo 99. Traveler's checks can be cashed at the Hotel El Castillo and Hotel Porto Santo.

For medical attention and a pharmacy, go to the **Clinica Internacional Baracoa,** Calle Martí, between Roberto Rey and Linvano Sánchez (📞 **21/64-1037-38;**
www.servimedcuba.com).

The main **post office** is on Calle Antonio Maceo 136, near Plaza Independencia;
it's open Monday through Saturday from 8am to 10pm and Sunday from 8am to 8pm.

Baracoa

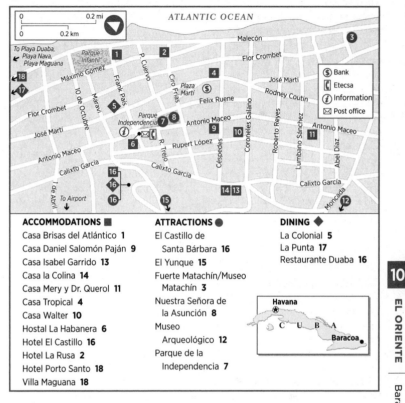

ACCOMMODATIONS ■

Casa Brisas del Atlántico **1**
Casa Daniel Salomón Paján **9**
Casa Isabel Garrido **13**
Casa la Colina **14**
Casa Mery y Dr. Querol **11**
Casa Tropical **4**
Casa Walter **10**
Hostal La Habanera **6**
Hotel El Castillo **16**
Hotel La Rusa **2**
Hotel Porto Santo **18**
Villa Maguana **18**

ATTRACTIONS ●

El Castillo de
  Santa Bárbara **16**
El Yunque **15**
Fuerte Matachín/Museo
  Matachín **3**
Nuestra Señora de
  la Asunción **8**
Museo
  Arqueológico **12**
Parque de la
  Independencia **7**

DINING ◆

La Colonial **5**
La Punta **17**
Restaurante Duaba **16**

10

EL ORIENTE | Baracoa

You can make local, long-distance, and international phone calls or use one of the computer terminals at the **Etecsa** office on Calle Antonio Maceo, opposite Plaza Independencia; it's open daily from 8:30am to 7:30pm.

What to See & Do

Baracoa is its own greatest attraction. Its bustling streets are lined with gaily painted clapboard houses, and the rivers, beaches, and mountains beyond the city are perfect for outdoor exploration.

In the 18th and 19th centuries, Baracoan settlers built three fortresses to protect the town from pirate attacks. **El Castillo de Santa Bárbara,** the oldest of the bunch, sits high above town, with splendid views of the bay and surrounding countryside; it has now been converted into a hotel. **Fuerte de la Punta,** facing the seaside promenade, is now a restaurant. The third, **Fuerte Matachín,** near the entrance to town, houses the municipal museum, **Museo Matachín,** Calle Martí s/n at the Malecón (ℂ **21/64-2122**). It holds a number of interesting historical exhibits related to the history of Baracoa and its legends and myths. The museum also has a collection of extraordinary, vividly colored and striped *polimitas* (snail shells), which locals used to make into necklaces sold to tourists before the supply dried up.

(It is now illegal to sell them.) The museum is open daily from 8am to noon, and from 2 to 6pm; admission is CUC$1 with a guide, and photo and video privileges cost an extra CUC$1 and CUC$5, respectively. Ask here about a city tour for CUC$5.

Nuestra Señora de la Asunción, Maceo 152 (© **21/64-3352**), the rather austere cathedral, was constructed in 1511, though it was burned by the French in 1652. The current structure was rebuilt at the beginning of the 19th century. It was in a considerable state of disrepair and was closed during 2010 for significant restoration work. The church is slated to reopening in time for the 500th anniversary of the city's foundation in August 2011. It is most notable for the **Cruz de la Parra,** a small wooden cross on display inside a glass case. Locals insist that Columbus himself planted the cross on the banks of the bay in 1492, shortly after disembarking on Cuban soil for the first time. Whether or not there's any truth to that claim, carbon dating has in fact established that the cross is more than 500 years old (making it one of the oldest Christian relics in the Americas, if not the oldest). The hardwood is native to Cuba, though, so if Columbus did leave it, the cross must have been fashioned in situ rather than having been brought with him, as was originally believed. The cross has greatly dwindled in size, due to the devout visitors over the years, who thought nothing of slicing off a memento for themselves. The church's opening hours are Tuesday through Saturday from 8am to noon and from 2 to 4pm.

Next to the church is **Parque de la Independencia** (also called Parque Central), a popular gathering spot for locals and tourists enjoying a few lazy days in Baracoa. A bust of the rebel Taíno Indian leader Hatuey (whose countenance today appears on beer bottles) adorns the square. Hatuey took up arms against the early conquistadores until he was caught by the Spanish and burned at the stake.

In the area around Baracoa are as many as 50 **pre-Columbian archaeological sites** related to the major Native American groups that inhabited the area (Siboney, Taíno, and Guanturabey). The only native group to survive is the Yateras, a small community that has succeeded in preserving its traditions, marrying only among each other and living along the Río Toa.

Above the town is the **Museo Arqueológico** in Reparto Paraíso, open Monday to Friday from 9am to 5pm and Saturday from 9am to noon; admission is CUC$3. It costs CUC$1 for a guide. The remains of Taínos can be seen in a cave, as well as in a random collection of ceramics and artifacts supposedly belonging to this pre-Columbian tribe. The museum is only really worth the entrance fee to climb to the *mirador* ★★★, where you can admire and survey the entire bay; on a clear day, the vista is stunning.

Outdoor Excursions Around Baracoa

Baracoa's potential as an ecotourism destination has just begun to be exploited. The spectacular area around Baracoa affords excellent opportunities for treks and whitewater rafting. The region features patches of secondary rainforest, and abounds in banana, yucca, mango, coconut, and tall royal palm trees, and at least 10 flowing rivers. The earth here is rich in iron, which gives it a red tone.

Distinctive **El Yunque** ★★, described in Spanish chronicles as an anvil-shaped, high (575m/1,886 ft.), and square mountain, dominates the landscape; Columbus wrote of seeing it on his approach to the bay. Frequently bathed in mist, the flat-topped limestone mountain is about 10km (6¼ miles) west of Baracoa, and its slopes can be climbed in 4 hours round-trip. The slopes have been declared a UNESCO Biosphere Reserve. El Yunque is part of the Parque Natural Duaba and is home to scores of bird species and unique plants. In fact, 16 of Cuba's 24 endemic bird species can be found in this area. You can also spot the endemic *coco thrinas* palms, which look like tall dandelions. The trek through tropical forest, with views of rare ferns and orchids, is beautiful, but it can be intensely humid and it is a challenging slog with a two-hour ascent. Those who aren't up for the hike can always drive, though it's rough going along the unpaved road. Tours are offered in town for CUC$16, including transport. Adventurers in search of rafting possibilities should check out **Río Toa,** the widest river in Cuba and part of a national park. Tours to Río Toa are CUC$18. Tours to the **Río Yumurí ★,** a beautiful, luscious deep river canyon 30km/19 miles east of Baracoa that can be accessed by boat and by walking on river islands cost CUC$22.

The UNESCO Natural World Heritage Site of **Parque Nacional Alejandro de Humboldt,** a mountainous rainforest area with karst scenery that extends for 32,560 hectares (80,458 acres) north of Baracoa, is rich in biodiversity. It is home to the ivory-billed woodpecker, Cuban parrot and parakeet, colorful *polimita* snails, Caribbean manatee, and rare Cuban *solenodon* (an insectivorous mammal). It also provides habitat for the world's smallest bat, smallest frog, smallest bird and smallest male scorpion. Tours are offered from town for CUC$24 and include a boat adventure into paradise—a slow tour around the **Bahía Taco ★★★,** where you can take in the mangroves, the stunning vista of royal and coconut palms, and search for manatee. If you have your own transport you can drive the 56km (35 miles) in 1¼ hours along the bad road. The park opens at 8am and guided walks can be bought from there too.

Alexander Domínguez at **EcoTur,** Coronel Cardoso 24 (*©* **21/64-3665**), organizes a variety of nature outings with transportation and guides, including rafting on the Río Toa, various treks, boating excursions along the Río Yumurí, and an exclusive 10km (6.2-mile) hike to Juncal-Rencontra in the Toa area, not offered by other agencies. **Havanatur** (*©* **21/64-5358**) and **Cubatur** (*©* **21/64-5306**) also offer organized excursions. Prices run between CUC$16 and CUC$24 per person, but there's often a six-person minimum.

Baracoa is blessed with a few superb beaches, which, due to the town's isolation, haven't yet been built up with huge all-inclusive hotels. **Playa Maguana ★** is about 22km (14 miles) from town on the road to Moa. It's a peaceful place with picture-perfect golden sands and is popular with local families and fishermen. There's a small hotel here (see "Where to Stay," below). Cubatur runs day excursions here from 10am to 4pm for CUC$5per person that can be organized on the morning you wish to go. There's a small restaurant, or you will find villagers who will also rustle up a fish lunch. A smaller and more isolated beach, **Playa Nava,** is another 6km (3¾ miles) west. It's not as pretty as Maguana, but you're likely to have it to yourself.

Playa Duaba is a black sand beach surrounded by wild vegetation and close to the mouth of the Río Duaba. There's a small monument here in the community which marks the exact spot where Antonio Maceo and the independence fighters landed on April 1st 1895. This 1924 monument has been replaced by a larger 1929 obelisk close to the Hotel Porto Santo and this is the monument to which the townsfolk process every year. Of mild interest, nearby, is the **Sendero del Cacao** at Finca Duaba (*©* **21/64-5339**), where a 270-meter (885-ft.) trail will lead you to the Casa del Cacaotero, where you'll learn about cocoa processing; entrance is CUC$3.

The **Parque Espeleo-Arqueológico Majayara** is a new protected area beyond the delightful fishing community of **Boca de Miel ★★★.** Walk out of town past the hurricane-damaged stadium along the black-sand beach of Playa Baracoa that curves around the Bahía de Miel until you reach the long wooden bridge that crosses the mouth of the River Honey. Here you can see locals fishing with nets against a scene of bucolic charm: mountains studded with thousands of coconut palms and, in the distance, the flat-topped El Yunque. After crossing the bridge, turn left before reaching the park kiosk. A 10-minute walk beyond is **Playa Blanca** (entrance CUC$2). The white sand is not silky, but the water is beautiful and there are rock pools and a shallow entrance for children. Further into the park is a stunning **Balcón Arqueolgico ★★**, a 500-meter- (1,640-ft.-) long limestone balcony with panoramic views of the entire coastline. Admission, which comes with a guide who can point out the flora and fauna in the park, varies from CUC$5–CUC$15; the park is open from 8:30am–5:30pm daily. (Guide Alejandro Correa Borges speaks English and is helpful.) Visitors should be fit and prepared to climb up a ladder and almost sheer rock face to the balcony. Before hiking stop at the house of Rodolfo Rodríguez, two doors down from the kiosk; he makes bars of chocolate and coconut (much rarer than you would imagine), as well as banana and almond *dulces*.

Where to Stay

There's nothing fancy or especially luxurious in easygoing Baracoa—except the spectacular views of the bay and surrounding mountains—but one of the main hotels, in the oldest fortress in town, is a charmer. The little town is populated by more than 150 *casas particulares*, most right within the old town; several are excellent and among the best deals of their kind in Cuba. A 14-bed Gaviota hotel, **La Liberación,** on Calle Ciro Frias between Antonio Maceo and Rubert López, was under construction in 2010.

MODERATE

Hotel El Castillo ★★ 🏨 Hovering on a hill with the best views of Baracoa and the bay, and a picture-perfect pool, this easygoing hotel—the lower part of which inhabits an old fort—is the top place in town to stay. Its simple rooms don't quite measure up to the privileged location and general ambience, though they're of pretty good size, have colonial-style furnishings, and are set around the pool. Ask for room no. 201, as it's a large corner room with a queen-size bed. In 2009, the hotel added a new block of rooms above the restaurant, which are spacious and hold double beds, but feel spartan and lack polish. The poolside snack bar was undergoing refurbishment during 2010. If we owned the place, we'd restyle it as a swank hotel. Advance reservations are essential in high season. Nonguests can use the pool for CUC$10, including CUC$8 worth of food and drink.

Calle Calixto García, Loma el Paraíso, Baracoa. ⓒ **21/64-5194.** www.gaviota-grupo.com. 62 units. CUC$56–CUC$60 double. Rates include breakfast. MC, V. **Amenities:** Restaurant; snack bar; 2 bars; outdoor pool. *In room:* A/C, TV.

Hotel Porto Santo Gaviota runs this hotel right on the bay near the spot where Columbus supposedly deposited the cross marking his arrival in the Americas. Slightly larger than Hotel El Castillo, this one gets more tour groups. It has a large pool with a deck and thatched-roof bar overlooking the bay and cute private-cove beach. In truth, rooms aren't very large or nicely decorated, and all have rather small bathrooms, but those in the last wing have the best bay views (something I'd request). Only four rooms have double beds. All come with a small balcony or private patio.

The location is somewhat isolated, though, and can be a pain if you're looking to make frequent trips into town.

Carretera del Aeropuerto, Baracoa.✆ **21/64-5106.** Fax 21/64-5339. www.gaviota-grupo.com. 83 units. CUC$56–CUC$60 double. Rates include breakfast. MC, V. **Amenities:** Restaurant; grill; bar; nightly show; outdoor pool. *In room:* A/C, TV, minibar (in 10 rooms).

Villa Maguana ★★ ⚓ ☺ 🎒   This little place, 21km (13 miles) from Baracoa, is a secluded and peaceful inn fronting a totally private, pretty cove next to a 2km (1¼-mile) white-sand beach. The four villas with 16 rooms are large and charmingly rustic, like private cabins, with dark-wood furniture; balconies with chairs overlook the transparent water. Note that villas nos. 1 and 2 face the beach. The villas would be a great place for a large family or a band of couples to rent and just hang out here on the beautiful outskirts of Baracoa. This kind of rustic (but equipped) cabin accommodation is a rarity in Cuba.

Carretera de Moa a Baracoa, Km 20, Baracoa. ✆ **21/64-1204.** www.gaviota-grupo.com. 16 units. CUC$73–CUC$83 double. Rates include breakfast. MC, V. **Amenities:** Restaurant; bar. *In room:* A/C, TV, minibar.

INEXPENSIVE

There are more than 150 *casas particulares* in Baracoa. Recommended *casas* include **Casa Daniel Salomón Paján** ★, Calle Céspedes 28, between Rubert López and Maceo (✆ **21/64-1443** or 529-17403; fifi@toa.gtm.sld.cu), which is one of the friendliest *casas* in Cuba. Daniel works at the museum and knows a lot about Baracoa's history. He has one comfortable room with a large bathroom and a central covered patio. Mountain bikes are also available for rent. **Casa Tropical** ★, Calle Martí 175 (✆ **21/64-3437**), has very comfortable rooms in a lovely colonial house with an enormous blue porch and courtyard, and is run by a friendly and welcoming family; the very tasty swordfish in coconut sauce is a good enough reason to stay. Adrian speaks excellent English. **Casa Isabel Garrido** ★, Calle Calixto García 164A (✆ **21/64-3515;** ysabel@toa.gtm.sld.cu), has a large terrace and a small balcony overlooking the street; there's also a separate entrance to the two upstairs bedrooms that share a sitting room and small kitchen. **Casa Walter,** Calle Rubert López 47, between Céspedes and Coroneles Galanos (✆ **21/64-2346;** wvazquez@enet.cu), is a central option with a third-floor terrace that has a high-pitched red-tile roof with dining tables and a bar. The two rooms share a sitting room and have independent entrances. **Casa Mery y Dr Querol,** Calle Maceo 222 between Limbano Sanchéz y Abel Diaz (✆ **21/64 2288;** querol@toa.gtm.sld.cu), is a modest home run by Mery and her son, an orthopaedic specialist. They have a large comfortable room, private dining room, and terrace upstairs. **Casa Brisas del Atlántico** ★, Calle Frank País 3, between Avenida Malecón and Máximo Gómez (✆ **21/64-3457**), has two rooms with a separate entrance and a huge rooftop terrace with sea views. At **Casa La Colina** ★, Calle Calixto García 158 altos, between Céspedes and Coroneles Gulano (✆ **21/64-2658** or 527-04365; proctologia@toa.gtm.sld.cu), which has a superb terrace, you'll want to take the large room fronting the terrace.

Hostal La Habanera ★   Fronting the Plaza de la Independencia, this renovated, downtown colonial structure is an atmospheric, affordable, and centrally located option. The rooms are all spacious, with high ceilings, rattan headboards, sparkling tile floors, and tubs in the bathrooms. All come with two twin beds. My favorite rooms are the four that share a long, broad veranda overlooking Calle Maceo.

Calle Maceo 68, at the corner of Calle Frank País. ✆ **21/64-5273.** www.gaviota-grupo.com. 10 units. CUC$35–CUC$40 double. Rates include breakfast. MC, V. **Amenities:** Restaurant; snack bar/bar. *In room:* A/C, TV, minibar.

Hotel La Rusa   This legendary little hotel was established by a Russian émigré (and princess) and former dancer ("La Rusa de Baracoa"), who, over the years, became active in Cuban revolutionary politics and later played host to Fidel, Che, and the poet Nicolás Guillén. Today, this big yellow house right by the sea has received a minor spruce-up by Gaviota, who run all the tourist spots in town, but it still doesn't really live up to its storied past. Rooms are small and if you stay you'll want a room overlooking the *malecón*.

Calle Máximo Gómez 161, Baracoa. ✆ **21/64-3011.** www.gaviota-grupo.com. 12 units. CUC$25–CUC$30 double. Rates include breakfast. MC, V. **Amenities:** Seafood restaurant; bar. *In room:* A/C, TV, minibar.

Where to Dine

Diners resigned to the plain, unimaginative food in the rest of Cuba are in for a treat in Baracoa. The town and region revel in a unique cuisine found nowhere else in Cuba, one that makes ample use of local coconut and chocolate. The region produces about three-quarters of Cuba's coconuts, so logically it plays a strong part in the local diet. Try *cucurucho,* a coconut pudding with fruit or almonds and honey wrapped in palm leaves; fresh fish embellished with coconut sauce; and the drinks *sacoco,* rum and coconut milk drunk from green coconuts, and *chorote,* chocolate with cornstarch. **Casa de Chocolate,** Maceo 121, is the place to get thick hot chocolate and locally made candies.

La Colonial ★ BARACOAN/CRIOLLAN   The only officially sanctioned *paladar* (private home restaurant) left in Baracoa, this well-run place in a lovely colonial home is good, and deserves to be supported by travelers. There's no fixed menu; ask about fresh dishes and catches from the daily roster of seven to eight main courses, including swordfish and shrimp cooked in *leche de coco* (coconut milk), shark, crab, and lamb. Once you get beyond the floral tablecloths, the decor and ambience here are actually somewhat romantic.

Martí 123. ✆ **21/64-5391.** Reservations recommended for large groups. Main courses CUC$8–CUC$9. No credit cards. Daily 11am–11pm.

La Punta BARACOAN/CRIOLLAN   On a covered terrace within the walls of one of the original three forts in Baracoa, this state-run restaurant is an elegant, tranquil spot that's perfect for lunch. It has good service and well-prepared dishes such as dorado and *pargo* (grilled fish). Typical Cuban dishes such as fish in coconut sauce, pork, and fried chicken are also available. The signature dish is fish fillet in a chocolate and coconut sauce. Spaghetti and beef fajitas are also served for those who want a bit of variety. Although the walls of the fort block most of the views, especially from the tables, if you walk around the grounds, you can peek through the cannon slots at the Atlantic Ocean, Baracoa bay, and some stunning scenery.

Fuerte de la Punta. ✆ **21/64-1480.** Reservations not accepted. Main courses CUC$2–CUC$6. No credit cards. Daily 10am–10pm.

Restaurante Duaba BARACOAN/CRIOLLAN   The restaurant within the Hotel El Castillo does big business serving Baracoa specialties to its guests but it's a good option for anyone in Baracoa. Try any of the locally flavored dishes, such as Santa Bárbara fish filet, or *cobo enchilado,* a huge shellfish. There are also some good options for vegetarians, including various salad plates. The daily set menu is pricey at CUC$12; try ordering a la carte instead.

In Hotel El Castillo, Calle Calixto García, Loma el Paraíso. ✆ **21/64-5106.** Reservations recommended. Main courses CUC$3–CUC$12. MC, V. Daily 7–10pm.

Baracoa After Dark

Baracoa has an amazingly lively, after-dark scene for a town so small. In fact, its nightlife ranks among the best in Cuba. Virtually all the clubs and live-music venues are conveniently located on a single street, **Calle Antonio Maceo,** making Baracoa throb most nights like a tiny, tropical New Orleans, with traditional Cuban and contemporary dance music and revelers spilling out into the street until the wee hours. The scene is especially buoyant on Saturday nights (*El Sabado Baracoese*), when Baracoans host a massive street party along Maceo. Unique to Baracoa are the enthusiastic *animadores,* or emcees, who introduce songs and bands and entertain audiences with florid language, poetry, and humor. Club cover charges are generally CUC$1 to CUC$3.

The first place to stop is the local **Casa de la Trova ★★**, Maceo 149, a comfortable, well-lit place loaded with locals and featuring good bands and a gregarious emcee. If you're lucky, you'll get to hear **Maravilla Yuqueña,** a wonderful group with a venerable old lead singer who should be far more famous than he is. Down the street is **485,** Maceo 141, with a *trova*-like covered patio and the livelier **el Paraíso** disco next-door (Tues–Sun only). Across the street, **La Terraza** is a huge, open-air terrace on top of a building. It has a nightly show (10pm–midnight) and full-throttle, decibel-busting music under the stars, with dancers and occasional dance contests as well as top comedians—if your Spanish is up to it. A more sedate spot, within shouting distance of the sound system of La Terraza, is **El Patio ARTex,** a cute, brightly colored cafe with red lamps and a corrugated tin roof. The live music is pure Cuban *son.*

Indigenous Baracoan music is called *Kiribá* and *Nengón.* It predates *son.* You can hear this music and see a dance performance by arranging a fiesta. It's a great day out in the countryside and you'll experience tasting a great spread of local food. Contact **Grupo Kiribá y Nengón** (Teresa Roché; ✆ **21/64-3447**). Three days' notice is required and the cost is by donation.

SANTIAGO DE CUBA

Santiago de Cuba ★★★ is the country's second-largest city, and it swings to the sound of son. Vibrant, tropical, and often sweltering, Santiago is the country's liveliest cultural showpiece, outside of Havana. With a population just under a half-million people, Santiago is a world apart, with a unique history and rhythms all its own. The city has produced some of Cuba's greatest contemporary musicians as well as several of its most stalwart revolutionaries, and it has served as the stage for some of the most storied events in Cuba's modern history. As the capital of the old Oriente province, it has the largest Afro-Cuban population in Cuba and a resolutely Afro-Caribbean feel that distinguishes it from the rest of Cuba.

Founded in 1515, Santiago was one of the first of seven towns in Cuba and the Spanish colony's capital until 1553. Diego Velázquez, the founder of the original seven *villas*, built his mansion here, and the house still stands in the heart of the historic quarter. The Spanish character of the city would soon be supplemented by other influences. After the 1791 revolution in Haiti, a large number of French coffee plantation owners fled with their African slaves and made their way to Santiago. Black Haitian workers followed, as did large contingencies of West African slaves, sold to work on the plantations.

While downtown Santiago has the requisite noise, traffic, and urban chaos of a large city, it retains the intimate, friendly feel of a provincial capital, with peaceful neighborhoods where men play dominoes outdoors on hilly streets.

Santiago continues to earn its reputation as one of the liveliest and most individualistic cities in Cuba. The city's annual Carnival celebrations in July are famous throughout Cuba, predated by the boisterous and entertaining Festival del Caribe and Fiesta del Fuego at the beginning of the month. Afro-Cuban religious traditions, including Santería and other forms of worship, have their strongest hold here. And Santiagueros are also recognized for their take on Cuban Spanish, with a unique vocabulary and singsong rhythm.

Santiago fans out from a large, deep natural bay—guarded by the 16th-century El Morro fortress—and sits at the base of low mountains. Interesting excursions await visitors with time to explore outside the city: **El Cobre** ★★ is a sacred shrine set in the beautiful foothills of the Sierra Maestra, while **Gran Piedra** is a rocky area just outside the city that invites hiking in its cool environs.

ORIENTATION
Arriving & Departing

BY PLANE Direct international scheduled and charter flights arrive at the **Aeropuerto Internacional Antonio Maceo** (✆ **22/69-8614;** airport code SCU). Airlines regularly servicing Santiago include **Aerocaribbean** from Santo Domingo and **Cubana.** Charter flights run between Miami and Santiago several times each week.

Daily flights connect Santiago with Havana via **Cubana** (✆ **22/65-1578** in Santiago, or 7/838-1039 in Havana; www.cubana.cu) for CUC$116. **AeroCaribbean** (✆ **22/68-7255** in Santiago, or 7/870-4965 in Havana) flies on Monday, Thursday, Friday, and Sunday for CUC$115. Flights are about 2 hours.

The airport is 8km (5 miles) south of the city. There are several car-rental agencies at the airport. The quickest and safest way to the city is by registered taxi; the trip into town is CUC$6 to CUC$9.

BY BUS Víazul's (✆ **22/62-8484** in Santiago, or 7/881-1413 in Havana; www.viazul.com) Havana–Santiago de Cuba line, with stops in Santa Clara, Sancti Spíritus, Ciego de Avila, Camagüey, Bayamo, and Holguín, is the best way to get to Santiago by bus, especially if you're planning to see any points of interest between Cuba's two main cities. For the trip from Havana, buses depart at 9:30am, 3:15pm, 6:15pm, and 10pm, and arrive at 1:20am, 7:20am, 7:15am, and 12:35pm respectively; the fare is CUC$51 one-way. From Trinidad (✆ **41/99-4448**), a bus leaves daily at 7:40pm and arrives at 7:05am; the fare is CUC$33 one-way. From Varadero, buses leave at 9:25pm and arrive at 12:10pm; the fare is CUC$49 one-way. (Buses depart Santiago for Havana at 9am, 3:15pm, 6:15pm, and 10pm).

Víazul also has once-daily service between Santiago and Baracoa, leaving Santiago at 7:45am and returning from Baracoa at 2:15pm. Duration is 4 hours and 50 minutes; the fare is CUC$15 one-way.

The **Terminal de Omnibuses** (✆ **22/62-8484**) for Víazul is located on Avenida de los Libertadores at the corner of Avenida Yarayó, about 2km (1¼ miles) from Parque Céspedes. A taxi to downtown costs about CUC$3, but the private *taxistas* who mob the exit will demand up to CUC$5. Only pay CUC$3.

BY TRAIN The Cuban *ferrocarril* (railway) is not dependable, and delays, midrun breakdowns, and other problems are quite common. Taking the train is a potentially adventurous experience for those who wish to see the "real Cuba," but can be frustrating for those who need to adhere to a schedule.

A special fast train, also known as the "French Train" or "Tren Francés," travels from Havana to Santiago when it can (12 hr. with stops in Santa Clara and Camagüey); check the schedule before you leave, since it varies. It offers *primera especial* (first-class) service for CUC$62 and *segunda clase* (second-class) service for CUC$50, featuring reclining seats, air-conditioning, and cafeteria services. Prices are discounted by 50% for children under 7 years old, and **Ferrotur** claims it will refund the fare if arrival is more than 1 hour late. Daily departure from Havana in the high season is at 6:05pm, arriving at 6:30am in Santiago.

In Santiago, the large, modern **Terminal Central de Ferrocarriles** is located on Avenida Jesús Menéndez at Paseo de Martí (✆ **22/62-2836**), across from the Caney rum factory.

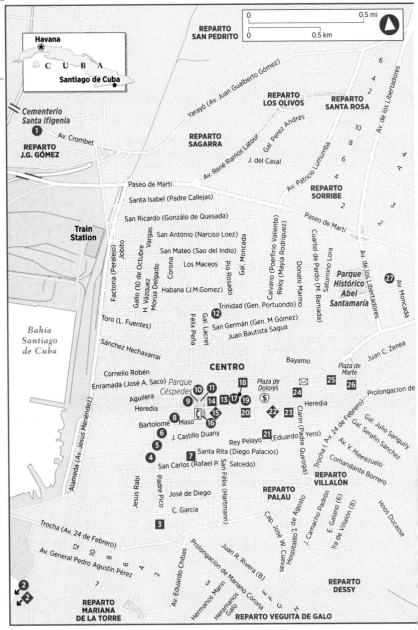

REPARTO SAN PEDRITO

0   0.5 mi
0   0.5 km

Havana
★
C U B A
Santiago de Cuba ●

Cementerio
Santa Ifigenia
❶
Av. Crombet
REPARTO
J.G. GÓMEZ

Yarayó (Av. Juan Gualberto Gómez)

REPARTO
LOS OLIVOS

REPARTO
SANTA ROSA

Av. de los Libertadores

6
4
2

Gal. Perez Andrés

REPARTO
SAGARRA

René Ramos Latour

10

J. del Casal

Av. René Ramos Latour

Av. Patricio Lumumba

8
6
4

REPARTO
SORRIBE

Paseo de Martí

Santa Isabel (Padre Callejas)

San Ricardo (Gonzálo de Quesada)

San António (Narciso Loez)

San Mateo (Sao del Indio)

Los Maceos

Habana (J.M.Gomez)

Paseo de Martí

Cuartel de Pardo (M. Bamada)

Calvario (Poerfirio Valiente)

Reloj (Mayía Rodríguez)

Donato Marmo

Saturnino Lora

Parque
Histórico
Abel
Santamaría

Av. de los Libertadores

Av. Moncada

❷❼

Train
Station

Factoria (Peralejo)

Jobito

Gallo (10 de Octubre)

Vargas

H. Vázquez

Morúa Delgado

Corona

Pío Rosado

Gal. Moncada

Trinidad (Gen. Portuondo)

❶❷

San Germán (Gen. M Gómez)

Juan Bautista Sagua

Toro (L. Fuentes)

Félix Peña

Gal. Lacret

Sánchez Hechavarrai

Bahía
Santiago
de Cuba

CENTRO

Bayamo

Plaza de
Marte

Juan C. Zenea

Cornelio Robén

Enramada (José A. Saco)

Aguilera

Heredia

Bartolomé   Masó

J. Castillo Duany

Santa Rita (Diego Palacios)

San Carlos (Rafael P. Salcedo)

Parque
Céspedes

❾ ❿ ⓫

⓮ ⓭ ⓱ ⓳

❽ ⓯

⓰

❻

❼

❺

❹

⓲

Plaza de
Dolores

✉

$

⓴

❷⓵

Rey Pelayo (Eduardo)

Clarin (Padre Quiroga)

Heredia

⓴⓶ ⓴⓷

⓴⓸

⓴⓹

⓴⓺

Prolongacion de

Gal. Julio Sanguily

Gal. Serafín Sánchez

Trocha (Av. 24 de Febrero)

Av. V. Hierrezuelo

Comandante Borrero

Jesús Rabí

Padre Pico

San Félix (Hartmann)

José de Diego

C. García

❸

REPARTO
PALAU

REPARTO
VILLALÓN

Hospitalito 2 de Agosto

J. Camacho Padrón

E. Galano (6)

1ra de Villalón (8)

Hnos Ducasse

Alameda (Av. Jesús Menéndez)

Trocha (Av. 24 de Febrero)

12

10

8

6

4

2

Av. General Pedro Agustín Pérez

7

Av. Eduardo Chibas

Prolongación de Mariano Corona

Juan R. Rivera (B)

Hermanos Marín

Hermanos Galo

REPARTO VEGUITA DE GALO

Cab. José W. Cuevas

REPARTO
DESSY

❷
❷

REPARTO
MARIANA
DE LA TORRE

❷⓻

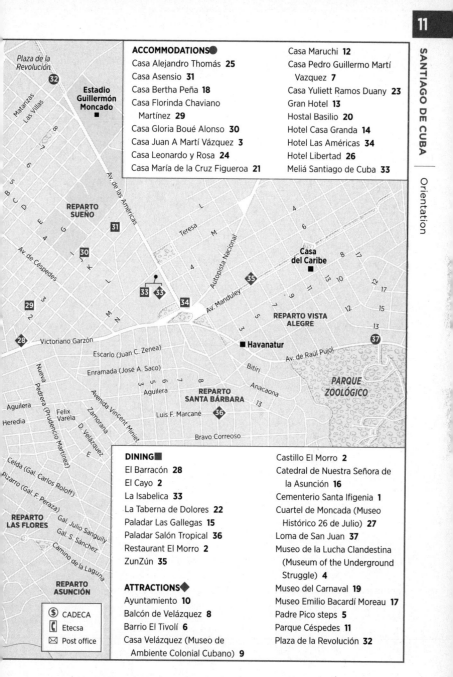

Plaza de la Revolución

Estadio Guillermón Moncado

REPARTO SUEÑO

Casa del Caribe

REPARTO VISTA ALEGRE

Havanatur

PARQUE ZOOLÓGICO

REPARTO SANTA BÁRBARA

REPARTO LAS FLORES

REPARTO ASUNCIÓN

ACCOMMODATIONS
Casa Alejandro Thomás **25**
Casa Asensio **31**
Casa Bertha Peña **18**
Casa Florinda Chaviano Martínez **29**
Casa Gloria Boué Alonso **30**
Casa Juan A Martí Vázquez **3**
Casa Leonardo y Rosa **24**
Casa María de la Cruz Figueroa **21**
Casa Maruchi **12**
Casa Pedro Guillermo Martí Vazquez **7**
Casa Yuliett Ramos Duany **23**
Gran Hotel **13**
Hostal Basilio **20**
Hotel Casa Granda **14**
Hotel Las Américas **34**
Hotel Libertad **26**
Meliá Santiago de Cuba **33**

DINING
El Barracón **28**
El Cayo **2**
La Isabelica **33**
La Taberna de Dolores **22**
Paladar Las Gallegas **15**
Paladar Salón Tropical **36**
Restaurant El Morro **2**
ZunZún **35**

ATTRACTIONS
Ayuntamiento **10**
Balcón de Velázquez **8**
Barrio El Tivolí **6**
Casa Velázquez (Museo de Ambiente Colonial Cubano) **9**
Castillo El Morro **2**
Catedral de Nuestra Señora de la Asunción **16**
Cementerio Santa Ifigenia **1**
Cuartel de Moncada (Museo Histórico 26 de Julio) **27**
Loma de San Juan **37**
Museo de la Lucha Clandestina (Museum of the Underground Struggle) **4**
Museo del Carnaval **19**
Museo Emilio Bacardí Moreau **17**
Padre Pico steps **5**
Parque Céspedes **11**
Plaza de la Revolución **32**

$ CADECA
C Etecsa
✉ Post office

11 SANTIAGO, CITY OF STRUGGLE & rebellion

Santiago has long demonstrated a fiercely independent streak. Among Cubans, the city is known affectionately as the *cuna de la Revolución,* or the cradle of the Revolution. The first slave uprisings in Cuba occurred in Santiago, and the city had prominent roles in the wars of independence against the Spanish in 1868 and 1895. Antonio Maceo rejected a pact with the colonial power, laying the foundation for continued resistance, and became one of the leaders of the rebel army. Each of the 29 generals during the 30-year war against the Spanish came from the city, and the Bay of Santiago was the site of the 1898 naval battles between the U.S. and Spain. Teddy Roosevelt and his Rough Riders stormed the Loma de San Juan, a low hill just east of the city, in battles against the Spanish, which led to Spain's imminent defeat and withdrawal from Cuba (though Cuba's independence was effectively usurped by the Americans in the years after the Spanish-American War).

In 1953, the young Fidel Castro and a band of insurgents attacked the Moncada military barracks in Santiago (the failed, but famous 26th of July episode). After many of his rebels were tortured and killed by the army, Castro was captured and he issued his famous declaration, "History will absolve me," in defense of his seditious actions. A local Santiago schoolteacher, Frank País, sparked an uprising of university students in 1957, attacking police headquarters. Assassinated by the Batista army in the streets of Santiago, he became a martyr of the Revolution. Castro returned from exile in Mexico in 1956 to wage war from the cover of the Sierra Maestra, west of Santiago, and 2 years later the rebel leader ultimately announced victory, on January 1, 1959, from the balcony of the governor's mansion (today Town Hall) in Parque Céspedes. Castro rewarded the city that supported him with the title "Heroic City of the Revolution."

BY CAR   Driving to Santiago is a good way to see the breadth of the country. The six-lane, toll-free Autopista Nacional (A1) and the Carretera Central run the length of Cuba, straight down the spine of the country from Pinar del Río to Santiago. However, east from Sancti Spíritus, it is just two lanes almost the entire way to Santiago, and the going can be slow at times, since there are equal numbers of cars, trucks, horse-drawn carriages, bicycles, and pedestrians making use of the Carretera Central. Santiago is 860km (534 miles) east of Havana, 127km (79 miles) east of Bayamo, and 134km (83 miles) southeast of Holguín.

Visitor Information

Santiago has a new **Infotur** desk inside the Cubatur office, Calle Lacret 701, corner of Heredia (© **22/66-9401**), that's open daily from 8am–5pm. There's another Infotur office at the airport (© **22/69-2099**). Most of the major tour agencies, including **Cubanacán,** Calle M, corner of Avenida Las Américas (© **22/64-1517**) and **Cubatur,** Calle Lacret 701, corner of Heredia (© **22/68-6033**) have offices in the airport and at several hotels in town. They all offer guided city and area tours for CUC$36 to CUC$70, excursions to El Cobre for CUC$15, La Gran Piedra for CUC$42, Baconao for CUC$61, and Tropicana for CUC$12–CUC$37. The best value tour takes you around the city, out to Cayo Granma, El Morro, and El Cobre for CUC$54.

City Layout

The historic center of the city rolls across low hills to the east of the **Bahía de Santiago.** The focal point of colonial Santiago is **Parque Céspedes.** This historic square boasts perhaps the oldest house in the Americas. **Calle Heredia,** which leads east from the square, is a popular street with plenty of foot traffic, and it is lined with live music venues, colonial houses and museums, and artisans selling their crafts. South of Parque Céspedes is the charming, hilly **El Tivolí** district and its emblematic Padre Pico steps. Heading east of Parque Céspedes is **Plaza de Dolores,** an attractive and shady little square that's a popular and easygoing hangout ringed by a handful of restaurants, bars, and cafes. **Plaza de Marte** marks the divide between old Santiago and the newer section, leading along the long and wide avenue Victoriano Garzón out toward the nicest suburbs in Santiago and districts of several hotels and *casas particulares,* **Reparto Sueño, Reparto Vista Alegre,** and **Reparto Santa Bárbara.**

Old and new street names (pre- and post-Revolution) are still sometimes used interchangeably in Santiago. The most common pre-Revolution street names used in the old colonial center are: Enramada (for José Antonio Saco); San Basilio (Bartolomé Masó); San Pedro (General Lacret); Santo Tomás (Félix Peña); Marina (Aguilera); and Carnicería (Pío Rosado).

GETTING AROUND

BY TAXI   Cubataxi (✆ 22/64-1965) and **Gran Car** (✆ 22/62-4328) congregate near the cathedral on Parque Céspedes and at the major tourist hotels. Be sure to ask prices before hiring one, as tourist gouging is a favorite local pastime (from the Meliá Santiago to Parque Céspedes, the fare should be CUC$3; from downtown to El Morro the fare is CUC$12–CUC$15). Gran Car charges CUC$0.80 a kilometer. Cheaper taxis, both registered and unregistered, can be found parked around Plaza Marte. With the latter, negotiate a price, but understand that the driver may be uncomfortable taking you directly to the door of your hotel if he's not officially licensed to carry foreigners.

There are also *bicitaxis* (bicycle taxis), which are convenient and inexpensive (usually CUC$1–CUC$3), but occasionally hair-raising for many passengers.

BY CAR   Cubacar (✆ 22/68-6107; www.transtur.cu) has offices at the airport, opposite the Cupet gas station on Carretera Central; Hotel Casa Granda; Hotel Las Américas; Meliá Santiago; and Hotel Villa San Juan. **Vía Rent a Car** (✆ 22/62-4646) is inside the Cubatur office, Lacret 701, corner of Heredia. Rates are CUC$60 to CUC$80 per day for a standard four-door compact car.

BY FOOT   The area of greatest activity and cultural interest to many visitors in the historic center—the few streets around Parque Céspedes—is easy to get around on foot, though some areas, such as the Tivolí district, are extremely hilly. However, many hotels are at least a couple of kilometers from the city center, and a good number of the city's foremost attractions, such as El Morro, are beyond the city and require transportation.

[FastFACTS] SANTIAGO DE CUBA

Airport See "Arriving & Departing," above.

Car Rentals See "Getting Around," above.

Currency Exchange A CADECA (✆ 22/65-1383) branch is on Calle Aguilera 508. The local branch of **Banco de Crédito y Comercio** (✆ 22/62-3316), where you can exchange traveler's checks and get cash advances, is on Félix Peña 614. **Bandec** (✆ 22/62-7581), with similar services, is on Félix Peña between Aguilera and Heredia with an ATM. Both are open Monday through Friday from 8am to 3pm and Saturday 8 to 11am. An ATM is at the **Banco Popular de Ahoro** (✆ 22/64-2454) on Plaza Dolores; it's open Mon–Sat 8am–7pm. You can also change money at the Meliá Santiago and most other hotels in the city.

Emergency Dial ✆ 106 for police or ✆ 185 for an ambulance.

Hospitals & Medical Assistance Clínica Internacional, Avenida Raúl Pujol at Calle 10 in Reparto Vista Alegre (✆ 22/64-2589), has 24-hour emergency services, a dentist, and English-speaking doctors. There are **pharmacies** at the clinic and along Calle José Antonio Saco.

Internet Access The **Etecsa** Multiservicios Céspedes on Heredia, corner of Sto Tomás (✆ 22/62-4784) provides telephone and Internet service daily from 8:30am to 7:30pm. You can also find Internet at the Meliá Santiago and Casa Granda.

Police The police station is located at Corona and San Gerónimo (✆ 106). However, the probability of finding an English speaker is remote. In case of an emergency, one of the better hotels (such as the Casa Granda or Meliá Santiago) should be able to help or at least interpret for the police.

Post Office The main post office is on Calle Aguilera 517 at Padre Quiroga (✆ 22/65-2397); it's open Monday through Saturday from 8am to 10pm. There are basic postal facilities in all the major hotels. A **DHL** office can be found at Calle Aguilera 310 at the corner of San Félix (✆ 22/68-6323).

Safety Santiago is one of Cuba's less safe cities, if only because the local *jineteros* are relentless in accosting foreigners. They are, for the most part, innocuous. Still, if you're attending a street festival, concert, or Carnival, put your money in a money belt and leave your watch, jewelry, and knapsack behind (these items will be safer in your hotel or *casa particular*). Also, be careful and keep an eye on your bags at the Santiago bus and train stations. That said, Santiago, as with the rest of Cuba, is still relatively safe for a large city.

Taxis See "Getting Around," earlier in this chapter.

Telephone You can make local, long-distance, and international phone calls with a phone card from **Etecsa** (see "Internet Access," above).

WHAT TO SEE & DO

Many visitors in search of what makes Cuba unique actually prefer the country's second city to the capital, even though Santiago is unpolished and has few grand examples of colonial architecture.

The Top Attractions

A major gathering spot day and night for Santiagueros, aggressive *jineteros,* and travelers alike, **Parque Céspedes** ★ is a menagerie of eclectic architecture, to put it mildly. Its benches, tall shade trees, and gas lamps are ringed by colonial, 19th-century, and modern structures, including the ancient mansion of Diego Velázquez (see "Casa Velázquez," below), as well as the handsome colonial governor's mansion (Town Hall), the baroque cathedral, and the city's oldest hotel, Casa Granda.

The **Ayuntamiento,** or Town Hall (also called the Palacio Municipal), a huge white building on the north side of the square with blue wooden grilles, was originally built in 1515. It was greatly renovated in the 1950s after an earthquake, but has retained its elegant colonial lines, balcony, and patio. Fidel Castro addressed the adoring masses here on January 1, 1959, after the rebel army had taken the city and announced the triumph of *La Revolución.*

Across the park, the early-19th-century **Catedral de Nuestra Señora de la Asunción** is a massive, ornate, pale-yellow-and-white basilica with twin towers—one of several churches to occupy the site since 1522. The frescoes on the arches and dome of the interior have been restored. Inside is a massive pipe organ, as well as the remains of the Spanish conquistador Diego Velázquez, although, since a 1678 earthquake, the whereabouts of those remains in the building are unknown. The graves of the first (Spanish) archbishop of Cuba and the first Cuban archbishop are clearly visible. The cathedral is open Tuesday through Saturday 8am to 12:30pm and 5 to 7:30pm, and Sunday 8 to 11am and 5 to 6:30pm.

Casa Velázquez (Museo de Ambiente Colonial Cubano) ★★

The mansion (ca. 1516) that once belonged to Diego Velázquez, founder of the original seven *villas* in Cuba, still stands despite the unrepentant fumes of tour buses and recent fires that have threatened it. The house has a notable Moorish influence, with a wonderful carved cedar ceiling (most of which had to be reconstructed after a fire). The top floor was the living quarters; the ground floor was the commercial part of the house, where Velázquez maintained offices and horse carriages were kept. The majority of the house's elaborate frescoes have been supplemented by very amateurish reproductions, a real sin against the authenticity that is so apparent elsewhere. The museum aims to depict the varied styles and epochs of colonial life, seen through period furnishings from the 16th to the 19th century. You'll find some splendid pieces of French, British, Spanish, and Cuban furniture; Spanish ceramics; carved chests; and French porcelain. Several dressers have extraordinary inlaid designs, proof of the wealth of the bourgeoisie in colonial Cuba. A second 19th-century house in back, blue, and white, with an attractive courtyard, is not part of the original Velázquez house.

Félix Peña 612 (corner of Aguilera), Parque Céspedes. ℰ **22/65-2652.** Admission CUC$2; CUC$1 to take photos, CUC$5 to take video. Guided tours in Spanish or English available. Sat–Thurs 9am–5pm; Fri 1–5pm.

Cuartel de Moncada (Museo Histórico 26 de Julio) ★

The yellow barracks of the Spanish army, east of downtown, represent a pivotal episode in modern Cuban history. The ocher-colored exterior is still pockmarked with bullet holes, a reminder of the day in July 1953 when Fidel Castro and a band of ragtag, but idealistic rebels launched an assault on the barracks, with the intention of stealing arms and jump-starting a revolution. First built by the Spanish in 1859, the barracks were burned

The **Balcón de Velázquez,** at the corner of Heredia and Corona at the edge of El Tivolí district, is a marvelous lookout over red-tile rooftops of the city as it slopes down to the Bay of Santiago. Named for the Spanish conquistador who founded the city, the terrace was reconstructed in the 1950s and now is a site of cultural goings-on on Fridays; it has been said that the original terrace in this very spot was used by Velázquez himself to observe incoming ships in the bay. An escape tunnel once ran from the spot, protected by cannons, all the way to the bay. Admission is free, but you'll have to pay CUC$1 or CUC$5, respectively, if you want to take photographs or videos.

down and then rebuilt in the late 1930s. Today, the Art Deco–style barracks house a museum focused on that day and the revolutionary struggle. For anyone interested in Cuban history, regardless of ideology, a visit to the museum is a must.

Fidel and his poorly funded troops, including his brother Raúl and Abel Santamaría, arrived in the early hours of July 26 dressed like army soldiers (though the street shoes they wore, rather than military boots, would give them away). Some 120 men attacked the barracks, but the plan failed miserably and 61 were killed. The others escaped, but were soon captured; many were tortured to death by Batista's army. Batista announced to the press that 500 well-funded militiamen had attacked the barracks and been killed in a gun battle. A young journalist succeeded in getting photographs of the tortured and murdered young revolutionaries out of Santiago and to Havana, where the pictures were published, galvanizing many Cubans against the Batista regime.

The museum exhibits the rebels' small rifles and pistols, bloodstained uniforms, photographs, letters, and other documents that tell the amazing story of the subsequent exile of the surviving rebels and guerrilla warfare in the Sierra Maestra. Exhibits are labeled in Spanish only, so a guide might be a good idea.

Calle Trinidad (corner of Moncada). ✆ **22/62-1157.** Admission CUC$2; CUC$1 to take photos; CUC$1 to take video. Free guided tours are available in English, French, and Italian. Tues–Sat 9:15am–5pm; Sun 9:15am–noon.

Museo Emilio Bacardí Moreau ★ Begun by Emilio Bacardí, the founder of the political and rum dynasty in 1899, this highly personal collection constituted one of the first museums in Cuba. Now a provincial museum, it remains an eclectic art and historical assembly. The grand, gleaming white neoclassical building was erected in 1928 to house the idiosyncratic collection. On the first floor is a wide variety of artifacts documenting indigenous peoples, slavery, and the wars of independence, including an extensive array of armaments and a peculiar coffin-shaped torpedo used by the Mambíses. Bacardí also collected personal items belonging to Cuban national heroes, including those of Antonio Maceo and Carlos Manuel Céspedes. Don't miss the tiny stage set of a colonial Santiago street (through a door on the south side of the first floor). In an annex, which must be entered from a side door on Calle Aguilera, is an archaeology room holding an Egyptian mummy (smuggled out of Egypt in 1913), a pair of Peruvian mummies belonging to the Paracas (pre-Inca) culture, various ceremonial objects, pre-Columbian ceramics, and an extraordinary decorated shrunken head from the Amazon. The second floor is an art museum exhibiting national and international paintings. There are several contemporary pieces, including a larger-than-life sculpture of Che Guevara in heroic pose. Allow an hour to see it all. All of the display information here is in Spanish, but English-speaking guides are available.

Calle Pío Rosado (at Aguilera). ☎ **22/62-8402.** Admission CUC$2. Free guided tours are available in English. Mon noon–4:15pm; Tues–Sat 9–4:15pm; Sun 9am–noon.

Other Attractions

Barrio El Tivolí 🏚️ A charming, hilly neighborhood just south of Parque Céspedes (loosely bordered by Av. Trocha and Calle Padre Pico), El Tivolí was once the most fashionable place to live in Santiago. Today, it's a relaxed place of steep streets, weathered and decrepit wooden houses, and a couple of attractions, but mostly it's a good place to wander.

The famous **Padre Pico steps** are named for a Santiaguero priest who aided the city's poor. Castro once roared fire and brimstone down on the Batista government here, but today you'll find more pacifistic chess and dominoes players who've set up all-hours tables on the steps. Take the steps up to the **Museo de la Lucha Clandestina (Museum of the Underground Struggle),** General Rabí 1 between Santa Rita and San Carlos (☎ **22/62-4689**), which is housed in a handsome 18th-century mansion on a hill, Loma del Intendente. Inside are disorganized exhibits related to the November 1956 attack on this former police headquarters, led by rebel leader and schoolteacher Frank País and his brother Josué, both executed by the army. Frank País's funeral was massively attended by Santiagueros, a signal that the Revolution would have significant local support. Other photos and documents attest to the phenomenal years of tension, rumors, and conflict that led to the rebels' triumph (labels are in Spanish only). The museum is open Tuesday through Sunday from 9am to 5pm; admission is CUC$1 (no photography is permitted).

Barrio El Tivoli, just south and west of Parque Céspedes.

Cementerio Santa Ifigenia ★★ Northwest of the city center, this sprawling cemetery, dating to 1868, is a small city of the dead, populated by elaborate marble tombs and sarcophagi, including several spectacular mausoleums (many of which are pre-1868, having been moved here from other cemeteries). By far the most famous is that of José Martí, a massive stone and marble circular structure built in 1951 (Martí died in 1895). Don't miss the solemn changing of the guard ceremony. The Lincolnesque mausoleum is near the entrance to the cemetery, at the end of a private path. Martí once wrote that he wished to die, "without a homeland, but without a master" and to be buried with "a bouquet of flowers and a flag." In addition to Martí, the remains of Emilio Bacardí, Carlos Manuel de Céspedes, Pedro (Perucho) Figueredo (author of the Cuban national anthem), and heroes of the Moncada 26th of July rebel attack are interred here. The newest addition to the celebrated figures buried here is the great musician and native son, Compay Segundo. In addition, the cemetery's palm-lined paths abound with a wealth of other fascinating tombs for families both famous and unknown.

Calzada Crombet. ☎ **22/63-2723.** Admission CUC$1, CUC$1 to take photos. Daily 7am–6pm.

Loma de San Juan This low-rise hill in the center of Reparto Vista Alegre, a leafy, upscale neighborhood, is where the decisive last battle of the Spanish-Cuban-American War was fought. Teddy Roosevelt and his army of an estimated 6,000 Rough Riders stormed the hill and defeated the Spanish troops. At the entrance to the park is the Arbol de la Rendención (Tree of Surrender), where the Spanish forces capitulated to the Americans. Something that still irks Cubans today, besides the commonly used name of the war that leaves them out, is that the Cubans were not even signatories to the surrender. While there are several plaques and monuments in the neatly manicured park, which pay tribute to the North Americans who participated and died in the war, there are few dedicated to the Cuban fighters (though the Tomb of the Unknown Mambi, or independence fighter, can be found there).

Reparto Santa Bárbara, at the intersection of Av. de Raúl Pujol and Carretera de Siboney Km 1.5 (next to the Hotel San Juan).

Museo del Carnaval ☺   Santiago's Carnival is the most famous in Cuba, and this small museum, in one of the oldest houses on Calle Heredia, aims to give visitors some historical perspective. Carnival counts centuries of tradition; the first published reference to the celebration was in 1669. It displays old costumes, black-and-white photographs, huge papier-mâché masks, and hand-painted and embroidered *mamarrachos* (capes). Percussion instruments show how popular the celebration is: They include old car parts and simple wood instruments. The final room displays a couple of the most recent winners of the costume contests—elaborate and huge affairs. **Folklore and music and dance events ★** are held at the museum if there is no rain Tuesday through Saturday at 4pm. Plan to spend about a half-hour viewing the displays.

Calle Heredia 303 (corner of Pío Rosado). ☏ **22/62-6955.** Admission CUC$1; CUC$1 for a guide; CUC$1 to take photos. Tues–Sun 9am–5pm.

Plaza de la Revolución   This massive, raised platform monument to Antonio Maceo features a startling equestrian statue of the great patriot surrounded by 23 enormous iron machetes slicing toward the sky, like daggers in the sides of the colonial power. Maceo, a Cuban of mixed blood, was called the "Bronze Titan" of the Cuban independence wars. Beneath the work is an eternal flame. The monument is an emphatic statement, to be sure. An underground room houses a small and rather uninspiring museum dedicated to the man.

Av. de las Américas (at Los Desfiles and Carretera Central). ☏ **22/64-3712.** Admission to museum CUC$1. Tues–Sat 9am–4pm; Sun 9am–1pm.

WHERE TO STAY

Santiago may not be blessed with the range of hotels that Havana has—in fact, it has less than a half-dozen hotels within easy reach of downtown—but it has enough variety among its few hotels that most guests shouldn't have trouble finding a decent place to stay at any price level. Only one of Santiago's major hotels is within the historic district, which is lively and fun, but too noisy and chaotic for many visitors. Most of the tourist hotels are on the outskirts of the city, an easy and inexpensive cab ride away.

Especially popular in Santiago are *casas particulares;* the city has hundreds of state-sanctioned private homestays, including some of the coolest *casas* in Cuba, several in historic homes in the heart of the old district and others in tranquil, leafy suburbs. Reparto Sueño alone has dozens of *casas.*

For those who might prefer to stay outside the city as an overnight excursion or even with plans to make a day trip out of Santiago, there are a couple of hotels along the coast and near some of the outlying attractions. Those hotels are listed in "Side Trips from Santiago de Cuba," later in this chapter.

Bay of Santiago

Santiago's deep natural bay is one of the city's defining characteristics. The narrow entrance to the Bahía de Santiago, past the Castillo El Morro, stretches 8km (5 miles). During the Spanish-American War, the contingency of Spanish ships was huddled within the bay, and the Americans were perched on the coast waiting to ambush them.

Today, Santiago's marina is popular with European and (believe it or not)

U.S. yachts. Visitors can book a 1-hour trip around the entire bay, scuba dive or kayak. If you just want to cross over to the fishing village on the tiny island of Cayo Granma for lunch, the ferry is CUC$5 round trip. For more information, contact the **Santiago Marina,** Calle 1 no. 4, Punta Gorda (✆ **22/69-1446;** marlin@nautica.scu.cyt.cu).

Centro Historico
MODERATE

Hostal Basilio ★ ✦ This little hotel is in a beautifully restored old home in the heart of downtown and now operates under the boutique Hoteles E brand. The good-size rooms have very high ceilings with ornate crown molding. Throughout the hotel, you'll find attractive tile work on the floors and wainscoting, nicely decorated and well-equipped bathrooms, and attractive blue bedspreads and curtains. Only two rooms here have anything besides two twin beds, and of these, no. 5 is the better bet, with a king-size bed. Still, my favorite room may just be no. 1, which has a lovely window overlooking the street—so this is not the room to choose for those easily bothered by street noise. The hotel has a small in-house restaurant serving reasonable local and international fare.

Calle Basilio 403 (btw. Calvario and Carnicería). ✆ **22/65-1702.** Fax 22/68-7069. www.hoteles cubanacan.com. 8 units. CUC$50-60 double. Rate includes breakfast. MC, V. **Amenities:** Restaurant; bar. *In room:* A/C, TV, minibar.

Hotel Casa Granda ★★ A large, elegant building right on Parque Céspedes, this hotel is a landmark in the city. Graham Greene's character Wormold, from *Our Man in Havana,* stayed in the 1914 hotel. Best known perhaps for its terrace bar with live music and its roof garden with great views over the cathedral and Santiago, the Casa Granda is one of the best places to stay in the city. Its location is superb, as long as you don't mind the hustle and bustle of travelers and *jineteros* in the square. The hotel features large rooms with high ceilings and restrained decor. As with most state-run hotels in Cuba, double beds are at a premium here; in fact, just 15 rooms come with a queen-size bed, and the rest have two twins. Rooms either have views of the park, Calle Heredia, or the interior—noise-sensitive guests should opt for the latter. The elegant a la carte restaurant on the first floor is handsome, with good food and service, but it's not cheap.

Heredia 201 (btw. San Félix and General Lacret). ✆ **22/65-3021.** Fax 22/68-6035. www.gran-caribe. com. 58 units. CUC$105–CUC$112 double; CUC$115–CUC$135 junior suite. Rates include breakfast. MC, V. **Amenities:** 2 restaurants; 2 bars room service. *In room:* A/C, TV, hair dryer.

INEXPENSIVE

There are scores of *casas particulares* in downtown Santiago; I've listed my favorites below. If these are full, you can also try **Casa Bertha Peña,** Calle Heredia 308 between Pío Rosado and Porfirio Valiente (☏ **22/62-4097**; co8kz@yahoo.es), a very centrally located house with two rooms. The second bedroom, dominated by a handsome, wood-and-marble dresser, is buried farther into the house and may be quieter. **Casa Pedro Guillermo Martí Vazquez,** Calle Corona 805 between Santa Rita and San Carlos (☏ **22/62-0101**; juan@music.santiagocaribe.com), a large house with an enormous front living room with original tiles and scarlet furniture, has two rooms. The one at the back of the house is larger. The house has large, unusual dado tiling of egrets catching fish. **Casa María de la Cruz Figueroa,** Calle Rey Palayo 83 between Reloj and Calvario (☏ **22/62-2152**; hospedajemaria@yahoo.com), is run by a very friendly family and has two rooms: one fairly spacious room upstairs at the back of the house with a decent-size bathroom that opens onto a shaded roof terrace, and the other room on the ground floor. **Casa Yuliett Ramos Duany** 🎁, San Basilio 513 between Clarin and Reloj (☏ **22/62-0546**; yuliett76@gmail.com), is a friendly household with young children. The two upstairs rooms are smartly furnished and are comfortable with plently of storage space. There's a front terrace and a roof terrace. **Casa Leonardo y Rosa,** Calle Clarín 9 between Aguilera and Heredia (☏ **22/62-3574**), is a large and colonial house with an ornate green-and-cream facade. The front room has extraordinarily high ceilings, chandeliers, and wainscoting on the walls, but we prefer the room at the back of the house.

Casa Alejandro Thomás ★ A nicely furnished and airy, colonial-style home, this conveniently located place is just a 5-minute walk from Parque Céspedes. It has two well-equipped rooms upstairs off a terrace. Each has its own bathroom, and one has its own independent terrace. The rooms share a small kitchen facility upstairs. Guests are welcome to lounge in the handsome family sitting room with leather club chairs, a sofa, and a TV. Good food is served.

Calle Aguilera 602 (corner of Barnada) btw. Barnada and Paraíso. ☏ **22/62-0844** or 52/90-0491. 2 units. CUC$15–CUC$25 double. No credit cards. *In room:* A/C, no phone.

Casa Juan A Martí Vázquez ★ 🎁 This lovely house has a plant-filled terrace with rocking chairs and a magnificent view up to the cathedral. The hotel is home to terrapin turtles and a peacock. One of the rooms has an attractive white wooden carved bed. Downstairs a 1910 French chandelier, a beautiful bronze Italian clock, and blue ceramics with matching candelabras grace the dining room. The *mamparas* (half-door screens inlaid with plain or decorative glass) are highly unusual with engraved French scenes compressed between the glass.

Calle Padre Pico 614 between Princesa y San Fernando. ☏ **22/62-2917.** juan@film.cineclubes.com. 2 units. CUC$25 double. No credit cards. *In room:* A/C, no phone.

Casa Maruchi ★ 🎁 This is a lovely colonial house with a wonderful patio covered with orchids and other plants. A striking fountain greets visitors at the tranquil patio. Two chic, comfortable rooms with exposed brickwork, Spanish colonial furniture, lace bedspreads, and candlesticks are located off the patio. The food, served on the patio, is good. This is a great place to meet a whole host of interesting locals and foreigners.

Calle Hartmann (San Félix) 357, corner of Trinidad and San Germán. ☏ **22/62-0767.** maruchib@yahoo. es. 2 units. CUC$20–CUC$25. No credit cards. *In room:* A/C, no phone.

Gran Hotel 🍴 This hotel, located on a major shopping street, offers good value and an excellent location in the heart of Santiago's historic center. The rooms themselves are rather uninspired and spartan, but they are clean and spacious (the triples are enormous and represent great value), with firm beds—although only two rooms here come with a double bed. A few rooms have tiny balconies overlooking bustling Calle Enramada. This hotel has historically been favored by local and visiting artists and musicians. There are plans to expand the hotel. *Be forewarned:* There's no elevator here, and all the rooms are on the second and third floors.

Calle Enramada 312 (corner of Calle San Félix), Santiago de Cuba. ℂ **22/65-3020.** 15 units. CUC$24–CUC$28 double. Children under 2 are free; children 3-12 are half price. **Amenities:** Restaurant; bar; cafeteria. *In room:* A/C, TV, minibar.

Hotel Libertad Fronting the busy Plaza de Marte, this hotel is another good budget option, run by the Islazul chain. Only half of the rooms here have windows, and you will definitely want a room with a window. No. 214 is the hotel's largest and best room. All have simple furnishings, and small, but functional bathrooms. About half the rooms here have double beds. Aside from its central location, the best feature here is the third-floor rooftop bar that was renovated in 2008.

Calle Aguilera 658 (across from Plaza de Marte), Santiago de Cuba. ℂ **22/62-8360.** www.islazul.cu. 17 units. CUC$28–CUC$38 double; CUC$36–CUC$46 suite (no. 214). Rates include breakfast. MC, V. **Amenities:** Restaurant; 2 bars. *In room:* A/C, TV.

The Outskirts

EXPENSIVE

Meliá Santiago de Cuba ★★ ☺ This unique, ugly postmodern high-rise, a mass of blue, red, and gray steel girders and glass, is the largest hotel in Santiago and easily its most luxurious. It's in a peaceful area about 2km (1¼ miles) from the historic core, which is perfect for guests who need a little bit more tranquillity and space. It has facilities and services in spades, including the best outdoor pool in the city. Rooms are attractive and large, with huge windows and excellent views, particularly from the higher floors. Royal Service, which includes a extras such as late check out, has been introduced. The hotel has a show on Saturday in its atmospheric **Santiago Café,** which is an indoor reconstruction of a miniature colonial city. Nonguests can use the pool facilities for a fee of CUC$10, which includes a CUC$5 discount at the poolside parrillada.

Av. de las Américas (at Calle M), Reparto Sueño, Santiago de Cuba. ℂ **22/68-7070.** Fax 22/68-7170. www.solmeliacuba.com. 302 units. CUC$110 double; CUC$135–CUC$165 junior suite. Children under 2 are free; children 3-12 sharing an adult's bedroom are half price. Royal Service rooms (standard, junior suite, master suite, and presidential suite) cost CUC$30 more for each type of room. MC, V. **Amenities:** 4 restaurants; 3 bars; gym; sauna; Saturday show; 3 outdoor pools; volleyball court; Wi-Fi in lobby (fee). *In room:* A/C, TV, minibar.

MODERATE

Hotel Las Américas ✦ A comfortable and friendly, older-style hotel just down the street from the Meliá Santiago, Las Américas isn't fancy, but it's a good place to stay, with plenty of services, attractive gardens, and a midsize pool. The rooms have been upgraded with new curtains, blackout shades, and bedspreads; they are a good size and have nice gray-marble bathrooms and cable television. The hotel dance club is quite popular with young Santiagueros. Nonguests here can use the pool facilities for a fee of CUC$10, which includes CUC$8 worth of food and drink.

Av. de las Américas (at General Cebreco), Reparto Sueño, Santiago de Cuba. ℂ **22/64-2011.** Fax 22/68-7075. www.islazul.cu. 70 units. CUC$40–CUC$50 double; CUC$48–CUC$58 minisuite. Rates include breakfast. MC, V. **Amenities:** 2 restaurants; 2 bars; dance club; outdoor pool. *In room:* A/C, TV, fridge.

INEXPENSIVE

Casa Asensio ★ 🖐   This fine house with an upstairs apartment is run by a friendly woman, Isabel. The huge apartment has an even larger, private rooftop terrace. There's an independent entrance and a separate kitchen, a large, comfortable bed, and good-size bathroom. Abstract art is painted on the walls, and you have access to the home's little garden.

Calle J no. 306 (btw. Calle 6 and Av. de las Américas), Reparto Sueño, Santiago de Cuba. ☎ **22/62-4600.** manuel@medired.scu.sld.cu. 1 unit. CUC$25 double. No credit cards. *In room:* A/C, kitchenette, fridge, no phone.

Casa Florinda Chaviano Martínez   This large and well-furnished house is impeccable. The lone bedroom for rent is big and meticulously maintained. It features a great rooftop terrace and breezy patio covered with vines.

Calle I no. 58 (btw. Calles 2 and 3), Reparto Sueño, Santiago de Cuba. ☎ **22/66-3660.** 1 unit. CUC$25 double. No credit cards. *In room:* A/C, TV, fridge, no phone.

Casa Gloria Boué Alonso   There is no shortage of nicely furnished 1950s-style houses in the Sueño district; this one has funky, overstuffed furniture and two rooms, one of which is upstairs with its own massive terrace. The other room is downstairs and is very spacious, with the largest private bathroom you're likely to find in Cuba. There's a common sitting room with a television showing only local channels.

Calle J no. 212 (btw. Calles 4 and 5), Reparto Sueño, Santiago de Cuba. ☎ **22/64-4969;** bony@recd.uo.edu.cu. 2 units. CUC$20–CUC$25 double. No credit cards. *In room:* A/C, fridge, no phone.

WHERE TO DINE

Santiago has a unique take on Cuban and Caribbean cuisine, but it isn't an especially great place for dining; there are few really good restaurants, and even fewer *paladares* (private home restaurants). A couple of the better restaurants are outside of downtown, and it's best if you plan ahead to combine them with sightseeing. The couple of officially sanctioned *paladares* and the state-run restaurants (many of which are concentrated around Plaza Dolores) are nothing to look forward to. Understandably, many visitors tend to eat at their hotel restaurants—as good an option as any. The Meliá Santiago de Cuba and Hotel Casa Granda have elegant restaurants that are worth a splurge even for nonguests (though you may want to skip the Italian restaurant La Fontana in the Meliá). Although you can only get sandwiches and simple dishes there, one of my favorite lunch spots is the **open-air terrace bar** at the Hotel Casa Granda. On a hot afternoon, this is the coolest place in town—in both senses of the word—but you should be prepared for laughably slow service. You can also get a decent pizza for CUC$4 on the **5th floor terrace** of the Casa Granda. This has affordable drinks and one of the best views in Cuba: the cathedral, bay of Santiago, and the mountains beyond. Around the corner on Aguilera is the new **pan.com**. Its ham and cheese paninis are tastier and cheaper than those of the Casa Granda's, but there's no view.

Café Ajedrez, Calle Enramada at Felix Peña (no phone), is located in a tiered 1966 art-deco building by architect Walter A. Betancourt. The café features stylized metal tresses, art-deco lamps, and stone tables with chess boards (*ajedrez*). It's open Tuesday to Sunday from 10am–3pm. Another great spot, if it's not overrun with *jineteros*, is the atmospheric **Café La Isabelica** on Plaza Dolores, corner of Calle Aguilera and Calvario. The two signature coffees are *rocio con gallo* (coffee with rum) and the Café Isabelica (coffee, rum, and honey). The cafe is reminiscent of an old inn with darkened furniture, leather-and-hide–covered chairs, and gossiping old men. It is open 24 hours daily. Santiago's Coppelia (the national ice cream chain) is known as **La Arboleda** and is on the corner of Av. Garzón y Av. de los Libertadores. Get your bargain ice cream *bolas* here in *moneda nacional*. There is no entrance fee. Splurge on the seven multi-flavored scoops of the Gran Piedra dish. It is open from 10am to 10pm daily.

Centro Historico
MODERATE
La Taberna de Dolores CRIOLLAN   This restaurant is located in an 18th-century house, with a courtyard with a well, that was formerly the home of Don Sebastian Kindelan, governor of Oriente province between 1800 and 1813. The prize tables are located on a small balcony overlooking bustling Plaza Dolores. Dine on roast pork, roast chicken, or fried fish. Dishes come with *moros y cristianos* (rice and beans), salad, and fried vegetables.

Calle Aguilera 468 (btw. Reloj and Calvario), Plaza Dolores. ℂ **22/62-3913.** Main courses CUC$8–CUC$15. No credit cards. Daily 11am–11pm.

Paladar Las Gallegas CRIOLLAN   Four sisters run this down-home place just a couple of blocks from Parque Céspedes. Portions are reasonable, the food is okay, and the spacious dining room—a cross between a living room and a salon—has a peaked beam ceiling, nine tables (including two on narrow balconies overlooking the street), an ornate chandelier, and red satin curtains. There's the predictable fried chicken, but also chicken fricasse, pork steaks, and ham. All dishes come with rice and salad. Go early or late; on many nights, the tiny place is full, though the wait usually isn't long.

San Basilio 305 altos (btw. General Lacret and San Félix). ℂ **22/62-4700.** Reservations not accepted. Main courses CUC$8. No credit cards. Daily 1–10:30pm.

INEXPENSIVE
El Barracón ★ 🍴 CRIOLLAN   This is a new restaurant memorializing the slave trade in Cuba. Two statues of slaves guard the entrance to the restaurant. Once inside, you'll see dark wood, exposed brick, paintings of slave plantations, and oversized decorations of bats and spiders. Ceramic mugs and plates add authenticity on the long wooden tables. Try the chef's choice, which changes regularly. *Carne pa' Chango* is a delicious lamb stew swimming in gravy (a rarity in Cuba). Carnivores will also delight in rump steak, pork chops, and pork in wine and honey. This is certainly good value.

Av. Victoriano Garzón. ℂ **22/66-1877.** Reservations not required. Main courses CUC$2.50–CUC$5.50. No credit cards. Daily noon–11pm.

The Outskirts
EXPENSIVE
La Isabelica ★★ INTERNATIONAL   This small, romantic restaurant serves up French-influenced cuisine in a tranquil and elegant setting. We recommend the fresh grouper in a saffron sauce, served over a bed of spinach. You also can't go wrong with the curried chicken breasts with plum and pineapple. There's a decent and reasonably priced wine list, and the service is attentive and efficient. Dinner here gets you a free entrance into the hotel's nightly cabaret show.

In the Meliá Santiago, Av. de las Américas (at Calle M), Reparto Sueño. ℂ **22/68-7070.** Reservations recommended. Main courses CUC$12–CUC$36. MC, V. Daily 7–11pm.

ZunZún ★★ CRIOLLAN This elegant and upscale restaurant occupies a handsome 1940s house in the Vista Alegre neighborhood. It has four private salons for intimate dining, and a couple of tables on a broad front veranda, which are my favorites. With relatively soft lighting, marble floors, and period furnishings—some original to the house—ZunZún (formerly Tocororo) is the place in town to splurge. Everything is very well prepared and nicely presented. It's especially good for seafood, such as a delicious mixed grill of fish and shellfish; medallions of lobster, shellfish, and shrimp; and garlic shrimp. Carnivores can opt for a beef filet in red-wine sauce or *ropa vieja* (shredded beef). The tables here have white tablecloths and candles—rarities in Cuba.

Av. Manduley 159, Reparto Vista Alegre. ℂ **22/64-1528.** Reservations recommended. Main courses CUC$6–CUC$21. Daily noon–10pm.

MODERATE

Paladar Salón Tropical ★ CRIOLLAN One of the most elegant *paladares* in Cuba—in fact, it's swankier than most state-owned and hotel restaurants—this attractively decorated place, with stained-glass windows, lovely tablecloths, and high-backed chairs, also has a terrific, breezy, plant-covered terrace. The views are excellent; it's a marvelous environment for having a couple of beers . . . and waiting interminably for your dinner. It's own popularity has overwhelmed this place, and service can be glacially slow at times. Depending upon what is available, the menu might offer a smorgasbord of choices, including chicken soup, shish kebobs, grilled fish, mixed grill, and barbecued chicken. The *paladar* is quite popular with smooching Cubans as well as bored *jineteras* with their romantic "dates." Reservations are highly recommended, and the operating hours listed below are not strictly enforced—this place often closes early or unexpectedly.

Luis Fernández Marcané 310 Altos (btw. Calles 9 and 10), Reparto Santa Bárbara. ℂ **22/64-1161.** Reservations recommended. Main courses CUC$5–CUC$6. No credit cards. Daily 12:30pm–midnight.

Bahia de Santiago

MODERATE

El Cayo 🍴 CRIOLLAN This relaxing spot for lunch is a boating excursion and dining outing rolled into one. In a pretty blue-and-white clapboard waterfront house on a tiny island in the middle of the Bay of Santiago—you have to take a CUC$5 round-trip ferryboat from the **Santiago Marina** (ℂ **22/69-1446**) to get there—is this breezy, tranquil restaurant that's popular with organized groups, but is perfect for independent travelers, too. Sit on the covered wraparound balcony overlooking the

---

📎 Bring on the *Béisbol*

Santiago is yet another baseball-mad Cuban city, and the local professional team is usually among the best in the national league. The *pelota* (as it's popularly known) season begins in late winter and continues through the spring. Games are held at the **Estadio** **Guillermo Moncada** on Avenida de las Américas (ℂ **22/64-5640**). Ask at your hotel about getting tickets (it's usually possible to purchase them right before game time at the stadium ticket booth).

water and try any of the specialties, which quite logically are seafood dishes: Spanish mackerel, lobster, red snapper, marlin, or fish soup.

Cayo Granma, Bahía de Santiago. ✆**22/69-0109.** Reservations recommended for lunch. Main courses CUC$6–CUC$18. MC, V. Daily 11am–6pm.

Restaurant El Morro ★ CRIOLLAN   A hugely popular and pleasant open-air place, perched on the coast near the fortress of the same name and boasting spectacular views of the sparkling blue Caribbean Sea, this restaurant, happily, isn't a tourist trap. It also serves a good-value lunch (with choices) for groups. Try the lobster if you're in a mood to splurge; otherwise, there's a fish filet stuffed with cheese, spicy shrimp, and chicken with pineapple. The long black tables are under a wood-beamed canopy thick with vines and hanging plants and white *tumbergia* flowers, a most welcome refuge from the scorching sun that makes midday at El Morro fortress a daunting proposition.

Carretera del Morro Km 8.5, Bahía de Santiago. ✆**22/69-1576.** Reservations recommended for lunch. Main courses CUC$5–CUC$12. V. Daily noon–4.30pm.

SHOPPING

Opportunities for shopping in Santiago, despite the city's cultural traditions, aren't that much better than in many smaller cities in Cuba. Your best bets, as elsewhere in Cuba, are handicrafts, music and musical instruments, and the always-dependable rum and cigars.

Art, Books & Handicrafts

Sellers and craftspeople line both sides of **Calle Heredia** from Parque Céspedes on up to Calle Porfirio Valiente. The informal daily market features a range of handicrafts and souvenirs, including sculptures of shapely (as well as rail-thin) women carved from ebony and other precious woods, paintings, masks, papier-mâché dolls, musical instruments, and jewelry. **Señor Aldo** sells books, postcards, records, and magazines inspired by the Revolution. A number of state-owned crafts and souvenir shops with similar merchandise, but inflexible pricing, occupy the storefronts at the base of the cathedral on **Parque Céspedes.** New crafts and souvenir shops line the road leading to the **El Morro** fortress (across from the El Morro restaurant).

Locally produced abstract and figurative art is available at a handful of galleries, including the **Galería de Arte Oriente** on Calle General Lacret 653, between Aguilera and Heredia.

Cigars & Rum

The **Barra de Ron Caney,** at the rum factory that used to be the original Bacardí plant before the Revolution (when the owners fled to the Bahamas and the U.S.), is a gift shop selling an array of types and vintages of Cuban-produced rum, as well as cigars, nice silver jewelry, and other souvenirs. You can taste before you buy. The factory and shop are on Av. Jesús Menéndez 703 between San Antonio and San Ricardo (✆ **22/62-5576**), across from the train station. The shop is open daily from 9am to 5:30pm. Alternately, you can check out the **Museo de Ron** (✆ **22/62-8818**), at San Basilio 358, which offers a brief illustrated guide to the history and process of rum production, with a pleasant bar next-door. (The museum was undergoing major renovation in 2010, and at press time, there was no slated reopening date.) When it does reopen, it will be worth visiting for the chandeliers——with delicately carved bronze flowers and cascading crystals.

Cigars can be purchased at hotel shops or **Casa del Habano,** next-door to the Caney rum factory (© **22/62-2366**), which even has a smokers' lounge and bar. *Note:* I'd be especially wary of the quality of cigars you are offered by *jineteros* on the street.

Music

Santiago is the capital of *son* and other indigenous forms of Cuban music, and there are a few good spots to pick up CDs and tapes of Santiaguero musicians (though overall, Havana has a much better selection of music stores). The **EGREM** music label has shops at the Antonio Maceo airport. The **Casa de la Trova** (p. 289) has an **ARTex** store, and there's a small record shop attached to the **Casa de la Música,** Corona (Mariano) 564, between Aguilera and José Antonio Saco. Of the artists you may have an opportunity to see perform live, most sell CDs at their performances.

SANTIAGO DE CUBA AFTER DARK
The Performing Arts

Besides the locally grown Cuban music scene, another nighttime draw is the **Cabaret Tropicana Santiago ★★**, Autopista Nacional Km 1.5, north of Santiago (© **22/64-2579**). It's second in size and fame only to Havana's internationally regarded Tropicana, but Santiago's show is no second banana. It's a slickly produced cabaret show—different from the one in Havana—with excellent singers and dancers and extraordinarily elaborate costumes. Dinner is available, and drinks aren't cheap, but the Tropicana is a must-see, only if you don't have an opportunity to catch the program in the capital. The show begins at 10pm on Saturdays; there's also a dance club on the premises, open until 3am. The show, including dinner and one drink, is CUC$20. Packaged excursions with dinner and transportation can be purchased at the larger hotels and all tour operators.

You'll find a much more scaled-down and less-expensive Saturday night show at the **Santiago Café ★** (© **22/68-7070**), in the Meliá Santiago. The cover here is just CUC$5, which includes two drinks.

The top spots for cultural events such as dance and theater (which inevitably take a back seat to live music) are the sleek **Teatro Heredia,** Avenida de los Desfiles, across from the Plaza de la Revolución (© **22/64-3178**). Keep an eye out for performances by **Ballet Folklórico Cutumba ★★★**, an extraordinary Afro-Cuban outfit that has toured in North America and Europe. Cutumba has returned to Santiago and has its base at the old Cine Galaxia, Calle Trocha corner of Santa Ursula (Av V. Hierrezuelo; © **22/65-5173;** www.cubanfolkloricdance.com/cutumba.php). At press time, the Ballet Folklórico Cutumba planned to have regular performances on Saturdays at 6pm, and Sundays at 11am (CUC$3). Rehearsals can be seen outside of festival times from Tuesdays to Fridays in the morning (CUC$1). Also keep an eye out for **Conjunto Folklórico de Oriente,** which often performs at Hotel Casa Granda. You may not catch all the spiritual and cultural elements embedded in their show, but the music and dance are infectious nonetheless. Teatro Heredia is the headquarters for the **Festival del Caribe ★★** in July, but the entertainment also takes place in the streets and the Casa del Caribe. Some events require reservations; contact **Agencia Paradiso** (© **22/62-0214;** paradisostgo@scsc.artex.cu) or the **Casa del Caribe** (see below).

Live Music

Santiago is all about the music. Some of the biggest personalities on the Cuban music scene, such as **Compay Segundo, Eliades Ochoa,** and **La Vieja Trova Santiaguera,** hail from Santiago. Although Compay died at 95 in 2003, Ochoa is still active, touring both in Cuba and internationally. Calle Heredia, just off Parque Céspedes, is Cuba's version of Bourbon Street, but much less commercialized. Four or five places burst with addictive live, traditional Cuban music on any given night, and several have bands during the day, too. Personal local favorites include **Los Jubilados,** a band of gregarious septuagenarians who often play at the Casa de la Trova; **Kokoyé,** a folkloric band playing traditional Afro-Cuban and Afro-Haitian music; and the **Vocal Divas,** a talented women's a cappella group.

Several of the spots below are not only great for hearing live music, but also for watching local patrons who make dancing to Cuban music a sultry art form all their own. Give it a try yourself and don't worry about looking foolish; unless you've had professional training, you simply can't compete with Cubans on the dance floor, so don't even try. If you're without a partner, there's usually no shortage of Cuban men and women (most of whom will invariably be *jineteros* and *jineteras*) willing to give you a whirl. At places like the Casa de la Trova and other spots around town, you're likely to find music throughout the day, beginning around noon, and well into the night. At most clubs, the music starts around 9pm and really heats up from around 10pm until 2am.

Casa de las Tradiciones ★★★   More cramped and heaps more intimate than the more touristy Casa de la Trova, this old house (called "La Casona" by locals) in the Tívoli section of town is loaded with character and decorated with dozens of paintings and photos on the walls. It gets perfectly steamy when there's a tight band playing and more than two couples working the dance floor. Calle Rabí 154. © **22/65-3892.** Cover CUC$1.

Casa de la Trova ★★★   Decades of raw and infectious Cuban music seep from the walls of this legendary live music venue, the greatest of the country's Casas de la Trova. Old-timers may complain that it doesn't have the character it once did, due to makeovers, but its long front room and back patio and the grand upstairs salon still outclass almost any other Cuban music joint. All the greats have played here; you may catch an up-and-coming star, or a band of octogenarians who rightly should be every bit as famous as the guys in Buena Vista. They aren't, but you'll enjoy their music all the more for their relative obscurity and chance to see them in such a welcoming environment. Heredia 206 (btw. San Félix and San Pedro). © **22/65-2689.** Cover CUC$1 daytime, CUC$3–CUC$10 at night.

Casa del Caribe ★   This cultural center has a full schedule of music events and other goings-on starting between 4 and 7pm Thursday to Sunday. The program is eclectic, ranging from poetry to folkloric dancing to rumba and steel bands. It would be best to call beforehand before hiking out here. Concerts are held on two leafy outdoor patios. There are also cultural conferences and workshops. Contact the *casa* for the Fiesta del Caribe program. Calle 13 no. 154 (corner of Calle 8), Vista Alegre. © **22/64-3609.** Cover CUC$1–CUC$2.

CARNIVAL & OTHER SANTIAGO festivals

Santiago is well known among Cuban cities for its sparkling music festivals, which thrust Afro-Caribbean culture and the local musical genius to the forefront of urban life. If you can stand the stultifying heat in late July, Carnival is the most exciting time to visit the city.

In Santiago, *Carnaval* is not a pre-Lenten celebration as it is in other Latin American countries. In the 17th century, slaves reshaped the traditional (and much more solemn) Catholic veneration of the city's patron saint, Santiago Apóstol, and the attendant religious processions, into a festive celebration. The slaves' revelry was much more raucous than that of the white Christians, who began to refer to the slaves' participation as the *Fiesta de Los Mamarrachos* (party of the Crazies). Gradually, the rest of Santiaguero society began to appreciate and even participate in Carnival. French and Haitian elements were incorporated after the 18th-century influx of those populations. By the 20th century, Santiago's Carnival had gone the way of samba and *Carnaval* in Brazil, which was appropriated from marginal black communities and transformed into a mainstream cultural affair.

Today, unsurprisingly, even Carnival is linked to politics. The 5-day celebration also serves to commemorate the 26th of July movement that was the foundation for the Revolution. At 5am on the 26th of July, a reconstruction of the Moncada attack is made, complete with a cavalcade of old cars and gun shots. It's a surreal event. Yet politics seems light-years away from the popular explosion that erupts on Santiago's sweltering streets. Garish floats, with parade queens atop, glide through the streets, frenetic drum-beating conga parades rock the neighborhoods (the biggest are the barrio congas of day 1), and masked *diablitos* (devils) dart daringly through the throngs. African elements, including representations of orishás (Yoruba gods), are omnipresent. *Comparsas,* the Carnival band processions, have marchers who don papier-mâché masks and brightly colored costumes.

Patio de ARTex   If there's not much happening at the Casa de la Trova, peek in here for live Cuban music every afternoon and night of the week; there's a gorgeous courtyard out back. Heredia 304 (btw. Pío Rosado and Porfirio Valiente). ✆ **22/65-4814.** Cover CUC$2 at night only.

Patio de los Dos Abuelos   This place on the Plaza de Marte is a good spot to listen to *boleros* and *filin* (feelin', a musical genre), daily from 9am to 2am. The scene is a little older and more sedate than most of the places listed above, but folks still get up and dance. Moreover, the patrons and players show real love for the romantic ballads and tragic love songs that are the staples here. Calle Pérez Carbó 5 (across from the Plaza de Marte). ✆ **22/62-3302.** Cover CUC$2 at night.

Bars & Clubs

In general, bars open around noon and stay open as long as there are patrons, usually between midnight and 2am. Dance clubs and music joints tend to get going around 10pm and stay open until at least 2am.

Bello Bar   This bar occupies the entire 15th floor of the Meliá Santiago hotel and has stunning 360-degree views of Santiago. Live jazz and Cuban tunes can be heard daily. In Meliá Santiago hotel. (Av. de las Américas at Calle M, Reparto Sueño). ✆ **22/68-7070.**

Today, Carnival manages still to be exuberant, even though funds for fancy costumes are tough to come by and homemade instruments predominate (during the years of the so-called Special Period in the mid-1990s, economic conditions were so tough that Carnival had to be canceled for a couple of years). Some conga ensembles, such as Los Hoyos, trace their origins back to the 19th century. Watch out for the following excellent dance troupes: Cabildos, La Placita, and Izuama y Olugo. The focal points of Carnival activities are along Avenida Jesús Menéndez and Victoriano Garzón, where the parade and float judging takes place. Tickets for the grandstand seating can be bought in wooden kiosks along Victoriano Garzón from one hour before the children's parades at 5pm and the adults' parades at 10pm ($2MN). If you can't bear the crush and need some space, pay for optimum viewing in front of the sealed-off El Barracón restaurant. It charges CUC$3 (including one *cerveza*) to sit down under its umbrellas with front row seats. Beware that you may be coaxed to sit in the foreigners' stand—and be charged a whopping CUC$5 for the privilege. If you've got the Spanish, argue against the discrimination.

Preceding Carnival is the **Fiesta del Fuego,** or **Festival del Caribe,** in the first week of July, which brings a cornucopia of cultural workshops, theater, and artistic performances to Santiago. On the last day of this festival, an effigy of the devil is burned (*Quema del Diablo*), and a conga line shimmies all the way from Parque Céspedes down to the water at 5pm—buy a bottle of rum, swing your hips, and join the end of the line. Another important date is the 24th of June (**Día de San Juan**) when the various congas from each barrio visit each other by snaking across the city in procession. Also worth catching, although not nearly as frenzied as Carnival, is the **Festival de Rumba** in mid-January, which is also celebrated with street dancing and music.

Discoteca La Iris   This sweaty dance club, extremely popular with young locals, pumps at all hours of the day, with ear-shattering disco, salsa, merengue, and Latin rock. The disco underwent a renovation in mid-2010. Calle Aguilera 617 (btw. Bamada and Plácido). © **22/65-4910.**

Hotel Casa Granda Terrace Bar   A great spot for people-watching over the Parque Céspedes, this convivial terrace/balcony bar is always hopping, with a good mix of foreigners and Cubans hoping to meet foreigners. The hotel also has a **Rooftop Garden** bar on the top floor with excellent views of the cathedral and Santiago Bay, although this pleasant open-air space almost always feels underused. Calle Heredia 201 (btw. General Lacret and San Félix). © **22/65-3021.**

La Taberna de Dolores 🍴   This local hangout—my favorite low-rent watering hole in Santiago—is in the pretty, leafy patio of an old colonial house. This joint always has cheap draft beer in plastic mugs. The crowd is mostly Cuban, with a few backpacker sorts. With a minimal bit of Spanish (like *cerveza*, meaning beer), you should be able to pay in Cuban pesos—be sure to ask about paying in *moneda nacional*, although be sure you have some *moneda nacional* in your pocket when they give you the bill. Calle Aguilera 468 (at Reloj), Plaza Dolores. © **22/62-3913.**

SIDE TRIPS FROM SANTIAGO DE CUBA

Excursions to all the places listed below, as well as to Guantánamo and Baracoa (see chapter 10), can be arranged at the tour desks found in most hotels, or with tour agencies. See Visitor Information p. 274.

Castillo El Morro ★★

15km (9 miles) S of Santiago de Cuba

Guarding the entrance to the Bahía de Santiago, this seemingly impregnable fortress is built atop a rocky promontory and entered across a formidable drawbridge. The medieval and Renaissance-style structure, a UNESCO World Heritage Site, is a warren of platforms, passageways, and cells spread across five levels and protected by 1.5m-thick (5-ft.) walls. It was engineered in 1638 by the Italian architect who built similar fortresses in Havana, as well as Cartagena, Colombia and San Juan, Puerto Rico, to protect against pirate attacks (which it didn't do so well, as pirates including Henry Morgan succeeded in ransacking the place).

The site, where the sun beats down unrelentingly, has magnificent views of the bay and the Caribbean coastline stretching all the way to the Sierra Maestra. Inside the fortress, built above a dry moat, is a sparse museum (with display explanations in Spanish only) detailing the history of piracy, El Morro, and Santiago de Cuba. One room contains artifacts related to the 1898 Spanish-American War—its principal naval battles were fought right in the Bay of Santiago. The 19 modern American ships sank all seven Spanish ships; ironically, the Spanish ship *Cristóbal Colón* was the last to sink, thus closing the door on the history of Spanish colonialism in the Americas.

A daily ceremony, called the Puesta del Sol, takes place at sunset daily (if it rains, it's cancelled), recalling the importance of the fortress in the 19th century. Youngsters dressed as *mambises,* or members of the Cuban rebel army, lower the flag and shoot off the ancient (ca. 1805) Spanish cannon to cries of "¡Viva Cuba Libre!" Visiting El Morro for the day-ending ceremony, when it has cooled off some, is an excellent idea. You'll need about an hour to tour the complex. Avoid the hours of 11am to 4pm at all costs.

To get there, an organized excursion or a car or taxi is required. The Castillo El Moro is open daily from 8am–7:20pm; admission is CUC$4, and an additional CUC$1 to take photos and CUC$1 to take video. Free guided tours are available in English, French, and Italian. For more information, call ⓒ **22/69-1569.**

Basílica del Cobre

18km (11 miles) W of Santiago de Cuba

The most important shrine for Cubans and the most famous church in the country is lodged in the foothills of the Sierra Maestra near the old copper mines that give it its name. The triple-domed church with the name of **El Santuario de Nuestra Señora de la Caridad del Cobre,** built in 1927, rises on Maboa hill and is photogenically framed by green forest. The faithful come from across Cuba on pilgrimages to pay their respects to (and ask for protection from) a black Madonna, the *Virgen de la Caridad* (Virgin of Charity). She is nothing less than the protectress of Cuba, and her image, cloaked in a glittering gold robe, can be seen throughout the country. Her parallel figure in Afro-Cuban worship is Ochún, goddess of love and femininity, who is also dark-skinned and dressed in bright yellow garments. In 1998, the pope visited and blessed the shrine, calling the Virgin "La Reina de los Cubanos" (Queen of Cubans), and donated a rosary and crown.

According to legend, the statue of Cuba's patron saint was discovered bobbing in the Bay of Nipe in 1611 by three young fishermen (or miners, depending on who's telling the story) about to capsize in a storm. The Madonna wore a sign that read YO SOY LA VIRGEN DE LA CARIDAD (I am the Virgin of Charity). With the wooden statue in their grasp, the fishermen miraculously made it to shore. Pilgrims, who often make the last section of the trek on their knees, pray to her image and place *votos* (mementos) and offerings of thanks for her miracles; among them are small boats and prayers for those who have tried to make it to Florida on rafts. Ernest Hemingway—whose fisherman in *The Old Man and the Sea* made a promise to visit the shrine if he could only land his marlin—donated his Nobel Prize in Literature to the shrine, but it was stolen (and later recovered, but never again to be exhibited here). The Virgin sits on the second floor, up the back stairs, encased in glass. When Mass is being said, the push of a button turns the Virgin around to face the congregation. The annual pilgrimage is September 8, and the patron saint's feast day is July 25. The Basílica is open daily from 6am to 6:30pm; admission is free.

You can take a taxi to El Cobre for CUC$25 round-trip, but an agency tour is cheaper. The no. 2 bus runs between Santiago and El Cobre four times daily, leaving from the main bus station in Santiago. To enhance the spiritual experience, or to merely have a serene and incredibly cheap overnight stay, there's an inn behind the church, **Hospedería de la Caridad,** which welcomes foreigners who abide by the strict rules (10pm curfew and repeated requests for quiet); a stay costs a mere 40 national pesos (CUC$1.60) a night. There are only 15 austere, but well-kept rooms; it's necessary to reserve by phone (© 22/34-6246) at least 15 days in advance as it's so popular. There's a large, breezy dining room too.

La Gran Piedra & La Isabelica

27km (17 miles) E of Santiago de Cuba

A tortuous coastal road east of Santiago ascends the mountains to **La Gran Piedra (The Big Rock)** ★★★, an enormous 25m-high (82-ft.) rock perched 1,200m (3,937 ft.) above sea level. You can climb a half-hour on foot to the top of the rock for a panoramic view of thickly wooded eastern Cuba and the majestic Sierra Maestra that extends to the Caribbean and as far as the eye can see. The air is much sweeter and cooler than in Santiago. Admission is CUC$2, which includes a drink. Near the foot of the trail is the modest **Gran Piedra** (© 22/68-6147; www.islazul.cu; CUC$20 double), a rustic little hotel with a restaurant, as well as the **Jardín Ave de Paraíso,** a small botanical garden with birds of paradise and other flowers. The garden is open daily 8am to 5pm, and admission is CUC$1.

About 2km (1¼ miles) beyond Gran Piedra, a passable dirt track leads to **Museo La Isabelica,** Carretera de la Gran Piedra Km 14, an early-19th-century coffee plantation *finca* (country house) that once was the property of newly arrived French immigrants who fled Haiti after the slave revolt there in 1791. The owner named La Isabelica for his mistress (and later wife), a beautiful slave. The house was a stone mansion built in the style of rural French manor houses in Haiti. It was one of about 60 coffee plantations in the area, which proved very hospitable for planting coffee beans. The 200 Arabica coffee plantations in the region helped Cuba become the number-one coffee producer in the world until 1850, when it was surpassed by Brazil.

These Franco-Haitian plantations were recently declared UNESCO World Heritage Sites. On the premises of La Isabelica is a workshop, along with the original furniture and slave instruments. The house has recently been renovated and provides a glimpse into the life of the period. It's open daily 8am to 4pm; admission is CUC$1.

Gran Parque Natural Baconao

25km (16 miles) SE of Santiago de Cuba

A UNESCO biosphere reserve, **Parque Baconao** is spread over some 40km (25 miles). The local dark-sand beaches are scruffy and the hotels are isolated, but the park hides a number of attractions, several of them man-made, for visitors with a couple of extra days in Santiago.

The road leading southeast out of Santiago is lined with 26 monuments to revolutionary heroes who died in the attack on the Moncada barracks. About 10km (6 miles) east is the **Valle de la Prehistoria,** Carretera Baconao Km 6.5 (© 22/63-9239), Cuba's very own Jurassic Park—a lifeless and cheesy attraction. Lodged on farmlands are 250 massive life-size statues of dinosaurs and a giant, club-wielding Stone Age man. The park is open daily from 8am to 5pm; admission is CUC$1.

Nearby, in a nod to more recent history, the **Museo Nacional del Transporte (Automobile Museum),** Carretera Baconao Km 8.5 (© 22/63-9197), has a decent number of old cars, some more valuable and in better shape than others. One vehicle, a 1951 Chevrolet, was driven by Fidel's brother Raúl to the Moncada attack (he got lost); a Cadillac on view belonged to the legendary singer Beny Moré. The museum's collection of vintage American cars has been built by the novel practice of offering Cubans new Russian-built Ladas for their old Cadillacs and Chevys. Next door is a collection of several thousand model and Matchbox cars. The museum is open daily from 8am to 5pm; admission is CUC$1; an extra CUC$1 is charged to take photos.

On the coast, at Km 27.5, is the **Acuario Baconao** (© 22/35-6264), a rather sad little aquarium that runs daily dolphin and sea lion shows. Admission is CUC$7. You can also swim with the dolphins for around 15 minutes for CUC$40.

> ## Beach Trips
>
> Tour operators can arrange day trips to some of the southern coastal resorts. As Siboney, the nearest beach, is not the most attractive, the best of these would be to the **Brisas Sierra Mar Los Galeones (p. 259).** A full-day trip at an all-inclusive resort, with transfers and food, costs CUC$23.

FAST FACTS

FAST FACTS: CUBA

Area Codes Area codes around the country range from one to two digits. See "Staying Connected," p. 58, for dialing instructions within area codes, from one area code to another, and from Havana to another area code.

Business Hours There are no hard-and-fast rules, but most businesses and banks are open Monday through Friday from 9am to 5pm. Some businesses and banks close for an hour for lunch. Shops and department stores, especially those that cater to tourists, tend to have slightly more extended hours, and are usually open on Saturday and Sunday.

Cellphones (Mobile Phones) See "Staying Connected," p. 58.

Drinking Laws Cuba has no firm or clear liquor laws. Beer, wine, and liquor are served at most restaurants and are available at most gift shops and hard-currency stores. Drinking and driving is against the law.

Driving Rules See "Getting There & Getting Around," p. 38.

Electricity You will find a mix of electrical currents and plug types used in Cuba. Around 90% of the hotels and *casas particulares* use a 110-volt current with standard U.S.-style two- or three-prong outlets. However, some outlets are rated 220 volts, particularly in hotels that cater to European clientele. These are usually marked and sometimes accept only two-prong round plugs. For all intents and purposes, you should have personal appliances rated for 110-volt current, with U.S.-style prongs, or the appropriate converters. It is also essential to carry a three-to-two-prong adapter for any appliance you have that has a three-prong plug.

Embassies & Consulates All major consulates and embassies are in Havana. Canada also has other locations.

The embassy of **Canada** is at Calle 30 no. 518, at the corner of Avenida 7, Miramar (© **7/204-2516;** fax 7/204-2044; http://havana.gc.ca). The Consulate of Canada is at Hotel Atlántico, Suite 1, Guardalavaca (© **24/430-320;** fax 24/430-321; honcongvaca@canada.com); and at Calle 13, corner of Avenida 1 and Camino del Mar, Varadero (© **45/61-2078;** fax 45/66-7395; honconvdero@canada.com).

The embassy of the **United Kingdom** is at Calle 34 no. 702, between Avenida 7 and 17, Miramar (© **7/214-2200;** fax 7/214-2268; http://ukincuba.fco. gov.uk).

Though neither an embassy nor a consulate, the **United States Interests Section,** Calle Calzada between Calles L and M, Vedado (© **7/833-3551;** http://havana.usint.gov/), is the official U.S. government representation on the island. There is no Australian embassy in Cuba. The Canadian embassy will officially assist.

Emergencies In most cases, you will want to dial © **106** for any emergency. This is the number for the police. Alternately, you can dial © **104** for an ambulance and © **105** for the fire department. At none of these numbers can you assume you will find an English-speaking person.

For legal emergencies, contact your diplomatic representation. All U.S. citizens can find assistance at the U.S. Interests Section (p. 35), with no questions asked about licenses.

Etiquette & Customs   Cubans are friendly, open, and physically expressive people. They strike up conversations easily and seldom use the formal terms of address in Spanish. However, be aware that as a foreigner, many Cubans who start a conversation with you in the street are hoping in some way to get some economic gain out of the relationship. *Jineterismo,* or jockeying, is a way of life in Cuba. This may involve anything from offers to take you to a specific restaurant or hotel (for a commission) to direct appeals for money or goods.

Dress is generally very informal, in large part due to the tough economic times faced by the broad population. Suits are sometimes worn in business and governmental meetings, although a simple, light, short-sleeved cotton shirt with a tie, or a *guayabera,* is more common. The *guayabera* is a loose-fitting shirt with two or four outer pockets on the front and usually a few vertical bands of pleats or embroidery. The *guayabera* is worn untucked, and is quite acceptable at even the most formal of occasions.

Perhaps the greatest etiquette concern is about what you say. Open criticism of the government or of Fidel or Raúl Castro is a major taboo. Don't do it—especially in open public places. The police, community revolutionary brigades, and reprisals for vocal dissent are an ongoing legacy of Cuba's political reality. One effect of this is that while Cubans you meet will often be very open and expressive with you, they tend to immediately clam up the minute another Cuban unknown to them enters the equation.

Gasoline (Petrol)   Gas costs about CUC$1.10 per liter (or about CUC$4.16 per gallon). See "Getting Around/By Car," p. 40.

Holidays   Cuba has a very limited number of official holidays, and aside from Christmas Day, no religious holidays are recognized by the state. The official holidays are **January 1** (Liberation Day), **May 1** (May Day, or Labor Day), **July 26** (Revolution Day), **October 10** (anniversary of the beginning of the 1868 War of Independence), and **December 25** (Christmas Day). However, the state has such total control that it's not uncommon for mass rallies or entire national mobilizations to be called as it sees fit. Other important dates that sometimes bring Cuba to a de facto state of national holiday include: **January 28** (Birth of José Martí), **February 24** (anniversary of the beginning of the 1895 War of Independence), **March 8** (International Women's Day), **April 19** (anniversary of Bay of Pigs victory), **July 30** (Day of the Martyrs of the Revolution), **October 8** (anniversary of the death of Che Guevara), **October 28** (anniversary of the death of Camilo Cienfuegos), and **December 7** (anniversary of the death of Antonio Maceo). For more information on holidays see "Calendar of Events," in chapter 3.

Insurance   In May 2010, Cuba implemented new insurance rules: All visitors and non-Cuban residents must hold a medical insurance policy. Failure to carry the correct documents could result in the visitor having to purchase mandatory coverage at the airport through Asistur. Visitors from the U.S. should take out their insurance policy from Cuban insurance companies that are affiliated with Havantur-Celimar Company. (American insurance companies do not provide coverage in Cuba.) For more information, contact the **Cuban Ministry of Foreign Affairs** (www.cubaminrex.cu/english/LookCuba/Articles/Others/2010/06-04.html). That said, it seems that visitors are not always asked to present proof of insurance documentation on entry. Still, to be safe, you should take out an insurance policy before you arrive in Cuba. If you do need to purchase insurance at the airport, contact **Asistur** (© **7/866-4499;** www.asistur.cu).

For information on traveler's insurance, trip cancelation insurance, and medical insurance while traveling, please visit www.frommers.com/tips.

Internet Access   See "Staying Connected," p. 58.

Language   Spanish is the official language of Cuba. English is spoken at most tourist hotels and some restaurants and attractions. Outside of the tourist orbit, English is not widely spoken, and some rudimentary Spanish will go a long way.

Indigenous and African languages have had a profound and lasting influence, and you will find many words—like *cigar, barbacoa,* and *conga*—tracing their origin to indigenous and African sources used widely across the island. Various African dialects are still widely used in the songs and ceremonies of Santeria and other syncretic religions, although almost no one speaks them conversationally. In a legacy from the Soviet days, some Cubans speak Russian. Also, see "Cuban Spanish Terms & Phrases," p. 301.

Legal Aid   If you get into legal trouble, immediately request to be put in touch with your embassy. All embassies have round-the-clock emergency numbers. **Asistur** (www.asistur.cu) may also be able to help. Its emergency numbers are *C* **7/866-8527,** *C* **7/866-8339,** and *C* **7/866-8920.**

Mail   A post office is called a *correo* in Spanish. You can get stamps at post offices, gift shops, and the front desk in most hotels. The Cuban postal system is extremely slow and untrustworthy. You can count on every parcel and piece of mail being opened and inspected. The cost of a postcard or letter to the U.S. or Canada is CUC$.75, and it takes about 3 weeks for delivery. A postcard and letter to Europe costs CUC$.70. A package of up to 1 kilogram (2.2 lb.) will cost CUC$10 to CUC$20 to ship, depending upon your destination country, but can only be dealt with at principal post offices.

However, it is best to send anything of any value via an established international courier service. **DHL,** Calle 26 and Avenida 1, Miramar, Havana (*C* **7/204-1876;** www.dhl.com), provides broad coverage to most of Cuba. *Beware:* Despite what you may be told, packages sent overnight to U.S. addresses tend to take 3 to 4 days to reach their destination.

Maps   Most car-rental agencies and many hotels will give you a copy of very basic nationwide and Havana road maps. The Cuban Geographic and Cartographic Institute publishes a couple of much more detailed maps; most tourist gift shops and Infotur kiosks carry these maps. If you're buying a map before your trip, try to get the **International Travel Map: Cuba** (ITMB Publishing; www.itmb.com). You'll also find good maps online at **www.cubaroutes.com**. Anyone doing any serious driving should purchase the indispensable **Guia de Carreteras** available irregularly in Havana (p. 89). Published by Limusa, it can be bought at **El Navegante,** Calle Mercaderes 115 between Obispo and Obrapía, La Habana Vieja.

Newspapers & Magazines   See "Staying Connected," p. 58.

Passports   See "Embassies & Consulates," above, for whom to contact if you lose your passport while traveling in the U.S. For other information, contact the following agencies:

For Residents of Australia   Contact the **Australian Passport Information Service** at *C* **131-232,** or visit www.passports.gov.au.

For Residents of Canada   Contact the central **Passport Office,** Department of Foreign Affairs and International Trade, Ottawa, ON K1A 0G3 (*C* **800/567-6868;** www.ppt.gc.ca).

For Residents of Ireland   Contact the **Passport Office,** Setanta Centre, Molesworth Street, Dublin 2 (*C* **01/671-1633;** www.foreignaffairs.gov.ie).

For Residents of New Zealand Contact the **Passports Office,** Department of Internal Affairs, 47 Boulcott Street, Wellington, 6011 (© **0800/225-050** in New Zealand or 04/474-8100; www.passports.govt.nz).

For Residents of the United Kingdom Visit your nearest passport office, major post office, or travel agency or contact the **Identity and Passport Service (IPS),** 89 Eccleston Square, London, SW1V 1PN (© **0300/222-0000;** www.ips.gov.uk).

For Residents of the **United States** To find your regional passport office, check the U.S. State Department website (travel.state.gov/passport) or call the **National Passport Information Center** (© **877/487-2778**) for automated information.

Police Nationwide, you can dial © **106** for police, although you shouldn't expect to find an English-speaking person on the other end of the line. In general, the police are quite helpful and not to be feared. Bribery is not an issue. In the event of robbery, the police are your best bet, but for physical emergencies or other threats of serious danger, you are probably best off contacting your embassy.

Smoking Although Fidel gave up smoking years ago, Cuba remains a major producer of tobacco and tobacco products. Many Cubans smoke. Cuba introduced a nonsmoking ban in enclosed public places in February 2005, but it is not really enforced. Most restaurants have nonsmoking areas.

Taxes There are no direct or specific taxes on goods or services in Cuba. However, some tourist restaurants and *paladares* have begun adding a 10% service charge onto their bills. However, this charge goes directly to the state restaurant and not the waiter, so you will need to leave a cash tip too. There is a CUC$25 departure tax that must be paid in cash upon leaving the country.

Telephones See "Staying Connected," p. 58.

Time Havana is 5 hours behind Greenwich Mean Time, or on a par with Eastern Standard Time in the United States and Canada. Daylight saving time is observed by setting clocks ahead 1 hour from one Sunday in March to one Sunday in October.

Tipping Most Cuban workers earn incredibly low salaries in dollar terms—around CUC$10 to CUC$15 a month—so tips are an extremely important and coveted source of supplemental income. With the rise in tourism, all sorts of workers now expect and work for tips, including taxi drivers, porters, waiters, guides, and restaurant musicians. Taxi drivers in particular are loath to give any small change on a fare. So if the meter reads CUC$4.30, you are expected to pay CUC$4.50, although you are certainly within your rights to ask for CUC$.20 or so. Taxi drivers, especially in Havana, tend to overcharge tourists. Porters should be tipped between CUC$.50 and CUC$1 per bag. Some state restaurants include a 10% service charge, although you should tip the waiter an additional 5% to 10% depending upon the quality of service, or even more (as this is how they actually survive, since they will not see any of that 10% service charge). If you stay in a resort, you should definitely tip the maid around CUC$1 a day, and also tip the waiters who serve you every day in the all-inclusive resorts, as they are on miserable salaries.

Toilets Public restrooms are hard to come by. You must usually count on the generosity of some hotel or restaurant, or duck into a museum or other attraction. Although it's rare that a tourist would be denied the use of the facilities, you should always ask first. In broad terms, the sanitary condition of public restrooms in Cuba is much higher than those found throughout the developing world, although at many establishments, toilet seats are sometimes missing. Always bring toilet paper with you wherever you go.

Many restrooms have an attendant, who is sometimes responsible for dispensing toilet paper. Upon exiting, you are expected to either leave a tip, or pay a specified fee. If the restrooms are not clean and you do not take the toilet paper, do not feel obliged to tip. Otherwise, leave up to CUC$.25

Visas All visitors to Cuba must have a tourist visa; however, tourist visas are generally issued by the ticketing airline or travel agent. Still, if you need more information on Cuban visas, visit the following sites:

Visitors from Australia should contact the Consulate General in Australia (© **02/9698-9797;** http://embacuba.cubaminrex.cu/Default.aspx?tabid=349).

Canadian visitors should visit **www.embacubacanada.net**, then under the "Embassies & Consulates" tab, click on "Consular Affairs," and then click on "Tourist Card." Or, contact the Cuban Embassy in Ottowa, Canada (© **613/563-0141**), or the Cuban consulates in Toronto (© **416/234-8181**) or Montreal (© **514/843-8897**).

Visitors from New Zealand should contact the Cuban Embassy in Wellington, New Zealand (© **04/472-3748;** http://embacuba.cubaminrex.cu/Default.aspx?tabid=5903).

Visitors from the U.K. should contact the Cuban Embassy in London, England (© **020/7240-2488;** www.cubaldn.com). **Cuba Direct** (www.visacuba.co.uk) is a reliable U.K. site where visitors can purchase travel visas.

See p. 34 in chapter 3 for more information on visas.

Visitor Information Tourism is Cuba's number-one source of hard currency, and the government is actively involved in promoting tourism internationally. As a result, there's a network of tourism boards and agencies in major cities around the world; some are better than others. Some offices are run by the Ministry of Tourism, others by one of the major state-run agencies like **Cubanacán, Havanatur,** or **Cubatur.** No matter the bureau, the focus is almost entirely on organized tours, but they can give you some basic information. Agencies to contact include **Cuba Tourist Board Canada,** 1200 Bay St., Suite 305, Toronto M5R 2A5 (© **416/362-0700;** www.gocuba.ca), or 2075, rue Université, Bureau 460, Montreal H3A 2L1 (© **514/875-8004**); **Cuba Tourist Board Great Britain,** 154 Shaftesbury Ave., 1st Floor, London WC2H 8HL (© **0207/240-6655;** www.travel2cuba.co.uk); and, in the United States, the **Cuban Interests Section** (© **202/797-8518;** http://embacu.cubaminrex.cu/sicw).

A host of other information is available online. The **Latin America Network Information Center** (http://lanic.utexas.edu/la/cb/cuba) is the best one-stop shop for helpful links to a wide range of travel and general information sites.

The Cuban government sponsors a number of websites, including **Cuba Travel** (www.cubatravel.cu), **CubaSi** (www.cubasi.cu), **Auténtica Cuba** (http://autenticacuba.com/uk) and **Directorio Turístico de Cuba** (www.dtcuba.com), the most useful. All provide a fair amount of travel-related information and links. State-run tourism agency websites—including **Cubanacán** (www.cubanacan.cu) and **Cubatur** (www.cubatur.cu)—are also good places to check for hotels, transportation, and package deals.

Infotur (www.infotur.cu), based in Cuba, also provides fairly detailed information on the country's provinces. Two interesting and informative sites are **Cuba Absolutely** (www.cubaabsolutely.com) and **Havana Journal** (www.havanajournal.com).

There are several interesting Cuba-related blogs, which offer an interesting perspective on life in Cuba, including **www.desdecuba.com/generationy, www.alongthemalecon.blogspot.com, www.sinevasionen.wordpress.com**, and **www.translatingcuba.com**.

Water Water is generally safe to drink throughout the country. However, since many travelers have tender digestive tracts, I recommend playing it safe and sticking to bottled water, sold as *agua mineral sin* or *con gas* and made by Ciego Montero. However, bottled water can be expensive, so if you have a strong stomach, you should ask for *agua hervida* (boiled water), always kept in fridges in *casas particulares.*

Wi-Fi See "Staying Connected," p. 58.

AIRLINE WEBSITES

MAJOR AIRLINES

Aerocaribbean
www.cubajet.com

Aeroflot
www.aeroflot.ru

Aeroméxico
www.aeromexico.com

Air Canada
www.aircanada.com

Air France
www.airfrance.com

Air Transat
www.airtransat.com

Bahamasair
www.bahamasair.com

Cayman Airways
www.caymanairways.com

Cubana
www.cubana.cu

Iberia Airlines
www.iberia.com

Lan Airlines
www.lan.com

Martinair
www.martinair.com

Taca
www.taca.com

Virgin Atlantic Airways
www.virgin-atlantic.com

BUDGET AIRLINES

Aerogaviota
www.aerogaviota.com

Air Europa
www.aireuropa.com

Blue Panorama
www.blue-panorama.com

Condor Airways
www3.condor.com

CUBAN SPANISH TERMS & PHRASES

Cubans speak fast and furiously. There's a very nasal and almost garbled quality to Cuban Spanish. Cubans tend to drop their final consonants, particularly the *s*, and they don't roll their *rr's* particularly strongly, converting the *rr* into an almost *l* sound in words like *carro* or *perro*. Cubans seldom use the formal *usted* form, instead preferring to address almost everyone (except those much older or of particular social or political stature) as *tú*. Likewise, you'll almost never hear the terms *señor* or *señora* as forms of address—Cubans prefer *compañero* and *compañera*. Cubans are also direct. They will almost always answer the phone with a curt *"Diga,"* which translates roughly as a mix of "Tell me" and "Speak."

BASIC WORDS & PHRASES

English	Spanish	Pronunciation
Good day	**Buenos días**	*Bweh*-nohss *dee*-ahss
How are you?	**¿Cómo está?**	*Koh*-moh ehss-*tah*?
Very well	**Muy bien**	Mwee byehn
Thank you	**Gracias**	*Grah*-syahss
You're welcome	**De nada**	Day *nah*-dah
Goodbye	**Adiós**	Ah-*dyohss*
Please	**Por favor**	Pohr fah-*vor*
Yes	**Sí**	See
No	**No**	Noh
Excuse me (to get by someone)	**Perdóneme**	Pehr-*doh*-neh-meh
Excuse me (to begin a question)	**Disculpe**	Dees-*kool*-peh

English	Spanish	Pronunciation
Give me	**Déme**	*Deh*-meh
Where is . . . ?	**¿Dónde está . . . ?**	*Dohn*-deh ehss-*tah*?
the station	**la estación**	lah ehss-tah-*seown*
a hotel	**un hotel**	oon oh-*tel*
a gas station	**una gasolinera**	*oo*-nah gasso-lyn-*air*-a
a restaurant	**un restaurante**	oon res-toh-*rahn*-teh
the toilet	**el baño**	el *bah*-nyoh
a good doctor	**un buen médico**	oon bwehn *meh*-thee-coh
the road to . . .	**el camino a/hacia . . .**	el cah-*mee*-noh ah/*ah*-syah
To the right	**A la derecha**	Ah lah deh-*reh*-chah
To the left	**A la izquierda**	Ah lah ees-*kyehr*-dah
Straight ahead	**Derecho**	Deh-*reh*-choh
I would like . . .	**Quisiera . . .**	Key-*syehr*-ah
to eat	**comer**	koh-*mehr*
a room	**una habitación**	*oon*-nah ah-bee-tah-*seown*
Do you have . . . ?	**¿Tiene usted . . . ?**	*Tyeh*-neh oos-*ted*?
How much is it?	**¿Cuánto cuesta?**	*Kwahn*-toh *kwehss*-tah?
When?	**¿Cuándo?**	*Kwahn*-doh?
What?	**¿Qué?**	Kay?
There is (Is there . . . ?)	**(¿)Hay (. . . ?)**	Eye?
What is there?	**¿Qué hay?**	Keh *eye*?
Yesterday	**Ayer**	Ah-*yer*
Today	**Hoy**	Oy
Tomorrow	**Mañana**	Mah-*nyah*-nah
Good	**Bueno**	*Bweh*-noh
Bad	**Malo**	*Mah*-loh
Better (best)	**(Lo) Mejor**	(Loh) Meh-*hor*
More	**Más**	Mahs
Less	**Menos**	*Meh*-nohss
No smoking	**Se prohibe fumar**	Seh pro-*hee*-beh foo-*mahr*

NUMBERS

English	Spanish	Pronunciation
1	**uno**	*ooh*-noh
2	**dos**	dohss
3	**tres**	trehss
4	**cuatro**	*kwah*-troh
5	**cinco**	*seen*-koh
6	**seis**	sayss
7	**siete**	*syeh*-teh
8	**ocho**	*oh*-choh
9	**nueve**	*nweh*-beh

English	Spanish	Pronunciation
10	**diez**	dyess
11	**once**	*ohn*-seh
12	**doce**	*doh*-seh
13	**trece**	*treh*-seh
14	**catorce**	kah-*tor*-seh
15	**quince**	*keen*-seh
16	**dieciseis**	dyess-ee-*sayss*
17	**diecisiete**	dyess-ee-*syeh*-teh
18	**dieciocho**	dyess-ee-*oh*-choh
19	**diecinueve**	dyess-ee-*nweh*-beh
20	**veinte**	*bayn*-teh
30	**treinta**	*trayn*-tah
40	**cuarenta**	kwah-*ren*-tah
50	**cincuenta**	seen-*kwen*-tah
60	**sesenta**	seh-*sehn*-tah
70	**setenta**	seh-*ten*-tah
80	**ochenta**	oh-*chen*-tah
90	**noventa**	noh-*behn*-tah
100	**cien**	*syehn*
200	**doscientos**	doh-*syehn*-tohs
500	**quinientos**	kee-*nyehn*-tohs
1,000	**mil**	meel

DAYS OF THE WEEK

English	Spanish	Pronunciation
Monday	**lunes**	(*loo*-nehss)
Tuesday	**martes**	(*mahr*-tehss)
Wednesday	**miércoles**	(*myehr*-koh-lehs)
Thursday	**jueves**	(*wheh*-behss)
Friday	**viernes**	(*byehr*-nehss)
Saturday	**sábado**	(*sah*-bah-doh)
Sunday	**domingo**	(doh-*meen*-goh)

MORE USEFUL PHRASES

English	Spanish	Pronunciation
Do you speak English?	**¿Habla usted inglés?**	*Ah*-blah oo-*sted* een-*glehss*?
Is there anyone here who speaks English?	**¿Hay alguien aquí que hable inglés?**	Eye *ahl*-gyehn ah-*key* keh ah-*bleh* een-*glehss*?
I speak a little Spanish.	**Hablo un poco de español.**	Ah-*bloh* oon poh-koh deh ehss-pah-*nyol*

English	Spanish	Pronunciation
I don't understand Spanish very well.	**No (lo) entiendo muy bien el español.**	Noh (loh) ehn-*tyehn*-do mwee byehn el ehss-pah-*nyol*
The meal is good.	**Me gusta la comida.**	Meh *goo*-stah lah koh-*mee*-dah
What time is it?	**¿Qué hora es?**	Keh *oh*-rah ehss?
May I see your menu?	**¿Puedo ver la carta?**	*Pweh*-doh vehr lah *car*-tah?
The check, please.	**La cuenta, por favor.**	Lah *kwehn*-tah, pohr fah-*vor*
What do I owe you?	**¿Cuánto le debo?**	*Kwahn*-toh leh *deh*-boh?
What did you say?	**¿Cómo? (colloquial expression for American "Eh?")**	*Koh*-moh?
I want (to see) . . .	**Quiero (ver) . . .**	*Kyehr*-oh (vehr)
a room	**un cuarto** or **una habit-ación**	oon *kwar*-toh, *oon*-nah ah-bee-tah-*seown*
with (without) bath-room	**con (sin) baño**	kohn (seen) *bah*-nyoh
We are staying here only . . .	**Nos quedamos aquí solamente . . .**	Nohs keh-*dahm*-ohss ah-*key* sohl-ah-*mehn*-teh
one night	**una noche**	*oon*-ah *noh*-cheh
one week	**una semana**	*oon*-ah seh-*mahn*-ah
We are leaving . . .	**Partimos (Salimos) . . .**	Pahr-*tee*-mohss (sah-*lee*-mohss)
tomorrow	**mañana**	mah-*nya*-nah
Do you accept . . . ?	**¿Acepta usted . . . ?**	Ah-*sehp*-tah oo-*sted*?
traveler's checks?	**cheques de viajero?**	*cheh*-kehs deh byah-*heh*-ro?
credit cards?	**tarjeta de crédito?**	tar-*hay*-ta de *kray*-dee-toe?

TYPICAL CUBAN WORDS & PHRASES

Ahí Namá   There it is, that's it!
Ay Mi Madre   Oh my mother! (exclamation of frustration)
Babalao   Afro-Cuban religious priest
Bachata   Informal party, hanging out
Bárbaro   Great, fabulous
Bicitaxi   Bicycle carriage
Bodega   Store
Bohío   Traditional, palm-thatched rural or indigenous dwelling
Botero   Private car with yellow plates not permitted to carry tourists
Cachito   Cuban-made sparkling lemonade; used to request all lemonade
CADECA   Acronym for *casa de cambio* (currency exchange office)
Carro particular   Privately owned car
Casa de la trova   Traditional music club
Casa del campo   A simple country house
Casa particular   A private home with rooms for rent
Cerveza   Beer
Chama   Child

Chavito   Cuban Convertible Peso
Chévere   Cool, excellent
Coche   Car
Coche de caballo   Horse-drawn carriage
Cola   Line or queue
Comida criolla   Cuban creole cuisine
Compañero/compañera   Literally, "partner," most common form of an address, as opposed to *señor* or *señora,* which are almost never used
Compay   Friend
Consumo   Price inclusive of food and drinks
Coppelia   National ice-cream chain, almost synonymous with ice cream
Cuba libre   Cocktail with rum and Coke
Diga   Literally, "speak"; this is a very common phone greeting
Divisa   U.S. dollar/Cuban Convertible Peso
Efectivo   Cash
Fanoso   Cheapskate
Fruta bomba   Papaya
Fula   U.S. dollar (slang)
Gallego/a   Foreigner
Guagua   Bus
Guarachar   To hang out or party
Guayabera   Loose-fitting, embroidered and pleated men's shirt
Hacer botella   To hitchhike
Jinetero/jinetera   Literally, "jockey"; used to refer to anyone hustling a foreigner for money
Mango   Good-looking person
Mangon   Exceptionally good-looking person
Mata   Tree
Mojito   A rum cocktail
Muchacho/a   Young man/young woman
Orisha   Santeria deity
Paladar   Private home restaurant
Paradero   Transport stop
Por nada   You're welcome
Puro   Cuban cigar/older respected man
¿Qué bolá?   "What's going on?" (slang)
Santero   Afro-Cuban Santeria religious priests
Sirilo   Yes or yeah
Socio/a   Literally, "member," used to address close friends
Transporte Chapa "T"   A type of taxi, marked by red license plates beginning with T, that are driven by Cubans and permitted to carry tourists
Villas   Towns or settlements
Yuma   Originally an American; now used as a term for all foreigners

Index

General Index